D1319923

KIERKEGAARD AS A CHRISTIAN THINKER

Eros and Self-Emptying: The Intersections of Augustine and Kierkegaard
Lee C. Barrett

Kierkegaard and the Paradox of Religious Diversity
George B. Connell

Kierkegaard and Spirituality
C. Stephen Evans

Recovering Christian Character
Robert C. Roberts

Beyond Immanence: The Theological Vision of Kierkegaard and Barth
Alan J. Torrance and Andrew B. Torrance

Kierkegaard's Concept of Faith
Merold Westphal

BEYOND IMMANENCE

The Theological Vision of Kierkegaard and Barth

Alan J. Torrance and Andrew B. Torrance

WILLIAM B. EERDMANS PUBLISHING COMPANY

GRAND RAPIDS, MICHIGAN

Wm. B. Eerdmans Publishing Co.
4035 Park East Court SE, Grand Rapids, Michigan 49546
www.eerdmans.com

Published 2023
Printed in the United States of America

29 28 27 26 25 24 23   1 2 3 4 5 6 7

ISBN 978-0-8028-6803-9

Library of Congress Cataloging-in-Publication Data

A catalog record for this book is available from the Library of Congress.

To C. Stephen Evans and Murray Rae

Contents

Foreword *by Paul Martens*   xi

Acknowledgments   xiii

Introduction   1
Barth's Reception of Kierkegaard   2
The "Phantom Kierkegaard"   3
Kierkegaard's Influence on Romans II   8
An Introductory Note on Kierkegaard's Theological Project   16
An Introductory Note on Barth's Theological Project   19
Overview of Chapters   24

1. **Kierkegaard's Audience and Approach**   28
    A "Christian" Nation   29
    Hegel   32
    Hans Lassen Martensen and Danish Hegelianism   44
    Kierkegaard's Approach   48

2. **Kierkegaard on Creation and Christology, against
    Hegelianism**   61
    God and Creation   62
    The Divine Incognito   70
    Paradoxical Christology   81
    Christ the Mediator   94
    Conclusion   104

3. **Karl Barth's Stand against Idealism, Cultural Religion,
    and Nationalism**   105
    Reasonable Religion, Pedagogy, and Incipient Idealism   106
    The Impact of Idealism on Biblical Scholarship   115
    Theology, Politics, and the Question of Criteria   118
    The Theological Impact of Neo-Kantian Idealism   127
    Conclusion   143

4. **The Theological Implications of God's Kinship in Time**   145
    *Liberating Christianity from Christianism and
        the Potential for Harm*   145
    Setting Theology Free   157
    Kinship, Covenant, and Creaturely Freedom   179
    Conclusion   191

5. **Barth's Appropriation of Kierkegaard**   192
    The Infinite Qualitative Difference   193
    Barth on God's Self-Revelation in History   201
    The Paradox of Faith   222
    Conclusion   245

6. **Engaging Secular Society**   246
    Barth's Debate with Brunner   247
    *"The Light of Natural Reason," the "Moral Sense,"
        and the Diversity of Epistemic Bases*   263
    The Moral Conscience as a Twofold Point of Connection   271
    *Dogmatics, Apologetics, and the Challenge of
        the Grounding Question*   273
    Christian Engagement in the Public Square   281
    Metanoia Again!   286
    *The Implications of the Kierkegaard-Barth Trajectory
        for Sociopolitical Ethics*   289
    "Either-Or," or "Both-And"   295
    From Solution to Plight   300
    Conclusion   302

7. **Beyond Immanence**   303

   The Divine Address and Human God-talk   303

   The Trinitarian Grammar of Revelation   310

   The Kierkegaard-Barth Trajectory and
   *   the Theologistic Fallacy*   314

   How Barth's Trinitarian Approach Obviates
   *   the Theologistic Fallacy*   321

   History and the Veiledness of Revelation   324

   The Age-Old Challenge of Idealism, and Two Parallel Gulfs   325

   Progressing beyond the Socratic in Biblical Scholarship   331

   Externalist Epistemology   334

   The Externalist Nature of Kierkegaard's and Barth's Accounts   339

   Fred Dretske on Recognition and Entitlement   340

   Semantic Externalism and Its Challenge of Descriptivist Theories
   *   of Reference*   346

   The De Re Character of Christian God-talk   351

   Conclusion   354

Conclusion   357

Bibliography   363

Index   385

FOREWORD

To state the obvious: Søren Kierkegaard's influence on twentieth-century thought is immense. Simone Weil, Ludwig Wittgenstein, Erich Przywara, Reinhold Niebuhr, Hannah Arendt, Emil Brunner, Paul Tillich, Albert Camus, Rudolf Bultmann, Abraham Joshua Heschel, Theodor Adorno, Yves Congar, and Jacques Derrida—to just scratch the surface—all wrestled with Kierkegaard as they sought to exist authentically in the face of the tragedies and challenges of the century. Karl Barth, arguably the defining Protestant theologian of the twentieth century, also claimed and exhibited debts to Kierkegaard.

More than merely a man of his times (though he certainly was that), Barth's idiosyncratic debts to Kierkegaard are deep and complex, and they evolve over time. Many have noted this; few have sought to parse the multilayered resonance and dissonance between the two; virtually none have attended to the overlapping theological visions of Kierkegaard and Barth in their respective contexts as carefully as the authors of this volume. In *Beyond Immanence*, Alan Torrance and Andrew Torrance deftly unpack the relationship between Kierkegaard and Barth as they elucidate (1) Barth's exposure to and familiarity with Kierkegaard's corpus, that is, his reception of Kierkegaard, (2) Barth's own articulation of his relationship to Kierkegaard, and (3) the common theological convictions that bind Kierkegaard and Barth together in what the authors refer to as the Kierkegaard-Barth trajectory. It is especially in this last part that *Beyond Immanence* makes its most significant and sustained contribution to contemporary scholarship and everyday Christian praxis.

In developing the Kierkegaard-Barth trajectory, Alan and Andrew remind us that Kierkegaard and Barth both understood that, all too often, our talk of God is complicit with our social, cultural, and political arrangements. Arguing forcefully against idolatries of nationalism in different forms, both sought to point toward an "infinite qualitative difference" between humanity and God that is bridged only in the incarnation, the revelation of God in the person of

Jesus Christ. Leaning heavily on Kierkegaard's *Philosophical Fragments* and Barth's *Church Dogmatics*, Alan and Andrew energetically argue that only the incarnation provides the critical and constructive epistemic and semantic conditions for Christian talk of God which, in turn, radically reshapes our social and political arrangements "beyond immanence." As such, this book about Kierkegaard and Barth is loaded, self-consciously, with contemporary ethical entailments.

When Stephen Evans and I first discussed this series many years ago, I could not imagine it without this volume. I feel the same today. Admittedly, I may be just a little biased, since it was Alan who first introduced me to Kierkegaard way back in the summer of 1995. In one sense, this book is the maturation and articulation of the themes and questions that exercised him in *Philosophical Fragments* and *Works of Love* already three decades ago. In another sense, this book is the natural outgrowth of Andrew's focused attention to Kierkegaard's account of what it means to become a Christian. In concert, Alan and Andrew have given us a gift of scholarship that points beyond itself to Kierkegaard and Barth and then beyond them to the self-giving God of grace that redeems and reconciles humanity through the incarnation.

Paul Martens

Acknowledgments

C. Stephen Evans's writings on both Kierkegaard and philosophical theology have inspired us both over very many years. At a personal level, he has been an enormous source of encouragement and support. Murray Rae supervised Andrew's doctoral research on Kierkegaard and Barth and has been an outstanding dialogue partner, colleague, and friend of Alan's over decades. It is a pleasure, therefore, to dedicate this book to two of the Christian thinkers we most admire and whose own contribution has such an immense amount to offer both the church and the academy.

Other people who have been a source of personal support, friendship, and intellectual inspiration include Lee Barrett, Richard Bauckham, Jeremy Begbie, Bruce Benson, Gijsbert van den Brink, Sarah Broadie, Douglas Campbell, Joshua Cockayne, Oliver Crisp, Kevin Diller, Aaron Edwards, David Gouwens, George Hunsinger, Peter van Inwagen, Paul Martens, Bruce McCormack, Christa McKirland, Jared Michelson, David Moffitt, Tim Pawl, Amy Peeler, Michael Rea, Jonathan Rutledge, Christoph Schwöbel, Eleonore Stump, Koert Verhagen, John Webster, Martin Westerholm, Gotthelf Wiedermann, and N. T. Wright along with numerous other colleagues, fellows, and students in the Logos Institute and in the University of St Andrews more widely as also further afield.

Mitch Mallary, Paul Martens, Jeremy Rios, Daniel Spencer, and David Stuart read an early draft of the manuscript providing incisive criticism and thoughtful theological suggestions. Over a period of weeks, it was a privilege to have four of our former supervisees serve as our supervisors! We are also indebted to Terry J. Wright, whose editing of the typescript was meticulously efficient and also insightful.

The Templeton Religion Trust provided us with a major grant to help establish the Logos Institute for Analytic and Exegetical Theology in the University of St Andrews. In addition to the intellectual environment the grant helped to create, the generosity of the Trust provided practical resources that helped to free up the time necessary for this research. One outstanding "resource" funded by the grant was Diana Verhagen. Her efficient and selfless commitment to the daily running of the grant and her sustained commitment to easing the administrative burden of the Institute were simply invaluable.

Finally, our wives, Margaret and Julie, along with the other members of the family have provided loving practical support, patient encouragement, and an all too necessary sense of humor. We are more grateful to them than words can easily express.

Introduction

Søren Kierkegaard is one of the Christian thinkers mostly widely read among contemporary philosophers, yet few of the philosophers who read Kierkegaard are drawn to the thought of Karl Barth. This is because these two figures are, in many respects, worlds apart from one another. Yet they are also united to a profound degree by the convictions they share and in their responses to the common challenges they faced. Both believe that the triune God not only explains the existence of the contingent order but also defines what it means to be human. Both maintain that God draws humans into loving union with Godself in and through the person of Jesus Christ. And both figures expounded and developed these convictions in contexts where the academy was characterized by idealist and romantic notions of Christianity, and where the church had become bound to oppressive forms of establishment religion.

The aim of this book is to offer a close examination of several key theological ideas that connect the two thinkers, with an eye to presenting their mutual vision for the theological task. Many books have been written, and many more could be written, on how these thinkers engaged with the theological ideas just mentioned. However, we shall attend specifically to those ideas that Barth developed (directly or indirectly) under the influence of Kierkegaard. In doing so, we shall highlight the ways in which Barth developed and extended Kierkegaard's trajectory, while also, in certain ways, departing from Kierkegaard. A key focus of this book is the profound sociopolitical relevance of the trajectory established by Kierkegaard and followed by Barth. Historically, this is especially relevant since Barth's thought was hammered out on an anvil of political engagement, in a context where cultural religion was complicit in unprecedented moral evil. Beyond our interest in Kierkegaard and Barth, reflection on this trajectory is invaluable for helping us to challenge the ongoing potential for religion to endorse oppressive and marginalizing social practices and political commitments.

As we reflect on the historical and theological relationships between these two thinkers, it is important to be open about the limits of such an endeavor. We are inhibited by the fact that there was very little depth to Barth's engagement with Kierkegaard; indeed, in many respects, his engagement with Kierkegaard was superficial. To lay out the obstacles facing this book, this introduction will begin with an analysis of Barth's flawed reception of Kierkegaard, while also introducing some of the ways that Barth accurately appropriated Kierkegaard. In the second part of this introduction, we shall offer a preliminary comparison of their different theological projects. This will set the scene for us to engage more deeply with their respective approaches, concerns, and commitments. Finally, we shall conclude with an overview of the chapters of this book.

Barth's Reception of Kierkegaard

Near the end of his life, Barth offered the following reflection on his relationship to Kierkegaard:

> I can at least tell you that I am as little an opponent of Kierkegaard now as I was earlier. On the other hand, not even in *Romans* was I a real friend of Kierkegaard, let alone a Kierkegaard enthusiast. I have seriously let his words be *spoken* to me—and let him who wants to be a theologian see to it that he does not miss him. But I have also let his words *be* spoken to me and then gone merrily on my theological way—for I still think that he who meets him and stays with him must take care that the Gospel does not become an irksome and legalistic thing.[1]

While this book will primarily be interested in the positive influence that Kierkegaard had on Barth, we should be candid, from the outset, that Barth's later attitude toward Kierkegaard was highly critical. Any positive impact that Kierkegaard once had on Barth came to be overshadowed by Barth's nervousness about (what he interpreted as) the more pietistic and existentialist

---

1. From a letter to Martin Rumscheidt on November 1, 1967. Karl Barth, *Letters, 1961–1968*, trans. Geoffrey W. Bromiley (Grand Rapids: Eerdmans, 1981), 273. In this letter, Barth responds to a comment that Rumscheidt makes on Alastair McKinnon's article "Barth's Relation to Kierkegaard" (see note 7 below) by saying, in vague terms, that Rumscheidt would be better to approach Eberhard Busch about their relationship.

elements in Kierkegaard's thought. These concerns can be found in Barth's earlier writings,[2] but became particularly pointed in his later view of Kierkegaard as the major influence behind the "anthropocentric" turn toward "the modern theological existentialism"—an existentialism that Barth associated with Rudolf Bultmann, on whom Kierkegaard was also a major influence.[3] This view led Barth to diverge so significantly from Kierkegaard that, in the end, he could no longer see himself as a devotee of his Danish counterpart.

THE "PHANTOM KIERKEGAARD"

The later Barth's apathy—even hostility—toward Kierkegaard was not based on a careful understanding.[4] According to Barth, Kierkegaard was a strong influence on him in his earlier years, but an influence that he left behind in his later years.[5] He saw Kierkegaard as "a teacher whose school every theologian must pass through once. Woe to him who fails to do so! Only that he does not stay sitting in it and would be better not to return to it!"[6] However, the "Kierkegaard" Barth came to know was a construct of mistranslation and misinterpretation. As Alastair McKinnon remarks, Barth's "Kierkegaard" was a "phantom Kierkegaard," a work of "historical fiction," and "the product of accident and animosity."[7] Or, as Philip Ziegler puts it, the target of Barth's critique was merely the "Danish 'ghost in the machine' of later varieties of theological

---

2. For example, in *The Epistle to the Romans*, Barth notes that "there proceeds . . . from Kierkegaard the poison of a too intense pietism." Karl Barth, *The Epistle to the Romans*, trans. Edwyn C. Hoskyns, 6th ed. (London: Oxford University Press, 1933), 276.

3. Karl Barth, *Church Dogmatics*, ed. Geoffrey W. Bromiley and Thomas F. Torrance, trans. Geoffrey W. Bromiley (Edinburgh: T&T Clark, 1956–1975), IV/3, 498; see also Barth, *Church Dogmatics* III/4, xii. It is worth noting that Barth would later acknowledge that Kierkegaard's focus on the existential character of the Christian "was an historically understandable and not unjustifiable reaction," even if "it led to a distortion of the whole complex of problems [*Problem-Komplexes*]." Barth, *The Christian Life: Church Dogmatics IV/4*, trans. Geoffrey W. Bromiley (Edinburgh: T&T Clark, 1981), 189.

4. This section draws freely on Andrew B. Torrance, "Beyond Existentialism: Kierkegaard on the Human Relationship with the God Who Is Wholly Other," *International Journal of Systematic Theology* 16, no. 3 (2014): 295–312.

5. Karl Barth, "A Thank You and a Bow: Kierkegaard's Reveille," in *Fragments Grave and Gay*, ed. Martin Rumscheidt, trans. Eric Mosbacher (London: Fontana, 1971), 98–99.

6. Barth, "Thank You and a Bow," 100–101.

7. Alastair McKinnon, "Barth's Relation to Kierkegaard: Some Further Light," *Canadian Journal of Theology* 13 (1967): 32.

existentialism."[8] It was this inaccurately constructed "Kierkegaard" that Barth had in mind when he sought to distance himself from Kierkegaard.[9]

While we cannot grasp all the intricacies of Barth's ambivalence—and, at times, hostility—toward "Kierkegaard," there are two things in particular that are worth pointing out. First, it has been well established that the German translations of Kierkegaard's works by Christoph Schrempf, Albert Dorner, and Hermann Gottsched were far from adequate—particularly in the case of Schrempf.[10] As Gerhard Schreiber points out, for example, Schrempf took it upon himself to simplify complex sentences, insert new sentences, and delete "what he took to be superfluous repetitions."[11] And he did this with a desire not only to translate Kierkegaard's words but to communicate them to a German audience: "Our goal, as far as possible, is to allow him to speak as he would have done if German had been his mother tongue."[12] As Schreiber notes, this aim inspired Schrempf to take "considerable liberties with the original text."[13] Consequently, it is clear that Barth, equipped and influenced as he was by these translations, would not have held the "real Kierkegaard" in his hands.[14]

Second, while it is unclear what exactly sparked Barth's initial interest

8. Philip Ziegler, "Barth's Criticisms of Kierkegaard: A Striking Out at Phantoms?," *International Journal of Systematic Theology* 9, no. 4 (2007): 438.

9. For example, Barth notoriously omitted Kierkegaard from his survey of *Protestant Theology in the Nineteenth Century*—mentioning him but three times in passing. Karl Barth, *Protestant Theology in the Nineteenth Century: Its Background & History* (London: SCM, 1972), 20, 386, 604. Contrary to what is sometimes suggested, however, this omission does not seem to be malicious. It is much more likely that this omission is due to his assessment that "Kierkegaard in particular did not have the slightest influence on 19th century theology, except, again, in the case of a few individuals." Barth, "Evangelical Theology in the 19th Century," in *The Humanity of God* (London: Collins, Fontana, 1967), 11.

10. See Gerhard Schreiber's extremely insightful "Christoph Schrempf: The 'Swabian Socrates' as Translator of Kierkegaard," trans. David D. Possen, in *Kierkegaard's Influence on Theology, Tome I: German Protestant Theology*, ed. Jon Stewart (Farnham: Ashgate, 2012), 297–306; and Habib Malik, *Receiving Søren Kierkegaard: The Early Impact and Transmission of His Thought* (Washington, DC: Catholic University of America Press, 1997), 311–15, 332–38.

11. Schreiber, "Christoph Schrempf," 298.

12. These words are found in the publisher's advertisement for the Schrempf edition of Kierkegaard's *Erbauliche Reden*. Quoted in Schreiber, "Christoph Schrempf," 297.

13. Schreiber, "Christoph Schrempf," 298. As Heiko Schulz also notes, "Schrempf's repeatedly revised, highly idiosyncratic, and at times breathtakingly free renditions of the Kierkegaardian texts soon became *the* authoritative voice at least for many German scholars." Heiko Schulz, "Germany and Austria: A Modest Head Start," in *Kierkegaard's International Reception, Tome I: Northern and Western Europe*, ed. Jon Stewart (Farnham: Ashgate, 2009), 316 (emphasis original).

14. McKinnon, "Barth's Relation to Kierkegaard," 32.

in Kierkegaard,[15] we can say with confidence that the troublesome figure of Emanuel Hirsch would have been a considerable influence on Barth's reception of Kierkegaard. Hirsch was a church historian and a scholar of both Johann Fichte and Martin Luther who, from the 1920s onward, grew to become one of the leading German experts on Kierkegaard—if not *the* leading German expert.[16] With Hirsch's advancement as a Kierkegaard scholar came what Heiko Schulz describes as the (further) "Germanization" (*Verdeutschung*) of Kierkegaard.[17] Driven by his strong nationalist and, post-1933, National Socialist convictions, Hirsch was instrumental in the German enculturation of Kierkegaard—a move that was colored by Hirsch's idealist and romantic vision of Kierkegaard.[18]

Barth's and Hirsch's paths crossed when they taught together at Göttingen in 1921—Hirsch in church history and Barth in Reformed theology. From early on, Barth found himself impressed by the breadth of Hirsch's understanding, rooted in "a profound knowledge of Luther and Fichte, an effete scholar of the kind to be found in books, German nationalist to his very bones, but a notable phenomenon."[19] He describes him as a "learned and perspicacious" man.[20] However, this did not hold him back from locking horns with Hirsch. In a 1922 letter to Eduard Thurneysen, Barth tells of one such exchange, written with

15. Barth notes that Kierkegaard "entered my thinking to a more serious and greater extent in about 1919, at a critical turning point between the first and the second editions of my *Epistle to the Romans*, and from that time onwards he played a more important role in my writing" (Barth, "Thank You and a Bow," 97). Originally published as "Dank und Reverenz," *Evangelische Theologie* 23 (1963): 339 (translation altered).

16. Notably, Hirsch was also a harsh critic of the Schrempf editions of Kierkegaard's works. See Schreiber, "Christoph Schrempf," 299, 301.

17. Heiko Schulz, "Die theologische Rezeption Kierkegaards in Deutschland und Dänemark: Notizen zu einer historischen Typologie," in *Kierkegaard Studies Yearbook 1999*, ed. N. J. Cappelørn and H. Deuser (Berlin: Walter de Gruyter, 1999), 229, quoted in and translated by Marcia Morgan, "Adorno's Reception of Kierkegaard: 1929–1933," in *Søren Kierkegaard Newsletter* 46 (Northfield, MN: Hong Kierkegaard Library, 2003), 9.

18. See also Alastair Hannay and Gordon D. Marino, Introduction to *The Cambridge Companion to Kierkegaard*, ed. Alastair Hannay and Gordon D. Marino (Cambridge: Cambridge University Press, 1997), 1; Matthias Wilke, "Emanuel Hirsch: A German Dialogue with 'Saint Søren,'" in *Kierkegaard's Influence on Theology, Tome I: German Protestant Theology*, ed. Jon Stewart (Farnham: Ashgate, 2012), 161.

19. Written in a letter to W. Spoendlin dated December 21, 1921, quoted in Eberhard Busch, *Karl Barth: His Life from Letters and Autobiographical Texts*, trans. John Bowden (Philadelphia: Fortress, 1976), 134.

20. Barth, *Church Dogmatics* IV/3, 20.

a report of Hirsch's theses and Barth's antitheses.[21] According to Barth's report, Hirsch believed that the Christian life is defined by self-transformation, guided by the reading of Scripture, and grounded in surrender to God. Furthermore, for Barth, Hirsch believed that one of the central ways in which we come to understand our relationship with God is by looking at how the exemplary figures of Scripture related to God. At the heart of Hirsch's understanding was an emphasis on how we appropriate *our ideas of* the Christian life to our own existence. Such an account was antithetical to Barth, who sought to stress the actuality of God's relationship with us and action toward us in and through Christ. For Barth, the Christian life is life *in Christ* for which God creates us and into which God reconciles us "under God and in accord with God."[22]

Barth's analysis of Hirsch is representative of the kind of account that came to be associated with Kierkegaard. As Lee Barrett points out, when Barth differentiates himself from Hirsch's position here, there is a sense in which he "was implicitly differentiating himself from what he took to be aspects of Kierkegaard's theological sensibility."[23] It is impossible to gauge how much Kierkegaard was in Barth's mind during his earlier conversations with Hirsch. But since they took place after the writing of the second edition of his commentary on Romans (hereafter *Romans II*)—the work of Barth's on which Kierkegaard's thought had the greatest influence—we know he was familiar with the Danish thinker. Barth would also have been alert to the "Kierkegaard" who was inspiring Hirsch, and Barth's friction with Hirsch may in turn have fueled his suspicion of Kierkegaard. Because Barth was not well versed in Kierkegaard's thought, he would have been more likely, of course, to trust the perceived expert.

What was wrong with Hirsch's Kierkegaard? The "Kierkegaard" of Hirsch was very much a construct that reflected the commitments of German idealism. As Matthias Wilke remarks, "Hirsch reads Kierkegaard as a Christian thinker who belongs to the 'idealist-romantic type in its superlative form.'"[24] This reading of Kierkegaard was undoubtedly influenced by Hirsch's disregard for the turn (in *Concluding Unscientific Postscript*) that Kierkegaard makes

---

21. Karl Barth, *Revolutionary Theology in the Making: Barth–Thurneysen Correspondence, 1914–1925*, trans. James D. Smart (Richmond, VA: John Knox, 1964), 1:82–88.

22. Barth, *Barth–Thurneysen Correspondence*, 1:83.

23. Lee C. Barrett, "Karl Barth: The Dialectic of Attraction and Repulsion," in *Kierkegaard's Influence on Theology, Tome I: German Protestant Theology*, ed. Jon Stewart (Farnham: Ashgate, 2012), 15.

24. Wilke, "Emanuel Hirsch," 173, quoting Hirsch, *Geschichte der neuern evangelischen Theologie*, 5:468. Wilke also notes here that Hirsch "sees a direct connection between Kierkegaard and the Pietism of Herrnhuter, German Romanticism, Schleiermacher, and German idealism."

in his later religious authorship—a turn that came with an emphasis on the decisiveness of the *real* God, revealed in Jesus Christ, for the Christian faith.[25] Hirsch, like so many other Kierkegaard scholars (and subsequent followers of these scholars), did not take this turning point seriously enough.[26] This led Barth to associate Hirsch's tendency to concentrate theology on anthropology with the "Kierkegaard renaissance" of the 1920s.[27]

However, there is a far more profound Christian realism in Kierkegaard's thought than was ever adequately communicated to Barth—a realism that associates the truth with the objective reality of God who lies beyond human subjectivity (i.e., beyond individual human experience, desire, knowledge, belief, etc.).[28] Furthermore, when we look at the debate between Hirsch and

25. See Schulz, "Germany and Austria," 345–46. It should be added that Hirsch did not totally disregard Kierkegaard's religious writings but did not distinguish them clearly enough from Kierkegaard's aesthetic writings. In appreciation for Kierkegaard's (or Anti-Climacus's) religious writing, Hirsch writes, "*The Sickness unto Death* and *Practice in Christianity*, his two masterpieces as a Christian writer, as well as *The Point of View*, . . . have greater prospect of being placed among the imperishable writings of the Christian Church than any other Christian-religious or Christian-theological productions of the nineteenth century." Emanuel Hirsch, *Kierkegaard-Studien*, 2 vols. (Gütersloh: 1933; repr. Vaduz, Liechtenstein: Topos Verlag, 1978), 1:229, quoted in Søren Kierkegaard, *Practice in Christianity*, ed. and trans. Howard V. Hong and Edna H. Hong (Princeton: Princeton University Press, 1991), xviii–xix.

26. In *The Point of View for My Work as an Author*, Kierkegaard asserts that *Concluding Unscientific Postscript* "constitutes the turning point in my entire work as an author, inasmuch as it poses the issue: becoming a Christian." Kierkegaard, *Point of View*, ed. and trans. Howard V. Hong and Edna H. Hong (Princeton: Princeton University Press, 1998), 63. At the heart of *Postscript*, we find Climacus turning to contemplate what it means (for the Christian) to be human before the reality of God—a focus that went on to characterize Kierkegaard's later religious authorship. Critical to this turn is the one whom Climacus refers to as "the god in time." For further discussion of this point, see Andrew Torrance, "Kierkegaard on the Christian Response to the God Who Establishes Kinship with Us in Time," *Modern Theology* 32, no. 1 (2016): 60–83.

27. Karl Barth, *Ethics*, ed. Dietrich Braun, trans. Geoffrey W. Bromiley (Edinburgh: T&T Clark, 1981), 8; see also 17. It is likely that Barth will have had Emanuel Hirsch in mind when he contends that "the *theologia naturalis vulgaris*" is a "depressing result [that] could be achieved even via Kierkegaard." Karl Barth, *No! Answer to Emil Brunner*, in *Natural Theology: Comprising "Nature and Grace" by Professor Dr. Emil Brunner and the Reply "No!" by Dr. Karl Barth*, trans. Peter Fraenkel (London: Centenary Press, 1946; repr., Eugene, OR: Wipf & Stock, 2002), 121.

28. For an excellent discussion of Barth's attitude toward Kierkegaard on the question of subjectivity, see Aaron Edwards, "A Broken Engagement: Reassessing Barth's Relationship to Kierkegaard on the Grounds of Subjectivity and Preaching," *International Journal of Systematic Theology* 16, no. 1 (2014): 56–78. Edwards draws the helpful conclusion that "it is evident from Barth's sermons and overall homiletical outlook that if Kierkegaard is to be labelled as a 'subjectivist' then Barth himself can be no less deserving of the same

Barth, we can safely say that there are many points where Kierkegaard would have sided with Barth. For Kierkegaard, as for Barth, it is the living God who awakens us into the Christian life by encountering us and drawing us into a life of faith and obedience, in and through Jesus Christ. For both thinkers, there is no faithful relationship with God that is grounded in our independent observations, reflections, decisions, or self-transformations.

Kierkegaard's Influence on Romans II

Where do Kierkegaard and Barth find alignment? For both of them, nineteenth-century theology was characterized by a tendency to treat God primarily as an object of human thought, a discrete facet of human experience, or merely a feature of human culture and society. Against this trend, Barth endeavored to think about God according to God's self-revelation—a revelation that makes known what otherwise transcends the immanent realm of human thought. He sought to do so by emphasizing that "men are men, and God is God"—a point that sought to stress God's transcendence over immanent human categories of thought and experience.[29] This statement was foundational not only to his thinking about God *in se* but also to his thinking about what creation is according to the God who creates it. It was Barth's appreciation for this point that led him to embrace Kierkegaard when writing *Romans II*, which is where he first acknowledges his indebtedness to Kierkegaard.

The primary work responsible for Kierkegaard's impact on Barth was *Practice in Christianity*, particularly the section entitled "The Impossibility of Direct Communication." We also find, in *Romans II*, quotes from Kierkegaard's *Journals*, his essay "The Difference between a Genius and an Apostle," *The Moment*, and *Concluding Unscientific Postscript*.[30] Furthermore, Lee Barrett

---

label. Ideally, of course, neither thinker would be tarred with such a brush. Rather, both should be seen, in their preaching, as taking the objective truths of Christian doctrine and seeking to make them temporally significant in the minds and lives of their congregations" (77). See also David J. Gouwens, *Kierkegaard as Religious Thinker* (Cambridge: Cambridge University Press, 1996), 149–50.

29. Barth, *Romans II*, 63. This statement finds earlier expression in Barth's oft-quoted statement: "World remains world. But God is God." Barth, "Kriegszeit und Gottesreich," a lecture delivered on November 15, 1915, cited in Herbert Anzinger, *Glaube und kommunikative Praxis: Eine Studie zur vordialektischen Theologie Karl Barths* (Munich: Chr. Kaiser Verlag, 1991), 120–22.

30. We know that Barth owned an abridged version of Kierkegaard's *Journals* (*Buch des Richters: Seine Tagebücher 1833–1855 in Auswahl*, trans. Hermann Gottsched [Jena: Die-

argues convincingly that we can see allusions to *Fear and Trembling* and *Works of Love* as well.[31] These references to Kierkegaard's works, however, are often somewhat incidental to *Romans II*; it is hard to know how much attention he actually gave to reading these writings. It is also difficult to determine the extent to which Barth's engagement with Kierkegaard was firsthand, as it is likely that some of Barth's references to Kierkegaard were secondhand, mediated to him by, among others, his good friend Eduard Thurneysen. Indeed, Barth himself notes that he only knew Kierkegaard "selectively."[32] However he encountered Kierkegaard's works, a handful of key ideas and quotes from Kierkegaard seem to have had a profound influence on Barth—not only on *Romans II* but also on his trajectory going forward. Last (and perhaps at risk of overqualification), we should acknowledge that many of Barth's thoughts that echo Kierkegaard had begun to form in his mind prior to his engagement with Kierkegaard. So, while Kierkegaard did have a critical impact on Barth, much of this influence may have involved Kierkegaard being used by Barth to articulate and make sense of his own nascent theological ideas.

What are the key ideas that Barth adopted from Kierkegaard? Prominent in the literature on Kierkegaard and Barth is a constant reference to Barth's statement:

> If I have a system, it is limited to a recognition of what Kierkegaard called the "infinite qualitative difference" between time and eternity, and to my regarding this as possessing negative as well as positive significance: "God is in heaven, and thou art on earth."[33]

Embedded in this statement is a point that is easily overlooked: for Kierkegaard and Barth alike, the emphasis on the infinite qualitative difference is not simply intended to stress humanity's inability to relate themselves to God. Instead, a critical purpose of it was to draw attention to the one mediator in

---

derichs, 1905]); *The Moment* (*Der Augenblick*, trans. Christoph Schrempf, 2nd ed. [Jena: Diederichs, 1909]); and *Practice in Christianity* (*Einübung in Christentum*, trans. Hermann Gottsched and Christoph Schrempf [Jena: Diederichs, 1912]).

31. Barrett, "Karl Barth," 11. We do know that the later Barth engages directly with *Works of Love*; see Barth, *Church Dogmatics* I/2, 385–86, where he references Søren Kierkegaard, *Works of Love*, ed. and trans. Howard V. Hong and Edna H. Hong (Princeton: Princeton University Press, 1995), 24–25.

32. *Karl Barth–Rudolf Bultmann Letters, 1922–1966*, ed. Bernd Jaspert and Geoffrey W. Bromiley (Grand Rapids: Eerdmans, 1981), 155.

33. Written in the preface to the second edition of Barth, *Romans II*, 10.

and through whom God makes it possible for persons to participate in right relationship with God: Jesus Christ through the power of the Holy Spirit. Accordingly, T. F. Torrance writes:

> What interested Barth in Kierkegaard's teaching was the emphasis upon the explosive force that the invasion of God in his Godness into time and human existence meant, which Kierkegaard sought to express by the paradox and dialectic. This is a point that has often been misunderstood in both Kierkegaard and Barth—for the emphasis upon the infinite qualitative difference between time and eternity . . . was not upon some abstract and distant Deity, but precisely upon the nearness, the impact of God in all his Majesty and Godness upon man—that is the significance of Jesus that had been lost, and which Barth as well as Kierkegaard sought to recover.[34]

While it would have been more accurate for Torrance to suggest that the emphasis on the infinite qualitative difference set the stage for Kierkegaard's and Barth's emphasis on the nearness of God in Christ, the point he is trying to make is correct. As we shall see, their commitment to the infinite qualitative difference was accompanied by a handful of other concepts that Barth picked up from Kierkegaard which had a more Christocentric focus: "the divine incognito," "paradox," "the moment," and "offense."

As we have mentioned, one of the main criticisms that Barth had of Kierkegaard was that his theology was overly pietistic and existentialist. Ironically, these criticisms could have been addressed if Barth had developed a better understanding of the very Kierkegaardian concepts that Barth embraced. While it is true that Kierkegaard stressed the importance of an authentic Christian life, this emphasis was undergirded by a deep appreciation for the grace of God, especially as it is revealed in Jesus Christ. Kierkegaard's references to "the divine incognito," "paradox," "the moment," and "offense" sought to stress the limitations of human

---

34. Thomas F. Torrance, *Karl Barth: An Introduction to His Early Theology, 1910–31* (London: SCM, 1962), 44. Torrance also notes that Barth was deeply indebted "to Kierkegaard's attack upon all direct communication." *Karl Barth*, 44. While Torrance makes a fair point here, it is an overstatement for him to add that "theologically and philosophically it was undoubtedly Kierkegaard who had the greatest impact upon him [Barth], far greater than the actual mentioning of his name, in the *Romans*, for example, indicates" (44). It is likely that Torrance's exaggeration was influenced by John Heywood Thomas's overestimation of Kierkegaard's influence on Barth's Christology in his essay "The Christology of Søren Kierkegaard and Karl Barth," *The Hibbert Journal* 53, no. 3 (April 1955): 280–88 (which Torrance had in his library).

understanding in order to deepen his readers' understanding of their need for God's grace; these concepts did not seek to turn individuals in upon themselves. Indeed, as we discuss in chapter 2, Kierkegaard interprets sin as a state of "in-closing reserve," a state of self-imprisonment in which the sinner "holds himself captive."[35] Moreover, this state of sin is addressed by a person being delivered into a life of faith in which he rests transparently in the power of God.[36]

"Subjectivity Is Truth"

Another contributing factor to Barth's critique of Kierkegaard was his super-ficial interpretation of the Kierkegaardian statement "subjectivity is truth." In a 1944 letter to Helene Barth, he writes, "I had to understand Jesus Christ and bring him from the periphery of my thought to the centre. Because I cannot regard subjectivity as being truth, after a brief encounter I have had to move away from Kierkegaard again."[37] By rejecting Kierkegaard on this issue, Barth joins the vast cohort of thinkers who misunderstand him.[38] What Kierkegaard—or, more accurately, his non-Christian pseudonym,[39] Johannes Climacus—is trying to communicate with the statement "subjectivity is truth" is a conviction that, because our internal perception of reality is the best we have to go by, we have no other option than to operate with our own beliefs.[40]

35. Søren Kierkegaard, *The Sickness unto Death: A Christian Psychological Exposition for Upbuilding and Awakening*, ed. and trans. Howard V. Hong and Edna H. Hong (Princeton: Princeton University Press, 1980), 63; Søren Kierkegaard, *Philosophical Fragments*, in *"Philosophical Fragments" and "Johannes Climacus,"* ed. and trans. Howard V. Hong and Edna H. Hong (Princeton: Princeton University Press, 1985), 17.

36. Kierkegaard, *Sickness unto Death*, 131.

37. Quoted in Busch, *Karl Barth*, 173.

38. Notably, in 1924 Barth shows an appreciation for Kierkegaard's view that "the subjec-tive is the objective." Karl Barth, *The Göttingen Dogmatics: Instruction in the Christian Reli-gion*, trans. Geoffrey W. Bromiley, ed. Hannelotte Reiffen (Grand Rapids: Eerdmans, 1991), 137, referencing *Concluding Unscientific Postscript* in Søren Kierkegaard, *Philosophische Brocken / Abschließende unwissenschaftliche Nachschrift*, ed. and trans. Hermann Gottsched and Christoph Schrempf (Jena: Diederichs, 1910), vols. 6–7, in *Gesammelte Werke*, 12 vols., ed. and trans. Hermann Gottsched and Christoph Schrempf (Jena: Diederichs, 1909–1922), 265–323. Also, in 1962 Barth comments that Kierkegaard's statement "subjectivity is truth . . . is at the very least open to misunderstanding." Barth, *Evangelical Theology: An Introduction* (London: Weidenfeld and Nicolson, 1963), 82.

39. We discuss Kierkegaard's pseudonymous authorship at the end of chapter 1.

40. See Søren Kierkegaard, *Kierkegaard's Journals and Notebooks*, ed. Niels Jørgen Cap-pelørn, Alastair Hannay, David Kangas, Bruce H. Kirmmse, George Pattison, Vanessa Rum-ble, and K. Brian Söderquist (Princeton: Princeton University Press, 2007–2020), 6:322.

But the fact that we cannot transcend our own subjectivity in order to know with pure objectivity (i.e., nonsubjectively) does not commit us to a Cartesian strategy of hyperbolic doubt. Instead, the Christian is called to place her faith in Christ, with a trust and a hope that, in Christ, God is at work in her life. If the Christian is not willing to "internalize" her faith in Christ, then Christianity is no longer possible.[41] Yet, in so doing, the Christian must believe that her faith is not simply a product of her own belief-forming imagination but is grounded in the reality of Christ;[42] she is called to believe that she cannot believe without the one in whom she believes. Without Christ, she can only generate unchristian beliefs.[43] Barth affirms precisely this point in 1928 when he writes: "That my faith is accepted as true faith is something again I can only believe—believe as I believe in the miracle of the divine mercy."[44]

There is more to say about the phrase "subjectivity is truth." As Eberhard Jüngel points out, the statement must be interpreted dialectically with Kierkegaard's further statement that "subjectivity is untruth."[45] For Kierkegaard, the suggestion that "I live" a Christian life needs to be qualified retrospectively by the statement "yet not I but Christ in me."[46] It is only in and through a

---

41. Søren Kierkegaard, *Concluding Unscientific Postscript to Philosophical Fragments*, ed. and trans. Howard V. Hong and Edna H. Hong (Princeton: Princeton University Press, 1992), 1:335-36.

42. Struggling with this paradox himself, Kierkegaard writes, "If I consider my own personal life, am I thus a Christian or is my personal existence not a purely poet-existence, with even an element of something demonic . . . perhaps, because it might turn out that I didn't become a Christian after all." Søren Kierkegaard, *Søren Kierkegaard's Journals and Papers*, ed. and trans. Howard V. Hong and Edna H. Hong, asst. Gregor Malantschuk (Bloomington: Indiana University Press, 1967-1978), 6:6431.

43. In this way, Christians are confined to the same way of life as every other subjective human being. But what distinguishes them, as Ingolf Dalferth points out, "is due not to what they do but to how they relate to what is done to them." Dalferth, "Becoming a Christian according to the *Postscript*: Kierkegaard's Christian Hermeneutics of Existence," in *Kierkegaard Studies Yearbook 1999*, ed. N. J. Cappelørn and H. Deuser (Berlin: Walter de Gruyter, 2005), 274.

44. Barth, *Ethics*, 103. Barth also writes, "There is no visible sanctification of man; no sanctification which can be seen, proved or measured; none which does not have to be *believed*." Karl Barth, "Church and Culture," in *Theology and Church: Shorter Writings, 1920-1928*, trans. Louise Pettibone Smith (London: SCM, 1926), 345.

45. Eberhard Jüngel, "Von der Dialektik zur Analogie: Die Schule Kierkegaards und der Einspruch Petersons," in *Barth-Studien* (Zurich: Benziger Verlag, 1982), 168-69.

46. See Søren Kierkegaard, *Christian Discourses*, in *"Christian Discourses" and "The Crisis and a Crisis in the Life of an Actress,"* ed. and trans. Howard V. Hong and Edna H. Hong (Princeton: Princeton University Press, 1997), 261; Kierkegaard, *Journals and Papers*, 4:3956.

relationship with the person of Jesus Christ—"the way, and the truth, and the life"—that a person can relate to the Truth of the Christian faith. This is not to suggest that Kierkegaard is contradicting himself. Without giving some kind of credence to the notion that subjectivity is truth, we are not able to believe that God is enabling us to relate faithfully to God; we are not able to be lifted beyond the suspicion that our faithful relationship with God is just another delusion of our subjectivity.

Kierkegaard's affirmation that "subjectivity is untruth" marks an appreciation of precisely the point Barth was making when he rejected the statement "subjectivity is truth." For Kierkegaard, becoming a Christian does not involve merely the inward transformation of our knowing; it involves reconciliation into a relationship with the Truth, into a relationship with the true God who defines who we truly are. This means that becoming a Christian is not grounded in a person's subjective relationship to God per se but, rather, in *God's* active relationship to that person, mediated in and through the God-human. Kierkegaard's Christian pseudonym Anti-Climacus writes:

> That the human race is supposed to be in kinship with God is ancient paganism; but *that* an individual human being is God is Christianity, and this particular human being is the God-man.[47]

As we argue in this book, both Kierkegaard and Barth are at pains to challenge the idealist and humanist visions of Christianity as defined by a society's immanent understanding of God.[48] They both seek to challenge the temptation to believe that we can talk about God without God, reducing God to the immanent realm of finite human understanding and language—a move that enables "God" to become a plaything to be employed for our own human agendas.[49] As we shall also see, however, Kierkegaard's and Barth's appreciation of the infinite

47. Kierkegaard, *Practice in Christianity*, 82; see also Kierkegaard, *Journals and Papers*, 4:4315; Kierkegaard, *Sickness unto Death*, 117, 126.

48. As Kevin Hector writes, "Since God is infinite, boundless, measureless, and so on, . . . concepts cannot possibly be applied to God without cutting God down to their size—without turning God into 'God,' in other words." Hector, *Theology without Metaphysics: God, Language, and the Spirit of Recognition* (Cambridge: Cambridge University Press, 2011), 49.

49. For Barth (and the same can be said for Kierkegaard), as John B. Webster notes, "the crucible for language about God is not its cultural or religious *use* nor willed or unconscious acts of *projection*, but *revelation*." Webster then notes, "Instead of human language reaching after its object, . . . revelation 'commandeers' language, *making* it into a fit instrument for God's self-articulation." Webster, *Barth's Ethics of Reconciliation* (Cambridge: Cambridge University Press, 1995), 179–80.

qualitative difference between God and humanity is held together with a concern to stress the reality of the union or kinship that God graciously establishes with humanity. They do not seek to challenge anthropocentric approaches by advancing the formula "*Gott Alles, der Mensch Nichts*" ("God everything and man nothing")—which Barth affirms is "not merely a 'shocking simplification' but complete nonsense."[50] For both, the distinction between God and humanity must always be accompanied by an understanding of God's affirmation of humanity in the God-human Jesus Christ. But on this point there is a slight parting of the ways between Kierkegaard and the later Barth. On the one hand, Kierkegaard refers to the disjunction between God and humanity in order to draw attention to the unique God-human in whom we are united with God. For Kierkegaard, by looking to Jesus Christ, we become free from any anxiety we might have over the division between humanity and God. Barth, on the other hand, starts with the unity that is in Jesus Christ, and he does so in a way that tells us from the outset that we do not need to worry about the disunity.

Many of the differences between Kierkegaard and Barth are rooted in their holding quite different theological views on a number of matters. However, their differences are also often rooted in context. As such, both need to be interpreted in light of the fact that they were developing their theologies within quite different contexts, with different concerns, and with subsequently different takes on how best to address their respective audiences. This is not to suggest that either of them was relativistic in their theology, but to recognize that they both approached the task of theology in an act of witness that would speak to and challenge the particular theological situations in which they found themselves. Accordingly, it is necessary to attend to the historical and theological concerns that motivated these two thinkers in their authorship. We shall now introduce some of these concerns in preparation for the deeper discussion that will unfold over the course of this book.

A Comparative Introduction to the Theological Projects of Kierkegaard and Barth

Kierkegaard and Barth stood as forces against the cultural endeavor to wed Christianity to the bankrupt agendas of this sinful world[51]—whether those

---

50. Barth, *Church Dogmatics* IV/1, 89.

51. The unity between them was acknowledged by Barth in his appreciation for "Kierkegaard's protest against *Weltkirchlichkeit* [worldly churchiness]." Barth, *Barth–Thurneysen Correspondence*, 1:336.

of the Danish government and bourgeois society, or of the National Socialist movement in Nazi Germany.[52] For both of them, this endeavor was undergirded by Christian leaders accommodating Christianity to the variety of idealisms, romanticisms, and post-Enlightenment humanisms that had become in vogue— each of which exalted the powers of immanent human reason over and above the reality of the eternal God. In stark contrast, Kierkegaard and Barth placed the reality of God in Jesus Christ at the center of their theologies. Although they did this in very different ways, both their approaches served to challenge the exaltation of corrupt human agendas and the abuse of religion to which it led.

In what ways were their approaches different? Kierkegaard's Christian ethic was concerned with the fact that we cannot move beyond our own subjective sphere of existence, a concern that prompts him to provide a more existentially concerned response to the question of what it means to be a Christian. To an extent, this meant taking our immediate context more seriously, albeit without neglecting the fact that we live our lives before God. For example, there are points where he deems it helpful to discuss the psychology of what it means to be a disciple of Christ in this world, and there are times when he elaborates on how the Christian life-view is relatively distinct from secular life-views. This does not mean, however, that he averts his attention from the priority of grace, which, he believes, is constantly at work in the world enabling Christians to share in a faithful relationship with God.

Barth's Christian ethic, however, was less accommodating to our immediate perspective. He continually returns to the question of what it means to be a human who is created by the triune God and elected in Jesus Christ. As John Webster writes, "Barth's ethics tends to assume that moral problems are resolv-

---

52. Questioning the use of the term "Christian" as an adjective, Barth asks, "What is meant by Christian worldview, Christian morality, Christian art? What, then, is meant by such phrases as 'Christian' view of the universe, 'Christian' morality, 'Christian' art? What are 'Christian' personalities, 'Christian' families, 'Christian' groups, 'Christian' newspapers, 'Christian' societies, endeavours and institutions? Who gives us permission to use this predicate so profusely?" He then asks, "Ought not a serious consideration of the office of the Holy Spirit to the pardoned sinner to have this small result, at least, namely: to make it more difficult in the future for such an adjective as this to drip from our lips and our pen?" Barth, *The Holy Spirit and the Christian Life: The Theological Basis of Ethics*, trans. R. Birch Hoyle (Louisville: Westminster/John Knox Press, 1993), 37–38; see also Barth, *Church Dogmatics* IV/2, 610. It was with this concern that Barth changed the title of *The Christian Dogmatics* to *The Church Dogmatics*. As he writes in the preface to *Church Dogmatics* I/1, "in substituting the word 'Church' for 'Christian' in the title, I have tried to set a good example of restraint in the lighthearted use of the great word 'Christian,' against which I have protested" (xiii, *Kirchliche Dogmatik* I/1, viii [translation revised]).

able by correct theological description of moral space. And such description involves much more than describing the moral consciousness of agents."[53] On the one hand, Barth focuses much more closely on a scriptural and creedal account of what it means to be human: to be someone who participates in Christ, by the power of the Holy Spirit, according to the will of the Father. On the other hand, he does not hesitate to apply what this means for our ethical lives in this world. This means taking seriously that the Christian is a self-determining human subject who is called to decide and act in obedience to God.

In short, whereas Kierkegaard is more concerned about what it means to exist as a Christian in this world, Barth is more concerned to consider what it means to be human in light of God's purposes, grounded in his understanding of who God is for us. Importantly, their different emphases are not mutually exclusive, and what will hopefully become clear is that both thinkers show a concern to steer between the Scylla of undermining the importance of human action (in this world) and the Charybdis of neglecting the grace of God. Yet Kierkegaard, faced with a situation in which utter passivity was embraced in the name of Christianity, was more concerned with Scylla; and Barth, facing a situation in which evil human action, or "militant godlessness," was being taken up in the name of Christianity, was more concerned with Charybdis. (Though this is not to suggest that Kierkegaard only faced the former problem, and Barth only faced the latter.) For us today, hearing from both thinkers provides us with a balanced guide for working our way between Scylla and Charybdis in a society where both Christian inactivity and evil human activity are commonplace problems.

In the rest of this section, we shall elaborate briefly on this initial comparison. By so doing, we will introduce their respective theological projects, in relation to one another, in preparation for the more in-depth examination that this book will offer.

An Introductory Note on Kierkegaard's Theological Project

Bruce McCormack asserts that "Kierkegaard's primary theological orientation was towards the problem of how revelation is subjectively appropriated by the

---

53. Webster, *Barth's Ethics*, 2. Webster continues: "A Christianly successful moral ontology must be a depiction of the world of human action as it is enclosed and governed by the creative, redemptive, and sanctifying work of God in Christ, present in the power of the Holy Spirit. Consequently, such an ontology is not centred on the human agent, and especially not on moral reflectivity."

individual."[54] In some respects, this is a fair assessment of Kierkegaard, who writes:

> My whole authorship pertains to Christianity, to the issue: becoming a Christian, with direct and indirect polemical aim at that enormous illusion, Christendom, or the illusion that in such a country all are Christians of sorts.[55]

Deeply perturbed by the situation of Danish Christendom, Kierkegaard saw it as his calling to "attempt to introduce Christianity into Christendom—but, please note, 'poetically, without authority.'"[56] The qualification that Kierkegaard makes here is important for understanding his authorship and is one that is often neglected. Kierkegaard was acutely aware that he was without authority in his authorship. He did not for a moment believe it was within his power to reveal the truth of the gospel and awaken persons to follow Christ.[57] He knew very well that the question of how humans appropriate the truth of revelation is beyond human comprehension and is a matter to be entrusted to the mysterious grace of God.[58] He was also adamant that grace should not be

---

54. Bruce L. McCormack, *Karl Barth's Critically Realistic Dialectical Theology: Its Genesis and Development, 1909–1936* (Oxford: Clarendon, 1995), 237–38. We would suggest that this issue is perhaps better understood as "Kierkegaard's primary theological concern"—a concern that arises *out of* his primary theological orientation toward the God revealed in Jesus Christ.

55. Kierkegaard, *Point of View*, 23.

56. Kierkegaard, *Journals and Papers*, 6:6317. Kierkegaard continues: "I am no apostle, I am a poetic-dialectical genius, personally and religiously a penitent." He also writes in another journal entry: "I was bound to the idea of trying to introduce Christianity into Christendom, albeit poetically and without authority (namely, not making myself a missionary)" (Kierkegaard, *Journals and Papers*, 6:6356); see also Kierkegaard, *Point of View*, 42, 123–24; Søren Kierkegaard, *The Moment*, in *"The Moment" and Late Writings*, ed. and trans. Howard V. Hong and Edna H. Hong (Princeton: Princeton University Press, 1998), 106–7.

57. To be clear, Kierkegaard understood that he was without authority both because he was never officially ordained in the Lutheran Church and also because he did not have the theological authority to reveal the truth of the gospel.

58. It is thus too simplistic for Niels Hansen Søe to write "Barth chooses to regard the matter 'theologically' and therefore speaks of God's free grace and of our constant dependence upon it. Kierkegaard, on the other hand, chooses to speak from a 'psychological' point of view and therefore dwells on man's 'passion' and his need to venture far out where reason is beyond its depth and where everything must be risked—where nothing is guaranteed or even regarded by 'probabilities.'" Here, Søe does not represent the decisively Christian element in Kierkegaard's thought. Søe, "Kierkegaard's Doctrine of the Paradox," trans. Margaret Grieve, in *A Kierkegaard Critique: An International Selection of Essays Inter-*

introduced "*as a matter of course*"—a mere step in the process of coming to faith—"which, after all, means that it [grace] is taken in vain."[59]

For Kierkegaard, when it comes to the question of how a person becomes a Christian in response to God's revelation, there is little more to say than that a person comes to faith when God mysteriously delivers her into fellowship with Godself, in and through the presence of God's Son, Jesus Christ. Yet he does show a certain concern for how a person appropriates revelation—but not in a way to which Barth is altogether allergic. Barth does not believe that the human appropriates revelation by God's simply cranking a person's cognitive faculties into gear. Indeed, there are several instances in which Barth—at least in the *Church Dogmatics*—acknowledges the role of the human subject "positing itself" (Barth uses "*selbst gesetzte*," "*selbst begriffen*," and "*Sichselbstsetzen*") in relationship with God.[60] For Barth, there is a rational human response to revelation that requires human action and reflection. Kierkegaard agrees. Neither believes that the Christian faith is a mere extension of divine action. For both, we are called to think and act as Christians by engaging with Scripture (as human subjects and agents), and doing so in the prayerful expectation that God is with us in our learning.

As we shall consider in chapter 1, it was the state of play in Lutheran Denmark that inspired Kierkegaard to stress the role that human reflection, decision, and action have in the Christian life. How did he stress these aspects? By redescribing what Christianity is (i.e., what Christianity should look like in this world), he set out to tell those in the established church that Christianity is not something that we should allow to be diluted by the ways of the world. As such, he sought to challenge Christians to reflect over and realize what they were proclaiming. This did not mean judging society, nor did it mean awakening or inspiring it; it simply meant proclaiming what Christianity is. He writes:

> "*Without authority*" **to make aware** of the religious, the essentially Christian, is the category for my whole work as an author regarded as a totality. From the very beginning I have enjoined and repeated unchanged that I was "without authority."[61]

preting Kierkegaard, ed. Howard A. Johnson and Niels Thulstrup (Chicago: Henry Regnery Company, 1962), 222–23.

59. Kierkegaard, *Point of View*, 16 (emphasis original).

60. See Barth, *Church Dogmatics* III/2, 195–96; III/4, 470.

61. Kierkegaard, *Point of View*, 12; see also 6n, 78, 87 (bold original).

Never have I fought in such a way that I have said: I am the true Christian; the others are not Christians, or probably even hypocrites and the like. No, I have fought in this way: *I know what Christianity is*; I myself acknowledge my defects as a Christian—but I do know what Christianity is. And to know this thoroughly seems in the interest of every human being, whether one is now a Christian or a non-Christian, whether one's intention is to accept Christianity or abandon it. But I have attacked no one, saying that he is not a Christian; I have passed judgement on no one.[62]

By seeking to redescribe what Christianity is, Kierkegaard was not under the impression that God needed a hand in Denmark.[63] But he did believe that God created humans to play a critical role in the Christian life. Consequently, he saw it as his calling to tell persons what the Christian life entailed and, furthermore, to upbuild them in their discipleship.

An Introductory Note on Barth's Theological Project

At the heart of Barth's theology is "the simple statement": "*Gott ist*" ("God is").[64] Barth's commitment to the statement did not, however, lead him to devote his attention primarily to who God is in Godself—who God is *in se*, as a perfect, eternal, transcendent being. Rather, he sought to draw our attention to *the triune God who is made known through God's incarnate Word, who is experienced through the presence of the Holy Spirit, and who is attested by Scripture.*

There are two things to acknowledge with regard to this italicized statement. First, Barth does not believe that we encounter God simply by reading Scripture. Scripture is not the literal embodiment of God's Word (in the way that Christ is), nor can its words directly represent God. For Barth, a person can only consciously encounter God by reading Scripture if God speaks to

---

62. Kierkegaard, *Point of View*, 15 (emphasis original); see also 16–20, 268. Kierkegaard also denies, contrary to Barth's critique of him, that he has ever attempted to be pietistically rigorous in his description of Christianity. Kierkegaard, *Point of View*, 17; see Barth, *Church Dogmatics* I/1, 20; II/2, 308; III/2, 21; IV/1, 150, 741; IV/3, 498.

63. We might add here that while Kierkegaard is primarily concerned with challenging the "Christian state" in Denmark, he also sees his attack on Danish Christendom as a starting point for "bursting open" the issue of what it means to be a Christian to the Christendom he "sees all over Europe." Kierkegaard, *Journals and Papers*, 6:6444.

64. Barth, *Church Dogmatics* II/1, 257, *Kirchliche Dogmatik* II/1, 288 (emphasis in the original German text).

her through *the medium of* Scripture, enabling her to begin to perceive it as a true witness to God's revelation. He insists, with Kierkegaard, that a person cannot come to know God merely by grappling with scriptural texts. Reading Scripture might enable one to learn many things, but unless God encounters a person in her learning, she will not become receptive to the reality of God and will only be able to form an understanding of others' thoughts about God. That God's immanence to creation cannot be known directly by human reason, in and of itself, was central to Barth's theology, and, as this book will argue, there are good reasons to believe that Kierkegaard influenced Barth's commitment to this point.

Second, Barth does not believe that we can simply learn about God by encountering God spiritually. The nature of a person's encounter with God is fuzzy to say the least. And because it is a spiritual encounter, it is all too easily blurred with ideas that we form in the realm of our imagination, which is why it is so easy for God to be reduced to a figment of our imagination. Yet, for Barth, this difficulty should not lead us into a state of despair in which we constantly question whether we ever actually encounter God. Barth is a positive theologian—particularly in his later writings—who constantly stresses that God is with us and for us, in Jesus Christ and by the Holy Spirit. Accordingly, he sought to inspire confidence that our faith in God is genuine and, moreover, that we can expect that God is really working with us in our lives—freely and constantly, albeit unpredictably and ambiguously. Nonetheless, the unpredictable and ambiguous nature of God's spiritual communication means that we cannot take the liberty of turning to our own minds—to our own "spirituality"—to know God. We must come to know God in the sphere of the church, where Holy Scripture is studied and proclaimed as the Word of God.

Barth's specific commitment to these two points about what it means to know God was in many respects motivated by his opposition to the kind of liberal, neo-Protestant theology of *Kulturprotestantismus*, which, he believed, opened the doors for the German Christian movement to attach itself to the Nazi regime.[65] That is, he was driven by a resistance to the politically dangerous theology that elevated human ideals over and above God's self-revelation.[66] When Barth sought to draw attention back to God, he made it

65. See Karl Barth, *Theological Existence Today! A Plea for Theological Freedom*, trans. R. Birch Hoyle (London: Hodder and Stoughton, 1933), 66; Barth, *Church Dogmatics* IV/3, 120–21.

66. The weakness and danger of this theology were epitomized for Barth on the infamous "black day" in October 1914 when "almost all" of Barth's theological teachers whom he "greatly venerated" signed up to Wilhelm II's war policy. "In despair," Barth writes,

clear that the world is not a place for God to be tamed. He is adamant that there is no room for tying God to society's own agendas. Yet this did not mean that he drew attention away from the importance of human thought and decision per se. In a lecture from 1939, in a passage that Kierkegaard would have warmly embraced, Barth remarks:

> We stand today in horror before the phenomenon of Europe, as so-called Christian Europe, which is threatened with the loss of its humanity. The problem lies not with those forces which would take its humanity away and would lead it to chaos. The problem lies in the fact that Europe has chosen not to decide, that it does not dare to choose and thereby has chosen evil, which means it has chosen inhumanity. But honest choice and decision, and thus a decision for humanity, exist only as a decision of faith, and the decision of faith, in turn, exists only under the sovereignty of God's Word. How has it come about that Europe has not been better instructed by the Christian church concerning the sovereignty of God's Word, and *thereby* seems to know so little of the sovereignty of God's Word? And therefore itself too little of the decision of faith? It is more essential than ever, for the sake of the Church of Jesus Christ as well as the just State, to ask, seek, and knock: *Veni creator spiritus!*[67]

It is noteworthy that Barth does not simply stress the role of human decision and action but also turns to the work of the Holy Spirit. He genuinely believed that if the Spirit is working in persons' lives, inspiring them to become faithful followers of Christ, then they will not be willing to commit crimes against humanity. Again, this belief did not lead him to overestimate our ability to read the work of the Spirit; he knew all too well how easy it is to confuse the work of the Holy Spirit with our own immanent spiritualities. As such, Barth also stresses that Christian decision and action must arise out of a prayerful engagement with Scripture, in the sphere of the "Confessing Church,"[68] and,

---

"I could not any longer follow either their ethics and dogmatics or their understanding of the Bible and of history." Barth, "Evangelical Theology in the 19th Century," 12–13; see also Busch, *Karl Barth*, 81–83.

67. Barth, "The Sovereignty of God's Word and the Decision of Faith," in *God Here and Now*, trans. Paul M. van Buren (London: Routledge & Kegan Paul, 1964), 26–27 (emphasis original); see also Barth, *Christian Life*, 182–83.

68. Barth contrasts the living congregations of the "Confessing Church" with the dead congregations of the "apparent Church," associating the latter with the established church of "the so-called 'German Christians' who co-operated with the Nazi government under

in particular, must arise from a devotion to the revelation of God's Word in Jesus Christ. Under these circumstances, Barth is happy to recognize the more existential side of the Christian life, particularly in his earlier works.[69] For example, in his lectures published in *Ethics* (1928), he provides the following definition of faith (one that would become scarce in his later works):

> With Luther we thus define faith as the trust and venture of the *heart* in relation to God, i.e., a trust and venture in which the center of our being is put in question and compromised, in which we exist, in which we must release and surrender and hazard no less than ourselves, letting God be in our heart and expecting all good things from him.[70]

As Wolf Krötke notes, "Barth greatly emphasized th[e] element of the independence of the human being, an independence that finds expression in an individual's own perceiving, thinking, willing, desiring, and active existence."[71] By acknowledging the role of the active individual, Barth, like Kierkegaard, was able to provide a further barrier against *Kulturprotestantismus*.[72] Yet, in contrast to Kierkegaard, this did not inspire him to focus on the psychological and existential dimensions of the Christian life in order to provide an account that is more directly applicable to human existence.[73] Barth was highly critical of (what he saw as) the Kierkegaardian focus on the "question of the individual experience of grace, . . . the question of individual conversion by it and to it, and of its

---

Hitler." Barth, "The Church," in *God Here and Now*, trans. Paul M. van Buren (London: Routledge & Kegan Paul, 1964), 74.

69. See Barth, *Ethics*, 16–17.

70. Barth, *Ethics*, 252–53 (emphasis original).

71. Wolf Krötke, "The Humanity of the Human Person in Karl Barth's Anthropology," trans. Philip G. Ziegler, in *The Cambridge Companion to Karl Barth*, ed. John Webster (Cambridge: Cambridge University Press, 2000), 170. As such, Krötke notes, "Every human being must be regarded as distinctive and unsubstitutable in the eyes of God and other people. A human being is never merely one number among many and may never be degraded into a mere object that others can treat like a thing." It is in the context of this understanding, he continues, that Barth makes his "strong statements about the capacity of the human person to encounter God, to hear him, and to answer him" (170).

72. See Barth, *Christian Life*, 182–204.

73. Barth does show a cautious appreciation for psychology in his *Ethics*, remarking that "the ethical question cannot in fact be asked without some attention being paid to the constancies of human behavior which the other sciences [psychology, cultural history, and jurisprudence] investigate." *Ethics*, 5. However, this appreciation has very much faded by the time we get to the *Church Dogmatics*.

presuppositions and consequences."[74] The result of this focus, for Barth, "was that the great concepts of justification and sanctification came more and more to be understood and filled out psychologically and biographically, and the doctrine of the Church seemed to be of value only as a description of the means of salvation and grace indispensable to this individual and personal process of salvation."[75] The reason for this, according to Barth, is that anthropology must start not with our immediate experience of being human but with the person of Jesus Christ, in whom we are elected to be human. As he stresses, "anthropological definition gains content only from the theological definition."[76]

> The reason why the theological definition of faith is so decisively important, and the reason why the decisive thing must be put here in Trinitarian formulae, is that everything depends on *God* being present where there is this trust and venture of the heart. This alone will prevent faith from being ontologically an illusion or a leap in the dark, even though phenomenologically it might and must seem to take this form. Faith is not irrational staggering but well-considered walking with unheard-assurance. Where faith is in God, there, as the trust and venture of the heart in and with the full surrender with which this is linked, and also in the uncertainty which is characteristic of this human action as it is of all others, faith takes place, so far as its object is concerned, with the firmness which is given by this object, with a certainty as hard as steel. Where there is faith, what is believed is that the Word has been spoken to us and that we have let it be spoken to us by the Spirit.[77]

To conclude our introductory comparison, how might we summarize the differences between Kierkegaard and Barth in preparation for the more in-depth comparison that will be offered over the course of this book? In the above passage, Barth emphasizes the assuredness, firmness, and certainty that characterizes the Christian faith, albeit while acknowledging the uncertainty that humans experience. What is the basis for Barth's confidence? His confidence is grounded in his theological commitment, *first*, to who God is for us in Christ, by the power of the Holy Spirit, and, *second*, to who we are in light of the fact that God is for us. In comparison to Kierkegaard, Barth is less interested in

---

74. Barth, *Church Dogmatics* IV/3, 150. Elsewhere, Barth is critical of Kierkegaard for his "ethical individualism" (*Christian Life*, 183) and "pronounced holy individualism" ("Thank You and a Bow," 99).

75. Barth, *Church Dogmatics* IV/3, 150.

76. Barth, *Ethics*, 253.

77. Barth, *Ethics*, 253.

the uncertainties of human faith and more focused on the concrete ways in which God is for us, based on *an objective theological perspective grounded in revelation and informed by Scripture*, whereas Kierkegaard's theology is more concerned about *the subjective human perspective of who we are before God*, albeit in a way that is grounded in his understanding of the Christian life as portrayed in Scripture. For Kierkegaard, this meant paying greater attention to the limitations, suffering, and uncertainty that Christians should expect as they struggle to live in tension with the sinful ways of the world.

Having offered this introductory comparison, we should qualify that the distinctions we have drawn here are far less clear-cut than our summary might suggest. As we unpack the nuances of their respective positions, we will find that the differences between them are far more complicated than any sketch can show. For example, we will find that there are many ways in which Kierkegaard emphasizes an objective theological perspective of who we are before God, grounded in revelation and informed by Scripture. And we will also find that there are many times when Barth (especially the early Barth) is highly attentive to a subjective human perspective of who we are before God, bound by uncertainty. So the general comparison that we have just offered will, at times, be questioned by some of what we have to say over the course of the book as a whole.

OVERVIEW OF CHAPTERS

In chapter 1, we begin with an account of the philosophical, theological, and contextual backdrop to the theology of Kierkegaard, particularly those areas in his theology that would impact Barth. This will involve a focus on the Hegelian ideas that were so formative of the theological landscape in which Kierkegaard worked, especially those ideas that encouraged Christians to become caught up within their own immanent thought worlds and cultures. This chapter will conclude with a brief analysis of the particular approach Kierkegaard took to challenging Hegelian theology in Denmark, expanding on some of the points we will introduce at the end of this chapter.

Chapter 2 offers an extended analysis of some of the core ideas in Kierkegaard's theology that he developed over against the Hegelian approaches that concerned him, especially those relating to creation and Christology. More specifically, we focus on some of the key theological concepts that would be picked up by Barth—such as "the infinite qualitative difference," "the divine incognito," "offense," "paradox," and "the moment." However, we will also paint a picture of their broader theological context which is critical to understanding the Kierkegaardian concepts that Barth employed. In so doing, we will offer a more accurate account of these concepts in Kierkegaard's thought than Barth was ever able to appreciate. This will enable us to show that Barth's perception of the weaknesses in Kierkegaard's theology in many respects missed the mark, and that Kierkegaard's views were actually much closer to Barth's theology than Barth realized.

Chapter 3 examines the religious, philosophical, sociocultural, and intellectual challenges that Barth faced. This exposes the stark parallels between the dynamics that Barth addressed and those to which Kierkegaard responded. We consider the impact of idealism on theology and, in particular, the interpretation of Christology as exemplified by David Friedrich Strauss's myth theory and Rudolf Bultmann's program of demythologizing. The chapter falls into three parts. The first discusses Barth's interpretation and critique of the impact of the Enlightenment on the church. The second looks at the failure of the church to recognize and address the dangers of cultural Protestantism and nationalism. The third considers the profound theological influence that the monist idealism of Barth's Neo-Kantian teachers in Marburg had on the shape of theology, an influence which was reflected in the thought of Rudolf Bultmann.

Chapter 4 considers the implications of Barth's approach which, like Kierkegaard's, is grounded in the recognition of the kinship or fellowship that God has established with humanity in time. For Barth, this generates a "turnabout" that stands to deliver the church and theology from those elements, stemming from the Enlightenment, which allow religion to acquiesce in and even endorse the kinds of oppressive cultural and political dynamics witnessed during the twentieth century. The chapter goes on to outline Barth's vision of theology when it has been set free from enslavement to the intellectual and sociopolitical commitments of the culture. It then considers the implications of this for the shape of human existence. Again, Barth's approach here is seen to develop a trajectory that reflects Kierkegaard's own vision.

In chapter 5, we focus on some of the particular ways in which Barth appropriated Kierkegaard's ideas in his earlier theology. We will draw particular attention to the concepts discussed in chapter 2. Additionally, we consider how Barth commandeered and developed these ideas in his own writings, particularly *Romans II*, using them in ways that went beyond Kierkegaard's use of them. In this chapter we also touch upon some of the reasons why Barth's early appreciation for Kierkegaard came to diminish.

Chapter 6 assesses the significance of Kierkegaard's and Barth's critique of immanentist approaches for the church's engagement with secular society. The focus of our discussion is the debate between Barth and Brunner on natural theology. This highlights a series of fundamentally important theological and methodological questions. On what grounds can there be shared sociopolitical and legislative decision-making between believers and nonbelievers? Is there a universal sense of God's moral and legal purpose that is presupposed by collaboration with secular society on matters of public policy? Does the outreach of the church presuppose universal "points of connection" between Christians and non-Christians? Brunner's utilization of natural theology to address these and related questions is explored at length. This leads us to engage a contemporary desire among Catholic and Reformed theologians to recover Brunner's insights in order to strengthen theology's engagement in the public square. In addition to evaluating the formal and material arguments used, we attend throughout the chapter to the potential of natural theology to serve politically harmful agendas. The discussion here makes reference to political developments in Nazi Germany, South Africa (during the apartheid years), and the "Deep South."

Our final chapter, entitled "Beyond Immanence," explores the key features that differentiate the "Kierkegaard-Barth trajectory" from theological approaches that operate along immanentist, "Socratic," or classical foundationalist lines. The chapter falls into three parts. The first examines Barth's account of how the language of finite, sinful human creatures can communicate the God who is infinitely qualitatively different from the created order. We consider Barth's interpretation of the divine initiative in this and his conception both of the form of the divine address and the means of its appropriation. This leads to an exploration of the Trinitarian nature of Barth's account of revelation and proclamation as the grounds of Christian God-talk. Given that the historical has decisive significance in Barth's account, this raises questions about the relationship between biblical scholarship, conceived as a historical discipline, and Christian theology. Specifically, we consider how to avoid the "theologistic fallacy" which constitutes a potential trap in any attempt to move from the conclusions of historical biblical scholarship to theological affirmation.

In the second part, we consider immanentist or idealist solutions to the problems raised above. In this connection, we revisit our discussion of Strauss and Bultmann and their perceptions of the gulf between historical statements and first-order theological statements—a gulf that shaped their differentiation between theology and mythology. This analysis not only highlights the stark contrast between their approach and that which characterized the Kierkegaard-Barth trajectory. It also spells out the full ramifications of their respective responses. We point out that far from the distinction between theology and mythology being a new discovery, this distinction stood at the heart of

Athanasius's Trinitarian account of hermeneutics—an account that prefigures the Kierkegaard-Barth approach.

The third and final part of the chapter asks about how the justification of theological beliefs and statements might be viewed and articulated by those holding to the Kierkegaard-Barth trajectory. Consequently, we explore the contribution of contemporary epistemological and semantic debates to attempts to move beyond immanentist and Socratic interpretations. This leads into a consideration of the relevance of recent philosophical insights for how we approach the role of history in theology. The chapter concludes with a discussion of the distinction between *de re* and *de dicto* beliefs, showing how the Kierkegaard-Barth trajectory opens the door to interpreting Christian theological beliefs and their attendant theological statements as *de re*. Fred Dretske's work on entitlement sheds light on how the Christian theologian might articulate within the public domain her entitlement to make the kinds of claims affirmed by both Kierkegaard and Barth.

KIERKEGAARD'S AUDIENCE AND APPROACH

Kierkegaard was an author of resistance, writing against those who sought a marriage between Christianity and the high culture of Danish society. In its bourgeois setting, Christian theology had become, in his view, little more than a form of knowledge-gathering that served to maintain the nominal Christian culture of the elite—a culture that had taken the divine into its possession and under its control. As such, Christianity had come to be identified with a cultural venture that was fixated on the compendium of Christian ideas, beliefs, images, and stories that gratified the Danish aesthetic.

In parallel with this, the Danish scholars of the Christian religion had devoted themselves to a form of "objective" scholarship that was not only removed from a life of faith but also actively encouraged such detachment. This scholarship aimed to distill the more "objectively certain" truths of Christianity by focusing on those truths that could be directly verified by empirical evidence—i.e., the empirical evidence that is directly accessible to us within the immanent frame of world-history. With this approach, for Kierkegaard, theology in Denmark was resisting its office as a form of faith seeking understanding, grounded in a subjective commitment to the transcendent God and expressed in a life of discipleship to Christ.

So, Kierkegaard was a contextual theologian, committed to helping society understand what it means to live before God. In this chapter, we shall paint a fuller picture of this context, especially as it was viewed by Kierkegaard. We begin with an introduction to his perception of the (overly) intimate relationship between Christianity and Danish society. We then survey some key themes in Georg Wilhelm Friedrich Hegel's thought, which undergirded Hegelian theology in Denmark. This will lead us into a specific discussion of the Danish theology of which Kierkegaard was so critical, particularly as it was advanced by Hans Lassen Martensen. In the final section, we give an overview of Kierkegaard's approach to challenging the problematic theology of his day. What we shall find in this chapter, and what will become clearer in the following chapter, is that Kierkegaard was committed to challenging those theologies that treated God as a being caught up in the immanence of this world as understood by human thought. It was the theology that accompanied this Kierkegaardian polemic that would go on to have a major impact on the early Barth.

A "Christian" Nation

In his time, Kierkegaard believed that the Danish Church had blurred the distinction between "Christianity" and Danish society. Nowhere was this more evident than in the rebranding of the State Church as the People's Church (*Folkekirke*).[1] With this development came the perception "that the people own the Church and, with it, God!"[2] Danish culture was shaping the "church" and "Christianity" for itself, thereby promoting "the delusion that the esthetic is the essentially Christian."[3] This led to what Kierkegaard describes as "the age of disintegration":[4]

> For many, many generations men have continually kept on trimming and reducing Christianity, made it milder and milder, more and more domesticated, until finally it is not Christianity at all. No wonder it is thought that Christianity must ultimately become identical with the world.

1. The term *Folkekirke* was firmly embraced and endorsed by Bishop Mynster, who writes, "We are happy . . . that we in this country dare call this church our People's Church. . . . Let us hold fast to the beautiful, living term 'People's Church'; it signifies that this is the Church to which the people cling, the Church whose confession is rooted in the people, the Church which is one of the strong bonds which holds the people together, and which connects the generations that follow with those that have gone before. Praise and thank God that we still have such a People's Church that holds together the vast preponderance of the people, so that those who deviate from it can quickly be added up. There are indeed people living among us who confess another faith . . . but everyone feels that they are in many respects guests and foreigners and that in essential ways they are not a part of our people." J. P. Mynster, *Prædikener holdte i Aarene 1846–1852: Sommer-Halvaaret*, 2nd ed. (Copenhagen: Gyldendal, 1854), 17–18, cited and translated by Bruce H. Kirmmse in "The Thunderstorm: Kierkegaard's Ecclesiology," *Faith and Philosophy* 17, no. 1 (2000): 88–89.

2. Kirmmse, "Thunderstorm," 88.

3. Kierkegaard, *The Point of View for My Work as an Author*, ed. and trans. Howard V. Hong and Edna H. Hong (Princeton: Princeton University Press, 1998), 54.

4. Søren Kierkegaard, *Søren Kierkegaard's Journals and Papers*, ed. and trans. Howard V. Hong and Edna H. Hong, asst. Gregor Malantschuk (Bloomington: Indiana University Press, 1967–1978), 6:6255.

Never in all eternity can Christianity become identical with the world. Christianity will never become identical with the world any more than the single individual's flesh and blood (natural drives, secular-mindedness) will ever as a matter of course ever [sic] become identical with the essentially Christian, so that the individual is perhaps born with self-renunciation instead of with flesh and blood (which on other grounds also would be nonsense, since self-renunciation presupposes something to fight against, specifically flesh and blood).

This everlasting nonsense about Christianity permeating the world more and more is a *quid pro quo*, a babbling of contradictions, for the truth of the matter is that the world is more and more wearing away and gnawing away the essentially Christian from Christianity.[5]

When Christianity became confused with the prevailing ideologies of his culture, ideas about God became merged with ideas about the world. Such confusion, for Kierkegaard, was fueled by the rise of Hegelianism in Denmark. For him, Hegel's philosophy emboldened society to act as though God belonged to creation, rather than the other way around. This freed up society to understand itself according to its own devices, thereby allowing it to make "God" in the image it made for itself. For Kierkegaard's Christian pseudonym Anti-Climacus (whom we shall discuss below), this "deification of the established order" meant, in fact, "the secularization of everything."[6]

How does one become a "Christian" in such a culture? According to such a cultural understanding, for Kierkegaard, it takes place at the beginning of a citizen's life; a person becomes a "Christian" *de nomine* by being baptized into the Danish Church as an infant. A person's "Christianity" is then sustained osmotically by attending church services on Sunday and being a member of the congregation. These activities themselves were taken to be sufficient to sustain persons in their faith. Consequently, Kierkegaard observed, there was no willingness to pursue a costly discipleship in response to the extreme demands of the New Testament. The result was that Danish Christianity became spiritless and apathetic, making very little difference to the lives of its adherents.

What made this situation particularly problematic, for Kierkegaard, is that the default ways of this world are not neutral with respect to Christianity. When the world goes off on its own trajectory, apart from God, it heads in a

---

5. Kierkegaard, *Journals and Papers*, 3:3334.
6. Søren Kierkegaard, *Practice in Christianity*, ed. and trans. Howard V. Hong and Edna H. Hong (Princeton: Princeton University Press, 1991), 91.

direction that is hostile to the truth of the gospel.[7] By contrast, when a person becomes a genuine witness to the Truth of Christianity, his or her life should be expected to renounce worldly ends and become characterized by suffering. As Kierkegaard writes:

> A truth-witness is a person who in poverty witnesses for the truth, in poverty [*sic*], in lowliness and abasement, is so unappreciated, hated, detested, so mocked, insulted, laughed to scorn—so poor that he perhaps has not always had daily bread, but he received the daily bread of persecution in abundance every day.[8]

Furthermore, for Kierkegaard, the idea that a person can be a Christian while embracing the baser pleasures of this world "is not only a monstrosity but an impossibility, like a bird that in addition is a fish, or an iron tool that in addition has the oddity of being made of wood."[9] To try to be a Christian under these circumstances is to pursue a life that is essentially unchristian.

Following this reasoning, and overstating matters in his own rhetorical way, Kierkegaard would often go so far as to question whether *anyone* in Denmark was a Christian. Paul Martens and Tom Millay set out the basic logic of this situation:

1. To be a Christian is to suffer for Christianity.
2. Nobody in Denmark is suffering for Christianity.
3. Therefore, nobody in Denmark is a Christian.[10]

While this logic is helpful, we should be wary of reading too much into point (1). Despite what some (or much) of Kierkegaard's rhetorical flourish

---

7. Søren Kierkegaard, *The Moment*, in *"The Moment" and Late Writings*, ed. and trans. Howard V. Hong and Edna H. Hong (Princeton: Princeton University Press, 1998), 11.

8. Kierkegaard, *Moment*, 5.

9. Kierkegaard, *Moment*, 11. This point was made in response to Professor Hans Lassen Martensen's claim that Bishop Mynster should be remembered "as one of the authentic truth-witnesses" (Kierkegaard, *Moment*, 3). For Kierkegaard, Mynster was "to a high degree . . . worldly-sagacious, but weak, self-indulgent, and great only as a declaimer" (*Moment*, 8).

10. Paul Martens and Tom Millay, "'The Changelessness of God' as Kierkegaard's Final Theodicy: God and the Gift of Suffering," *International Journal of Systematic Theology* 13, no. 2 (2011): 173. As they also note, this logic of Kierkegaard's is a response to the logic of his Danish contemporaries: "(A) all who live in Christendom are Christians; (B) all Danes live in Christendom; therefore (C) all Danes are Christians. Consequently, because all Danes are Christians, no one in Danish society can suffer for Christianity at the hands of his or her fellow Danes" (173n12).

suggests, particularly in his later authorship,[11] it is not straightforwardly the case that his theological vision equates the Christian faith with suffering for Christianity. The latter is not the former, but an inevitable consequence of it. This means that we need to be careful about how we interpret Kierkegaard's position that suffering is "the prerequisite for Christianity."[12] When he makes statements such as these, they should be read as a commentary about the health of Christianity as it expresses itself as a human religious movement. Christianity, for Kierkegaard, will not be truly Christian unless it is characterized by suffering in this pagan world. Yet this does not make suffering a prerequisite for becoming a Christian. Rather, it is a consequent experience that is inseparable from a life of following Christ.

Hegel

Underlying many of the problems that Kierkegaard saw with Danish Christianity was the scholarly approach of Hegel and the Hegelianism that followed in its shadow. To understand what motivated Kierkegaard's project, careful attention needs to be given to the Hegelian ways of thinking that encouraged the dynamics he witnessed both in Denmark and in Europe more widely.

We do not have space here to offer an in-depth analysis of Kierkegaard's interpretation of Hegel. Such a task is well beyond the scope of this book and has been given plenty of worthy attention by others to whom we defer.[13] Nonetheless, it is important to say something about Kierkegaard's response to the problematic trends that he saw as an accompaniment to Hegelianism. This response is particularly relevant for our purposes because the primary constructive influence that Kierkegaard had on Barth is closely connected to the former's critique of Hegel.

11. See Kierkegaard, *Moment*, in particular.

12. Martens and Millay, "'Changelessness of God,'" 174.

13. See, for example, Jon Stewart, *Kierkegaard's Relations to Hegel Reconsidered* (Cambridge: Cambridge University Press, 2003); Mark C. Taylor, *Journeys to Selfhood: Hegel and Kierkegaard* (Berkeley: University of California Press, 1980); and Niels Thulstrup, *Kierkegaard's Relation to Hegel*, trans. George L. Stengren (Princeton: Princeton University Press, 1980). On Stewart's momentous study, it is worth taking note of Robert Perkins's critical comments in *International Journal for the Philosophy of Religion* 56, no. 1 (2004): 55–57. Perkins, we think rightly, critiques Stewart for not having a sufficient appreciation for Kierkegaard's paradoxical understanding of Christianity. That said, these comments should not be taken to diminish the value of Stewart's work, which would be our primary recommendation from these three books.

When we explore Kierkegaard's relationship to Hegel, we find that many of his concerns relate to Hegel's project of mediation. In the process of mediation, the pursuit of truth is successful when false oppositions are united through human reasoning. Nicholas Adams argues insightfully that Hegel's philosophy of mediation operates with a "Chalcedonian logic": one that views such concepts as self/other, subject/object, and divinity/humanity as pairs of concepts that do not identify a competitive relationship but which, when apprehended by human thinking, are bound up in a relationship of unity.[14] For Hegel, it is by mediating between such polar concepts that we can come to understand how they find integration within a coherent whole: the whole that he conceives as the one world-historical system. This project of mediation is bound up with humanity's direct experience of the historical world such that, for Hegel, it is through our conscious experience that the world can come to be represented as thought and conceptualized in a manner that facilitates a systematic understanding of truth. In this way, human reason mediates between thinking and being. As we shall see, this was not how Kierkegaard understood matters.

The Mediation of the Truth

With respect to Hegel's account of truth, there are two points to mention briefly that are relevant to our discussion.

First, Hegel was committed not only to a coherence theory of truth but also, within the constraints of his system, to a correspondence theory of truth in that an assertion is true insofar as it corresponds to our experience of the world.[15] For Hegel, the truth is known when human knowledge corresponds to the world, thereby making manifest "the immediate *unity* of *thought* and *being*."[16] It is through our experience of the world that human reason progresses in its understanding of the truth.

Second, our comprehension of the phenomenal world—the world as it appears to us—is not only how human reason progresses; it is also one of the ways in which the world, as a whole, progresses. Since human reason is united with the world, within the one world-historical system, the progress of human understanding contributes to the progress of the system as a whole. For Hegel,

14. Nicholas Adams, *The Eclipse of Grace: Divine and Human Action in Hegel* (Oxford: Wiley-Blackwell, 2013), 17–116.

15. For an excellent discussion of this, see H. S. Harris, "Hegel's Correspondence Theory of Truth," *Bulletin of the Hegel Society of Great Britain* 29 (1994): 1–13.

16. Georg Wilhelm Friedrich Hegel, *The Phenomenology of Spirit*, trans. Terry Pinkard (New York: Oxford University Press, 2018), 463.

"the true is the whole," and "the whole is only the essence completing itself through its own development."[17]

In and through the perpetual process and progress of human understanding, a spiritual journey unfolds. In a specific sense, for Hegel, the world develops a consciousness of itself as "Spirit" (*Geist*): it develops a consciousness of itself as a systematic whole that, by way of observation and philosophical speculation, progresses to become an ever more integrated whole. The further it progresses in this task, the further it manifests itself as Spirit. For Hegel, Spirit is world-history as it progresses in a process of self-understanding and self-realization. In this process, thoughts about the nature of reality are formed, and through this process, a mediation between being and thinking unfolds.

The World-Historical Theology of Hegel

For Hegel, another mediation that transpires in this process is the mediation between God and humanity. This mediation emerges through the historical development of religion, in which human society reflects on the eternal truth. Uncontroversially, Hegel notes that "God is supposed to be the ground absolutely of everything."[18] However, this leads him to the view that all things exist in union with God, albeit without being a manifestation of God. On this view, when the world becomes progressively conscious of itself—when the world, as Spirit, comes to think of itself as the world that it is—this development takes place as a divine act of reasoning. Additionally, those who progress furthest in their systematic thinking about God are those who progress furthest in their relationship with God. Or, to put it in terms more appropriate to Hegel, the religious scholars who progress furthest in their systematic theology are those in and through whom God's relationship with the world is made most manifest. It follows, for Hegel, that the powers of human reason have a form of redemptive significance by opening the door to union with God.

To be clear, Hegel does not think God is human, nor does he identify God with the world or with reason—points that Kierkegaard sometimes fails to appreciate.[19] The Hegelian project of mediation was able to avoid confusing these

---

17. Hegel, *Phenomenology of Spirit*, 13.

18. Georg Wilhelm Friedrich Hegel, *Encyclopedia of the Philosophical Sciences in Basic Outline, Part I: Science of Logic*, trans. Klaus Brinkmann and Daniel Dahlstrom (Cambridge: Cambridge University Press, 2010), 77.

19. As Peter Hodgson rightly notes, "The charge of pantheism is implicit in Kierkegaard's critique of what he regards as the totalizing tendency of Hegel's system, which (he says) identifies thought and being (existence), abolishes the principle of contradiction, introduces

things by holding them together in a relationship of union-in-distinction. For Hegel, God is the absolute Spirit that unites being and thinking in a coherent whole, without conflating the two. How, then, are we to understand the relationship between God and humanity? The more that the union or reconciliation between being and thinking becomes manifest through the progress of human recognition, the more humanity, the world, and reason participate in and make manifest the absolute Spirit that Hegel associates with God. It is in and through this process that the world comes to correspond more fully to God, and it is in and through this becoming that the world finds fulfillment. Further, to the extent that God is bound up with this process, this process also involves a divine becoming; it involves God becoming manifest in the history of the world.

For those familiar with Kierkegaard and Barth, it is easy to see how these features in Hegel's thought would clash with their commitments. Yet there are also points of resonance between Hegel's theology and that of Kierkegaard and Barth. For example, all three believe that God is the one to whom all persons must correspond if they are to find fulfillment. However, whereas this position is grounded for Hegel in an understanding of inherent unity between God and creation, for Kierkegaard and Barth, this position flows from a deep respect for God's freedom and transcendence over creation. A further point of resonance is that all three believe that the triune God is foundational to the being of world-history, in which God makes Godself known. In contrast to Hegel, however, Kierkegaard and Barth are adamant that God's relationship to creation is grounded in the free and personal agency of the triune God. For them, the knowability of God is tied to the particular way in which God communicates Godself to the world both as a personal being and also in and through a personal human being (Jesus Christ). The capacity to know God is dependent upon God's free communicative action because God is both beyond and incomprehensible to human reason, in and of itself, since humans are both distorted by sin and limited in their ability to conceptualize God. It is precisely because human reason in and of itself is unable to mediate God into the world that Kierkegaard views the human relationship with God as paradoxical. What does Kierkegaard mean by a paradox?

C. Stephen Evans offers a helpful description of Kierkegaard's view in a passage that is worth quoting at length, given that Kierkegaard's use of paradox had a major impact on Barth: "A paradox is something that may appear to us to be a

---

becoming into logic, and excludes the possibility of the offence of reason." Hodgson, *Hegel and Christian Theology: A Reading of the Lectures of Philosophy of Religion* (Oxford: Oxford University Press, 2005), 249.

contradiction. In general, the discovery of a paradox is the result of an encounter with a reality which our concepts are inadequate to deal with, a reality that ties us in a conceptual knot. When we try to understand it we may find ourselves saying self-contradictory things, but of course this does not mean that the reality we have encountered is itself self-contradictory. It means that there is a problem with our conceptual equipment."[20] For Kierkegaard, since we do not possess an inherent ability to mediate conceptually between God and creation, our minds will (or, at least, should) encounter what appears to be a contradiction when they attempt to do so.[21] Against Hegel's philosophy, Kierkegaard therefore notes: "Philosophy's idea is mediation—[Christianity]'s is the paradox."[22]

Nevertheless, neither Kierkegaard nor Barth, as we shall see, rules out a place for mediation between God and humanity. For them, this mediation is not achieved by way of finite human reasoning; rather, it is located in the person of Jesus Christ, the one "mediator . . . who leads us to God."[23]

By contrast, how does Hegel conceive of Christ? For him, God and humanity are bound up in a noncompetitive relationship of union, a position that finds fullest expression in the Christian image of the incarnation. As such, Hegel viewed Christianity as the absolute religion; it is the religion that most fully recognizes the divine-human union that is affirmed by his concept of religion.[24] However, this union is not unique to Christ; rather, the person of Christ exemplifies a general union between God and humanity—the God-human union that is represented in Christ is true for all persons. Indeed, Hegel goes so far as to say that "the divine nature is the same as the human nature, and it is this unity which is intuited [in the incarnation of the divine being]."[25] At the same time, while God is bound up with the history of the

20. C. Stephen Evans, *Passionate Reason: Making Sense of Kierkegaard's Philosophical Fragments* (Indianapolis: Indiana University Press, 1992), 104.

21. What do we mean by "contradiction" here? As C. Stephen Evans helpfully elucidates, Kierkegaard's use of contradiction "may seem sloppy to a contemporary reader, but he is here, as at so many points, following the Hegelians, who notoriously used the term 'contradiction' in a very broad manner." Evans references, for example, Hegel's view of nature as a contradiction. See *Hegel's Philosophy of Nature*, trans. A. V. Miller (Oxford: Clarendon, 1970), 17–22. As Evans argues, when Kierkegaard is referring to a contradiction, he is referring "to what might today be designated as an 'incongruity'" (Evans, *Passionate Reason*, 100).

22. Søren Kierkegaard, *Kierkegaard's Journals and Notebooks*, ed. Niels Jørgen Cappelørn, Alastair Hannay, David Kangas, Bruce H. Kirmmse, George Pattison, Vanessa Rumble, and K. Brian Söderquist (Princeton: Princeton University Press, 2007–2020), 3:207.

23. Kierkegaard, *Journals and Papers*, 2:1432.

24. Hegel, *Phenomenology of Spirit*, 435–36; see also James Yerkes, *The Christology of Hegel* (Missoula, MT: Scholars Press, 1978), 164–73.

25. Hegel, *Phenomenology of Spirit*, 436.

world, the God-human union is yet to be fulfilled. Such a union would only be achieved if world-history were to develop a complete self-understanding, in and through the objective pursuit of knowledge—a fulfillment that Hegel might have construed, in his own unique way, as the beatific vision.

In summary, how is God mediated to the world according to Hegel? By way of the scientific and philosophical thinking of the community. With the progression of our understanding of the world-historical whole, human society advances into fuller participation in God—a progression that, again, takes place both on the divine side and the human side. As humans grow in their knowledge of God, God becomes embodied in and identified with the community, leading to a more fully conscious realization of the God-world relationship.

For the remainder of this section, we shall focus our examination by highlighting three concepts in Hegelian mediation that were deeply concerning for Kierkegaard: (1) the subjective and the objective, (2) the individual and the community, and (3) God and humanity.

The Subjective and the Objective

Central to the process of Hegelian mediation is a resistance to the oft-perceived opposition between subject(ive) and object(ive)—that is, between the subjective knower and the object known. For Hegel, such dualistic ways of thinking do not track with the way that subjects think about the objects they experience. When a given subject experiences an object, the thoughts that emerge involve a synthesis between the subject who experiences and the object that is experienced. In this process, the more a subject experiences and reflects on that object, the more that subject's thoughts come to correspond to the object. As Hegel reflected on human thought, he believed that his philosophy spoke to a scientific-philosophical (or empirical-rational) system of thought that could hold together the subjective and the objective as they progress in the development of human thinking about the world. This system of reason, known as speculative reason, not only corresponds to but is also at the heart of Hegel's one world-historical system of reality in which all things cohere.

For Kierkegaard, a major problem with this approach is that it encourages a hesitancy and disinterestedness with respect to the process of decision-making. Why is this? It is because it commits subjective thinkers to an unending process of striving for ever greater objective certainty about the nature of things. Such striving precedes commitment to a particular view of reality—that is, to a metaphysical foundation suitable to guide persons in their decision-making. This cripples the thinker because, to the extent that a subject cannot transcend the limits of her own subjective perception, she will only ever be able to know objective truth to a certain degree. Therefore, she will find herself obliged to resist drawing conclusions until there has been further progress in her objective understanding of the truth. On such an approach, a better understanding of reality always awaits her in the future, which means she is invariably obliged to hesitate to commit to a particular position.

When the time comes for a person to make a decision about the truth, that decision will be filled with trepidation because her decision will be tied to an objectivity that she can only ever know provisionally. Positively, this can encourage an attitude of deep humility. Negatively, however, it can also cultivate an apathy about committing to a way of life that is objectively uncertain. For Kierkegaard, this is particularly disastrous when it comes to Christian thinking, which requires a bold and faithful commitment to truths that, objectively speaking, do not attain to the kind of demonstrable certainty that the protégés of the Enlightenment desired.

For Kierkegaard, it is not only the Christian life that is restrained by objective uncertainty. Any way of life that seeks to be true to objective reality will be characterized by uncertainty. This is because each and every life-view will require metaphysical assumptions that are beyond what a person can learn from the empirical evidence that derives from observing the natural world. Therefore, a consistent commitment to a Hegelian approach will always hold a person back from committing to a particular way of life. Indeed, it should hold a person back from committing to the Hegelian approach itself. This is because a person's subjective existence is always bound up with, and therefore held back by, the problem of objective uncertainty.

Against Hegel, Kierkegaard's non-Christian pseudonym Johannes Climacus (whom we shall discuss below) insists that the "essential truth" for an existing subject does not concern objective certainty but a subject's uncertain commitment to what she (provisionally) perceives to be the object to which she commits herself.[26] And he provides the following well-known account of truth: "*An objective uncertainty, held fast through appropriation with the most passionate inwardness, is the truth*, the highest truth there is for an *existing* person."[27] It is with this in mind that Climacus famously insists that "subjectivity is truth."[28] For Kierkegaard, the existing person must always be ready to commit to a par-

---

26. Søren Kierkegaard, *Concluding Unscientific Postscript to Philosophical Fragments*, ed. and trans. Howard V. Hong and Edna H. Hong (Princeton: Princeton University Press, 1992), 1:199–201.

27. Kierkegaard, *Concluding Unscientific Postscript*, 1:203 (emphasis original).

28. Kierkegaard, *Concluding Unscientific Postscript*, 1:203.

ticular way of life as a true way of life, despite the objective uncertainty that surrounds such a commitment. Now it may be that a person will come to discover that she was mistaken about her chosen way of life and so will need to be open to adapting her life-view, or even having her life-view transformed. However, it is better to be willing to take such a risk and live a life in which one can resolve to become something—to make something of oneself—rather than to live a life that is bound up with a hesitancy to commit to a particular life-view because it may not correspond to the objective fact of the matter.

Again, Kierkegaard insists that we will never be able to transcend our subjective lives and access objective truth *sub specie aeternitatis*, thereby understanding how everything holds together within the one system of existence. Whereas on a Hegelian view this encourages noncommitment (at least according to Kierkegaard), on a Kierkegaardian view it encourages commitment to an objective uncertainty. Human minds can never transcend the limits of their capacity to demonstrate what is true by rational means in order to view the world objectively. Such a system is something that only God can know. Climacus writes:

> A system of existence cannot be given. Is there, then, not such a system? This is not at all the case. Neither is this implied in what has been said. Existence is a system—for God, but it cannot be a system for any existing spirit.[29]

So, to be clear, Climacus does not deny that there is a system in which the subjective and objective hold together. The key word in the above quotation is "given"; he is simply denying the "givenness" of any such unity for the human mind. Only the eternal God knows this system. Therefore, any commitment to such a system must be grounded in a commitment to God's revelation: to the revelation of the one whose existence is not bound up within the world-historical system but is the transcendent Creator of it.

The Individual and the Community

The commitment to a mediation of subjectivity and objectivity is paralleled by a commitment to a mediation of the individual and the community. For Hegel, the subjective/objective mediation is mirrored in the relationship between the individual and the community, such that an individual's *subjective* pursuit of knowledge must be mediated with the *objective* progress that takes place in the knowledge of the community. The individual must assess the progress of her

---

29. Kierkegaard, *Concluding Unscientific Postscript*, 1:117.

knowledge with the assistance of the community, and the knowledge of the community is constituted by the voices and understandings of individuals. It is as a collective whole that humanity progresses in its self-understanding—both in its understanding of world-history and its understanding of who (or what) it is within that history.

This progression contributes not only to human self-understanding but also, as noted above, to the self-understanding of the system as a whole. To be clear, Hegel is here postulating a self-awareness that is possessed by the world-historical system itself. In his thinking, the more fully that society's mind corresponds to reality, the more fully there is an embodiment of the union between ideality and reality, thought and being, and so the more fully the world realizes itself. Again, for Hegel, this embodiment is the incarnation of Spirit or of God in the world. Because God is immanent within this system, this progression not only involves the world working itself out in its relationship with God, but it also involves God working Godself (or itself) out in the history of the world.

Now, because individuals are bound up with the community, individuals must always be cognizant of how their learning is derivative from, accountable to, and refined by the knowledge of the community. Even the scholar who isolates herself in her own little office is required to (and will have had to) draw on the learning of others in order to make progress in the world's quest for knowledge. It is by gathering together a collection of insights and synthesizing them into a system of understanding that the world progresses in its self-understanding. And it is the resulting systematic understanding of these insights that constitutes true knowledge. This means that scholars and learners, generally speaking, should seek to be accountable to communal practices, to customs and laws that have been established by and are embodied in modern society, as the fullest expression of the progress of society.

While there may be ways in which this emphasis could be seen to discourage individual creative thinking—thinking that pushes against the grain of society—it does not rule it out altogether. Hegel does not deny the possibility that there are intellectual pioneers who serve to innovate our understanding of the world. If, however, their thinking does in fact correspond to the truth, this will eventually be confirmed by its coming to be recognized by and appropriated within the community. It is in this way that conjecture is confirmed as knowledge; to quote Climacus, "[Hegelian] speculative thought is always wise afterward."[30]

30. Kierkegaard, *Concluding Unscientific Postscript*, 1:33.

Nonetheless, the Hegelian culture of Denmark put strong pressure on individuals to doubt themselves before they doubted the community. For Kierkegaard, this message was particularly problematic in the life of the church. In Denmark, the Hegelian influence encouraged a synthesis between the church's pursuit of truth and society's pursuit of truth—a synthesis that, in practice, resulted in the church conforming to society more than Danish society conformed to the church. Accordingly, any sense of calling to follow Christ in a way that moved against the dominant trends of "Christian" society (the church-society synthesis) was likely to be quashed. Since it is easy to adapt Christianity to the world, and unappealing to conform to a true and costly Christianity, it is not surprising that such a theology was quick to catch on not only in Denmark but also across Europe

A commitment to the synthesis of the individual and community also meant that objective "Christian" culture ended up playing a more central role in shaping a person's Christian life than her own individual commitment to following Jesus Christ. A person was able to know that she was a Christian simply by observing that she lives in a "Christian" country, by noticing that she participates in a "Christian" community, and by recognizing that she had grown up in a "Christian" family. She was a "Christian" because she was a part of the mass of "Christian" culture. Against this approach, Kierkegaard emphasized the decisive role that the single individual plays in determining the true nature of their existence, a way that did not bend to the ever-progressing ways of modern society. Rather, the individual is called to decide for herself what it means to follow Christ, according to the witness of the New Testament, and according to the particular way in which she believes she should respond to God's call in her life.

In ecclesial terms, according to Hegelian theology, the church is perceived as the religious community that embodies God's relationship to the world. In this respect, the church is not only the body of Christ but also the body of God, and the church progresses by coming to recognize itself as such. For Kierkegaard, by contrast, reconciliation between God and humans is worked out by particular persons collectively responding to the grace of God. It is a consequence of the work of Jesus Christ and the Holy Spirit, who are not bound up with the church, but who are actively creating the lives of faith that give rise to the life of the church. It is only by God freely and personally creating a relationship with the world in time, and by delivering persons into this relationship, that persons can come together as Christians: as persons who are united with God and thereby united as a community.

God and Humanity

As we have indicated, for Hegel, God and humanity exist in a noncompetitive relationship of union; they exist in a unity wherein God's being and agency do not displace that of humanity, nor vice versa. This religious understanding of Hegel finds its fullest expression in Christianity. In light of its commitment to an incarnational unity between God and humanity, Hegel viewed Christianity as the absolute religion; it is the religion that most fully recognizes the divine-human union that is affirmed by his concept of religion.[31] Once again, however, according to Hegelian theology this union is not unique to Christ. Rather, Jesus Christ testifies to or exemplifies a general union between God and humanity—the God-human union that is made apparent in Jesus Christ is true for all persons. Indeed, Hegel goes so far as to say that "the divine nature is the same as the human, and it is this unity that is beheld [in the incarnation of the divine being]."[32] At the same time, while God is immanent within the history of the world, for Hegel, the God-human union is yet to be fulfilled. This union only finds fulfillment when world-history develops its complete self-understanding, in and through the objective pursuit of knowledge.

So how do human beings relate to God according to Hegel's philosophy? As we have suggested, they relate to God from within. By progressing in their understanding of the world, human society progresses in its participation in God, and, again, this progression takes place both on the divine side and the human side. As humans grow in their knowledge of God, God becomes embodied in and identified with the community, leading to a more conscious realization of the God-world relationship. Accordingly, as Nicholas Adams writes, "knowledge of God is a matter of God dwelling in humanity rather than being what Hegel would call an object of consciousness."[33] Talk about God should not be seen as straightforwardly objective, as though God transcends human subjectivity. Nor should it be seen to be purely subjective, as though the God of Christian theology could be reduced to a figment of human thought. Under the influence of Hegel's mediation, we need to deny any suggestion of opposition between God and humanity, albeit without conflating the two.

By incorporating Christian terminology into his thinking, Hegel's method sought to deconstruct historical Christianity and provide a philosophical re-

---

31. Hegel, *Phenomenology of Spirit*, 461–63; *The Phenomenology of Mind*, trans. J. B. Beillies (London: George Allen & Unwin, 1949), 758–85; see also Yerkes, *Christology of Hegel*, 164–73.

32. Hegel, *Phenomenology of Spirit*, 460.

33. Adams, *Eclipse of Grace*, 224.

construction of what he perceived to be its actual truth—its truth aside from superstitious beliefs in the miraculous activity of a transcendent God, and aside from the belief that there is a truth that can only be accessed through a historical event of reconciliation. In a sense, he sought to sublimate the historical message of Christianity into his modern scientific philosophy so that Christian concepts could progress beyond their historical context and find fuller expression in the modern world. Hegel sought to realign Christianity with the progress that was being made with modern rationalistic ways of thinking. As such, for Kierkegaard, it was hard to see how Hegel's engagement with Christianity constituted more than a form of wordplay in which Christian concepts were commandeered to fit Hegel's systematic method.

It is not all that surprising that Hegel would seek to commandeer Christianity into his thinking. In a certain sense, Christianity poses a puzzle for Hegelianism: How could it be that so much of society's progress is bound up with the Christian belief in a transcendent God and the superstition that goes along with it? How could it be that so much of enlightened modern society is Christian? Do these things not urge the reflection that Christianity (or at least the spirit of Christianity) might, in some way, contribute to our understanding of the world? While Hegel did not hold an orthodox view of Christianity, the pressure of these kinds of questions urged him to find a place for Christian concepts within his scientific philosophy. He saw Christian concepts as corresponding, in various ways, to the nature of reality. Nonetheless, to make sense of them within his speculative framework, Christianity needed to be made to fit within the world-historical process as it could be observed by natural empirical science. It also needed to find an ever fuller expression in the progressive culture of the Christian community.

A critical theological difference between Hegel and Kierkegaard is that Hegel gives no credence to the possibility that human reason is limited by being in a state of alienation from God—a state from which it needs to be delivered. Rather, the Christian idea of the incarnation (as interpreted through Hegelianism) speaks to the fact that God is eternally reconciled with the world.[34] The human relationship with God is therefore increasingly being worked out and realized in the progression of the Christian community. In order to understand reconciliation with God, the Christian community must seek to recognize the

---

34. This position is described derogatorily by Climacus when he notes that if "the coming into existence of the eternal in time is supposed to be an eternal coming into existence, then Religiousness B [a term Climacus later uses to describe what he presents as the true account of Christianity] is abolished, 'all theology is anthropology,' [and] Christianity is changed from an existence-communication into an ingenious metaphysical doctrine addressed to professors" (Kierkegaard, *Concluding Unscientific Postscript*, 1:579).

ways in which the relationship with God is unfolding in and being embodied by its own life and culture. For Kierkegaard, "there is nothing about which I have greater misgivings than about all that even slightly tastes of the disastrous confusion of politics and Christianity."[35] This is why so much of his theology stressed God's transcendence and was accompanied by a strong emphasis on the entirely unique mediatory activity of Jesus Christ, the absolute paradox. Once again, there is a stark contrast between Hegel and Kierkegaard. For Hegel, the ideas of "relationship" and "reconciliation" between "God" and "humanity" are conceived in metaphorical and essentially impersonal terms. For Kierkegaard, God is to be conceived in irreducibly personal terms.

In this section, we have only been able to offer a very limited account of Hegel's thought, but let us conclude by noting that while it can often come across as abstruse, perhaps even idiosyncratic, there is a certain genius to his approach. For the patient and persistent reader, his philosophy possesses a remarkable ability to track with the thinking of modern society (particularly in the West). Few thinkers offer a more comprehensive analysis of how we think about reality. He achieved this success by paying careful attention to the manner in which our lives are bound up with our immediate surroundings— by concentrating on the ways in which immediacy (the world as we directly understand it) shapes not only our scientific judgment, but also our moral, philosophical, and religious imagination. This enabled him to captivate a large audience across Europe and, thereby, have a profound influence on the shape and direction of so much theology over the last two hundred years. As we shall see, however, for both Kierkegaard and Barth, the source of Hegel's success points also to his greatest weakness. Hegel's fixation with immediacy—or more specifically unmediatedness—distracted him from recognizing what it means to exist before the God who is both transcendent and free.

But first, let us turn to consider the influence that Hegel had on Christian thought in Denmark, particularly insofar as we see a pronounced integration between Hegel's philosophy of religion and the theology of the church. In so doing, some of the dangers of Hegel's thought will become evident.

Hans Lassen Martensen and Danish Hegelianism

While Kierkegaard was often critical of Hegel, he rarely focused his attacks on Hegel directly. He was far more concerned about the speculative theolo-

---

35. Søren Kierkegaard, *The Corsair Affair and Articles Related to the Writings*, trans. Howard V. Hong and Edna H. Hong (Princeton: Princeton University Press, 1982), 53.

gians who, while not strict followers of Hegel, quite definitely fell under his influence. A prime target in this respect was the Lutheran theologian Hans Lassen Martensen, the professor of theology in Copenhagen who would become bishop of Zealand.

In Martensen, Hegel's thought was developed in a way that brought it into much closer alignment with Christian orthodoxy, enabling it to be more readily embraced by the church. In this respect, Martensen saw himself as someone who sought to "go beyond Hegel."[36] So, for example, he placed a greater emphasis on how the incarnation provides the decisive revelation of God—a revelation that was particular to the historical person of Jesus Christ and his mediatory role between God and humanity. Still, much of his thought continued to follow Hegel closely. He saw the revelation of Jesus Christ as inaugurating a new stage of religiousness for civilization; Christ was the fulfillment of sacred history and thereby established a new paradigm for understanding our relationship with God. This paradigm was embodied in the life of the church such that it was by participating in the culture of the church that persons could grow in their relationship with God. For Martensen, however, it was not solely the church that was called to embody the image of Christ; this was also the task of society. The church, therefore, was called to help society conform to the revelation of Christ—to help society imagine a culture for itself that was informed by revelation. In so doing, it becomes possible for society to assume its true identity as Christendom. He writes:

> For a nation to become Christian, means that its heathenism and national selfishness are ended, and that it is to submit itself to the guidance and purification of the Spirit of Christ. It means that the nation is to partake, by Christian faith, of the blessings of the gospel, and under all dispensations, whether of weal or woe, to find in it a refuge and support. It means that the nation is to cultivate, under the fertilizing influences of the Spirit of Christ, the gifts God has bestowed upon it, the pound with which it has been entrusted, and thus to occupy its God-ordained position in the entirety of the human race, when all nations shall be comprised under Christ in one Christendom. Hence the relation of Christianity to nationality is not only a purifying, but a cultivating or perfecting one.[37]

---

36. H. L. Martensen, *Af mit Levnet: Meddelelser* (Copenhagen: Gyldendal, 1882–83), 2:4–5, cited in Stewart, *Kierkegaard's Relations to Hegel*, 308–10.

37. H. L. Martensen, *Christian Ethics: Special Part; Second Division: Social Ethics*, trans. Sophia Taylor (Edinburgh: T&T Clark, 1882), 93.

This passage presents Martensen as a theologian who was deeply committed to thinking about God's relationship to the world according to the image of Christ, a relationship that ought to be reflected in the culture of the church. More precisely, he believed that the revelation of Christ could be appropriated by society in a way that would bring about a synthesis between the kingdom of God and the kingdom of the world. For Martensen, society was able to aid the mission of the church because it operated as a "kingdom of freedom" in which God's providence and goodness are "realised in history as the development of the freedom of the race"—that is, in "the progress made by the creatures themselves in the course of their natural self-development."[38] Space does not allow us to explore the finer details of Martensen's position, which are not always clear. But what is clear is that he saw in modern Danish society the possibility of a Christian culture that could advance the cause of the church. This story of advancement was one that began with "the advent of Christ, the revelation of the highest good," and developed with the enlightenment of society. For him, if society could allow itself to be informed by Christian values, it would be able to embody "the idea of the *Kingdom of God*."[39]

While figures such as Martensen wed Christianity to Danish society, Kierkegaard noticed that it was being sold to a niche market. In accord with a Hegelian vision of progress, Christianity was being tied to a way of life that favored the intellectual elite; it became a religion that was most fitting for the well-educated and most appealing to the aesthetic tastes of a bourgeois upper class. Under these circumstances, it was the job of the pastor to educate persons about how they should participate "Christianly" in Danish culture. Christians were called to focus their attention on doctrine and those qualities, virtues, and habits that doctrine inspires: the beauty of church architecture, the chanting of the liturgy, the singing of hymns, the learning of the creeds by rote, and so on. To be clear, Kierkegaard was not primarily worried about these facets of church life in and of themselves. What did worry him were the ways in which this focus facilitated the squeezing of Christianity "into the sphere of the intellectual."[40] Indeed, speaking as Climacus, he hyperbolizes, "Christian scholarship has abolished Christianity by confusing what it is to be an apostle with what it is to be a person of intellectuality."[41] Such scholarship diminished

---

38. H. L. Martensen, *Christian Dogmatics*, trans. William Urwick (Edinburgh: T&T Clark, 1886), 382, 117.

39. Martensen, *Christian Dogmatics*, 215 (emphasis original).

40. Kierkegaard, *Journals and Papers*, 4:4953.

41. Kierkegaard, *Journals and Papers*, 4:3865.

Christianity into "an object for passive, brooding meditation" about "scholarly nonessentials."[42] Subtly but surely, Christianity was being hijacked by the variety of idealisms, romanticisms, and post-Enlightenment humanisms taking shape in the intellectual culture of his day.

With so much attention being given to the (perceived) betterment of Christian culture, Kierkegaard felt that the Danish Church was failing to teach individuals what it truly means to follow Jesus Christ. For many, the Christian faith had become just another part of their busy lives, a pursuit among other pursuits that could be embraced without inconvenience. There was little sense in which so-called Christians were willing to die to the sinful ways of the world. For Kierkegaard, this evidenced a serious confusion about the nature of Christianity. For him, the person who earnestly seeks to follow Christ will find herself being drawn into a life that does not simply progress with but runs counter to the grain of society. Her life will become filled with uncertainty, and what makes sense to her will often appear incoherent or even delusional to the prevailing intellect of society.

It is not difficult to see why Kierkegaard's account of the Christian life sat in tension with the Hegelian faith in the organic progress of human reason (particularly that of modern Western reason). With a Hegelian hope, many systematic theologians had come to prioritize those features of the Christian tradition that were more palatable to modern systems of scholarship—that is, those features that were most edifying to contemporary culture and most acceptable to the standards of current empirical science. Commenting on this situation, Kierkegaard notes that when such scholarship treats Christianity like any other object of study, "the scholarly is the most dangerous of all for essential Christianity."[43] Among the most disturbing of problems with this approach was that it gave scholars far too much self-confidence—a confidence that showed no fear of God. He writes:

> But there is no one who *fears* God: we do not hear him in the thunder, our notions are too intellectual for that; we do not see him in the fates—and we have nothing of inwardness. But just as everything has been trained in the conventions of finitude, so has God himself been trained: With the help of various rules, the priests have put him on a leash.[44]

---

42. Kierkegaard, *Journals and Papers*, 4:3864, 1:318.
43. Kierkegaard, *Journals and Papers*, 3:3581.
44. Kierkegaard, *Kierkegaard's Journals and Notebooks*, 2:252.

For Kierkegaard, God was not being taken seriously for who God is. When one considers what Abraham was willing to sacrifice, what the martyrs were willing to give up, he thought it was shameful that persons were not willing to sacrifice far more in the name of God. Instead, God was reduced to a concept to be used in service of the so-called progress of society; this was cultural Christianity's God, treated as a conceptual postulate by philosophers, a part of Christian doctrine by theologians, and the inaugurator of religious culture by society.

By contrast, how did Kierkegaard view God?

> God is the sole bestower of grace. He wants every person (educated up to it through proclamation of the requirement) to turn, each one separately, to him and to receive, each one separately, the indulgence which can be granted to him. But we men have turned the relationship round, robbed or tricked God out of the royal prerogative of grace and then put out a counterfeit grace.[45]

For Kierkegaard, God is first and foremost a personal agent who delivers us from error, who calls us to die to ourselves and be born anew. Humans are called to relate to God as one who cannot be reduced to an object of their speculation—a datum or factoid that is best understood with the scrutiny of a scholarly mind. Instead, faith in God must be characterized by a humble recognition of its inability to command God in the way that a person might develop an intellectual command over worldly phenomena. In sum, what the Hegelian theology of Denmark invited, in Kierkegaard's less-than-subtle judgment, was (functionally) an "impious, pantheistic, self-worship," according to which God ends up being worshiped as an object of society's mind.[46] What had emerged was the disastrous confusion of a worldly vision of progress with Christianity's development.[47] This happened because society, particularly its "upper" echelons, had become so absorbed in immediacy that it was failing to revere God, allowing God to be worshiped as something akin to the Spirit of the immanent order.

KIERKEGAARD'S APPROACH

Despite the many concerns that Kierkegaard expressed regarding Christian scholarship in Denmark, there are nevertheless many ways in which his own

---

45. Kierkegaard, *Journals and Papers*, 2.1476.
46. Kierkegaard, *Concluding Unscientific Postscript*, 1:124.
47. See Kierkegaard, *Kierkegaard's Journals and Notebooks*, 8:36.

approach mirrored the style of this scholarship—almost in an exaggerated way. Ever the ironist and humorist, Kierkegaard sought to challenge the intellectualization of Christianity by providing what is nothing short of a profoundly scholarly account of Christianity. Nonetheless, insofar as he denied that Christianity is ultimately a scholarly pursuit, he performed this task with a deep awareness of his limitations. Furthermore, the careful reader of Kierkegaard's theological writings will notice that there is always a sense in which they are pointing away from themselves, both to the Christian life and to the God who enables this life. His scholarship could never, in and of itself, truly communicate *who* Jesus Christ is, and, therefore, could never truly communicate what it means to follow him. Accordingly, he never intended to provide anything more than a witness—an indirect form of communication—to the one who is the true object (or subject) of the Christian faith. This witness to Christ essentially sought to correct those intellectuals who were distorting Christianity in Denmark. He took it upon himself to challenge this scholarly perception of Christianity by playing intellectuals at their own game.

Kierkegaard's Task of Translation

Central to Kierkegaard's task was his attempt to offer an authentic account of Christianity to the intellectuals who were interpreting it through Hegelian-tinted glasses.[48] He sought to restate what it means to be and to become a Christian to those who were allowing "Christianity" to be pushed around and distorted by "objective" forms of scholarship.[49] To correct their perception of Christianity, Kierkegaard did not think he could simply insist on his own theological position without regard for the particularity of his audience. So he sought to speak the language of those who had fallen under the influence of Hegelian ways of thinking—to embark on what could be described as a task of translation.[50] This did not mean that he believed he could use his intellectual powers of persuasion to translate the Truth of Christianity into the language of the rationalists. Again, he was fully aware that human reason cannot, in and of itself, bring a person to know the Truth of Christianity. Such knowledge requires a person to come to faith in response to God's working in that person's

---

48. Kierkegaard, *Journals and Papers*, 2:1962.

49. As he remarks in a journal entry from 1849, Kierkegaard had his "sights on a brash scientific scholarship, a brash scholarship, etc., which wants to go farther than Christianity" (Kierkegaard, *Journals and Papers*, 6:6531).

50. Kierkegaard, *Journals and Papers*, 6:6498.

life; it requires a person to be transformed by a gracious activity that is not subject to human thought or agency.[51] In short, Kierkegaard was aware that he could not himself transmit the grace of God to others, and that no human reasoning could draw persons into a spiritual relationship with God. To claim this would be to suggest that the grace of God depended somehow on human skill. He, therefore, did not see himself as somehow paving the way for grace.

Yet Kierkegaard did believe that God speaks to the world through particular forms of human communication—forms that directly engage the human audience. To seek to converse with the scholars of his day, he translated (insofar as he could) the "what" of Christianity into a message that both engaged and challenged the subjective mindset of a particular group of people. He did this because he recognized that to become a Christian, a person must develop an understanding of what Christianity is. For example, he appreciated that "a person first must gain some knowledge of Christ."[52] Without doing so, a person cannot know what it means to follow Jesus Christ; without it, a person cannot make the difficult decisions to which Christ calls her, and she cannot appreciate the extent to which she needs God in her life. In Kierkegaard's view, it is with a Christianly informed and Christianly active existence that a person comes to participate in the Christian life—and this takes place in and through a relationship with God, who is with us and for us in Jesus Christ.

By taking this approach, Kierkegaard sought to question scholars in a way that might penetrate their speculative shields and challenge them to rethink how they were relating to Christianity. He sought to undercut the intellectual foundations that strengthened their resistance to the notion that the Truth is to be found through a relationship with the free and transcendent God. He did this by playing them at their own game, exposing the limits of their position via their own methods. We see this, for example, in the "thought experiment" of *Philosophical Fragments*, which we shall discuss further in the following chapter. In this "imaginative construction," he questions his intellectual audience by showing them the coherence of an alternative way of understanding how a person might relate to the Truth—an alternative that bears a striking

51. "Before God," Kierkegaard writes, "the moment when humanly speaking I have come furthest, I have not come one inch, not one millionth of an inch, closer to God than the person who strove, indeed, than the one who strove with all his might for the opposite." Søren Kierkegaard, *Judge for Yourself!*, in *"For Self-Examination" and "Judge for Yourself!,"* ed. and trans. Howard V. Hong and Edna H. Hong (Princeton: Princeton University Press, 1990), 152.

52. Kierkegaard, *Journals and Papers*, 1:318.

resemblance to the gospel message.[53] Through this account, he questions their unyielding confidence in the power of human reason, opening the door to the notion that the Truth is to be found through a relationship with God that is *beyond* the scope of unredeemed human reason, the God who cannot be conjured up from the human mind's own resources. Kierkegaard thus drew attention to the gospel message that God can only be known in and through a relationship with God as God discloses Godself to us *personally* in history in a reconciling act—that is, in Jesus Christ, who is the way, the truth, and the life, and who is thus, in himself, the condition for our being brought into relationship with the Truth. Naturally, this required a reorientation of his audience's focus back to the one who can truly draw persons into the Christian life. It meant creating an opportunity to focus again on the *revelation* that alone defines what Christianity is. In this way, Emil Brunner remarks, Kierkegaard "used his great philosophical powers in the service of faith."[54]

Kierkegaard and His Pseudonyms

Kierkegaard regularly utilized pseudonyms to engage his audience, and it is therefore important to say something about the role that this practice played in his authorship. These pseudonyms permitted him to adopt a perspective very different from his own, but they also create challenges for the reader. The reader, approaching these different voices, should understand that they represent "poeticized personalities, poetically maintained so that everything they say is in character with their poeticized individualities."[55] Kierkegaard was quite clear that his pseudonymous authorship should not be confused with his own authorship. This did not mean that he completely disagreed with the accounts of Christianity put forward by his pseudonyms; indeed, we often find extensive continuity between their respective accounts. The major difference between Kierkegaard and his pseudonyms concerns how the pseudonym perceives his own relationship to the account of Christianity under consideration. This perspective, consequently, has a critical impact on the way the pseudonym presents his respective account. In our discussion of Kierkegaard, we shall be engaging extensively with two of these pseudonyms:

53. Kierkegaard, *Journals and Papers*, 6:6859. An upper case "T" is being used here and throughout to signify that, for Kierkegaard and Barth, to be brought into relation with the Truth is to be brought into relation with the person of the Word, that is, with God.

54. Emil Brunner, *Revelation and Reason: The Christian Doctrine of Faith and Knowledge*, trans. Olive Wyon (Philadelphia: Westminster Press, 1946), 377.

55. Kierkegaard, *Journals and Papers*, 6:6786.

Anti-Climacus, who was most influential on Barth's thinking, and Johannes Climacus, who provides the clearest articulation of some of the key themes that are picked up by Barth.

Johannes Climacus

Kierkegaard conceived the character of Johannes Climacus as an outsider to the Christian faith. He was someone who did not recognize the Truth of Christianity for himself but was very interested in the question "How can I, Johannes Climacus, share in the happiness that Christianity promises?"[56] Exploring this question from his particular perspective, Climacus was able to develop what could be perceived to be a more "objective" account of what Christianity is. Kierkegaard presents him as an outsider to the Christian faith, but he also views him as someone who could be an insider to some of the groups that he sought to critique. Climacus was a dialectician, a humorist, and a psychologist who could have found himself welcomed to the table of the Danish elite.

As we have argued, the brand of "Christianity" that found favor with the cultural and intellectual elite of Denmark was characterized by a rationalistic commitment to Christian doctrine and teaching. Climacus was someone who could speak the language of the rationalisms that were in vogue across Europe. What he was able to do (and which Kierkegaard in his own voice could not) was function as a mere observer of Christianity, one who could offer a more detached analysis of what Christianity is. Nonetheless, as a character whose existence was determined by Kierkegaard's project, Climacus also wrote as someone who served Kierkegaard's cause. In particular, his writing presented a strong challenge to the confidence that scholars had in a Hegelian vision of Christianity, in which Christianity was interpreted according to the world's ever-progressing self-understanding.[57] Climacus criticizes this perspective by pointing to the coherence of an alternative way of understanding the Truth of Christianity—one that is contrasted with Hegel's absolute idealism. This alternative bears a much more striking resemblance to orthodox Christianity than its idealist alternative. By using Climacus to point this out, Kierkegaard was able to challenge his readers with a familiar voice (i.e., that of the intellectual elite) who could help them recognize the problematic nature of their approach.

---

56. Kierkegaard, *Concluding Unscientific Postscript*, 1:17.

57. Against a Hegelian view of progress, Kierkegaard presents the process of history as one of digression. Kierkegaard, *Moment*, 219.

We must be clear, however, that Kierkegaard was not under the impression that he could use Climacus to translate the Truth of Christianity into the language of the rationalists. Once again, he did not believe that the grace of God depended upon his particular communication skills. But by speaking to the rationalists in their own terms, through Climacus, Kierkegaard was able to penetrate their speculative strategies and challenge them to rethink how they were relating to Christianity. This is how he attempted to expose the limits of their position via their own methods.

Anti-Climacus

Of all Kierkegaard's writings, it was *Practice in Christianity* that had the greatest impact on Barth. This was a work signed by the pseudonym Anti-Climacus whom Kierkegaard conceived as an extraordinary Christian.[58] In contrast to Climacus, Anti-Climacus devoted himself to asserting what Christianity is, from an authentic Christian perspective—a perspective that Kierkegaard saw as not only higher than Climacus's, but also higher than his own. To a certain extent, therefore, Anti-Climacus was employed to present Christianity in a way that Kierkegaard did not think that he could own for himself. Of himself (and as himself), Kierkegaard writes:

> Never have I fought in such a way that I have said: I am the true Christian; the others are not Christians, or probably even hypocrites and the like. No, I have fought in this way: *I know what Christianity is*; I myself acknowledge my defects as a Christian—but I do know what Christianity is. And to know this thoroughly seems in the interest of every human being, whether one is now a Christian or a non-Christian, whether one's intention is to accept Christianity or abandon it. But I have attacked no one, saying that he is not a Christian; I have passed judgement on no one.[59]

By employing Anti-Climacus to make his case, Kierkegaard was able to distance himself from the pietistic critiques that Anti-Climacus would offer of Christendom. That said, as we shall see, Anti-Climacus was not simply committed to offering condemnation and exhortation. His writings were much more concerned about clarifying that it is God in Jesus Christ who is the

---

58. Kierkegaard, *Journals and Papers*, 6:6349.

59. Kierkegaard, *Point of View*, 15 (emphasis original). Kierkegaard also denies that he has ever attempted to be pietistically rigorous in his description of Christianity (17).

proper object of Christianity and who determines what Christianity is. In *Practice in Christianity*, Christianity is not primarily defined by the persons who call themselves Christian, but by the God-human: "Jesus Christ, the infinitely highest one, true God and true man," who, "from on high, . . . will draw all to himself."[60]

The Kierkegaardian Approach to Changing the State of Play

Deeply perturbed by the theology of Danish Christendom, Kierkegaard saw it as his task to "attempt to introduce Christianity into Christendom."[61] With his pseudonyms, he set out to redescribe Christianity, proclaiming that Christianity is not something that can be brought into alignment with the world's own cultures. Being a Christian cannot be reduced to a set of mundane practices, defined solely by one's infant baptism and church attendance. Christianity calls for an earnest following of Christ, which will inevitably lead one's life to clash with the ways of the world. Kierkegaard felt that the appropriate course of action was for him to challenge self-proclaimed but complacent Christians to reflect on and realize what it was they were proclaiming. This was the motivation for Kierkegaard's proclamation of a true vision of Christianity (to the extent that it can be directly proclaimed) to the nominal Christians in Denmark. He hoped that his words might challenge the ways in which the Danish Church was confusing Christianity with the ways of the world.

One way that Kierkegaard sought to do this was by "upbuilding" Christians in their discipleship. In the preface to *The Sickness unto Death*, Anti-Climacus writes, "From the Christian point of view, everything, indeed everything, ought to serve for upbuilding. . . . Everything essentially Christian must have in its presentation a resemblance to the way a physician speaks at the sickbed."[62] In the cozy sickbed of establishment Lutheranism, Christianity had become, as Kierkegaard puts it, "a familiar, good-natured, decent chap" who comforts the life of the bourgeois.[63] He believed that those who lay in their sickbeds needed

---

60. Kierkegaard, *Practice in Christianity*, 160.

61. Kierkegaard, *Journals and Papers*, 6:6317; see also Kierkegaard, *Moment*, 106–7. In a journal entry from 1849, he clarifies this statement by writing, "I was bound to the idea of trying to introduce Christianity into Christendom, albeit poetically and without authority (namely, not making myself a missionary)." Kierkegaard, *Journals and Papers*, 6:6356.

62. Søren Kierkegaard, *The Sickness unto Death: A Christian Psychological Exposition for Upbuilding and Awakening*, ed. and trans. Howard V. Hong and Edna H. Hong (Princeton: Princeton University Press, 1980), 5.

63. Kierkegaard, *Journals and Papers*, 2:1816; see also Kierkegaard, *Moment*, 28.

to be told that they were sick, and they needed to be told that those with whom they lay were not the standard of good health, but patients in an epidemic. Kierkegaard felt that his fellow Danes needed to become a community that knew "that to need God is a human being's perfection"—a community fully expressive of the "feeling of absolute dependence."[64]

A significant and controversial move that Kierkegaard made was to bring focus to the individual. His work, he tells us, was committed to the "*single individual*, with polemical aim at the numerical, the crowd, etc."[65] It is difficult to make this move without opening oneself up to criticism. For example, Martensen contended that Kierkegaard's Christianity was in no way a social faith, "but a private religion pure and simple, a Christianity in which the Christian church and the activity of the Holy Spirit has been left out."[66] However, Kierkegaard had good reason for doing this. The socialization or communalization of Christianity, a situation furthered by Martensen, led to the "confusion that whole states, countries, nations, kingdoms are Christian."[67] And under the influence of Hegel, the Holy Spirit became confused with the Hegelian concept of the divine Spirit, thereby serving to further the confusion of Christianity with Danish culture. The result was that Danish Christians perceived their participation in "Christianity" as coterminous with their participation in Danish Christian culture. Moreover, for Kierkegaard, the Danish Church had "managed to make being a Christian almost synonymous with being a human being."[68]

It was in order to address this situation that Kierkegaard believed that there needed to be a transformation in the minds of individual Christians. To help facilitate this transformation, Kierkegaard had the following five aims throughout his authorship: (1) to help individuals to grasp the costliness of

64. Søren Kierkegaard, *Christian Discourses*, in *"Christian Discourses" and "The Crisis and a Crisis in the Life of an Actress,"* ed. and trans. Howard V. Hong and Edna H. Hong (Princeton: Princeton University Press, 1997), 64.

65. Kierkegaard, *Point of View*, 18 (emphasis original). This concern of Kierkegaard's led Barth to associate Kierkegaard with an "ethical individualism." Karl Barth, *The Christian Life: Church Dogmatics IV/4*, trans. Geoffrey W. Bromiley (Edinburgh: T&T Clark, 1981), 183. That said, Barth does acknowledge that Kierkegaard's focus on the existential character of the Christian "was an historically understandable and not unjustifiable reaction," although he also remarks that "it led to a distortion of the whole complex of problems [*Problem-Komplexes*]" (*The Christian Life*, 189).

66. H. L. Martensen, *Berlingske Tidende*, December 28, 1854, cited and translated by Kirmmse, "Thunderstorm," 89.

67. Kierkegaard, *Journals and Papers*, 2:2056.

68. Kierkegaard, *Journals and Papers*, 2:2054; see also 4:4176.

the decision to follow Jesus Christ—for example, when deciding to become baptized or confirmed (if one has been baptized as an infant); (2) to encourage persons to struggle as witnesses to God in the world, with the understanding that God upholds them in their struggles, working behind them and with them; (3) to tell individuals to follow Christ with the knowledge that when they fall infinitely short, Christ is not only their prototype but also their redeemer; (4) to foster an attitude of earnest repentance, with which Christians continually turn to God for renewal—for example, by coming to encounter God in the Eucharist (in the presence of Christ); and (5) to teach persons to lead prayerful lives so that they could learn to talk about their struggles with God.[69] With these emphases, Kierkegaard envisioned the church as a community of Christians united by the fact that they each individually embraced an active relationship with the one God revealed in Jesus Christ, not because they were all a part of the same cultural phenomenon.

These five aims sought to shift attention "*from* the public *to* 'the single individual.'"[70] They sought to persuade persons to develop their own convictions about the Christian life, guided by a prayerful reading of Scripture, giving particular attention to the calling of Jesus Christ. In Kierkegaard's thinking, without such reflection, there is no Christian life. This is because individuals cannot live by truths that are not appropriated by them personally in a way that inspires a life of faith.[71] Such was his appreciation for individual Christian reflection that he writes, "My relationship to God is a relationship of reflection, inwardness in reflection, since reflection is the predominant quality of my individuality; this is also why in praying my strength is in giving thanks."[72] This statement is easily misunderstood but, despite its Hegelian connotations, Kierkegaard does not suggest that Christianity is grounded in a synthesis between God and human reflection. Rather, he is saying that his relationship with God led him into a life of reflection—a life with regard to which he would not "dare to say that it is God who directly contributes the thoughts to me."[73] Kierkegaard continues:

69. Kierkegaard, *Christian Discourses*, 75.

70. Kierkegaard, *Point of View*, 10.

71. Importantly, this does not mean that we should keep rereading Scripture until it aligns with our prior human worldviews. To paraphrase Kierkegaard, we must not keep interpreting Christ's words until we get our own banal meaning out of them, a meaning that we can then use to support our easygoing lives in this world (Kierkegaard, *Moment*, 221).

72. Kierkegaard, *Point of View*, 74.

73. Kierkegaard, *Point of View*, 74.

One does not become a Christian through reflection, but in reflection to become a Christian means that there is something else to discard. A person does not reflect himself into being a Christian but out of something else in order to become a Christian, especially when the situation is Christendom, where one must reflect oneself out of the appearance of being a Christian.[74]

Kierkegaard here affirms the importance of the individual making an authentic decision to become a Christian.[75] What does he mean by this? When a person becomes a Christian, she must make a conscious decision to struggle to live as a Christian—to strive to follow Christ in obedience to God and to discard the distraction of the secular world. It is in this way that she becomes a *Christian Christian*—a Christian both in name and in life, within and without. That is, she becomes a person who not only believes and states that she is in a relationship with God but, through reflection, is awakened to live a life that practically expresses her relationship with God.

For Kierkegaard, it was through his own life of reflection that he "served the cause of Christianity."[76] He did not believe he could know how and to what extent God had used him.[77] Nevertheless, he trusted that it was God who governed him in his authorship and impelled him to speak.[78] Thus, at the heart of his authorship, we find a sincere Christian realism—a belief that his authorship was inspired by the governance of a real God.[79] He carried this belief into his work, writing that "it was religiously my duty that my existing and my existing as an author express the truth, which I had daily perceived and ascertained—that there is a God."[80]

The Place of Christian Doctrine

As will hopefully become clear in the following chapters, Kierkegaard did not believe that the Christian is faced with an either-or choice between God and Christian doctrine. He knew all too well how dependent his own thinking

---

74. Kierkegaard, *Point of View*, 93.

75. Kierkegaard, *Point of View*, 93.

76. Kierkegaard, *Point of View*, 93.

77. Kierkegaard, *Point of View*, 76.

78. Kierkegaard, *Point of View*, 71.

79. Kierkegaard writes, "Without a doubt Governance has supported me beyond telling; that I myself knew best of all, but not in such an extraordinary way as if I had a special relationship to God" (Kierkegaard, *Journals and Papers*, 6:6317).

80. Kierkegaard, *Point of View*, 72n.

was on the development of Christian doctrine. Yet he remained adamant that there is a proper order to Christian thought, according to which primacy must be given to the God who reveals Godself personally to us, in and through Jesus Christ, rather than to the doctrinal information that God's revelation inspires. Christian doctrine is a means to serve the living God, not the other way around. Consequently, the Christian theologian must be characterized by a humble longing both to know God and to follow God's guidance. The Christian theologian must yearn for God's will to be done to the extent that she is inspired to point to God's will and shout enthusiastically: "Look! Here is the only, the one and only joy, the one and only happiness."[81]

The Christian theologian, therefore, must always be aware that, at best, her vocation is to be a witness to the Truth who transcends the limits of her finite understanding—the Truth who has made and is making Godself known in Christ by the power of the Holy Spirit. That is, she is called to be a witness to the God who is, in an ultimate sense, the Truth. The vocation of a Christian thinker, therefore, must not be driven by scholarly ambition but by a call to service—that is, to serve that personal reality that is the Truth. While the theologian may have much to say about Christianity from the wealth of Scripture and the tradition of the church, she will also find that she continually arrives at a point where she must pronounce "enough said" and point away from the Christianities of this world to God in Jesus Christ. When she does this, she does so with the hope that God can enliven her mind so that she might be guided in her theological pursuit by the attentiveness of faith.

At the same time, Kierkegaard did not think that the primary object of Christian theology could be simply an invisible or spiritual God. At the heart of Christian theology is the recognition that God assumes humanity in Jesus Christ and thereby makes a visible person the primary object of the Christian faith. In and through this act, God endorses the world as a place where God has made, is making, and will make Godself known in a visible way. This is not to say that God reduces Godself to an object of this world, but that this world has been created as a stage in which the elements of creation can serve to proclaim the glory of God. However, this affirmation comes with the qualification that we cannot directly discern God from the surface appearance of the world without God's help. Instead, God communicates Godself to the world, not simply by way of a written or spoken message but by assuming a human form—someone who personally and humanly relates God to everyone, regardless of a person's literateness or intellectuality. For Kierkegaard, when

81. Kierkegaard, *Journals and Papers*, 1:757.

the theological task treats complex Christian principles, nuanced church history, and elaborate philosophical arguments as the primary objects of the faith (rather than as ways to direct our attention to God) it ceases to be Christian theology—that is, Christian reflection on God. Instead, it becomes a form of philosophy of religion, history of religion, or sociology of religion. In such a mode, theology directs attention back to human ideas and beliefs about God; it turns persons back upon themselves rather than to God.

Kierkegaard was not so inconsistent as to deny that serious theological work can be undertaken within the created order, but he was convinced that this work must be accompanied by a deep appreciation for the limits and proper end of Christian thinking and knowing. In so many ways, Kierkegaard was a Christian thinker who embodied what it means to do theology positively, insofar as that is possible. That is, he was committed to thinking about what a Christian really can say, while also recognizing the ways in which our finitude and sinfulness limit the extent to which we can engage in positive theology. This led him to develop a theological vision that centered on God's self-revelation in Jesus Christ, and on what it means to exist before God faithfully, prayerfully, and scripturally. The positivity of his theology, however, came with a fear and trembling which knew that positive theology requires a mediator to relate human thoughts about God to the living Truth of God—indeed, he would see this fear and trembling as itself a positive expression of faithfulness. Taking this approach, he saw it as his task to describe Christianity in a way that limited speculation and focused attention on what has been made known.

When we read through Kierkegaard's writings as a whole, we do not find anything like a fully fledged systematic theology. Instead, we find a somewhat fragmentary collection of theological responses to the hurdles that were preventing persons from living the lives to which God was calling them. For him, a more systematic understanding of Christian doctrine was not what was most needed by the Lutheran Church in Denmark, which found itself increasingly caught up in the system building of Hegelian philosophy. The much bigger problem was a failure to be attentive to the person of Jesus Christ and his call to discipleship. For Kierkegaard, it was the person of Jesus Christ and who he is for us that should be the cornerstone of Christian theology. He writes:

> Christian dogmatics, it seems to me, must grow out of Christ's activity, and all the more so because Christ did not establish any doctrine; he acted. He *did not teach* that there was redemption for men, but *he redeemed men*. A Mohammedan dogmatics (*sit venia verbo*) would grow out of Mohammed's teaching, but a Christian dogmatics grows out of Christ's activity.

Through Christ's activity (which actually was the main thing) his nature was also given; Christ's relationship to God, man, nature, and the human situation *was conditioned by his activity*. Everything else is to be regarded only as introduction.[82]

As we shall see in the following chapter, it was not only Christ's activity but also the person of Christ who was foundational to Kierkegaard's theology. Kierkegaard did not simply challenge the Hegelian attempts to bring God down to earth—to synthesize the eternal and the temporal—by countering them with an emphasis on the transcendence of God, in a way that invited a purely mystical theology. Rather, he responded by foregrounding the one in whom the eternal God establishes kinship with us in time, in an entirely unique way. As we go on to consider in chapter 5, it was certain key Christological concepts in Kierkegaard's theology that would have a major impact on Barth's early theology.

---

82. Kierkegaard, *Journals and Papers*, 1:412 (emphasis original).

Kierkegaard on Creation and Christology, against Hegelianism

A central aim of this book is to explore those elements in Kierkegaard's theology that would influence the trajectory of Barth's thought. As we shall find, it was the contra-Hegelian elements of Kierkegaard's thought that would have the most formative impact. In this chapter, we shall describe four such elements: (1) Kierkegaard's emphasis on the distinction between God and creation,[1] (2) his account of Jesus Christ as the divine incognito, (3) his paradoxical Christology, and (4) his understanding of Jesus Christ as the one mediator between God and humanity. As we shall see in chapter 5, these elements are taken up in Barth's writings in various ways, particularly his earlier writing. This is especially evident in the way that Barth commandeers several Kierkegaardian concepts that relate closely to these elements— Kierkegaardian concepts such as the infinite qualitative difference, the divine incognito, the moment, and the paradox, all of which will be discussed in this chapter. However, we shall also demonstrate that Barth was not merely influenced by a grab bag of Kierkegaardian concepts but also by the broader Kierkegaardian theology that surrounded them.

Another aim of this chapter will be to contribute to the argument that the later Barth was far more dismissive of Kierkegaard than he needed to be. As we saw in the introduction, Barth became highly disparaging of Kierkegaard. While he may have had some justifiable concerns, much of his resistance to Kierkegaard was based on misunderstanding. By engaging with Kierkegaard's theology more carefully than Barth ever did, this chapter will also present a vision of Kierkegaard's theology that is very different from the later Barth's interpretation of it.

---

1. For further discussion of Kierkegaard's account of the relationship between God and creation, see Andrew B. Torrance, "Creation: By, For, and Before God," in *The T&T Clark Companion to the Theology of Kierkegaard*, ed. David J. Gouwens and Aaron Edwards (London: Bloomsbury T&T Clark, 2020), 223–40.

GOD AND CREATION

Creation Out of Nothing

As we saw in chapter 1, Kierkegaard was committed to critiquing the Hegelian confusion of God with the world—a confusion that he went so far as to associate with pantheism.[2] A doctrine that Kierkegaard saw as fundamental to addressing this confusion is the doctrine of creation out of nothing, which has historically played a critical role in maintaining the Creator-creature distinction.[3] In addition to making this distinction clear, this doctrine also makes it plain that every facet of creation is dependent on and objectively defined by God. It is foundational to the assertion that, in every respect, God is Lord over creation.[4] When this is affirmed alongside the belief in God's benevolence, this doctrine also undergirds the conclusion that creation is "all very good."[5] More specifically, as that which God lovingly wills into existence, creation lives and moves and has its being as a reflection of God's love. Its existence is grounded in the love of God such that "every one of [God's] works seems to bear the appendage: *Praise, thank, worship the Creator*."[6] Creation is the beloved of God that finds its true meaning in loving union with God.

Within creation, however, there is not a simple uniformity to how creation relates to God. God creates a world in which there is a diversity of things that relate to God in a variety of ways. For the nonhuman things of creation, this generally involves their relating to God according to their basic nature as it is determined by God—that is, they cannot make self-conscious choices to define themselves against their created purpose. But for human beings, the

---

2. Søren Kierkegaard, *Concluding Unscientific Postscript to Philosophical Fragments*, ed. and trans. Howard V. Hong and Edna H. Hong (Princeton: Princeton University Press, 1992), 1:122–23. As we argued in chapter 1, the accusation that Hegel was a pantheist is based on a misreading.

3. While Kierkegaard makes very little reference to this doctrine in his formally published writings, his deep respect for this doctrine is clear from his journals and notebooks.

4. Kierkegaard writes, "A beautiful word to express that all creation serves but one Lord and looks to only One: *uni-versum* (the universe)." Søren Kierkegaard, *Kierkegaard's Journals and Notebooks*, ed. Niels Jørgen Cappelørn, Alastair Hannay, David Kangas, Bruce H. Kirmmse, George Pattison, Vanessa Rumble, and K. Brian Söderquist (Princeton: Princeton University Press, 2007–2020), 5:333.

5. Søren Kierkegaard, *Christian Discourses*, in *"Christian Discourses" and "The Crisis and a Crisis in the Life of an Actress,"* ed. and trans. Howard V. Hong and Edna H. Hong (Princeton: Princeton University Press, 1997), 291.

6. Kierkegaard, *Christian Discourses*, 291 (emphasis original).

situation is different. God creates humans with an autonomy that allows them to behave as though they are lords over their existence—authors of their own meaning. Further, Kierkegaard insists, God "refuses to intervene forcibly" in their life journeys.[7] This means that humans have the chance either to take offense at both God and their createdness, or to choose to align themselves with God's creative purposes. If, on the one hand, persons take offense at God, they become caught up in a life of sin, which is a state of imprisonment wherein they hold themselves captive.[8] But on the other hand, if humans embrace their createdness before God, they engage in "the true worship of God."[9] By so doing, they not only praise, thank, and worship God in and through their created being, but they also do these things by the choices they make within their existence. This is the choice to be true to their created nature. Kierkegaard saw it as a testimony to "the wondrousness of creation" that God created beings who could choose their own life direction—beings who do not simply concur with God by natural instinct but by voluntary choice.[10] This means that a two-way relationship between God and humans is possible.

To be clear, he did not see this relationship as a symmetrical relationship between equals. He was also adamant that the reciprocity of this relationship does not compromise God's aseity.[11] God's omnipotence is such that God can create out of nothing both "without giving up the least bit of its power" and

---

7. Søren Kierkegaard, *Søren Kierkegaard's Journals and Papers*, ed. and trans. Howard V. Hong and Edna H. Hong, asst. Gregor Malantschuk (Bloomington: Indiana University Press, 1967–1978), 2:1450.

8. See Søren Kierkegaard, *Philosophical Fragments*, in *"Philosophical Fragments" and "Johannes Climacus,"* ed. and trans. Howard V. Hong and Edna H. Hong (Princeton: Princeton University Press, 1985), 17. That said, we can find some places in Kierkegaard's writings where he sees sin as having its own kind of power. For example, in a journal entry from 1850, drawing on Romans 7, he writes, "Take courage, it is not you who wills the evil, it is the power of sin in you; console yourself in Christ" (Kierkegaard, *Kierkegaard's Journals and Notebooks*, 7:92). Yet, in making this statement, he would not want to deny that it is human beings themselves who hold themselves in sin.

9. Kierkegaard, *Concluding Unscientific Postscript*, 1:246.

10. Kierkegaard, *Concluding Unscientific Postscript*, 1:246–47.

11. Climacus ponders that the god "must move himself and continue to be what Aristotle says of him, ἀκίνητος πάντα κινεῖ [unmoved, he moves all]. But if he moves himself, then there of course is no need that moves him, as if he himself could not endure silence but was compelled to burst into speech. But if he moves himself and is not moved by need, what moves him then but love, for love does not have the satisfaction of need outside itself but within" (Kierkegaard, *Philosophical Fragments*, 24). See note 43 below for a summary of what Climacus means by "the god."

without becoming "ensconced in a relationship to another."[12] How is this possible? Kierkegaard did not think he could begin to explain how God creates such an arrangement. He thought it was "inconceivable" that God could create "a being that is independent vis-à-vis omnipotence"—that "omnipotence, with its mighty hand, can take hold of the world so powerfully and can also make itself so light that what has been brought into being has independence."[13] Yet what he does say is that it is made possible by an act of creation out of nothing.

> If a [human] being had the least bit of independent existence vis-à-vis God beforehand (with respect to *materia*), he [God] could not make him free. Creation out of nothing is, once again, an expression of the capacity of omnipotence to make someone independent. He to whom I owe absolutely everything—even while he has just as absolutely retained everything—this is the person who has in fact made me independent. If in creating a [human] being God himself had lost a little of his power, he would indeed be unable to make a [human] being independent.[14]

Despite denying that humans can explain how God's omnipotence enabled God to create such an asymmetrical relationship, Kierkegaard did recognize that the doctrine of creation out of nothing was fundamental for thinking through the nature of this relationship.

As we discussed in the previous chapter, one of the core elements of Danish Hegelianism that Kierkegaard set out to critique was its overconfidence in the human ability to comprehend God—to incorporate God into a systematic understanding of the world in which "God does not play the role of the Lord."[15] Such confidence, for him, exuded a lack of respect for God—a lack of fear and trembling. Instead of revering God in God's transcendence, it allowed God to be treated as one who finds a home in the bourgeois setting of Danish society. This laid the ground for a conventional Christianity in which God's revelation becomes entangled with world culture. For Kierkegaard, it was not only the case that Christian symbols were playing a decisive role in shaping Danish culture,

12. Kierkegaard, *Kierkegaard's Journals and Notebooks*, 4:57.
13. Kierkegaard, *Kierkegaard's Journals and Notebooks*, 4:57.
14. Kierkegaard, *Kierkegaard's Journals and Notebooks*, 4:57.
15. Kierkegaard, *Concluding Unscientific Postscript*, 1:156. Kierkegaard writes, "Father in heaven! You are incomprehensible in your creation; you live afar off in a light which no one can penetrate, and even if you are recognized in your providence, our knowledge is still only weak and obscures your clarity. But you are still more incomprehensible in your grace and mercy" (Kierkegaard, *Journals and Papers*, 3:3409).

but that Danish culture was also playing an outsized role in shaping, distorting, and diluting "Christianity." By drawing "God" into "the world-historical process," "God" came to be "metaphysically laced in a half-metaphysical, half-esthetic-dramatic, conventional corset, which is immanence."[16] Aside from the obvious doctrinal difficulties with such an approach, Kierkegaard also saw it as inviting a forgetfulness of God's overarching and unsurpassable authority.

When God's transcendent sovereignty is disregarded, for Kierkegaard, it becomes all too easy to confuse God with creation and confuse human life before God with life before the world. Such confusion emboldens us to think about God according to the limits of our creaturely imaginations. This leads not only to a forgetfulness of God qua Creator out of nothing but also to a forgetfulness of creation's createdness. Creation becomes something that is not objectively defined by God but by the (subjective) imagination of the creatures who live within it and are part of it. We thereby come to relate to creation as something that can be known on its own terms—or, more precisely, on our terms. Under these circumstances, God is rendered a projection of human belief, and theology becomes mythology—"mythology in the proper sense, [which] is the creation of God in human form."[17] In response to this dynamic, Kierkegaard implores:

> Recall that you are created in his image and according to his likeness, and this is the highest and the most glorious thing that can be said—and you wilfully and arbitrarily want to create him in your image and form him according to your likeness.[18]

While the danger of persons forgetting their createdness was not always an explicit concern for Kierkegaard, it was always an implicit concern—one closely tied to his ongoing emphasis on God's transcendence. This concern was essential to his critique of Hegelianism. And this critique was rooted in a commitment to the doctrine of creation out of nothing, as the fundamental doctrine for clarifying the proper place of humans in relation to God.

The Power Who Established Creation

With his commitment to the doctrine of creation out of nothing, Kierkegaard was adamant that it is God alone who establishes and fixes the meaning of

---

16. Kierkegaard, *Concluding Unscientific Postscript*, 1:156.
17. Kierkegaard, *Journals and Papers*, 3:2700.
18. Kierkegaard, *Kierkegaard's Journals and Notebooks*, 1:267–68.

creation, which entails that, ultimately, it is not up to humans to define who they are.[19] Indeed, he devoted an entire book to this point. In *The Sickness unto Death*, Kierkegaard employed Anti-Climacus to give a detailed account of what it means for humanity to be defined according to "the power that established it"—that is, God the Creator.[20]

For Kierkegaard, the ultimate task for humans is not to create their own distinctive identities but to become who God creates them to be.[21] Indeed, as Anti-Climacus argued, it is futile to attempt to define oneself apart from God.[22] No matter how hard we try to recreate ourselves (e.g., by attempting to define ourselves by our own hopes and dreams), and no matter how much we might believe we have successfully done so, our true self will always be defined "by that directly before which it is a self," which is "the power that established it."[23] For Anti-Climacus, a person's created nature always holds true; it cannot be lost, no matter how much a person embraces a life that goes against her createdness.[24] This also means that God's criteria are definitive for determining what it means to be a "vital" and "healthy" self, irrespective

19. Kierkegaard associates the contentment that creation makes for itself, apart from God, with an "arbitrary merit." He writes, "[A self-made contentment] is a sign of your miserable state that only witnesses against you! There is really nothing in the wide world that is able (no more than the whole world is able) to compensate a person for the harm he would inflict on his soul if he gave up the thought of God." Søren Kierkegaard, *Eighteen Upbuilding Discourses*, ed. and trans. Howard V. Hong and Edna H. Hong (Princeton: Princeton University Press, 1990), 235.

20. Søren Kierkegaard, *The Sickness unto Death: A Christian Psychological Exposition for Upbuilding and Awakening*, ed. and trans. Howard V. Hong and Edna H. Hong (Princeton: Princeton University Press, 1980), 14.

21. This meant that Kierkegaard denied that true freedom was to be found by focusing on "freedom of choice"; indeed, he believed such focus leads to "the loss of freedom" (Kierkegaard, *Kierkegaard's Journals and Notebooks*, 7:62–63). In agreement with Augustine, he insists that "abstract freedom of choice (*liberum arbitrium*) is a phantasy," and alongside Gottfried W. Leibniz and Pierre Bayle, he asserts "a perfectly disinterested will (equilibrium) is a nothing, a chimera" (Kierkegaard, *Journals and Papers*, 2:1268). Concrete human freedom is not grounded in a state of being equally disposed to go one way or another. Human lives are swayed by their subjective content; indeed, in one journal entry, Kierkegaard notes that this content is "so decisive" that a person can only ever choose to go one way (Kierkegaard, *Kierkegaard's Journals and Notebooks*, 7:62–63). For him, true human freedom is realized by aligning with the order for which God established creation. Any so-called freedom to choose between obeying and disobeying God is in fact a freedom to choose between freedom and unfreedom, between humanity and inhumanity, between truth and untruth.

22. Kierkegaard, *Sickness unto Death*, 20.

23. Kierkegaard, *Sickness unto Death*, 20–21, 79–80.

24. Kierkegaard, *Sickness unto Death*, 20–21.

of whether a person is conscious of her createdness.[25] More specifically, true human identity finds its home in a life of faith in which "the self in being itself and in willing to be itself rests transparently in God."[26]

The rest that a person finds in God, for Kierkegaard, is by no means generally restful. Indeed, for Kierkegaard, resting in God inspires a life of physical and emotional struggle. When a person faithfully seeks to obey God, she will find her life at odds with the sinful trends of society. The preponderance of humans is absorbed in a pursuit of immediate pleasures, which leads them astray from God's purposes. Anti-Climacus diagnoses such pursuits as characterized by despair and symptomatic of the "sickness unto death" (John 11:4). By falling into sin, humans end up pursuing life in non-life-giving ends. When they think that they are breathing healthy air, they are actually inhaling toxins that are gradually suffocating them. Consequently, they find themselves on a path to death, the condition that results from seeking life where there is none—none, that is, apart from the Creator and Sustainer. It is only by being delivered into a life of faith that a person can discover the despair of sin and be cured of it. This requires a person to die to her untrue self (the self that embraces sin) and be drawn (or dragged) into a relationship with God, who gives her life.[27] When a person finds rest in God, she discovers the most profound sense of belonging—a belonging that is only discovered when she learns that she is a beloved child of God. Reflecting on this experience, Kierkegaard comments:

> When I go out under the heavens' vault and see the many stars—then I do not, after all, feel myself a stranger in this vast world—for of course it is my father's. Still less do I feel myself abandoned in face of life's changes, its wretchedness, for indeed my father's eyes are always upon me.[28]

Belonging to God, for Kierkegaard, generates the truest and deepest sense of belonging. This is because we are all children of God "not by birth but by creation out of nothing," which means that we "belong to God in every thought,

---

25. Kierkegaard, *Sickness unto Death*, 7–8; see also Søren Kierkegaard, *The Point of View for My Work as an Author*, ed. and trans. Howard V. Hong and Edna H. Hong (Princeton: Princeton University Press, 1998), 88–89n.

26. Kierkegaard, *Sickness unto Death*, 82. Anti-Climacus ends *The Sickness unto Death* by noting that "the definition of faith" is "in relating itself to itself and in willing to be itself, the self rests transparently in the power that established it" (131).

27. Kierkegaard, *Sickness unto Death*, 6.

28. Kierkegaard, *Kierkegaard's Journals and Notebooks*, 4:378.

the most hidden; in every feeling, the most secret; in every movement, the most inward."[29] As a part of God's creation, there is no other way for us to be. God has set boundaries in place that prevent us from being able to define ourselves for ourselves. Kierkegaard says:

> As God has limited a human being physically, so he has also set bounds to him in a spiritual sense, if in no other way, simply by his being a creature, one who has not created himself. . . . By means of abstract imaginative thinking a person wishes to transform himself (although if this self-creation were to succeed, it would simply mean his annihilation); yet at the same time he does continue to exist, to be present, and therefore it can never succeed.[30]

God's authority, therefore, is far more radical than any form of earthly authority. On this matter, Kierkegaard is explicit: "God's relationship to the world is not like that of an earthly government; God has, after all, the Creator's right to demand faith and obedience from what is created, as well as that every created being in his heart dare think only all that is agreeable to him."[31] As Creator, God knows what is best for us from beyond our own immediate perception of what we think might be best. Also, since creation is bound to God in a bond of love,[32] any demands that God makes of us are not those of a tyrant but of a loving parent. In the relationship between God and creation, it is out of love that God calls creation to order. This means that a person's proper response to this creative love ought to be to follow God on God's terms and for God's reasons. Kierkegaard writes:

> We talk about being obliged to love God by virtue of being created by God—and the only one who truly loves God is the apostle, he who in order to become an instrument is absolutely unconditionally shattered by God.
>
> To love God because he has created you is to love yourself. No, if you want to love God in truth, you must show it by gladly, adoringly letting yourself be totally shattered by God in order that he can unconditionally advance his will.[33]

29. Søren Kierkegaard, *Works of Love*, ed. and trans. Howard V. Hong and Edna H. Hong (Princeton: Princeton University Press, 1995), 115.

30. Kierkegaard, *Journals and Papers*, 2:1348.

31. Kierkegaard, *Kierkegaard's Journals and Notebooks*, 2:273.

32. Kierkegaard, *Works of Love*, 115.

33. Kierkegaard, *Journals and Papers*, 2:2098.

Knowing how inclined humans are to want to define their relationship with God in their own terms, it became a kind of theological mantra for Kierkegaard that it is not God who belongs to creation but creation that belongs to God. One of the ways he sought to differentiate sharply between these two (perceived) sources of meaning was to insist that God and creation are distinguished by what he referred to as an infinite qualitative difference. By insisting on this, he sought to discourage theological ambitions that sought to go further than is possible for finite human thought, thereby venturing into idolatry—namely, theologizing that treats the distinction between God and creation as a finite quantitative difference.

The Infinite Qualitative Difference

Kierkegaard's emphasis on the "infinite qualitative difference" or "infinite qualitative distinction"[34] was elevated when the early Barth offered a firm endorsement of this language—a point that we will consider later in this book.[35] Both thinkers used this enigmatic term to emphasize that there is "nothing whatever" that human beings can do, in and of themselves, to relate themselves directly or positively to God.[36] For both, it must be "God who gives everything; it is he who makes a [human being] able to have faith, etc. This is grace, and this is the major premise of [Christianity]."[37] The infinite qualitative difference between God and humanity "always remains,"[38] and, therefore, humans are wholly dependent on God to know God.

While Kierkegaard used the concept of the "infinite qualitative difference" to make this point, he offered very little analysis or explanation of this concept, which invites speculation precisely as to how he understood the Creator-creature distinction. Yet it would be a mistake to view this term as having a meaning that can be clearly articulated. Kierkegaard does not use this term

34. See Kierkegaard, *Sickness unto Death*, 99, 117, 121–22, 126–27; Kierkegaard, *Practice in Christianity*, ed. and trans. Howard V. Hong and Edna H. Hong (Princeton: Princeton University Press, 1991), 28–29, 63; Søren Kierkegaard, *Without Authority*, ed. and trans. Howard V. Hong and Edna H. Hong (Princeton: Princeton University Press, 1997), 100, 102.

35. See Karl Barth, *The Epistle to the Romans*, trans. Edwyn C. Hoskyns, 6th ed. (London: Oxford University Press, 1933), 10.

36. Kierkegaard, *Kierkegaard's Journals and Notebooks*, 5:244.

37. Kierkegaard, *Kierkegaard's Journals and Notebooks*, 5:244; see also Kierkegaard, *Journals and Papers*, 3:2910.

38. Kierkegaard, *Kierkegaard's Journals and Notebooks*, 4:73, 5:298; Kierkegaard, *Journals and Papers*, 3:3087.

positively to try to say something about the precise nature of the relationship between God and creation.[39] Its primary purpose was negative: to rebuke conversations and cultures that try to incorporate God into a systematic understanding of the world-historical process. Against Hegel and his followers, the "infinite qualitative difference" served to stress that God cannot be synthesized with human understanding. There is little more to say. Indeed, to try to say too much more would be to miss the point. Kierkegaard referred to the "infinite qualitative difference" to steer Christians away from trying to represent God for themselves—an endeavor that, for Kierkegaard, always ends up dragging God down to the level of creaturely speculation.

In what other ways did Kierkegaard seek to redirect theological reflection, in light of his strong appreciation for divine transcendence? Following Luther, he directed attention to the one mediator in and through whom God makes Godself known: Jesus Christ, the God-human. Yet he does not present Jesus Christ as one in whom God is known directly—as if God were on display. For Kierkegaard, when God makes Godself known in Jesus Christ, God makes Godself known in the divine incognito. In other words, God veils Godself in a humanity that hides God's nature from the eyes of the world. It is only when God gives us the eyes to see that we can see Jesus as the embodiment of the one true God. When this happens, the infinite qualitative difference that separates us from God ceases to function as an alienating difference. In and through Christ, we are given to know ourselves in relationship with God. That is, humans come to relate to God in faith by sharing in a loving relationship with the *person* of Jesus Christ, the God-human, in and through whom there is both mediation between God and humanity, and redemption from the sin that alienates human beings from God.

THE DIVINE INCOGNITO

The Incarnation as God's Free Act of Love

One of Kierkegaard's best-known reflections on Christology is given by Climacus in *Philosophical Fragments*. In "The God as Teacher and Savior (A Poetical Venture)," Climacus asks readers to imagine that "there was a king who loved a maiden of lowly station in life."[40] This king wrestles with the question of how he would ever be able to approach the lowly maiden in a way that would

---

39. Kierkegaard, *Journals and Papers*, 2:1340.
40. Kierkegaard, *Philosophical Fragments*, 26.

not overwhelm her. He struggles with the thought that his power and majesty would be so mesmerizing that it would cause her to forget herself and lose her own identity. If this happened, "she would indeed have been happier if she had remained in obscurity, loved by one in a position of equality . . . boldly confident in her love."[41] Climacus continues:

> The king could have appeared before the lowly maiden in all his splendor, could have let the sun of his glory rise over her hut, shine on the spot where he appeared to her, and let her forget herself in adoring admiration. This perhaps would have satisfied the girl, but it could not satisfy the king, for he did not want his own glorification but the girl's, and his sorrow would be very grievous because she would not understand him; but for him it would still be more grievous to deceive her. In his own eyes just to express his love incompletely would be a deception, even if no one understood him, even if reproach sought to vex his soul.[42]

Building from the foundation of this story, Climacus goes on to tell a further story about the god who loves the learner.[43] In this familiar tale, deliberately adapted from the narrative of the Gospels, the god lovingly seeks to relate to the human learner without overwhelming him.[44] To do this, the god seeks to "bring about equality."[45] Without equality, "the love becomes unhappy and the instruction meaningless, for they are unable to understand each other."[46] So, he suggests, the god must become the servant: "The god must suffer all things, endure all things, be tried in all things, hunger in the desert, thirst in his agonies, be forsaken in death, absolutely the equal of the lowliest of human beings."[47] By so doing, the form of the servant becomes "his true form,"[48] and

---

41. Kierkegaard, *Philosophical Fragments*, 27.

42. Kierkegaard, *Philosophical Fragments*, 29.

43. When Climacus refers to "the god," he is referring to "the god" that is constructed for his speculative thought project (in chapter 1 of *Philosophical Fragments*) and imagined for his poetical venture (in chapter 2), in contrast to the transcendent God who truly reveals Godself in time.

44. Kierkegaard, *Philosophical Fragments*, 28.

45. Kierkegaard, *Philosophical Fragments*, 28.

46. Kierkegaard, *Philosophical Fragments*, 28; see also Kierkegaard, *Practice in Christianity*, 13–14; Kierkegaard, *Journals and Papers*, 3:2402.

47. Kierkegaard, *Philosophical Fragments*, 32–33. Climacus does not think that it would work for the god to first elevate the learner into equality with the divine, because "love . . . does not change the beloved but changes itself" (33).

48. Kierkegaard, *Philosophical Fragments*, 33.

thus, by way of a god-humanward movement, the god establishes a genuinely mutual relationship with the learner.

Climacus's "imaginary construction" echoes Kierkegaard's own understanding of the incarnation.[49] For Kierkegaard, the incarnation is an expression of God's self-giving love for creation. He writes, "God loved us first; and again the second time, when it was a matter of the Atonement, God was the one who came first—although in the sense of justice he was the one who had the furthest to come."[50] It is through a "free decision" that God descends into this world to be with us so that we might become reconciled into a reciprocal relationship with God—a human-to-human relationship with God.[51]

Kierkegaard further considers the intimate nature of the God-human relationship established in Jesus Christ in his discourse entitled "High Priest," which explores Hebrews 4:15: "We have not a high priest who is unable to have sympathy with our weaknesses, but one who has been tested in all things in the same way, yet without sin." What does it mean, Kierkegaard asks, for God to put Godself completely in the place of the sufferer by becoming human in Jesus Christ? It means that by entering fully into the human situation, God can have true empathy with us in the trials of our human experience. Not only that, when God "became a human being, he became the human being who of all, unconditionally all, has suffered the most."[52] By so doing, God "opens his arms to all sufferers" with an empathy that enables God "to be able really to comfort."[53] This does not mean that God becomes like us in every way. Jesus Christ is without sin and so remains "the Holy One" who, as God, is infinitely qualitatively different from the sinner.[54] Nonetheless, as our vicarious redeemer, Jesus takes to himself the suffering and death that is a consequence of our sin. Kierkegaard writes:

> If he, if the Redeemer's suffering and death is the satisfaction for your sin and guilt . . . did he not and does he not then put himself completely in your place? . . . My listener, this is the kind of high priest of sympathy we have. Whoever you are and however you are suffering, he can put himself completely in your place. . . . Whoever you are, O sinner, as we all are, he puts himself completely in your place.[55]

49. Kierkegaard, *Concluding Unscientific Postscript*, 1:362.
50. Kierkegaard, *Works of Love*, 336.
51. Kierkegaard, *Practice in Christianity*, 131, 171.
52. Kierkegaard, *Without Authority*, 117.
53. Kierkegaard, *Without Authority*, 117, 116.
54. Kierkegaard, *Without Authority*, 123.
55. Kierkegaard, *Without Authority*, 123–24.

Divine Hiddenness

Due to the hiddenness of God, Kierkegaard insisted, when we first encounter Jesus (whether in person, through written record, through spoken testimony, or otherwise), we cannot directly tell that he is divine; we cannot know him as the one true mediator between God and humankind. Based on our unaided sense perception, Jesus appears as just another human. In God's visible human form, God is clothed in "absolute unrecognizability"; the invisible God is veiled in visibility, in a form that is not essential to who God is eternally and antecedently in Godself.[56] This is not simply because God chooses to make Godself unrecognizable. Since God, by God's very essence, is not a physical part of creation, "the true God *cannot* become directly recognizable."[57] By assuming human flesh, God becomes "the most profound incognito or the most impenetrable unrecognizability that is possible, because the contradiction between God and being an individual human being is the greatest possible, the infinite qualitative contradiction."[58]

How, then, is it possible to know Jesus Christ as divine? Again, to know Christ's divine identity, beyond immediate appearances, Kierkegaard affirmed that a person needs to be given the eyes of faith.[59] This is not a special kind of "theo-vision" with which a person's perception can directly penetrate the humanity of Jesus Christ to see a visible divinity. Rather, faith involves its own unique form of perception, one with which a person comes to recognize and believe that Jesus Christ is the God-human without being able to see Christ's divinity directly. From our finite perspective, this means recognizing Christ as "the divine incognito" and a "sign of contradiction": a visible (human) sign that reveals an invisible (divine) reality in a way that is not only unfathomable to our limited minds but also appears incongruous or paradoxical.[60]

How, then, does a person come to have this faith? When a person directly encounters Jesus Christ, they encounter a visible sign of the invisible God, which draws them into a life of faith. Yet they will not immediately be able to view Jesus as a sign. A sign, Anti-Climacus explains, "is only for the one who knows that it is a sign and in the strictest sense only for the one who knows

---

56. Kierkegaard, *Practice in Christianity*, 127.

57. Kierkegaard, *Practice in Christianity*, 137.

58. Kierkegaard, *Practice in Christianity*, 131. As we have discussed, Anti-Climacus does not have in mind a logical contradiction here but an apparent contradiction.

59. See Kierkegaard, *Journals and Papers*, 4:3916.

60. Kierkegaard, *Practice in Christianity*, 124.

what it means; for everyone else, the sign is that which it immediately is."[61] So, not only do we need faith to recognize Jesus Christ as the God-human, we also need faith to recognize that Christ's humanity is a sign that points to God. This requires us to be earnestly attentive to Jesus Christ as the yet-to-be-known sign so that, in and through this sign, God can give us the eyes to see that Jesus is not merely human. When transformed, we not only come to know who Jesus truly is but will also find ourselves being drawn into a new life before God in which we come to see the rest of the world in a new way. We will find ourselves unsettled by the dynamics of the sinful world, where we once felt a sense of belonging, and will instead discover that our belonging lies with God.

From what we have said so far, there could appear to be a certain order to this transformative process: a person (1) encounters the visible Jesus (or, at least, a witness to his visible form), is (2) drawn by God into a relationship with God, leading her to (3) respond to God in a life of faith, which (4) results in a new life of faith and discipleship. However, such ordering is not at all clear-cut or straightforward. Due to the hiddenness of God, there is no way for a person to know precisely how God is involved in this process. Moreover, this taxonomy wrongly suggests that we have a certain systematic control over how we involve ourselves in (or exclude ourselves from) this process.

Once again, Kierkegaard believed that a Hegelian approach encourages us to overestimate our control over Christianity. This was particularly evident in the (Hegelian-inspired) Christendoms of this world that stirred up undue confidence among their citizens, prompting them to assume a certain mastery over their Christian faith, and encouraging them to synthesize "Christian" culture with world culture into what Kierkegaard calls a "hodgepodge." Under these circumstances, "Christianity" becomes distorted by the sinful ways of the world.[62] This is why Kierkegaard viewed Christendom as pagan: a culture in which Christians worship a god of their own making. When Christianity becomes mixed up with human culture, "god" also becomes mixed up with human culture, and this "is a self-contradiction" that leads to "something mythical."[63]

Again, as we have seen, Kierkegaard did not think all contradictions concerning the relationship between God and humanity were a problem; he recognized that there is both a good and a bad form of contradiction. On the one hand, there is the (apparent) contradiction at the basis of Christian theology:

61. Kierkegaard, *Practice in Christianity*, 124.
62. Kierkegaard, *Kierkegaard's Journals and Notebooks*, 7:139.
63. Kierkegaard, *Kierkegaard's Journals and Notebooks*, 7:139.

the God-human in whom kinship is created between the eternal God and temporal humanity. On the other hand, there is the idolatrous contradiction at the center of pagan mythology, according to which the human treats the eternal God as a projection of his human imagination, thereby making "god a man (the man-god)."[64] It is this latter contradiction that characterizes the distorted worship of Christendom, whereby humans think they can worship God directly but end up worshiping a finite god who is a projection of human society—a god who is wholly different from the eternal God. Again, humans cannot work out their relationship with God in and of themselves; it is God alone who provides the true conditions for this relationship, in and through the sole God-human, Jesus Christ.

Accordingly, it was a major source of frustration for Kierkegaard that the Danish people were acting as though they could see straight through Christ's incognito, so to speak—enabling them to treat Christ's divinity as an object of Christian culture. The Danish Church had come under the delusion that Christ could be known directly as the God-human—that he could be known in a way that is "inadmissible and illicit."[65] This made it all too easy to synthesize—or, more accurately, confuse—God with the world. Rather than viewing Christ as the eternal one who should be elevated on high—beyond human objectification—Christ was treated as one who could be incorporated into society as a means toward cultural progress. In Denmark, the direction of the pressure of interpretation ran from culture to Christ, when it should have been the other way around. This meant that the gospel message did not present a challenge to Danish culture but simply a divine stamp of approval.[66] To challenge the backwardness of this approach, Kierkegaard would emphasize the offensiveness of the incarnation.

The Offensiveness of Jesus Christ

For Kierkegaard, when we hear the claim that Jesus is God, we should be taken aback. The suggestion that the almighty and transcendent God became a lowly human should be shocking, a "sign of offense."[67] This is not just another piece of historical information but a complete game changer. This claim is then made all the more offensive because Jesus brings a message that is an affront to the

---

64. Kierkegaard, *Sickness unto Death*, 126.
65. Kierkegaard, *Practice in Christianity*, 95.
66. Kierkegaard, *Practice in Christianity*, 91.
67. Kierkegaard, *Practice in Christianity*, 24.

engrained cultures of this world—a message that challenges persons and calls them to an entirely new way of life before God. For Kierkegaard, Christ should interrupt us as an intruder in the sinful wilderness we have made our home.

Why did Kierkegaard emphasize that Jesus Christ is offensive to the eyes of the world? For those committed to spreading the gospel, this may seem like a strange move. He was prompted to do this because Christ had become inoffensive to Danish society for the wrong reasons; he had been turned into an altogether different reality from who he is in truth. Denmark was not embracing Christ because it had been transformed by the grace of God to see the Truth of Jesus Christ; it was embracing Christ because he had become a part of Danish culture and thereby transformed into "something different from what he is."[68] Consequently, his message had been distorted into one that would appeal to the Danish people. In short, the former scenario is a goal of Christ's revelation as it is presented in the New Testament, according to which God's kingdom comes to be on earth as it is in heaven. By contrast, the latter scenario is a goal of mediation in Hegelian theology, whereby the relationship with God unfolds in the cultural and intellectual progress of society. In the Hegelian theology of Denmark, "Jesus Christ" was being "remodeled" into an image that played into the intellectual and cultural games of Danish theology.[69] The offensiveness of Christ was neutered, and "Christ" was tailored to fit the procrustean bed of Danish society. For Kierkegaard, this amounted to blasphemy, that is,

> blasphemy, contained in the non-sensical-undialectical climax of clerical roaring: *to such a degree* was Christ God that one could immediately and directly perceive it, instead of: he was true God, and therefore *to such a degree* God that he was unrecognizable—thus it was not flesh and blood but the opposite of flesh and blood that inspired Peter to recognize him.[70]

This is a complex passage that is worth unpacking, especially since Barth would draw attention to the first half of it in the second edition of his commentary on Romans.[71] By assuming that we can know Jesus Christ directly as the God-human, Danish theology was operating on the "non-sensical-undialectical" assumption that God had assumed a form that made God directly knowable according to the (distorting) limits of immanent human reason. Danish theo-

---

68. Kierkegaard, *Practice in Christianity*, 94.
69. Kierkegaard, *Practice in Christianity*, 128 (emphasis original).
70. Kierkegaard, *Practice in Christianity*, 128; Matt. 16:17; Gal. 1:16.
71. Barth, *Romans II*, 279.

logians were under the impression that we can reason our way up to God, degree by degree, by way of our own "flesh and blood"—that is, our own immanent cognitive faculties. Such a perception, for Kierkegaard, got things the wrong way around and thereby allowed God to be treated as an object which effectively belonged to the furniture of the world. For Kierkegaard, it is the spiritual reality of God—"the opposite of flesh and blood"—that gives us the capacity to see the God-human for who he is, thereby delivering us from our inability to do so.

To analyze Kierkegaard's position more precisely, there are primarily two ways in which he considered Christ to be offensive. The more obvious of the two ways is that Christ proclaims a deeply countercultural message. While Jesus ultimately brings good news to the world, not everything he says will be immediately appealing, especially to elite members of society. For Kierkegaard, this point should be obvious to any sincere reader of Scripture. The reason Christ's message is unsettling is that so many of us are content with the shape of our sinful lives. In the grip of "the sickness unto death," we define ourselves according to our own finite ends in a way that is dead to God and in "the state of deepest spiritual wretchedness."[72] As Climacus puts it, the sinner exists in a state of imprisonment in which he "holds himself captive,"[73] and in this state, he is oblivious to the sickness that accompanies his overly positive view of his life. When caught up in sin, it is extremely difficult to notice, let alone take seriously, our state of despair. We are happily sick, so when the true world-changing gospel message is spoken into this situation, it cannot simply be taken as a message that supports us in our daily lives. When God assumes human form, God does not settle in with us in our "sickbed," nor does God comfort us in our sinful ways.[74] Rather, God reveals Godself by acts of revelation that seek to deliver us from our sickness. Anti-Climacus writes:

> Christianity did not come into the world as a showpiece of gentle comfort, as the preacher blubberingly and falsely introduces it—but as the absolute. It is out of love that God so wills but it is also God who wills it, and he wills as he wills. He will not be transformed by human beings into a cozy human god; he wills to transform human beings and he wills it out of love.[75]

72. Kierkegaard, *Sickness unto Death*, 6.

73. Kierkegaard, *Philosophical Fragments*, 17; see also Kierkegaard, *Concluding Unscientific Postscript*, 1:208; Kierkegaard, *The Concept of Anxiety*, ed. and trans. Reidar Thomte (Princeton: Princeton University Press, 1980), 22; Kierkegaard, *Practice in Christianity*, 151.

74. Kierkegaard, *Sickness unto Death*, 5.

75. Kierkegaard, *Practice in Christianity*, 62.

There is a second offensiveness, more decisive and absolute, which Anti-Climacus refers to as the "real offense, that which is related to becoming a Christian."[76] This offense "is related to the God-man . . . to Christ *qua* God-man,"[77] and it comes in two forms: offense at loftiness and offense at lowliness. The *offense at loftiness* occurs when a person takes offense at the claim that the historical Jesus is God; in Anti-Climacus's words, "The offense comes in such a way that I am not at all offended at the lowly man, but at his wanting me to believe that he is God."[78] The *offense at lowliness* occurs when a person is offended at the claim that God would appear in the form of a lowly servant, that "the loftily exalted one, the Father's only begotten Son, . . . should suffer in this manner, [and] be surrendered powerless into the hands of enemies."[79] Summing up the difference between these two forms of offense, Anti-Climacus writes, "In the one case the qualification 'man' is presupposed and the offense is at the qualification 'God'; in the second case, the qualification 'God' is presupposed and the offense is at the qualification 'man.'"[80]

In both situations, the God-human is offensive because he challenges our expectations of how God should be revealed in this world. Apart from the revelation of Jesus Christ, for Kierkegaard, we would not expect the eternal and transcendent God to reveal Godself to us in and through a visible, historical form, let alone in the form of a lowly human servant.[81] This is why it was so hard for so many Jews and Greeks to accept the gospel message (see 1 Cor. 1:23). But there is more to be said here. That God would reveal Godself in human form is not only difficult to anticipate by sinful forms of human knowing, but impossible. For Kierkegaard, God cannot directly make Godself known to us (as the true God) in the form of a visible historical person because the finite and sinful human mind is incapable of imaging or conceptualizing God. For Anti-Climacus, "A revelation, the fact that it is a revelation, is recognized by its opposite, that it is a mystery. God reveals himself—this is known by his hiding himself. Thus there is nothing of the direct."[82] So again, offense

---

76. Kierkegaard, *Practice in Christianity*, 111. Anti-Climacus also refers to this form of offense as the "essential offense" (94).

77. Kierkegaard, *Practice in Christianity*, 94; see also 81.

78. Kierkegaard, *Practice in Christianity*, 82.

79. Kierkegaard, *Practice in Christianity*, 103.

80. Kierkegaard, *Practice in Christianity*, 82.

81. Although, to be clear, for Kierkegaard, even the most impressive and pleasing spectacle of a human being would not be able to communicate God directly—"for God it is always an abasement to be a human being" (Kierkegaard, *Practice in Christianity*, 40).

82. Kierkegaard, *Journals and Papers*, 3:3110. It is also for this reason that Anti-Climacus

at the incarnation is the appropriate response, which should caution us against treating God as an objectifiable part of this world—especially as we represent this world to ourselves with minds that are alienated from God.

Be that as it may, Kierkegaard does not think that the revelation of Christ's divinity is tied to a person's response to it. While he does think that it is only by faith that we can perceive the reality of the God-human, he is also clear that, objectively, Jesus Christ is always revealing God to the one who has the eyes to see. In the face of that revelation, we are always confronted with the objective reality of the one in whom God is with us.

Given Kierkegaard's emphasis on the offensiveness, paradoxicality, and uncertainty of Jesus Christ, the question arises as to how we should approach Jesus Christ. This question will be addressed more fully in the rest of this chapter. When we do, we shall find Kierkegaard stressing that we must not approach Jesus as a "what" but as a "who." As soon as we reduce Jesus Christ to an object of human thought, we depersonalize him and thereby cease to relate to him as the God-human. What inevitably happens is that we abstract Jesus's humanity (as that which we can objectify—i.e., represent to ourselves in a concrete form) from his true identity as a divine person (as that which we cannot objectify). Consequently, once again, we end up with an idol of our own making—a God-human made in our own image of "God," according to the metrics of "worldly or earthly loftiness."[83] As such, Kierkegaard insists that we must not view Christ primarily as an object of Christological debate, a model for art and poetry, an inspiration for ethical reflection, and so on.[84] For him, when God speaks to us in Jesus Christ, God's Word speaks to us in the personal form of a human, and it is in and through this person that God draws us to Godself and calls us to discipleship.

As strange as it may sound, for Kierkegaard, when the Word becomes flesh, the God-human speaks *as* the Truth—as a personal Truth who transcends those truths that persons can conceptualize for themselves. This fundamentally personal mode of communication is yet another Christological act that clashes with how we often think about the pursuit of reason. Kierkegaard's position— that a faithful relationship with a historical person is the proper foundation for human reason—pushed squarely against the idealisms of his day. To be clear,

---

goes so far as to say (in a statement that is easily misunderstood) that Christ is not "a merely historical person, since as the paradox he is an extremely unhistorical person" (Kierkegaard, *Practice in Christianity*, 63). That is to say, the God-human is not reducible to his historical appearance; he is always characterized by an eternality that does not appear to us directly.

83. Kierkegaard, *Practice in Christianity*, 238.

84. See Kierkegaard, *Journals and Papers*, 2:1904.

his view does not degrade human reason per se but simply grounds it in right relationship with Jesus Christ. For Kierkegaard, it is because of the authority of the *person* of Jesus Christ that an individual should submit to his teachings; it is not out of a respect for his teachings that we should admire Jesus Christ.[85] Rather, he stops us in our tracks, offends us, unsettles us, and challenges us to rethink our understanding of reality.[86]

There is a final aspect to clarify regarding Kierkegaard's view of Christ's offensiveness. With respect to the offense of lowliness, there is a way to question the extent of Jesus's unextraordinary and abased life on earth. In response to Anti-Climacus, one could contend that Jesus did in fact reveal his divinity when he walked this earth as a miracle worker, as someone who attracted the attention of the whole country, became a sensation, and revealed himself remarkably in his encounter with Saul on the road to Damascus.[87] Far from being offensive, one might think that many of these acts of revelation fit expectations we might have of how God would reveal Godself in human form.

Kierkegaard does not suggest that we should disregard the miraculous performances of Jesus. But neither does he think that such performances directly reveal that Jesus is God.[88] They could, for example, simply point to the idea that Jesus had been empowered by the Spirit, much like many other figures we read about in Scripture. More importantly, Kierkegaard was of the view that miracles cannot directly lead persons to recognize Jesus Christ as the true God.[89] Anti-Climacus notes that when a person in the Gospels was confronted by the miraculous, "*directly* there was nothing to be seen except a lowly human being who by signs and wonders and by claiming to be God continually constituted the possibility of offense."[90] He continues: "You see

85. Anti-Climacus notes that if "someone says that Christ's life is extraordinary because of the results, then this is again a mockery of God because Christ's life is the in-itself-extraordinary." He also adds: "The emphasis does not fall upon the fact that a human being has lived. Only God can attach that much importance to himself, so that the fact that he has lived is infinitely more important than all the results that are registered in history" (Kierkegaard, *Practice in Christianity*, 32).

86. Kierkegaard, *Practice in Christianity*, 82, 105.

87. For Kierkegaard, this event of revelation was decisive for Saul's becoming an apostle—"a man who is called and appointed by God and sent on a mission." Kierkegaard, *The Book on Adler*, ed. and trans. Howard V. Hong and Edna H. Hong (Princeton: Princeton University Press, 1998), 176.

88. In Second Temple Judaism, impressive acts performed by humans were certainly not understood to be a surefire revelation of divinity.

89. See Matt. 24:23–24.

90. Kierkegaard, *Practice in Christianity*, 65 (emphasis original). As a side note, the suggestion that Jesus Christ claimed to be God in his earthly ministry is highly disputable.

something inexplicable, miraculous (but no more); he himself says that it is a miracle—and you see before your eyes an individual human being."[91] The most that can be derived from a direct encounter with the wonder-working Jesus, therefore, is an opportunity to know the God to whom Jesus *witnesses* but whom he *does not demonstrate* to us directly.[92] This point is critical. If a person were to accept Jesus's divine status based purely on his impressive performances, there would be a confusion on that person's part about who God is—the confusion that Christ's divinity can be recognized simply by generating human astonishment.

So, for Kierkegaard, it is not miracles per se that reveal Jesus Christ as the God-human. Rather, it is through spiritual encounter with the presence of the risen and ascended Jesus Christ today that he communicates the truth of who he is to a potential disciple. If this happens, it is not because a person has happened upon a theological account of the risen and ascended Christ. It is because Jesus Christ freely presents himself to that person; he encounters that person in a way that enables her to know him as God. Without Christ's mediatory presence, there is no revelation—it is not possible to know Christ for who he is, beyond what may be known of his humanity. In this way, as Sylvia Walsh suggests, the "proper way of relating oneself to Christ . . . [is] to learn to know him first in his lowliness, and then through that come to behold his loftiness."[93]

PARADOXICAL CHRISTOLOGY

As we have seen, Kierkegaard felt that the Christological views of his contemporaries kept trying to stretch beyond the boundaries of what we are immediately able to know.[94] In response, he sought to cultivate a more cautious posture, characterized by a deeper reverence before the eternal God. This caution did not preclude positive statements about Christology, and we find a positive

91. Kierkegaard, *Practice in Christianity*, 97.

92. Accordingly, Anti-Climacus notes, "The miracle can demonstrate nothing, for if you do not believe him [Christ] to be who he says he is then you deny the miracle" (Kierkegaard, *Practice in Christianity*, 97).

93. Sylvia Walsh, *Living Christianly: Kierkegaard's Dialectic of Christian Existence* (University Park: Pennsylvania State University Press, 2005), 71.

94. This section is a based on Andrew B. Torrance, "Kierkegaard's Paradoxical Christology," in *The Vicarious Humanity of Christ and Ethics*, ed. Todd Speidell, supplement, *Participatio*, vol. 5 (2019): 60–82.

message throughout much of Kierkegaard's later authorship. He maintains, for example, that Jesus Christ is fully God and fully human, insisting that we must not confuse these two natures—thereby avoiding any suggestion that the incarnation involves a synthesis or confusion of God and the world.[95] Kierkegaard also explicitly denies that the incarnation involves a divestment of Christ's divinity, as certain kenotic Christologies risk suggesting. In the incarnation, there is no competitive relationship between humanity and divinity, no zero-sum game between Christ's divine and human natures. Jesus Christ is "true God and true man," "the lowly human being, yet God, the only begotten of the Father,"[96] and, as such, is a single person who "is in lowliness and in loftiness one and the same."[97] Yet Kierkegaard remained adamant that we are extremely limited in our ability to understand such Christological statements.

Kierkegaard's belief that the logic of the incarnation sits beyond the limits of finite human comprehension—that the incarnation is absolutely paradoxical—places him in company with much of Christian orthodoxy. Cyril of Alexandria recognized this paradox in "the strange and rare paradox of [Christ's] Lordship in servant's form and divine glory in human abasement."[98] And in 1 Timothy 6:16, we read that Christ "dwells in unapproachable light, whom no one has ever seen or can see." In Kierkegaard's words: "God dwells in a light from which flows every ray that illuminates the world, yet no one can force his way along the paths in order to see God since the paths of light turn into darkness when one turns toward the light."[99] In his emphasis on the paradoxical nature of Christology, it is important to recognize that Kierkegaard was not endorsing a logical contradiction. Rather, he simply affirmed that Christology appears contradictory to us from our limited, finite perspective. Again, therefore, Kierkegaard's understanding of the God-human as absolute paradox sought to emphasize that humans should not place too much faith in their own systematic understanding of the incarnation.[100]

95. See Kierkegaard, *Journals and Papers*, 2:1349, 3:3087, 1:236.

96. Kierkegaard, *Practice in Christianity*, 160, 75.

97. Kierkegaard, *Practice in Christianity*, 161.

98. Cyril of Alexandria, *On the Unity of Christ*, trans. John Anthony McGuckin (Crestwood, NY: St. Vladimir's Seminary Press, 1995), 101.

99. Kierkegaard, *Works of Love*, 9.

100. Kierkegaard, *Practice in Christianity*, 82. It has been well established by C. Stephen Evans (and widely acknowledged in Kierkegaard scholarship) that, for Kierkegaard, the paradox is not a formal or logical contradiction, but just appears to be so to speculative forms of natural human reason. See Evans, *Passionate Reason: Making Sense of Kierkegaard's "Philosophical Fragments"* (Indianapolis: Indiana University Press, 1992), 97–104; Evans, *Kierkegaard's "Fragments" and "Postscript": The Religious Philosophy of Johannes Climacus* (Atlantic Highlands, NJ: Humanities Press, 1983), 212–22.

For Kierkegaard, however, the fact that God assumed a form that is paradoxical does not simply expose the limits of human comprehension; it also facilitates theological understanding. When God becomes human, God reveals Godself in a form that is familiar to us. Naturally, there will always be features of God's inner life that remain hidden to us, and this is because there are qualities that are essential to God that we cannot directly represent for ourselves through reference to creation. But in the humanity of Jesus Christ, God provides the world with a finite object through which God communicates the fullness of Godself to creation. Despite the paradox created by God's absolute otherness, in Christ God is united with creation, and through Christ God positively communicates Godself to the world. By the work of the Holy Spirit, this communication can be received by us in faith.[101]

To provide more theological context for this paradoxical Christology—and to show how it finds expression in his broader theology—we shall now turn to consider how Kierkegaard holds together the suffering, omnipotence, and changelessness of the God-human.

The One Who Suffers Omnipotently

In a view reminiscent of Cyril of Alexandria's articulation of Mary as *Theotokos*, mother of God, Anti-Climacus affirms that once God allows Godself "to be born," God "has in a certain sense bound himself once and for all."[102] Indeed, he goes so far as to say that there is a sense in which the God-human

> is in the power of his own incognito, in which lies the literal *actuality* of his
> pure human suffering, that this is not merely appearance but in a certain

---

101. We do not find much reference to the Holy Spirit in Kierkegaard's writings. This is likely because of the way in which the Spirit had come to be associated with the Hegelian theologies of which he was so critical. That said, he does note that "the Spirit brings faith, the faith—that is, faith in the strictest sense of the word, this gift of the Holy Spirit." Søren Kierkegaard, *For Self-Examination*, in *"For Self-Examination" and "Judge for Yourself!,"* ed. and trans. Howard V. Hong and Edna H. Hong (Princeton: Princeton University Press, 1990), 81. Also, he maintains that the Spirit must help us to know the Son, the Mediator, who directs us to the Father: God "becomes my Father in the Mediator by means of the Spirit" (Kierkegaard, *Journals and Papers*, 2:1432).

102. Kierkegaard, *Practice in Christianity*, 131. Earlier, Anti-Climacus writes, "When God chooses to let himself be born in lowliness, when he who holds all possibilities in his hand takes upon himself the form of a lowly servant, when he goes about defenceless and lets people do to him what they will, he surely must know well enough what he is doing and why he wills it; but for all that it is he who has people in his power and not they who have power over him" (Kierkegaard, *Practice in Christianity*, 34).

sense is the assumed incognito's upper hand over him. . . . He is not, therefore, at any moment beyond suffering but is actually in suffering. . . . [The
divine incognito] was maintained to such an extent that [the God-man]
himself suffered purely humanly.[103]

Kierkegaard makes it clear that the God-human subjects himself to human
suffering in such a way that he is caught up in the suffering of creation. This
is possible because with "everything divinely in his power," Christ is free "to
suffer humanly, every moment divinely capable of changing everything."[104] In
other words, the God-human suffers omnipotently. Kierkegaard's perspective
on Christ's omnipotent suffering is reminiscent of Cyril of Alexandria's belief
that the incarnate Word suffered impassibly.[105] For Cyril, as Paul Gavrilyuk
writes, "both qualified divine impassibility and qualified divine passibility were
necessary for a sound theology of incarnation. That affirmation of the impassibility was a way of protecting the truth that the one who became incarnate was
truly God. Admitting a qualified passibility secured the point that God truly
submitted himself to the conditions of the incarnation."[106] The words of Philippians 2:5–11 also resonate throughout Kierkegaard's depiction of Jesus Christ.
For example, in one of his upbuilding discourses, he writes: "He who was
equal with God took the form of a lowly servant, he would command legions
of angels, indeed could command the world's creation and its destruction, he
walked about defenceless; he who had everything in his power surrendered
all power and could not even do anything for his beloved disciples but could
only offer them the very same conditions of lowliness and contempt. . . . If
this is not self-denial, what then is self-denial?"[107] What does Kierkegaard

---

103. Kierkegaard, *Practice in Christianity*, 131–32.

104. Kierkegaard, *Journals and Papers*, 4:4610. Based on his interpretation of Matt. 26:53,
Kierkegaard asserts "that [Christ], the abased one, at all times had it in his power to ask
his Father in heaven to send legions of angels to him to avert this most terrible thing [his
death]" (Kierkegaard, *Practice in Christianity*, 177).

105. For further discussion of the notion that Christ suffered impassibly, see Thomas
Weinandy, "Cyril and the Mystery of the Incarnation," in *The Theology of Cyril of Alexandria*,
ed. Thomas Weinandy and Daniel Keating (Edinburgh: T&T Clark, 2003), 49–53.

106. Paul Gavrilyuk, *The Suffering of the Impassible God: The Dialectics of Patristic
Thought* (Oxford: Oxford University Press, 2004), 150.

107. Søren Kierkegaard, *Upbuilding Discourses in Various Spirits*, ed. and trans. Howard V. Hong and Edna H. Hong (Princeton: Princeton University Press, 1993), 224–25.
Kierkegaard also writes that Jesus Christ "learned obedience and was obedient, obedient in
everything, obedient in giving up everything (the glory that he had before the foundation of
the world was laid), obedient in doing without everything (even that on which he could lay

mean by "self-denial" here? He does not think that the Son (the one "who was equal with God") denies or divests himself of his essential divinity (or Godness) by taking the form of a lowly servant.[108] Rather, God chooses to express God's power through a (paradoxical) powerlessness that we might not (but should) naturally associate with God. Moreover, for Kierkegaard, God cannot express God's power through an apparent "powerlessness" without assuming a new form. God reveals Godself in an act that is not characterized by the kind of transcendent glory that characterizes the other acts of God which we read about elsewhere in Scripture. When "divine glory . . . take[s] on a lowly form,"[109] God gives Godself to relate personally to human beings in a new way, such that there would seem to be a sense in which the incarnation involves "something new for God."[110] Indeed, Kierkegaard says that "God suffers" in and through the humanity of Jesus Christ.[111] What we see here, in the words of Cyril, is a paradoxical understanding of Jesus Christ as one "who as God transcends suffering, [yet] suffered humanly in his flesh."[112] For Kierkegaard, this is possible by way of an omnipotence that "can withdraw itself at the same time it gives itself away."[113]

The Changelessness of God

Kierkegaard approaches the changelessness of God without getting caught up in systematic debates about the extent of God's attributes, their mutual compatibility, or their precise definition. For him, debates about God's attributes tend

---

his head), obedient in taking everything upon himself (the sin of humankind), obedient in suffering everything (the guilt of humankind), obedient to subjecting himself to everything in life, obedient in death" (Kierkegaard, *Christian Discourses*, 85).

108. Reflecting on John 12:32, Kierkegaard refers to the uplifted one as "God's only begotten Son, our Lord, who from eternity was with God, was God, came to the world, then ascended into heaven, where he now sits at the Father's right hand, glorified with the glory he had before the world was" (Kierkegaard, *Practice in Christianity*, 222).

109. Kierkegaard, *Eighteen Upbuilding Discourses*, 303.

110. Paul R. Sponheim, "Relational Transcendence in Divine Agency," in *International Kierkegaard Commentary: Practice in Christianity*, ed. Robert L. Perkins (Macon: Mercer University Press, 2004), 53.

111. Kierkegaard, *Journals and Papers*, 4:4610. Kierkegaard also notes that "Christ entered into the world *in order to suffer*" (Kierkegaard, *Concluding Unscientific Postscript*, 1:597 [emphasis original]).

112. Cyril of Alexandria, *De symbolo*, 24, in *Cyril of Alexandria: Selected Letters*, ed. and trans. L. R. Wickham (Oxford: Clarendon, 1983), 123.

113. Kierkegaard, *Journals and Papers*, 2:1251.

to veer beyond the remit of human theologizing, which, he believed, should hesitate to advance overly systematic doctrines of God or overly rigid descriptions of God's attributes. This is especially the case if such theological schematics risk obscuring elements that Kierkegaard took to be central to Christian orthodoxy. With this attitude, Kierkegaard was nevertheless clear that there was an important sense in which we need to affirm divine changelessness.

Kierkegaard gives particular attention to this concept in his sermon "The Changelessness of God." Here he offers a reflection on James 1:17–21, focusing especially on verse 17: "Every good and perfect gift is from above and comes down from the Father of lights, with whom there is no variableness or shadow of turning."[114] The content of this sermon closely corresponds to its title, so Kierkegaard does not surprise us by questioning the immutability of God. In the opening prayer of this sermon, he starts as he intends to go on by referring to God as the "Changeless One, whom nothing changes!"[115]

Yet Kierkegaard's approach to immutability is not straightforward. Later in the same opening prayer, he writes, "You who in infinite love let yourself be moved, may this our prayer also move you to bless it so that the prayer may change the one who is praying into conformity with your changeless will, you Changeless One!"[116] Kierkegaard does not suggest that God changes who God essentially is or what God essentially wills, but he does suggest that God can allow Godself to be moved by human prayers. For him, God is free to interact with what God creates, albeit without exhibiting the kind of arbitrary and capricious reactiveness that characterizes human behavior. And he does not believe that this ability diminishes God's immutability in any way.

But again, Kierkegaard is not interested in developing a systematic account of how God's changelessness aligns with God's interactions with creation. Predictably, this is because he does not think that the complexities of divine providence are within the purview of human understanding, since we neither possess divine changelessness ourselves nor have any other access to it. Indeed, he was highly critical of those who sought to think abstractly about God's changelessness, who get into "a phantom-battle about the predicates of God."[117] When Kierkegaard emphasizes God's changelessness, his primary concern was to recognize that God is unchangeably good, true, and

114. Søren Kierkegaard, *The Moment*, in *"The Moment" and Late Writings*, ed. and trans. Howard V. Hong and Edna H. Hong (Princeton: Princeton University Press, 1998), 263–82.

115. Kierkegaard, *Moment*, 269.

116. Kierkegaard, *Moment*, 269.

117. Kierkegaard, *Journals and Papers*, 2:1348.

loving. God's changelessness is not "an abstract something."[118] If God existed changelessly in some abstract way, then there would not be any possibility of a reciprocal relationship with God. For Kierkegaard, Scripture presents God as constant and changeless, albeit in a way that does not prevent God from being personally free to be responsive to human life.

The Role of Paradoxical Christology

In his theology, Kierkegaard primarily used the language of paradox functionally to maintain that God's relationship to creation not only transcends but also challenges what we can comprehend with our limited minds. This is not to imply that his use of paradox was merely functional; it was also theological—grounded in an understanding of who God is and who we are before God. Nevertheless, as we shall consider in this section, he did deploy his paradoxical Christology to address some of the key problems that he associated with Danish cultural Christianity.

What problems did he set out to address? One problem Kierkegaard sought to challenge was the kind of abstract speculating about Jesus Christ that distracted persons from lives of discipleship.[119] For him, this was not only a problem in his immediate context, but one that hindered much of the history of Christological reflection, right from the very beginning when Jesus's contemporaries—including the disciples—struggled to understand his true identity and vocation due to their predetermined theological commitments. From Kierkegaard's perspective, this penchant for abstraction is especially evident in theologians who act as though the heart of Christianity is to be found in doctrinal statements. Not only did this move tend to take Christianity out of the hands of less-educated members of society, but it turned Christianity against them—it changed Christianity into an intellectual luxury that was barely within their means. He writes:

> Theory and doctrine are a fig leaf, and by means of this fig leaf a professor or clergyman looks so portentous that it is terrifying. And just as it is said of the Pharisees that they not only do not enter into the kingdom of heaven themselves but even prevent others from entering, so also the professor prevents the unlearned man by giving him the idea that it depends on doctrine and that consequently he must try to follow along in a small way. This, of

118. Kierkegaard, *Journals and Papers*, 2:1348.
119. Kierkegaard, *Kierkegaard's Journals and Notebooks*, 1:247.

course, is to the professor's interest, for the more important the doctrine becomes, the more important the professor becomes as well, and the more splendid his occupation and the greater his reputation. Generally speaking, the professor's and pastor's spiritual counselling is a hoax, for it is calculated to prevent people from entering the kingdom of heaven.[120]

For Kierkegaard, there is a tendency in Christian scholarship to become so preoccupied with transposing Christian truths "into the sphere of the intellectual" that Christians ignore the Truth who stands right in front of them, calling them to leave their nets and follow him.[121] For him, this tendency distracted persons from understanding the essence of Christianity. As he saw it, where there is no Christian living, there is no Christian understanding: "When the truth is the way, being the truth is a life—and this is indeed how Christ speaks of himself: I am the Truth and the Way and the Life."[122] If a particular kind of theological discourse becomes detrimental to the liveliness of a person's discipleship, then something has gone very wrong.

At various points in his writings, Kierkegaard became so caught up in his critique of the intellectualization of Christianity that he ended up being critical of any amount of reflection on Christian doctrine. Indeed, in one journal entry, he goes so far as to write "I do not have a stitch of doctrine—and doctrine is what people want. Because doctrine is the indolence of aping and mimicking for the learner, and doctrine is the way to sensate power for the teacher, for doctrine collects men."[123] From what we have seen, he clearly had more than a stitch of doctrine, and he did not want to advance a theology that fell out of line with Christian orthodoxy. Nevertheless, he believed that the intellectual emphasis on theological digging and probing was a misplaced priority. In Kierkegaard's perception, there was no immediate need for so much attention to be given to progressing theological understanding. In many respects, he seemed to think that we would be fine with nothing more than what Richard Baxter referred to as "mere" Christianity.[124] Indeed, in his view, the ongoing speculative pursuit of theological progress was leading to regression.

---

120. Kierkegaard, *Journals and Papers*, 4:3870.
121. Kierkegaard, *Journals and Papers*, 4:4953.
122. Kierkegaard, *Practice in Christianity*, 207.
123. Kierkegaard, *Journals and Papers*, 6:6917.
124. While this phrase originated with Richard Baxter's *Church History of the Government of Bishops* (1680), it received new popularity through C. S. Lewis's *Mere Christianity* (London: Collins, 2012). See N. H. Keeble, "C. S. Lewis, Richard Baxter, and 'Mere Christianity,'" *Christianity and Literature* 30, no. 3 (1981): 27–44.

It should come as no surprise that a prime target that Kierkegaard had in his sights was the systematic Christology of Hegelianism. To put matters simply, Hegel's project attempted to advance Christology by applying his project of philosophical mediation to the doctrine of the incarnation, a form of mediation that sought to hold the divine and human together within a single system of human understanding.[125] For Kierkegaard, this pursuit turned the theological task on its head. Rather than seeing Christology as a witness that directs our attention to Jesus Christ, the person of Jesus Christ was being treated as a person who directs our attention to speculation over Christological puzzles. In Kierkegaard's words, "It is not a doctrine that [Jesus Christ] communicates to you—no, he gives you himself."[126] He continues:

> The Savior of the world, our Lord Jesus Christ, did not come to the world in order to bring a doctrine; he never lectured. Since he did not bring a doctrine, he did not try by way of reasons to prevail upon anyone to accept the doctrine, nor did he try to authenticate it by proofs. His teaching was really his life, his existence. . . . One does not become a Christian by hearing something about Christianity, by reading something about it, by thinking about it, or, while Christ was living, by seeing him once in a while or so by going and staring at him all day long. No, a *setting* (*situation*) is required— venture a decisive act; the proof does not precede but follows, is in and with the imitation that follows Christ.[127]

God speaks as a person to creation, and that person (the God-human) bespeaks God. This person is to be loved and followed, and it is by so doing that we come to know God. In this relationship, we must resist reducing Jesus Christ to a set of human ideas or principles, lest we lose out on the essential truth of who he is.[128]

This theological focus on the person of Jesus Christ is not often associated with Kierkegaard and is more commonly associated with Dietrich Bonhoeffer. In his 1933 lectures on Christology, Bonhoeffer stresses that when we approach Jesus Christ, we must resist the temptation to reduce the person of Jesus to the limits of our own preconceived Christologies—ideas that are bounded by human systems of understanding. When Christ is displaced by Christology, our

125. See Kierkegaard, *Practice in Christianity*, 136.

126. Kierkegaard, *Without Authority*, 187.

127. Søren Kierkegaard, *Judge for Yourself!*, in *"For Self-Examination" and "Judge for Yourself!,"* ed. and trans. Howard V. Hong and Edna H. Hong (Princeton: Princeton University Press, 1990), 191.

128. Kierkegaard, *Journals and Papers*, 2:1904.

commitment to Christ becomes fixated on "how" questions. We focus, for example, on questions such as "How is it possible for Jesus Christ to be both divine and human?" As a result, Christ becomes an object whom we seek to define in the light of our prior commitments, rather than the one who seeks to transform our modes of interpretation, our prior understanding. Caught up in pursuing our own systematic ideas about Christology, we become distracted from allowing Christ to transform us. Consequently, for Bonhoeffer, the task of Christology must begin by asking the "who" question of Christ: "Who are you?"—a question that recognizes the "otherness of the other."[129] As we ask this question, we are led to look beyond ourselves to the risen and ascended Jesus Christ and allow that personal reality to transform our conceptual systems and allegiances.

Kierkegaard had a decisive impact on Dietrich Bonhoeffer. Indeed, when Bonhoeffer emphasizes the "who" question, he is, in fact, channeling Kierkegaard.[130] By so doing, he gave Kierkegaard's Christology a voice that it did not previously have.[131] Why did Kierkegaard's position not receive a greater hearing? There are many possible reasons for this, but one in particular is worth reflecting upon. Arguably, Kierkegaard's greatest weakness was his tendency to overstate his case, and, as we have seen, this tendency was particularly evident when it came to his critique of Christian doctrine. His disdain for theology in Denmark, particularly in his later life, made it difficult for him to be taken seriously. Simultaneously, and partly because of his particular tack, Kierkegaard's theology was overshadowed by the dominance of Hans Lassen Martensen who, Kierkegaard comments, "sits there arranging a system of dogmatics . . . while the whole of existence is disintegrating."[132]

129. Dietrich Bonhoeffer, *Berlin: 1932–1933*, in *Dietrich Bonhoeffer Works*, ed. Larry Rasmussen, trans. Isabel Best and David Higgins (Minneapolis: Fortress, 2009), 12:303; see also 12:300–308.

130. Dietrich Bonhoeffer, *Christ the Center*, trans. Edwin Robertson (New York: Harper & Row, 1978), 27. Notably, the more recent translation of Bonhoeffer's lectures on Christology (cited above) does not show Bonhoeffer's reference to Kierkegaard because, as Christiane Tietz explains in her excellent chapter on Kierkegaard and Bonhoeffer, "this new edition follows only one student's notes instead of being a compilation of several like the earlier edition was." Christiane Tietz, "Dietrich Bonhoeffer: Standing in the Tradition of Christian Thinking," in *Kierkegaard's Influence on Theology, Tome I: German Protestant Theology*, ed. Jon Stewart (Farnham: Ashgate, 2012), 47n14.

131. Also, on a related note, it was not only Kierkegaard's emphasis on the person of Jesus Christ that had such a major impact on Bonhoeffer; his emphasis on the importance of following and imitating Jesus Christ was also a cornerstone for Bonhoeffer's *The Cost of Discipleship*.

132. Kierkegaard, *Kierkegaard's Journals and Notebooks*, 6:151.

One of the driving factors behind (what Kierkegaard saw as) the excessive investment in systematic theology is the existence of theological puzzles. Ironically, in affirming a paradoxical Christology, Kierkegaard was aware that there was a danger that a paradoxical presentation of Jesus Christ could incite the very speculation he sought to subvert—paradoxes are, after all, apparent contradictions that are prone to dispute. Fallen human reason, curious and controlling as it is, is stubborn about letting go of the desire to see theological matters explained in terms that satisfy human systematic frameworks—that satisfy our "how" questions.[133] In this respect, paradoxical Christology veritably begs "how" questions about the union between Christ's divinity and humanity. And yet the history of such projects has been fraught with confusion. Kierkegaard writes:

> In the first period of Christendom, when even aberrations bore an unmistakable mark of one's nevertheless knowing what the issue was, the fallacy with respect to the God-man was either that in one way or another the term "God" was taken away (Ebionitism and the like) or the term "man" was taken away (Gnosticism). In the entire modern age, which so unmistakably bears the mark that it does not even know what the issue is, the confusion is something different and far more dangerous. By way of didacticism, the God-man has been made into the speculative unity of God and man *sub specie aeterni* [under the aspect of eternity] or made visible in that nowhere-to-be-found medium of pure being, rather than that the God-man is the unity of being God and an individual human being in a historically actual situation. Or Christ has been abolished altogether, thrown out and his teaching taken over, and finally he is almost regarded as one regards an anonymous writer: the teaching is the principal thing, is everything.[134]

As this passage suggests, systematic approaches to Christology have led to (1) zero-sum games between Christ's human and divine natures, (2) the development of a "speculative unity of God and man" that directs our attention to an overarching system within which God and humanity are united, and (3) the setting aside of the person of Christ to focus on his teachings.

How did Kierkegaard respond to such approaches? He insisted that we cannot teach persons to comprehend Christ in the way that we can teach persons to solve philosophical problems, writing that "[Christ] knows that

133. Kierkegaard, *Philosophical Fragments*, 42–43.
134. Kierkegaard, *Practice in Christianity*, 123.

no human being can *comprehend* him, that the gnat that flies into the candlelight is not more certain of destruction than the person who wants to try to comprehend him or what is united in him: God and man."[135] Nonetheless, he was completely clear that we do need to come to know him because "he is the Savior, and for no human being is there salvation except through him."[136] With this concern in mind, Kierkegaard's paradoxical Christology sought to direct our attention toward knowing the person rather than explaining the doctrine—as someone to be loved and respected, not simply observed and speculated over. Kierkegaard's alternative approach to Christology, therefore, sought to encourage a primarily personal, rather than speculative, relationship with Christ. For Kierkegaard, we must trust in the person who unites God and humanity and simply accept that his divine-human identity is unexplainable by finite human minds. By focusing on the person rather than abstract doctrine, Kierkegaard's paradoxical Christology avoids directing our attention to a puzzle to be solved; instead, it seeks to halt speculation over matters that we cannot (and should not try to) explain in our own finite terms. Faith in Christ "does not consist in choosing either one side of the contrast [his lowliness/humanity or his loftiness/divinity] but in choosing a unity of both sides."[137] It consists in believing and trusting in a person and giving him the kind of attention that was given to him by his apostles.

> In the conversation of the apostles one continually gets the impression that they had been personally in the company of Christ, had lived with him as with a human being. Therefore their speech is very human, although they never do forget the infinite qualitative difference between the God-man and other human beings.[138]

Kierkegaard thus directs our attention to the person of Christ who can be known personally in a way that is comparable to how the apostles related to him.

The Paradoxical Mediator

It is difficult to imagine another verse from Scripture that better captures Kierkegaard's Christological vision than 1 Timothy 2:5: "There is one God; there is also

---

135. Kierkegaard, *Practice in Christianity*, 77.
136. Kierkegaard, *Practice in Christianity*, 77.
137. Kierkegaard, *Practice in Christianity*, 161.
138. Kierkegaard, *Journals and Papers*, 2:1385.

one mediator between God and humankind, Christ Jesus, himself human." Yet he never cites this verse and only rarely refers to the mediation of Jesus Christ. Why is this? There are many significant theological topics, such as the Holy Spirit, the Trinity, the mediation of Christ, participation in Christ, and reconciliation, which receive surprisingly little attention in Kierkegaard's writings. In many cases, these topics are avoided because of how they were treated in Hegelian theology. They were being used by Hegelianism to show how "God" is immanent in the world-historical process. As we have seen, this was particularly problematic when it came to Christology, where, especially through Martensen's work, the Hegelian synthesis of God and humanity had become a cornerstone of the cultural Christianity of Denmark. This situation not only allowed but encouraged the gospel to be chopped and changed to fit its particular milieu.

As we have seen, Kierkegaard pushed back against the Hegelianism of his context by insisting on the "infinite qualitative difference between God and man."[139] Indeed, at one point, he insists so strongly on this qualitative difference that he suggests "we cannot speak of fellowship with God, and man cannot endure the fellowship, cannot endure continually having only the impression of God's presence."[140] This statement may seem out of place for Kierkegaard, given his emphasis on the decisiveness of a loving relationship with God. One could even put these words down to rhetorical flourish, especially since they appear in a journal entry. But it is also possible to interpret this statement in a way that is in keeping with his theological vision. For Kierkegaard, direct fellowship with God, in all God's transcendent glory, really is beyond the scope of human possibility—the infinite qualitative difference "always remains."[141] This means that right relationship with God always requires the mediation of the incarnate Son. Drawing on John 6:45, Kierkegaard writes, "God directs us to the Son, to the Mediator," and pronounces: "In the Mediator I can be a father to you."[142] By assuming human flesh, the eternal Son mediates God to humanity, thereby allowing human beings to know God according to the limits of their finitude. In this way, "the glory is not directly known as glory but, just the reverse, is known by inferiority, debasement."[143] In the person of Christ, the glory of God is mediated to the lowliness of the world—to a world that is unable to contain God in God's transcendent glory.

---

139. Kierkegaard, *Journals and Papers*, 2:1416.
140. Kierkegaard, *Journals and Papers*, 2:1416.
141. Kierkegaard, *Journals and Papers*, 2:1349.
142. Kierkegaard, *Journals and Papers*, 2:1432.
143. Kierkegaard, *Judge for Yourself!*, 161.

But again, Kierkegaard hesitated to use the language of mediation to talk about God's relationship to creation. Instead, he primarily chose to talk about Christ's mediatorial role in terms of Christ's paradoxicality. As we have seen, he presented Jesus Christ as one who incomprehensibly and unsettlingly brings God and humanity together in a way that does not confuse the Creator-creature distinction. For Kierkegaard, it is a paradoxical Christology that best draws attention to this message. The presentation of Jesus Christ as absolute paradox halts those systematic and depersonalizing attempts to comprehend the logic of Jesus Christ and focuses attention instead on the person who invites us to come and follow him. Importantly, however, as soon as the language of paradox has served this purpose, it can be dropped from discussion. This is the case with many of the complex, extrabiblical terms that line the pages of Kierkegaard's writings; as soon as they had helped to get persons (particularly the more intellectually elite) to a place where they could earnestly follow Jesus Christ with a personal, loving, and devoted faith, they had served their purpose.

While Kierkegaard emphasized paradox more than mediation, the mediatorial role of Jesus is fundamental to his theology. So, in our concluding section, we shall turn to consider this more positive ground to his theology. It was Barth's failure to understand and appreciate this core element in Kierkegaard's theology that allowed Barth to become unduly critical of Kierkegaard.

Christ the Mediator

As we have seen, Kierkegaard's paradoxical Christology sought to emphasize the limits of human understanding when it comes to knowing Christ. However, as we also indicated, Kierkegaard had many positive things to say about Christ's role as mediator—as the one who "walked the infinitely long way from being God to becoming man."[144] In this section, we turn to the more positive side of Kierkegaard's Christology. We shall begin by elaborating on why he thinks there is a need for a mediator between God and creation. We then consider his emphasis on the role of the teacher rather than the teaching, looking more closely at Kierkegaard's emphasis on the "who" question. Last, we think about how we should understand what it means to encounter Jesus Christ in his contemporaneity—Kierkegaard's account of how the Jesus of history continues to be with us and for us today.[145]

144. Kierkegaard, *Practice in Christianity*, 171.
145. For an excellent discussion of the theme of "Christ for us" in Kierkegaard and

The Need for a Mediator

Kierkegaard acknowledges that there is a sense in which all humans, by virtue of being created, are naturally related to God. Yet, it does not follow, for him, that humans have an inherent ability to relate themselves back to God. When we try to relate ourselves to God by way of our own powers, he cautions, our eyes "turn toward heaven," we are "astonished at the infinite distance," and our eyes cannot "find a resting place between heaven and earth."[146] This is because God does not create humans with an inherent ability to bring themselves into relationship with God in a way that is true to who God is. Rather, God creates humans to relate to God *with God*; it is only by the grace of God that human minds can become truly oriented toward God and thereby become all that God creates them to be.

How does God make this possible? This is possible, for Kierkegaard, because "we have a mediator."[147] What we cannot know for ourselves is made known by God coming to be with us in Christ. It is in Christ that God gives us "a resting place between heaven and earth"; in Christ, God meets us in the midst of this world and utters the words: "Come here to me, all you who labor and are burdened, and I will give you rest."[148] And in Christ, God "involves himself with us human beings" so as to establish the basis for an interpersonal relationship between two infinitely qualitatively different parties.[149] For Kierkegaard, it is "necessary" for us to have a mediator so that we can be made "aware that it is God with whom, as we say, I have the honor of speaking; otherwise a man can easily live on in the indolent conceit that he is talking with God, whereas he is only talking with himself."[150] It is by coming to know Jesus Christ, the God-human, that our lives can become responsive to God in a reciprocal way that would not otherwise be possible.

The Teacher Rather Than the Teaching

Earlier in our discussion of Kierkegaard's Christology, we turned to Climacus's poetic account of the incarnation in *Philosophical Fragments*, which is the work

---

Bonhoeffer, we highly recommend Philip Ziegler's essay "Christ for Us Today: Promeity in the Christologies of Bonhoeffer and Kierkegaard," *International Journal of Systematic Theology* 15, no. 1 (2013): 27–45.

146. Kierkegaard, *Journals and Papers*, 2:1200.

147. Kierkegaard, *Journals and Papers*, 2:1200 (Heb. 3:6).

148. Kierkegaard, *Practice in Christianity*, 13–14 (Matt. 11:28).

149. Kierkegaard, *Journals and Papers*, 2:1425; see also 4:4517.

150. Kierkegaard, *Journals and Papers*, 2:1424.

in which Kierkegaard makes a decisive move toward a more Christological vision of theology. He then later cements this move in *Concluding Unscientific Postscript*, which he describes as the "turning point" in his authorship—as the work that turns to focus more specifically on "the *issue*: becoming a Christian."[151] At the heart of this development was a new focus on Jesus Christ as the mediator of Christian Truth—as the one who is not simply a *means* for human beings to receive certain truths but also the one who *is* the Truth-for-human-beings. It follows that it is not a person's inward transformation that is the ground of her relationship with God, but rather an interpersonal relationship with God. As such, the living *person* of Jesus Christ is more fundamental than the *message* he communicates; that is, primacy is given to the teacher over the teaching. To gain a better understanding of this transition, we will look more closely at Climacus's position in *Philosophical Fragments*.

In *Fragments*, Kierkegaard deploys Climacus to expose the implications of interpreting Christian experience from an idealist perspective. His concern is to show the irreducible incompatibility between the New Testament account of the Christian faith and the absolute idealism of Hegel. This task gets underway with an account of the Socratic approach. On Climacus's rendering of the Socratic account, human beings can only recognize the truth—that is, the universal truths that are the objects of knowledge—to the extent that the truth is already inherent in the mind, either explicitly or subliminally. We can only recognize the truth because, in a certain sense, we already know it. Accordingly, for Socrates, knowledge of universals cannot be confused with the knowledge of particularities. Particularities, as this includes historical events, are only significant to the extent that they exemplify universals and universal truths. On this view, the particular moment when an individual "discovers" the truth and the particular teacher who prompts an individual to recollect the truth neither have nor, indeed, can have any significance. On a Socratic account, "any point of departure in time is *eo ipso* [in and of itself] something accidental, a vanishing, an occasion. Nor is the teacher anything more."[152] For Socrates, truth resides within the mind; it cannot enter the mind, and no condition can be gained that leads the mind to discover something new or outside the mind. All that the learner needs to realize the truth is a "Socratic midwife"—a teacher who can "bring to birth" what is immanently there.[153] On this schema, the particular identity of the midwife is irrelevant to the learner's

151. Kierkegaard, *Point of View*, 63 (emphasis original).
152. Kierkegaard, *Philosophical Fragments*, 11.
153. Kierkegaard, *Philosophical Fragments*, 9–13.

relation to the truth just as the identity of the school teacher who happened to bring one to discover a mathematical truth is irrelevant to one's knowledge of that truth. Moreover, the particular historical moment when the discovery was apparently made is no less relevant.

Climacus then considers, hypothetically, how our relationship to the truth might look if the idealist (Socratic) model were to be altered.[154] He writes, "If the situation is to be different, then the moment in time must be of decisive significance."[155] If a moment in history is to be decisive to an individual's capacity to access the truth, then that would mean that "the seeker up until that moment must not have possessed the truth. . . . Consequently, he has to be defined as being outside the truth."[156] The learner, therefore, would be in a state of untruth. The absence of the condition of being in relation to the truth would mean, therefore, that the learner's mind was enslaved to untruth, captive until a new condition could be provided that would liberate the learner's mind from the alienated forms of thought that conditioned their thinking. Climacus decides to refer to this state of untruth as a state of sin.[157] Under such conditions, he suggests that, for the mind to be set free from sin to learn the truth, the learner would require much more than a mere midwife to bring the learner to the recognition of the truth. Why? It is because if the moment is of decisive significance, the truth cannot be inherent within the learner—there would be no truth within the learner for the midwife to deliver. Consequently, for the learner to be brought into relationship with the truth, he would need someone who could "provide him with the condition for understanding it." This teacher would have to have the ability to transform the learner and to

154. As the Hongs point out, "No distinction is made here between Socrates and Plato. Nor is a distinction made in *Fragments* between Socrates-Plato and philosophical idealism nor between them and naturalism and scientific humanism, inasmuch as all of them presuppose an immanental possession of genuine knowledge or of the condition for acquiring it" (Kierkegaard, *Philosophical Fragments*, 277n8).

155. Kierkegaard, *Philosophical Fragments*, 13. As we shall see, under the influence of Kierkegaard, the "moment" becomes a critical theme in the second edition of Barth's commentary on Romans.

156. Kierkegaard, *Philosophical Fragments*, 13.

157. Kierkegaard, *Philosophical Fragments*, 15. Climacus contends that it would be a contradiction to suggest that the loss of the condition was due to an act of the god. As Evans explains, "Presumably Climacus is here simply assuming that whatever else God may be, God must be seen as good, as the source of our true humanness, and it would thus be contradictory to think of God as the destroyer of that humanness" (Evans, *Passionate Reason*, 35). Climacus also thinks it would be a contradiction to suggest that the condition was lost by way of an accident on the part of the learner.

create within the learner something radically new, that is, a condition that would otherwise be absent. To do so would far surpass the powers of a mere human teacher. In Climacus's words, "No human being is capable of doing this; if it is to take place, it must be done by the god himself."[158] Climacus considers what we should call "the god who gives the condition and gives the truth."[159] He continues:

> Let us call him a *savior*, for he does indeed save the learner from unfreedom, save him from himself. Let us call him a *deliverer*, for he does indeed deliver the person who had imprisoned himself, and no one is so dreadfully imprisoned, and no captivity so impossible to break out of as that in which the individual holds himself captive! And yet even this does not say enough, for by his unfreedom he had indeed become guilty of something, and if the teacher gives him the condition and the truth, then he is, of course, a *reconciler* who takes away the wrath that lay over the incurred guilt.[160]

This savior, deliverer, and reconciler, Climacus goes on to propose, must be not only a divine teacher but he must also be human. "In order for the teacher to be able to give the condition, he must be the god, and in order to put the learner in possession of it, he must be man."[161] The teacher must be "the god in human form."[162] To be clear, Climacus does not think that "the condition" is simply a one-off gift that the god-man implants in the learner, which then allows the learner to relate to the truth for himself apart from the teacher. For the learner to continue to exist in truth, he "must constantly cling firmly to the teacher." This is because the possession of the condition for being in relation to the truth is inseparable from the relationship to the teacher who, on this understanding, has decisive significance for recognition of the truth.[163] It is only by surrendering (and continuing to surrender) his life to the teacher that the learner becomes transformed in and through a relationship to the truth—and finds himself living out the "happy passion" of faith.[164]

Through the agnostic voice of Climacus, Kierkegaard demonstrates two things in *Philosophical Fragments*. First, he demonstrates the radically either-or

158. Kierkegaard, *Philosophical Fragments*, 14–15.
159. Kierkegaard, *Philosophical Fragments*, 15.
160. Kierkegaard, *Philosophical Fragments*, 17 (emphasis original).
161. Kierkegaard, *Philosophical Fragments*, 62.
162. Kierkegaard, *Philosophical Fragments*, 55.
163. Kierkegaard, *Philosophical Fragments*, 62.
164. Kierkegaard, *Philosophical Fragments*, 54, 59.

nature of the choice between, on the one hand, a Socratic endorsement of the immanent way of knowing the truth, or, on the other, an alternative way of knowing that is analogous to that presented by the New Testament. Second, he shows the coherence of this alternative approach. In so doing, he questions the undue confidence that is placed in the immanent powers of human reason, opening the door to the suggestion that the truth may be found in a faithful relationship with the God-human *teacher* which cannot be delivered by human reason operating exclusively with the ideas and suppositions inherent within our minds. This is a teacher whose existence and nature cannot be conjured up from the mind's own resources, by philosophical argumentation or the analysis of *teaching*. If such a teacher fell within the scope of human reason, then the totality of the Christian witness would collapse into Socratic immanence. The message that the gods gave Socrates at Delphi, "Know thyself" (*gnōthi seauton*), would be sufficient to present us with the totality of the Christian witness to God. Instead, Climacus's account draws attention to the gospel message that God can only be known in and through a relationship, a relationship in which God discloses Godself to us personally, in history, in the person of Jesus Christ who is the way and the truth and the life. It is by encountering God in the presence of the "God in time" that our minds are delivered from error and reconciled to the truth, enabling us to discern in truth that Reality for which we were created to be in relationship. Because of this, faithful theology must reject any attempt to operate with an account of an "immanental underlying kinship between the temporal and the eternal, because the eternal itself has entered into time and wants to establish kinship there."[165] The object of faith, in short, is "not the *teaching* but the *teacher*," who presents himself to us in space-time, in history.[166]

Now, there is a danger that the *Fragments* be read as an attempt to demonstrate the Truth of the Christian faith. However, if it is read in this way, Kierkegaard would be hoist with his own petard, since it would be the result of an exercise in immanence. Instead, *Fragments* is simply a "thought project" that explores the question of what would be necessary for knowledge of ultimate truth apart from the Socratic package. What emerges from Climacus's picture is a profound questioning of every facet of the Socratic framework. The alternative picture, in turn, looks remarkably like the knowledge of God that we find in the New Testament. To reiterate again, *Fragments* is not an argument for the New Testament account; it is simply an attempt to show that it has

---

165. Kierkegaard, *Concluding Unscientific Postscript*, 1:573.
166. Kierkegaard, *Philosophical Fragments*, 62 (emphasis original).

its own radical coherence, a coherence that makes it different from Socratic idealism at every nodal point.

This theme is picked up more forcefully in *Practice in Christianity*. Here, Anti-Climacus—a firmly Christian voice—takes readers beyond the merely conjectural approach of Climacus. He argues that the Christianity of Christendom had become so focused on the teachings concerning Jesus Christ that it was failing to give primacy to his personal reality. The result was that Jesus Christ was regarded (at least in practice) as no more essential for communicating the truth than any merely human prophet. While a prophet may serve to provide new information about God's purposes for the world, the direct way that she does this is no different from the way of the preacher who delivers the Sunday sermon or the professor who teaches Christian doctrine.

The subjugation of the person of Jesus Christ to Christian teaching, for Anti-Climacus, was a sign that "the modern age has abolished Christ."[167] By incorporating "Jesus Christ" into "the imaginative medium of abstraction," society was abstracting "Christ" into a place where "God does not exist or is not *present*."[168] Against the Hegelian theologies of his day, he believed that the idealization of Jesus Christ—turning Jesus Christ into an idea—entailed the paganization of Christianity. It resulted in the displacing of Christianity's proper object of worship, the person of Jesus, with human Christological constructs. For Anti-Climacus, it is always the person of Jesus Christ who must determine not only how he should be understood but also, more generally, how we should come to understand what it means to be human. For him, no matter how much we may think that we have progressed in our scientific, philosophical, moral, aesthetic, and historical understanding of the world, if we move away from the person of Jesus Christ, we fall away from the ultimate truth who defines who we are.

In Danish Christendom, by contrast, Christians grow into a deeper relationship with the Truth of Christianity as their understanding of Christ's teachings grows and develops. So, for example, the ability to know the truth of who Jesus Christ is (qua God-human) was seen to be a result of (Hegelian) progress whereby society's citizens were more readily willing to embrace the (so-called) teachings of and about Jesus Christ. Anti-Climacus comments on this situation:

---

167. Kierkegaard, *Practice in Christianity*, 128.
168. Kierkegaard, *Journals and Papers*, 2:347.

Everything is made abstract and everything personal abolished: we take Christ's teaching—and abolish Christ. This is to abolish Christianity, for Christ is a person and is the teacher who is more important than the teaching.—Just as Christ's life, the fact that he has lived, is vastly more important than all the results of his life, . . . so also is Christ infinitely more important than his teaching. It is true only of a human being that his teaching is more important than he himself; to apply this to Christ is blasphemy, inasmuch as it makes him into only a human being.[169]

Again, direct teaching about Jesus Christ is unable to represent who Jesus Christ is qua the God-human; because the God-human "is a paradox, . . . all direct communication is impossible."[170] The divine-human identity is wholly unique to the person of Jesus Christ and therefore always transcends our own finite and sinful systems of thought. For the teaching to be true to the teacher, we must always recognize it is first and foremost a witness to the teacher. The Christian's relationship to Jesus Christ (and therefore to the Truth of Christianity that he mediates to the world) must always be understood to derive from the teacher "who is inseparable from and more essential than the teaching."[171] As Kierkegaard himself writes:

> Since he [Jesus Christ] is the Truth, you do not find out from him what Truth is and now are left to yourself, but you remain in the Truth only by remaining in him; since he is the Way, you do not find out from him the way you are to go and now, left to yourself, must go your way, but only by remaining in him do you remain on the way; since he is the Life, you do not have life handed over by him and now must shift by yourself, but you have life only by remaining in him.[172]

To summarize, the Truth of Christianity cannot be contained within a human worldview or a set of beliefs, as an idea that can then be redeployed as an object of intellectual discourse or a source of inspiration for culture-shaping. Christianity cannot simply be grounded in the assumption or acceptance of orthodox

---

169. Kierkegaard, *Practice in Christianity*, 123–24.

170. Kierkegaard, *Practice in Christianity*, 123.

171. Kierkegaard, *Practice in Christianity*, 123.

172. Kierkegaard, *Without Authority*, 188; see also Kierkegaard, *Practice in Christianity*, 34–35, 207–9, 238.

Christian teachings (whatever they may be). How, then, does a person relate to the Truth of Christianity? This happens by following Jesus Christ, by hearing his call to discipleship and responding with a life of faith and love. Within this life, a person gradually becomes transformed in conformity to the reality of Jesus Christ, the one and only God-human mediator.

Contemporaneity with Jesus Christ

It is all well and good to say that we need to give more attention to the person of Jesus Christ—to say that our relation to the Truth is tied up with a personal relationship with Jesus Christ himself. However, this raises the difficult question as to how we relate to the person of Jesus Christ today without, at the very least, relating ourselves to a belief, idea, or image that is held in our minds. For Kierkegaard, however, we are not simply left to relate to Christ by way of our imagination or reason. There is a sense in which we can still encounter Jesus Christ today, contemporaneously, and it is this encounter that serves as the foundation for the Christian life.

How does Kierkegaard understand this? He is not under the illusion that Christ shows up immediately to persons on the street or in a church and thereby draws them into a life of faith (as he did with Saul on the road to Damascus). For Climacus, the risen and ascended Christ encounters persons today by way of a "nonimmediate" contemporaneity[173]—that is, Christ encounters persons spiritually and in this way draws them to himself. Nervous about Hegelianism, Kierkegaard does not describe this encounter in "spiritual" terms. Nonetheless, the nonimmediate nature of a person's encounter with the presence of Christ is probably best described as a "spiritual" encounter. That is to say, the reality of Jesus Christ encounters us from beyond our immediate perception, transforming us without our being able to apprehend the occurrence of this transformation. At best, we only see in retrospect that Jesus Christ has encountered us.

When a person encounters the presence of Jesus Christ, that person interacts with the reality of the God-human. He then draws her into faith in his presence, such that, in faith, he becomes "a contemporary in the *autopsy*"— that is, in the personal act of seeing.[174] In and through this encounter, a person

---

173. Kierkegaard, *Philosophical Fragments*, 67–68.

174. Kierkegaard, *Philosophical Fragments*, 70. As the Hongs helpfully note, *autopsy* is literally the personal act of seeing (in the Greek: *autos* [self] + *optos* [seen]) (Kierkegaard, *Philosophical Fragments*, 296n39).

will not only find herself contemporary with the God-human, she will also find herself being drawn to become a follower of Jesus Christ.[175] This is decisive for Anti-Climacus. Indeed, he contends: "If you cannot prevail upon yourself to become a Christian in the situation of contemporaneity with him, or if he cannot move you and draw you to himself in the situation of contemporaneity, then you will never become a Christian."[176] It is only in and through contemporaneity with Christ that a person is drawn into a personal relationship with Jesus Christ and thus a life of faithful discipleship. Faith, for Kierkegaard, expresses that a person is participating in a two-sided relationship with the reality of Jesus Christ. Anti-Climacus writes:

> It is indeed eighteen hundred years since Jesus Christ walked here on earth, but this is certainly not an event just like any other events, which once they are over pass into history and then, as the distant past, pass into oblivion. No, his presence here on earth never becomes a thing of the past, thus does not become more and more distant. . . . As long as there is a believer, this person, in order to have become that, must have been and as a believer must be just as contemporary with Christ's presence as his contemporaries were. This contemporaneity is the condition of faith, and, more sharply defined, it is faith.[177]

At the same time, this life of faith does not come from nowhere as if there were no worldly phenomena serving to occasion the life of faith. As Climacus acknowledges, the communication of faith does await a particular form of teaching, namely, "a believer's report."[178] However, unlike the report of the historian or philosopher, the testimony of the believer draws attention to the "object of faith."[179] The believer's testimony generates an "ambiguity of awareness," one that Climacus views as an essential feature of the mindset of the person who is reconciled into faith. This mindset does not look to its own

---

175. Kierkegaard, *Philosophical Fragments*, 100. The Hongs translate "follower" from the Danish term *Discipel*. This can also be translated "disciple," which has clearer Christian connotations and, therefore, finds much more alignment with some of the other "Christian" terms that Climacus uses allusively in *Fragments* (Kierkegaard, *Philosophical Fragments*, 281). This point is made in Murray A. Rae, *Kierkegaard's Vision of the Incarnation: By Faith Transformed* (Oxford: Clarendon, 1997), 89n21; and Evans, *Passionate Reason*, 96n3.

176. Kierkegaard, *Practice in Christianity*, 64.

177. Kierkegaard, *Practice in Christianity*, 9–10.

178. Kierkegaard, *Philosophical Fragments*, 104.

179. Kierkegaard, *Philosophical Fragments*, 104.

powers of reasoning for assurance but humbly turns toward God.[180] Important though it might be, the believer's report only provides an occasion, "an historical point of departure," for Jesus Christ to draw a person to himself and thereby deliver that person into a life of faith. Ultimately, it is only through God's active mediation that a person can truly encounter the Truth of God in Jesus Christ and thereby participate in the Christian life.[181]

CONCLUSION

The aim of this chapter has been to introduce some of the core elements of Kierkegaard's theology that would go on to impact Barth. These elements hold together in a theological project that sought to think carefully and critically about how God relates to humans from beyond their immanent thought worlds. Negatively, we have seen that Kierkegaard was fully committed to exposing the limits of human knowing when it comes to understanding the Christian faith. Yet we have also seen that his theology was not wholly negative. Indeed, Kierkegaard's Christocentric understanding gave him a profoundly positive basis for thinking about God's relationship with humans. Unfortunately, Barth never really saw beyond the more negative side of Kierkegaard's theology, which was the side that had the most constructive impact on him. This meant that when Barth's theology went in a more positive direction, he felt he had to leave Kierkegaard behind. As we shall consider in chapter 5, had Barth developed a better understanding of Kierkegaard's emphasis on the mediatorial role of Christ, he may not have felt a need to become so dismissive of Kierkegaard.

---

180. Kierkegaard, *Philosophical Fragments*, 104.
181. See Kierkegaard, *Philosophical Fragments*, 93.

3

Karl Barth's Stand against Idealism, Cultural Religion, and Nationalism

In this chapter, we discuss the religious, sociocultural, and intellectual developments that Barth sought to challenge, developments which provided the context for his distinctive theological path. The chapter is divided into three parts. The first focuses on Barth's analysis of certain features of the Enlightenment and the impact of these on the church and theology. The second looks at the ensuing sociopolitical developments—most notably, the impact of cultural Protestantism, the impact of nationalism, and the failure of the church and the theology of the time to address these. The third explores the nature and character of Neo-Kantian idealism that was the prevailing philosophical influence in the University of Marburg, where Barth studied. This sets the scene for appreciating the radical nature of Barth's break with the philosophical, religious, and sociopolitical commitments of his teachers. What should be apparent from this survey are the striking parallels between the intellectual context that Barth confronted in twentieth-century Germany and that which Kierkegaard addressed in nineteenth-century Denmark. The concluding section will discuss Barth's contemporary, Rudolf Bultmann, who also studied in Marburg and who has been viewed as the theological heir of Kierkegaard. However, whereas Barth's theological approach constituted a repudiation of the monist idealism of the Marburg school, Bultmann's approach remained, in its key elements, a product of the Neo-Kantian idealism of his Marburg teachers.

Like Kierkegaard, Barth challenged, first, the Enlightenment approach to pedagogy and the attendant assumptions about our relation to the truth and the nature of discovery; second, the extent to which a cultural agenda determined the shape and direction of the church's theological commitments; and, finally, the impact of monist idealism on the church and its interpretation of the faith. Due largely to the existentialist element in his rendering of the New Testament, Bultmann is often regarded as reflecting Kierkegaard's theological agenda. We shall argue, however, that it was Barth rather than Bultmann who was true to the trajectory that Kierkegaard had established almost a century earlier.

REASONABLE RELIGION, PEDAGOGY, AND INCIPIENT IDEALISM

In Barth's view, the assumptions and affiliations that emerged in the seventeenth and eighteenth centuries shaped the religious culture of Germany not only throughout the nineteenth century but also during the period leading up to the First World War and beyond. The Enlightenment was not merely a philosophical movement; in his view, it was a "spiritual" movement characterized by a passion and commitment that went well beyond impartial philosophical beliefs. What characterized it was the optimistic conviction that it is possible for human beings "to master life" by means of a process of illumination and clarification that involved a corresponding rejection of whatever is perceived to lack sufficient rational or evidential support.[1] Advocates saw themselves as championing a stand against "prejudices and passions, against vice and hypocrisy, ignorance and superstition, intolerance, partiality and fanaticism." Consequently, they committed themselves to honoring "wisdom and virtue, reason and nature."[2] Related to this was what Barth perceived to be a utilitarian concern for human welfare that required society to be delivered from superstition, fanaticism, and the like. Although this did not involve the rejection of religion per se, it shaped the kind of religion that was deemed compatible with human flourishing. The exemplar of enlightened religion was, in Barth's words, "a somewhat tepid, but always very assured and busy believer in God, freedom and immortality."[3] The result was "Christianism," that is, the kind of establishment religion that Kierkegaard had critiqued in Denmark.[4]

The vision of rationality that shaped this environment was epitomized by the philosophy of Christian Wolff. Standing between Gottfried Leibniz and Immanuel Kant, Wolff adopted a demonstrative-deductive method which, he believed, shed light on almost every scholarly subject of his time. To engage in *rational* theology involved rejecting divine revelation in favor of a more empirical and rationalistic form of religion. Echoing John Locke's concern that religion be "reasonable,"[5] Wolff's most famous work was entitled *Reasonable*

---

1. Karl Barth, *Protestant Theology in the Nineteenth Century: Its Background & History* (London: SCM, 1972), 11. The reference here to "mastering life" appears to mean both taking control and ownership of one's life and realizing one's latent potential.

2. Barth, *Protestant Theology*, 11.

3. Barth, *Protestant Theology*, 11.

4. Karl Barth, "A Thank You and a Bow: Kierkegaard's Reveille," in *Fragments Grave and Gay*, ed. Martin Rumscheidt, trans. Eric Mosbacher (London: Fontana, 1971), 98.

5. John Locke's major monograph on religion, published in 1695, was entitled *The Reasonableness of Christianity*. A century later, in 1793, Kant published his immensely influ-

Thoughts on God, the World and the Human Soul, and All Things in General Communicated to the Lovers of Truth. Barth comments amusingly on how the frontispiece reflects the Enlightenment vision by exhibiting

> a sun whose powerful rays pierce a mass of black clouds, and spread light upon mountains, forests, towns and villages. The aureole of this sun is obviously not considered to be insupportable to the human gaze, for it takes the form of an exceedingly friendly and pleasantly smiling human face, whose owner seems to be extremely pleased to see the clouds in the heavens and the shadows on the earth dissipate everywhere.[6]

One of the greatest contributions of the Enlightenment was its passionate commitment to a rigorous program of education as evidenced, for example, by the establishment of Europe's first teacher-training colleges. Despite its strengths, however, the philosophy of education inherent in this program was not problem-free especially with regard to its theological implications. There was, in Barth's view, an overly confident assumption that a comprehensive education could provide children with an all-embracing philosophy of "actual life" or "real life." The enlightenment that attended this would ultimately deliver society from the prescientific ignorance that characterized the Dark Ages.[7]

---

ential *Religion within the Limits of Reason Alone* (*Die Religion innerhalb der Grenzen der bloßen Vernunft*).

6. Barth, *Protestant Theology*, 11; cf. John Hoyles, *The Waning of the Renaissance 1640–1740: Studies in the Thought and Poetry of Henry More, John Norris and Isaac Watts* (The Hague: Martinus Nijhoff, 1971), 161n50.

7. How prescientific and "dark" the Dark Ages actually were—along with the question of whether attitudes toward that period by representatives of the Enlightenment were justified—is the subject of a great deal of research. Suffice it to say that it was a period characterized by advances in philosophy, mathematics, architecture, and the arts, and the research of David Lindberg, Ronald Numbers, and Edward Grant into scientific progress in the Middle Ages does a great deal to challenge the mythical assumptions that this was a period of scientific bankruptcy and that the role of the church was fundamentally antiscience. One such myth was the view that medievals believed in a flat earth—a view invented by Washington Irving in the early nineteenth century that has been completely discredited. One might add that the influence of monasticism during this period had a profound impact on shaping later Western values and, indeed, the ideals adopted by the Enlightenment itself. See David C. Lindberg, "The Medieval Church Encounters the Classical Tradition: Saint Augustine, Roger Bacon, and the Handmaiden Metaphor," in *When Science and Christianity Meet*, ed. David C. Lindberg and Ronald L. Numbers (Chicago: University of Chicago Press, 2003); Edward Grant, *Physical Science in the Middle Ages* (New York: John Wiley, 1971); and Grant, *The Foundations of Modern Science in the Middle Ages* (Cambridge: Cambridge University Press,

The self-confidence that characterized this vision of rational pedagogy carried risks of its own, however. Although Barth had no desire to return to a bygone age, he recognized that the endorsement of "reasonable" religion, and the optimistic confidence in a certain model of pedagogy as the key to human progress, paved the way in a scientifically advanced Europe to a Dark Age of a different kind, one characterized by unthinkable atrocities and unprecedented bloodshed. What the Enlightenment and its concept of "reasonable religion" lacked were the critical criteria to recognize, let alone challenge, the nationalistic aspirations in which it found expression.

So what precisely was the nature of Barth's objection to the academic ideals of that period? His concerns were twofold. First, the commitment to trusting what is "reasonable" and the attendant appeal to experience were less innocent than its advocates assumed. What persons perceive to be reasonable is likely to be prescribed by the canons of reason, that is, cultural and other affiliations that are not delivered by reason but which, it is assumed, should direct it.[8] A similar problem emerges with appeals to experience. As Kant himself famously recognized, there is no such thing as *uninterpreted* experience.[9] It is inevitably the case, therefore, that the appeal to "experience" will be, in large measure, an appeal to the *subjective grid* through which we interpret our experience. So when, in the assessment of theological claims, we appeal to what is "reasonable" or to what "experience teaches,"[10] we inevitably find ourselves submitting the claims of

---

1996). On the myth of the flat earth, see Jeffrey Burton Russell, *Inventing the Flat Earth: Columbus and Modern Historians* (Westport, CT: Praeger, 1997).

8. The "Western canon" denotes those works of philosophy, literature, music, and art identified at a particular time as the epitome of "high culture." John Searle defines our contemporary Western canon as "a certain Western intellectual tradition that goes from, say, Socrates to Wittgenstein in philosophy, and from Homer to James Joyce in literature." John Searle, "The Storm over the University," *New York Review of Books* 37, no. 19 (Dec. 6, 1990): 34–42.

9. "Intuition and concepts . . . constitute the elements of all our cognition, so that neither concepts without intuition corresponding to them in some way nor intuition without concepts can yield a cognition. Thoughts without [intensional] content (*Inhalt*) are empty (*leer*), intuitions without concepts are blind (*blind*). . . . The understanding can intuit nothing, the senses can think nothing. Only from their unification can cognition arise." Immanuel Kant, *Critique of Pure Reason*, A50–51/B74–76, translation taken from Robert Hanna, "Supplement: The Togetherness Principle, Kant's Conceptualism, and Kant's Non-Conceptualism," in *Stanford Encyclopedia of Philosophy*, article published 2017, https://plato.stanford.edu/entries/kant-judgment/supplement1.html.

10. See, for example, Thomas Aquinas, "What Experience Teaches Us about God," in *Commentary on the Book of Job*, trans. Brian Mulladay, ed. Joseph Kenny, OP, chap. 12, accessed September 21, 2020, https://isidore.co/aquinas/SSJob.htm. It can also be found in

Christian theology to the procrustean bed of our prior epistemic affiliations and assumptions. These in turn serve (whether we realize it or not) as court and jury in determining the conclusions we draw. The same applies not only to our theological conclusions but to our ethical, cultural, and sociopolitical conclusions as well. As we shall see in chapter 6, this is a problem highlighted in Barth's critique of Brunner's appeal to reason and experience in discerning the divine "ordinances of creation": "On the basis of instinct and reason one person may proclaim one thing to be an 'ordinance of creation,' another person another thing—according to the liberal, conservative or revolutionary inclinations of each."[11] In Barth's view, the elements integral to the Enlightenment project risked elevating the human subject and its affiliations to the point where it was the self, rather than God, who became the arbiter and measure of all truth. When this happens, "reasonable" does not mean "rational." Rather, it means "reasonable within my cultural domain," that is, within my sphere of values and the collective suppositions shaped by the fleeting fashions of the time. When theologians appeal to experience (*Experientia docet!*), the same applies. How one interprets what experience teaches about God's purposes is likely to be different depending on whether one is a "German Christian" or a persecuted Jew during the 1930s, whether one is a white Afrikaner in South Africa during the apartheid years or one of the forty million disenfranchised persons of color, or whether one is male rather than female in a patriarchal context.[12] Barth did not play down religious experience but interpreted it theologically by recognizing that experience is inevitably theory-laden. Consequently, he refused to interpret it as an autonomous capacity that allowed a dichotomy between its subjective component and its object. Rather, Christian experience for Barth was interpreted as our all-embracing "acknowledgment" of the Word. As such, it was inseparable from faith in which

---

John Calvin's *Institutio*; see Anthony N. S. Lane, *John Calvin: Student of the Church Fathers* (London: A&C Black, 1999), 21n52.

11. Karl Barth, *No! Answer to Emil Brunner*, in *Natural Theology: Comprising "Nature and Grace" by Professor Dr. Emil Brunner and the Reply "No!" by Dr. Karl Barth*, trans. Peter Fraenkel (London: Centenary Press, 1946; repr. Eugene, OR: Wipf & Stock, 2002), 87.

12. Barth was critical of Simone de Beauvoir's *Le Deuxième Sexe* (1949), but he was considerably more open to the challenges she articulated than might have been expected of a male raised in Switzerland, where women were not granted the right to vote until 1971; that is, they did not have the right to vote during Barth's lifetime! He writes, "Woman is still faced with the task of bringing her destiny as an autonomous human individual into accord with her special human conditioning, of getting to grips with her situation and mastering it, of abolishing that very myth of femininity which man has devised only for the purpose of maintaining his own control." Karl Barth, *Church Dogmatics*, ed. Geoffrey W. Bromiley and Thomas F. Torrance, trans. Geoffrey W. Bromiley (Edinburgh: T&T Clark, 1956–1975), III/4, 161.

God is experienced as addressing each of us as a "thou" and thereby in a manner that includes our reasoning, our will, and our emotions.[13]

An additional concern of Barth's was the Enlightenment's approach to education. To this, he raised four specific objections. First, he rejected the assumption that education was something over which we should seek to have complete control—as if humanity in its *enlightened* state knows in advance where truth is to be found and is able, therefore, to ensure access to it. Second, he objected to the conviction that a comprehensive education informed by Enlightenment values was the medium through which the pupil is best introduced to the ultimate realities of human life—to "real life." Third, he rejected the assumption that when there is divergence of opinion between religious and secular approaches to education, ultimate responsibility and control should reside with the secular educators. Fourth, he objected to the assumption that there was a single "method of correct education" which educators were obliged to enact and disseminate. Mirroring the philosophical doctrine that dominated the age, they looked to the Socratic method as paradigmatic. There, knowledge was elicited by a process of questioning, operating on the assumption that the answer was already present or immanent within the mind of the pupil. The essence of education was "maieutic";[14] that is, pupils were helped to "give birth," to use the Socratic metaphor, to what "they already knew."[15]

Enlightenment education's self-confidence and sense of conviction with respect to its aims meant that, despite claiming to serve the church, it "progressively dared to esteem itself more and more independent of, nay even superior to, the revealed gospel; the school, in fact, felt superior to the Church. 'What's more exalted than the teacher?'"[16] What the teacher had to offer was deemed considerably more important than anything that could be offered by the church. The real nub of the problem, however, was that the church of the time appeared to concur with this. Where the church had initially made room for the school to operate alongside, the church became so captivated by this vision of education that it began to assume "its own superfluity."[17] This loss of confidence in its Lord and the personal Reality that is the focus of the faith meant that it submitted itself to the Socratic immanentism that defined Enlightenment pedagogy. Consequently, as the church lost its distinctive identity

13. Barth, *Church Dogmatics* I/1, 227–28.
14. In Greek, *maieuesthai* means "to act as a midwife."
15. Barth, *Protestant Theology*, 38–39.
16. Barth, *Protestant Theology*, 39–40.
17. Barth, *Protestant Theology*, 40.

and ceased to bear witness to Jesus Christ, its capacity to critique the religious and sociocultural affiliations of the age was also lost. When this happened, the opportunity was there for religion to go awry. An enfeebled and impoverished church had neither the categories nor the confidence to challenge this.

It is in their shared analysis of the nature and root of the problem facing the church that we find one of the most significant and important parallels between Barth and Kierkegaard. We discussed in chapter 2 how Kierkegaard, through his pseudonym Johannes Climacus, exposes with analytic clarity the fundamental incompatibility between the Socratic understanding of our relationship to the truth and that radically different relationship to the Truth to which the New Testament bears witness. Like Barth after him, Kierkegaard saw that the sine qua non of a Christian critique of society was that the Christian vision of our relationship to the Truth should not be submitted to the pedagogical suppositions of the Enlightenment. If the historical component of the Christian faith no longer has decisive significance, then there is nothing left to the gospel other than to provide illustrations of what is already known. Moreover, there is no reason to privilege illustrations of the relevant truth that are found within Christian resources as opposed to any other resources found outside the domain of the church. For Kierkegaard, either our thinking is informed by the kinship that the eternal God establishes personally in time, or we return to the Socratic, to the Delphic oracle: "Know thyself" (*gnōthi seauton*). When we adopt the Socratic, maieutic approach, no individual teacher and no moment in time can ever have *decisive* significance. The most a teacher or an occasion can do is to prompt us to recall what we already know subliminally. What this means is that the sole source of religious and cultural critique lies in our self-understanding and the assumptions inherent within it. The result was that the Enlightenment debates concerning the Bible, miracles and religion per se manifest the approach satirized by Alexander Pope in the opening lines of his "Essay on Man" (1733–34): "Know then thy-self, presume not God to scan; / The proper study of Mankind is Man."[18]

Barth never departed from the belief, which he reiterated again toward the end of his life, that the problem with the theologians of the nineteenth century was that they "proceeded fundamentally along the lines of the 18th-century Christian Enlightenment."[19] Is this to deny that the Enlightenment had any benefits to offer theology? No! Many of the Enlightenment's ideals and intentions

18. Alexander Pope, "An Essay on Man: Epistle II," cited in Alasdair I. C. Heron, *A Century of Protestant Theology* (Cambridge: Lutterworth Press, 1980), 11.

19. Karl Barth, "Evangelical Theology in the 19th Century," in *The Humanity of God*

were profoundly important.[20] With respect to theology and its service of society, however, there was one fundamental problem with its legacy for the theologians who followed in its wake. That was the belief that it was their duty to establish and justify the possibility of Christian faith and that to do so involved appealing to the worldviews that were normative for their contemporaries and which, ultimately, became normative for them.[21] The problem was not simply that they sought to operate from within these worldviews. Rather, it was that they sought to draw theological conclusions from these worldviews. A subliminal effect of this was the uncritical endorsement of their validity. This was inevitably the case, in Barth's view, given that acceptance of the prevailing philosophy was an essential presupposition of their broader approach. The result of this was that the direction of interpretation ran *from* the prevailing worldview *to* the subject matter of theology and did so, moreover, in a manner that excluded the possibility of any critique running in the opposite direction. This precluded the capacity of theology, and with it the church and society, to learn from the distinctive content of the Christian faith and to allow the relevant worldviews to be challenged, revised, or even supplemented in light of this content. The outcome was that any unique contribution that theology might have to offer became redundant. It was no surprise, therefore, for Barth, that when a theologian such as Friedrich Schleiermacher (a colleague of Hegel's in Berlin) sought to present the Christian religion in a way that would prove attractive to its "cultured despisers,"[22] he failed miserably to have any impact on the culture of the time.

> The efforts of Schleiermacher and of his successors did not acquire any significance for the broad mass of the "cultured" to whom Schleiermacher had addressed himself so impressively with his proof of the roots of religion in the structure of man's spiritual life. . . . If this does not necessarily undermine the "excellence" of what these philosopher-theologians did, it is clearly a problem given the explicit intention of their work.[23]

(London: Collins, Fontana, 1967), 21. This address, delivered in 1957 as "Panorama of a Century," should not be confused with Barth's *Evangelical Theology: An Introduction*.

20. For example, the Enlightenment brought political modernization to the West and introduced the democratic ideals that gave rise to our modern, liberal democracies. It encouraged religious tolerance, highlighted the importance of education, and challenged oppressive forms of superstition.

21. Barth, "Evangelical Theology in the 19th Century," 21.

22. Schleiermacher published an apology for the Christian faith, entitled *On Religion: Speeches to Its Cultured Despisers* (Über die Religion: Reden an die Gebildeten unter ihren Verächtern), in 1799.

23. Barth, "Evangelical Theology in the 19th Century," 22.

As Barth puts it, the prevailing assumption during the nineteenth century was that the primary task of theology was to establish how carefully selected theological affirmations, ideals, and principles, detached from their historical context, can be shown to harmonize with the worldviews of the time. The most obvious question this raised for Barth was how they could avoid rendering impotent Christianity's distinctive contribution to the fundamental questions of the day. The very nature of such an approach is that anything that is specific to the Christian message or that does not fit with the worldviews of the time is bracketed out to ensure the Christian faith can be accommodated by the commitments and agendas of the contemporary culture. Barth's response to this is worth quoting at length:

> Could the Christian message and the Christian faith be a subject for debate while the validity of a general world view was presupposed? Is there any proof that acceptance of a particular world view will make Christianity generally accessible or even possible? Even granted the existence of [humanity's] religious disposition, can the Christian faith be called one of its expressions, in other words, a "religion"? Nineteenth-century evangelical theology assumed that this was so. But it could not do so without subjugating the Christian message and the Christian faith to that interpretation and form by which Christianity could achieve validity and general accessibility for the proponents of the prevailing world view. The Christian faith had to be understood as a "religion" if it was to be generally accepted as valid. What if it resisted this classification? What if acceptance was so eagerly sought that Christian faith ceased to be Christian faith as soon as it was interpreted as "religion"? What if the attempt to give it the "firm" basis actually removed the real ground from under it? Nineteenth-century theology did not raise these questions.[24]

The failure even to raise these fundamental questions highlighted for Barth the pathos of nineteenth-century Protestant theology.[25] The thinking of the theologians shaped by the Enlightenment was driven by a "general assumption"—that the primary task of theology was "relatedness to the world"—and a "specific assumption"—that it was possible for there to be a general acceptance of the Christian faith. The consequence of this was that when theologians sought to fulfill their "proper task in and for the Church," they became more interested in Christianity as a religion than in the one whom it proclaims and from whom it lives—"more interested in the Christian faith than in the Christian message."[26]

24. Barth, "Evangelical Theology in the 19th Century," 23.
25. Barth, "Evangelical Theology in the 19th Century," 23.
26. Barth, "Evangelical Theology in the 19th Century," 23.

Here the profound parallels between Barth's analysis of the problem and Kierkegaard's come to the fore. Both Kierkegaard and Barth saw with penetrating clarity the incompatibility between, on the one hand, the conceptions of our discovery of the truth and our relationship to it that define Christian faith and, on the other hand, the assumptions about knowledge and discovery that define the pedagogy of the Enlightenment. For Kierkegaard's Climacus, the Socratic account of learning makes two assumptions with respect to theology's outreach into the culture. First, it assumes that the culture has the inherent ability to confirm the truth of Christian claims by making recourse to the immanent or inherent assumptions that define the self-understanding of its adherents. This entails that the only valid form of theological outreach makes explicit what the adherent of the culture already knows subliminally. Second, it is obliged to demonstrate that the relevant truths or ideas that are recognized to be true are not only exemplified in the relevant Christian teaching but define it in toto. In sum, the only valid form of theological education on this Enlightenment model is maieutic. The theologian is called, like Socrates, to be a midwife (*maieuesthai*) who helps persons to "give birth" to the religious insights inherent in their cultural self-understanding. If a person is not able to *recognize* in the light of her own immanent suppositions that a claim is true, then there is no basis on which she can be expected to accept that claim. Still further, if the claim cannot be accommodated within the framework through which she interprets the world, then she has a duty to reject it because it cannot be true. The totality of religious knowledge can be defined, therefore, as the explicit expression of what is subliminally known by all. Any facet of the Christian faith that cannot be recalled through a process of self-discovery on the part of the learner (anamnesis) is to be rejected. The significance of Pope's allusion to the Delphic oracle could not be plainer.

Barth saw the irony: their concern to accommodate Christian thought to the procrustean bed of cultural affiliation was directly responsible for the theologians' failure to achieve their intended goal. As he wryly points out, theology could hardly elevate its position in relation to other academic disciplines when the only reason it could provide for its existence was its ability to express some chosen element already present in their self-understanding! Such a strategy was not merely self-defeating folly; it gave rise to a "religious anthropocentrism" which reduced the Christian gospel to "a statement, a religion, about Christian self-awareness," thereby losing sight altogether of the God who "in His sovereignty confronts humanity, calling it to account, and dealing with it as Lord."[27] The desire to be perceived to be relevant nullified the Christian faith and thereby its distinctive contribution and relevance.

27. Barth, "Evangelical Theology in the 19th Century," 27.

For Barth, as for Kierkegaard, if God's address to humanity is identified with a historical event of decisive significance, then it cannot, by its very nature, be subsumed within a general or abstract category of religion or reduced to expressions of humanity's inherent, religious self-understanding. When the latter takes place, the gospel is changed (to adopt an expression Climacus uses) into something of a completely different kind (*metabasis eis allo genos*).[28] The clarity on this matter which Kierkegaard and Barth shared was lost, with only a few exceptions, to the whole army of nineteenth- and early-twentieth-century theologians, as these include Friedrich Schleiermacher, Albrecht Ritschl, Rudolf Otto, Adolf von Harnack, and Ernst Troeltsch—a clarity that, too often, is still lacking in contemporary theology and philosophy of religion.

The Impact of Idealism on Biblical Scholarship

The same Enlightenment weaknesses found parallel expression in biblical scholarship. The function of historical analysis of the life of Jesus was the illustration of prior philosophical and religious suppositions. As Barth commented, the so-called historical Jesus served to represent "certain religious phenomena."[29] What phenomena these were depended on the particular moral, aesthetic, and religious fashions and affiliations that characterized the value system of the relevant biblical exegetes. George Tyrrell famously wrote of Harnack, "The Christ that Harnack sees, looking back through nineteen centuries of Catholic darkness, is only the reflection of a Liberal Protestant face, seen at the bottom of a deep well."[30] Although this was a criticism of Harnack's Christology, Tyrrell's comment could be applied to much New Testament scholarship of that period. Why? Because self-knowledge was key to Enlightenment pedagogy and consequently the mode of interpretation it inspired. "Recognition" of the truth

---

28. Climacus took over the phrase *metabasis eis allo genos*, originally coined by Aristotle, from Lessing's *Über den Beweis des Geistes und der Kraft*, quoted in Alastair Hannay, *Kierkegaard: A Biography* (Cambridge: Cambridge University Press, 2003), 469n55. The phrase means literally "shifting from one genus to another" or a "change into something of a different kind." Both Lessing and Climacus are agreed on the discontinuity to which this phrase refers. For Climacus, to cross between the two would involve a "leap." Søren Kierkegaard, *Concluding Unscientific Postscript to Philosophical Fragments*, ed. and trans. Howard V. Hong and Edna H. Hong (Princeton: Princeton University Press, 1992), 1:194-95. See M. Jamie Ferreira's discussion in "Faith and the Kierkegaardian Leap," in *The Cambridge Companion to Kierkegaard*, ed. Alastair Hannay and Gordon D. Marino (Cambridge: Cambridge University Press, 1997), 213.

29. Barth, "Evangelical Theology in the 19th Century," 30.

30. George Tyrrell, *Christianity at the Crossroads* (London: Longmans, Green, 1909), 44.

assumes one knows subliminally (immanently) the fundamental truths that will be "discovered." Again, the genius of Kierkegaard and Barth was the way in which they traced the theological problems of nineteenth-century Denmark and Germany to the Enlightenment's philosophy of education.

Nowhere are these underlying issues illustrated more clearly than in the work of the foremost New Testament scholar of the nineteenth century and father of "myth theory." The approach of David Friedrich Strauss had its roots in the epistemology of Leibniz with its dichotomization between necessary truths supplied by reason (to which epistemic access is a priori) and contingent truths mediated by sense perception. Baruch (Benedictus de) Spinoza compounded the impact of this dichotomy by arguing that the truth of a historical narrative cannot provide knowledge of God, the latter deriving solely from general ideas that possess epistemic certainty. This, in turn, constituted the background of Gotthold Ephraim Lessing's famous ditch which reflected his insistence that events and truths belong to different and, indeed, logically unconnected categories. Historical truths concern contingent facts that can be doubted; as such, they cannot establish metaphysical truths of any kind and so cannot establish truths about God. This incapacity of the contingent truths of history to establish eternal truths was what generated for him "the ugly great ditch which I cannot cross, however often and however earnestly I have tried to make that leap."[31] The outcome of the Leibniz–Spinoza–Lessing trajectory was that the theological significance of the historical and the "contingent" was displaced (annihilated!) in favor of necessary truths of reason. The subsequent turn to (Hegelian) idealism led Strauss to dismiss out of hand any suggestion that a particular individual or a particular series of events in history might have a *decisive* role with respect to the mediation of the divine. The full implications of Strauss's idealism come to full expression when, toward the end of his monumental investigation into the life of Jesus (*The Life of Jesus, Critically Examined*), he considers whether Jesus's life has any "dogmatic import" and, more specifically, whether the divine "must actually have been once manifested, as it never had been, and never more will be, in one individual." He responds: "This is indeed not the mode in which Idea realizes itself; it is not wont to lavish all its fullness on one exemplar, and be niggardly toward all others—to express itself perfectly in that one individual, and imperfectly in all the rest."[32]

31. Gotthold Ephraim Lessing, "On the Proof of the Spirit and of Power," in *Philosophical and Theological Writings*, trans. and ed. Hugh Barr Nisbet (Cambridge: Cambridge University Press, 2005), 87.

32. David Friedrich Strauss, *The Life of Jesus, Critically Examined*, trans. George Eliot

In short, his emphasis on the Idea and the ideal precludes any possibility that a single individual or a particular point in history could have decisive significance in mediating the divine. The belief in an individual incarnation reflects mythological thinking and requires translation, therefore, into categories that the idealist can embrace. "Is not the idea of the unity of the divine and human natures a real one in a far higher sense, when I regard the whole race of mankind as its realization, than when I single out one man as such a realization?"[33]

Strauss's adoption of Hegelian idealism resulting in his endorsement of myth theory would find significant parallels a century later in Bultmann's adoption of Neo-Kantian idealism and his subsequent program of demythologizing. In short, Kierkegaard's and Barth's critique of Hegelian and Neo-Kantian idealism addressed not only the theology of the time but also the major developments that shaped the direction of New Testament scholarship from the nineteenth century onward. Both expose the incompatibility between idealist commitments and the recognition that a particular individual or a particular moment in time should have decisive theological significance; idealism rules out any such recognition tout court.

The legacy of the Enlightenment found expression, in Barth's view, in a form of theological arrogance; he asks:

> Did not the whole [theological] enterprise, from beginning to end, suffer painfully from the fundamental mistake that, in the words of Schleiermacher, productive theologising was possible only from a lofty place "above" Christianity?[34]

The effect of idealism and the Socratic was to exclude a priori (that is, "from a lofty place 'above' Christianity") the possibility of affirming any of the following, all of which are essential to the proclamation that characterizes the New Testament:

1. God addresses humanity through a particular person who lived at a particular point in time.

(London: SCM, 1973), 779. By "Idea," Strauss was referring to ideas and ideals. Universals possess reality in a way that the spatiotemporal particulars that exemplify them do not.

33. Strauss, *Life of Jesus*, 780. The following sentence runs: "Is not incarnation of God from eternity, a truer one than an incarnation limited to a particular point of time?"

34. Barth, "Evangelical Theology in the 19th Century," 30.

2. To be related to the Truth of God is to be related to that particular historical person.
3. God addresses persons individually.
4. The condition for the recognition of the divine address involves the redemption of our minds and thus the provision of criteria that are not immanent.

What both Kierkegaard and Barth recognized with unparalleled clarity was that the criteria for the recognition of God's self-disclosure and God's purposes were *included* in the actuality of God's self-disclosure. When God addresses the church and its participants, God provides the eyes to see what could not otherwise be seen and ears to hear what could not otherwise be heard.

If that is not the case, then our immanent criteria are ultimately identified with divine revelation. That is because to the extent that these criteria constitute the grounds for the *recognition* (re-cognition) of God's purposes, the content of God's self-disclosure is necessarily identical with them. As Climacus comments, "Understanding the truth is like being able to ask about it—the condition and the question contain the conditioned and the answer."[35] For both Kierkegaard and Barth, there is an unambiguous pedagogical either-or: *either* all that could ever be known about God is already inherent within the human subject, *or* the moment of disclosure in time—the occasion of the discovery, the person of the teacher, and the transformation of the mind of the individual hearer—possesses decisive significance for one's relation to the Truth. For both Kierkegaard and Barth, the latter is recognized (a posteriori) to be the case. What that means is that the message of the Christian faith is irreducibly incompatible with the fundamental presuppositions of the Enlightenment and the idealism to which its heirs found themselves committed.

THEOLOGY, POLITICS, AND THE QUESTION OF CRITERIA

The history of the twentieth century includes graphic testimony to the potential of Christian God-talk (talk about God) either to foster or to acquiesce in oppressive, racist, and sexist social and political programs and practices. This highlights two recurring themes throughout this book. First, it underscores the dangers of "criterial immanentism," that is, the assumption that the criteria for

35. Søren Kierkegaard, *Philosophical Fragments*, in *"Philosophical Fragments" and "Johannes Climacus,"* ed. and trans. Howard V. Hong and Edna H. Hong (Princeton: Princeton University Press, 1985), 14.

theological assessment are inherent or immanent within our natural conceptuality, that is, the current state of play in our thinking. Second, it stresses the importance of approaching the nature of the criteria we use *theologically*. That is, the way in which we interpret the *where* and the *what* of God's revelation, that is, its locus and content, should not be decided in the light of criteria determined *in advance of* or *independently of* God's self-disclosure.[36] This was a recurring theme in Barth's response to the tragic history of events during this period and the failures of both the church and the theology of the time. What this analysis also highlights is the timeless relevance of the theological trajectory that Kierkegaard had established and that Barth developed. The challenges that they addressed during their lifetimes are no less relevant today!

Barth did not regard political or ethical criteria as playing a role in determining the shape of faithful theology. At the same time, he was insistent that the gospel had profoundly important sociopolitical ramifications. When the church is wedded to oppressive or exclusive practices, this indicates a failure to be true to the one whom the gospel proclaims. Even when in the 1920s, as he later admitted in a letter to Eberhard Bethge, he exercised a degree of political constraint, he still refers to the direction which, at that time, he "silently took for granted or emphasized only in passing: ethics, fellow-humanity, a serving church, discipleship, socialism, peace movement, and in and with all these things, politics."[37] These commitments stem directly, for Barth, from his belief that at the center of the Christian faith stands "the one Word of God whom we have to hear, and whom we have to trust and obey in life and in death."[38] The writings of Friedrich-Wilhelm Marquardt, Helmut Gollwitzer, Hermann Diem, and George Hunsinger are an important corrective, therefore, to those interpreters of Barth who were misled by his care not to allow theological commitments to be driven by political commitments. Barth never ceased to be engaged with the sociopolitical relevance of the gospel.[39] What is important to appreciate is that, for Barth, sociopolitical engagement is not an additional task; it belongs

---

36. See Alan J. Torrance, "*Auditio Fidei*: Where and How Does God Speak? Faith, Reason and the Question of Criteria," in *Reason and the Reasons of Faith*, ed. Paul Griffiths and Reinhard Hütter (New York: T&T Clark, 2005), 30–33.

37. Karl Barth's letter to Eberhard Bethge, Basel, 22 May, 1967, in *Letters, 1961–68*, trans. and ed. Geoffrey W. Bromiley (Grand Rapids: Eerdmans, 1981), 251. Cf. H. Gollwitzer, "Kingdom of God and Socialism in the Theology of Karl Barth," in George Hunsinger, ed., *Karl Barth and Radical Politics* (Philadelphia: Westminster, 1976), 99–100.

38. This is taken from the first thesis of the Barmen Declaration.

39. See George Hunsinger's edited collection of essays, *Karl Barth and Radical Politics*, 2nd ed. (Eugene, OR: Cascade, 2017).

to the very essence of being faithful to the one whom the church confesses. The church is never more sociopolitically relevant than when it has the courage to be the church, that is, to think from the center of the faith.[40] But when sight of this is lost, as it was in the nineteenth century, the Christian gospel is "changed into a statement, a religion, about Christian self-awareness." Such loss "blur[s] the sight horizontally" and is "fatal" for the witness of the church.[41]

> The Christian was condemned to uncritical and irresponsible subservience to the patterns, forces, and movements of human history and civilisation. Man's inner experience did not provide a firm enough ground for resistance to these phenomena. . . . It was fatal for the evangelical Church and for Christianity in the 19th century that theology in the last analysis had nothing more to offer than the "human," the "religious," mystery and its noncommittal "statements," leaving the faithful to whatever impressions and influences from outside proved strongest.[42]

When a Christologically driven recognition of God's inclusive affirmation of human beings—whatever their race, social class, or gender—ceases to inform the church's thinking, the door is opened to forms of civil religion that endorse the vested interests and political agendas of those in power, with all the consequences that this brings. Later in life, Barth commented that what had opened his eyes as a young man had been an experience resulting from what he famously referred to as that "black day" in "early August," 1914.[43] As war broke out, a group of ninety-three German intellectuals "impressed public opinion" by signing a declaration in support of the Kaiser's war policy that was both nationalistic and, indeed, racist.[44] "Among these intellectuals," Barth reports,

---

40. Alasdair Heron comments, "[Barth's] early concerns as a parish minister and his active involvement in the cultural and political turmoil of Germany in the 1920s and 1930s are of direct relevance for his theology, and in particular for the passionate conviction that ran through all his work from 1918 to 1968: that Christian faith rests solely on the revelation of God in Jesus Christ, and that the task of theology is to allow that revelation to shine in its own light and stand on its own authority as the Word of God to us" (Heron, *Century of Protestant Theology*, 74).

41. Barth, "Evangelical Theology in the 19th Century," 27.

42. Barth, "Evangelical Theology in the 19th Century," 27.

43. Bruce McCormack points out that although Barth thought the "black day" occurred in early August, the relevant manifesto actually appeared on October 5. Bruce L. McCormack, *Karl Barth's Critically Realistic Dialectical Theology: Its Genesis and Development, 1909–1936* (Oxford: Clarendon, 1995), 112.

44. The nationalistic and racist tone of the declaration is epitomized in the following:

I discovered to my horror almost all my theological teachers whom I had greatly venerated. . . . I suddenly realized that I could not any longer follow either their ethics and dogmatics or their understanding of the Bible and of history. For me at least, 19th-century theology no longer held any future.[45]

And as he commented in a letter to W. Spoendlin on January 4, 1915, cited by Eberhard Busch, "'It was like the twilight of the gods when I saw the reaction of Harnack, Herrmann, Rade, Eucken and company to the new situation,' and discovered how religion and scholarship could be changed completely, 'into intellectual 42 cm cannons.'"[46]

The theological teachers whom Barth had so revered were seen to have been "hopelessly compromised by what I regarded as their failure in the face of the ideology of war."[47] Such an ethical failure in the face of the clear message of the gospel could only mean, for the young Barth, that "their exegetical and dogmatic presuppositions could not be in order."[48] The bankruptcy of cultural Protestantism (*Kulturprotestantismus*) together with the principle of "reverence for history" (*Ehrfurcht vor Geschichte*) were laid bare not least by the fact that Germany's leading theologians saw no tension between the subject matter with which they were engaged on the one hand and Germany's war policy on the other. Frank Gordon's analysis of the preaching of the time graphically illustrates this. D. G. Goens, for example, proclaimed that "Germany was the focal point of world Protestantism and that when Germans fought for the Fatherland, they were 'fighters for Jesus Christ.'"[49] Friedrich Lahusen proclaimed, "We are fighting for the Rule of God, . . . for the free and liberating Gospel."[50]

"Those who have allied themselves with Russians and Serbians and present such a shameful scene to the world as that of inciting Mongolians and negroes against the white race, have no right whatever to call themselves upholders of civilization. . . . Have faith in us! Believe, that we shall carry on this war to the end as a civilized nation, to whom the legacy of a Goethe, a Beethoven, and a Kant is just as sacred as its own hearths and homes. For this we pledge you our names and our honour." The signatories include Adolf Deissmann, Adolf von Harnack, Wilhelm Herrman, Adolf von Schlatter, and a similar number of leading Catholic theologians and church historians.

45. Barth, "Evangelical Theology in the 19th Century," 14.

46. Eberhard Busch, *Karl Barth: His Life from Letters and Autobiographical Texts*, trans. John Bowden (Philadelphia: Fortress, 1976), 81.

47. *ABT* I, cited in Busch, *Karl Barth*, 81.

48. *ABT* VII, 4, cited in Busch, *Karl Barth*, 81.

49. Frank J. Gordon, "Liberal German Churchmen and the First World War," *German Studies Review* 4, no. 1 (1981): 41, https://doi.org/10.2307/1428755.

50. Gordon, "Liberal German Churchmen," 41.

Gordon has documented that in 1914 a wide range of pastors—from military chaplains to the highest-ranking clergy—preached along similar lines, secure in the recognition that "virtually all German churchmen supported their country as it embarked upon the war."[51] Senior Court Chaplain (*Oberhofprediger*) Ernst von Dryander believed humanity had found its fulfillment when patriotism and Christianity finally came together. When he was invited to preach at the opening of the German Parliament on August 4, 1914, he chose as his text Romans 8:31: "If God is for us, who can be against us?" It is no coincidence that only two decades later, and in the context of the run-up to another world war, those events in August 1914 would be recalled by Otto Dibelius when he preached on that same text at the "Day of Potsdam" ceremony on March 21, 1933. The ceremony opened with Hitler shaking hands with Hindenburg, the purpose of which was to symbolize the unity of the old Prussia and the new Germany. In his sermon, Dibelius referred to those "halcyon days of August 1914 when 'the call went through the masses: one empire, one people, one God (*ein Reich, ein Volk, ein Gott*).'"[52] This motto would morph into one of the most-repeated Nazi slogans: "*Ein Volk, ein Reich, ein Führer!*" ("One people, one empire, one leader!"). August Pott called upon the Germans to unite God's Holy Spirit with the spirit of hate and to direct this mixture against the English.[53]

As witnessed in so many contexts since (e.g., in apartheid South Africa, in the history of segregation in the southern United States,[54] and in Northern Ireland during "the troubles"), the combination of a romantic nationalism, ethnic allegiance, and exclusive religious loyalty opens the door to identifying the spirit of the people—or the spirit of a nation or a particular ethnic or religious group—with the Holy Spirit. The result, as we have already suggested, is the alleged divine endorsement of social and political programs driven by self-

---

51. Gordon, "Liberal German Churchmen," 41.

52. Cited in Jeffrey Verhey, *The Spirit of 1914: Militarism, Myth, and Mobilization in Germany* (Cambridge: Cambridge University Press, 2000), 224. "*Ein Reich, ein Volk, ein Gott*" was famously proclaimed by the Kaiser in 1896 in celebration of the twenty-fifth anniversary of the Reich, appearing on postage stamps and medallions issued around that time. It then reappeared in the form of a call for national unity in Germany during the First World War.

53. Gordon, "Liberal German Churchmen," 41.

54. As recently as September 3, 2019, BBC News reported from Booneville, Mississippi, that a couple had been refused a wedding venue as they were mixed race. When the person responsible for refusing the couple was asked why, the BBC reported her as having explained that "she had been taught as a child that people were meant to stay 'with your own race.'" "Mississippi Wedding Venue Refuses Interracial Pair over Owner's Christian Faith," *BBC News*, September 3, 2019, https://www.bbc.com/news/world-us-canada-49571207.

serving agendas—too often a toxic recipe for violence in the name of religion.[55] It is against these kinds of associations— these expressions of immanence— that the third thesis of the Barmen Declaration stands: "We reject the false doctrine that the Church could have permission to hand over the form of its message and of its order to whatever it itself might wish or to the vicissitudes of the prevailing ideological and political convictions of the day."

The False Alternative of Religious Socialism

During the years preceding the First World War, Barth was introduced by his friend, Hermann Kutter, to the emerging Religious Socialist movement in Switzerland. It contrasted dramatically with the "cultural optimism" of Liberal Protestantism and was committed to challenging the pietism of church-centered Christianity, which had lost, in their view, the understanding of hope at the heart of the New Testament. This central message was being diluted by the church such that it came to be interpreted as "a purely individual hope of a future life for the soul."[56] What needed to be recovered was the New Testament's confident and unsettling expectation of the kingdom of God which will "rectify the whole world and all life even to its deepest recesses."[57] This new "fight for the kingdom of God" with which Christoph Blumhardt, Hermann Kutter, and especially Leonhard Ragaz identified themselves took a radical and, for Barth, a "particularly surprising turn" when they "linked it with the eschatology and hope of the Socialist Labour movement."[58] He comments, "They expressly approved this movement and contrasted it with the Church, theology and Christendom, as the representative realisation for our time of the faith that Jesus did not find in Israel."[59] Under the leadership of Kutter and Ragaz (who was pastor of Basel Cathedral and then professor of theology in Zurich), this led, in 1906, to the establishment in Switzerland of the Religious Socialist movement. The launch of the journal *Neue Wege* (*New Ways*) gave it its voice. The resulting

55. For an informed analysis of the political ambiguities of religious affiliation in Northern Ireland during the "troubles," see R. Scott Appleby, *The Ambivalence of the Sacred: Religion, Violence, and Reconciliation* (Lanham, MD: Rowman and Littlefield, 2000). See also Ronald A. Wells, "Northern Ireland: A Study of Friendship, Forgiveness, and Reconciliation," in *The Politics of Past Evil: Religion, Reconciliation, and the Dilemmas of Transitional Justice*, ed. Daniel Philpott (Notre Dame: University of Notre Dame Press, 2006), 189–222.

56. Barth, *Church Dogmatics* II/1, 633.

57. Barth, *Church Dogmatics* II/1, 633.

58. Barth, *Church Dogmatics* II/1, 633.

59. Barth, *Church Dogmatics* II/1, 633.

highly influential dynamic was indicative, in Barth's view, of the extent to which the theological culture in Switzerland contrasted with that in Germany: "Any young Swiss pastor of the time who wasn't asleep, or didn't live somewhere on the other side of the moon, or hadn't been corrupted in some way, was a Religious Socialist in the narrower or wider sense."[60] Although influenced by this in a number of ways, Barth retained his distance from the movement. Moreover, the ensuing debate between Ragaz and Kutter served to clarify still further for Barth the importance of refusing to allow the Word of God to be confused with any philosophical or political agenda, socialist or otherwise, and to ensure that we never identify the kingdom of God with any prior set of sociopolitical commitments. What Kutter had intended to be simply an interpretation of the signs of the times, rather than a program, was developed by Leonhard Ragaz into a "system of religious Socialism" where socialism in general was identified as "a pioneer manifestation of the Kingdom of God."[61]

In Barth's view, there is a wide range of resources to help Christian theologians interpret the signs of the times. When a political theory is deemed *foundational* to theology, however, that inevitably leads persons to attach divine ratification to the deliverances both of the relevant theory and of the worldview it expresses. When our affiliations, intellectual and otherwise, are not "metamorphosed" by the gospel but "schematized" by a secular theory or set of commitments, this can only obstruct our discernment of the truth.[62] That is, it distorts our perception of God's relation to the world and God's purposes for it. If the *Kulturprotestantismus* of the liberal theologians was to be criticized for submitting the Word of God to one procrustean bed, Religious Socialism was simply submitting it to another. It was for these reasons, Barth explains, that he and Ragaz found themselves heading in very different directions: "Ragaz and I roared past one another like two express trains: he went out of the church, I went in."[63]

Such a description could apply equally well to the trajectory of Barth's own theology in contrast to the trajectory of his Marburg teachers. As we have suggested, the dogmatic slumber from which Barth was awoken during the period prior to the First World War (represented by that dramatic "black day" in 1914) had a far wider impact than simply generating disillusionment with his teachers' political stance. It brought to his attention the incompatibility between their socioreligious agendas on the one hand, and the clear witness of

60. Cited in Busch, *Karl Barth*, 77.

61. Barth, *Church Dogmatics* I/1, 74; cf. Busch's discussion of this in *Karl Barth*, 78.

62. We are appropriating here the language of Romans 12:2. The terms "metamorphosed" and "schematized" are literal translations of the Greek terms Paul uses in this passage.

63. M. Matmüller, *Ragaz* II, 229, cited in Busch, *Karl Barth*, 92.

the New Testament on the other. Still further, it forced him to critique the theological methods that were in play and that explained how this situation came about. The consequence was a growing clarity that to be faithful to the God of the New Testament means that our thinking about every facet of life should take the form of a "thinking after" (*Nachdenken*) in faithfulness to the divine address rather than a "forward thinking" (*Vordenken*) which predetermines how God's address will be heard. That is, whereas our natural inclination is to seek to interpret and appropriate God's self-disclosure with reference to prior frameworks of thought, to be faithful to God's self-disclosure requires us, conversely, to submit our prior commitments, assumptions, and frameworks of thought to it so that these commitments might be questioned, critiqued, revised, and transformed accordingly. In sum, our thinking requires to be shaped "after" (*nach*), that is, in the light of God's self-disclosure, rather than "before" (*vor*), that is, in advance of it. This does not apply only to the content of theology but also to our interpretation of theological method. As Barth puts it in his *Göttingen Dogmatics*, "All reflection on how God can reveal himself is in truth only a 'thinking after' (*Nachdenken*) of the fact that God has revealed himself."[64] Indeed, as David Ford argues in his essay on Barth's method,[65] and as Rowan Williams has also argued,[66] the entire theological enterprise is to be understood, on Barth's account, as an exercise in *Nachdenken*.[67] We see here once again how Barth's approach reflects Kierkegaard's contrast between Socratic approaches (where theological discovery simply constitutes the outworking of what is known immanently in advance) and those approaches that recognize God's engagement with humanity in time (which cannot be anticipated) as having decisive significance.

The Logos as Counter-Logos with Respect to the Immanent

Barth's methodological insights find vivid and socially pertinent expression in lectures that Dietrich Bonhoeffer gave on Christology in 1933 which, as

---

64. Karl Barth, *The Göttingen Dogmatics: Instruction in the Christian Religion*, trans. Geoffrey W. Bromiley, ed. Hannelotte Reiffen (Grand Rapids: Eerdmans, 1991), 151.

65. David F. Ford, "Barth's Interpretation of the Bible," in *Karl Barth: Studies of His Theological Method*, ed. S. W. Sykes (Oxford: Clarendon, 1979), 55-87.

66. Rowan Williams, "Barth on the Triune God," in *Karl Barth: Studies of His Theological Method*, ed. S. W. Sykes (Oxford: Clarendon, 1979), 149.

67. For Ford's analysis of Barth's account of *Nachdenken*, see Ford, "Barth's Interpretation of the Bible," 81-86. For further discussion of this, see Alan J. Torrance, *Persons in Communion: An Essay on Trinitarian Description and Human Participation, with Special Reference to Volume One of Karl Barth's "Church Dogmatics"* (Edinburgh: T&T Clark, 1996), 74.

we argued in the previous chapter, also reflect the influence of Kierkegaard. Bonhoeffer opens his lectures by quoting Kierkegaard:

> Teaching about Christ begins in silence. "Be still, for that is the absolute," writes Kierkegaard. That has nothing to do with the silence of the mystics, who in their dumbness chatter away secretly in their soul by themselves. The silence of the church is silence before the Word.[68]

Bonhoeffer advocates a methodological silence that refuses to start with a prior series of suppositions. Consequently, he argues, the Logos requires to be seen from our perspective as the "counter-logos"—as the one who stands over against our assumptions and agendas. The counter-logos confronts, transforms, redefines, and reconciles our prior commitments and categories of interpretation. Our speech must be a response, therefore, to his prior speaking, and this must be evident at both the material and formal levels. He explains:

> The ultimate presupposition of man is given to him in his human, classifying logos. What happens when doubt is thrown upon this presupposition of his scientific activity? What if somewhere the claim is raised that this human logos is superseded, condemned, dead? What happens if a counter-logos appears which denies the classification? Another logos which destroys the first? What if the older order of the first logos be proclaimed as broken up, superseded and in its place a new world has already begun?[69]

One of the fundamental points that unites not only Kierkegaard and Barth but also Bonhoeffer in challenging the culture and politics of their respective contexts is their shared opposition to all attempts to interpret God's self-disclosure with reference to a predetermined system of thought. This is exemplified, Bonhoeffer argues, in the Hegelian idealism where "the logos has assimilated the counter-logos into itself."[70] This brings us back to what is perhaps the most significant element in Barth's development, namely, how his commitment to theological *Nachdenken* led him to depart so radically from the idealist system of his teachers. To appreciate this, we shall consider the Neo-Kantian idealism of the Marburg school in which Barth completed his theological studies and to

---

68. Dietrich Bonhoeffer, *Christ the Center*, trans. Edwin Robertson (New York: Harper & Row, 1978), 27; see the earlier discussion of Bonhoeffer in chapter 2.

69. Bonhoeffer, *Christ the Center*, 29.

70. Bonhoeffer, *Christ the Center*, 29.

which he had transferred in order to study under the Neo-Kantian theologian Wilhelm Herrmann.

The Theological Impact of Neo-Kantian Idealism

In his magisterial monograph *The Origins of Demythologizing*, Roger Johnson states that "the philosophical roots of mid-twentieth-century theology as a whole are firmly embedded in Marburg Neo-Kantianism."[71] He argues that its influence on Rudolf Bultmann was immense and that it had a profound impact on the whole shape of modern and contemporary theological debate. While Marburg Neo-Kantian idealism must be distinguished from Hegelian idealism, there are profoundly important parallels between them. Appreciating these similarities highlights the all-important methodological parallels between Kierkegaard's critique of Hegelian idealism (as it underpinned cultural Lutheranism in Denmark) and Barth's critique of Marburg Neo-Kantianism (as it served to underwrite cultural Protestantism in Germany).

It is rare for a university to be taken over almost entirely by systematic adherence across all faculties to a single philosophy. This, however, is essentially what took place in the University of Marburg at the end of the nineteenth and the beginning of the twentieth centuries. When Hermann Cohen and Paul Natorp launched the journal of the Marburg school in 1906, they sought to articulate and to promote the all-embracing philosophical system that was being adopted across their university. The mission of the journal was clear: "Whoever is bound to us stands with us on the foundation of the transcendental method. . . . Philosophy, to us, is bound to the fact of science, as this elaborates itself. Philosophy, therefore, to us, is the theory of the principles of science and therewith of all culture."[72]

The transcendental philosophy they endorsed was panlogistic in the sense that reality was seen as the construct of thought—a position which, although different, was not unrelated to that of Hegel, who also eroded any dichotomy between reason, logic, and ontology. The Neo-Kantians, however, sought to elevate science (somewhat ironically, perhaps) within a framework that rejected a priori

---

71. Roger A. Johnson, *The Origins of Demythologizing: Philosophy and Historiography in the Theology of Rudolf Bultmann* (Leiden: Brill, 1974), 40–41.

72. *Philosophische Arbeiten* 1, no. 1 (1906), cited in Lewis White Beck, "Neo-Kantianism," in *The Encyclopedia of Philosophy*, ed. Paul Edwards (New York: Macmillan and Free Press, 1967), 5:470.

any suggestion that truth could be "given" from beyond the realm of thought. As Lewis White Beck observes, for Cohen the key to all knowledge is logic "in which any assertion gains its status as true solely by virtue of its systematic position in a body of universal laws that, in turn, require each other on methodological grounds." He continues, "Thought, Cohen taught, accepts nothing as given and is not true of anything independent of it—certainly not of intuitional data, as Kant believed. Thought generates content as well as form, and the content of self-contained thought is reality itself as object and goal of knowledge."[73]

The differential calculus, which Cohen interpreted as grounding mathematical physics, served as a model of discovery in their panlogistic approach; it illustrated the capacity of thought to *generate* the objects of knowledge.[74] The differential calculus was not *given* for thought but was, rather, *created* by pure thought and constituted in turn the necessary means of the creation of nature as a whole as an object of possible experience. In Cohen's words, "This mathematical generation of motion (by integration of the derivative) and thereby nature itself is the triumph of pure thinking."[75] Beck argues that the method of the calculus offered a paradigm of the category of origin (*Ursprung*) and also the logical process of production (*Erzeugung*) to which every fact owes its reality, that is, its position in a logically necessary scheme. The capacity for the activity of thought to engage exclusively with its own material is such that, in Cohen's view, we are free to dispense altogether with the assumption that there are any independent givens in knowledge. Nothing is "given" to thought from beyond. "Facts" are completely determined by thought. So what place does this allow for Kant's category of the *Ding-an-sich* (thing-in-itself)? Quite simply, none! That is because the *Ding-an-sich* is not a *thing* at all. As Beck explains, "It does not exist, but is only a thought of a limit (*Grenzbegriff*) to our approach to a complete determination of things as they are; that is, as they would fully satisfy systematic thought."[76]

In drawing parallels between Kierkegaard's and Barth's rejection of the Socratic, it is pertinent to note that Cohen's pupil, Ernst Cassirer, described him as

---

73. Beck, "Neo-Kantianism," 471.

74. Commenting on Cohen's *Logik der reinen Erkenntnis*, David Congdon rightly comments that "law is here understood in the sense of mathematical laws." He adds that this is also the case in his earlier writings on mathematics and epistemology. David W. Congdon, *The Mission of Demythologizing: Rudolf Bultmann's Dialectical Theology* (Minneapolis: Fortress, 2015), 371.

75. Hermann Cohen, *Logik der reinen Erkenntnis* (Berlin, 1902), 20, cited and trans. in Beck, "Neo-Kantianism," 471.

76. Beck, "Neo-Kantianism," 471.

"one of the most resolute Platonists that has ever appeared in the history of philosophy."[77] Even more significant for appreciating parallels between the monist idealism of Hegel and that of the Marburg Neo-Kantians is Beck's comment: "Cohen had moved so far from Kant toward Hegel that it was for him an almost insignificant accident that individual men and women know anything."[78]

Frederick Beiser has shown the extent to which the monism that characterized Cohen's epistemology and metaphysics also found expression in his political thought. Cohen was a vehement advocate of patriotism and the importance of "the bond of unity," arguing that "people should have the same religion, the same morals, the same culture, and indeed the same ethnic background."[79] There is a profound poignancy here given that he was a German who was committed to Judaism. "People who want political or national unity [*Staats und Volks-Einheit*] have to strive for unity," he argued, "with all the power of their spirit and soul in every dimension of their political existence."[80] In other words, his monist idealist vision found expression in a passion for the all-embracing unity of the political system and thus of the state. As subsequent history would illustrate, however, the nationalistic desire for unity is disinclined to tolerate difference. The extent to which "the idealizing tendency in Cohen's epistemology and hermeneutics" found sociopolitical expression in his work is analyzed insightfully by Edward Skidelsky, who argues that it is in Cohen's writings on Germany and Judaism that we discover the "emotional source" of his thought. "Cohen's concept of reason as fundamentally idealizing reflects a cultural *persona* that was itself the product of idealization."[81] The tragic irony here is that Cohen's driving desire to see a "German-Jewish synthesis" failed to survive the rise of ethnic-chauvinist *völkisch* nationalism. Indeed, in denigrating his Kant scholarship, the academic guild would cruelly blame his perceived misinterpretation of Kant on his Jewishness.[82]

---

77. "Hermann Cohen, 1842–1918," *Social Research* 10 (1943): 231, cited in Edward Skidelsky, *Ernst Cassirer: The Last Philosopher of Culture* (Princeton: Princeton University Press, 2011), 39; and Frederick C. Beiser, *Hermann Cohen: An Intellectual Biography* (Oxford: Oxford University Press, 2018), 122.

78. Beck, "Neo-Kantianism," 471. Despite the stark parallels between Hegelian and Neo-Kantian idealism, the two should not be confused. As Roger Johnson rightly points out, "The Neo-Kantian *Geist* [spirit] is more akin to mathematical *Vernunft* [reason] than it is to a dialectical movement in history" (*Origins*, 49).

79. Beiser, *Hermann Cohen*, 122.

80. Beiser, *Hermann Cohen*, 122.

81. Skidelsky, *Ernst Cassirer*, 39 (emphasis original).

82. Skidelsky describes how Bruno Bauch, coeditor of *Kant-Studien*, would soon critique Cohen's failure to appreciate that "the truly revolutionary significance of Kant's philosophy"

The philosophical and cultural context of Barth's theological studies constituted, therefore, a rarefied form of idealism. As we have argued, the Neo-Kantians rejected both Kant's category of the thing-in-itself and the dualism to which that gave rise in his thought in favor of an unfettered, monist idealism. In order to appreciate the extent of Barth's own break with the idealist allegiances of his teachers, it is necessary to consider, albeit briefly, the extent to which Paul Natorp developed Marburg's theological appropriation of Neo-Kantianism when he took over the reins from Hermann Cohen. Natorp taught in Marburg from 1881, when he was appointed to the position of *Dozent*, right through until his death in 1924, and his influence was immense—due, not least, to his success in expanding the transcendental method into the domain of the social sciences, most notably psychology. Mariano Campo argues that, for Natorp, the importance of Kant lay in the discovery of the transcendental method as a critical foundation and justification not only of the great "facts" of science but also of "morality, art, and religion and of the generative laws of logic immanent in the various forms of objectification" evident there. What we find is that the application of the transcendental method constituted "an unending progressive undertaking" which showed itself able to subsume *every* field of inquiry within the Neo-Kantian system.[83]

This broader compass, which now included psychology, led Natorp to move away from the extreme panlogism of Cohen and focus on upholding and applying the transcendental method. Importantly, despite his commitment to psychology, Natorp did not believe there existed anything in the neighborhood of a pure ego which might be regarded as an object for study. The concept of the ego, like that of the *Ding-an-sich*, was nothing more than a *Grenzbegriff*—a boundary concept or the concept of a limit to our experience. Indeed, Beck explains how consistently idealist his account of the self was: "For Natorp the objective and the subjective were not two realms. . . . Rather, they were two directions of knowledge, objectification and subjectification, each starting from the same phenomenon and each employing the transcendental method of categorical constitution, resolution into *Ursprung* [origin] and *Erzeugung* [generation]."[84] That is, Natorp reiterated Cohen's view that "objects" were not the referents of thought. They constituted, rather, the goal of thought—as

---

is to be found in its discovery of "the sphere of 'validity and value'"—something which, he believes, Cohen as a Jew could not possibly comprehend (Skidelsky, *Ernst Cassirer*, 39–40).

83. Mariano Campo, "Natorp, Paul," in *The Encyclopedia of Philosophy*, edited by Paul Edwards (New York: Macmillan and Free Press, 1967), 5:446.

84. Beck, "Neo-Kantianism," 471.

products of thought that displaced Kant's conception of the "thing."[85] "Objects are not 'given,'" he explains; "consciousness forms them. . . . All objectifying [is] the creative deed of consciousness."[86] One implication of this, which we shall see in Bultmann, is that it is not possible on this account to speak about God or God's involvement in the world as an "objective reality." That is quite simply because all that belongs to the realm of objective knowledge is the result of a process of objectification (*Objektivierung*) in accordance with law. To suggest that God was objectively "known" would be to suggest (within Neo-Kantian epistemology) that God was a law-governed construct of the mind.

The Significance of Law for the Neo-Kantians

Roger Johnson summarizes the essence of Marburg Neo-Kantian epistemology in a single sentence: "To know is to objectify in accordance with the principle of law."[87] The construction of objects was anything but arbitrary. It would be profoundly mistaken, therefore, to think that the approach of Natorp and his colleagues was subjectivist in any individualistic sense. The process of objectification took place in accordance with universal laws.[88] This meant that, as Johnson explains, the principle of law replaced sensory data "as evidence for the objective validity of any cognitive judgement."[89] The Neo-Kantians moved well beyond Kant, therefore, in that they understood reason as both beginning and ending with itself—"thinking begins from its own concepts (not a plurality of data) and ends with the object as the product of thought." The object given for thought became "the objectified construct of thought."[90] As William Werkmeister explains, "There is no longer any need for the assumption that objects exist in and by themselves. All we need accept now is the possibility of an orderly progress of cognition, the possibility of establishing an

---

85. Johnson, *Origins*, 47.

86. Paul Natorp, *Religion innerhalb der Grenzen der Humanität* (Leipzig, 1894), cited in Johnson, *Origins*, 39.

87. Johnson, *Origins*, 49–50.

88. Anthony Thiselton cites Beck: "Any assertion gains its status as true solely by virtue of its systematic position in a body of universal laws that, in turn, require each other on methodological grounds." Anthony C. Thiselton, *The Two Horizons: New Testament Hermeneutics and Philosophical Description with Special Reference to Heidegger, Bultmann, Gadamer, and Wittgenstein* (Grand Rapids: Eerdmans, 1980), 210. The quotation is taken from Beck, "Neo-Kantianism," 471.

89. Johnson, *Origins*, 49.

90. Johnson, *Origins*, 50.

all-comprehensive context according to law, the method of securing scientific cognition. The 'object' becomes the ultimate goal of that process."[91]

The effect of these developments was to attach overwhelming significance to the place of law. It is law that governs thought and objectification and which ensures, therefore, that objects are not arbitrary constructs. It is law and not some inaccessible realm of things as they are in themselves that facilitates the "orderly progress of cognition" and ensures that "reality" is constructed (objectified) coherently and cogently.

Monist Idealism and the Construction of Reality

To reiterate, for the Neo-Kantians, objective reality is a construct of thought—a process governed by the rule of law. In Cohen's words, "Only thinking may produce that which may be regarded as Being (*Sein*)."[92] And in a telling allusion to the Johannine Prologue, which anticipates Bultmann's appropriation of it, Natorp writes:

> In the beginning was the act, the creative act of the formation of the object, in which alone man built up himself, his human nature, and as he objectified himself in this, the stamp of his spirit was fundamentally and in a completely unified manner impressed upon his world.[93]

One final element requires to be grasped in order to appreciate the radical nature of Barth's break with the Neo-Kantianism of his teachers. This concerns the interpretation of law. As Anthony Thiselton has argued so convincingly, nineteenth-century Lutheranism adopted a strongly dualistic understanding of the relationship between law and grace on the one hand, and between works and faith on the other.[94] The sphere of grace and faith was distinguished radically, therefore, from that of law and works. Now, to the extent that Neo-Kantian epistemology saw "objective" reality as "constructed" in accordance with "law," every reference to objective (objectified) reality constituted a reference to the sphere of works and law. The marriage of nineteenth-century Lutheranism and Marburg Neo-Kantianism in the thought of both Wilhelm Herrmann and Rudolf Bultmann meant, therefore, that to suggest that God was "objectively known" in

91. William H. Werkmeister, "Cassirer's Advance Beyond Neo-Kantianism," in *The Philosophy of Ernst Cassirer*, Library of Living Philosophers 6, ed. Paul Arthur Schilpp (Evanston, IL: Library of Living Philosophers, 1949), 765.

92. Cited in Johnson, *Origins*, 48.

93. Cited in Johnson, *Origins*, 48.

94. See Thiselton, *Two Horizons*, 212–17.

any sense was precluded not merely by the tenets of Neo-Kantian epistemology but also by the Lutheranism of the time. Given that, for the nineteenth-century Lutherans, God was to be conceived in terms of the domain of grace and faith in contrast with that of law and work, this compounded their insistence that God was emphatically not to be found within the sphere of human knowing. That would make God a construct—a product of human work (construction) in accordance with law! This Lutheran attitude to law, therefore, added further weight to the Neo-Kantian dichotomization between faith and objective knowledge of God and this is evident in the direction of Bultmann's thought. Here, moreover, the contrast with Barth's approach could not be more clear-cut. For Barth, there is no dualism, as we shall see, between grace and law or between faith in God and knowledge of God. To appreciate Barth's exposition of these themes, therefore, is to recognize how radically Barth broke with both Lutheranism, particularly in its nineteenth-century form, and also the Marburg school. In both these respects, Barth pursued a radically different direction from Bultmann, his fellow Marburg protégé.

We shall now focus on the extent to which Marburg Neo-Kantianism found expression in the theology of Bultmann, its true heir. This will set the scene for an appreciation of the theological and epistemological moves that define the Kierkegaard-Barth trajectory and how radically it breaks with monist idealism which so profoundly influenced the direction of modern New Testament scholarship and theology.

The Impact of Neo-Kantian Idealism on the Approach of Rudolf Bultmann

Rudolf Bultmann was one of the most influential biblical scholars and theologians of the twentieth century and, as we have already suggested, his approach can be seen as a development of the Neo-Kantian commitments of his Marburg teachers. Just as the work of David Friedrich Strauss, the father of myth theory, was shaped by the monist idealism of Hegel, so the work of Rudolf Bultmann, the father of "demythologization," was shaped by the monist idealism of the Marburg Neo-Kantians. What we shall see is that just as Kierkegaard's work challenged the idealism of Hegel and its outworking in the church, so Barth's theology broke radically with the monist idealism of the Marburg school and the influence it had on theological scholarship and, indeed, the church of the time, not least through Wilhelm Herrmann, Barth's teacher.[95] The discussion that follows should highlight the extent to which Barth's career exemplified

95. As mentioned above, Herrmann was one of the ninety-three signatories of the dec-

the "turnabout" (*Wende*) that he advocated and which we shall discuss further in chapter 4.

Roger Johnson's account of the genetics of Bultmann's program of de-mythologization and the extent to which it was shaped by Marburg Neo-Kantianism is carefully documented and, in general, convincing. Bultmann's appropriation of Heideggerian categories allowed him to present Neo-Kantian anthropological categories in innovative, existentialist terms. However, as Johnson and Thiselton both show, Heidegger's influence does not alter the fact that, during his academic career, Bultmann remained true to the fundamental metaphysical and epistemological commitments of Marburg Neo-Kantianism and to its interpretation of modern science. Indeed, the Johnson-Thiselton thesis may help to explain why Bultmann's approach deviated so little from the key elements that characterized his early writings. Walter Schmithals, for example, observes that Bultmann's essay on myth in 1941 summarized "in a systematic way what Bultmann had been teaching and publishing for twenty years." He adds, "All his work had been 'demythologizing,' even when this term did not occur."[96] Schubert Ogden further emphasizes the consistency in Bultmann's commitments. There is, he suggests, "complete agreement between Bultmann's book *Jesus*, first published in 1926, and his later *Jesus Christ and Mythology*, published in 1958."[97]

The Neo-Kantian legacy can be spelled out with reference to several inter-related features of his thought. First, as we have suggested, his fundamental epistemological suppositions, his identification of objective knowledge with objectification, reflect his Neo-Kantian commitments. These are evident in his understanding of the physical world and what the modern scientific worldview entailed. More significantly, it also had profound theological implications. His commitment to the principle of "non-objectifiability" led him to deny a priori the possibility that God could *freely choose to be known* by human beings in such a way that God was not an objectified construct. The suggestion that God could be miraculously known by creaturely minds by means of an event of incarnation was inevitably dismissed, therefore, as mythology.[98] It would involve identifying

---

laration in support of the Kaiser's war policy, the declaration which so disillusioned the young Barth.

96. Cited in Thiselton, *Two Horizons*, 205.

97. Schubert M. Ogden, introduction to *Existence and Faith: Shorter Writings of Rudolf Bultmann*, by Rudolf Bultmann (n.p.: Collins, 1964), 11.

98. Bultmann writes, "A miracle in the sense of an action of God cannot be thought of as an event which happens on the level of secular (worldly) events. It is not visible, not capable of objective scientific proof which is possible only within an objective view of the world. To

the "unworldly" presence of God with "worldly" events, that is, with events within what Neo-Kantian science required him to conceive as a closed continuum of cause and effect.[99] To include the unworldly within an "objective view of the world" is to engage in mythology.[100] "*Der Mythos objektiviert das Jenseitige zum Diesseitigen*" ("Myth objectifies the other-worldly as this-worldly").[101] Moreover, to identify God with what one has "objectified" amounts to idolatry. It is to treat a human construct as God. The vocation of the theologian is, therefore, to demythologize the myths we find in the New Testament. That does not mean that we reject them. Rather, we seek "to recover the deeper meaning behind the mythological conceptions" that we find.[102] This is a process, he suggests, that we find taking place within the New Testament itself.[103]

So what are the implications of this for the life of faith in the modern world? It means we assume that we live in a closed causal continuum while, at the same time, accepting the "nevertheless" of faith:

> The worldview given by science is a necessary means for doing our work within the world. Indeed, I need to see the worldly events as linked by cause and effect not only as a scientific observer, but also in my daily living. In doing so there remains no room for God's working. This is the paradox of faith, that faith "nevertheless" understands as God's action here and now an event which is completely intelligible in the natural or historical connection of events.[104]

---

the scientific, objective observer God's action is a mystery." Rudolf Bultmann, *Jesus Christ and Mythology* (New York: Scribner, 1958), 23. It is pertinent to our discussion to note the parallel between the expressions "objective view of the world" and "capable of objective scientific proof." It is possible for there to be "objective" recognition of facets of reality that is not necessarily susceptible to scientific proof. For example, a woman can know that her husband is truthful in the way he communicates what he is thinking.

99. Faith is not to be confused with "an objective view of the world" (Bultmann, *Jesus Christ and Mythology*, 23). Moreover, faith does not confuse the "natural" and the "supernatural." Bultmann writes, "In faith I deny the closed connection of the worldly events, the chain of cause and effect as it presents itself to the neutral observer. I deny the interconnection of the worldly events not as mythology does, which by breaking the connection places supernatural events into the chain of natural events; I deny the worldly connection as a whole when I speak of God" (25).

100. Bultmann, *Jesus Christ and Mythology*, 23.

101. Bultmann, *Jesus Christ and Mythology*, 19. The English translation runs, "gives worldly objectivity to that which is unworldly." We have translated it literally to reflect Bultmann's use of the term "objektiviert."

102. Bultmann, *Jesus Christ and Mythology*, 5.

103. Bultmann, *Jesus Christ and Mythology*, 32.

104. Bultmann, *Jesus Christ and Mythology*, 65.

This "nevertheless," this "living as if" is integral to faith. What we must not lose sight of here is that faith, for Bultmann, does not (and cannot) include an epistemic relation to its "object." For that reason, "faith" can never, on Bultmann's account, mean anything in the neighborhood of "faith in" or "trust in." That, however, raises the question as to how far Bultmann's interpretation of faith is compatible with how "faith" is construed in the New Testament. In Paul's letters, for example, faith clearly does have an epistemic component. This is evident in the *pistis Christou* language (e.g., Rom. 3:22; Gal. 2:16; Phil. 3:9). Indeed, both those who interpret *pistis Christou* in objective genitive terms (faith in Jesus Christ) and those who interpret it in subjective genitive terms (the faith or faithfulness of Jesus Christ) agree that faith entails some form of knowledge, whether it refers to our faith in God, Christ's faith in God, or Christ's faithfulness in relation to God. As Douglas Campbell argues, for Paul, faith possesses a cognitive and an affective component and is functionally equivalent to the portrayal of the mind in Philippians 2:6–8.[105] The pressure of Marburg epistemology, in other words, means that the meaning of the word "faith" also requires to be demythologized or, to use a favorite phrase of Climacus's, to undergo *metabasis eis allo genos*.[106]

The New Testament aside, it is hard to understand how this understanding of faith is compatible with approaches that recognize God as possessing explanatory power with respect to the contingent order. It is commonplace, for example, to regard the "object" of Christian faith as the God who explains why anything contingent exists at all. For Bultmann, however, it is epistemologically confused to think of God as causally related, in such a way, to the contingent order. Rather, we are obliged to live with a radical dichotomy between what faith appears to "tell us" and what we objectively "know" to be the case. That is, faith calls us to live "as if" what faith tells us were true while, at the same time, recognizing that, objectively, it is false and necessarily recognized (known) to be so.

Here we see the outworking of the harmonization of nineteenth-century Lutheranism and Neo-Kantian epistemology which so compounded the dichotomization between gospel and law, and between faith and works. To live by faith is to refuse to live from any supposed "objective knowledge of God" since that would be to ground one's faith in law and works. To recall Natorp's

---

105. Cf. Douglas A. Campbell's recent *Pauline Dogmatics: The Triumph of God's Love* (Grand Rapids: Eerdmans, 2020), chap. 13. For further literature on the topic, see *Pauline Dogmatics*, 325–26.

106. "Transformation into something of a different kind." See note 28.

account of knowledge, "The creative ground of such a deed as the formation of the objects is the law: that fundamental law which one still designates as Logos, Ratio, *Vernunft*."[107] If knowledge is grounded in a work of objectification in accordance with universal law, then to conceive of faith as cognitive "knowing" *in any sense* would be to interpret faith and the gospel in terms of the categories of both law and also work. To avoid this, faith requires to be reinterpreted, therefore, as nonobjective and noncognitive. To fail to do so is to reduce faith and the freedom integral to it to the mechanisms of law-governed objectification that define human knowing. Similarly, and in parallel with this, if theology is to be scientific (*wissenschaftlich*), it cannot contradict what Bultmann refers to as "the modern worldview," which, again, requires to be defined in terms of the determinist suppositions that characterized Newtonian science, and which were essential to the broader Kantian system.[108]

Faith and Fictional Living

As we have already suggested, Bultmann's conception of living by faith in the context of the "modern worldview" commits him to living "as if," that is, to a form of "fictional living." In 1911 the Kantian Hans Vaihinger wrote an influential monograph, *Die Philosophie des Als Ob*, advocating the Kantian philosophy of the "as if."[109] This operated from the assumption that we do not know the underlying reality of the world as it actually is. Consequently, we construct models or systems of thought to enable us to live "as if" they reflected the way things actually are. As a result, he argued for a pragmatic "principle of fictionalism":

107. Johnson, *Origins*, 48, citing August Messer.

108. It is relevant here to recognize that Kant originally established his transcendental method out of a concern to secure the scientific advances of his time against the threat of skepticism. Whereas David Hume had awoken Kant from his dogmatic slumbers by challenging the influential metaphysics of Christian Wolff and his followers, Kant was concerned about the disarray in which metaphysics now found itself and the capacity of Hume's skepticism to undermine not only morality but the science of the time. It was these apologetic concerns that were the major driving force behind Kant's "Copernican revolution" and establishment of the transcendental method. Immanuel Kant, preface to the second edition, *Critique of Pure Reason*, B xix. See W. H. Walsh, *Kant's Criticism of Metaphysics* (Edinburgh: Edinburgh University Press, 1975), chap. 1, especially pages 2–3.

109. Hans Vaihinger, *The Philosophy of "As If": A System of the Theoretical, Practical and Religious Fictions of Mankind*, trans. C. K. Ogden, 2nd ed. (London: Routledge & Kegan Paul, 1935; 1st ed. 1924).

An idea whose theoretical untruth or incorrectness, and therewith its falsity, is admitted, is not for that reason practically valueless and useless; for such an idea, in spite of its theoretical nullity[,] may have great practical importance.[110]

Bultmann's appropriation of the Neo-Kantian dichotomy between the sphere of the *Individuum* (individual) and that of *Vernunft* (reason) served to accommodate the dichotomy between the sphere of faith and that of objectification. This in turn led him to embrace a "Kantian" conception of fictional living as it defined the life of the individual believer. In the conclusion of *Jesus Christ and Mythology*, Bultmann argues that "our relation to the world as believers is paradoxical." The concluding paragraph of the book summarized and commandeered the language of Paul to advocate living "as if":

> As Paul puts it in 1 Cor. 7:29–31, "Let those who have wives live as though they had none, and those who mourn as though they were not mourning, and those who rejoice as though they were not rejoicing, and those who buy as though they had no goods, and those who deal with the world as though they had no dealings with it." In terms of this book, we may say, "let those who have the modern worldview live as though they had none."[111]

This raises an obvious question: What are the implications of the interpretation of faith as fictional living for how we understand religious experience? And what place, if any, can the epistemology and metaphysics of the Marburg Neo-Kantians provide for it?[112] As William Dennison rightly points out, for the Neo-Kantians, "all culture is the objectification of human thought, and, thus, every component of its construct is subject to explanation (*Erklärung*) by

---

110. Vaihinger, *Philosophy of "As If,"* viii.
111. Bultmann, *Jesus Christ and Mythology*, 85.
112. Jos de Mul argues that Wilhelm Dilthey takes "the distinction between *inner* and *outer experience* as the criterion for the demarcation of the natural and human sciences. Outer experience (*aujiere Erfahrung*) is the process by which, through collaboration of the senses and discursive understanding, an image of reality, subject to laws outside ourselves, is created (GS I, 15–17, cf. GS V, 243). In the lived experience (*innere Erfahrung* or *Erlebnis*) we experience—without the co-operation of the senses—an independent world of mind, characterized by a sovereignty of the will and a responsibility for actions." Jos de Mul, "Das Schauspiel des Lebens: Wilhelm Dilthey and Historical Biography," *Revue Internationale de Philosophie* 226, no. 4 (2003): 407–24, https://www.cairn.info/revue-internationale-de -philosophie-2003-4-page-407.htm.

means of scientific investigation, analysis, and criticism."[113] This means that it must be possible to provide a full scientific explanation of *every facet* of religious experience to the extent that it is manifest in the cultural milieu. But how is it possible, if that is the case, to avoid a radically reductionistic account of religion and thus of human spirituality? Are we simply to accept that religious experience is to be subsumed within *Erfahrung*, that is, the generic form of experience that characterizes human participation in science, morality, aesthetics, and religion? If so, it is hard to see how there can be any place at all for the transcendent in experience given that, to the extent that experience is rational, it is completely determined by the laws constitutive of our processing of reality.

In order to try to counteract the reductionist implications of interpreting religious experience in this way, Cohen, a practicing Jew, and Natorp, a Protestant thinker (albeit an atheist in practice), set out to uphold the integrity of religion by postulating a special kind of individual experience which they allocated to the sphere of ethics. The leading Marburg theologian Wilhelm Herrmann, however, saw that this would inevitably subsume the individual and the experience of the transcendent within the category of culture, thereby making every facet of religion completely explicable in terms of the law-governed processes of objectification. Herrmann insisted that if the realm of true religion were to possess any credibility, the reality of the individual (*Individuum*) would have to remain a distinct and isolated sphere—a *Gegensatz* (an "antithesis") in relation to every sphere of objectification in accordance with law. Consequently, he sought to commandeer and introduce an older concept of experience, namely, that of *Erlebnis*. *Erlebnis* was taken as denoting "the immediacy with which something real is grasped"[114] by the individual—in effect, the essence of the experience of encounter. This allowed for a category of religious experience which would not be subject, it was suggested, to scientific investigation in that the sense of the immediacy of encounter was taken as transcending culture (science, ethics, and aesthetics). Instead, it came to denote, as Dennison explains, "an independent revelation which the individual could only understand in its immediacy, i.e., a revelation that is received in an isolated moment of pure religious truth—feelings without objects. When *Erlebnis* includes an encounter with God, it is an encounter without any preconceived idea of who God is."[115] He concludes: "The terms

113. William D. Dennison, *The Young Bultmann: Context for His Understanding of God, 1884–1925* (New York: Peter Lang, 2008), 55.

114. Dennison, *Young Bultmann*, 55.

115. Dennison, *Young Bultmann*, 56.

Erfahrung and *Erlebnis* are descriptive, therefore, of Herrmann's neo-Kantian dualism. *Erfahrung* (active, controlling life) is a rational experience of culture, the objectified construct of the mind. In this realm, true religion cannot be found. In contrast, *Erlebnis* (passive, absolute dependence) is an immediate encounter with the essence of religious truth. As an occurrence purely within the individual, it transcends culture; it is not subject in any way to the objectifications of human thought."[116] It is no surprise, therefore, that Bultmann found Heidegger's characterization of *existentiell* awareness so congenial theologically.[117] The underlying conceptuality was already present, in embryo, in Natorp's thought and became even more prominent in Herrmann's concept of *Erlebnis*, which appeared to open the door to the language of "encounter" in theology.[118] Bultmann's underlying conceptuality was rooted in the Neo-Kantian conception of the *Individuum*, but filled out by means of Heideggerian categories. His subsequent account of the self and encounter furnished his program of demythologizing with its all-important anthropological categories. This enabled him to adopt the language of divine address, encounter, vocation, and experience without departing from his Neo-Kantian frame of reference. What should be clear, however, is that this did not allow him to avoid the bullet he was obliged to bite. If there were any divine subject or free divine initiative in the encounter at the heart of theology, it would never be possible to *know* that reality. In order for it to be known or recognized in any "objective" sense, it would have to be "objectified" in accordance with the laws of thought. As we have argued at length, no such constructed *Objekt* could ever be identifiable as the transcendent God without our being guilty of idolatry. For precisely

116. Dennison, *Young Bultmann*, 56.

117. In *Being and Time*, Martin Heidegger distinguished between "ontological" and "existential" on the one hand and "ontic" and "*existentiell*" on the other. The former concepts are essentially analytic and theoretical in function, whereas the latter refer to the interaction of particular beings with the world and the experience that attends everyday life. As such, they are the basis of ontological and existential interpretation which denotes modes of theoretical analysis. "Existential" refers to the being of the human individual (or *Dasein*), whereas "*existentiell*" pertains to the human being as a particular entity. William D. Blattner provides the following example: "It is an existential feature of Dasein that it understands, but an existentiell feature of Jones that she understands herself as a basketball player, say." Blattner provides further helpful definitions on his page "Some Terminology in *Being and Time*," updated September 2, 2011, *Heideggeriana*, https://faculty.georgetown.edu/blattnew /heid/terms.htm.

118. Roger Johnson comments, "For a reader familiar with the 'later Heidegger,' it is impossible to read the 'later Natorp' without the strange sensation of *déjà vue*" (Johnson, *Origins*, 41).

the same reason, the experience at the heart of the Christian faith could not be conceived as "objective" either. Consequently, it could have no "objective" content as it could have nothing to do with "knowledge" of God. The result is theological terminology which, when analyzed, appears fluid at best and vacuous at worst. What is "experience" if it is necessarily devoid of any element of cognition or recognition? And what is "encounter" when there can be no recognition of what or whom one is *encountering*?

It comes as no surprise that Herrmann and Bultmann shared an admiration for Friedrich Schleiermacher.[119] The influence on Bultmann of both Schleiermacher and Herrmann is evident in a sermon he preached in 1917 in which he claimed that "the feeling of absolute dependence is in and of itself God's co-presence in self-consciousness."[120] Significantly, there is justification for interpreting Schleiermacher's own approach as reflecting a "transcendental move."[121] For Schleiermacher, the key to theology was neither a form of knowing nor of doing but, rather, of feeling. The feeling of absolute dependence (or nonultimacy, given that the sense is intransitive) is the universal condition under which we experience the world. In more modern parlance, one might say it constitutes an "existential a priori" in that it is constitutive of our orientation to the world as a whole—though Schleiermacher found its supreme expression in Christian doctrine.

A parallel move is also found in Karl Rahner, who, from his early publication *Spirit in the World*, set out on his path of integrating Kant's philosophy with Thomism. Rahner's interpretation of the transcendental method interpreted the human preapprehension of being (*Vorgriff auf esse*) as constitutive of the self's orientation to the world.[122] Like Schleiermacher, he too sought to

---

119. Dennison suggests "Herrmann admitted freely that his thought was built upon the legacy of Schleiermacher, who had placed the religious experience of God within the individual" (*Young Bultmann*, 2; cf. 56–57); cf. Judy Deane Saltzman, *Natorp's Philosophy of Religion within the Marburg Neo-Kantian Tradition* (New York: Georg Olms Verlag, 1981), 194.

120. Dennison, *Young Bultmann*, 96.

121. Cf. Alan J. Torrance, "Christian Experience and Divine Revelation in the Theologies of Friedrich Schleiermacher and Karl Barth," in *Christian Experience in Theology and Life*, ed. I. Howard Marshall (Edinburgh: Rutherford House, 1988), 83–113.

122. By means of our preapprehension of being (*Vorgriff auf esse*) the human spirit "reaches out toward what is nameless and by its very nature is infinite." Karl Rahner, *Foundations of Christian Faith: An Introduction to the Idea of Christianity* ([New York?]: Crossroad Publishing, 1976; rev. ed., 1982), 62.

argue that the highest expression of this is found in Christian doctrine.[123] The moves he makes here are spelled out clearly in his *Foundations of Christian Faith*, which he presents as an introduction to the "idea" of Christianity.[124] The key influence on Rahner's adoption of Kant was Joseph Maréchal, the founder of transcendental Thomism, the intention of which was to seek to merge the theology and philosophy of Aquinas with the thought of Kant.

Space does not allow us to explore these developments further. Suffice it to say, the impact of idealism (in its Hegelian, Kantian, and Neo-Kantian forms) on Lutheran, Reformed, and Catholic theology is far more pervasive than is widely recognized. When Roger Johnson suggested that "the philosophical roots of mid-twentieth-century theology are firmly embedded in Marburg Neo-Kantianism," he may have been overstating his case.[125] What cannot seriously be questioned, however, is that radical idealism underpinned by Kant's transcendental method was to become the dominant influence on the shape of Lutheran, Reformed, and Catholic theology in the later nineteenth and twentieth centuries.

Whereas his fellow protégé of the Marburg school adopted Herrmann's amalgam of nineteenth-century Lutheranism and Neo-Kantianism and applied it to the theological interpretation of the New Testament, Karl Barth broke with it at every point. McCormack was right to describe Barth as a "critical realist." What has to be grasped, however, is how radical such a position was, given the philosophical developments of the previous two centuries. When one appreciates the extent to which the intellectual, cultural, and political pressures on the church and theology were grounded in the radically immanentist and idealist agendas represented by Hegel and the Neo-Kantians, one recognizes not only how radical Barth's "about turn" was but also the courage it took to seek, *contra mundum*,[126] to reinterpret the Christian message in its own light and on its own grounds and then to go on, as he did, to explore the full implications of doing so. The cost of the failure of Protestant

123. Perceptively, Nicholas Lash used to refer to Karl Rahner in lectures as the "Catholic Schleiermacher."

124. See Karen Kilby's thorough analysis and critique of Rahner's concept of the *Vorgriff* (30–31) and also of his "problematic" (71) use of transcendental arguments in *Karl Rahner: Theology and Philosophy* (London: Routledge, 2004). Kilby goes on to suggest if his philosophical demonstration of *Vorgriff* is "fundamentally flawed," it is at least "thinkable" that one can "read his theology with a certain degree of separation from his philosophy" (71). See also Fergus Kerr's telling critique, "Rahner Retrospective III: Transcendence or Finitude," *New Blackfriars* 62 (1981): 370–79.

125. Johnson, *Origins*, 40–41.

126. *Contra mundum*, meaning "against the world"; Athanasius of Alexandria was known as "Athanasius *contra mundum*."

and Catholic theology to challenge the philosophical, cultural, political, and religious assumptions of the age was the horrific moral evils witnessed during the first half of the twentieth century. It is worth reading Barth's reflections later in life with that in mind.

> A free theologian will not be hindered by traditional conceptions from thinking and speaking in the direction from God to humanity. . . . His ontology will be subject to criticism and control by his theology and not conversely. He will not necessarily feel obligated to the philosophical *kairos*, the latest prevailing philosophy. The gratitude of the Royal House of Austria will, in any event, not be showered upon him.[127]

As we discuss the shape of Barth's theology under the influence of Kierkegaard, this should highlight the radical difference between the Kierkegaard-Barth trajectory, on the one hand, and the Hegelianism-Strauss and Neo-Kantianism-Bultmann trajectories on the other. What should also become clear is the stark nature of the choices with which Christian thought is presented and the implications of these.

CONCLUSION

This chapter focused on three related topics. First, we explored the ways in which Barth challenged central features of the Enlightenment and the impact they had on the church and its theological agenda. Second, we turned to Barth's perception of the impact of cultural Protestantism not least on religion and nationalism in Germany and his analysis of the failure of the church's theological commitments to address this. Third, we examined the nature and influence of Marburg Neo-Kantianism and the extent to which Barth broke with the philosophical, religious, and sociopolitical commitments that characterized this.

When one recognizes the extent to which Barth challenged the idealism of his teachers, the culturally driven religion of the time, and the political agendas it served, one appreciates not only how radical and intellectually courageous he was but also the sociopolitical significance of the theological decisions he made. What is no less apparent is the extent to which, in all these respects, it

---

127. Barth, "Evangelical Theology in the 19th Century," 93. The reference to the Royal House of Austria is an allusion to the House of Hapsburg's support for Germany in World War I and Emperor Franz Joseph's signing of the declaration of war on Russia in August 1914.

was Barth and not Bultmann who was the heir of Kierkegaard. Like Kierkegaard before him, he had the intellectual clarity to recognize that if the Christian faith finds itself "ill-wed"[128] to monist idealism, not only is it left without anything distinctive or constructive to contribute but by endorsing "religion" and the "immanent" it also opens itself to serving the ends of the culture wherever they lead. What Barth would witness during his lifetime was precisely how dangerous that can be.[129]

On a more positive note, what Kierkegaard and Barth also grasped, and which will become plain in the chapters that follow, is that when Christian theology has been set free from philosophical, religious, and cultural constraints to recognize the kinship that the eternal God has established in time, not only does its cogency and explanatory power become apparent, so too does its profound personal and sociopolitical relevance.

128. On the frontispiece of *Philosophical Fragments*, Kierkegaard placed a quotation from Shakespeare: "Better well-hanged than ill-wed."

129. "It is hard to resist the conclusion that the uniqueness of the Christ event needs to be elucidated by a more positive treatment of dogmatics than we find in Bultmann's thought. The historical necessity and soteriological finality of Jesus Christ can only be articulated by a return to many of the themes relating to the person and work of Christ that are dismissed by Bultmann." David Fergusson, *Bultmann* (London: Geoffrey Chapman, 1992), 141. Fergusson's conclusion is unconvincingly challenged by David Congdon, who comments, "It is unclear why Fergusson thinks we can 'only' make sense of the ultimate significance of Christ by returning to dogmatic themes" (*Mission*, 369).

The Theological Implications of God's Kinship in Time

In the previous chapter, we discussed Barth's critique of three factors that he saw as undermining the church and its ability to serve the culture and the state. The first was the influence of certain features of the Enlightenment, the second was cultural Protestantism, and the third was the monist (Neo-Kantian) idealism of Barth's theological teachers. What became clear from this were the striking parallels between the challenges that Barth confronted in Germany and those that Kierkegaard had confronted in Denmark. In this chapter, we explore the trajectory initiated by Kierkegaard and which came to characterize Barth's response—a trajectory that reflected their shared commitment to set the church, the academy, and the society free from the constraints of idealism and cultural religion. Chapter 5 will then proceed to focus on three areas in which Barth appropriated central themes in Kierkegaard's theology, namely, his understanding of the "infinite qualitative difference," his theology of history, and his concept of "paradox."

This chapter is divided into three parts. The first explores the significance of the Kierkegaard-Barth trajectory for addressing cultural Christianity and its potential to underwrite social and political evil. The second sets forth Barth's vision of theology freed from the legacy of the Enlightenment and its constraints. Part three examines Barth's interpretation of the nature of human existence—how the covenantal kinship that God has established defines who we are, underpins social relations, and establishes human freedom.

Liberating Christianity from Christianism and the Potential for Harm

Early in his career, Barth famously issued young theologians with the following exhortation: "Take your Bible and take your newspaper, and read both.

But interpret newspapers from your Bible."[1] Not only did Barth advocate this message, he exemplified what it means to enact it—to engage with the world rigorously as a theologian, but to ensure that the agenda is established not by the world but from another source.

The news reports that confronted him during his career included the emergence of German nationalism prior to the First World War and the war itself, the emergence of Communism and the rise of both fascism and anti-Semitism during the 1920s and 1930s, and the horrors of the Second World War followed by the hideous reports of the Holocaust and other atrocities that took place in the 1940s. During his later years, he witnessed the erection of the wall separating East and West Germany, the Cold War, the threat of nuclear holocaust, and the further implication of Christian churches in racism and colonialism across the globe. Barth was painfully aware of the complicity of Christendom in all these events, and one fails to understand him if one ignores the extent to which he sought to interpret these events in the light of Scripture, and thereby to discern how the church should respond.

In recent years, the capacity of religion to underpin harmful policies and practices has been overplayed, not least by the four horsemen of modern atheism. That is, it is easy to forget the atrocious record in this regard of atheist leaders and regimes: Mao Zedong, Emperor Hirohito, and Stalin. Of course, Hitler, too, was an atheist.[2] That said, Christian theology cannot ignore the fact that forms of "Christian" establishment religion and what might be referred to as "Christianism" (or *Christlichkeit*, to use Barth's language) have been culpable both by commission and omission for appalling moral evils—the complicity of Christians and, indeed, of Christian churches in slavery during the nineteenth century is just one example.[3] At times, this complicity in moral evil has been

---

1. "Barth in Retirement," *Time Magazine*, May 31, 1963, http://content.time.com/time/sub scriber/article/0,33009,896838,00.html. In the same interview in which he recalled that exhortation, he stressed the importance of the newspaper, commenting, "I always pray for the sick, the poor, journalists, authorities of the state and the church—in that order. Journalists form public opinion. They hold terribly important positions. Nevertheless, a theologian should never be formed by the world around him."

2. It is important not to forget that tens of millions died under atheist leaders such as Mao Zedong, Adolf Hitler, Emperor Hirohito, and Joseph Stalin, not to mention those responsible for smaller scale atrocities, such as Pol Pot, Slobodan Milošović, Mengistu Haile Mariam, and Khorloogiin Choibalsan. In short, atheist leaders have been responsible for far more numerous and larger scale atrocities than religious leaders.

3. "By 1860, the final census taken before the American Civil War, there were four million slaves in the South, compared with less than 0.5 million free African Americans in all of the US." Aaron O'Neill, "Black and Slave Population in the United States, 1790–1880,"

explicit; at other times, subliminal. In order to challenge the weaponization of god-talk where it is used to endorse exclusive vested interests—be they racist, nationalist, androcentric, or homophobic—the theologian is obliged to ask the following: Given the radically inclusive nature of the gospel, what has led church theologians to relativize and distort the Christian message? Whereas Barth had this question in view throughout his career, it came to the fore during the 1930s when he, along with Dietrich Bonhoeffer, Martin Niemoeller, Marga Meusel, Elizabeth Schmitz, Gertrud Staewen, and other members of the *Bekennende Kirche* (the Confessing Church) challenged the anti-Semitic and nationalistic distortion of the faith that characterized the German Christian movement, a movement whose "undoing" of Christian theology is directly apparent in their documents.[4] What heightened Barth's horror at what was happening among the German Christians was that they sought to justify their embrace of Nazism by appeal to the Protestant Reformation, which sought to affirm the lordship of Jesus Christ and the authority of the Bible over against every area of life—including national politics.[5]

March 19, 2021, Statista, https://www.statista.com/statistics/1010169/black-and-slave-popu lation-us-1790-1880/. Richard Reddie observes, "The Christian Church was involved in the trade at many levels." Specifically, the Church of England had links to slavery—the Bishop of Exeter was one leading churchman who personally owned slaves. "The Church: Enslaver or Liberator?," last updated February 17, 2011, BBC News, https://www.bbc.co.uk/history /british/abolition/church_and_slavery_article_01.shtml.

4. See *A Church Undone: Documents from the German Christian Faith Movement, 1932–1940*, selected, translated, and introduced by Mary M. Solberg (Minneapolis: Fortress, 2015), which is an extensive collection of writings by leading German Christians. In addition to *The Handbook of the German Christians*, it includes essays by prominent theologians and church leaders representing the agenda of the German Christians. Among these are Emanuel Hirsch, Gerhard Kittel (*The Jewish Question*), Ludwig Müller, and Paul Althaus. She also includes Karl Barth's essay *Theological Existence Today!*, which was written in June 1933 as a response to these developments, urging the church and its theologians to "stay *awake*"—or if it *had* gone to sleep, to wake up. "Even in a totalitarian state the people live from the Word of God, whose content is 'the forgiveness of sins, the resurrection of the body, and life everlasting.' The church and theology must serve this Word, for the sake of the people. In so doing they are the limit of the state. This they are for the health and salvation [*Heil*] of the people, which neither the state nor the church can create but which the church is called to proclaim" (99).

5. Despite impressive efforts, not least by several prominent and courageous women such as Marga Meusel, Elizabeth Schmitz, Gertrud Staewen, and Helene Jacobs, Wolfgang Ger lach argues that Barth believed the Confessing Church could have done more. He writes, "In his farewell letter to Pastor Hermann Hesse, Karl Barth (who had accepted a professorship in Basel) arrived at the verdict that the Confessing Church 'still has no heart for millions suffering under injustice. It still has found nothing to say on the simplest questions of public honesty. It still speaks—when it speaks—always and only on its own behalf.'" Wolfgang

It was not only the Lutheran Church, however, that was compromised by the fusion of religion, nationalism, and racism. During the 1930s, a third of the German population was Catholic, many of whom supported the Nazi Party—although it should be added that support among Catholics for the Nazi Party in 1933 was lower than the national average.[6] The problem did not lie simply with Catholic adherents. In his study of Pope Pius XI and the rise of fascism, David Kertzer has shown that the relationship between the Roman Catholic hierarchy and Nazism in Germany, as also with fascism in Italy, was characterized by cynical diplomatic compromise driven by vested interests. This was manifest, for example, in the many concordats signed out of a strategic concern to safeguard the church's interests.[7]

It is not only in Europe that the Christian church has been compromised by racist ideology. As we shall discuss in chapter 6, the apartheid regime in South Africa, supported and endorsed by the Dutch Reformed Church, and the racist policies of segregation in the southern United States are just two examples of racism that were upheld in two of the world's most devoutly "Christian" contexts.[8] If we turn from racism to sexism, we also find that, for over two

---

Gerlach, *And the Witnesses Were Silent: The Confessing Church and the Persecution of the Jews* (Lincoln: University of Nebraska Press, 2000), 95, citing Kurt Dietrich Schmidt (ed.), *Die Bekenntnisse und grundsätzlichen Äußerungen zur Kirchenfrage - Band* 3: Das Jahr 1935. (Göttingen: Vandenhoeck & Ruprecht, 1936), 64. Barth's comments are also cited in Daniel Jonah Goldhagen, *Hitler's Willing Executioners: Ordinary Germans and the Holocaust* (New York: Knopf, 1996), 437.

6. The lower average notwithstanding, the Nazi Party first developed in Munich, a city that was largely Catholic.

7. David Kertzer's *The Pope and Mussolini: The Secret History of Pope Pius XI and the Rise of Fascism in Europe* (Oxford: Oxford University Press, 2014) is the result of an in-depth study of a trove of archives released in recent years, providing an informed and scholarly assessment of the extent of the compromise of the Vatican in Italy. Kertzer argues that in 1933, for example, fascist rallies would begin with morning mass celebrated by a priest, and both churches and cathedrals were important props in the pageantry. His extensive documentation of Pope Pius XI's close cooperation with Mussolini suggests that, for more than a decade, the Vatican lent his regime organizational strength and moral legitimacy. See Dave Davies, "'Pope and Mussolini' Tells the 'Secret History' of Fascism and the Church," NPR, Fresh Air, January 27, 2014, https://www.npr.org/2014/01/27/265794658/pope-and-mussolini-tells-the-secret-history-of-fascism-and-the-church.

8. For a scholarly analysis of the history of the church's involvement in South Africa, see the first two chapters of John de Gruchy, *The Church Struggle in South Africa* (Grand Rapids: Eerdmans, 1979), 1–101; and for a similar study of the history of the church's involvement in segregation in the United States, see Michael Emerson and Christian Smith, *Divided by Faith: Evangelical Religion and the Problem of Race in America* (Oxford: Oxford University Press, 2000), 21–50.

thousand years, women have borne an enormous burden at the hands of the marginalizing power structures of an androcentric and patriarchal church. What is clear from the above is the following: To fail to question critically the purported access to the divine will is to open the door to the misappropriation of theology in the service of oppressive and dehumanizing social and political agendas. While Barth recognized the extent to which the gospel stands to redeem our social, cultural, and political allegiances, he also grasped, with unparalleled clarity, how theological reasoning can fail the church by diluting or, indeed, corrupting its recognition of the sociopolitical implications of God's all-inclusive purposes in Jesus Christ.

Here, as elsewhere, Barth's insights into the conditions whereby this happens were anticipated by Kierkegaard's analysis of the capacity of theological immanentism to subvert Christian faith such that it serves the ends of the cultural status quo. As we saw in chapter 3, the insights of both men found vivid expression in Dietrich Bonhoeffer's insistence that Jesus Christ requires to be seen as the "counter-logos" with respect to all our immanent conceptualities (*logoi*), biases, and "systems of classification." That is, the Logos does not endorse our immanent *logoi* but stands to redefine them, along with all our sociopolitical agendas and allegiances.[9]

So how should the theologian respond to those betrayals of the Christian faith that have been complicit in social evils? For many, the answer is to encourage greater ethical or critical sophistication when it comes to religious affirmations. But that inevitably invites the responses, Whose ethics and whose critical theory? and, How precisely does religion clarify which criteria to select? It is here that the distinctive approaches of Kierkegaard and Barth stand out. For them, the freedom to challenge the culture of the day lies not in our opting for an alternative ideology. Rather, it is grounded in a transformative recognition, namely, the recognition of that kinship or fellowship that God has established with us in time and which redefines our orientation toward God and others. Integral to this is the affirmation that both the historical moment and the person of the teacher possess decisive significance. As such, the object

---

9. "But what happens if the counter Logos suddenly presents its demand in a wholly new form, so that it is no longer an idea or word that is turned against the autonomy of the [human] logos, but rather the counter Logos appears, somewhere and some time in history, as a human being, and as a human being sets itself up as judge over the human logos . . . ? Here it is no longer possible to fit the Word made flesh into the logos classification system. Here all that remains is the question: Who are you?" Dietrich Bonhoeffer, *Berlin: 1932–1933*, in *Dietrich Bonhoeffer Works*, ed. Larry Rasmussen, trans. Isabel Best and David Higgins (Minneapolis: Fortress, 2009), 12:302.

of faith is not a religious program or set of ideals (moral, spiritual, political, or otherwise). Rather, it is the personal reality of God who establishes a *relationship* in and through which our interpretation of the world undergoes a process of transformation, through which we are delivered from error—from a state of continual departing from the truth, as Climacus suggests.

The effect of Kierkegaard's argument is to deny us the possibility of affirming loyalty to God *alongside and in addition to* loyalty to the state or the culture. The vision of Christian discipleship that emerges stands in radical tension, therefore, with upholding any supplementary allegiance such as, for example, to the Nazi "*blut und boden*" ("blood and soil"—i.e., race and country). Any religious bondage to idolatrous forms of exclusive loyalty defined by race, culture, and vested interests is radically challenged by the kinship that defines Christian faith—a kinship established in the one in whom there is neither Jew nor gentile, black nor white, bond nor free, male and female.[10]

Duality and the Problem of Dual Allegiance

In chapter 3, we considered ways in which the Enlightenment subverted the gospel message. Whereas Kierkegaard exposed the impact of post-Enlightenment construals of reason on Danish theology, Barth exposed a parallel confusion in German cultural Protestantism (*Kulturprotestantismus*)—one that provided fertile soil for the emergence of German nationalism. A key factor in this was the two kingdoms doctrine that was inherent in nineteenth-century Lutheranism and had shaped Christian thought in both Denmark and Germany. Its effect was to inoculate the people's cultural and political commitments against any challenge from acknowledging the lordship of Jesus Christ and it did this by dichotomizing allegiances into the sphere of personal piety and the spheres of the state and culture.[11] Christ's lordship belonged to the former, the effect of which was to make it a spiritual lordship. This gave rise to an attitude of dual allegiance which was supported by a series of parallel dichotomies between law and grace, state and church, the secular and the spiritual—distinctions that would find further support, as Anthony Thiselton has argued, in Neo-Kantian dualism.[12] The resulting division of

---

10. Gal. 3:28. The switch from "nor" to "and" is present in the text and appears to be an allusion to "male and female created he them" (Gen. 5:2).

11. What was originally a less radical *Zwei-Regimenten-Lehre* (two regiments doctrine) in Luther would become a more radical *Zwei-Reiche-Lehre* (two kingdoms doctrine) in nineteenth-century Germany.

12. See Anthony C. Thiselton's important analysis of this and how it shaped later German theology in *The Two Horizons: New Testament Hermeneutics and Philosophical Description*

allegiances meant that the lordship of Jesus Christ found itself circumscribed by more foundational loyalties to the state, to the nation, to the realm of the law, and thus to the culture.

But why did this separation of the realm of the church from that of the state and culture not weaken rather than strengthen cultural Protestantism? After all, cultural Protestantism held to a synthesis and confusion between faith and cultural affiliation. Their separation, one might assume, should encourage persons to avoid any syncretism. It is important to recognize why this is not the case. As Barth saw with such clarity, when theologians endorse a system of dual loyalties with different sets of obligations (in this case, to the state and also to the church), what is perceived to be the broader field of obligation tends to become foundational, constituting thereby a procrustean bed that determines the extent or boundaries of faith and thus the lordship of Christ. What the history of cultural Protestantism and "civil religion" illustrates is that when it is assumed that the "spiritual" is *not* allowed to inform the "worldly," or that participation within the church should *not* interfere with political allegiances (i.e., that we should "keep Christianity out of politics"[13]), the person of Christ and the Bible are bracketed out of the evaluation of the so-called worldly sphere and thereby the duties and obligations that characterize everyday life. The problem is then compounded when this dual allegiance finds *theological* endorsement in the insistence that Jesus Christ is Lord only over the spiritual realm of personal piety, but that God has a separate and different purpose for the sociopolitical domain. That has the effect of ascribing divine endorsement to the dictates that emerge within the political or secular realm. Romans 13 is frequently cited, eisegetically, in support of this move.[14]

For Barth, however, following the trajectory established by Kierkegaard, there is no sphere of life where our thinking and decision-making does not take place *coram Deo*—before the one God who has established fellowship

---

with Special Reference to Heidegger, Bultmann, Gadamer, and Wittgenstein (Grand Rapids: Eerdmans, 1980), 212–16.

13. This Jeffersonian principle has been the dictum of those who believe the church should not interfere with state policies, whether they concern apartheid, segregation, the death penalty, or, in earlier times, whether women should have the right to vote!

14. "Let every person be subject to the governing authorities; for there is no authority except from God, and those authorities that exist have been instituted by God." (Rom. 13:1 NRSV) What is easily overlooked in superficial exegeses of this text is the question, What are the characteristics of an authority that is "from God"? If the "powers that be" exercise their authority in ways that are contrary to God's will as we know it in Jesus Christ, then it is far from clear that their exercise of power can be claimed to have divine authority. If their exercise of power does not possess divine authority, then on what grounds should it be endorsed by those who bend their knee before the one Lord?

with us in time and addressed us as the incarnate Word. Every facet of life is to be interpreted in light of that all-transforming fact. "In the totality of their existence as human beings, they should and must live with the fact that not only sheds new light on but materially changes all things and everything in all things—the fact that God is."[15] And who is this God? "God is who He is in the act of His revelation. God seeks and creates fellowship between Himself and us."[16] Kierkegaard's reference to the eternal God establishing kinship with humanity in time became in Barth God's establishing fellowship with humanity in history.[17] Consequently, as Kierkegaard argues in his late writings, Christ is to be regarded as both the "pattern" who defines the orientation of our lives and our redeemer.[18] To seek to bracket out the decisive reality of the incarnation by choosing *not* to interpret God and all things related to God from that center could only constitute an act of disobedience and faithlessness—a repudiation of what Climacus refers to as our redemption from error and, for Barth, God's act of reconciliation in Christ. Foundational to both Kierkegaard's and Barth's approaches stands God's redemptive and self-authenticating act of self-disclosure. As we shall argue in chapter 7, that foundational recognition takes the form of properly basic and (potentially) warranted beliefs—beliefs, in other words, that do not require to be justified by inference from other beliefs or propositions that are more basic.[19] As such, the object of these beliefs is an "all-transforming fact" which, as the phrase suggests, bears on every facet of our understanding of the world and our allegiances within it.

15. Barth, *Church Dogmatics* II/1, 258. Jürgen Moltmann picks up Barth's understanding here when he argues that a "trinitarian understanding of the history of Christ with God and of God with Christ . . . leads faith and practice away from the pragmatic trivializing of the concept of God, setting them both face to face with that divine reality which the young Barth rightly called 'the all-transforming fact.'" Moltmann, *The Future of Creation: Collected Essays* (Minneapolis: Fortress, 2007), 81.

16. This is the opening sentence of chapter 6, "The Reality of God," §28, "The Being of God as the One who Loves in Freedom." Barth, *Church Dogmatics* II/1, 257.

17. Cf. Søren Kierkegaard, *Practice in Christianity*, ed. and trans. Howard V. Hong and Edna H. Hong (Princeton: Princeton University Press, 1991), 9–10, and the discussion of this in chap. 1.

18. See especially Søren Kierkegaard, *Judge for Yourself!*, in *"For Self-Examination" and "Judge for Yourself!,"* ed. and trans. Howard V. Hong and Edna H. Hong (Princeton: Princeton University Press, 1990), 145–209. Here we are following C. Stephen Evans, who translates the Danish term used by Kierkegaard "pattern," whereas the Hong translation uses the term "prototype."

19. As Plantinga argues, moreover, such beliefs are warranted if they are "produced by cognitive faculties functioning properly in a congenial epistemic environment according to a design plan successfully aimed at truth." Alvin Plantinga, *Warranted Christian Belief* (New York: Oxford University Press, 2000), 178.

A Brief Consideration of Two Potential Objections

We have emphasized that the incarnation is central to the thought of Kierkegaard and Barth. Too often, a stress on the centrality of the incarnation is dismissed, by liberals and conservatives alike and without clear argument, as "Barthian" or "Christomonist," thereby giving them permission to function as epistemological Arians. Consequently, before we return to consider Barth's arguments in detail, it is worth considering, albeit briefly, what kind of response might be offered to this objection.

The Kierkegaard-Barth Trajectory Overplays the Significance of the Incarnation

It belongs to the very nature of the case that those who cannot personally identify with the "recognition" of who Christ is are unlikely to find such an approach to the theological task convincing. What is less easy to appreciate, however, is why those who self-identify as participants within the church, and who adhere to the Nicene tradition (for which this "recognition" is a constitutive feature of orthodoxy), would reject such an approach. It may be helpful, therefore, to present the argument here in conditional form, that is, as a loosely syllogistic argument with a conditionalizing general premise.

> *Premise 1*: If God chooses to reveal Godself in a once-and-for-all event of incarnation for the purposes of redemption and reconciliation, then it follows that God deems this event to be of decisive significance for the full and veridical discernment of God's nature and purposes.
>
> *Bridge premise to the conclusion*: If God deems something to be of decisive significance for the full and veridical discernment of God's nature and purposes, then theologians have a duty to discern God's purposes in accordance with it.
>
> *Premise 2*: God has chosen to become incarnate as Jesus Christ for the purposes of redemption and reconciliation (and here we keep in mind that there may be yet further purposes not mentioned in the argument).

Therefore:

> *Conclusion*: Theologians ought (have a duty) to discern God's nature and purposes in accordance with the incarnation, that is, through primary recourse to Jesus Christ.[20]

---

20. We are grateful to Jonathan Rutledge for refining the formulation of this argument.

In short, the implication of Kierkegaard's and Barth's approach here is that the incarnation presents theologians with an "exclusive or" (referred to in logic as an XOR): either we affirm this all-important event in history and take on board the theological and epistemological implications of doing so, or we deny, in practice, that it has taken place. To affirm the incarnation but to reject the suggestion that it has decisive significance (to use Climacus's expression) appears to involve a refusal to acquiesce in God's intentionality. In Barth's language, this constitutes an act of disobedience.

Is this to suggest that God is incapable of addressing persons independently of the incarnation? Clearly not! In the Hebrew Bible, the Christian Old Testament, God addresses persons prior to the incarnation—even if one rightly affirms that the validity of their proclamation ultimately finds confirmation through the incarnation.[21] Nor is it to suggest that God is not capable of communicating with persons outside the Judeo-Christian tradition. As C. Stephen Evans argues, Kierkegaard takes natural theology for granted to the extent that we have a general awareness that God exists and also an awareness of God's requirements by means of our moral consciences—although Evans also explains that Kierkegaard regards natural religious knowledge as usually inadequate and unreliable.[22]

And Barth is clear that God does indeed have the power to speak to us quite independently of Christian sources, while he also makes clear how the Christian theologian should bear this in mind.

> If the question what God can do forces theology to be humble, the question what is commanded of us forces it to concrete obedience. God may speak to us through Russian Communism, a flute concerto, a blossoming shrub, or a dead dog. We do well to listen to Him if He really does. But, unless we regard ourselves as the prophets and founders of a new church, we cannot say that we are commissioned to pass on what we have heard as independent proclamation. God may speak to us through a pagan or an atheist, and thus give us to understand that the boundary between the church and the secular world can still take at any time a different course from that which we think we discern. Yet this does not mean, unless we are prophets, that we ourselves have to proclaim the pagan or atheistic thing which we have

---

21. It is too often overlooked here that temporal/historical priority does not entail logical/epistemological priority.

22. See C. Stephen Evans's particularly helpful and nuanced analysis of Kierkegaard's attitude towards natural theology in "Kierkegaard, Natural Theology, and the Existence of God," in *Kierkegaard and Christian Faith*, ed. Paul Martens and C. Stephen Evans (Waco, TX: Baylor University Press, 2016), 45, 48, 58.

heard. Finally, we may truly and rightly think that we have heard the Word of God in the worship and active love and youth education and theology of the church known to us. This does not mean, however, that we have received a commission to pursue these things as proclamation.[23]

Contrary to what is widely assumed, Barth has no interest in denying a priori that God can and does speak through sources that are not clearly connected to the church. And he does not rule out the possibility that there might be true insights into God's nature and purposes that philosophers, religious thinkers, and others may rightly come to believe—although he does not suggest that this would deliver personal knowledge of God. In short, God can commandeer any medium in order to disclose who God is and what God wills for the world. What he is clear about, however, is that if we believe that the light of the world has come and the day has dawned, it is neither faithful nor, indeed, rational to try to find one's way by the reflected light of the stars. Moreover, in the one who is the "light of the world," we have a criterion by which we can test the spirits of the age and associated religious claims as they find expression in cultural, political, and religious agendas. This enables us to determine what is consonant with God's purposes, what is in tension with them, and what is opposed to the kingdom of God.

The Kierkegaard-Barth Trajectory Introduces a Christomonist Focus

So how does one respond to the criticism that the Kierkegaard-Barth trajectory displaces a theology grounded in the doctrine of God with "Christocentric" or even "Christomonist" piety? What informs and drives the Kierkegaard-Barth trajectory is not a one-sided interest in Christology. It is emphatically a concern with who God is. As Evans observes concerning Kierkegaard, "Few have a deeper appreciation of the necessity for God to reveal himself to us if we are to know God truly and relate to him as we ought."[24] In the case of Barth, his concern with the doctrine of God is spelled out in the first two lengthy volumes of his *Church Dogmatics*, the second of which is explicitly on the doctrine of God. Driving Barth's approach is, quite simply, the recognition that God is Lord and that God is free. Consequently, God is only known and grasped by the human mind to the extent that God freely gives Godself to be known. "This means that we cannot discern the being of God in any other way

23. Karl Barth, *Church Dogmatics*, ed. Geoffrey W. Bromiley and Thomas F. Torrance, trans. Geoffrey W. Bromiley (Edinburgh: T&T Clark, 1956–1975), I/1, 55.
24. Evans, "Kierkegaard, Natural Theology," 59.

than by looking where God Himself gives us Himself to see."[25] Barth's account of the doctrine of God begins with God's Word. This recognizes, first, that God freely enables human creatures to speak about God, second, that God intends creatures to speak about God, and third, that God determines the way in which we should speak about God. Barth refuses, therefore, to engage in any description of who God is independently of God's free and sovereign self-giving to be known and spoken of. This in turn implies that God should not be spoken of in abstraction from God's act.[26] It is worth pointing out here that the heart of Barth's exposition of "the reality of God" lies in his analysis of "the being of God in act," where he reminds the reader that "our subject is God and not being." To speak of the "being" of God is to recognize right from the start that it is "filled out in a quite definite way."[27] We require therefore to think in terms of the "concretion" of God, recognizing that there can be no dichotomy between God's being and God's act, between who God *is* and who God is *toward us*.[28] God is known, therefore, *where* and *as* God freely, sovereignly and concretely determines to be known.

> What or who "is" God? If we want to answer this question legitimately and thoughtfully, we cannot for a moment turn our thoughts anywhere else than to God's act in His revelation. We cannot for a moment start from anywhere else than from there.[29]

This, of course, does little to assuage the fears of those struggling with the foundationalist inclinations that emerged during the Enlightenment. How can such counterintuitive epistemic claims be regarded as warranted? Wherein lies the epistemic entitlement for Barth's and, indeed, Kierkegaard's claims about specific divine actions in history? If Barth perceives Christian theology to be "set free" from the forms of ideological, cultural, and political bondage associated with developments stemming from the Enlightenment, does that also mean he is entitled to sidestep such questions? Clearly not—especially given the potential of god-talk for harm! So how are the vexed questions of warrant, entitlement, and accountability to be addressed without our being misled into that farrago of missteps whereby persons seek to provide justification for god-talk in ways that misrepresent the very nature of faith? The inclination is to

25. Barth, *Church Dogmatics* II/1, 261.
26. Barth, *Church Dogmatics* II/1, 257–59.
27. Barth, *Church Dogmatics* II/1, 260–61.
28. Barth, *Church Dogmatics* II/2, 51.
29. Barth, *Church Dogmatics* II/1, 261.

seek to ground faith in what "flesh and blood" can both deliver and confirm, rather than in that defining recognition at the heart of the Christian faith which gives rise, moreover, to its very doctrine of God.[30]

The first thing that has to be recognized is that to seek to ground faith elsewhere than in the God who has assumed flesh can only change faith into something of a radically different kind—to force it to undergo a *metabasis eis allo genos*.[31] Second, this is not to suggest that faith sets the theologian free from accountability with respect to her God-talk. Quite the opposite! For Barth, however, to ask about theological accountability is to ask to whom we are accountable and only then and in that light what the nature of that accountability is. What is immediately clear is that it is not possible for Christian God-talk validly to underwrite harm and suffering precisely because the one to whom it is accountable is the God who has become flesh as Jesus Christ and in whom is manifest God's unconditional love for and commitment to every human being. For Barth, moreover, there is a tight correlation between the accountability of theology, its being "scientific," and, importantly, its being "free." When theology fails in its responsibilities to the church, to the culture, and, indeed, to the state, too often it is because it has lost sight of what it means to be "set free," to think from that center that is God incarnate. It is to Barth's understanding of the liberation of theology, therefore, that we turn next.

SETTING THEOLOGY FREE

In 1953 Barth gave a profoundly important lecture to a meeting of the Society for Protestant Theology. It was entitled "The Gift of Freedom: Foundation of Evangelical Ethics."[32] In it, he spelled out his vision of the theological task, outlining what it means to be set free from bondage to philosophical, religious,

---

30. The reference here is to Simon Peter's recognition of who Jesus was. "Simon Peter answered, 'You are the Messiah, the Son of the living God.' And Jesus answered him, 'Blessed are you, Simon son of Jonah! For flesh and blood has not revealed this to you but my Father in heaven'" (Matt. 16:16–17).

31. This is to adopt a favorite phrase of Climacus, which means literally "shifting from one genus to another" or a "change into something of a different kind." Again, see chapter 3, note 28.

32. Karl Barth, "The Gift of Freedom: Foundation of Evangelical Ethics," in *The Humanity of God* (London: Collins, Fontana, 1967), 67–96. This is the English translation of "Das Geschenk der Freiheit: Grundlegung evangelischer Ethik," a lecture delivered at the Society for Protestant Theology (*der Gesellschaft für evangelische Theologie*) on September 21, 1953, in Bielefeld.

cultural, and sociopolitical agendas—constraints which, for over a century, had evacuated theology's capacity to serve the church faithfully.

The lecture begins by focusing on the freedom of God: "*God's freedom is His very own. It is the sovereign grace wherein God chooses to commit Himself to man [Menschen³³]*. Thereby God is Lord as *man's* God."[34] He then turns to consider human freedom: "*Man's freedom is his as the gift of God. It is the joy wherein man appropriates God's election*. Thereby man is God's creature, His partner, and His child as *God's* man."[35] Finally, he turns to explore "evangelical ethics," which he interprets as "reflection upon the *divine call to human action* which is implied by the gift of freedom."[36]

Highlighted in the essay are what he considers to be the five characteristics of "free theology." These summarize the vision of theology we find in his *Church Dogmatics*. They also articulate with unusual clarity and simplicity the characteristics of the Christian alternative to Socratic or immanentist approaches to theology.

The Directionality of Thought and the "About Turn"

A free theologian will be found ready, willing, and able always to begin his thinking *at the beginning*. This means his recognition of the resurrection of Jesus Christ as the directive for his reasoning.[37]

To "begin at the beginning," Barth goes on to explain, means that the theologian's reflections (*Nachdenken*) and statements "always first proceed from God's relationship to humanity and only then continue with humanity's relationship to God."[38] The Christian theologian should not approach God-talk, therefore, on the basis of epistemological foundations that she establishes in advance. Contrary to the assumptions that defined the Enlightenment, to start with the human subject—that is, with reference to reason, will, or emotion, for example—constitutes a refusal to start "at the beginning." What Barth is advocating here is what Kevin Diller refers to as a "theo-foundational epistemology" in contrast to the "anthropo-foundational" epistemologies of the

---

33. The language of the original German text is gender neutral.
34. Barth, "Gift of Freedom," 69 (emphasis original).
35. Barth, "Gift of Freedom," 69 (emphasis original).
36. Barth, "Gift of Freedom," 69 (emphasis original).
37. Barth, "Gift of Freedom," 89 (emphasis original).
38. Barth, "Gift of Freedom," 89; "Das Geschenk der Freiheit," 22.

nineteenth century.[39] Christian theology emerges *in response to* the recognition of the divine initiative in the incarnation and the resurrection and is thus reflection (*Nachdenken*) on a divine act that is free and that is pure grace.

Although the theoretical force of Barth's commitment to a post-factum theological approach may be presented in a conditionalizing form—by showing what conditional premises necessarily involve, as set out in the XOR above—Barth himself does not utilize arguments of this kind. Why? Because to engage in hypothetical or conditionalizing argumentation would be to stray from post-factum argumentation. This would be to refrain from starting "at the beginning," that is, in light of the given facticity of God's initiative. For Barth, the interpretation of Christian faith takes place within the sphere of the recognition of God's self-disclosure and consequently within the body of Christ. It was for this reason that he did not proceed with his original plans while he was teaching in Münster to write a *Christian* dogmatics and wrote instead a *Church* dogmatics.[40] For Barth, it is as participants within the redeemed community that we are given to recognize the veracity and propriety (or otherwise) of theological claims. Their confirmation, moreover, lies with God's self-disclosure rather than external criteria. Why? Because the criteria for veridical knowledge of God are necessarily *integral* to God's self-disclosure itself—and are only recognized, therefore, within the community of faith. Such a suggestion will inevitably generate "offense" within our contemporary culture—not least because of its apparent circularity.[41] It appears to suggest that religious persons consider themselves entitled to mark their own homework. The counterintuitive nature of the suggestion that recognition of the veracity of revelation belongs to the event of revelation itself is something to which we shall return when we look at the paradox of faith in chapter 5.

We have suggested that it is not our duty to confirm the truth of theological statements by making recourse to secular convictions or assumptions. Why? Because theology operates on the basis of the actuality of God's self-

---

39. Kevin Diller, *Theology's Epistemological Dilemma: How Karl Barth and Alvin Plantinga Provide a Unified Response* (Downers Grove, IL: InterVarsity Press Academic, 2014), 42–47, and chap. 3.

40. When Barth moved to Münster in 1925, he started writing a multivolume "Christian dogmatics in outline." He regarded his "Münster dogmatics," however, as a false start and "the attempt of a beginner in this area," and they remained unfinished. See Christiane Tietz, *Karl Barth: A Life in Conflict*, trans. Victoria J. Barnett (Oxford: Oxford University Press, 2021), 161.

41. Cf. 1 Cor. 1:23, which describes the gospel as *ethnesin de mōrian* ("foolishness to the gentiles").

disclosure to alienated minds—a reconciling self-disclosure constitutive of a new humanity whose understanding undergoes thereby a process of *metanoia* or *metamorphosis*, as Paul puts it, *for the sake of* discernment of the truth. For Climacus, this deliverance from error generates an "about turn" from an orientation that involves a continual departing from the truth. It makes no sense, therefore, to suggest that we should seek to confirm the validity of God's self-disclosure with reference to a state of error.

What Barth is reiterating here is that, as we discussed in the previous chapter, the theological task requires to be seen as *Nachdenken*. It is prompted by and is a response to a prior event of God's self-disclosure that could never have been anticipated. This continues to have unsettling implications for the child of the Enlightenment, for the advocate of "reasonable" religion. Not only are we obliged to understand *who* God is by means of God's self-disclosure, but it is also in the light of this (and not in advance of it) that we are to understand *how* God reveals Godself, and thus *how* God intends us to know God. As we shall discuss in chapter 6, for Barth, even the recognition of the impossibility of knowing the Word of God outside its reality is possible only on the presupposition of this "real knowledge."[42] Superficially, this appears to imply a circularity which may be interpreted by the Enlightenment mind as involving a *sacrificium intellectus*. It offends the conviction that the valid assessment of what is reasonable requires autonomy, detachment, and "objective" criteria that are independent of that which is known. On Barth's approach, however, God's reconciling self-disclosure is the sine qua non of our being restored to the only means of knowledge of God that can be said to be free, rational, and scientific.

Intrinsic to Barth's argument here is what he continually refers to as an "about turn" or "turnabout" (*Wendung*).[43] This "about turn" refers to the conversion and, indeed, liberation from forms of theology that are grounded in our prior, unreconciled self-understanding and which operate on that basis. An "about turn" is thus a necessary condition, provided by God, whereby the learner is set free to operate in the light of God's self-disclosure. It is necessary, therefore, not simply so that we might find valid solutions to the problems we perceive as confronting humanity, but also—and more importantly—so that we might understand these problems aright, that is, understand the true nature and location of the challenges that confront us. Consequently, for Barth, "it is only by grace that the lack of grace can be recognised as such."[44] He

42. Barth, *Church Dogmatics* I/1, 197.
43. See, for example, Barth, "Gift of Freedom," 90.
44. Barth, *Church Dogmatics* II/2, 92. For the relevance of this for the interpretation

argues, therefore, for a grace-nature or solution-plight approach rather than a nature-grace or plight-solution approach. To interpret grace in the light of a prior account of nature and sin inverts the "turnabout" that is integral to the true recognition not only of God's grace but also of sin. Its effect is to ratify our prior, unreconciled accounts of law and sin.

Again, Barth's account of the turnabout echoes Climacus's interpretation of conversion and repentance in *Philosophical Fragments*.[45] As we discussed in chapter 2, the transition facilitates the recognition of what cannot be grasped from an immanent basis in oneself and, for Climacus, involves nothing less than "a transition from non-being to being," the "birth" of one who previously did not exist. Climacus is engaging here in the "shabbiest plagiarism ever to appear," to use his terminology, in drawing on the language, analogies, and metaphors integral to the New Testament sources: the New Testament language of metanoia, the reference in the Synoptics to the fact that new wine requires new wineskins and cannot be accommodated by the old,[46] the Synoptic description of the transition of Simon to become Peter,[47] and what is portrayed in the New Testament as "rebirth," where one is not only reborn but "reborn *of God*."[48] The same conceptuality finds further expression in the language of "new creation" and the creation of a new humanity.[49] In short, while the language of "conversion" and the metaphor of "being born again" may have been dismissed by theologians and sections of the church because of their association with certain styles of evangelical outreach, there are few themes more central to the Synoptic, Johannine, Pauline, and so-called deutero-Pauline sources. Whereas Enlightenment pedagogy has led theologians to ignore or

---

of Paul, see Douglas A. Campbell, *Pauline Dogmatics: The Triumph of God's Love* (Grand Rapids: Eerdmans, 2020), esp. 13–48, 72–78, 95–97, 127–31, 653–55, 672–75, 689–700. In addition, Samuel V. Adams provides an insightful discussion of the plight-solution debate in the Pauline scholarship of J. Louis Martyn and Douglas Campbell; see *The Reality of God and Historical Method: Apocalyptic Theology in Conversation with N. T. Wright* (Downers Grove, IL: InterVarsity Press, 2015), 112–22.

45. Søren Kierkegaard, *Philosophical Fragments*, in *"Philosophical Fragments" and "Johannes Climacus,"* ed. and trans. Howard V. Hong and Edna H. Hong (Princeton: Princeton University Press, 1985), 21. See Murray A. Rae's analysis of Kierkegaard's account in chap. 6 (*"Metanoia"*) of his *Kierkegaard's Vision of the Incarnation: By Faith Transformed* (Oxford: Clarendon, 1997), 140–71.

46. Kierkegaard, *Philosophical Fragments*, 35. Cf. Matt. 9:16–17; Mark 2:21–22; Luke 5:36–39.

47. See Matt. 16:13–18.

48. See, for example, John 3:3–6; 1 John 4:7, 5:4; 1 Pet. 1:3, 1:23; Titus 3:5.

49. See 2 Cor. 5:17.

demythologize this language, it is impossible to deny its central place in the New Testament witness. Both Kierkegaard and Barth held such a "conversion" or "turnabout" to have decisive theological relevance. The conversion to which they refer, Barth argues, denotes our being placed "under the Word" and thus under the transformative influence of a "very definite power."

> The power on which it counts is the power to set us, the recipients of its witness, in a very definite freedom: the freedom to appropriate as our own conversion the conversion of humanity to God as it has taken place in Jesus Christ, the translation of humanity from a state of disobedience to one of obedience; the freedom to keep to the fact and orientate ourselves by it, that the alteration of the human situation which has taken place in Him is our own; the freedom, therefore, to set ourselves in the alteration accomplished in Him.[50]

The freedom to which Barth refers is given by God, but it is also a freedom that we make our own: "It is the power in whose operation we are motivated and impelled from within, of ourselves, to be in this freedom, and to us it is our own. It is the power to call us effectively to positive decision in relation to what is said to us, to that freedom of accompanying and following, of conversion."[51]

When we attempt to engage in theology without this "turnabout" and the associated freedom it brings, we inevitably find ourselves "cut off from the fresh air." We cease to breathe the oxygen that fuels faithful Christian reflection and discernment. When that happens, Barth adds with astute insight, the theologian "considers it his bounden duty not to let others breathe fresh air either."[52] The implication is that theology is presented with two further exclusive alternatives, in the shape of two contrasting forms of discipleship: either our thinking is informed by our participation in the church conceived as the body of Christ, or our thinking is governed by our membership in the "church" conceived as a religious club. The first way of thinking bears witness to Jesus Christ, whereas the second lives for whatever cultural commitments and agendas happen to be in vogue. On the second approach, Jesus Christ is used as an exemplar to illustrate and confirm our cultural values and predilections. Here, as Kierkegaard sees, Jesus is reduced to his teachings to the point where he is regarded "as one regards an anonymous writer: the teaching is the principal thing, is everything."[53] But the situation is even more problematic in

50. Barth, *Church Dogmatics* IV/2, 304–5.
51. Barth, *Church Dogmatics* IV/2, 305.
52. Barth, "Gift of Freedom," 90.
53. Kierkegaard, *Practice in Christianity*, 123. The fuller quotation appears in chap. 2, page 91.

that the teachings are selected to endorse prior ethical, cultural, and spiritual commitments by human beings who are "in error" to the extent that they fail to recognize that reality which has decisive significance.[54] The risk is that God's address is silenced and Jesus's teachings are commandeered in the name of religion defined by the vested interests of the culture.

So what precisely does this "turnabout" denote? It refers to the change of direction from what Helmut Thielicke refers to as the "Cartesian"[55] orientation of modern theology, where the human subject stands at the center of our worldview, toward what Diller refers to as a "theo-foundational" orientation. This takes place when the theologian is set free from the constraints upon her of contemporary cultural and philosophical allegiances to interpret God's purposes in the light of the resurrection and God's inauguration of a new creation—set free, that is, from modes of thought in which the primary reference is her prior suppositions as to what it is "reasonable" to affirm and accept.

Is this to suggest that the theologian is free to "choose" where to start—free, therefore, to choose to start with the resurrection? For Barth, there is no arbitrary choice here, just as there is no "dialectical trick to be learned and then used merrily again and again."[56] The relevant methodological decisions are not the consequence of any capricious, subjective decision. The turnabout through which the theologian is set free is the rational response to an event of personal address discerned with the eyes of faith, one which recognizes that the subject matter is not in our possession. "God is in heaven and we are on earth. God is Lord and we are his servants."[57]

One further element in Barth's stress on the directionality of thought is that our thinking runs from God's self-disclosure to our categories of interpretation. The "about turn" recognizes that the essential form of Christian discourse is not third-person description but second-person response.[58] God does not sim-

---

54. Tom Greggs rightly objects to the reduction of Barth's *Nachdenken* approach to the adoption of a principle, namely, a *Christological* principle: "It is in a person and not a principle that humanity is elected." He then cites Barth's emphasis that the focus of theology is the free act of a person who cannot be "grasped" in the sense of "conceptual apprehension and control." Greggs, *Theology against Religion: Constructive Dialogues with Bonhoeffer and Barth* (London: T&T Clark, 2011), 112, citing Barth, *Church Dogmatics* IV/3, 176.

55. Cf. Helmut Thielicke's analysis of "Cartesian theology" ("Theology A") in *The Evangelical Faith, I: Prolegomena; The Relation of Theology to Modern Thought Forms* (Grand Rapids: Eerdmans, 1974).

56. Barth, "Gift of Freedom," 90.

57. Karl Barth, *God in Action: Theological Addresses* (Eugene, OR: Wipf & Stock, 2005), 102.

58. It is not irrelevant here that in Barth's volume on the doctrine of God, the section entitled "God's Being in Act" is preparatory for his section on the love of God: "The Being of God as the One who Loves" (Barth, *Church Dogmatics* II/1, 272-97).

ply communicate detached information; God elects to address us individually and personally, and the election of the individual takes the form of the divine address: "Thou art the one!"[59] To hear and acknowledge God's address in this second-personal form is to recognize that the primary form of Christian speech is not speech *about* God so much as speech *to* God. Christian theology must recognize and reflect this. Just as it was historically the case that theological statements developed out of doxological statements, so third-person God-talk derives from a context of second-personal address and acknowledgment.[60] Faith is grounded in a reciprocal I-Thou relationship between God and the human person such that the claims the theologian makes about God in the third person reflect this and articulate the ground and grammar of this relationship.

This "about turn" in the direction of thought is no less critical to the doctrine of soteriology and, indeed, theological ethics. Space does not allow us to explore this as fully as it deserves. Suffice it to say that for Barth the recognition of our ethical obligations before God and thus the nature of sin also needs to be reinterpreted in light of this "about turn" and with a "backward look." Here again, he challenges the whole tradition of Western thought which has operated on the basis of an appeal to immanent ethical and legal suppositions—the effect of which has been to press the good news to fit a foreign procrustean bed.

One of the foundations of the Western understanding of salvation has been, and remains, the nature-grace model. This has given rise to a specific ordering of the key elements in salvation— what is referred to as the Western *ordo salutis*.[61] Foundational here has been the view that built into human nature is a moral conscience which provides innate knowledge of God's moral law. This conscience (interpreted as a natural "with-knowing"[62] with God of God's legal purposes[63]) was seen as generating the awareness of sin and sense of guilt

---

59. Barth, *Church Dogmatics* II/2, §35, 323.

60. The primary purpose of theology is, as we have seen, to ensure that the church remains a faithful and responsible witness to the personal address that is constitutive of it; cf. Barth, *Church Dogmatics* II/2, 323.

61. The most incisive and sophisticated critique of the key ingredients of the Western *ordo salutis* (namely, its account of law, its contractualism, and its misappropriation of Paul) is to be found in the work of the Pauline scholar Douglas A. Campbell. See *The Deliverance of God: An Apocalyptic Rereading of Justification in Paul* (Grand Rapids: Eerdmans, 2009), chap. 1, "The Heart of the Matter: The Justification Theory of Salvation," 11–35. His analysis and critique of the textual base of this in Paul is found in chaps. 10 and 11. For a brief theological critique that discusses the covenant-contract distinction, see chap. 6, "Beyond Old and New Perspectives," 203–18.

62. Greek *suneidēsis* or Latin *conscientia* (from *cum scientia*), from which "conscience" derives.

63. We shall revisit this in discussing Barth's debate with Brunner in chap. 6.

that necessitate the requisite conditions of forgiveness and reconciliation with God—namely, confession, contrition, and repentance. In certain contexts, not least those influenced by Anselm, reconciliation and atonement require a further condition, namely, the "satisfaction" of divine justice.[64] This generally refers to Jesus Christ's redeeming humanity through his suffering and death on the cross in a manner that ensures the requirements of God's justice are satisfied.

The Western *ordo salutis* takes various forms, but it is widely characterized by certain key features. First, it assumes a conditional or contractual schema whereby God's forgiveness of the guilty is conditional upon metanoia on their part—and where this is interpreted as an essentially self-initiated act of repentance. Second, it assumes that human beings possess a prior and immanent knowledge of God's moral or legal purposes; that is, innate knowledge of the divine law constitutes the foundation of God's plan of salvation in that it provides the capacity of human beings to satisfy the conditions of forgiveness—an awareness of sin, contrition, and repentance. Third, it generally assumes a retributive conception of justice whereby retribution is enacted in order that the conditions of atonement be met. In sum, the essential ingredients of this whole schema assume a natural, innate, and prior knowledge of God's law and the requirements of God's justice, including divine punishment—that is, of the conditions which have to be met for there to be just atonement between God and humanity.

In sharp contrast to the Western ordering of salvation, forms of which are present in both Catholic and Protestant thought, Barth approaches each element of the doctrine of salvation from the opposite direction—reflecting, in short, a turnabout. First, foundational for Barth is God's "Yes" to humanity, which faith recognizes as having been enacted in Jesus Christ. What this holds forth is God's prior, unconditioned love for and forgiveness of humanity. For Barth, God's purposes for humanity are discerned by consideration of God's Word to humanity, and the key to understanding these is located *in that same Word* rather than in prior categories that are immanent within the self.

Second, for Barth, the perception of our plight and the conditions under which we recognize our sin prove to be very different when they are interpreted in the light of what Jesus Christ discloses about the nature of God's

---

64. This can be traced to Anselm's *Cur Deus Homo*, although his account there has been widely misrepresented. For a particularly incisive and informed analysis of these issues by an Anselm scholar, see Oliver Crisp, *Approaching the Atonement: The Reconciling Work of Christ* (Downers Grove, IL: InterVarsity Press Academic, 2020), esp. chap. 10. Aquinas also uses the term "satisfaction" in his account of Christ's atonement but stresses that this is not to be conceived in penal terms. See Aquinas, *Summa Theologiae* (London: Eyre & Spottiswoode; New York: McGraw-Hill, 1964–80), II-I, q. 87, a.8.

purposes and the nature of human sin as compared with what our unenlight-ened consciences are likely to dictate. (Do the latter tell us that it is God's will that we love and forgive our enemies, for example?)

Third, it is the recognition of God's "Yes!" namely, God's Word of grace and forgiveness issued to sinners—and where each is addressed as a beloved "thou"—that generates metanoia. Repentance expresses our response to the good news rather than to the subjective sense of guilt generated by whatever happens to constitute our innate suppositions as to the nature and compass of God's law.

Fourth, it is God's "Yes!" to humanity that holds forth the essential shape of God's law, namely, that we are to love God and our neighbors as ourselves—that, as those created in the image of God, we are to "image" God's orientation toward humanity.[65] By contrast, to trust in the deliverances of a (supposedly universal) innate conscience risks identifying God's legal purposes in cultur-ally conditioned ways.[66]

Finally, the acknowledgment of God's "Yes!" generates true recognition of the nature of sin. Sin is seen for what it is—rebellion against God's will as we recognize it in Jesus Christ and the refusal to "image" the God who loves creatures unconditionally and forgives them seventy times seven.

It is appropriate to add here that there are parallels between Barth's en-dorsement of a grace-nature approach over against a nature-grace model and what amounts to a vivid "about turn" metaphor used by Luther. As Luther expresses it, God's grace generates an *excurvatus ex se* orientation (where we are turned outwards and away from ourselves) as opposed to an *incurvatus in se* orientation (where we are turned inwards into ourselves), which defines the essence of sin. Luther's contrast here parallels that between interpreting sin with a "backward look" in the light of God's grace and the reconcilia-tion and unconditional forgiveness manifest in Jesus Christ, and interpret-ing sin with recourse to our immanent preconceptions as to the nature of God's moral law, divine justice, and the juridical requirements of God's law, including punishment.[67]

Barth views metanoia as taking place in response to grace rather than in response to any words of law or condemnation that derive from an immanent

---

65. See Mark 12:28-31.

66. One example of this would be the disapproval and banning of mixed marriage based on the perceived deliverances of moral conscience as contravening God's perceived will for diverse ethnic groups. Another might be the extent to which the consciences of the "first world" have tended to focus on certain "private" sins rather than a lack of concern for the suffering and poverty of the majority of the world's population.

67. For a full and insightful analysis of this, see Matt Jenson, *The Gravity of Sin: Augus-tine, Luther and Barth on "homo incurvatus in se"* (New York: T&T Clark, 2007).

sense of what is right or wrong. It is God's gracious second-personal address that generates that metanoia, the all-embracing "about turn" that is intrinsic to Christian existence *coram Deo* and everything that attends it.[68] To use Calvin's language, later reiterated by F. D. Maurice, Barth's approach endorses *evangelical* repentance as opposed to *legal* repentance.[69] That is, repentance is interpreted as a response to the good news of God's grace rather than to legal exhortations and the condemnations implicit in them. That is, it is the recognition of God's faithful covenant commitment that is transformative. Particularly pertinent to this is the importance of understanding law in terms of the Torah, as it affirms and spells out the implications of God's *ḥesed*, rather than in the impersonal and contractual terms in which Western concepts of *lex* are presented.

In sum, the question of the directionality of thought is key to every dogmatic locus and thus to the very character of human existence. In radical contrast to the (Socratic) suggestion that self-knowledge (the Delphic *gnōthi seauton*) provides the foundation for our knowledge of God and of God's purposes for us, it is only when we are given to know God through the kinship that God has established in time—and the second-personal fellowship which this generates by the Spirit—that we are given to grasp who we are in truth and who we are created to become, and thereby enabled to commence the journey toward that end.

The Role of the Bible in Free Theology

The means through which we have access to the all-transforming fact of the divine address, the incarnation, and God's triune life is the witness of the Bible. That is the starting point for free theology—but it is not because orthodoxy requires it, or because there is some law that asserts theology must begin there. Nor is it because doctrines of the canon or the verbal inspiration of Scripture are deemed foundational.[70] Rather, the Bible is the key to free theology because it is through the unique testimony of this book that the theologian comes to know the free action of God and the personal nature of God's address to humanity. Its witness sets the theologian free, therefore, from the constraints and pressures of her culture to speak and think about God in a manner that is faithful to God's free decision to make Godself known. In short, the proclama-

---

68. Barth, *Church Dogmatics* IV/1, 390.

69. See Alan J. Torrance's analysis of the distinction between evangelical repentance and legal repentance in "The Theological Grounds for Advocating Forgiveness and Reconciliation in the Sociopolitical Realm," in *The Politics of Past Evil: Religion, Reconciliation, and the Dilemmas of Transitional Justice*, ed. Daniel Philpott (Notre Dame: University of Notre Dame Press, 2006), esp. 53–57.

70. Barth, "Gift of Freedom," 90–91.

tion and testimony that constitute Scripture testify to the "kinship" (Kierke-gaard[71]) or "fellowship" (Barth[72]) that the eternal God establishes with us in time. The Bible's collective witness to God's grace means that acknowledging its role is "a privilege."[73]

But is this not to usher in, by sleight of hand, a conveniently selected founda-tional text that has been adopted on fideistic grounds and which we are thereby entitled to interpret uncritically? Any suggestion that Barth has opened the door to uncritical interpretation of the Bible is explicitly rejected. To study the Bible out of an eagerness to understand it involves, he argues, a refusal to despise the "many ways" through which we come to understand the biblical writings better. These include, not least, the "analytic, historical-critical method."[74] So does this mean theology cannot begin its task until we have what Barth refers to as "the so-called 'ascertained results' of historical-critical research, or the so-called 'exegetical findings'"?[75] Barth rejects this on two grounds. First, the results of critical research do not in and of themselves provide the sure grounds on which theological interpretation is based. Its results "have a tendency to change every thirty years and from one exegete to another,"[76] so it is not appropriate to assume that the latest developments in biblical scholarship constitute a firm and indubi-table foundation. Second, and more importantly, we must not assume that the analysis of either biblical or secular texts will either guarantee or presuppose the act of listening that theology requires, despite the fact that this is "a *conditio sine qua non* of attentive listening to their message."

> We listen when we read and study synthetically. The free theologian com-bines in one single act analysis and synthesis in his reading and studies. . . . The free theologian, taking the Bible as his starting point, is led by the testimony of the Bible or, more precisely, by the origin, object, and content of this testimony.[77]

71. Søren Kierkegaard, *Concluding Unscientific Postscript to Philosophical Fragments*, ed. and trans. Howard V. Hong and Edna H. Hong (Princeton: Princeton University Press, 1992), 1:573.

72. Barth, *Church Dogmatics* II/1, 257.

73. Barth, "Gift of Freedom," 90.

74. Barth, "Gift of Freedom," 91. Indeed, in his *Church Dogmatics*, Barth comments, "There is no reason why historico-critical Bible research should not contribute to the in-vestigation and exposition of this historical Christ of the New Testament." Barth, *Church Dogmatics* I/2, 65.

75. Barth, "Gift of Freedom," 91.

76. Barth, "Gift of Freedom," 91.

77. Barth, "Gift of Freedom," 91.

The implication here is that the forms of proclamation that constitute the biblical witness mean that God's self-disclosure possesses what John Baillie refers to as a "mediated immediacy."[78] That self-disclosure is not identical with the medium itself—the only mediator between God and humanity is the person of the incarnate Word who is not to be confused with the written *words* of the Bible. At the same time, that one Word elects to be known in and through the mediating witness and forms of proclamation that the body of Christ has collated as its canon.

There is a series of open questions regarding the status of Scripture that this raises. We shall return to these in chapter 7. The key point here is that the "turnabout" that Barth perceives as the liberation of theology reposes on the witness of Scripture.

Setting Theology Free for an Appropriate Interaction with Philosophy

A recurring theme throughout Barth's theology is that the theologian is set free to be faithful when, by means of an "about turn," the directionality of her thinking runs *from* God's free self-disclosure as the incarnate Word rather than *to* it. This denotes a process wherein her prior suppositions and assumptions about God and all things related to God are surrendered to God's self-disclosure such that they can be corrected and revised by it, rather than the other way around.

This means that when it comes to interpreting God's self-disclosure and the biblical witness to it, a hermeneutical circularity emerges—to borrow Heidegger's expression, a "relatedness backward and forward"—but one in which the pressure of interpretation runs from God's self-disclosure to our interpretive processes and not the other way around.[79] The implication of this is that the status of the suppositions we bring to this task of interpretation is provisional. Although they provide the temporary ground on which we stand in interpreting Scripture, they will require to be reassessed and reinterpreted *retrospectively* in the light of the reality to which Scripture bears witness. Integral to God's self-disclosure, therefore, are the transformation and reconciliation of the categories of interpretation that we bring to the process of understanding.

The recognition that God's self-disclosure stands to revise our categories of interpretation challenges the age-old temptation of regarding the supposi-

---

78. John Baillie, *Our Knowledge of God* (London: Oxford University Press, 1939), "A Mediated Immediacy," chap. 4, §16, 178–98.

79. Martin Heidegger, *Being and Time*, trans. John Macquarrie and Edward Robinson (New York: Harper & Row, 1962), 28. Heidegger uses this expression in discussing the relationship between the ontic and the ontological in his analysis of the human being.

tions that we bring to the hermeneutical task (suppositions about the nature of reason, our human capacities, assumptions about the divine nature, moral categories, and so on) as constituting a foundational grid for the interpretation, assessment, and affirmation of divine revelation. The seductive and problematic effect of this temptation, which reposes on a form of the naturalistic fallacy,[80] is that it reverses the direction of interpretation in such a way that our prior philosophical affiliations and interpretive apparatus become foundational to God's self-disclosure, constituting a return to immanence. In short, if these prior suppositions predetermine what revelation can and cannot disclose, they risk becoming a Trojan horse which, once admitted into the theological Ilium, can subtly overpower our abilities to interpret God's revelation *in its own light*.[81]

What Barth, following Kierkegaard, saw with such clarity is that a failure to accept the provisional nature of these assumptions can blind us to the extent to which God provides new wineskins into which the new wine is poured. What the theologian who is set free from the constraints of her former suppositions recognizes is that God's self-disclosure commandeers our categories of interpretation and not the other way around. This means, for example, that our established terminology will require to undergo a process of semantic transformation or metanoia. Precisely this is highlighted in the account of Peter's confession and his ensuing interaction with Jesus. When asked about who people thought Jesus was, the disciples recounted the prevailing popular theories. When invited to address the "who" question, however, Peter confessed that Jesus was the Messiah, the Son of the living God. He had been given to recognize what flesh and blood, we are told, could not disclose. It is what happens next, however, that illustrates the full implications here of the Kierkegaard-Barth trajectory. Jesus began to explain to his disciples that he must go to Jerusalem, suffer greatly at the hands of the elders, chief priests, and scribes, and then be killed (Matt. 16:21). To this Peter objected strongly, going on, indeed, to rebuke Jesus, saying that he would forbid it (Matt. 16:22). Jesus's response to this apparent act of loyalty on the part of the first person to confess who he was, was uncompromisingly direct: "Get behind me, Satan!" (Matt. 16:23). Peter's recognition and affirmation that Jesus was the Messiah had involved the transformation of his categories of interpretation—given that

80. I.e., it constitutes a move from "is" to "ought": assuming X is how we initially make sense of Scripture and therefore assuming X is how we *ought* to make sense of Scripture.

81. This is an allusion to Barth's use of that metaphor in Barth, *Church Dogmatics* I/1, 335–36.

Jesus did not meet the prevailing criteria for how the term "Messiah" should be used. It was not long, however, before the direction of Peter's thinking, for whatever commendable reason, began to revert such that his prior conceptions of what was appropriate for a Messiah came into play. There was, in short, a reversal in the direction of interpretation, the result of which was that he began to dictate to the Messiah how the Messiah should and should not act, and what was and was not appropriate. What this account illustrates is that God's self-disclosure involves an ongoing semantic metanoia (or "about turn") such that the language we use can faithfully *track* this new reality rather than continue to be defined by its former associations and rules of use.[82] To reverse this directionality and impose one's prior conceptuality on God's revelation is to subvert God's self-disclosure. To do that, as Peter was so brutally reminded, is satanic. As Jesus explained to Peter, "You are setting your mind not on divine things but on human things" (Matt. 16:23).

In his exposition of Barth, making the same point, Eberhard Jüngel argues that how we respond to God's self-disclosure involves either a gain to language or a loss of revelation.

> But the language in which revelation should be able to come to speech must, "as it were, be commandeered"[83] by revelation. Where such "commandeering" of the language by revelation for revelation takes place, then there is a *gain to language*. The gain consists in the fact that God comes to speech as God. Over against this, in the opposite case, one would have to speak of a *loss of revelation* if revelation were commandeered by language.[84]

---

82. As Stewart R. Sutherland argues, there is something "new" in revelation that must be more than simply "a matter of information or facts which have so far eluded us." Sutherland, "The Concept of Revelation," in *Religion, Reason and the Self: Essays in Honour of Hywel D. Lewis*, ed. Stewart R. Sutherland and T. A. Roberts (Cardiff: University of Wales Press, 1989), 43. This is a point that both Kierkegaard and Barth grasped with utmost clarity, and it is exemplified in Barth's approach here.

83. Barth, *Church Dogmatics* I/1, 340.

84. Eberhard Jüngel, *God's Being Is in Becoming: The Trinitarian Being of God in the Theology of Karl Barth; A Paraphrase*, trans. John B. Webster (London: Bloomsbury, 2001), 23. Bruce D. Marshall (*Journal of Theological Studies* 50 [1999]: 434–36) and Andrew Louth (*Heythrop Journal* 42 [2001]: 529–31) have expressed nervousness over appropriating Jüngel's metaphor in the way that we are doing here. Bruce Marshall is concerned lest we conceive of these transformed meanings as "totally disconnected from other uses and senses the words have" (436). What should hopefully be clear from the text is that neither Barth nor Jüngel nor we ourselves are seeking to play down the fact that God's self-disclosure engages with (and does not replace) the language we use. It interacts with the language-games in the light

So what are the implications of this? Does Barth expect free theologians to evacuate all prior semantic, philosophical, and ontological assumptions from their minds? Is the theologian expected to dismiss from her thinking any insights that might derive from classical theism or perfect being theology, for example, that might be inherent in the language we use? Emphatically not! Barth is quite clear: "A free theologian does not deny, nor is he ashamed of, his indebtedness to a particular *philosophy* or ontology, to ways of thought and speech."[85] Christian theology does not operate with a language or with thought-forms that descend untainted from above. The biblical authors themselves, he explains, spoke in diverse earthly languages and not in some pure "celestial language."[86] In short, the free theologian uses all the conceptual tools she has to hand and recognizes that it is not possible to escape philosophical suppositions. Consequently, Barth argues, the theologian should feel free to speak "from within his philosophical shell."[87] That said, in and through that process, the philosophical shell and the suppositions integral to it stand to be challenged and, where necessary, undergo a process of revision and transformation.

Barth is eager to affirm the need for semantic and conceptual humility if the theologian is to exegete faithfully the biblical testimony to God's self-disclosure. At the same time, he is also concerned that the theologian avoid any inclination to elevate the status of her claims or conclusions. In a manner that echoes Kierkegaard's telling distinction between a genius and an apostle (which we shall discuss in chapter 5), the authority of the theologian lies not in any authority that she attaches to her own claims nor to any validity that she might attach to her system of thought. Rather, the theologian's "listeners must sense it [her authority] without [her] explicit affirmation."[88]

---

of which we interpret God and the world. What the metaphor of *Eroberung* ("commandeering" or "conquest") seeks to emphasize, however, is that God's self-disclosure adapts and reschematizes, as Paul understands it, our language and thought forms so that they might be true to the reality of God in God's reconciling self-disclosure.

When we use the word *theos*, for example, it is obliged to undergo a process of redefinition so that it comes to track faithfully who God is in God's self-disclosure. Otherwise, we will find ourselves requiring that God's self-disclosure be reconceived so that it "tracks" the diverse assumptions that happen to characterize our preunderstanding (*Vorverständnis*) of the word *theos*.

We are grateful here to comments made by Gijsbert van den Brink.

85. Barth, "Gift of Freedom," 92.
86. Barth, "Gift of Freedom," 92.
87. Barth, "Gift of Freedom," 92.
88. Barth, "Gift of Freedom," 92.

In sum, Barth points to three features of the free theologian's utilizing philosophical tools in the process of interpreting God's self-disclosure.

> First, he is aware of his condition. Secondly, he stands ready to submit the coherence of his concepts and formulations to the coherence of the divine revelation and not conversely. Thirdly, to mention the inevitable slogan, he is a philosopher "as though he were not," and he has his ontology "as though he had it not." A free theologian will not be hindered by traditional conceptions from thinking and speaking in the direction from God to humanity, as affirmed at the outset of this address. His ontology will be subject to criticism and control by his theology, and not conversely. He will not necessarily be obligated to the philosophical *kairos*, the latest prevailing philosophy.[89]

So what is Barth's attitude to philosophy here?

> If we visualise for a moment the ideal situation of the free theologian, we may foresee the possibility not of theology recognising itself in any form of philosophy, but of free philosophy recognising itself in free theology.[90]

This invites the question: What kind of philosophy recognizes itself in free theology? This could mean a number of things, but was Barth more open in his later years to the possibility of a Christian philosophy? If so, how would this relate to Barth's statement early in the *Church Dogmatics*, that "there never has actually been a *philosophia christiana*, for if it was *philosophia* then it was not *christiana*, and if it was *christiana* it was not *philosophia*"?[91] The following comments by Nicholas Wolterstorff on Barth's relationship to philosophy summarize widely held assumptions: "Barth had little direct influence on philosophy. There is, in that, a certain historical justice: Barth made clear that in his theology he had little use for philosophy. He regarded philosophical theology as idolatrous; and as to philosophy of religion, he insisted that Christianity is not a religion."[92] Others go further than Wolterstorff and suggest that Barth denounced the very possibility of fruitful dialogue with philosophy. Kevin Diller summarizes these attitudes as follows: "It is commonly held that, in his

---

89. Barth, "Gift of Freedom," 92–93.
90. Barth, "Gift of Freedom," 93.
91. Barth, *Church Dogmatics* I/1, 6.
92. Nicholas Wolterstorff, "The Reformed Tradition," in *A Companion to Philosophy of Religion*, ed. Philip L. Quinn and Charles Taliaferro (Cambridge, MA: Blackwell, 1997), 166.

zeal to preserve the character and freedom of theology, Barth says a resounding 'No!' to any role for philosophy." Citing H. L. Stewart, Diller continues, "Barth's injunction is taken to be an absolute parting of the ways, philosophy is 'excommunicated as not merely an alien but an enemy.'"[93] What should be clear from our argument up to this point and, indeed, our quotation from "The Gift of Freedom," is that Barth's view of philosophy has been misinterpreted, and Kevin Diller is right to redress these misconceptions.

> Barth's denunciation is levelled against philosophy's presumed competency, based on an ungrounded ontological assumption to regulate and establish from below truth about God independent of revelation. It was this presumed competency that inveigled the theology of the nineteenth and twentieth centuries to accept the demands of Enlightenment foundationalism without notice of the cost. And yet, Barth still holds out the possibility for a Christian philosophy or philosopher who also works in the light of and strives for obedience to the revelation of God. Philosophy can and must be employed in a way that observes the dependence of human theological knowing on the grace of the miracle and mystery of God's self-revelation.[94]

To conclude that Barth has no time for philosophy is like presuming he had no time for science because he considered it confused to think that the physical sciences could determine (by applying their own methods) what can be deduced about God's self-disclosure. If a philosopher adopts methods of inquiry that exclude the possibility of divine self-disclosure, it is neither rational nor "scientific" for the Christian theologian to acquiesce in her conclusions concerning God's existence, nature, and action. If a particular philosophical approach has not set free from the shackles of Enlightenment humanism or "creative anti-realist" presuppositions, then it is not appropriate for the theologian to endorse it.[95] That is no reason, however, for the theologian to dismiss philosophy in toto! And the theologian should not be misled into

---

93. Kevin Diller, "Karl Barth and the Relationship between Philosophy and Theology," *Heythrop Journal* 51, no. 6 (2010): 1035, citing H. L. Stewart, "The 'Reverent Agnosticism' of Karl Barth," *Harvard Theological Review* 43, no. 3 (1950): 231.

94. Diller, *Theology's Epistemological Dilemma*, 92–93.

95. See Alvin Plantinga's critique of those approaches to philosophy that he refers to as "Enlightenment humanism" or "creative anti-realism" in *The Twin Pillars of Christian Scholarship* (Grand Rapids: Calvin College, 1990). For further discussion of Dewey, Rorty, and the question as to whether human beings "construct" the truth, see Plantinga, *Warranted Christian Belief*, 429–37.

assuming the term "philosophy" denotes a single, unified enterprise in which all philosophers agree on its epistemic and ontological assumptions. A cursory glance at the history of philosophy shows that there is no common series of foundational assumptions. Consider, for example, Plato, Aquinas, Hume, Kant, Hegel, Nietzsche, Wittgenstein, Foucault, Derrida, Rorty, and Swinburne![96]

Barth has no interest in any a priori dismissal of the possibility that one or other form of philosophy might contribute to the theological task. If he had done so, he would have been hoist with his own petard! Certainly, Barth had been critical of the ease with which the "Christian" theology of his time had adopted contemporary Enlightenment philosophy and treated it as foundational. And this generated a certain disillusionment with those forms of theology which sought to interpret themselves as Christianized (or quasi-Christian) philosophy. As we have seen, however, Barth was happy to affirm that there could be a "free philosophy" liberated from Enlightenment constraints. Such a philosophy would be able to ask the questions appropriate to its own specific field in the light of God's self-disclosure and thereby "thinking and speaking in the direction from God to humanity."[97] Had the philosophers of the time been approaching their task in the way that Alvin Plantinga, Nicholas Wolterstorff, Peter van Inwagen, Marilyn McCord Adams, C. Stephen Evans, Eleonore Stump, Trenton Merricks, Dean Zimmerman, Paul Moser, Hud Hudson, and Michael Rea do, he would doubtless have questioned or challenged them on individual issues and commitments, but there is no reason to think he would have dismissed their work as irrelevant to the theological task any more than he dismissed the contribution of the Christian analytic philosophers of the medieval period with whom he engaged extensively. And we should not forget Kierkegaard, of whom Barth was a qualified admirer and whose influence on Barth was even greater, perhaps, than he was aware. Kierkegaard can be regarded, albeit cautiously, as a Christian philosopher. This has to be qualified, however, given that Kierkegaard considered the fact that the essential pursuit of the truth involves following and loving another person to be a cross that natural philosophy cannot bear; it is "an offense to the Jews, foolishness to the Greeks—and an apparent absurdity to the understanding."[98] Natural philosophy, in his view, is limited therefore to a "purely human view of

---

96. Alvin Plantinga exposes the confused assumption by some theologians that philosophy is a unified discipline pursuing the dictates of reason in his critique of the papal encyclical *Fides et Ratio*, "Faith and Reason," *Books & Culture* 5, no. 4 (July/August 1999): 32–35.

97. Barth, "Gift of Freedom," 93.

98. Kierkegaard, *Concluding Unscientific Postscript*, 1:213; see also Kierkegaard, *Practice in Christianity*, 154.

the world—the humanistic standpoint."[99] This does not mean that Kierkegaard rules out philosophy per se. He writes, "I can conceive of such a philosophy after Christianity, or after a person has become Christian, but then it would be a Christian philosophy. The relationship would not be one of philosophy to Christianity but of Christianity to Christian knowledge, or, if you absolutely must, Christian philosophy."[100] He explains this point more fully in the rest of the journal entry. Suffice it to say, Kierkegaard's main point here is that philosophy, as with the imagination, can operate within the redeemed sphere of Christianity.

The Christian Community as the Locus of Free Theology

A free theologian thinks and speaks within the Church, within the communion of saints.[101]

Just as there is no such thing, in Barth's view, as private Christianity, there is also no such thing as a private theology: "Private theology is not free theology; it is not theology at all."[102] For Barth, theology takes place *coram Deo* and thus within the context of the communion of saints—it is neither a private nor an individualistic enterprise and is undertaken in a context of respect for church theologians, past and present. Barth's convictions are particularly evident in a pastoral letter he wrote to a young Reformed doctoral student. After sponsoring the student to study theology in Edinburgh, Barth received a letter from him expressing "high-flying plans for the reformation of dogmatics" and his intention to "spin a heap of straw into gold." Barth reminded the student in the strongest possible terms that theology begins with listening and attentive reading, before adding that "if you cannot or will not learn this, you had better keep your fingers out of not merely academic theology but theology in general."[103] He concludes by urging him to begin at the beginning and thus with "the fear of the Lord that is the beginning of wisdom."[104]

So what are the implications of operating within the context of the communion of saints? For Barth, it means loving respect for the church's confessions as

---

99. Søren Kierkegaard, *Kierkegaard's Journals and Notebooks*, ed. Niels Jørgen Cappelørn, Alastair Hannay, David Kangas, Bruce H. Kirmmse, George Pattison, Vanessa Rumble, and K. Brian Söderquist (Princeton: Princeton University Press, 2007–2020), 1:208.

100. Kierkegaard, *Kierkegaard's Journals and Notebooks*, 1:25.

101. Barth, "Gift of Freedom," 93.

102. Barth, "Gift of Freedom," 95.

103. Karl Barth, "Letter 11: To a Theological Student," in *Letters, 1961–1968*, trans. and ed. Geoffrey W. Bromiley (Grand Rapids: Eerdmans, 1981), 19.

104. Barth, "Letter 11," 20.

this facilitates its reading, explanation, and application of Scripture. However, although the theologian sits at the feet of the confessions, she is not bound by them: "She doesn't owe them the freedom of her thought and speech."[105] To operate within a particular church tradition, as every Christian theologian does and must, does not mean that adherence should be uncritical. There is no place for any "club mentality" within the new humanity. Consequently, there is no place for identifying theology with the uncritical reiteration of those claims that define one's particular tradition. Nor is it appropriate to interpret the Christian community as a group composed of oneself and one's "closest theological friends."[106]

> A free theologian is not a [member] of a sect. He speaks and he thinks his definite "Yes" or "No." He is a person of action, not of reaction. His freedom is not primarily "freedom from" but "freedom for." He bewares of becoming enmeshed in a friend-foe relationship.[107]

The theologian who has been set free does not define her loyalties, therefore, with exclusive reference to the demands of a particular church tradition any more than the exclusive demands of a particular culture. The first thesis of the Barmen Declaration challenged sectarian and culture-specific loyalty: "Jesus Christ, as he is attested to us in Holy Scripture, is the one Word of God whom we have to hear, and whom we have to trust and obey in life and in death."[108] To live from this Word is to refuse to identify uncritically with a particular religious or theological tradition.

Thus, whereas the free theologian operates within the community of faith, her vocation is not simply to voice the thinking of her community as one of its members. Rather, she is called to serve it not least through faithful, "scientific" critique. Her calling in this regard is a high one: "The Christian community, its gathering, its nurture, and mission in the world, are at stake."[109]

Free Theology and the Academic Theological Community

A free theologian works in communication with other theologians. She grants them the enjoyment of the same freedom with which she is en-

---

105. Barth, "Gift of Freedom," 93. The gender of the personal pronouns has been altered.
106. Barth, "Gift of Freedom," 93.
107. Barth, "Gift of Freedom," 94. The language of the original German text is gender neutral.
108. Thesis I of the Barmen Declaration. See also note 134 below.
109. Barth, "Gift of Freedom," 94–95.

trusted. Maybe she listens to them and reads them with only subdued joy, but at least she listens to them and reads them.[110]

Barth's opposition to "private theology" is further manifest in his approach to academic theology, which he envisions as a community of scholars characterized by mutual respect. His injunction to act accordingly, that is, to listen and read fairly and carefully those theologians with whom one disagrees, was something he sought increasingly to enact in his writing and in his teaching. In the seminar he ran on Schleiermacher, for example, he insisted there be no criticism of this, the greatest theologian of the nineteenth century, throughout the first semester until it was clear that they had heard and understood faithfully what Schleiermacher was saying. Even then, he urged people not to be too quick to criticize him—despite the fact that Barth profoundly disagreed with his fellow Reformed theologian and implored his students not to follow the voice from the cave.[111] Barth's emphasis on the importance of listening carefully to those with whom one disagrees informed his frustration with fellow Christian theologians whose criticism of his own work failed to exhibit the same sense of duty. When, at the request of the editor of *Christianity Today*, Geoffrey Bromiley invited Barth to respond to critical questions raised by Gordon Clark, Fred Klooster, and Cornelius van Til, Barth refused to do so, explaining that, in addition to his heavy commitments, "such a discussion would have to rest on the primary presupposition that those who ask the questions have read, learned, and pondered the many things I have already said and written about these matters. They obviously have not done this."[112] Citing the words of an eighteenth-century poem on "those who eat men up," Barth concludes, "These fundamentalists want to eat me up. They have not yet come to a 'better mind and attitude' as I once hoped. I can thus give them neither an angry nor a gentle answer but instead no answer at all."[113]

110. Barth, "Gift of Freedom," 95. The gender of the personal pronouns has been altered.

111. "I have indeed no reason to conceal the fact that I view with mistrust both Schleiermacher and all that Protestant theology essentially became under his influence, that in Christian matters I do not regard the decision that was made in that intellectually and culturally significant age as a happy one, that the result of my study of Schleiermacher thus far may be summed up by Goethe: 'Lo, his spirit calls to thee from the cave: Be a man and do not follow me.'" Karl Barth, *The Theology of Schleiermacher: Lectures at Göttingen, Winter Semester of 1923–24*, trans. Geoffrey W. Bromiley, ed. Dietrich Ritschl (Grand Rapids: Eerdmans, 1982), xvi.

112. Karl Barth, "Letter 3: To Dr. Geoffrey W. Bromiley, Pasadena, California," in *Letters, 1961–1968*, trans. and ed. Geoffrey W. Bromiley (Grand Rapids: Eerdmans, 1981), 7.

113. Barth, "Letter 3," 8. By contrast, he profoundly respected the seriousness with which

Barth is not simply endorsing the academic values and virtues that characterize the modern university. His response to how the theologian operates within the academic community reflects fundamental convictions that derive from his theological anthropology and it is to this that we now turn. What should become apparent is that, for Barth, the kinship that God has established in time shapes our whole interpretation of the nature of the human person.

KINSHIP, COVENANT, AND CREATURELY FREEDOM

At the heart of the third volume of Barth's *Church Dogmatics* stands one of the most extensive expositions of theological anthropology since the Reformation. Like Kierkegaard, Barth was committed to exploring in depth what it means to exist *coram Deo* and thus in the light of the fellowship that God has established with us. The key to this for Barth is to understand the nature of the covenant—what he refers to as "God's eternal covenant with man as revealed and operative in time in the humanity of Jesus."[114] His whole approach to theological anthropology, indeed, develops out of his exegesis of God's covenant commitment to humanity. For Barth, moreover, this belongs to the doctrine of God. The following passage on the fellowship between God and humanity distills the very heart not only of Barth's theological anthropology but also and simultaneously of his doctrine of God—the reason for quoting this exceedingly important passage in full.

> In the true Christian concept of the covenant of God with man the doctrine of the divine election of grace is the first element, and the doctrine of the divine command is the second. It is only in this concept of the covenant that the concept of God can itself find completion. For God is not known and is not knowable except in Jesus Christ. He does not exist in His divine being and perfections without Jesus Christ, in whom He is both very God and very man. He does not exist, therefore, without the covenant with man which was made and executed in this name. God is not known completely—and therefore not at all—if He is not known as the Maker and Lord of this covenant between Himself and man. The Christian doctrine of God cannot have "only" God for its content, but since its object is *this*

Gerrit Cornelis Berkouwer studied him and then made his criticisms—and he answered these in detail (7).

114. Barth, *Church Dogmatics* III/2, 219.

God, it must also have man, to the extent that in Jesus Christ man is made a partner in the covenant decreed and founded by God. We dare not encroach on the freedom of God by asserting that this relationship of His with man is essential, indispensable, and inalienable. But we cannot avoid the free decision of His love in which God has actually put Himself into this relationship, turning towards man in all the compassion of His being, actually associating Himself with man in all the faithfulness of His being. We cannot try to go behind that. Of course, man in himself and as such has no place in the doctrine of God. But Jesus Christ has a place. God's compassion and faithfulness towards man have a place. A God without Jesus Christ, without this compassion and faithfulness towards man, would be another God, a strange God. By the Christian standard He would not be God at all. The God of Christian knowledge, the only true and real God, is as surely the Lord of the covenant between Himself and man as He is "the God and Father of our Lord Jesus Christ."[115]

God's covenant commitment to humanity is a *free* expression of God's love— God is under no obligation to humanity. At the same time, given that this covenantal commitment has been actualized in Jesus Christ, it is inappropriate to bracket this out when offering an account of the being of God. To do so would be to cease to refer to the "real" or "actual" God to whom Scripture bears witness. The same applies a fortiori to the incarnation. It is no longer appropriate to define who God is in a manner that brackets the incarnate Son out of the definition. This event is of decisive significance for understanding who God is.

To be faithful to the biblical witness regarding God's orientation toward God's creatures means that we are obliged to expound the entirety of God's purposes in covenantal terms. For Barth, creation is the "external basis of the covenant," meaning that the covenant is enacted within creation—God's covenantal commitment to creatures presupposes a contingent order. Now to recognize this is widely taken to suggest that we should engage in a theology of creation first and only then turn to the interpretation of the covenant. For Barth, however, while creation may be the "external basis of the covenant," the covenant requires to be seen as "the internal basis of creation." That is, internal to creation we find a commitment and relationship established by God that presents us with the underlying purpose behind God's bringing the contingent order into existence. Consequently, although the covenant takes place within creation, it is the covenant and not creation per se that presents us with the

---

115. Barth, *Church Dogmatics* II/2, 509–10.

rationale for God's creative purposes. In short, the covenant provides the key to understanding God's creative purposes as a whole: God created human creatures for covenantal communion. The argument that God's covenant commitment defines God's creative purposes receives the most profound confirmation in the new covenant in Jesus Christ. What is signified here, for Barth, is that God elects *not* to be God *without* the human creature. Indeed, due to an act of gracious "becoming"[116] that transcends anything human creatures would be likely to imagine or predict, we are now obliged to confess that "the Creator is creature and the creature Creator."[117]

Moreover, as this passage from *Church Dogmatics* indicates, to understand God's covenantal commitment to humanity is also to understand the divine command as it spells out our reciprocal obligations to God and to one another. The command that requires our response to the covenant is apodictic in that the obligations that stem from the covenant are not conditional—or contractual—in nature. As God is unconditionally committed to humanity in (or as) Jesus Christ, so humanity owes God unconditional obedience in gratitude. This is evident in the structure of Exodus 20: God's relationship to God's people is characterized by covenant faithfulness (*ḥesed*; Exod. 20:2, 6). Therefore, just *as* the Lord is faithful to the people of Israel, *so* they are to be faithful *both* to God (Exod. 20:3–11)[118] and *also* to each other (Exod. 20:12–17).[119] To be faithful to God is to be faithful also to all those to whom God is faithful. There is an order to these three elements whereby each leads directly into the next. The same dynamic that we find in the Pentateuch is reiterated in the New Testament in the summary of the law as it is presented in all four Gospels. God loved us first, and this leads us (and should lead us) to love God in response.[120] This response is articulated in the law which is summarized (and fulfilled) as

116. Colin E. Gunton summarizes, "Because revelation is God taking place, rational theology is forced to the conclusion that his being consists in his becoming." Gunton, *Becoming and Being: The Doctrine of God in Charles Hartshorne and Karl Barth*, 2nd ed. (Eugene, OR: Wipf & Stock, 2011), 152. For an extensive discussion of this, see chaps. 6 and 7 in Gunton, whose primary aim in the book is to explore the differences between the approaches to divine becoming in Barth and Hartshorne. Moreover, Eberhard Jüngel gave his "paraphrase" of the first volume of Barth's *Church Dogmatics* the title *God's Being Is in Becoming* (*Gottes Sein ist im Werden*).

117. Barth, *Church Dogmatics* III/2, 159; cf. John 1; Col. 1:16.

118. These are the commandments numbered one to four, following the order in the lxx.

119. Commandments five to ten.

120. "We love because God first loved us" (1 John 4:19). The logic of God's love means that it is valid to move from a description of who God is to prescriptions as to how humanity should behave.

loving God and our neighbors as ourselves.[121] Consequently, "Those who say, 'I love God,' and hate their brothers or sisters, are liars."[122] What God's covenant commitment implies, therefore, is that co-humanity belongs to the very essence of our humanity as God intends it.

Discerning the True Nature of Humanity

What does this mean for how we understand what it is to be human in truth? When we seek to define humanity, Barth suggests, Scripture presents us with a serious problem. This concerns the "theological standpoint" from which we are to understand our being and the nature of humanity as created by God.[123] The fact that our natures are sinful and corrupt influences our understanding and interpretation.

> The revelation of God does not show us man as we wish to see him, in the wholeness of his created being, but in its perversion and corruption. The truth of man's being as revealed in the Word of God and attested generally by Holy Scripture shows us man as a betrayer of himself and a sinner against his creaturely existence. It accuses him of standing in contradiction to God his Creator, but also to himself and the end for which he was created. It presents him as the corrupter of his own nature. It is no doubt true that this does not mean that God ceases to be God for him or that he ceases to stand before God. But his real situation in the sight of God is that he is the one who contradicts the purpose of God and therefore himself, distorting and corrupting his own being. What is sinful and strives against God and himself is not just something in him, qualities or achievements or defects, but his very being.[124]

For Barth, it is only when we know grace that we can understand sin aright, and it is when we look beyond our sin to the grace of God that we discern who we are created to be. Second, God knows what it is to be human in truth and imparts this knowledge to us in Jesus, God's revealing Word.[125] He is the source, therefore, of our knowledge of human beings as God created them to be.

---

121. Matt. 22:35–40; Mark 12:28–31; Luke 10:25–28; John 13:31–35.

122. 1 John 4:20 NRSV.

123. Barth, *Church Dogmatics* III/2, 26.

124. Barth, *Church Dogmatics* III/2, 26. The word translated "man" is gender-ambiguous in the German.

125. Barth, *Church Dogmatics* III/2, 31.

The nature of the man Jesus alone is the key to the problem of human nature. . . . He alone is primarily and properly man. If we were referred to a picture of human nature attained or attainable in any other way, we should always have to face the question whether what we think we see and know concerning it is not a delusion, because with our sinful eyes we cannot detect even the corruption of our nature, let alone its intrinsic character, and are therefore condemned to an unceasing confusion of the natural with the unnatural, and *vice versa*. We do not have to rely on these vague ideas, and we are not therefore condemned to this confusion, because true man, the true nature behind our corrupted nature, is not concealed but revealed in the person of Jesus, and in His nature we recognise our own, and that of every man.[126]

As Geoffrey Bromiley summarizes Barth here, "Both noetically and ontically, anthropology rests on Christology. We do not first know man and then understand Jesus relative to this general knowledge. We first know the man Jesus and then understand all men relative to this special knowledge."[127] What we are given in the true Adam constitutes an "Archimedean point" from which we can view humanity generally and our own humanity in particular. "It is not yet or no longer theological anthropology if it tries to pose and answer the question of the true being of man from any other angle."[128]

Two radical affirmations are entailed by this Christological basis to theological anthropology. First, it means recognizing that this fellow human being—Jesus Christ—is also the divine other. He is not this in the abstract but *as this particular human being*. Second, it means recognizing that "every human being as such is the fellow human being of Jesus."[129] Barth concludes that "the ontological determination of all men is that Jesus is present among them as their divine Other, their Neighbour, Companion and Brother."[130] The implication of the kinship that God has established is that "to be a human is to be with God."[131] But what precisely does this mean? Formally, it means that although the human being "is distinct from and to that extent independent of the being of God," it is also a being that is "absolutely grounded" in the being of God "and therefore

---

126. Barth, *Church Dogmatics* III/2, 43.

127. Geoffrey W. Bromiley, *Introduction to the Theology of Karl Barth* (Grand Rapids: Eerdmans, 1979), 123.

128. Barth, *Church Dogmatics* III/2, 132.

129. Barth, *Church Dogmatics* III/2, 134.

130. Barth, *Church Dogmatics* III/2, 135.

131. Barth, *Church Dogmatics* III/2, 135.

absolutely determined and conditioned by it."[132] Materially, it means that all human beings are chosen for kinship or fellowship with God as the "fellow-elect" of Jesus Christ who is simultaneously both the one who *elects* humanity and also the one who *is elected* on behalf of humanity, chosen by God.[133] It also means that we are to hear God's incarnate Word as the sum of God's address.[134]

To recognize the kinship that God has established with humanity is to recognize not only that our fellow Christians have Jesus as their brother but also that those of other religions and none do as well—human beings are his kin whatever their race, gender, or affiliations, and they are to be treated accordingly. The social, cultural, political, and ethical obligations of this are profound. Suffice it to say, Barth's theological vision of human existence shapes the entirety of his sociopolitical agenda but also, as we saw in the previous section, his vision for how the academic theologian engages with the world, not least those with whom she profoundly disagrees. The kinship established in time defines the shape and character of human existence.

The Imago Dei *Reconceived*

It is commonplace to look to the *imago Dei* as the basis for theories of rights, justice, and the like. The problem is that throughout the history of thought this expression has been construed in disparate and diverse ways. It has been taken as denoting the capacity for reason, our moral capacities, our capacity for transcendence, the sense of the divine, and, indeed, whatever human capacity is deemed to set *Homo sapiens* apart from other animals. In short, despite the fact that this affirmation is so prominent in the history of theology (considerably more so, indeed, than it is in the Bible!), there appears to be little agreement on what precisely it delivers theologically.[135]

Reflecting the emphasis on the infinite qualitative difference that he inherited from Kierkegaard, Barth insists that we not forget the limitation implicit in the expression. There is a radical "disparity" between the divine and human which should not be diluted—there is a radical "disparity," therefore, between the relationship between God and humanity on the one hand, and the prior

132. Barth, *Church Dogmatics* III/2, 140.

133. Barth, *Church Dogmatics* III/2, 147.

134. Barth, *Church Dogmatics* III/2, 147–49; cf. Thesis 1 of the Barmen Declaration (see note 108 above).

135. See Ryan Peterson, *The* Imago Dei *as Human Identity: A Theological Interpretation* (Winona Lake, IN: Eisenbrauns, 2016). There Peterson provides a helpful analysis of substantialistic, relational, and functional approaches to the *imago Dei*. His discussion points to the diversity with which this expression has been interpreted anthropologically.

relationship of the Father to the Son and of the Son to the Father—that is, of God to Godself—on the other. At the same time, Barth argues, the humanity of Jesus can accurately and truthfully be defined as the image of God: "The humanity of Jesus is not merely the repetition and reflection of His divinity, or of God's controlling will; it is the repetition and reflection of God Himself, no more and no less."[136] To the extent, therefore, that we participate in Christ (*en Christo*) as members of Christ's body, we are given to share in his humanity, that is, in the new humanity. In sum, we are reconciled to become the image of God—something that is only fully realized in the *eschaton*. What this means is that we can indeed treat the *imago Dei* as providing justification for respecting the dignity of others. However, if an appeal to the *imago Dei* is to be foundational in our formulation of ethics and provide the grounds for our treatment of others, it is imperative that we appeal to the one who is the image of God in truth and not see it as justification for reading God's purposes out of our own independent and distorted interpretations of our own humanity.

To grasp the *imago Dei* in truth, therefore, requires us to look to the one in whom God has established kinship with us in time. When we interpret God's purposes from that center, then it is profoundly appropriate to appeal to the notion of the image of God—Jesus Christ is the true image of God as the true human. In him we discern God and God's purposes in the person of our fellow human. To allow our interpretation of humanity to be shaped by the true image, that is, by Jesus Christ, is to recognize, however, that the image provides no warrant for endorsing prior, immanent anthropological assumptions as foundational to the interpretation of God's purposes. When the image is used in this latter way, the results can be profoundly dangerous. John Kilner has explored the extent to which it has been used to wreak havoc throughout history.[137] What Karl Barth offers is an interpretation of the image that transforms our "natural" self-understanding, our vision of society, and our sociopolitical obligations.

Covenantal Kinship and the Question of Analogy

For Barth, if "'God for man' is the eternal covenant revealed and effective in time in the humanity of Jesus," then the decision of the Creator for the crea-

---

136. Barth, *Church Dogmatics* III/2, 219.

137. In the first chapter of *Dignity and Destiny: Humanity in the Image of God* (Grand Rapids: Eerdmans, 2015), John Kilner argues that misappropriations of this concept have provided support for the advocacy of slavery in the United States, genocide in Nazi Germany, and the demeaning of women everywhere. He then goes on to argue for the importance of the image's being interpreted Christologically.

ture is "not alien to the Creator, to God as God."[138] Rather, he adds, one might almost describe it as "appropriate and natural to Him." God's relationship *ad extra* (that is, to that which is not God) "repeats," in Barth's view, a relationship proper to God and God's inner divine essence. When God enters into this covenantal relationship with humanity, God "makes a copy of Himself."[139] Although there is a dissimilarity (*Ungleichheit*) between God's relationship with human creatures and the inner Trinitarian relationships, there is a "correspondence" and even a "similarity." He explains:

> For all the dissimilarity, . . . there is a correspondence and similarity between the two relationships. This is not a correspondence and similarity of *being*, an *analogia entis*. The being of God cannot be compared with that of man. . . . It is a question of the *relationship* within the being of God on the one side and between the being of God and that of man on the other. Between these two relationships as such—and it is in this sense that the second is the image of the first—there is correspondence and similarity. There is an *analogia relationis*.[140]

So, God's relationship toward us in the covenant is a real reflection of who God is eternally and antecedently in Godself. Consequently, Barth affirms an analogy between the two kinds of relationship, between God's internal relations and God's relationship to creatures. He will not, however, do anything to undermine the "infinite qualitative difference" between God and creatures, nor will he allow theological affirmations to be subsumed within a general metaphysic. Consequently, he rejects the notion of an analogy of being (*analogia entis*), but he is happy to affirm an analogy of relations (*analogia relationis*)—an analogy that upholds God's freedom and the fact that God's relationship to humanity is an act of grace.[141]

Despite Barth's rejection of the *analogia entis*, he is considerably less critical of its formulation by the Roman Catholic theologian Gottlieb Söhngen than of

---

138. Barth, *Church Dogmatics* III/2, 218.

139. Barth, *Church Dogmatics* III/2, 218.

140. Barth, *Church Dogmatics* III/2, 220 (emphasis added). We have changed the translation of *Ungleichheit* from "disparity," which is too strong, to "dissimilarity": "Es besteht aber—und das ist der positive Sinn des Begriffes 'Bild'—bei aller Ungleichheit doch Entsprechungund Ähnlichkeit zwischen dieser zweiten und jener ersten Beziehung." Barth, *Die Kirchliche Dogmatik* (Munich: Chr. Kaiser Verlag, 1932; and thereafter Zurich: EVZ, 1938–1965), III/2, 264. Barth later reiterates that "there can be no question of an analogy of being, but of relationship" (*Church Dogmatics* III/2, 324).

141. This might be described as an *analogia communionis sola gratia*.

previous versions and withdraws his former statement that it was "the invention of anti-Christ."[142] As Keith Johnson rightly argues, Barth does not endorse Söhngen's formulation, but he does recognize that it is based on theological foundations and requires, therefore, to be given due consideration.[143]

So where does this leave us? First, Barth is opposed to any dichotomization between being and relationship in God, as well as between God's being and act in the person of Jesus Christ. Given, further, the significance of participation for Barth's theology, his endorsement of an analogy of relations opens the door to further exploration of the language of analogy—so long as it is interpreted Christologically, that is, in terms of the kinship that God has established by pure grace and not, as Erich Przywara and the Neo-Thomist tradition interpreted it, in terms of an overarching philosophy or metaphysics of being. What Barth's exposition of the *imago Dei* and the analogy of relations bear witness to is his determination, on the one hand, to uphold the divine freedom and the infinite qualitative difference between God and creatures, while affirming the incarnation on the other—that God has not simply come to us "in" a human being but "as" a human being.

Barth's endorsement of an analogy of relations is relevant for how we understand not only the nature and shape of human existence but also the ground and grammar of Christian ethics. What his argument suggests can be formulated in the following way:

1. As the Father is related to the Son, so the Father is related to the incarnate Son, namely, Jesus Christ.
2. As the Father is related to the human Jesus, so Jesus (the incarnate Son) is related to his disciples and the world.
3. As Jesus is related to the world, so the church is related to the world in him.

142. Barth, *Church Dogmatics* I/1, Preface, xiii (*Kirchliche Dogmatik* I/1, Preface, viii). Following a careful discussion of two articles published by Gottlieb Söhngen on the doctrine of analogy, Barth concludes, "If this is the Roman Catholic doctrine of *analogia entis*, then naturally I must withdraw my earlier statement that I regard the *analogia entis* as 'the invention of anti-Christ'" (Barth, *Church Dogmatics* II/1, 82). There has been some considerable discussion within Catholic theology as to whether Barth is closer to endorsing the *analogia entis* than he realizes, or whether there are ways of presenting the *analogia entis* that would be more palatable for him. See, for example, Colm O'Grady, *The Church in the Theology of Karl Barth* (London: Geoffrey Chapman, 1968), 93, as well as his *The Church in Catholic Theology: Dialogue with Karl Barth* (London: Geoffrey Chapman, 1969), 7-8.

143. See Keith Johnson's magisterial analysis in *Karl Barth and the Analogia Entis*, T&T Clark Studies in Systematic Theology (New York: T&T Clark, 2010). Particularly pertinent here is his discussion of Barth's engagement with Söhngen (170-81).

4.   As the church is related to the world in Jesus Christ so the church *ought* to relate to the world.

Whereas (1), (2), and (3) are descriptive, (4) is prescriptive—or, one might add, eschatologically descriptive. That is, the analogy of relations leads us from the descriptive to the prescriptive, and the key here lies in its Christological axis: *as* God loves the world and is "with" us in Jesus Christ (despite our sin and dysfunctionality), *so* we are to love one another and be "with" our fellow human beings (not least our enemies and the socially dysfunctional).[144] There is no divine will that does not uphold God's eternal covenant commitment to humanity as it is enacted in the incarnation, in the new covenant, and there is no divine law that is not consonant with this.

The anthropological implications are clear. To be human in truth is defined in the light of God's covenant commitment to humanity, and what defines this is the kinship that God has established in Jesus Christ. In Jesus Christ we see, therefore, the integral connection between the image and the covenant. He is the true image of God, given that *in his humanity* he is the repetition and reflection of God and precisely as such embodies God's covenant commitment to God's creatures.[145] If the Creator has become creature, where else do we look to determine who we are created to be! To be human in truth is to be set free by God and God's covenantal commitment for relationship with God and with the other. Here the covenant has its "inviolable correspondence" in the fact that our creaturely being is a being in encounter—between I and Thou. The humanity of our creaturely being lies in this encounter, and in this it is a likeness of the being of its Creator.[146]

Barth's exposition provides, therefore, a Trinitarian, incarnational, and covenantal account of the fact that our humanity requires to be interpreted as co-humanity. As Mark McInroy rightly comments, although Barth's use of the conceptuality of encounter, co-humanity, and I-Thou relations shares a great deal in common with the language of the personalist philosophy of the time, his approach cannot simply be construed as the product of the influence of that school. Its roots are profoundly theological, and the conceptuality of the personalist philosophers is reconceived in covenantal terms.[147]

144. See John 15:9–10.
145. Barth, *Church Dogmatics* III/2, 219.
146. Barth, *Church Dogmatics* III/2, 203.
147. Mark J. McInroy rightly argues that when Barth uses personalist categories, these have not simply been taken over from Buber, Brunner, and Gogarten and the so-called Patmos Circle. Rather, when Barth took over the notions of encounter (*Begegnung*), co-

In a rather poetic exposition of the "four constant elements" in the encounter between human beings, Barth describes the form that our co-humanity takes in real life. Drawing on the metaphors of the eye, mouth, ear, hands, and heart, he expounds these constant elements as (1) looking the other in the eye,[148] (2) speaking and listening to the other in the giving and receiving of address,[149] (3) rendering mutual assistance,[150] and, most importantly, (4) doing all these things gladly.[151] In these elements, he argues, we see how mutual relationships, properly conceived, underwrite human freedom. That is because the dignity of the other is affirmed in such a way that there is neither absorption of one into the other, nor the manipulation of one by the other.[152] Evident throughout his exposition is the extent to which Barth's *koinonial* vision of human relations breaks with the more individualistic accounts that have characterized so much European thought not only since the Enlightenment but also much earlier—as evidenced by the thought of Aquinas and, much earlier still, that of Boethius who was to become so influential in the Middle Ages.[153] The essence of humanity is to be found, for Barth, not in some particular individual capacity or capability, but in our free and glad encounter with the other and being-with-the-other. The *koinonia* for which human beings were created and which defines the new creation testifies not only to God's covenantal purposes but to God's very being.

The Freedom of the Theologian Revisited

What should be apparent from the above discussion is the extent to which Barth's understanding of what it is to be a free theologian reflects a wider theological and anthropological vision. His repudiation of attempts to view

---

humanity (*Mitmenschlichkeit*), and the I-Thou relation (*Ich-Du-Beziehung*), these personalist categories were comprehensively criticized, restructured, and grounded in his Trinitarian and Christological account. McInroy, "Karl Barth and Personalist Philosophy: A Critical Appropriation," *Scottish Journal of Theology* 64, no. 1 (2011): 45–63.

148. Barth, *Church Dogmatics* III/2, 250–52.

149. Barth, *Church Dogmatics* III/2, 252–60.

150. Barth, *Church Dogmatics* III/2, 260–65.

151. As we saw in chap. 2, Kierkegaard also emphasizes "gladness" as characterizing our second-personal relationship with God.

152. Barth, *Church Dogmatics* III/2, 265–70.

153. Famously, Boethius defined the person as *rationalis naturae individual substantia* (an individual substance of a rational nature). Under his influence, Thomas Aquinas was to define the person as *subsistens distinctum in natura rationalii* (a distinct subsistent in a rational nature); see *Summa Theologiae* Ia, q. 29, a.3.

theological engagement as essentially private is not driven simply by the rec-ognition that the theologian happens to operate within and for the church. Rather, it reflects his perception that how we approach the privilege of engag-ing in talk about God should reflect our recognition of who God is toward us. That recognition, moreover, should inform every facet of the life of the free theologian—not only in her academic relationships but also in her service of the church, society, culture, and the state.

Is this to advocate a sentimental inclusiveness in theological interaction? Quite the opposite! For Barth, it may require the theologian to "oppose and sharply contradict many, if not most, of his co-workers."[154] His critique (in his essay *No!*) of his friend and fellow Swiss Reformed theologian Emil Brunner is an illustration of this, as is his vehement opposition to Emanuel Hirsch and the theology of the German Christians. The free theologian, he argues, is "not afraid of the *rabies theologorum* [the madness or rage of theologians]" in con-fronting opposing theologians.[155] At the same time, the theologian "refuses to part company with them, not only personally and intellectually but, above all, spiritually, just as he doesn't want to be dropped by them. He believes in the forgiveness of both his theological sins and theirs, if they are found guilty of some."[156] This sets the theologian free to "dispense with the hard, bitter, and contemptuous thoughts and statements about each other, with the bitter-sweet book reviews and the mischievous footnotes we throw at each other, and with whatever words of darkness there are."[157]

When Barth famously stated that "dogmatics is ethics and ethics is dog-matics,"[158] this was indicative of his recognition that when we understand who God is and the nature of God's relation to the contingent order, we are given to know what it is to be human in truth, and therein to understand the nature of the obligations placed upon us. In Barth's emphasis on responsibility, there emerges an even stronger emphasis on human freedom which Barth sees as going to the very heart of what it is to be human. "Freedom is given to the human being as every other creature is given its peculiar gift by God. It is his creaturely mode. . . . In the first place God alone is free. Then He alone wills and creates a free being as His creature."[159] The gift of freedom (which he describes as "the foundation of evangelical ethics") finds its fulfillment

154. Barth, "Gift of Freedom," 95.
155. Barth, "Gift of Freedom," 95.
156. Barth, "Gift of Freedom," 95.
157. Barth, "Gift of Freedom," 95–96.
158. Barth, *Church Dogmatics* I/2, 793.
159. Barth, *Church Dogmatics* III/2, 194.

in the capacity of finite creatures to respond to God's summons by acting as responsible witnesses to the grace of God.

Barth's vision of what it is to be a "free theologian" shared a great deal in common with Kierkegaard's vision of the Christian vocation. Both saw the academic task as taking place *coram Deo*. For both of them, this meant operating in the presence of, under the authority of, and to the honor and glory of the God who has established fellowship with us, and who addresses us in the second person. Both, moreover, saw the self as defined by the gift of freedom. For Barth, God alone is originally free. True human freedom is a gift from God that "constitutes the being of man and woman and therefore real humanity."[160] As such, it is ultimately "actualised and exercised only in the knowledge of God, in obedience to Him and in asking after (*nach*) Him."[161]

CONCLUSION

In this chapter we sought to do three things. First, we set out to explore the sociocultural relevance of Kierkegaard's and Barth's shared theological and epistemological commitments. Specifically, we considered the extent to which their shared trajectory challenges the failure of culturally driven Christianity to address the social and political evils of our age and, further, its inherent potential to underwrite such evils. Second, we explored Barth's vision of the theological task when it has been set free from the distortive elements of the Enlightenment's legacy. Finally, we assessed Barth's constructive vision of the nature of human existence—how the covenantal kinship that God has established serves not only to define who we are as persons and to ground our social relationships but also how it serves to establish and uphold human freedom.

---

160. Barth, *Church Dogmatics* III/2, 194. The original German text uses gender-inclusive language.

161. Barth, *Church Dogmatics* III/2, 194. The German reads "nur in der Erkenntnis *Gottes*, nur im Gehorsam gegen *ihn*, nur im Fragen nach *ihm* aktualisiert und gebraucht werden kann." Barth, *Die Kirchliche Dogmatik* (Munich: Chr. Kaiser Verlag, 1932; and thereafter Zurich: EVZ, 1938–1965), III/2, 231 (emphasis original). By "Fragen nach," Barth means asking questions *in the light of* God's self-disclosure. There appears to be an allusion here to his concept of theology as *Nachdenken* ("thinking after").

Barth's Appropriation
of Kierkegaard

In the opening two chapters, we presented an account of the theology of Kierkegaard that would go on to influence Barth, of its background, its motivations, and its content. The following two chapters drew attention to the background concerns of Barth that prepared him to embrace Kierkegaard and also explored some of the remarkable parallels between their theologies. Building on key themes in the previous four chapters and drawing them together, this chapter will offer an in-depth analysis of three specific ways in which Barth appropriated Kierkegaard's theology, especially in his writing of *Romans II*. This will serve to provide more detailed insight into the influence Kierkegaard had on Barth, while also considering the significance of the actual and perceived differences between them.

In section one, we look at the impact that Kierkegaard's concept of the "infinite qualitative difference" had on Barth's theology, with a brief discussion of Barth's later reservations regarding the overly negative theology that this concept invited. Section two focuses on Kierkegaard's influence on Barth's theology of history, seen especially in Barth's embrace of two key Kierkegaardian concepts: "the moment" and "the divine incognito." Then, in section three, we shall examine Barth's appropriation of Kierkegaard's concept of "paradox," while also reflecting on how and why Barth's appreciation for this concept dwindled in his later years.[1] These three sections, which could be read as

---

1. Readers familiar with Kierkegaard and Barth may be surprised at the absence of a discussion of the term "dialectic" and its cognates. The reason for this omission is that we do not consider it to be the most helpful of terms for understanding the relationship between Kierkegaard and Barth. This is not to deny that this term can be helpful when carefully defined—e.g., one helpful way to define it, among others, is as a "method which calls for every theological statement to be placed over against a counter-statement, without allowing the dialectical tension between the two to be resolved in a higher synthesis." Bruce L. McCormack, *Karl Barth's Critically Realistic Dialectical Theology: Its Genesis and Development, 1909–1936* (Oxford: Clarendon, 1995), 11 (following Michael Beintker, McCormack offers a range of definitions of

stand-alone sections, will highlight some of the critical ways in which Barth was influenced by Kierkegaard. Along the way, we shall also consider some of the reasons why the later Barth felt a need to part ways with Kierkegaard (albeit based on his flawed interpretation of Kierkegaard's theology).

THE INFINITE QUALITATIVE DIFFERENCE

The most oft-quoted passage in the literature on Kierkegaard and Barth is Barth's statement, "If I have a system, it is limited to a recognition of what Kierkegaard

---

"dialectic"). Christiane Tietz also provides an extremely clear and precise account of how Barth understood dialectical theology in her section "What is Dialectical Theology?," in *Karl Barth: A Life in Conflict*, trans. Victoria J. Barnett (Oxford: Oxford University Press, 2021), 133–36. However, the diversity of ways in which this has been used (including by Kierkegaard and Barth) has rendered it somewhat ambiguous and slippery, with the result that its currency for academic discourse has been devalued. Toward the end of his career, Barth responded to a student struggling with the use of the term "dialectical" by describing it as an "unfortunate term" before going on to say that "I have long ago lost interest in the word." Karl Barth, *Table Talk*, in *Scottish Journal of Theology Occasional Papers* 10, ed. John D. Godsey (Edinburgh: Oliver and Boyd, 1963), 24 (spoken early in the period between 1953 and 1956). Moreover, in 1925, Barth noted that once the word "dialectic" "is thrown into conversation," it "immediately becomes a bogy with which one frightens children, as if some kind of horror of sub-Christian philosophy lurked behind it." Importantly, however, he then notes that he uses this term in recognition that "our talking, speaking, or arguing in theology can only be an appeal to God's speaking to men which happened and is continually happening in Christ." Karl Barth, "Church and Theology," in *Theology and Church: Shorter Writings, 1920–1928*, trans. Louise Pettibone Smith (London: SCM, 1926), 302. That is, by drawing attention to the disunity between God and humanity, Barth, as well as Kierkegaard, sought to draw attention to the only one in and through whom there can be union, Jesus Christ. For those who want to learn more about the role of the "dialectic" in relation to Kierkegaard and Barth, we strongly recommend the following works on this topic: Lee C. Barrett, "Karl Barth: The Dialectic of Attraction and Repulsion," in *Kierkegaard's Influence on Theology, Tome I: German Protestant Theology*, ed. Jon Stewart (Farnham: Ashgate, 2012); Aaron Edwards, "A Broken Engagement: Reassessing Barth's Relationship to Kierkegaard on the Grounds of Subjectivity and Preaching," *International Journal of Systematic Theology* 16, no. 1 (2014): 56–78; Edwards, "The Paradox of Dialectic: Clarifying the Use and Scope of Dialectic in Theology," *International Journal of Philosophy and Theology* 77 (2016): 273–306; Edwards, *A Theology of Preaching and Dialectic: Scriptural Tension, Heraldic Proclamation, and the Pneumatological Moment* (London: Bloomsbury T&T Clark, 2018); Heiko Schulz, "From Barth to Tillich: Kierkegaard and the Dialectical Theologians," in *A Companion to Kierkegaard*, ed. Jon Stewart (Oxford: Wiley-Blackwell, 2015), 209–22; Christophe Chalamet, *Dialectical Theologians: Wilhelm Herrmann, Karl Barth, and Rudolf Bultmann* (Zurich: TVZ, 2005); David Congdon, "Dialectical Theology as Theology of Mission: Investigating the Origins of Karl Barth's Break with Liberalism," *International Journal of Systematic Theology* 16, no. 4 (2014): 390–413; McCormack, *Barth's Critically Realistic Dialectical Theology*, esp. chaps. 3, 5, and 8.

called the 'infinite qualitative difference' [*unendlichen qualitativen Unterschied*] between time and eternity": "God is in heaven, and thou art on earth."[2] In the first part of this section, we shall examine how Barth applies this statement to his theology in *Romans II* in a way that sought to challenge anthropomorphizing tendencies in the theology of his day. The second part will then consider why his early appreciation for this concept would later become more qualified.

Setting Theology Free from Anthropomorphism

One of the first things to note about Barth's emphasis on the infinite qualitative difference is its irony—an irony that is often overlooked. By referring to the qualitative nature of the distinction between God and humanity, he is affirming that God cannot be known by simply maximizing human terms such as goodness, strength, or knowledge to an infinite degree. God can neither be understood nor directly represented by means of various metaphysical concepts such as "the infinite," "the absolute," or "the supernatural." Rather, there is a quality to who and what God is *a se* that is beyond any human system of understanding. In the same way that we cannot describe the color of a red rose with recourse to its fragrance, we cannot reduce the essence of God to an idea containable by human thought. There is an explanatory gap between human understanding and the holy being of God.

What Kierkegaard's and Barth's emphasis on the infinite qualitative difference primarily sought to encourage was a reverent silence and humility, a fear and trembling, when it comes to the task of theology. As Lee Barrett points out, this term "was not an ontological category but rather a rhetorical trope used to communicate a sense of the destabilizing impact of God's self-revelation upon human existence."[3] This did not, however, lead them to advocate for a hesychastic theology in which humans turn inwardly to their own silence and humility. As Barth writes (with unfortunate insensitivity to Jewish thought), to "think of silence as the final leap of human piety is the triumph of Pharisaism in a new and more terrible form; for it is the Pharisaism of humility taking the place of the Pharisaism of self-righteousness."[4] Before God, even

---

2. Written in the preface to Karl Barth, *The Epistle to the Romans*, trans. Edwyn C. Hoskyns, 6th ed. (London: Oxford University Press, 1933), 10. The translation of "*unendlichen qualitativen Unterschied*" has been altered from the original English translation of "infinite qualitative distinction" to bring it into alignment with the Hongs' translation of the Danish (*uendelige qvalitative Forskjel*) while remaining true to the German.

3. Barrett, "Karl Barth," 30.

4. Barth, *Romans II*, 109.

our efforts to be silent need to be silenced, and our efforts to be humble need to be humbled.[5] Kierkegaard's and Barth's emphasis on the infinite qualitative difference, therefore, affirmed that no human hustle can directly find God, and no human noise (or silence) can directly represent God. Christian theology is wholly dependent on God making Godself known in and through Jesus Christ by the power of the Holy Spirit. The infinite qualitative difference, therefore, directs us away from ourselves and toward God's personal revelation in Christ, the one mediator in and through whom we are called to relate to God.

To be clear, however, Christ's mediatory activity does not somehow abolish the infinite qualitative difference between humanity and divinity. Rather, in Christ, God forms a union with humanity that creates a real yet mediated correspondence between God and human beings across the infinite qualitative difference, a correspondence that, as Barth would go on to write, "will not mean abolition of 'the infinite qualitative difference' between God and man."[6] No human becomes a "second Christ"; no general identity is created between God and human beings; and (apart from Christ's activity) no human acts can be construed as a repetition of divine acts.[7] Thus, for Barth, despite the "closest fellowship" that God establishes with human beings in and through Christ, it is still the case that "God and man are in clear and inflexible antithesis."[8]

What was it that motivated their emphasis on the infinite qualitative difference? As we have seen, Kierkegaard and Barth both had serious concerns about the anthropomorphizing of God. More specifically, they were targeting those idealist and romantic theologies that over-exalted human concepts of and attitudes toward God. At the same time, they were not naive to some of the underlying motivations for idealism and romanticism. Both were very aware that we cannot escape our subjective human perspective and thereby come to know God from some Archimedean point beyond our finite minds—some neutral space or, indeed, some divine perspective.[9] Nonetheless, this aware-

---

5. See Søren Kierkegaard, *Søren Kierkegaard's Journals and Papers*, ed. and trans. Howard V. Hong and Edna H. Hong, asst. Gregor Malantschuk (Bloomington: Indiana University Press, 1967–1978), 6:6837.

6. Karl Barth, *Church Dogmatics*, ed. Geoffrey W. Bromiley and Thomas F. Torrance, trans. Geoffrey W. Bromiley (Edinburgh: T&T Clark, 1956–1975), II/2, 577.

7. Barth, *Church Dogmatics* II/2, 577.

8. Barth, *Church Dogmatics* II/2, 578, 577.

9. This is evident, for example, in Barth's appreciation of Kierkegaard's insight that "the subjective is the objective" (in 1924). Karl Barth, *The Göttingen Dogmatics: Instruction in the Christian Religion*, trans. Geoffrey W. Bromiley, ed. Hannelotte Reiffen (Grand Rapids: Eerdmans, 1991), 137, referencing *Concluding Unscientific Postscript* in Søren Kierkegaard, *Philosophische Brocken / Abschließende unwissenschaftliche Nachschrift*, ed. and trans. Her-

ness did not lead them to think that we should reduce reality (functionally or otherwise) to what is immediately accessible to us within the constraints of our immanent understanding. Rather, it should urge us to seek to know God and all things in relation to those ways in which God does reveal Godself—we should seek to know God and creation according to those ways in which God invites us to know God and creation. On the one hand, this means hoping, trusting, and praying that God's Spirit is at work guiding our knowing in ways that are beyond what we can fathom—that is, in ways that are hidden from us. On the other hand, this also means trusting in the visible words of Scripture through which God genuinely makes Godself known to us in accordance with our human limitations.[10]

Another relevant point to note here is that Kierkegaard's and Barth's emphasis on the infinite qualitative difference points to an asymmetry in God's communication with creatures. For Barth, "No bridge, no continuity, links the potter and the clay, the master and his work, they are incommensurable."[11] This point also sought to draw attention to the revelation of Jesus Christ. Turning attention to Christ, however, is by no means straightforward. This is because, as we saw in chapter 2 and will discuss later in this chapter, even in God's incarnate state, the divine nature is not directly visible. God reveals Godself in an act that Barth (quoting Kierkegaard) calls the "divine cunning"—that is, through a medium in which God remains hidden.[12] Barth elaborates, quoting Kierkegaard again:

---

mann Gottsched and Christoph Schrempf (Jena: Diederichs, 1910), vol. vi–vii, in *Gesammelte Werke*, vols. 1–12, ed. and trans. Hermann Gottsched and Christoph Schrempf (Jena: Diederichs, 1909–1922), 265–323; see also Karl Barth, *The Christian Life: Church Dogmatics IV/4*, trans. Geoffrey W. Bromiley (Edinburgh: T&T Clark, 1981), 189.

10. Barth writes further, "The whole greatness and the whole tragedy of human life together is enclosed in the fact that as we make ourselves known to one another we are unknown to one another. Woe to us if it is not the hiddenness of *God* that we then come up against! If God's concealment is really to be his revelation, if the barrier before which we stand is also to be a door that opens, if God is to make himself known, then this must take place by God's concealing his pure deity, by his emptying himself of the *morphē theou* [form of God], as Phil. 2:6 puts it, by his becoming human" (*Göttingen Dogmatics*, 77–78 [emphasis original]).

11. Barth, *Romans II*, 356.

12. Barth, *Romans II*, 279; Barth, *Der Römerbrief*, 2nd ed. (Zurich: TVZ, 1922), 262 (translation altered), quoting Søren Kierkegaard, *Concluding Unscientific Postscript to Philosophical Fragments*, ed. and trans. Howard V. Hong and Edna H. Hong (Princeton: Princeton University Press, 1992), 1:245.

If this be so [that God's revelation is hidden by the humanity of Christ], the mission of the Son is recognizable only by the revelation of God [by the outpouring of the Spirit]. We must therefore be on our guard against that "blatant, undialectical climax of clerical crying: to such a degree was Christ God that one could perceive it immediately and directly." May we be preserved from the blasphemy of men who "without fear and trembling before the deity, without the agony of death which is the birth-pang of faith, without the trembling which is the beginning of worship, without the fear of the possibility of offense, hope to immediately and directly come to know what cannot be directly known . . . instead of saying that He was truly and verily God, and therefore to such a degree that He was unrecognizable" (Kierkegaard). There is then no mission of the Son except—in the likeness of sin-controlled flesh, except in the form of a servant, except in His impenetrable incognito.[13]

By communicating Godself in this way, God makes Godself known through a visible object, albeit without enabling humans to know God by way of their own unaided perception. God does not give God's revelation over to humans to interpret for themselves. Consequently, they continually need to turn to God and to God's revelatory activity for help in theological discernment. As such, Kierkegaard's and Barth's emphasis on the infinite qualitative difference stressed that the theological task must not only be taken up before God but also *with* God and *by* the grace of God.

While Barth's appreciation for the infinite qualitative difference would wane in his later years, he never ceased to maintain our need for God's help when it comes to theology. He was especially adamant that the theological task is never handed over to humans to commandeer for themselves, thereby allowing it to be diluted by an array of human agendas. So even when Barth was at his most critical of Kierkegaard's emphasis on the infinite qualitative difference, he would still write:

What attracted us particularly to [Kierkegaard], what we rejoiced in, and what we learned, was the criticism, so unrelenting in its incisiveness, with which he attacked so much: all the speculation that blurred the infinite qualitative difference between God and man, all the aesthetic playing down

13. Barth, *Romans II*, 279; *Der Römerbrief*, 262 (translation altered), quoting Kierkegaard, *Practice in Christianity*, ed. and trans. Howard V. Hong and Edna H. Hong (Princeton: Princeton University Press, 1991), 136, 135–36.

of the absolute claims of the Gospel and of the necessity to do it justice by personal decision; in short, all the attempts to make the scriptural message innocuous, all the excessively pretentious and at the same time excessively cheap Christianism and churchiness of prevalent theology from which we ourselves were not yet quite free. . . . I believe that throughout my theological life I have remained faithful to Kierkegaard's reveille as we heard it then, and that I am still faithful to it today. Going back to Hegel or even Bishop Mynster has been out of the question ever since.[14]

Beyond the Infinite Qualitative Difference

So why did Barth's appreciation for the infinite qualitative difference fade in his later years? The main reason, as Lee Barrett suggests, is that Barth became concerned that an emphasis on the infinite qualitative difference "tended to make descriptive language about God impossible."[15] This risked discouraging God-talk altogether, with the result being that theology would become functionally anthropocentric. Any positive theological statements would end up needing to be qualified (or countered) by mystical statements about the hiddenness of God and the mysteriousness of God's ways—to the extent that negative qualifications would risk overshadowing any positive statements theologians hoped to make. As such, Barth writes:

Was it permissible to bring into focus the contrasts, contradictions, and precipices that Kierkegaard had sketched so masterfully? Was it permissible to formulate more strictly still the conditions for thinking and living in faith, in love, and in hope? Was it permissible to make and thus again and again effect the truly necessary *negations* about the subject of theology and thereby to cause poor wretches who become Christians, or might want to think of themselves as such, to taste again and again the bitterness or the training required? Was that permissible, if the aim was to proclaim and to interpret the Gospel of God and thus the Gospel of his free grace? It is odd how easily one is caught in the wheels of law that can only deaden and make one sour, gloomy, and sad.[16]

14. Karl Barth, "A Thank You and a Bow: Kierkegaard's Reveille," in *Fragments Grave and Gay*, ed. Martin Rumscheidt, trans. Eric Mosbacher (London: Fontana, 1971), 98.
15. Barrett, "Karl Barth," 20.
16. Barth, "Thank You and a Bow," 99. In this paragraph, Barth appears to be alluding to *Practice in Christianity* (or *Training in Christianity*, as it is sometimes translated).

For Barth, the overly negative emphases, which he associated with the infinite qualitative difference, risk leading theologians into "a state of suspension" in which "they seek neither to stand up nor to lie down."[17] In such a state, theologians can become "surrounded by nothing but threatening negations," and the "salvation of human existence is their concern in their ever fresh awareness of its absolute questionableness."[18] Barth felt that Kierkegaard could not "break with the narrowness of Schleiermacher's anthropological horizon."[19] Indeed, he went so far as to claim that Kierkegaard was caught up "in conformity with the spirit of the middle of the nineteenth century."[20]

One of the contributing factors to Barth's growing unease with (what he saw to be) Kierkegaard's negative theology was a deeper appreciation for the

17. Karl Barth, "Kierkegaard and the Theologians," in *Fragments Grave and Gay*, ed. Martin Rumscheidt, trans. Eric Mosbacher (London: Fontana, 1971), 103. Barth is referring to theologians whom he describes as having "worked themselves deeper and deeper into Kierkegaard," embracing his commitment to the "infinite qualitative difference between God and man, with all its consequences" (103).

18. Barth, "Kierkegaard and the Theologians," 103.

19. This quote comes from a lecture that directly alludes to Kierkegaard: Barth's "Concluding Unscientific Postscript on Schleiermacher," in *The Theology of Schleiermacher: Lectures at Göttingen, Winter Semester of 1923–24*, trans. Geoffrey W. Bromiley, ed. Dietrich Ritschl (Grand Rapids: Eerdmans, 1982), 271. The question of how close Kierkegaard's theology was to Schleiermacher's has been a subject of debate. On the one hand, Murray Rae argues that, for Kierkegaard, "there is a fundamental problem with Schleiermacher's romantic presumption of a relation between the highest reach of human consciousness (the first immediacy) and the reality and presence of the divine." Murray A. Rae, *Kierkegaard's Vision of the Incarnation: By Faith Transformed* (Oxford: Clarendon, 1997), 43. Rae argues this point in close engagement with Kierkegaard's own critique of Schleiermacher, evident, for example, in the following passage from Kierkegaard's *Journals*: "What Schleiermacher calls 'religion' and the Hegelian dogmaticians 'faith' is, after all, nothing else than the first immediacy, the prerequisite for everything—the vital fluid—in an emotional-intellectual sense the atmosphere we breathe—and which therefore cannot properly be characterized with these words [*faith* and *religion*]." Kierkegaard, *Journals and Papers*, 2:1096. On the other hand, George Pattison contends that "Kierkegaard's theological position . . . remained closer to Schleiermacher's affirmation of religion as a 'feeling of absolute dependence' than to the Barthian denial of any 'point of contact,' with which he is often associated." George Pattison, *Kierkegaard and the Theology of the Nineteenth Century: The Paradox and the "Point of Contact"* (Cambridge: Cambridge University Press, 2012), back cover; see also Pattison, *Kierkegaard and the Quest for Unambiguous Life: Between Romanticism and Modernism; Selected Essays* (Oxford: Oxford University Press, 2013), 115–16; and Pattison, *The Philosophy of Kierkegaard* (Montreal: McGill-Queen's University Press, 2005), 149–50. As our discussion of Kierkegaard would suggest, our reading of the relationship between Kierkegaard and Schleiermacher would be closer to Rae's rather than Pattison's.

20. Barth, *Theology of Schleiermacher*, 271.

humanity of God—that is, the humanity that God assumes in Christ. This led Barth to foreground God's "Yes" to the world rather than that which separates us from God—for example, the infinite qualitative difference. To be clear, this shift did not signal an increasing confidence in some inherent human capacity for revelation—a capacity to represent or perceive God in and through our own positive theological or, indeed, Christological statements.[21] His Christocentric approach was firmly grounded in, and emboldened by, a faith in the faithfulness of Jesus Christ, who stands behind our proclamation of God's self-revelation, sending the Spirit to empower our proclamation as a witness to God. It was on this basis that Barth found the confidence to proclaim that God is with us and for us in the theological task as it is taken up prayerfully within the domain of the church. With this emphasis, Barth does not turn to stress the givenness of God's self-revelation but, one might say, the givenness of the givingness of this revelation; that is, Barth sought to stress the givenness of God's promise to be with us, persistently communicating Godself to us through the power of the Holy Spirit. When a theologian trusts in this promise, Barth writes, they "are permitted to learn to walk" out of "a state of suspension" (between the negative and the positive), and thereby to graduate from Kierkegaard's school.[22]

Was Barth justified in his concern that Kierkegaard's emphasis on the infinite qualitative difference risked inviting a more anthropocentric theology? Did the more mystical side of Kierkegaard's theology push him toward the existentialist and pietistic theology that Barth associated with him? As we have seen and will continue to see, there were many shortcomings to Barth's reading of Kierkegaard. To be fair, Barth's concern was not entirely unfounded, and his assessment would gain particular support from his reading of *The Moment*—one of the writings of Kierkegaard with which he was most familiar. However, although Kierkegaard did have a greater concern than Barth for waking up his audience to a more earnest piety and authentic commitment to Christianity, he did not advocate for a view of faith that is "founded in and moved by itself and thus groundless and without object."[23] What Barth overlooked, as our opening chapters have hopefully shown, is that Kierkegaard's theology was decisively

---

21. As Barth later writes, "We cannot view [revelation] in such a way that propositions may be taken from it which, isolated from the giving of God's Word in revelation, Scripture and proclamation, can be known as general truths by man . . . so that they for their part can then be made—and this is the decisive point—the presupposition of an understanding of God's Word or the basis of theology" (Barth, *Church Dogmatics* I/1, 165).

22. Barth, "Kierkegaard and the Theologians," 104.

23. Barth, "Thank You and a Bow," 100.

Christocentric, grounded in a profound understanding of the kinship that God establishes with us in time.[24]

BARTH ON GOD'S SELF-REVELATION IN HISTORY

In this section, we turn to consider Kierkegaard's impact on Barth's understanding of God's self-revelation in history, giving special attention to Barth's use of the Kierkegaardian concepts of "the moment" and "the divine incognito" in *Romans II*. However, before we consider these specific concepts, we shall provide some context for our discussion with a brief subsection on Barth's theological and Christological account of history. Under Kierkegaard's influence, Barth developed a theology of history that sought to challenge (what he saw to be) overly reductive phenomenological renderings of history: descriptions of events, insofar as any event can be directly experienced within the *temporal* and *visible* world, that resist any consideration in relation to the *eternal* and *invisible* God. This discussion will pave the way for a discussion of "the moment" that unites time and eternity, of the frontier between God and creation, and of Jesus Christ as "the divine incognito" in whom God united the visible and the invisible. In these four subsections, we shall see that, for Barth, God's self-revelation in Christ requires more than our direct perception of visible phenomena. Without the help of God's Spirit, our knowing is limited to the "immanent frame" of creation, to borrow Charles Taylor's language, and thereby held back from relating to the reality of God.[25] This is because, for Barth, "the power of God can be detected neither in the world of nature nor in the souls of men."[26]

---

24. In the *Göttingen Dogmatics*, Barth quotes *Concluding Unscientific Postscript*, which is the work in which Kierkegaard (through Climacus) insists on the Christological ground for theology. Bruce McCormack contends that Barth had read *Postscript* by the time of his writing the *Göttingen Dogmatics* (*Barth's Critically Realistic Dialectical Theology*, 360–61n105). While this may be right, it is not clear that Barth ever read *Postscript* closely. If he had, Barth should have been much more aware of the Christological grounding of Kierkegaard's theology. For further discussion of the Christological basis for Kierkegaard's theology advanced in *Concluding Unscientific Postscript* (e.g., in Kierkegaard's emphasis on God's establishing kinship with us in time), see Andrew B. Torrance, "Kierkegaard on the Christian Response to the God Who Establishes Kinship with Us in Time," *Modern Theology* 32, no. 1 (2016): 60–83.

25. Charles Taylor, *A Secular Age* (Cambridge, MA: Belknap Press of Harvard University Press, 2007), 539–93.

26. Barth, *Romans II*, 36.

The History of Jesus Christ

At the heart of *Romans II* is a commitment to a Christological view of history. Reflecting on Romans 1:3, Barth writes:

> **Jesus Christ our Lord.** This is the Gospel and the meaning of history. In this name two worlds meet and go apart, two planes intersect, the one known and the other unknown.[27]

It is easy to glance at this statement and see it as an instance of the rhetorical flourish that, as we shall see, is characteristic of Barth's expressionistic style in *Romans II*—his bold and emotive, unnuanced and provocative style that is apparent to even the most inattentive of readers. However, readers should avoid being too quick to dismiss these more grandiose statements, lest they overlook key parts of Barth's argument. In the case of the above statement, to refer to "Jesus Christ our Lord" as the very meaning of history is precisely what Barth intends to say. So what does he mean by this?

Barth develops his theology of history as a polemic against some of the prevailing treatments of history that shaped eighteenth- and nineteenth-century theology, many of which had been embraced by his teachers and colleagues. What had taken root in this period was a so-called scientific approach to history that reduced history to the chain of events we directly perceive in the visible world—what we shall term *phenomenal history*. This way of interpreting history, for Barth, reflected the patterns of a world that had settled into its fallen existence. He writes, "The known plane is God's creation, fallen out of its union with Him, and therefore the world of the 'flesh' needing redemption, the world of men, and of time, and of things—our world."[28] By interpreting the world according to its phenomenal history (or the "known plane") and thus apart from the invisible God, theologians were prioritizing ways of thinking that bracketed out God (functionally or otherwise). This approach, for Barth, encouraged a forgetfulness of God and, consequently, a forgetfulness of the true meaning of history—history as it is purposefully created and sustained by God.

One of the main problems with this approach was how it inadvertently influenced persons' thinking about God's relationship to the world—that is, of God as a being who was made to fit alongside our phenomenal accounts of history (i.e., accounts based on history as it is directly experienced by us). On

27. Barth, *Romans II*, 29 (bold text original).
28. Barth, *Romans II*, 29.

the one hand, for those who followed a Hegelian line of thinking, this approach encouraged persons to think about God in a way that pulled God down into the immanence of the phenomenal world, rendering it all too easy for God to be treated as a pawn in the maneuverings of society. On the other hand, for those who followed a more Kantian way of thinking, a phenomenal account of history was accompanied by an abstract or impersonal view of God, who is separated off from the phenomenal world and located in the noumenal realm. So, for Barth, the lack of a robust theological understanding of history invited confused ways of thinking about God's relationship to creation, according to which God was either synthesized with phenomenal history or wholly abstracted from any relationship to it.

Returning to the above quote, how does Barth distinguish between the "known plane" and the "unknown plane"? The *unknown plane* is "the world of the Father, of the Primal Creation, and of the final Redemption."[29] What this means is not entirely clear (in either English or German). However, contextual clues suggest that the unknown plane is the plane according to which creation is known in relation to the unknown God (that is, the God who is not reduced to the observable plane of phenomenal history). In order to know the unknown plane, a person needs to be awakened to faith so that they can have the eyes to see history as created history. Since the unknown plane refers to a theological construal of history, it is especially attentive to those invisible features of history—such as its true meaning and purpose—that go unnoticed when one's interpretation of history is based simply on observations of visible phenomena. The *known plane*, in contrast, is distinguished from the unknown plane as the plane where history can be known directly, apart from God, by modern scientific-historical methods. These two planes intersect in the person of Jesus Christ, thereby making the unknown God knowable through (directly) knowable phenomena—albeit without God's merging with such phenomena. In and through Jesus Christ, therefore, a new and redeemed history of unity with God is inaugurated and made known. And, for Barth, this reveals the true meaning of created history.

The Intersection between God and Creation

A concern that can arise with Barth's (and Kierkegaard's) view of divine transcendence is that it creates problems for how we think about the eternal God's

---

29. Barth, *Romans II*, 29.

interactions with created history.[30] How could the transcendent God cross the "broad ugly ditch" between eternity and history—to appropriate Lessing's famous phrase?[31] Despite the difficulties with thinking about how God could interact with the inner workings of history, Barth is clear that God does in fact do so. How does he interpret such activity? For the early Barth, God's interaction with creation involves a movement between God and creation that is not contained within the immanence of creation. It is a movement that "cannot be enclosed in a system or a method or a 'way.' It rests in the good pleasure of God, and its occasion is to be sought and found only in Him."[32] Metaphorically speaking, God does not interact with creation by way of a horizontal movement on the contingent historical plane but by way of a vertical movement of eternity that breaks forth into the horizontal.[33]

The central event that Barth associates with this vertical-to-horizontal movement is the resurrection. So, in *Romans II*, he calls into question the attempt to "thrust Resurrection into history."[34] That is, he questions approaches that treat the resurrection as just another event among other events—one that can be explained in the same way that a historian would explain any other historical event. For Barth, the miraculous nature of the resurrection means that it requires a theological explanation that cannot simply be based on direct empirical evidence. Barth recognizes that if the resurrection is merely interpreted phenomenally, it will appear as an "abnormal event."[35] However, to affirm that God raised Jesus Christ from the dead is to refer to a divine action, that is, it refers to activity that comes from beyond the visible stage of phenomenal history. Without God, the essential source of life, Barth asserts, "resurrection ceases to be resurrection."[36] It becomes nothing more than resuscitation: a return from apparent death. For Barth, it is only the life-giving power of God that can raise someone who is truly dead to life, in a movement from the old to the new.

---

30. See, for example, N. T. Wright, *History and Eschatology: Jesus and the Promise of Natural Theology* (London: SPCK, 2019), 106–8.

31. Gotthold Ephraim Lessing, "On the Proof of Spirit and of Power," in *Lessing's Theological Writings*, ed. and trans. Henry Chadwick (Stanford: Stanford University Press, 1956), 55.

32. Barth, *Romans II*, 110.

33. To clarify, when Barth uses the term "vertical" metaphorically, he is not positing a relative dimensional relationship between God and creation. He asserts that the line of intersection between the horizontal and the vertical must be recognized as "undimensional." All he intends to say is that this movement involves a starting point that is beyond the realm of created history. See Barth, *Romans II*, 60.

34. Barth, *Romans II*, 115.

35. Barth, *Romans II*, 115.

36. Barth, *Romans II*, 115.

It is important to be clear here, however, that Barth's resistance to a phenomenal view of God's relationship to history neither presupposes nor commits him to a competitive understanding of the God-creation relationship. He is simply resisting those modern approaches that reduce history to a series of past events that can, in principle, be fully explained with recourse to that which is directly perceivable. By deliberately taking such an approach, Barth contends that scholars refuse to interpret creation as a "witness to the *everlasting divinity* of God."[37] Further, they make a choice to forget that it is God in whom "*we live, and move, and have our* being (Acts xvii. 27, 28),"[38] and that "all human being and having and doing" is subject to God.[39] For Barth, the theologian must never cease to interpret history according to the transcendent author who not only defines it but who also interacts with it.

As a final consideration, it is worth mentioning another metaphor that the early Barth uses to depict the intersection between God and the history of creation: the metaphor of a tangent that touches a circle, yet without being touched by it.[40] With this image, Barth sought to communicate that the intersection between God and creation is not a straightforward meeting between two parties in which creatures can immediately experience God. Rather, it involves an encounter in which God is present to (that is, touches) creation but cannot be directly experienced (that is, be touched) by human beings as a phenomenon that is contained within the immanence of creation.

Why can God not be experienced in this way? One reason is that human experience is essentially diachronic; it involves encountering an object over a period that is extended in time. Humans, therefore, cannot experience an object that they encounter in a moment that has no temporal extension. The problem here is that when God interacts with creation, visibly impacting it, the eternal God's activity is not reducible to an activity that is temporally extended through created history. God's activity cannot be located within the causal stream of creation and, therefore, cannot be directly experienced by humans as God's activity per se.[41] So, with the metaphor of the tangent and a circle, Barth is again emphasizing that when we think theologically about history, we must not reduce history to that which is directly accessible to us in our immanent frame of reference. While Barth's theology of history underwent some major

---

37. Barth, *Romans II*, 47 (emphasis original).
38. Barth, *Romans II*, 47 (emphasis original).
39. Barth, *Romans II*, 116.
40. Barth, *Romans II*, 30.
41. See Barth, *Romans II*, 29.

developments throughout his career, he never ceased to hold to this point. In so doing, Barth maintained a commitment to a key Kierkegaardian concept that he originally commandeered in *Romans II*: the moment.

The Moment

Kierkegaard's Influence on Barth's Use of the Moment

The first book of Kierkegaard's that Barth purchased was *The Moment*, in 1909. Writing in 1963 about this purchase, he asserted that "it cannot have had a deep impression on me then."[42] Yet, if we turn to a letter Barth wrote to Eduard Thurneysen on June 24, 1920, we find him reporting that he had devoted an entire evening to reading this work.[43] This took place in the very period when he was writing *Romans II*. Subsequently, we find that "the moment" (*Augenblick*) at the very least becomes a critical part of his vocabulary in *Romans II*—a notable change since the writing of his 1919 edition of *Romans*. While Barth does not explicitly connect his use of this term to Kierkegaard, it is difficult to imagine that this connection is merely coincidental—especially when his use of "the moment" bears such a striking resemblance to Kierkegaard's. Before discussing Barth's use of this term, let us briefly reconsider Kierkegaard's use of it, focusing specifically on how he deploys it in *The Moment*.

To summarize our discussion in chapter 2, Kierkegaard refers to "the moment" as a decisive point in time in which the eternal God encounters a person in a way that delivers that person into a relationship with the eternal truth.[44] As Climacus reflects in *Philosophical Fragments*, the fact that such a moment involves a relationship of God in time is paradoxical, meaning that he did not think there was much to say about the specific nature of the moment. When

42. Barth, "Thank You and a Bow," 97.

43. Karl Barth, *Revolutionary Theology in the Making: Barth–Thurneysen Correspondence, 1914–1925*, trans. James D. Smart (Richmond, VA: John Knox, 1964), 1:400. A couple of weeks earlier, on June 7, Barth reported to Thurneysen that he was often starting his day "with a little private morning devotion [*Morgenandacht*] from Kierkegaard." Barth, *Barth–Thurneysen Correspondence*, 1:51. (Originally published as *Karl Barth–Eduard Thurneysen: Briefwechsel*, ed. Eduard Thurneysen, 2 vols. [Zurich: TVZ, 1973], 1:395.)

44. It is worth acknowledging that Kierkegaard's use of this term is not wholly consistent. As Howard and Edna Hong point out, "'the moment' has two meanings: the moment of decision and newness when time and eternity meet . . . and the ordinary meaning of actual present time." Søren Kierkegaard, *The Moment*, in *"The Moment" and Late Writings*, ed. and trans. Howard V. Hong and Edna H. Hong (Princeton: Princeton University Press, 1998), 630n1. It is the former meaning that aligns with Barth's use of this term.

we turn to *The Moment*, we find very little discussion of the moment per se—indeed, it is unclear how Kierkegaard understands the moment simply from reading this text.

Is there anything we can learn about "the moment" from *The Moment*? While *Fragments* offers a clearer picture of this concept, there is nevertheless a strong connection between its use in these two writings. In *The Moment*, Kierkegaard echoes *Fragments* by noting that the moment "is not something ephemeral. . . . It was and is something eternal."[45] He then adds that it is on this basis that he reserves for himself "in *every* regard the *most unconditional freedom*" in his work.[46] The first of these quotes shows that he views the moment as having its basis beyond time—that is, with the eternal God. In the second quote, he states that it is on the basis of this moment that he finds the freedom to live out his Christian calling as an author. Why is this? It is because it draws attention to the fact that God is with him in time, governing him in his authorship—even though he could not always experience God's presence.[47] Kierkegaard's trust in the eternal God enabled him to experience a freedom from the despair that consumes this finite world; he felt a sense of deliverance from anxiety over the morrow.[48] And, for him, his sense of peace was grounded in the God who is not locked into the happenstance of world-history but who, in eternity, is present with us at every moment to upbuild us in faith. In an appendix to *The Moment*, he writes, "The moment is heaven's gift to . . . the believer. . . . To have faith, this and only this relates itself as possibility to the moment."[49]

Again, there is very little mention of "the moment" (as the meeting point between time and eternity) in *The Moment*. So why does Kierkegaard give it

---

45. Kierkegaard, *Moment*, 101. Also, in an appendix to *The Moment* Kierkegaard refers to the moment as "the new thing, the woof of eternity" (338).

46. Kierkegaard, *Moment*, 101.

47. Kierkegaard insisted, "Governance has supported me indescribably much"—although he is quick to clarify that he did not experience God's governance "in any extraordinary fashion, as if I had a special relationship to God." Søren Kierkegaard, *Kierkegaard's Journals and Notebooks*, ed. Niels Jørgen Cappelørn, Alastair Hannay, David Kangas, Bruce H. Kirmmse, George Pattison, Vanessa Rumble, and K. Brian Söderquist (Princeton: Princeton University Press, 2007–2020), 5:243; see also Søren Kierkegaard, *The Point of View for My Work as an Author*, ed. and trans. Howard V. Hong and Edna H. Hong (Princeton: Princeton University Press, 1998), 72n.

48. See Søren Kierkegaard, *The Sickness unto Death: A Christian Psychological Exposition for Upbuilding and Awakening*, ed. and trans. Howard V. Hong and Edna H. Hong (Princeton: Princeton University Press, 1980), 50; Barth, *Romans II*, 367.

49. Kierkegaard, *Moment*, 339.

this title? He notes that his intention in this work is to "introduce something decisive": something that would make a decisive difference to how persons relate to Christianity.[50] For him, Christianity calls persons to a wholly new way of life that is to be sharply distinguished from the ways of the world: a life that cannot be synthesized with the (sinful) ways of society and must be awakened by an eternal act of God. To become a Christian, therefore, a person must experience a moment of decision wherein they decide between the ways of the world and following God—a decision that is not a product of any movement of this world but is grounded in that moment where God encounters a person in time. Kierkegaard's language of "the moment" emphasizes that Christianity requires a decisive, all-embracing, and wholehearted commitment in response to an eternal act of God—as opposed to a lukewarm commitment that only characterizes us "to a certain degree."[51]

Barth also embraces the concept of "the moment" as referring to a decisive event in which God interacts with a person in time and calls her to follow Jesus Christ. But Barth goes further than Kierkegaard in his use of the moment, developing a theology of the moment that sharply challenges theologies that portray "God" as part of creation—theologies which prove to be susceptible to the prevailing trends of societies. Like Kierkegaard, Barth was meticulous in his endeavor to develop a theology that neither synthesizes God with the world-historical process (à la Hegel) nor denies God's personal involvement with the world (à la Kant). Again, for Barth, God—and, therefore, a relationship that includes God—cannot be contained within phenomenal history. God always remains free, unconstrained by the history of creation. And it is according to God's transcendent freedom that God reveals Godself to creation.

While Barth uses the concept of the moment to make some clear points, it is also the case that his references to the moment are often ambiguous and obscure. This is partly because, like Kierkegaard, he views the moment as paradoxical, meaning that certain unresolvable tensions appear when trying to conceptualize what is united in the moment—for example, the polarities of time and eternity. Yet if we survey his use of this term, we can paint a clearer picture of what he is intending (and not intending) to say. In discussing Barth's theology of the moment, we shall focus on three features of it: the positive message it provides about the relationship between God and creation, its paradoxical nature, and the human response it expects.

---

50. Kierkegaard, *Moment*, 92.
51. Kierkegaard, *Moment*, 94.

The Positive Nature of the Moment

For understandable reasons, *Romans II* is often viewed as a primarily nega-tive reflection on the relationship between God and creation. While it is true that this work is consistently negative about humans' ability to relate to God by their own means, it also has some positive things to say. This is particu-larly the case in Barth's theology of the moment, which focuses on the eternal God's unity with us in time. To come to terms with the positive nature of the moment, let us first turn to a passage where the moment is not explicitly men-tioned but which certainly speaks to his theology of the moment.

> The positive relation between God and man, which is the absolute paradox, veritably exists. This is the theme of the Gospel, proclaimed in fear and trembling, but under pressure of a necessity from which there is no escape. It proclaims eternity as an event. We declare the knowledge of the Unknown God, the Lord of heaven and earth, who does not dwell in temples made by hands, who needs no one, seeing as He himself gives to all life and breath and all things.[52]

In this passage, Barth uses the language of absolute paradox to speak to the positive fact that God really is with us in and through a moment in time—"eter-nity as an event." Yet, in speaking of eternity as an event, he affirms that God relates to us in time from beyond time, and therefore without becoming caught up in created time—even though we relate to God from within time. Follow-ing Kierkegaard, Barth does not think we can begin to resolve the absolute paradoxicality of this eternal-temporal relationship due to the conceptual dif-ficulties that we face when trying to hold together our concept(s) of time with our concept(s) of eternity (as that which transcends our concept[s] of time). Yet, he remains clear that this positive relationship veritably exists, and so can be known and proclaimed as good news.

While it is not difficult to find a positive message in the above passage, it is also true that the positive statement is well clothed in negative statements about the limits of human knowledge. Throughout *Romans II*, Barth's positive statements are constantly overshadowed by negative statements, sourced as they are in his unrelenting emphasis on divine transcendence. This emphasis is expressive of the core theological message that we have seen in *Romans II*: that the positive nature of the relationship between God and creation cannot

---

52. Barth, *Romans II*, 94; *Der Römerbrief*, 2nd ed. (Zurich: TVZ, 1922), 69 (translation altered).

be captured within a human system of thought and thereby used to advance creaturely agendas in the name of God. Yet Barth also did not want readers to become so fixated on the negative that they ended up worshiping their own notions of mystery or transcendence, which would be every bit as idolatrous as the worship of (other) created things. This latter point is critical for understanding the early Barth who, even in *Romans II*, persistently makes the positive point that God is with us and for us as we exist in the history of this world. For this positive message to be truly appreciated, however, Barth understood it must not be seen as something we can grasp for ourselves. Rather, positive theology must be construed as a proclamatory witness that endlessly points away from ourselves to God's movement toward creation. As soon as we try to define God's relationship to us in our terms, we are likely to end up focusing on the question of *how we are for God* in the history of this world, which, for Barth, is the very thing we must not do.

An additional positive point that comes up in Barth's discussion of the moment is that the unity that God establishes between eternity and time is a unity with the whole of time—a unity that holds together the past, present, and future in the oneness of God's historical narrative.[53] The idea that moments such as the moment of resurrection and the moment of faith are interconnected in the whole of time is again incomprehensible to us. This is because our thinking is caught up in and conditioned by the "stream of time," preventing us from seeing the bigger theological picture *sub specie aeternitatis*.[54] Insofar as we reduce history to our immediate experience of it, we close history off from the one who unites it as a whole. In so doing, we hold ourselves back from seeing that we are living in "the invisible New Age" in which "each moment in time is a parable of the eternal 'Moment.'"[55] As hard as this is to fathom, the fact that God, for Barth, unites Godself with history means that "every moment in time bears within it the unborn secret of revelation, and every moment can be thus qualified."[56] Time, he writes, "is swallowed up in eternity," which means that flesh is swallowed up "in the infinite victory of the Spirit."[57] Therefore, every event in history must be understood according to the unity that the eternal God establishes with history and for history.

---

53. Barth, *Romans II*, 497.
54. Barth, *Romans II*, 499.
55. Barth, *Romans II*, 516.
56. Barth, *Romans II*, 497, 499.
57. Barth, *Romans II*, 285.

The Human Response to the Moment

If God's positive communication to the world must always be construed as having the character of "the moment" (that is, as being eternal-historical), then the question arises as to how humans can experience God in time. We touched upon this question above, but it is worth thinking further about it here. The first point to clarify is that, for Barth, the wrong way to answer this question is to ask how it is that *we* can be for God—a question that urges us to think about how *we* can relate to God in our own finite terms. Simply put, we do not know how to answer this question. When we attempt to probe for an answer according to the best of our knowledge, we keep bumping up against the paradox that emerges when we try to unite our limited concepts of time and eternity. The very appearance of this paradox, for Barth, should serve as a reminder that it is not our place to define our relationship with God. We are to leave the precise logic of this relationship in God's hands. How exactly we can experience and relate to God is something that only God knows. For our part, therefore, we should simply proclaim that the Holy Spirit unites us (and our experiences) with God in and through Jesus Christ.

How, then, should we think about how human beings relate to God in faith? This is once again a question that we cannot answer in our own terms. What we can say is that human faith is grounded in the faithfulness of God who, through the eternal-historical movement of the Holy Spirit, unites us to Christ and thereby communicates the God-human unity to us in a way that elevates us into communion with God. That this elevation takes place on the basis of the momentary (eternal-historical) movement of the Spirit means that it elevates us in a way that cannot be comprehended by our temporal systems and methods:

> The "Moment" of the movement of men by God is beyond men, it cannot be enclosed in a system or a method or a "way." It rests in the good pleasure of God, and its occasion is to be sought and found only in Him. The law of the spirit of life is the point of view—which is no point of view!—by which all human boasting is excluded.[58]

The logic of the moment, therefore, can only be comprehended from God's eternal point of view, which can never become our point of view.

Is there anything more that Barth can say about what it means for us to respond to the moment in faith? For Barth, faith involves participation in "the

---

58. Barth, *Romans II*, 110.

advent of the 'Moment' which is beyond all time, by which everything before and after is set in a new context."[59] Consequently, when a person is drawn into a life of faith by the Spirit uniting her to Christ, she begins to see creation anew. With faith, she starts to see the world according to God's perspective; she begins to know as she is known.[60] This becomes possible on the basis of the God-humanward movement that draws us to participate in a human-Godward movement. Faith, therefore, involves "we—but not 'we'" (*wir [nicht wir!]*); it involves a union with God that we cannot bring about for ourselves but which we only trust to God to create.[61]

If we cannot claim our faith for ourselves, then how can we seek to live out our relationship with God? For Barth, we seek to live our lives before God by turning to those places where we can trust that God is at work—especially the church. While Barth recognizes a decisive role for the single individual, he places much greater confidence in the role that the church plays in God's mission to the world—a confidence that distinguishes him from Kierkegaard. Nonetheless, his confidence in the church—at least in its visible form—was not absolute. As the church exists in this world, he was very aware that it is haunted by an uncertainty about how best to go about its mission. Consequently, it can also experience an anxiety over how to respond to God's calling—an anxiety, for example, over how to interpret Scripture, how to discern the guidance of the Spirit, and what theological views and practices to adopt. Against such anxiety, Barth insists that the church must continually be reminded of three certainties:

> The Lord, Resurrection, and Faith. LORD denotes the unconditional imperative; RESURRECTION the utterly strange; and FAITH the free initiative of the absolute Moment [*des absoluten Moments*] of the righteousness of God.[62]

59. Barth, *Romans II*, 125.
60. Barth, *Romans II*, 303.
61. Barth, *Romans II*, 303-4; *Der Römerbrief*, 287.
62. Barth, *Romans II*, 381-82 (capitalization original). To clarify, Barth's language of the "absolute Moment"—which is not language that Kierkegaard uses—is very different from the account of the absolute moment that we find in Hegel. Georg Wilhelm Friedrich Hegel, *Lectures on the Philosophy of Religion*, vol. 1, "Introduction" and "The Concept of Religion," ed. and trans. Peter C. Hodgson (Berkeley: University of California Press, 1984), 194-95n28. In contrast to Hegel, Barth insists that a relationship with God is conditional upon the personal and transcendent God creating a union (in the temporal-eternal moment) between God and creation—a union that is not immanent to world-history, but which is conditional upon God's movement toward it. While Barth insists that the eternal moment in which

In this passage, Barth's allusive language makes him once again difficult to follow. In context, however, he seems to be saying that the church can know assuredly (1) that the Lord is the unconditional imperative for salvation, (2) that the resurrection points to a reality that is utterly strange (or utterly new) alongside the regular phenomena we experience in this world, and (3) that faith initiates persons into a unity with the righteousness of God. Together, these three basic and essential points should give the church confidence to proceed beyond any anxiety that might paralyze it. On the basis of these points, the church can boldly proceed to seek God's message and guidance by prayerfully engaging with Scripture, together as the church past and present. These points give the church this confidence because they speak to the fact that God is behind us, with us, and ahead of us, leading the church onward, despite the challenges that Christians experience when embracing a message that is so strange and uncertain amid the dominant (sinful) cultures of this world.

Along with his insistence in *Romans II* on the transcendent basis for unity with God, Barth also affirms that in Christ we are given a historically particular, contingent, and finite ground in and through whom to respond positively to God in this world.[63] For Barth, the gospel does not draw our attention away from creation toward some transcendent uncreated realm. Rather, it draws our attention to the particular ways in which God reveals Godself in history. We are called to respond to God's revelation in time as it is made known to us in and through the historical ministry of Jesus Christ. He writes:

> [We] live in the flux of time; and if we do not love within a succession of moments, we love not at all. Jesus was the Christ, not somewhere outside this flux but within it, not outside this succession of moments but within it. For us, too, knowledge of the eternal "Moment" must occur within the same flux. For us, too, there must be within this knowledge a place, a time, an occasion for love. The knowledge of the "Moment" must occur in a moment: the turning back to eternity must occur in a time. This present moment, this present time, is the high time for us to awake out of sleep.[64]

God relates positively to creation "can be compared with no moment in time," he does not deny its unity with time (Barth, *Romans II*, 498). What he does deny, however, is that we can positively relate ourselves to the eternal God on the basis of our existence within time. Again, for Barth, God relates to us in history in an event that is entirely new, without historical precedent—i.e., without any precedent that we can construe independently of the eternal God's relationship to us in time.

63. Barth, *Romans II*, 381–82.
64. Barth, *Romans II*, 498.

Concluding Remarks on the Moment

By referring to the moment as the point of unity between the eternal God and the temporal creation, Barth echoes Kierkegaard's account of the moment as an event that speaks to God's contemporaneity with us in the here and now—"the 'Moment' when men stand naked before God and are clothed by Him."[65] For both thinkers, we are created to be clothed by God—that is, the content of our lives is to be shaped by God's authority over us. In contrast, the story of the fall speaks to our desire to seek to determine the content of our lives for ourselves, over against God's authority. Barth's theology of the moment in *Romans II* opposes this fallen tendency, stressing that humans are incapable of crossing the line that separates them from God. This line, he describes, "is the line of death, which is, nevertheless, the line of life; it is the end, which is, nevertheless, the beginning; it is the 'No,' which is, nevertheless, the 'Yes.' It is God who pronounces and speaks and renders, who selects and values according to His pleasure."[66]

What does Barth mean by this? He means that the fallen and idolatrous attempts of humans to cross this line from their side—to relate to God on their own terms—have no endurance; they end in death. He also means that this end is not simply accidental; it expresses the "No" that God utters to the waywardness of creation, a "No" that is accompanied by a "Yes." Insofar as creation belongs to God, it is God who determines and has determined its end. For Barth, the end of creation is new creation; it is "Yes." On the other side of the line, which from our side is a boundary, is the God who is for us in a way that we cannot be for God, in and of ourselves. From this other side, God gives life to creation. This is not simply a future possibility but is one that meets us today when we encounter God in the eternal-historical moment. When God, in the moment, unites Godself with us across this line (which is emphatically not a boundary for God), God restores life to this world.

---

65. Barth, *Romans II*, 111. In *Göttingen Dogmatics*, Barth more explicitly echoes Kierkegaard's account of God's contemporaneity with us in Christ, although Barth does not associate his use of this concept with Kierkegaard. For example, Barth refers to the "contemporaneity [that] is exclusively that of faith" (*Göttingen Dogmatics*, 148). Also, in his section entitled "Direct Witness to Revelation," Barth elaborates on the concept of contemporaneity in a way that bears a striking resemblance to Kierkegaard's use of it (*Göttingen Dogmatics*, 201–11). Given Barth's reading of *Practice in Christianity*, it is hard to imagine that the connection between his and Kierkegaard's use of the concept of contemporaneity is purely coincidental.

66. Barth, *Romans II*, 111.

The Frontier between God and Creation

As we have just discussed, the moment in which God's "vertical" activity intersects with "horizontal" history is, for Barth, a moment of union-in-distinction—a moment in which God unites Godself with creation, albeit without creating a synthesis. This lack of synthesis means that any impressions God leaves on creation cannot, in and of themselves, provide a direct window into the eternal life of God.[67] Instead, God reveals Godself to us at the frontier between the heavenly realm and the created order. As we observe God's revelation from our immediate perspective within creation, revelation appears no different from any other feature of creation. However, there is always more to God's revelation than directly meets the eye. In Christ, for example, all that we can directly see from our side of the frontier between God and creation is a human being; we cannot directly see his divinity. For Kierkegaard and Barth, this frontier between creation and God, time and eternity, is not one that we can cross for ourselves. It is, however, possible for us to relate to the other side of the frontier indirectly, in and through the one who unites God and creation.

When Jesus stands at the frontier between God and creation, he does not stand as one divided between the human side and the divine side. Like Kierkegaard, Barth manages to avoid any systematic pull toward Nestorianism, or any other heresy that would separate Christ's two natures. He does so simply by accepting "the divine contradiction that is in Christ"—the contradiction that is not a logical contradiction but the apparent contradiction or paradox of Christ being fully God and fully human.[68] It is only when we try to resolve this paradox with our limited concepts of divinity and humanity that we end up playing those zero-sum games that divide and separate Christ's two natures. Such a temptation, for Barth, can be overwhelming because "men shall continue to prefer their 'No-God' to the divine paradox."[69] By this, Barth means that humans are reluctant to embrace a God who does not conform to their idea of what God should be or can be. Such a "God," however, is a "No-God," a mere projection of our own ideals. The appeal of this "No-God" is especially strong in the modern world, which is characterized by a presumptiveness that everything that can be known is in principle knowable directly to us. This world, he writes, is "a world without paradox and without eternity, of knowing

67. Barth, *Romans II*, 29.
68. Barth, *Romans II*, 40.
69. Barth, *Romans II*, 41.

without the background of not-knowing, of a religion without the unknown God."[70] Yet the appeal of such a world is not without reason. Barth writes:

> It evokes confidence, for it is simple and straightforward and uncramped; it provides considerable security and has few ragged edges; it corresponds, generally speaking, with what is required by the practical experiences of life; its standards and general principles are conveniently vague and flexible; and it possesses, moreover, a liberal prospect of vast future possibilities.[71]

In the contemporary world, it can seem strange, even delusional, to believe that there is a being who exists beyond the limits of our immediate perception—an unknown God who defines what the world truly is.[72] This is partly because of the growing dominance that the empirical sciences play in shaping society's metaphysical intuitions, leading many in society to reduce the ultimate nature of reality to that which we immediately know (or think we know).

For Barth and Kierkegaard alike, this modern temptation is not only confused but sinister. Having fallen into sin, human beings have fallen into untruth. Therefore, to reduce our perception of reality only to those things that are immanent to creation—without God opening our hearts and minds to God's ultimate truth—is to embrace "vanity of mind and blindness of heart."[73] And to do this before God—in a way that is unconscious or forgetful of our fallenness, and unconscious or forgetful of the one to whom we truly belong—is to make fools out of ourselves.[74] When this becomes as commonplace as it has, we slip further and further into disordered ways of thinking that become self-perpetuating. The hidden God becomes displaced by the visible world, and we turn the light of God into darkness. Left to ourselves, we end up thinking about God according to "the dominion of the meaningless power of the world."[75]

To know in truth the relationship that God has with the world, we require the "memory of the eternal breaking in upon our minds and hearts."[76] This memory is not one we can possess or maintain for ourselves but is one that can only be created and sustained within us by the grace of God. It is a memory that harkens back to the original prelapsarian creation. Without this memory,

70. Barth, *Romans II*, 48.
71. Barth, *Romans II*, 49.
72. Barth, *Romans II*, 48.
73. Barth, *Romans II*, 49.
74. Barth, *Romans II*, 49.
75. Barth, *Romans II*, 48.
76. Barth, *Romans II*, 48; *Der Römerbrief*, 23 (translation altered).

"our thought remains merely empty, formal, critical and unproductive, incapable of mastering the rich world of appearance and of apprehending each particular thing in the context of the whole."[77] Without this memory, we not only forget God, but we also forget who we are.

The Divine Incognito

Another Kierkegaardian concept in *Romans II*, which is closely connected to Barth's understanding of the frontier between God and creation, is that of Jesus Christ as *the divine incognito*. This concept communicates that there is no "direct and observable manifestation of divinity" in the humanity of Jesus Christ.[78] God is Spirit and therefore (Barth writes, quoting Kierkegaard) "the denial of direct immediacy. If Christ is true God, He must be unrecognizable. Direct recognizability is characteristic of the idol."[79] So when the invisible God veils Godself with visible humanity, God appears to us as the divine incognito. Jesus Christ is the image of the invisible God, the one in whom God is concealed by that which is not God. The name of Jesus Christ, therefore, speaks to us of our Lord in whom "two worlds meet and go apart."[80]

When Barth employs this concept, he often does so with a number of other Kierkegaardian terms—for example, the infinite qualitative difference, paradox, the moment, and indirect communication. In a passage that Kierkegaard himself could have written, Barth writes:

> Faith is awe in the presence of the divine incognito; it is the love of God that is aware of the qualitative distinction between God and man and God and the world; it is the affirmation of resurrection as the turning-point of the world; and therefore it is the affirmation of the divine "No" in Christ, of shattering halt in the presence of God.[81]

Commenting on Barth's use of Kierkegaard, Lee Barrett observes that Barth tended to put "Kierkegaard's words to a use somewhat different from their original employment."[82] While this is certainly true, it is also the case that

77. Barth, *Romans II*, 48.
78. Barth, *Romans II*, 279.
79. Barth, *Romans II*, 38; *Der Römerbrief* 14 (translation altered), quoting Kierkegaard, *Practice in Christianity*, 136.
80. Barth, *Romans II*, 29.
81. Barth, *Romans II*, 39.
82. Barrett, "Karl Barth," 29.

when the Kierkegaardian terms Barth adopts are held together within his theological framework, they invite a theological understanding that resonates closely with Kierkegaard—despite Barth's somewhat superficial understanding of him. This is certainly the case when it comes to Barth's understanding of the divine incognito, which clearly echoes Kierkegaard, and whose view we discussed in chapter 2.

In the rest of this section, we shall focus on Barth's account of what it means for God to reveal Godself in and through the divine incognito. As we have already discussed many of the key issues relating to Barth's account of the divine incognito, we shall keep this section short to avoid unnecessary repetition.

The Revelation of the Divine Incognito

Perhaps the driving concern of *Romans II* is what humans can and cannot know about God and God's relationship to creation. On the one hand, Barth, like Kierkegaard, fought against the merging of theology with human culture, which led them both to emphasize the limits of human thought. On the other hand, Barth did not want to leave the theologian with nothing to say—with an overbearing hesitancy to engage in theological description when it comes to those things that God does make known. When Barth refers to Jesus Christ as the divine incognito, he views him as one who unites what humans can and cannot know theologically and, in so doing, communicates theological truths to us that we could not otherwise know. In this section, we consider how Barth addresses a question that he poses early on in *Romans II*: "Is there any connexion between those impressions of revelation which may be discovered in the events of history or in the spiritual experiences of men, and the actual revelation of the Unknown God Himself?" We shall conclude by considering how Barth views Jesus Christ as the central answer to this question.

So what does Barth think we can say with any confidence? For starters, Barth believes we can affirm the following fundamental points about God's relationship to creation:

1. God is transcendent.
2. God communicates Godself to the world in a way that makes it possible for humans to begin to align with God's purposes for it.
3. God communicates Godself to the world in a way that reveals who God is *ad extra*, according to the outworking of God's relationship to creation.
4. Who God is *ad extra* is grounded in who God is *ad intra*.

While God cannot be reduced to who God is relative to creation, Barth is also clear that God cannot be abstracted from God's actions toward creation. God's actions are true to who God is, which means that they are revelatory of God. However, for God's works to be known as revelatory, they need to be interpreted by minds that can track their revelatory meaning—by minds that have been transformed by the Holy Spirit and thereby attuned to the meaning of God's works. One of the implications of this, for Barth, is that theological understanding should always be unsettled; theologians should hesitate to hold too firmly to their doctrines out of an awareness of their limitations, along with a readiness to be guided in a different direction by God.

It is because God's actions are true to who God is that theologians are able to develop a network of beliefs, doctrines, and theological documents (including Scripture) according to which they can know and understand things about God and all things in relation to God. For Barth, while Scripture and other theological works are not sacred in their own right, and while worshiping them as sacred would be idolatrous, they can nonetheless serve as media through which God speaks—as "sign-posts to the Holy One."[83] These signposts give us something positive to work with in the pursuit of theological understanding. Yet as signposts to God's revelation, they do not enable us to commandeer God's revelation for ourselves; they point away from themselves to Christ who, through the Spirit, is persistently revealing God through these signposts, and who, as God's Word, is foundational to our interpretation of them.[84] This ongoing revelation of God's Word, for Barth, is the power of the gospel; it is a power that "speaks of God as he is: it is concerned with Him Himself and Him only. It speaks of the Creator who shall be our Redeemer and of the Redeemer who is our Creator."[85] For the theologian to be faithful in her task, therefore, she must engage with theological signposts (such as Scripture and other theological works) *as signposts* that bear witness to the ongoing ministry and mission of the gospel—to the mission of God's incarnate Word, and to the empowering work of his Spirit. On this point, Barth warns:

> If anything Christian (!) be unrelated to the Gospel, it is a human by-product, a dangerous religious survival, a regrettable misunderstanding. For in this case content would be substituted for a void, convex for concave,

83. Barth, *Romans II*, 36.
84. See Barth, *Romans II*, 215–16.
85. Barth, *Romans II*, 37.

positive for negative, and the characteristic marks of Christianity would be possession and self-sufficiency rather than deprivation and hope. If this be persisted in, there emerges, instead of the community of Christ, Christendom, an ineffective peace-pact or compromise with that existence which, moving with its own momentum, lies on this side of the resurrection. Christianity would then have lost all relation to the power of God.[86]

The Christian faith, therefore, is not simply grounded in collective Christian beliefs or doctrines but in the power of the gospel. It rests upon a transformative relationship with the divine incognito who, by uniting the visible and the invisible, provides us with a theological basis for understanding what God actually reveals to us. So, by becoming united with Christ, by the power of the Spirit, a person's "imagination is filled with the picture of a divine plan of God's purpose."[87] It is on this basis that the theologian can be emboldened to take up her task, despite the uncertainties she faces. He writes:

At the incredible point where we discover the question-mark which is set against us—set against us manifestly by One that we are not—we encounter eternity; united with Christ, we are apprehended and known by God, and we possess the possibility which is beyond all possibility, the impossible possibility of walking *after the Spirit*.[88]

In this passage, Barth's emphasis on what is *impossible* for humans could, once again, risk inviting an apathy toward the theological task. When focusing on what is impossible for us to know about God, theology can come to resemble a task that is forever bound to failure—a task of speaking meaningless words which do little more than witness to the unknown. And even when Barth emphasizes the positive role that Jesus Christ and the Spirit play in directing us to God, this could come across as highly mystical in a way that leaves us with little concrete help—indeed, for some, this emphasis could be seen as an invitation to put one's head in the clouds. After all, as the divine incognito, Jesus's divinity remains "in its final hiddenness and its most profound secrecy."[89] He stands on "the frontier of what is observable";[90] his human disguise is on the

---

86. Barth, *Romans II*, 36.
87. Barth, *Romans II*, 72.
88. Barth, *Romans II*, 278 (emphasis original).
89. Barth, *Romans II*, 98.
90. Barth, *Romans II*, 327.

horizon for all to see, while his divinity is on the other side of that frontier, beyond what we can see.

Yet, in the above passage, Barth also stresses what is *possible* for us when united with Christ. For Barth, when we see Jesus Christ on the horizon, we actually do see that "*God is for us* (Rom. 8.31), and we are by his side."[91] Moreover, the visible life of Christ provides us with a clear and concrete "parable" of what it looks like to live before God, and to pursue the very real "possibility of walking *after the Spirit*."[92] While the humanity of the divine incognito may disguise the Son's divinity, it also bears a "*likeness*" to the Son of God; the incarnation literally and figuratively puts flesh on God's Word.[93] It is of course true that the "parable" and "likeness" are open to misinterpretation. Indeed, Barth asks rhetorically, "Is there any historical occurrence so defenceless against brilliant and stupid notions, against interpretations and misinterpretations, against use and misuse; is there any historical happening so inconspicuous and ambiguous and open to misunderstanding—as the appearance in history of God's own Son?"[94] Yet again, Barth remains confident in God's promise to send the Spirit to give us the eyes to see and ears to hear, so that we can become faithful interpreters of the visible side of revelation.

One of the most pivotal pieces of good news revealed by the humanity of Christ is that humanity, for Barth, has been deprived of its alienating independence. Christ "exposes the gulf which separates God and man, and, by exposing it, bridges it."[95] In and through Christ, therefore, the flesh's "independent might and importance and glory have been condemned, and thereby its glory and significance as the creation of God have been restored."[96] In short, in the incarnation, God rejects human independence from God by uniting Godself with humanity. Consequently, humanity is shown to be something "vastly more important" because it has become a part of something much greater than it could ever be in and of itself.[97]

While the doctrine of the incarnation is foundational to much of Barth's thinking in *Romans II* (as the doctrine that testifies to the invisible God assuming human visibility in the divine incognito), we should be careful not to overemphasize the role this doctrine plays in this work. Interestingly, his

---

91. Barth, *Romans II*, 327 (emphasis original).
92. Barth, *Romans II*, 281, 278 (emphasis original).
93. Barth, *Romans II*, 281–82 (emphasis original).
94. Barth, *Romans II*, 280.
95. Barth, *Romans II*, 31.
96. Barth, *Romans II*, 281; *Der Römerbrief*, 264.
97. Barth, *Romans II*, 281; *Der Römerbrief*, 264.

understanding of the revelation of Jesus Christ in *Romans II* is not grounded in Christology per se; the more Christological grounding would not emerge until later in his authorship. Indeed, the doctrine of the incarnation receives very little explicit attention until the *Göttingen Dogmatics*. In the place of an emphasis on the incarnation, *Romans II* puts a greater emphasis on the resurrection. This is perhaps not surprising given that Barth is writing a commentary on Romans, albeit in an idiosyncratic way. While Barth's vision of what a commentary can look like may be dismissed by many contemporary biblical scholars, it is still the case that he is being guided (however loosely) by the text. And whereas the resurrection is a central and explicit theme in Romans, the incarnation is more implicit. What is especially significant about the resurrection is that it reveals and confirms to us who Christ always was and is, as the incarnate Son of God. Barth writes:

> Resurrection is the revelation: the disclosing of Jesus as the Christ, the appearing of God, and the apprehending of God in Jesus, . . . the reckoning with what is unknown and unobservable in Jesus, the recognition of Him as Paradox.[98]

When we reflect on Barth's early use of some of the Kierkegaardian terms in *Romans II*, what is striking (and perhaps surprising for those who are primarily familiar with the later Barth) is that Kierkegaard's use of these terms had a much firmer grounding in Christology than Barth's did. In a significant respect, therefore, some of the ways in which Barth's theology would become more firmly grounded in the incarnation actually drew him closer to Kierkegaard's theology, rather than the opposite. So while Barth saw himself as moving away from Kierkegaard, this is not as true as he seemed to think.

The Paradox of Faith

Over the course of his career, Barth had a complicated attitude toward the concept of paradox. During the writing of *Romans II*, he embraced it wholeheartedly. But in his later years, he became apprehensive about it, particularly his earlier use of it. How readers of Barth feel about his early use of paradox can make a big difference to whether they are drawn more toward the earlier or the later Barth. For example, Martin Westerholm asserts that the early Barth "leaves himself

98. Barth, *Romans II*, 30.

with little space to develop an account of divine presence that does not reduce to paradox and negation," adding that this difficulty has "partial roots in the absence of a theology of creation."[99] In stating this view, Westerholm aligns himself with Erich Przywara's and Hans Urs von Balthasar's critiques of the early Barth. As he interprets them, Przywara and von Balthasar saw Barth as following

> the idealist tradition in speaking of creation as the antithesis of the divine rather than following the broader tradition in speaking of creation as a fundamentally good counterpart to God, and the lack of an adequate theology of creation prevented Barth from developing a coherent Christology and theology of revelation. Because the creature appeared simply as the antithesis of the divine, the christological union could only be described as paradox.[100]

Westerholm makes the case that Barth became aware of this "shortcoming . . . and worked assiduously to correct this difficulty."[101] He did this by replacing "the notion of paradox with the notion of promise as the proper category for understanding divine presence."[102] And he "worked his way to an understanding of the relation of God and creatures that does not reduce relations between them to paradox and negation."[103] On Westerholm's account,

99. Martin Westerholm, "Creation and the Appropriation of Modernity," *International Journal of Systematic Theology* 18, no. 2 (2016): 229, citing Hans Urs von Balthasar, *The Theology of Karl Barth: Exposition and Interpretation*, trans. Edward T. Oakes (San Francisco: Ignatius, 1992), 66; see also Martin Westerholm's superb book, *The Ordering of the Christian Mind: Karl Barth and Theological Rationality* (Oxford: Oxford University Press, 2015), 14, 106, 189.

100. Westerholm, "Creation," 229. It is worth pointing out that neither von Balthasar nor Przywara critiques Barth for having a paradoxical account of the relationship between God and creation in the works that Westerholm cites: von Balthasar's *Theology of Karl Barth* and Erich Przywara's "Gott in uns oder über uns? (Immanenz und Transzendenz in heutigen Geistesleben)," *Stimmen der Zeit* 105 (1923): 343–62. Indeed, Przywara had a deep affinity for the use of the concept of paradox in theology. In particular, Przywara had a deep appreciation for the way in which Kierkegaard's paradoxical account of the relationship between God and humanity stresses "unity" (*Einheit*) and "absolute equality" (*absoluten Gleichheit*), while also recognizing that sin absolutely separates humanity from God. Erich Przywara, *Das Geheimnis Kierkegaards* (Munich: Verlag von R. Oldenbourg, 1929), 66. That said, as we discuss in this chapter, there are understandable reasons for Westerholm to interpret Barth in the way that he does. There is also more sophistication to Westerholm's concerns than we can consider here. We encourage readers to take their own look at his arguments.

101. Westerholm, "Creation," 230.

102. Westerholm, "Creation," 230.

103. Westerholm, "Creation," 231.

it is in thinking about creation that we come to see that the creature is not the antithesis of the divine, that God's presence is not simply paradox, and that living with God is not a matter of lurching between union and difference. Where the creaturely is understood as antithesis, the divine can appear only as paradox and negation; but God's answer appears as an answer precisely because it reminds us of the goodness of our creatureliness, which in turn permits the divine answer to appear positively as an indication of peace and rest.[104]

It is not difficult to see why Westerholm might arrive at such conclusions. As we have seen, Barth certainly makes radical comments, bursting with rhetorical flourish, which invite this critique. Yet one of Westerholm's concerns is worth questioning: that the early Barth's references to paradox suggest an "antithesis" between God and creation. As we have suggested, it makes more sense to view Barth as using the concept of paradox to refer to an *apparent* antithesis that arises when humans struggle to unite their concepts of God and creation, as these concepts are interpreted by minds that are constrained by finitude and distorted by sin.[105] Accordingly, Barth understood "paradox" to refer to a mere *appearance* of contradiction; it did not, therefore, refer to an essential or logical antithesis between the two.[106]

What reason is there to think that Barth follows Kierkegaard in his paradoxical account of the God-human relationship? In the first edition of Barth's commentary on Romans, there is no reference to paradox, but there is in the second edition. Again, it was between the writing of these two editions that Barth became more familiar with the work of Kierkegaard. Also, Barth explicitly associates his use of the concept of paradox with Kierkegaard.[107]

How did Barth's attitude toward the concept of paradox develop in his later thought? Did his attitude change? Westerholm is certainly right that Barth lost his fondness for this concept, and we shall elaborate on why this hap-

104. Westerholm, "Creation," 232.

105. In a particularly helpful and relevant discussion of paradox in theology, Aaron Edwards defines paradox as "a unified juxtaposition of seemingly incompatible polarities" ("Paradox of Dialectic," 286).

106. Barth refers to a paradox as "a communication which is not only made by a *doxa*, a phenomenon, but which must be understood, if it is to be understood at all, *para ren doxan*, i.e., in antithesis to what the phenomenon itself seems to be saying" (*Church Dogmatics* I/1, 166).

107. For a more focused discussion from Barth on the concept of paradox, see his discussion of Tillich's "positive paradox": Barth, "The Paradoxical Nature of the 'Positive Paradox,'" in *The Beginnings of Dialectic Theology*, ed. James Robinson, trans. Keith Crim and Louis De Gratzia (Richmond, VA: John Knox, 1968), 142–54.

pened later in this section. But first we shall return to think more about the role that "paradox" played in Kierkegaard's theology. Earlier, we discussed Kierkegaard's use of paradox in *Practice in Christianity*—the book that had the clearest impact on *Romans II*. Another place where Kierkegaard uses this concept is in his essay "The Difference between a Genius and an Apostle." While it is unclear how much Barth engaged with this essay, his use of paradox in *Romans II* strongly echoes Kierkegaard's use of paradox in this work. Furthermore, in the very opening paragraph of *Romans II*, he cites the following sentence from it:

> The apostolic calling is a paradoxical fact that in the first and the last moment of his life is outside of his personal self-identity (Kierkegaard).[108]

Once we have elaborated further on Kierkegaard's use of paradox, we will turn to Barth's attitude toward paradox throughout his writings. As we shall suggest, Barth's growing disinterest in a paradoxical theology appears to have been motivated by a greater emphasis on the *ontological nature of the God-human relationship* in contrast to his earlier emphasis on the *human understanding of this relationship*; that is, Barth's understanding of epistemological questions (which were the basis of his emphasis on paradox) became refashioned around his growing interest in the ontology of the God-human relationship (which is not itself contradictory).

The Difference between a Genius and an Apostle

In "The Difference between a Genius and an Apostle," written under Kierkegaard's pseudonym H. H., the genius is a creature of immanence, someone who defines himself according to the progress of his own intellect.[109] "The genius is

108. Barth, *Romans II*, 27 (translation altered); quoting Søren Kierkegaard, *Without Authority*, ed. and trans. Howard V. Hong and Edna H. Hong (Princeton: Princeton University Press, 1997), 95. Further evidence of Barth's engagement with this essay is evident from his direct reference to it in Barth, *Church Dogmatics* I/1, where he notes that "we cannot reflect assiduously enough 'on the difference between an apostle and a genius' (Kierkegaard, 1847)" (112). He then adds on the same page: "Kierkegaard very rightly says that mistaking an apostle for a genius is to be seen not only on the side of heterodoxy but also on that of hyperorthodoxy, and that of thoughtlessness in general."

109. The understanding of genius here is closely echoed by Barth's polemical words, "In the midst of such great possibility of genius, men are able to dress themselves up in the festal wedding-garments of their own beloved EGO and to feel that they are unassailable, unbroken, and secure" (*Romans II*, 435 [capitalization original]).

what he is by himself, that is, by what he is in himself."[110] This self-definition is crafted according to the philosophies that the genius and his peers construct for themselves; it is measured according to an "immanent teleology," which is informed by whatever intellectual criteria are exalted by society—the genius is someone whom Hegel would have put on a pedestal. For Kierkegaard, therefore, the ultimate goal for the genius is to embody whatever his intellectual peers consider to be intellectual brilliance. And his endeavor toward this end unfolds through his own self-development, over which he takes ownership.[111]

The apostle, by contrast, "is what he is by divine authority."[112] His pursuit of truth is not led by guiding principles that have emerged spontaneously within the immanent history of this world.[113] Rather, he pursues the truth in response to the transcendent God. In contrast to Hegel, the apostle does not believe that the pursuit of truth is a story about him and society advancing the world-historical system. Rather, the apostle's story is one of faithfully responding to the personal God who created him. The apostle is measured according to God's criteria, which have a transcendent basis, but which are communicated to the world by God's revelation.

Additionally, the apostle finds fulfillment as a character in the story of Jesus Christ. For the apostle, Jesus possesses an entirely unique authority as the God-human. His teachings are known to be true simply because he teaches them; so, to judge his teaching according to worldly categories would be blasphemous. Further, as the teacher whose existence grounds the truth of his teaching, Jesus Christ exists as a unique mediator of the Truth. That is, he is the one who most fully communicates the Truth of God to us; he is the positive act of God's self-revelation. This does not mean that he creates a channel through which the Truth of God simply flows into the history of this world, as we directly experience it. The theological truth that he mediates is bound up with who he is, such that any reception of this Truth must be grounded in an interpersonal relationship with him. Furthermore, because Christ's mediation is grounded in a God-humanity that appears contradictory when we try to conceptualize it for ourselves, he exists as a paradoxical mediator. What is held together in him is not something that we can hold together in our minds, representatively or otherwise. This is because the Truth he communicates to this world is not *of* this world. We therefore depend upon him to mediate God to us. In Kierkegaard's words:

110. Kierkegaard, *Without Authority*, 94.
111. Kierkegaard, *Without Authority*, 106.
112. Kierkegaard, *Without Authority*, 94.
113. For consistency, we follow Kierkegaard in using masculine pronouns to refer to the apostle.

> *A Mediator* is necessary for me, among other reasons, simply to make me
> aware that it is God with whom, as we say, I have the honor of speaking;
> otherwise a man can easily live on in the indolent conceit that he is talking
> with God, whereas he is only talking with himself.[114]

A key component of Kierkegaard's position is his conviction that Christ's message must always be understood as *Christ's* message—in other words, Christ's message must always be interpreted according to the one by whom it is spoken and to whom it refers. The Christian culture that grows out of Christ's message, therefore, must always direct our attention to the person of Jesus Christ, not the other way around. For the apostle who receives the call to follow Christ, the value of his response is measured according to the extent to which it reflects Jesus Christ and thereby reiterates his message to the world.

There is more to say here. For now, however, let us turn specifically to consider the Kierkegaardian use of paradox that had such a decisive impact on Barth.

Kierkegaard on the Paradox of Faith

Kierkegaard's theology of paradox is often tied to an emphasis on the absolute newness of faith—when he is not referring to the paradox of the incarnation. What is it that makes faith so very new for us? It is that faith is enlivened by God who is not reducible to or directly identifiable with the familiar phenomena of the immanent order. Because human experience is confined to the immanent order, we cannot become accustomed to God in God's transcendence (that is, it cannot become old for us). We can only know God according to God's free self-communication in and through (but never as) the world-historical phenomena that witness to God. Hence, revelation and the faith it awakens are always characterized by a qualitative newness. Since the apostle is identified by and with this newness, he is qualitatively different from the genius.[115]

This emphasis on the newness of faith had a pivotal impact on Barth's theology. Barth's opening quote in *Romans II*—that "the apostolic calling is a paradoxical fact that in the first and the last moment of his life is outside of his personal self-identity (Kierkegaard)"[116]—is a testimony to a critical realism

---

114. Kierkegaard, *Journals and Papers*, 2:1424.

115. H. H., it should be noted, is happy to recognize that a genius (or anyone, for that matter) can make new discoveries relative to the collective knowledge of society. However, as soon as this happens, the newness of this information "vanishes in the human race's general assimilation"—in contrast to God's communicative activity, which never tires by being dragged into the familiarity of immediacy (Kierkegaard, *Without Authority*, 94).

116. Barth, *Romans II*, 27 (translation altered), citing Kierkegaard, *Without Authority*, 95.

that runs throughout *Romans II*, and this critical realism reflects the Kierke-gaardian themes we find throughout this work. What do we mean by "critical realism"? Bruce McCormack helpfully summarizes it as a system of thought in which the object of knowledge is acknowledged as an objective reality that transcends and precedes human thoughts but is also seen as a reality that can be truly known by humans.[117] Theologically, this means that a person acknowledges that God truly reveals Godself to persons in a way that can be received by creaturely knowing, albeit without God's revelation becoming re-ducible to an object of human thought. Further clarity on this position emerges when we place Kierkegaard's words in their original context.

> Prior to becoming an apostle, there is no potential possibility; every hu-man being is essentially equally close to becoming that. An apostle can never come to himself in such a way that he becomes aware of his apostolic calling as an element in his own life-development. The apostolic calling is a paradoxical fact that in the first and the last moment of his life stands paradoxically outside his personal identity as the specific person he is. . . . By this call he does not become more intelligent, he does not acquire more imagination, greater discernment etc.—not at all; he remains himself but by the paradoxical fact is sent by God on a specific mission. By this paradox-ical fact the apostle is for all eternity made paradoxically different from all other human beings. The new that he can have to proclaim is the essentially paradoxical. However long it is proclaimed in the world, it remains just as new, just as paradoxical; no immanence can assimilate it. . . . Even if thought considered itself capable of assimilating the doctrine, it cannot assimilate the way in which the doctrine came into the world, because the essential paradox is specifically the protest against immanence.[118]

Here, H. H. stresses that more intelligence, more imagination, or greater dis-cernment is no advantage to becoming an apostle; the apostle cannot develop by the "fertility of his ideas."[119] This is because apostleship is neither grounded in inward self-reflection nor built up by human teachings alone. It is rooted in the free grace of God, which, for Kierkegaard, "cannot be *proved, demon-strated, comprehended*" since the human mind has no inherent capacity to

---

117. McCormack, *Barth's Critically Realistic Dialectical Theology*, 67.
118. Kierkegaard, *Without Authority*, 95–96.
119. Kierkegaard, *Journals and Papers*, 3:3088.

explain, observe, or imagine the operations of grace.[120] As Barth remarks—drawing on an entry from Kierkegaard's *Journals*—it is the grace given to Paul that "constitutes the peculiarity of his position [as an apostle] and the paradox of his apostolate."[121] Barth also writes, again drawing on Kierkegaard, "So new, so unheard of, so unexpected in this world is the power of God unto salvation, that it can appear among us, be received and understood by us, only as contradiction."[122] It appears to us as a contradiction because of the distortive impact of our shortsightedness as confined by and to the finitude of this world.

What, more precisely, is paradoxical about God's self-communication? In our finite understanding, we lack the categories to understand how God could at once be both transcendent and yet also participate within the history of this world. This is evident from the fact that many of the orthodox words we use to talk about God's transcendence are, in our finite language, contradictory to many of the orthodox words we use to refer to God's self-revelation. Take the following biblical paradoxes, for example: that an image could represent the invisible God (Col. 1:15), that objects made with human hands could provide a stage for God's self-communication (Acts 17:24), and that our thoughts and ways could witness to the thoughts and ways of God (Isa. 55:8–9). Paradox is also evident in the incongruities that appear to us when we try to understand how Jesus Christ could at once be fully divine and fully human, impassible and passible, omniscient and ignorant, immutable and mutable, and so on. From God's perspective, there are no contradictions; but from the human perspective, numerous paradoxes appear to us due to the limits of our finite and sinful understanding.[123]

What does Kierkegaard's and Barth's emphasis on transcendence mean for how we construe the apostle's relationship with God? For Kierkegaard, the apostle is identified by his being called by God and sent on a mission. How should we understand this calling? While it is a spiritual calling that addresses

---

120. Kierkegaard, *Kierkegaard's Journals and Notebooks*, 3:388 (emphasis original).

121. Barth, *Romans II*, 439.

122. Barth, *Romans II*, 38 (Barth is here drawing on Kierkegaard, *Practice in Christianity*, 136); see also Barth, *Romans II*, 97–98.

123. Kierkegaard makes this point when he asks the following rhetorical question in a journal entry: "Is it not a self-contradiction on your part that you accept Holy Scripture to be the word of God, accept Christianity as divine teaching—and then when you bump up against something which you cannot square with your ideas and feelings—then you say that it is a self-contradiction on the part of God, rather than that it is self-contradiction on your part?" (*Journals and Papers*, 3:2888).

the apostle within his subjective existence, it is also a transcendent call that comes to him from beyond the sphere of his contingent reality. These two features of divine calling mean that it cannot be anticipated in advance; it can only be known to have occurred retrospectively, when the apostle comes to respond to the God who calls him. For Kierkegaard, an "apostle can never come to himself in such a way that he becomes aware of his apostolic calling as an element in his own life-development."[124] Here we find another key paradox: the "I, yet not I" paradox of faith[125]—a paradox that both Kierkegaard and Barth associate with the grace of God.[126] Although the apostle is aware of his own agency, he is also aware that every move he makes qua apostle is empowered by the grace of God. Paradoxically, the life of the apostle is grounded in a shared agency that involves both God's activity and his own activity working together in a noncompetitive manner. So, when it comes to understanding the identity of the apostle, there is no way in which "the primitive, the original, the primeval" mode of human existence, as it operates *"within immanence,"* can be seen to develop naturally into an apostolic existence *"within transcendence."*[127] Again, "the qualification 'an apostle' belongs in the sphere of the transcendent."[128] To become an apostle, a person needs to be reborn from above according to the witness of the Spirit and thereby become "a new creation" (John 3:3-8).[129] In so doing, God delivers the apostle to participate in a life that rests in God, is transformed by God, and is oriented toward God. On this point, Barth quotes a selection from Kierkegaard's *Journals* approvingly.

124. Kierkegaard, *Without Authority*, 95–96.

125. Or, again, as Barth puts it, the "we—but not 'we'" (*wir [nicht wir!]*)(*Romans II*, 303–4; *Der Römerbrief*, 287).

126. This paradox is depicted in Kierkegaard's famous illustration of the mother and her son, little Ludvig. Here, he famously describes a situation in which a mother wants to give her child, little Ludvig, the delightful perception of pushing the stroller for himself. Such a feat, however, is not one that is possible for Ludvig, and so while the mother allows Ludvig to struggle to push the stroller for himself, it is actually she who is doing the pushing. Such a situation, he considers, is comparable to the person who struggles to live out the Christian life, while all the time it is God who is enabling her to live out the Christian life. Søren Kierkegaard, *Judge for Yourself!*, in *"For Self-Examination" and "Judge for Yourself!,"* ed. and trans. Howard V. Hong and Edna H. Hong (Princeton: Princeton University Press, 1990), 185. For Barth's discussion of this paradox, see Barth, *Romans II*, 152.

127. Kierkegaard, *Journals and Papers*, 3:3088 (emphasis original).

128. Kierkegaard, *Without Authority*, 101.

129. Christian rebirth is required, which, Kierkegaard writes, involves "a relationship not between man and man but between God and man," in which man becomes "a new creation" (Kierkegaard, *Journals and Papers*, 1:649:19).

"God cannot be refashioned according to thy good pleasure: thou it is that must be refashioned according to His good pleasure. . . . As the arrow, loosed from the bow by the hand of the practised archer, does not rest till it has reached the mark; so men pass from God to God. He is the mark for which they have been created; and they do not rest till they find their rest in Him. . . . The moment I make of my words an existential thing—that is to say, when I make of Christianity a thing in this world—at that moment I explode existence and have perpetrated the scandal" (Kierkegaard).[130]

For both Kierkegaard and Barth, it would be scandalous for the apostle to conflate his apostolic identity with his immediate experience of being an apostle. The apostle who seeks to respond to God hopes, prays, and trusts that God is with him and, as such, that there is always more going on in and with his life than he can immediately perceive. Unlike the genius, the apostle lives in this world with a calling that is both beyond and hidden from the ways of this world. As Barth quotes Kierkegaard, the apostle is "commissioned and seconded to be a spy in the highest service (Kierkegaard)."[131] Like the divine incognito, the apostle's immediate appearance to the world does not directly reveal who he truly is.

The Place of Paradox in Kierkegaard's Theology

An important question arises here—one that keeps cropping up. Does Kierkegaard's emphasis on paradox call into question the positive task of systematic theology? Kierkegaard does not rule out a systematic approach to theology per se—even if he was highly critical of the systematic theology that prevailed across nineteenth-century Europe. As we laid out earlier, his goal was to challenge those systematic theologies that echoed Hegel by daring to weave God into our immanent systems of thought. This is why Kierkegaard urged theologians to be mindful of the limits we face when seeking to understand God and all things before God.

There is another closely related question that also arises here: Does Kierkegaard's concept of paradox grant permission for intellectual laziness on the part of the theologian? No; theologians should not be too quick to cry "paradox"

---

130. Barth, *Romans II*, 438–39; Kierkegaard, *Kierkegaard's Journals and Notebooks*, 4:341, 6:319.

131. Barth, *Romans II*, 439; *Der Römerbrief*, 424 (translation altered), quoting Kierkegaard, *Journals and Papers*, 6:6192.

when confronted by complexity. Such hastiness would compromise the work that Kierkegaard's use of paradox does to encourage reverence before the transcendent God. It could also short-circuit the positive and practical role that intellectual reflection on revelation can have—especially in a way that serves God's mission in the world. For example, such reflection might facilitate a clearer proclamation of revelation in a particular context. And there can be little doubt that Kierkegaard sought to use his intellectual abilities in response to God's calling in his own life. With these abilities, he sought to be careful, analytic, and systematic in the way that he used paradoxical language in the service of philosophical theology.

So when does Kierkegaard think it is appropriate for the theologian to claim paradox? He does not set out clear guidelines on when to make theological reference to paradox. Generally, however, he uses this concept to describe how God could at once be fully transcendent and yet also reveal Godself in this world. Positively, his emphasis on paradox encourages us to pursue theology without anxiety or despair over paradoxical conclusions; they are to be expected. Again, the fact that theologians continually stumble across paradoxes provides a constant reminder of the limits of human thought. Paradox, therefore, is a "protest against immanence" that holds humans back from becoming too confident in their capacity to comprehend the unity that God establishes with the world.[132] This confidence becomes especially problematic, for Kierkegaard, when it allows us to try to unravel the Christian message to fit our immanent philosophical systems. Such an approach elevates the authority of human reason over against the authority of God by trying to "defend and uphold Christianity . . . in the wrong categories."[133] For H. H., "the one called by revelation [that is, the apostle], to whom doctrine is entrusted, argues on the basis that it is a revelation, on the basis that he has authority."[134] And this calling gives the apostle an incredible confidence. The apostle is emboldened by a recognition that, although he cannot fully understand how everything holds together, he can nonetheless participate in the coherent picture of the whole (as it is known by God) by aligning himself with the revelation that God speaks into the world. When Kierkegaard questions our sense of coherence, he does not pave the way for an anarchical or irrational vision of Christianity. Rather, he seeks to draw attention to the only one who can, and does, bring true coherence into the world: to God and, in particular, to the person of Jesus Christ, in whom all things on heaven and on earth hold together.

132. Kierkegaard, *Without Authority*, 95–96.
133. Kierkegaard, *Without Authority*, 102.
134. Kierkegaard, *Without Authority*, 96.

Barth's Appreciation for the Concept of Paradox

As we noted in the opening to this section, over the course of his career, Barth both appreciated and repudiated Kierkegaard's theology of paradox. While the later Barth grew increasingly critical of his earlier use of paradox, it is also the case that his departure from a paradoxical understanding of the God-human relationship was never clear-cut. To show this, we shall first seek to demonstrate that Barth's appreciation for a paradoxical account of the God-human relationship continued throughout his authorship, right into *Church Dogmatics*.

Let us first consider a few places in Barth's later writing where he was happy to use the concept of paradox to refer to God's self-revelation. In *Church Dogmatics* I/1, Barth refers to "the great and irremovable paradox of divine revelation."[135] Here, Barth is referring to the paradox associated with God sending God's Spirit to be experienced by persons and thereby awaken them to faith: the paradox in which "[God] becomes theirs and makes them His."[136] This is paradoxical because we cannot begin to comprehend what it means for God to be ours and for us to be God's. Therefore, human attempts to work out the relationship between divine and human agency when it comes to human faith tend to summon up the appearance of contradiction (as in the case of paradox)—or, worse, they prompt a zero-sum-game approach when trying to make sense of the relationship between these two agencies.

Yet again, although our theologizing will frequently fall short when it comes to thinking about God's revelatory activity, this does not imply that the theological task is futile. Barth makes this clear in the following passage from *Church Dogmatics* II/1:

> [God] is primarily and properly all that our terms seek to mean, and yet of themselves cannot mean, that He has revealed Himself to us in His original and proper being, thus remaining incomprehensible to us even in His revelation, yet allowing and commanding us to put our concepts into the service of knowledge of Him, blessing our obedience, being truly known by us within our limits.[137]

Barth's emphasis here—that there is promise to our theological words, despite the appearance of contradiction—could be seen to connect with Westerholm's

135. Barth, *Church Dogmatics* I/1, 450.
136. Barth, *Church Dogmatics* I/1, 450.
137. Barth, *Church Dogmatics* II/1, 287.

suggestion that Barth replaces "the notion of paradox with the notion of prom-ise as the proper category for understanding divine presence."[138] The prob-lem with suggesting that promise displaces paradox in Barth's later theology, however, is that Barth's earlier use of paradox also sought to draw attention to a theology of promise. In *Romans II*, he is explicit that the limitation of paradox does not bring an end to the theological task. He did not think that the theologian should strive to a point where she throws up her hands and cries out "God's relationship to creation is only mystery," leaving her to wallow "in the whole dim world of mythology and mysticism."[139] As we have seen, it is certainly true that *Romans II* presents revelation as paradoxical, so it should therefore inspire silent and prayerful contemplation. However, he also believed that such contemplation should be directed toward the ordained media through which God positively gives Godself to be known. Barth be-lieved that, by trusting in God's faithful commitment to the church, we can trust the human words of the Bible to bear witness to the Word of God through the work of the Holy Spirit. Accordingly, he resisted the temptation to stress the transcendence of God by simply emphasizing silence and humility. To be "under grace," for him, is not to be reduced to silence but to be made "aware of the message of Christ" and thereby "exposed to the full and unavoidable earnestness of His demand, claim, and promise."[140] It is to be awakened and mobilized for discipleship by the power of the gospel—by the power of God's Word and Spirit.[141] When we encounter and are empowered by the gospel, we "are in a position to see that our own position in time is pregnant with eternal promise."[142]

The connection between Barth's theology of paradox and promise is evi-dent not only in *Romans II* but also in the *Church Dogmatics*, albeit to a lesser extent. In *Church Dogmatics* II/1, for example, he refers to paradox in a way that draws attention to a theology of promise. By exposing the limitations of our immediate understanding, he suggests that a recognition of paradox urges

---

138. Westerholm, "Creation," 230; see also Barth, *Church Dogmatics* I/1, 339.

139. Barth, *Romans II*, 141. Kierkegaard was also of the view "that the conception of God's sublimity, of Christ's sublimity, has become so infinite that it has really become fantastic and that there remains no actual Christian life to speak of, at best a little Jewish piety." He continues, "To Christians both God and Christ have become all too infinitely distant majesties for the single individual to associate thought of them with life's minor details" (*Journals and Papers*, 2:1385).

140. Barth, *Romans II*, 229.

141. Barth, *Romans II*, 162.

142. Barth, *Romans II*, 96.

us to find peace in the promise that God is at work through our theological reflection, as it emerges out of Scripture, despite our confused tendency to see contradiction where there is none.[143] On this point, Barth distinguishes between the knowledge that puffs up (1 Cor. 8:2), which finds confidence in our own intellectual powers, and the knowledge that is grounded in the love of God, with which we can trust in theological matters that we cannot fully understand and, as such, appear contradictory.[144] So, even in the later Barth, we find that the concept of paradox continues to occupy the same place as it did in his earlier theology.

Yet we should not overstate the continuing role that the term "paradox" played in Barth's later work. There, we do find a departure from his earlier emphasis on paradox. Right from the outset of the *Church Dogmatics*, when acknowledging that "the Word of God alone fulfils the concept of paradox in full rigour," Barth is quick to recommend that theologians use the term "paradox" sparingly, "now that it has played its part, and also caused all manner of confusion."[145] And, as we shall see, there are several points in the *Church Dogmatics* where Barth is critical of a paradoxical account of the God-world relation, making this criticism more than a mere anomaly.

Barth's Departure from the Concept of Paradox

What was it that concerned Barth about his earlier use of the concept of paradox? Barth was particularly nervous about how it led him to be misunderstood as calling into question the positive nature of revelation, and there was one person in particular who led Barth to see how this language was open to confusion: Erik Peterson.

In his booklet "What is Theology?," Peterson stresses that if "revelation is paradox, then there is also no theology," and, if this is the case, "there is also no revelation."[146] While Barth had frustrations with Peterson's reading of him, he still took his words seriously. In response to Peterson, he writes:

143. In relation to this point, Barth qualifies that paradoxes concerning the nature of God do not involve "a logical tension between two concepts which we can perceive and control as such." He then adds on the same page that such paradoxes appear as a result of "the combination of His grace and our lost condition, not the paradox of the combination of two for us logically irreconcilable concepts" (Barth, *Church Dogmatics* II/1, 287).

144. Barth, *Church Dogmatics* II/1, 42; see also 198–99, 287.

145. Barth, *Church Dogmatics* I/1, 166.

146. Erik Peterson, "What is Theology?," in *Theological Tractates*, ed. and trans. Michael Hollerich (Stanford: Stanford University Press, 2011), 5.

The revelation of which theology speaks is not dialectical, is not paradox. That hardly needs to be said. But when theology begins, when we humans think, speak, and write . . . on the basis of revelation then there is dialectic. Then there is a stating of essentially incomplete ideas and propositions among which every answer is also again a question. All such statements reach out beyond themselves towards the fulfilment of the inexpressible reality of the divine speaking.[147]

This passage is an early indication of Barth's growing reluctance to use the concept of paradox in reference to God's self-revelation.[148] Peterson's concern that Barth's use of paradox clashed with a positive account of revelation would become Barth's primary concern with a Kierkegaardian use of paradox—even if such a danger was not a strict entailment.[149]

Barth also had other concerns with his earlier use of paradox. He worried that the language of paradox could be misinterpreted to suggest an ontological contradiction between God and humanity rather than a merely apparent contradiction, which emerges due to the inadequacy of human knowledge.[150] At one point, for example, when reflecting on the hypostatic union, Barth stresses that Jesus Christ "is without tension, dialectic, paradox, or contradiction."[151] He then adds: "If the opposite seems true to us, it is our mistaken thinking, not God, which is to blame."[152] Barth is here denying that there is anything inherently paradoxical (whatever that means) about God's unity with humanity in Christ.[153] Instead, as Christophe Chalamet rightly notes, he sought "to speak

147. Barth, "Church and Theology," 299–300.
148. The extent to which it was Peterson who prompted this turn in Barth's choice of language is open for debate. See Christophe Chalamet, *Dialectical Theologians*, 181; Eberhard Jüngel, "Von der Dialektik zur Analogie: Die Schule Kierkegaards und der Einspruch Petersons," in *Barth-Studien* (Zurich: Benziger Verlag, 1982; repr., Gütersloh: Gütersloher Verlagshaus Gerd Mohn, 1982), 178. However, there is no question that he had some impact.
149. It is relevant to note that several criticisms Peterson makes of Kierkegaard would come to be echoed in Barth's later writings—particularly the connection Peterson draws between Kierkegaard's paradoxical account of revelation and the "melancholic" pietism reflected in Kierkegaard's personal life (Peterson, "What is Theology?," 6). See Barth, *Church Dogmatics* I/1, 20; II/2, 308; III/2, 21; IV/1, 150; IV/1, 741; IV/3, 498. Against this reading of him, Kierkegaard writes, "Never, even in the remotest way, have I made as if I wished to develop a pietistic severity, which is a thing alien to my soul and nature" (*Point of View*, 17).
150. Jüngel, for example, is concerned that Kierkegaard's paradoxical Christology suggests that, by becoming human, God "contradicts himself" ("Von der Dialektik," 178).
151. Barth, *Church Dogmatics* II/1, 663.
152. Barth, *Church Dogmatics* II/1, 663.
153. As we indicate in the brackets, it is hard to know what it means to describe something as paradoxical in itself. As we have been referring to paradox in this chapter, a paradox is an

primarily about the good news of Jesus, who is 'Yes' and 'Amen' and not an ambiguous yes and no."[154] This is not because Barth was becoming increasingly confident in the human capacity to conceptualize God's union with humanity. Rather, it was because he believed we should proclaim the ontological truth of this union in a way that overshadows our epistemological confusion and inadequacy. Consequently, rather than stressing the paradox of this union (from our epistemological perspective), he prioritizes the noncontradictory ontological nature of this union (from God's perspective).[155] As Michael Beintker and Cornelis van der Kooi argue,[156] there is a sense in which Barth seeks to approach the task of theology from God's perspective (*Schauen von Gott aus*)—not that Barth thinks we can actually assume God's perspective.[157] In taking this approach, Barth followed a certain reading of 2 Corinthians 5:16, according to which we should no longer think about anyone from a worldly point of view. Instead, "we begin with the insight that God is 'not a God of confusion, but of peace' (1 Cor. 14:33)."[158] It was with this shift in emphasis that Barth would begin to move away from his Kierkegaardian emphases in *Romans II*. Whereas the early Barth's negative theology sometimes risked overshadowing his positive theology, his later theology would do precisely the opposite. Accordingly, in a passage worth quoting at length, Barth writes:

---

apparent contradiction rather than an essential or logical contradiction. As such, something is only paradoxical if it appears contradictory to someone who seeks to understand that thing, albeit with an understanding that cannot (yet) see beyond the appearance of contradiction.

154. Chalamet, *Dialectical Theologians*, 280.

155. Carl Hughes makes a similar point in his comparison of Kierkegaard and Barth when he writes: "Barth understands theology as proclaiming divine truth from the vantage point of eschatological victory. Kierkegaard, in contrast, insists that theology always emerges from the theological half-light of finitude." Carl S. Hughes, "Renewing Theology—Kierkegaard beyond Barth," in *Kierkegaard and the Staging of Desire: Rhetoric and Performance in a Theology of Eros* (New York: Fordham University Press, 2014), 197.

156. Michael Beintker, *Die Dialektik in der "dialektischen Theologie" Karl Barths: Studien zur Entwicklung der Barthschen Theologie und zur Vorgeschichte der "Kirchlichen Dogmatik"* (Munich: Chr. Kaiser Verlag, 1987), 190; Cornelis van der Kooi, "Karl Barths zweiter Römerbrief und seine Wirkungen," in *Karl Barth in Deutschland (1921–1935): Aufbruch—Klärung—Widerstand*, ed. Michael Beintker, Christian Link, and Michael Trowitzsch (Zurich: TVZ, 2005), 66; Cornelis van der Kooi, *Anfängliche Theologie: Der Denkweg des jungen Karl Barth (1909 bis 1927)* (Munich: Chr. Kaiser Verlag, 1987).

157. Barth does come close to suggesting this when he declares that "our possibility of knowing God's Word is the possibility of a clear and certain knowledge, not equal but at least similar to the clarity and certainty with which God knows Himself in His Word" (*Church Dogmatics* I/1, 243). Here, he is making the point that revelation draws us into an epistemic participation in the triune life of God, in Christ and by the power of the Holy Spirit.

158. Barth, *Church Dogmatics* IV/1, 186.

[If God] has revealed Himself in Jesus Christ as the God who does this [becomes a creature, man, flesh], it is not for us to be wiser than He and to say that it is in contradiction with the divine essence. . . . It is not for us to speak of a contradiction and rift in the being of God, but to learn to correct our notions of the being of God, to reconstitute them in the light of the fact that He does this. We may believe that God can and must only be absolute in contrast to all that is relative, exalted in contrast to all that is lowly, active in contrast to all suffering, inviolable in contrast to all temptation, transcendent in contrast to all immanence, and therefore divine in contrast to everything human, in short that He can and must be only the "Wholly Other." But such beliefs are shown to be quite untenable, and corrupt and pagan, by the fact that God does in fact be and do this in Jesus Christ. . . . Our ideas of His nature must be guided by this, and not *vice versa*.[159]

Any appearance of contradiction, he writes,

is because our concept of God is too narrow, too arbitrary, too human—far too human. Who God is and what it is to be divine is something we have to learn where God has revealed Himself and His nature, the essence of the divine. And if He has revealed Himself in Jesus Christ as the God who does this, it is not for us to be wiser than He and to say that it is in contradiction with the divine essence. We have to be ready to be taught by Him that we have been too small and perverted in our thinking about Him within the framework of a false idea of God.[160]

For Barth, we should not allow our "small and perverted" understanding of God's unity with the world to shape our theological judgment. When all that Christ accomplishes is fully appreciated, there is no need to describe the unity between God and creation as paradoxical. For those who participate in the body of Christ, he writes, "the fact that 'Jesus lives, and I in Him,' this unknown attribute, the new subject of human life may be very hard to see or demonstrate in ourselves, yet it is no mere paradox, but the most obvious and natural truth."[161] The witness of Christ, therefore, calls us to give priority to the one who tells us the way things are, over against our confused minds that keep seeing contradiction where there is none. When we think we see contradiction,

---

159. Barth, *Church Dogmatics* IV/1, 186.
160. Barth, *Church Dogmatics* IV/1, 186.
161. Barth, *Church Dogmatics* II/2, 761.

for Barth, the actual paradox is not God's relationship with creation. Rather, the paradox (or "terrible paradox," as he calls it) is

> that man is the being whose attitude not only does not correspond to the attitude of God as revealed and active in Jesus Christ, but contradicts it and actively opposes it, that the two attitudes move in a diametrically opposite direction, and that no other view seems to be possible than that they never seem to coincide.[162]

More precisely, he writes, "the contradiction of the being of the man in sin . . . [is where] we see the real paradox and absurdity of his being."[163]

In brief, what concerned Barth was that an emphasis on paradox granted too much precedence to the confusion of human minds; it prioritized human epistemology (and the paradox it perceives) over the (noncontradictory) ontological reality of God-with-us that we are given to proclaim.[164] For Barth, when a person shares in the faith of the church, they participate in a new community that is constituted as and united by the one body of Christ, in and through whom there is unity between divine action and human action. Accordingly, there can be true correspondence within the church between God's action and human action, between God's Word and human words. In response to the revelation of this unity, humans are called to proclaim that God is wholly with us (undistracted by any appearance of contradiction) and live our lives with a confident trust and hope in this reality.

With this development in his thinking, there is an extent to which Barth further diverges from Kierkegaard. In this, he gives even less precedence to the way things immediately appear to us—according to our inadequate knowledge—in favor of proclaiming the way things are according to the revelation of the transcendent God (despite any appearance to the contrary). While Kierkegaard's theology is often shaped by his critique of the priority that Hegelian theology gave to the immediate world, there was an extent to which Kierkegaard ended up allowing the immediate appearance of paradox to play a major role in his thinking. He ended up responding to the (overly) positive theology that the Hegelians were advancing on the basis of immediacy by endorsing a somewhat negative theology, also on the basis of immediacy. This point, however, should not be overstated. Within the limits of what Kierkegaard thinks is

---

162. Barth, *Church Dogmatics* IV/1, 418.
163. Barth, *Church Dogmatics* IV/1, 502.
164. See Barth, *Church Dogmatics* III/2, 66.

possible for human theologizing, he was often a very positive theologian and had an enormous amount to say about what it means to exist before God. Yet against figures such as Martensen, as we discussed in chapter 1, Kierkegaard devoted himself to emphasizing the limits of human reason when it comes to talking about God's self-revelation—limits that Barth would continue to acknowledge, albeit while giving them less attention. Whereas Barth would turn to emphasize the positive message for a theology of proclamation, Kierkegaard would stress the paradox of faith and the limits of our knowledge of God's self-revelation.

Concluding Comments on Paradox

When taking an approach to Christian theology that prioritizes the revelation of Jesus Christ, it is easy to see the appeal of Barth's reasoning, and there is much that Kierkegaard could have learned from Barth's approach. Yet, as we have seen in our discussion of Hegelian theology in Denmark, there are also risks with treating the revelation of God's unity with creation (when considered apart from Jesus Christ) as the standpoint from which to speak and reason about God's relationship to the world. It can generate a false confidence in our ability to mediate God to the world by way of our own intellectual, aesthetic, and moral reasoning.

Now it is true that if theologians are to have anything to say, they need to talk positively about how the gospel is expressed through human concepts, practices, and images. However, if these human expressions are left to take on a life of their own—giving us too much freedom to (re)define Christianity in our own categories—then their primary role is easily forgotten. That is, it becomes all too easy to forget that, first and foremost, these expressions should serve to point beyond themselves to God and God's self-revelation in Jesus Christ. The primary task of Christian theology, therefore, is not to gain a knowledge of the Christian tradition but to help us to know God by aiding us in loving and following the person of Christ. All other theological knowledge is, at its best, derivative from knowledge gained in this way. This is precisely what Kierkegaard's and Barth's uses of paradox sought to affirm. For both of them, we are called to confess the union of Christ without trying to make sense of this union for ourselves. This is because the God-human unity of the person of Christ gives coherence to our faith that we can never give to him. The asymmetry of this relationship is precisely why paradox emerges when we try to conceptualize God's relationship to creation in our own terms. So, to try to understand the unity between God and humanity by mediating between our own concepts of God and humanity will always involve an overly reductive move—one that will be misrepresentative and contradictory. We are warned against such reduction by the fact that our best attempts to speak truthfully about God's union with creation conjure up paradox.

While Barth became less attached to the language of paradox, he remained as clear as anyone about the risks of overestimating human thought. And while the later Barth may have avoided the language of paradox by continuing to maintain the givenness and nongivenness of revelation, much of his earlier theology of paradox continues to find a place in the *Church Dogmatics* (albeit with very little reference to the word "paradox").[165] It is also present in his other later writings, not least those that correlate with his concerns about the political dangers of natural theology. Additionally, while the later Barth fervently resists any suggestion that God's revelation is ontologically contradictory (which, as we have seen, the language of paradox can be taken to suggest), he continued to insist that we recognize a proper distinction and, indeed, tension between our human conceptions of God and who God really is—between our formulations of the truth and the Truth itself, as witnessed to by Scripture. For Barth, as George Hunsinger points out,

> the field of tension . . . was something to be respected and worked within, not something to be explained away or resolved for the sake of achieving a tidier conceptual outcome. No possible tidier outcome could be achieved except at the expense of hermeneutical adequacy. Any gains in technical consistency at the conceptual or doctrinal level could be had only by suffering unacceptable losses of coherence with the subject matter of scripture.[166]

Yet, instead of acknowledging this "field of tension" by utilizing the concept of paradox, the later Barth replaces the concept of paradox with the concept of mystery—thereby evading any suggestion of ontological contradiction. As Henning Schröer affirms, "the concept of mystery now [in the *Church Dogmatics*] plays the central role that the concept of paradox used to hold."[167] In

165. For example, Barth would continue to view Christ as one in whom "[God] unveils Himself as the One He is by veiling Himself in a form which He Himself is not" (Barth, *Church Dogmatics* II/1, 52).

166. George Hunsinger, *How to Read Karl Barth: The Shape of His Theology* (New York: Oxford University Press, 1991), 107.

167. Henning Schröer, *Die Denkform der Paradoxalität als theologisches Problem: Eine Untersuchung zu Kierkegaard und der neueren Theologie als Beitrag zur theologischen Logik* (Göttingen: Vandenhoeck & Ruprecht, 1960), 150.

other words—and to make a point that almost goes without saying—the later Barth continues to believe that human theologies are both limited and compromised in their attempts to witness to the nongiven source of revelation: the transcendent God.

Given the similarities between their theologies of revelation, it is difficult to know precisely why Barth departed from a Kierkegaardian use of paradox to the extent that he did. This is why our account of Barth's relationship to the concept of paradox has needed such nuance. Yet, as we have suggested, this departure was motivated by Barth's later commitment to give primacy to the reality of God's unity with creation, as revealed in Jesus Christ, which is the basis for the church's proclamation. To draw attention to paradox, for Barth, is to draw attention away from the reality of Christ and toward the inadequacy of human knowledge. As Aaron Edwards writes, Barth became "unwilling to allow the antithetical nature of theological polarities to undermine or overrule proclamation."[168]

However, it is not straightforwardly a commitment to a theology of proclamation that led Barth to depart from Kierkegaard. Such a commitment is also foundational to Kierkegaard's use of paradox. The fact that Kierkegaard dedicated himself to proclaiming theological truths that are paradoxical is precisely because of his commitment to the authority of revelation, which, for him, confronts us with paradox. Where the later Barth differs from Kierkegaard, however, is in his reluctance to allow our shortsighted perception of revelation's contradictoriness to have an overly determinative impact on what we proclaim in our theology. Barth sought to foreground the revelation of Jesus Christ as a reality that is essentially noncontradictory, despite how it might appear given our immanent categories of understanding. We can find a few points where Kierkegaard is also willing to take such an approach.[169] However, due to his resistance to Hegelianism, he is far more nervous about attempts to speak dogmatically from the perspective of God's self-revelation

---

168. Edwards, "Paradox of Dialectic," 284–85.

169. For example, when talking about the apparent absurdity of God's relationship to creation, Kierkegaard notes that "when the believer has faith, the absurd is not the absurd—faith transforms it" (Kierkegaard, *Journals and Papers*, 1:10). See also Kierkegaard, *Kierkegaard's Journals and Notebooks*, 7:20–21; and Kierkegaard, *Journals and Papers*, 6:6598. This is because faith enables a person's mind to correspond to God—albeit in a humble manner that is appropriate to the creature. This takes place when one walks hand in hand with one's "savior under the eye of the heavenly Father, that is under the eye of a truly loving father, strengthened by the testimony of the spirit" (Kierkegaard, *Kierkegaard's Journals and Notebooks*, 7:471; see also 6:105). Kierkegaard, like Barth, understands that revelation is not inherently contradictory. In this respect, we think there are ways in which Kierkegaard would agree with Barth that "'paradox' cannot be our final word in relation to Jesus Christ" (Barth, *Church Dogmatics* IV/2, 348).

in Jesus Christ. Instead, he is more preoccupied with our inability to escape the inadequacy of our finite and sinful perspective.

In suggesting that Kierkegaard's resistance to Hegelianism was a factor in distinguishing him from Barth, we are not suggesting that Barth was heading in a Hegelian direction. Barth steers clear of this trajectory by maintaining many elements of his earlier theology—albeit making them less of a center-piece. On the one hand, he affirms that the revelation of Christ "finds a way of becoming the content of our experience and our thought; it gives itself to be apprehended by our contemplation and our categories."[170] On the other hand, he insists (in a passage that could have come from *Romans II*) that Christ mediates himself to us from

> beyond the range of what we regard as possible for our contemplation and perception, beyond the confines of our experience and our thought. It comes to us as a *Novum* which, when it becomes an object for us, we cannot incor-porate in the series of our other objects, cannot compare with them, cannot deduce from their context, cannot regard as analogous with them. It comes to us as a datum with no point of connexion with any other previous datum. . . . We can understand the possibility of it solely from the side of its object, i.e., we can regard it not as ours, but as one coming to us, imparted to us, gifted to us. In this bit of knowing we are not the masters but the mastered.[171]

Barth remains adamant that Christ does not reveal any inherent or general unity between God and creation; the mediation of Christ is always wholly new to us.

While Barth did not follow Hegel, a case can be made that there were ways in which elements of Barth's theology echo Hegel, albeit within Barth's very different framework. That such resonances exist is not controversial; indeed, Barth is well known for admitting, in 1953, that he had "a certain weakness for Hegel and [was] always fond of doing a bit of 'Hegeling.'"[172] But a little more requires to be said if we are to be quite clear about the relationship between Barth and Hegel.

As mentioned in chapter 1, the image of God's reconciliation with human-ity, as revealed in Jesus Christ, is foundational to Hegel's philosophy of religion. As Barth interprets Hegel, this gives Hegel the self-confidence to deny any

---

170. Barth, *Church Dogmatics* I/2, 172.

171. Barth, *Church Dogmatics* I/2, 172.

172. This comment was recorded from a conversation that Barth had with pastors and lay persons from the Pfalz in September 1953. Cited in Eberhard Busch, *Karl Barth: His Life from Letters and Autobiographical Texts*, trans. John Bowden (Philadelphia: Fortress, 1976), 387.

opposition between God and reason—to affirm that there is nothing offensive or foolish about the idea that God is revealed in the history of this world.[173] For Hegel, Jesus Christ testifies that God's union with creation is foundational to how we reason about the nature of reality. In this respect, Barth saw in Hegel a strong affirmation of history as the stage of God's revelation. What elevates Hegel above Kant, in Barth's mind, is Hegel's understanding that the truth is not simply grounded in a priori reason but also in our a posteriori understanding of history, through which God reveals Godself. On this point, it is not only Hegel and Barth who are on the same page; there are ways in which Kierkegaard is also in basic agreement.

Where Kierkegaard and Barth depart sharply from Hegel, however, is in their shared belief that God's revelation communicates something wholly new to us—something we have no inherent ability to recollect or comprehend. For Hegel, revelation does not involve an event of free divine action, an event in which God freely communicates divine truth(s) that we are unable to access in and of ourselves. Rather, according to Hegel, God is bound up with the history of this world and with the thinking that goes on within it. Without going into more detail than we have already, Barth affirms that this "is the basis of Hegel's confidence in God."[174] Because our relationship with God is inherent within us, we can, without hesitation, proclaim the coherence of God's relationship with creation. No special divine activity is needed to restore creation to right relationship with God.[175]

Let us conclude by returning to a question that was raised in the beginning of this section. Does a paradoxical account of God's relationship to creation call into question the goodness of creation and suggest a cosmic dualism between God and creation? It does not, at least not in the work of Kierkegaard and the early or, indeed, the late Barth. It simply serves to recognize that, as creatures, we do not have it within ourselves to develop a unified understanding of our relationship to the transcendent God by reflecting on our own created existence. We are called instead to entrust such unity to the one in, through, and for whom all things are created, the only one in whom all things hold (cohere) together (Col. 1:16-17). It is in Christ alone that we are given to find peace by knowing the one true source of unity in our interpretation of reality and, indeed, in our self-understanding.

173. Karl Barth, *Protestant Theology in the Nineteenth Century: Its Background & History* (London: SCM, 1972), 394.

174. Barth, *Protestant Theology*, 420.

175. Barth, *Protestant Theology*, 420.

CONCLUSION

This chapter has offered a close analysis of Kierkegaard's influence on Barth, while also considering some of the ways in which Barth would move beyond this influence. As we have seen, Kierkegaard played a critical role in helping Barth to resist those approaches that sought to capture God within the immanent frame of human perception and understanding. In so doing, he had a major impact on how Barth came to think about the relationship that the eternal God establishes with human beings in time. For both thinkers, this relationship finds its fulfillment in the person of Christ who unites divinity and humanity, albeit without creating any confusion between God and the world. For Barth, this unity and distinction was highlighted by commandeering such Kierkegaardian concepts as the moment, the divine incognito, and the paradox. However, as Barth's thinking evolved, he became increasingly concerned that Kierkegaard's theology was overly preoccupied with the limits of human understanding. The risk with such a preoccupation, in Barth's view, was that it can generate a state of anxiety that can undermine the human confidence to proclaim the gospel message of God with and for us. While some of Barth's concerns about Kierkegaard were not entirely unfounded, there is no question that Barth failed to appreciate the profoundly positive side to Kierkegaard's theology that shines through many of his writings. This is especially evident in the way in which Kierkegaard's emphasis on human limitations led him to affirm, like Barth, the centrality of Jesus Christ for the theological task. It is certainly the case that there are differences between the Christocentric emphases in Kierkegaard's and Barth's theologies. For example, Kierkegaard's Christocentric theology led him to focus more sharply on *who we must become* by following Christ, whereas Barth's Christocentric theology was more devoted to proclaiming *who we are in Christ*. Yet these emphases were by no means mutually exclusive in the thinking of either of them. Kierkegaard was entirely clear that it is only by participating in an intimate relationship with Christ that we come to discover who God created us to be. And Barth was adamant about the inseparability of theology and ethics, which, for him, means that we cannot discover who we are in Christ without experiencing a radical calling to take up our crosses and follow Christ into a life that stands against the sinful ways of this world.

Engaging Secular Society

Kierkegaard and Barth were committed to repudiating any tendency to fuse or, indeed, confuse the divine address with the dictates of culture. This has been a key theme in the preceding chapters. We now turn to consider the implications of their approach for the church's engagement in the public square. This will lead us to ask about the theological, methodological, and epistemological grounds on which such engagement stands to take place. To this end, we shall compare two alternative approaches. The first approach assumes that all persons—theists, agnostics, and atheists alike—possess an innate awareness of the moral law or, at least, the ability to distill its essential shape. This common (immanent) awareness or capacity is regarded, moreover, as foundational to engagement with secular society. Such an approach reflects the "nature-grace model" which has played a key role both in apologetics and also in the interpretation of salvation within the Western theological tradition. The second approach is the one we shall associate with the "Kierkegaard-Barth trajectory" (KBT). This regards the redemptive kinship that God has established in Jesus Christ as foundational to engagement with secular society. Our analysis will be based on an extended discussion of the debate between Barth and Emil Brunner on natural theology. This will serve to highlight the fundamental challenges of grounding engagement with secular society in our immanent capacities and suppositions and will set the scene for considering the alternative approach that stems from the KBT.

It is important to emphasize from the outset that reference to the KBT is not intended to play down, let alone ignore, the significant differences between Kierkegaard and Barth's respective projects. What it seeks to recognize, however, is that they shared several critical theological insights and convictions. Consequently, at key nodal points they made parallel moves in their interpretation of the Christian faith and what it involves. We shall assess the significance of these with an eye to their ongoing, contemporary significance.

So what exactly was this common ground, and what do we mean by the KBT? First, as indicated above, it denotes their shared recognition that the eternal God has established kinship or fellowship with humanity in time, in a unique event of divine self-disclosure. Second, it refers to their shared recognition that this event has decisive significance for how we should think and talk about God and all things in relation to God. Thus, the KBT challenges the Socratic supposition that the criteria that bear on our assessment of the Christian message and our engagement with society at large are immanent within each of us. It rejects, therefore, any approach that regards the primary theological function of the narratives concerning Jesus Christ as being to *illustrate* or to *remind* persons of religious, philosophical, and ethical assumptions that are inherent within them, that is, that already belong to their epistemic base. Third, the KBT interprets the kinship established by God as a *reconciling* event through which alienated creatures are redeemed from erroneous interpretations of God and the world and, a fortiori, the relationship between the two. To endorse the KBT, therefore, is to recognize that it is in and through the recognition of that kinship that persons are set free for a properly functioning interpretation of the world and our social, ethical, and political obligations—an interpretation that is in accordance with God's purposes.

BARTH'S DEBATE WITH BRUNNER

Reference to the Barth-Brunner debate denotes two publications: Emil Brunner's *Nature and Grace* and Karl Barth's response to it, entitled, quite simply, *No!* (*Nein!*). Both were published in 1934, which was a critical year in European history. The previous year had seen Adolf Hitler appointed chancellor, which was followed by a series of anti-Semitic and other measures which defined the direction in which Germany was headed: the Reichstag Fire Decree, the establishment of the Dachau concentration camp (to incarcerate political opponents), the anti-Jewish boycott, the introduction of limits on the number of Jewish students in public schools, the burning throughout Germany of books deemed "un-German," and the Editors' Law, which forbade non-"Aryans" from working in journalism. In addition, the Law for the Prevention of Offspring with Hereditary Diseases was passed mandating the forced sterilization of certain individuals with physical and mental disabilities. On August 30 the Fifth Nazi Party Congress commenced in Nuremberg inspiring Leni Riefenstahl to make a film entitled, ominously, *The Victory of Faith* (*Der Sieg des Glaubens*). In April 1934, all Germany's police forces outside Prussia came under the command of *Reichsleiter* Heinrich Himmler of the SS, and in August, following the death of von Hindenburg, Hitler declared himself Führer of Germany, becoming head of state as well as chancellor. Less than three weeks later, Hitler's assumption of the powers of head of state was ratified in a referendum with 89.9 percent voter support. The result of this was that he became, in effect, the absolute dictator of Germany. In September, the Nazi Party Congress was held in Nuremberg, attended by seven hundred thousand Nazi Party supporters. Leni Riefenstahl made a further film of the rally, entitled *Triumph of the Will* (*Triumph des Willens*).

It was also in 1934 that the Confessional Synod of the German Evangelical Church (*Deutsche Evangelische Kirche*) met in Barmen to produce the Barmen Declaration. Less than two weeks later, however, a group of leading theologians and church representatives wrote and signed the *Ansbacher Ratschlag* (Ansbach Counsel) in repudiation of the Barmen Declaration and attempting to provide theological vindication of support for the Führer.

It would be hard to overstate, therefore, the political challenges that faced the church at that time. How we assess the church's response and the way in which it was framed has continuing significance, moreover, for how we interpret the theological task. An analysis of the debate between Barth and Brunner stands to shed a great deal of light on how the theologian engages with society more generally. The context of that debate highlights in particular the impropriety of making claims about God's purposes for society that fail to address the following fundamentally important questions. On what basis is a theologian entitled to make sociopolitical statements? Does their justification lie with "public reason," and, if so, what does this involve?[1] Does the entitlement to make such claims lie within divine revelation, and, if so,

---

1. It is pertinent to consider the theological justification of morality in comparison with secular attempts to justify morality. Bernard Gert, for example, provides an account that generates ten moral rules by appealing to "public reason." Although there is some overlap between the Ten Commandments and this secular equivalent delivered by public reason, there are significant differences. Gert defines morality quite simply as "a public system that applies to all rational persons"—a definition which he spells out in terms of what all impartial rational persons could advocate in public. Justifying a moral system, he writes, "requires providing a public system that incorporates the moral rules and that applies to all rational persons and then showing that all impartial rational persons would advocate adopting that system as the public system that all rational persons should use as a guide for their conduct and a basis for their judgements." Gert, *Morality: A New Justification of the Moral Rules* (New York: Oxford University Press, 1988), 6, 131. (The ten moral rules are outlined in chaps. 6 and 7.)

Gert's analysis leaves one asking how referencing the divine will would alter the moral rules as he defines them and where the grounds of these changes would lie. This, in turn, raises the question why reference to the content of the divine will accessed by "natural theological means" is essential. If it is indeed necessary, would it introduce changes that differ from the deliverances of "public reason," as Gert understands them, and if so, then on what grounds—and are these grounds that are *not* accessible to all rational persons?

where is the content of that revelation to be found—is it located in the Bible, in the person of Jesus Christ, or in the deliverances of a "general" revelation or "natural theology"? Does the ability to recognize God's revelation presuppose that there are corresponding and innate capacities for discernment within the human being such as a sense of the divine (*sensus divinitatis*), a moral sense (*sensus moralis*), or a more general "innate sense of God's purposes"? Does the capacity to provide theological endorsement of social policies require the concept of a general revelation to which all persons have epistemic access? And if one refuses to endorse general revelation, how is it possible to support ethical or sociopolitical claims without endorsing special pleading from a religiously exclusive base? Is it not the case that to make sociopolitical claims on the basis of theological grounds to which epistemic access is restricted or "exclusive" establishes a dangerous precedent? That is, does it open the door to the justification of problematic sectarian claims made on the basis of special or exclusive access to the divine will?

The reference to a "dangerous precedent" points to a host of strategic questions that emerge. If Barth, however, were asked whether strategic considerations should shape our engagement with revelation, his reply would be a decisive "No!" Moreover, any explanation he provided for this response would itself be a posteriori in nature. Questions bearing on (1) epistemic access to God's will, (2) the veracity of the claims that stem from revelation, and (3) the propriety and significance of the resulting affirmations require to be addressed post factum, that is, in the light of God's self-disclosure and not in advance of it. That means that, for Barth, the answers do not lie in ideological, philosophical, epistemological, or pragmatic considerations that are assessed prior to dogmatic considerations.

Barth's antipathy to attempts to explain, independently of revelation, whether revelation is veridical and whether God's revelation might be generally accessible is based on what he believes God's self-disclosure itself requires us to affirm. As we saw in chapter 4, for Barth, attempts to explain how knowledge of God is possible must unfold from reflection (*Nachdenken*) on how God is *actually* known. To fail to recognize this is to assume that the historical does not possess decisive significance for the knowledge of God and God's purposes. The issues here are not simply theoretically or dogmatically important; they are critically important for how we understand the *grounding* of the sociopolitical claims that theologians make—and thus for theology's engagement in the public square.

Famously, these questions came to a head in the confrontation between Barth and Brunner over the place and validity of natural theology—one of the most high-profile but also most important theological debates of the twentieth century. Brunner was a friend of Barth and a fellow Swiss academic theologian. Both, moreover, were Reformed, strongly incarnational and Trinitarian in their convictions, and both were associated with the so-called dialectical school of theology. Brunner's approach, however, was shaped by strategic apologetic concerns—most specifically, how we interpret the "point of connection" (*Anknüpfungspunkt*) between God and humanity, a question that Brunner considered to be critically important for how we approach the whole engagement between Christians and the secular world.

For Brunner, the key to answering this question lay in the fact that human beings are created in the image of God. In his view, this doctrine was vital to understanding the connection both between God and humanity, and between church and society. Central to his interpretation was his distinction between the formal image and the material image.[2] The *formal* image constitutes our *humanum*[3] and distinguishes the human from the rest of creation. As such, it denotes the essential form of human subjectivity, namely, the universal human capacity for language, rationality, and moral responsibility.[4] But although the formal image remains in place despite human sin, the *material* image, he argues, has been eviscerated as a result of the fall. "The human being is a sinner through and through and there is nothing in him or her which is not defiled by sin."[5] Despite, however, the devastating impact of sin on the material image, "formally the *imago* is not in the least touched—whether sinful or not, man is a subject and is responsible."[6] For Brunner, therefore, no one (not least Barth)

2. Emil Brunner, *Nature and Grace: A Contribution to the Discussion with Karl Barth*, in *Natural Theology: Comprising "Nature and Grace" by Professor Dr. Emil Brunner and the Reply "No!" by Dr. Karl Barth*, trans. Peter Fraenkel (London: Centenary Press, 1946; repr. Eugene, OR: Wipf & Stock, 2002), 23.

3. Brunner, *Nature and Grace*, 24.

4. Gary Dorrien comments that Barth interpreted Brunner's concept of *Wortmachtigkeit* ("capacity for words") as *Offenbarungsmächtigkeit* ("capacity for revelation"). "Since 'Word' functioned as a near synonym for 'revelation' in both of their theologies, Barth undoubtedly reasoned that the two compound terms had identical meanings." Dorrien adds that despite the fact that, in the ensuing discussion between Barth and Brunner, Brunner clarified what he did and did not mean by the term, "he did not answer Barth's main argument." As Dorrien rightly explains, Barth held that "Brunner usually spoke of this attribute as the capacity to *recognise* revelation," meaning that "'something very material' [had] been added to what was supposedly a purely formal category." Dorrien, *The Barthian Revolt in Modern Theology: Theology without Weapons* (Louisville: Westminster John Knox, 2000), 124 (emphasis original).

5. Brunner, *Nature and Grace*, 24.

6. Brunner, *Nature and Grace*, 24.

is in a position to deny that "even sinful and unredeemed man is capable of doing and thinking what is reasonable."[7] Nor is it possible to deny that human beings have a "conscience," that is, a sense of responsibility that includes a knowledge of God's will:

> Only because human beings somehow know the will of God are they able to sin. A being which knew nothing of the law of God would be unable to sin—as we see in the case of animals. Responsibility of the sinner and knowledge of the will of God as the source of law (the knowledge also being derived from the law) are one and the same thing.[8]

Consequently, for Brunner, the "legal knowledge of God" is constitutive of humanity in its natural state.[9] Not only does this underpin personal morality, but it also sustains order in society and grounds social policy. That this legal knowledge of God's will is inherent in our natures means, further, that there exists common ground between Christians and non-Christians. This is necessary if there is to be shared, rational consensus on ethical and legislative matters.

Creation and the Self-Communication of God

So what is the basis of this innate access to God's legal will and moral purpose? Adopting a long-standing emphasis inherent in the Aristotelian-Thomist tradition, Brunner argues that "wherever God does anything, he leaves the imprint of his nature upon what he does. Therefore, the creation of the world is at the same time a revelation, a self-communication of God."[10] Here Brunner echoes Aquinas's maxim *omne agens agit sibi simile*: "every agent acts in a manner similar to itself," or "every agent produces its like."[11] Cited over 220 times in the Thomistic corpus, this is employed, as Daniel Pierson argues, in the service of Aquinas's natural theology, natural philosophy, and the philosophy of knowledge.[12] For Brunner, this likeness between God's effects and

7. Brunner, *Nature and Grace*, 22.
8. Brunner, *Nature and Grace*, 25.
9. Brunner, *Nature and Grace*, 25.
10. Brunner, *Nature and Grace*, 25.
11. Thomas Aquinas, *On Creation* [*Quaestiones Disputatae de Potentia Dei*, Q. 3], trans. S. C. Selner-Wright (Washington, DC: Catholic University of America Press, 2011), 5.
12. Daniel Pierson, "Thomas Aquinas on the Principle *Omne Agens Agit Sibi Simile*" (PhD diss., Catholic University of America, 2015), chap. 1.

God serves the task of natural theology by supporting general revelation. This likeness or imprint means that the act of creation is "a self-communication of God." Brunner's reasoning appears to run along the following lines:

> Major Premise: Everything that an agent causes is similar to that agent.
> Minor Premise: God belongs to the class of agents.
> Conclusion: Everything that God causes is similar to Godself.

When this axiom is applied to God's relationship to human creatures, it generates a further categorical syllogism:

> Major Premise: If God creates human agents, they will be similar to God with respect to their defining attributes.
> First Minor Premise: God is, by definition, intrinsically rational, good, and morally responsible.
> Second Minor Premise: God created human agents.
> Conclusion: There is a similarity between human subjects and God in respect of their defining attributes (as these include the capacity for reason and moral responsibility).

As the first syllogism highlights, these arguments rely on subsuming God within the genus (class) of agents with the consequence that the "likeness" believed to hold universally between all effects and the agents who caused them is applied to the relation between God's effects and God. It is on the basis of arguing from the "likeness" between those created in God's image and their Creator that Brunner draws natural-theological conclusions.

The arguments here are influential not only for Brunner but for the Christian tradition more widely, and it is worth considering their implications. What immediately strikes one is that it appears to be in tension with two fundamentally important principles that are stressed, ironically, by Thomas Aquinas. First, Aquinas insists that God does not belong to any class (*Deus non est in genere*). For this reason, he insists that theological predication should never assume the analogy of "two to a third" (where one subsumes two entities under a third class concept) or "many to one" (where one subsumes many entities under a class concept). Both treat God as if God were on the same level as other finite entities and lower than some other reality, namely, the relevant "idea" or genus (class concept).[13] Second, and related to this, it is in tension

---

13. Cf. Battista Mondin, *The Principle of Analogy in Protestant and Catholic Theology* (The Hague: Martinus Nijhoff, 1963). Mondin seeks to recover what he perceives to be Suarez's more cogent interpretation of Aquinas's account of analogy over the much more influential

with Aquinas's principle that the use of human language to speak of God
must invariably recognize the ontological priority of God and the posterior
or derivative nature of the contingent order. Consequently, if we are to use the
principle of analogy to apply the same attribute (for example, "goodness") to
God and also to Mother Teresa, the predication of the term must recognize
that its *primary* application is to God, who is *perfectly* good, but predicated
analogically and thus in a derivative and subsequent way (*per posterius*) of
Mother Teresa, thus acknowledging that her goodness derives from God. So,
for Aquinas, the direction of interpretation in analogical predication should
always be from God to humanity—if goodness is to be predicated of Mother
Teresa, the analogy should recognize the property is predicated properly of
God alone and only derivatively of Mother Teresa. Consequently, any account
of the grounding of theological statements must reflect, for Aquinas, the order
of being—human speech about God and the contingent order must reflect the
fundamental ontological priority of God over all that is contingent upon God
and thus ontologically derivative. All analogical predication must consequently
function *per prius et posterius* (acknowledging priority and posteriority).

Now the response might be given that the principle "God does not belong
to a class" is not one Brunner needs to worry about given the challenges involved in adhering to it. Platonists, for example, would point out that to attribute any property to God is to suggest that God belongs to the class of objects
to which that property applies but in a manner that does not denigrate God.[14]
The more challenging issue for Brunner's utilization of the likeness principle,
however, would appear to stem from Aquinas's second dictum, namely, that
every account of theological language must recognize the *priority* of God and
the *posteriority* of the contingent. As we have seen, this is a concern that is
reiterated in Barth. The major thrust of Barth's methodological concerns is
precisely that we safeguard this *directionality* in theological thought and pred-

---

account provided by Cajetan (34–53). In the light of this discussion, he goes on to provide
his own reclassification of Aquinas's account. See also Alan J. Torrance, *Persons in Communion: An Essay on Trinitarian Description and Human Participation, with Special Reference
to Volume One of Karl Barth's "Church Dogmatics"* (Edinburgh: T&T Clark, 1996), 135–42.

14. To say that "God is one," for example, is to suggest that God belongs to the class
of objects that are "one." This appears to be in tension with Aquinas's ruling because it
appears to subsume God within the genus of objects that possess the attribute "oneness."
Plato's advocacy of the *sumplokē tōn eidōn*, that is, of the eternal intercommunion or inter-
weaving of the forms, is testimony to his willingness to countenance an ultimate plurality
of universals—something that Aquinas, like Parmenides before him, appears unable to
accommodate. See A. K. Rogers, "Plato's Theory of Forms," *The Philosophical Review* 44,
no. 6 (Nov. 1935): 515–33.

ication. In this respect, Barth's insistence that we "let God be God" and not treat the terms we use of God as if they apply preeminently to the contingent appears consistent with Aquinas's commitments although Aquinas's approach is, arguably, driven by his Aristotelian metaphysic. Both affirm that all our theological statements must take radically seriously the priority of God and the posteriority of the contingent.

That said, Brunner's conclusion that "the creation of the world is at the same time a revelation" raises further questions. First, does this approach take sufficiently seriously God's freedom in creation? Is God free to choose *not* to leave pointers to God's nature and purposes that can be read off the created order by contingent beings? Is Brunner suggesting that, like all other agents (for example, rabbits, pigeons, or slugs, who are unable not to leave traces of their presence in a vegetable patch), God cannot but leave "traces" of God's nature and purposes in all that God creates—with the result that creation is *inevitably* inherently revelatory of God? Moreover, how are these supposed likenesses within creation to be interpreted given, not least, the apparent ambiguities in nature—the suffering and, indeed, cruelty that seem to be part of its warp and weft? Might it not be argued that certain key features of nature point at best to an "ananthropocentric purposivism," to use Tim Mulgan's expression. He argues that there is evidence of purpose in the cosmos but that there are no grounds to assume that *Homo sapiens* located in this infinitesimally small corner of the universe features in this overarching purposiveness.[15] Or might it not be argued that horrendous moral evil points to a god who, as Jim Garrison argues, is dipolar in nature and thus very different from the God of traditional expressions of Christian faith?[16] This is certainly not to suggest that Brunner's

15. Tim Mulgan, *Purpose in the Universe: The Moral and Metaphysical Case for Ananthropocentric Purposivism* (Oxford: Oxford University Press, 2015).

16. In *The Darkness of God: Theology after Hiroshima* (London: SCM, 1982), Jim Garrison argues that moral evils of the kind exemplified by Hiroshima require us to interpret God as "dipolar." "We must be willing at long last to give up our monopolar prejudice concerning God's being merely an expression of the *Summum Bonum* and capable of only love and mercy and 'goodness.' We must recognise that God is the God of all possibilities; that is to say, God utilizes all the instruments of power, including the blinding of those involved in the divine plan, including the deliberate and intentional committing of what we experience as intrinsic evil, and including the ruthless disregard for any claims of covenantal morality" (5). Thinking in this way is required if we are to recognize that "evil is objectively and intrinsically real." Taking seriously the "profound and startling assertion of Isaiah 45:7 that God creates evil," he states, "I hold that evil, like good, comes from God and is therefore an objectively real phenomenon" (22). In his specific way, Garrison is developing Charles Hartshorne's dipolar conception of God, which is outlined in Hartshorne, "The Dipolar

arguments are demonstrably false. It is simply to point out that if it is thought that the "likeness" principle serves to deliver a doctrine of "general revelation" that opens the door to a Christian understanding of God, then there are critically important questions that require to be addressed.

John Calvin and the Kierkegaard-Barth Trajectory

Brunner's adoption of the "likeness principle" together with his emphasis on the formal capacities that define the image were foundational to his belief that creation can provide a basic knowledge of God as Creator. This led him to affirm a *duplex cognitio*, that is, a twofold knowledge of God—the knowledge of God as Creator and the (salvific) knowledge of God as Redeemer. Brunner believed, moreover, that this reflected the views of John Calvin. After the Second World War, there was a perception that Barth's concerns about the sociopolitical dangers of natural theology had been vindicated by the course of events. This served to heighten interest in the nature and implications of Calvin's own views. For example, T. H. L. Parker endorsed Barth's interpretation of Calvin and, against Edward Dowey's defense of Brunner,[17] argued that Calvin believed God *freely* places traces or pointers to God's glory and goodness in the created order but these were to be interpreted by faith and in the light of the frame of reference that faith provides.[18] Calvin also believed, Parker continued,

---

Conception of Deity," *Review of Metaphysics* 21, no. 2 (1967): 282–84. Hartshorne goes on to add, "Neither [Alfred North] Whitehead nor I has ever suggested that God's existence 'guarantees the triumph of good over evil'" (285).

17. In *The Knowledge of God in Calvin's Theology* (New York: Columbia University Press, 1952; repr., Grand Rapids: Eerdmans, 1994), Edward Dowey argues that Calvin taught a *duplex cognitio*, that is, a twofold knowledge of God from creation and redemption. Suffice it to say, the debate over whether it was Parker or Dowey who interpreted Calvin correctly continues; see, for example, Stephen Grabill's appropriation of Richard Müller's arguments on this matter in *Rediscovering the Natural Law in Reformed Theological Ethics* (Grand Rapids: Eerdmans, 2006), 25–29. It is hard not to conclude that the recent eagerness to vindicate Dowey is driven by the desire to recover a strong doctrine of natural law within Reformed circles, in opposition to Karl Barth's suspicion of attempts to relativize God's self-disclosure in Jesus Christ. It is surprising that Calvinists appear so slow to recognize the extent to which the misappropriation of natural theology in Calvinist contexts such as South Africa resulted in the betrayal of affirmations that lie at the heart of the gospel.

18. "On each of his works he has inscribed unmistakable marks of his Glory" (John Calvin, *Institutio* 1.5.1). These signs or testimonies to God's craftsmanship (*opificium Dei*) constitute a mirror or an image or an "effigy of God" (*effigies Dei*) in which the glory of God can be seen. T. H. L. Parker, *Calvin's Doctrine of the Knowledge of God* (Edinburgh: Oliver and Boyd, 1952; repr., Eugene, OR: Wipf & Stock, 2015), 18. It is important to note

that God had placed within us an innate awareness of God (*notitia Dei*) or sense of the divine (*sensus divinitatis* or *sensus deitatis*), which Calvin describes as the seed of religion (*semen religionis*), but that this awareness of God did not constitute knowledge of God (*cognitio Dei*).[19] Given this God-given sense of the divine and given the testimonies to God's glory that God has freely placed in the created order, Parker argues that, in Calvin's view, we would have been able to interpret these signs and pointers aright "if Adam had remained whole/upright" (*si integer stetisset Adam*).[20] However, he did not, and so, as Calvin argues in his *Commentary on Colossians*, human beings are "altogether, and in the whole of their mental system, *alienated from God*, that no one may imagine, after the manner of philosophers, that the alienation is merely in a particular part."[21] In sum, what separates Barth's interpretation of Calvin from Brunner's is the all-important "if" in "if Adam had remained whole." This denotes a condition that, for Calvin, is not met due to the alienation of the human mind.[22] In parallel with Kierkegaard's argument in *Philosophical Fragments*, without the condition for being in relation to the truth, we remain in a state of error and are unable, therefore, to process aright the nature and purposes of God and all things in relation to God. As Calvin understands it, we are unable to interpret veridically that semiotic system of pointers to God's glory and purposes that is evident in the created order to the reconciled mind, that is, to the eyes of faith. Referring back to the Barth-Brunner debate, Parker argues, "This conditional phrase, as Karl Barth points out in *Nein!*, is definitive of the early chapters (and indeed, of the first book) of the *Institutio*."[23]

For Calvin, the innate awareness of the divine that God has given us does not lead us into faithful recognition of God's goodness and glory, despite the

---

here that God *did this freely*; that is, the signs are not a necessary consequence of God's creative agency. Parker writes, "*Effigies Dei* is equivalent to the *certae notae gloriae suae* which God has inscribed on His workmanship. Thus, in creating the universe God made it a representation of Himself. This he did freely; He need not have left these marks upon His work. For they are not like the adventitious evidences that enable us to 'date' or 'place' a poem or a concerto" (18–19).

19. Parker, *Calvin's Doctrine*, 8.

20. Parker, *Calvin's Doctrine*, 27.

21. John Calvin, *Commentaries on the Epistles of Paul the Apostle to the Philippians, Colossians, and Thessalonians*, trans. John Pringle (Edinburgh: Calvin Translation Society, 1851), 158.

22. Cf. Calvin's use of the expression *alienati mente* in his *Praelectiones in librum prophetiarum Jeremiae et lamentationes* (1576), 289. This is the Vulgate's translation of the Greek phrase *echthroi tē dianoia*, which appears in the accusative (*echthrous*) in Col. 1:21.

23. Parker, *Calvin's Doctrine*, 27.

pointers to his glory that God has freely placed in creation. Due to the alienation of our minds, the innate seed of religion leads us into idolatry, superstition, and false theological construction.[24] It is not out of a purist concern for
Calvin scholarship that Barth objects so strongly to Brunner's perceived misappropriation of Calvin. It is that Brunner failed to appreciate the importance
of a point that Calvin grasped with profound clarity. As a result, Brunner was
unable to recognize the extent to which natural theology threatened to deliver
the church in Europe into the most dangerous forms of idolatry. It is this that
provides the background to Barth's response here:

> When he speaks of the God who can be and is "somehow" known through
> creation, Brunner does unfortunately mean the one true God, the triune
> creator of heaven and earth, who justifies us through Christ and sanctifies
> us through the Holy Spirit. It is he who is *de facto* known by all human
> beings without Christ, without the Holy Spirit, though knowledge of him is
> distorted and dimmed and darkened by sin, though he is "misrepresented"
> and "turned into idols."[25]

Barth saw Brunner as turning this "idolatry" into "a somewhat imperfect preparatory stage of the service of the true God," with the result that the critically
important connection between revelation and the reconciliation of our minds
is dangerously eroded.[26] In stark contrast to this, in Barth's view, to know God
is to be reconciled into a true relationship with God through the personal
reality of God's address. This involves nothing less than the redemption of our
categories of interpretation. That is, God is known in a reconciling act. Consequently, "How can Brunner maintain that a real knowledge of the true God,
however imperfect it may be (and what knowledge of God is not imperfect)
does not bring salvation?"[27] The rhetorical question that follows goes to the
nub of our present discussion:

> Has not Brunner added to humanity's "capacity for revelation," to what we
> have been assured is purely "formal," something very material: humanity's

---

24. Parker, *Calvin's Doctrine*, 31, 38.
25. Karl Barth, *No! Answer to Emil Brunner*, in *Natural Theology: Comprising "Nature
and Grace" by Professor Dr. Emil Brunner and the Reply "No!" by Dr. Karl Barth*, trans. Peter
Fraenkel (London: Centenary Press, 1946; repr., Eugene, OR: Wipf & Stock, 2002), 81–82.
26. Barth, *No!*, 82.
27. Barth, *No!*, 82.

practically proved ability to know God, imperfectly it may be, but nevertheless really and therefore not without relevance to salvation?[28]

For Barth, writing in 1934, the suggestion that political collaboration with non-believers in the interpretation of the state's purpose and function should be grounded in unreconciled, natural (idolatrous) interpretations of God's purposes was anathema. Here, but not only here, Calvin would have endorsed the KBT.

The Struggle for the Soul of the Reformed Tradition

So why did Calvin scholarship become such a significant issue during this debate and then again after the war? Why the eagerness to determine the precise nature of Calvin's arguments? How significant is it if T. H. L. Parker was correct in thinking that Barth rather than Brunner was the more faithful representative of Calvin's thought?[29] And, conversely, if Edward Dowey was right in thinking that Brunner was the more accurate interpreter of Calvin, how important is that?

As we have indicated, Barth's disagreement with Brunner on the interpretation of Calvin was not an exercise in the niceties of Calvin scholarship. Barth saw himself as fighting for the soul of the Reformed tradition, having seen the Lutheran and Roman Catholic Churches become profoundly compromised by their commitments to forms of general revelation and natural theology. The debate, after all, was taking place between the two leading Swiss representatives of Reformed theology in a strongly Christian country with a large Reformed population. In 1934, the political implications of these theological issues could hardly have been writ larger. The "German Christians" were now an influential force supporting Nazism and affirming God's endorsement of the superiority of the German *Volk* and the so-called Aryan race—a natural-theological argument that the Nazis saw as confirmed by Germany's uniquely rich culture and traditions. During the 1930s, this led to the emergence of Positive Christianity (*Positives Christentum*), which was a movement advocating a new understanding of revelation and a reformulation of Christian thought that made the history and culture of the Aryan race central to the theological task. Consequently, it sought to adapt the Bible to fit its Aryan (and hence anti-Semitic and anti-Gypsy) theological agenda by appealing to the conclusions of its natural-theological reflections. This led it to reject the Christian Old

28. Barth, *No!*, 82.
29. Parker, *Calvin's Doctrine*, 29–30, 37.

Testament and those elements of the Bible that were "Jewish."[30] Accordingly, it claimed Aryanhood for Jesus and set out to establish a new unitary form of postdenominational "Christian religion." In 1937, Hans Kerrl, the Nazi Minister for Church Affairs, explained that Positive Christianity was dependent neither on the Apostles' Creed nor on faith in Jesus Christ: "God's will reveals itself in German blood." When someone objected that Christianity was about "faith in Christ as the Son of God," his response was that any such suggestion made him "laugh": "True Christianity is represented by the party, and the German people are now called by the party and especially by the Führer to a real Christianity. . . . The Führer is the herald of a new revelation."[31]

In short, Barth would not countenance any appeal to an intrinsic "likeness" between God and what were perceived to be the highest and purest expressions of humanity as a means of interpreting God's purposes. The attempt to go behind the back of Jesus Christ and appeal to the likeness between God and what they perceived to be the supreme expression of humanity—to appeal to an intrinsic likeness between God's will and the German will—was pure idolatry. It was antichrist. Barth had no desire to see the Reformed Church validate, on the basis of confused dogmatic considerations and an erroneous reading of Calvin, the kind of idolatrous natural theology in which the various church denominations in Germany were becoming complicit.

Whereas the German Christian movement was most closely associated with the Protestant church, the theological issues here penetrated beyond the Lutheran or Protestant tradition—something that explains, in part, the intensity of Barth's concerns about the Catholic endorsement of natural theology and the analogy of being (*analogia entis*).[32] Given the serious theological failings within the Catholic and Protestant traditions in Germany, Austria, and

---

30. On antiziganism, see, for example, Henry Friedlander's discussion of Eva Justin's work on the Romani in *The Origins of Nazi Genocide: From Euthanasia to the Final Solution* (Chapel Hill: University of North Carolina Press, 1997), 250, 294.

31. William L. Shirer, *The Rise and Fall of the Third Reich: A History of Nazi Germany* (London: Secker and Warburg, 1960), 211–12.

32. Robert Ericksen argues, "The explicit endorsement of 'positive Christianity' in the Nazi Party Program actually had Catholic roots, with nationalistic, disaffected Catholics in Munich, Catholics suspicious of ultramontanism and political Catholicism, helping give it shape." Ericksen, *Complicity in the Holocaust: Churches and Universities in Nazi Germany* (New York: Cambridge University Press, 2012), 50n44. In *Catholicism and the Roots of Nazism: Religious Identity and National Socialism* (Oxford: Oxford University Press, 2010), Derek Hastings comments, "Although the central principle of Positive Christianity remained explicitly interconfessional, it was envisioned and implemented first and foremost within a local context that was overwhelmingly Catholic" (14). Chaps. 2–3 contain his argument in full.

then Italy, it was imperative, in Barth's view, that the potential of the Christian church to foster idolatry be challenged with theological clarity and consistency. When he saw the waters being muddied in Switzerland, his reaction was a passionate "*Nein!*" The kind of natural theology that Brunner was endorsing undermined the commitment to interpret the gospel in its own light and thereby threatened to distort its message. It also risked being used by those who embraced Positive Christianity and the like. That is because it undercut and relativized central themes in the gospel that challenged and opposed the developments integral to it. In short, Barth wanted the Reformed Church to be a faithful, theological witness to the affirmations that defined the gospel, and he certainly did not want it to acquiesce in, let alone become complicit in, the moral evils being witnessed in the heart of Europe.

So where, for Barth, did the fundamental theological problem lie? In the final analysis, it concerned, quite simply, the *directionality* of their theological thinking—the church risked succumbing to a "false movement of thought" whereby theologians operated *from* prior cultural, religious, philosophical, and political commitments *to* the interpretation of divine revelation, rather than the other way around. This concern is explicit in his reference to Emanuel Hirsch in the preface to *No!* Hirsch was dean of the theology faculty in Göttingen University during the Third Reich and the intellectual leader of the "German Christians" who sought to promote the central ideological principles at the heart of Nazism, most notably its commitment to anti-Semitism, racism, and the *Führerprinzip*.[33] Barth writes:

> I can hardly say a clear "No" to Hirsch and his associates, but close my eyes in the case of Brunner, the Calvinist, the Swiss "dialectic theologian." For it seems to me that at the decisive point he takes part in *the false movement of thought by which the Church to-day is threatened.* . . . My polemic against Brunner is more acute than that against Hirsch because his position is more

33. The *Führerprinzip* refers to the "leader principle" that affirmed the Führer had complete and total authority in government, and that his word was above all written law. In a speech broadcast at Cologne on June 25, 1934, Rudolf Hess proudly affirmed the position of the Führer as "above all criticism": "He was always right and will always be right. The National Socialism of us all is anchored in the uncritical loyalty, in the devotion to the Fuehrer that does not ask for the wherefore in the individual case. . . . We believe that the Fuehrer is fulfilling a divine mission to German Destiny! This belief is beyond challenge." Hess, *Speeches* [*Reden*], Munich, 1928, 25; radio speech at Cologne, 25 June, 1934, at Yale Law School, *The Avalon Project: Documents in Law, History and Diplomacy*, accessed August 8, 2021, https://avalon.law.yale.edu/imt/2373-ps.asp.

akin to mine, because I believe him to be in possession of more truth, *i.e.*
to be closer to the Scriptures. . . . For that very reason he seems to me just
now to be much more dangerous than a man like Hirsch.[34]

It is sometimes thought that Barth's rejection of Brunner's natural theology
was indicative of a refusal to take humanity and culture seriously in the interpretation of revelation. But even Brunner acknowledges that "Barth himself
does not deny that . . . humanity and culture are not simply to be dismissed
as of no value from the point of view of revelation."[35] It would be utter folly
to deny Barth's love of culture.[36] Indeed, he was happy to acknowledge that
God can speak to us through culture—a Mozart flute concerto, for example.[37] Moreover, no one can deny the central place he gives to anthropology
in his dogmatics. So where precisely does the problem lie? To reiterate, the
disagreement with Brunner boils down to a concern with the *directionality*
of our thinking about God. Brunner's insistence that "formally the image is
not in the least touched"[38] by sin opened the door to the Socratic and what
amounts, therefore, to an inverse metanoia—a reversal of the "turnabout"
that characterizes Christian conversion. When the historical ceases to possess
decisive significance for knowledge of God, then it is difficult to see how this
does not open the door to the Christian message's being relativized, rejected,
or transformed into something of a radically different kind (*metabasis eis allo
genos*), allowing divine endorsement to be given to agendas that are in error,
that are fundamentally opposed to the reconciling and transforming pressure
of interpretation that stems from confessing Jesus Christ as Lord. It is for
precisely this reason that Barth used the term "antichrist" of approaches to
natural theology. They reversed the direction of interpretation that stemmed
from attaching decisive significance to the historical.[39]

34. Barth, *No!*, 67–68 (emphasis added).

35. Brunner, *Nature and Grace*, 22–23.

36. This is clear from his near infatuation with the music of Mozart and his extended
correspondence with the Catholic author and playwright Carl Zuckmayer; see Zuckmayer,
A Late Friendship: The Letters of Karl Barth and Carl Zuckmayer, trans. Geoffrey W. Bromiley (Grand Rapids: Eerdmans, 1972).

37. Karl Barth, *Church Dogmatics*, ed. Geoffrey W. Bromiley and Thomas F. Torrance,
trans. Geoffrey W. Bromiley (Edinburgh: T&T Clark, 1956–1975), I/1, 55.

38. Brunner, *Nature and Grace*, 24.

39. "I regard the *analogia entis* as the invention of Antichrist" (Barth, *Church Dogmatics* I/1, xiii). This (in)famous statement reflects Barth's perception of any and every attempt
to invert and therefore to operate against (*anti*) the direction of thought that reflects God's
self-disclosure in Jesus Christ. Barth was no less opposed to that inversion when he found

From the perspective of the KBT (a trajectory which, as we have suggested, not only Athanasius but also Calvin would endorse), the nonnegotiable "either-or" does not concern a particular doctrine per se. It concerns the *direction of the pressure of interpretation* in our thinking about God. If it is the case that "the eternal itself has entered into time and wants to establish kinship there," what justification could there possibly be for our choosing to find the "point of connection" between God and humanity elsewhere and then electing to think from that basis?[40] The response that Brunner's likeness maxim and its Thomistic progenitor invite from Barth is the same one he gave to the Augustinian suggestion that traces of God's being could be found in nature. Are we not being presented here with an "ancient Trojan horse" that has been "unsuspectingly allowed entry into the theological Ilium, and in whose belly . . . we can hear a threatening clank?"[41]

The "threatening clank" that Barth discerned in the use of natural theology in the run-up to and during the First World War and then again in the 1930s cannot be dismissed as an extended one-off. Recent history provides further graphic illustrations of a "false movement of thought" within the Reformed tradition leading it to support nationalist and racist forms of civil religion. The Dutch Reformed Church appealed to the deliverances of their formal capacities to provide divine ratification for apartheid in South Africa. The same was no less apparent in the endorsement of segregation in the largely Reformed American Deep South during the period up to the late 1960s. Those contexts provide further examples of how natural predilections relating to race, gender roles, and sexual orientation, which at various points were deeply engrained within our culture, received apparent divine ratification through the appeal to "natural law" and the "orders of creation," the discernment of which was provided by the "light of natural reason." It is to the light of natural reason, perceived as one of the God-given *formal* capacities that define the image, to which we shall turn now. The rationale for our pursuing this question is because of the potential that the appeal to the light of natural reason has to reverse the direction of thought in theology so that the interpretation of God's purposes becomes defined by prior assumptions and convictions integral to our (alienated) worldviews.

---

it in the theology of a fellow Swiss Reformed theologian than in the endorsement of the *analogia entis* within Roman Catholic thought.

40. Søren Kierkegaard, *Concluding Unscientific Postscript to Philosophical Fragments*, ed. and trans. Howard V. Hong and Edna H. Hong (Princeton: Princeton University Press, 1992), 1:573.

41. Barth, *Church Dogmatics* I/1, 335-36.

"The Light of Natural Reason," the "Moral Sense," and the Diversity of Epistemic Bases

Aquinas famously argued that there is a "twofold mode of truth in what we profess about God."[42] Some truths exceed the ability of human reason, such as the truth that God is triune. Others, however, such as the truth that God exists and that God is one, have been "proved demonstratively by the philosophers, guided by the light of natural reason."[43] For Aquinas, the scope of this "natural light" is not restricted to demonstrations of God's existence or divine simplicity.[44] It is also a means by which we are able to make moral judgments. The reason for this is that it constitutes an "imprint" within the human creature of God's light. In Aquinas's words, "the light of natural reason, whereby we discern what is good and what is evil, which is the function of the natural law, is nothing else than an imprint on us of the Divine light."[45] As Maria Elton explains:

> This light of natural reason, by which we discern what is good and what is bad, is not a discursive light but the light of reason judging by connaturality on the basis of the human inclinations of our nature. It is the impression of the divine light in us, which transmits the practical truth to us. The divine reason impresses its light on human reason by the channel of natural inclinations.[46]

This same notion also played a key role in the thought of René Descartes. In his early essay *Rules for the Direction of the Mind*, he argues that a person should focus on "increasing the natural light of reason . . . in order that in every particular situation of his life his intellect may show his will what choice to make."[47] Descartes was not unaware, however, that this light could be darkened, and

---

42. Thomas Aquinas, *Summa Contra Gentiles, Book One: God*, trans. Anton C. Pegis (Notre Dame: University of Notre Dame Press, 1975), chap. 3, para. 2.

43. Aquinas, *Summa Contra Gentiles, Book One*, chap. 3, para. 2.

44. Maria Elton notes that this concerns a natural capacity and not, therefore, a "supernatural light." Elton, "Moral Sense and Natural Reason," *Review of Metaphysics* 62, no. 1 (2008): 108n149.

45. Thomas Aquinas, *Summa Theologiae* (London: Eyre & Spottiswoode; New York: McGraw-Hill, 1964–80), I-II, q. 91, a. 2.

46. Elton, "Moral Sense and Natural Reason," 108.

47. René Descartes, *Rules for the Direction of the Mind* [Regulae ad Directionem Ingenii], 1701, repr. in *Philosophical Essays and Correspondence*, ed. Roger Ariew (Indianapolis: Hackett, 2000), 3.

in his *Discourse on Method*, he comments, "I learned not to believe anything too firmly of which I had been persuaded only by example and custom; and thus I little by little freed myself from many errors that can darken our natural light and render us less able to listen to reason."[48] John Locke was also aware of the shortcomings of this concept and skeptical about how effectively it could serve either religious or ethical claims.[49] Despite that, its legacy is evident throughout the seventeenth and eighteenth centuries in both the secular and religious contexts—not least in ethics, where the light of natural reason came to be conceived as a natural instinct that could discern what was right and wrong. This was evident in the shift in the interpretation of the related concept of *synderesis*, which originally denoted the natural capacity of practical reason to recognize intuitively the first principles of human action. As Robert Greene argues, Aquinas's synderesis was reinterpreted as a natural "instinct": "During the bilingual early modern period an increasingly secularized, internalized, and reified *instinctus naturae*, together with its abbreviated vernacular cognate, 'instinct,' came to serve as a substitute and synonym for the obsolescent synderesis." He continues, "Edward Herbert's attention to *instinctus naturae* in his *De Veritate* (1624), Sir Matthew Hale's speculations about the place of rational instinct in the natural law, and Francis Hutcheson's theory of a moral sense all exemplify this semantic legacy."[50] Maria Elton supports Robert Greene's view that in the modern period the "moral sense" came to serve as a substitute and synonym for Aquinas's concept of synderesis. There are, she argues, "analogies between the relevant moral faculties of Hutchesonian 'moral sense' and Thomistic 'natural reason.'"[51]

It is not simply in the more secular academic contexts of Scotland and England that we witness a conflation of these faculties. This is evident, for example, in the preaching of the New England Puritan Cotton Mather—one of

48. René Descartes, *Discourse on the Method for Conducting One's Reason Well and for Seeking the Truth in the Sciences* [Discours de la Méthode pour bien conduire sa raison, et chercher la vérité dans les sciences], 1637, repr. in *Philosophical Essays and Correspondence*, ed. Roger Ariew (Indianapolis: Hackett, 2000), 50.

49. "Natural religion, in its full extent, was nowhere that I know taken care of by the force of natural reason. It should seem, by the little that has hitherto been done in it, that it is too hard a task for unassisted reason to establish morality in all its parts, upon its true foundation, with a clear and convincing light." John Locke, *The Works of John Locke* (London: Thomas Tegg, 1823), 7:139. For a discussion of this, see John C. Ford, "Natural Law and the Pursuit of Happiness," *Notre Dame Law Review* 26, no. 3 (1951): 443.

50. Robert A. Greene, "Instinct of Nature: Natural Law, Synderesis, and the Moral Sense," *Journal of the History of Ideas* 58, no. 2 (1997): 173–74.

51. Elton, "Moral Sense and Natural Reason," 82–83.

the most important intellectuals of the period. Mather appears to conflate the moral sense with the workings of reason, which he refers to as the "candle of the Lord." It is not simply that "the light of this precious and wonderful candle" enables us to assess what is true and false mathematically; it also enables us to judge "as often, and as clearly, what is morally good, or what is morally evil; what is right and what is wrong, in morality too."[52]

In short, the notions of moral sense, conscience, human instinct, and the light of natural reason had a profoundly significant place in Reformed and Puritan thought in New England. Jennifer Herdt comments that, within the context of commonsense philosophy in America, "intuitionist accounts of conscience and providentialist accounts of human instincts were easily conflated, with both placed in service of the nation-building project."[53]

For the towering intellectual of the era, Jonathan Edwards, the "moral sense" also played an important role.[54] Stephen Wilson argues that his belief that God has provided all human creatures with natural instincts including moral conscience was a manifestation of his metaphysics of emanation, in addition to the influence of John Calvin's epistemology.[55] Whatever the genetics of his thinking, at the heart of his treatise *The Nature of True Virtue* is a chapter entitled "Of Natural Conscience and the Moral Sense." There he argues that God has established a principle of natural conscience that "approve[s] and condemn[s] the same things that are approved and condemned by a spiritual sense or virtuous taste."[56] The same applies, moreover, to the "moral sense" which is also "natural to mankind."[57] All persons, therefore, possess a God-given "natural conscience" and "moral sense," and the deliverances of these do not require a "spiritual" or "virtuous" sense—the deliverances are natural and universal. In his subsequent chapter, "Of Particular Instincts of Nature," Edwards develops further his argument that we possess natural "dispositions

52. Cotton Mather, *A Man of Reason: A Brief Essay to Demonstrate That All Men Should Hearken to Reason* [. . .] (Boston: 1718), https://teachingamericanhistory.org/document/mather-a-man-of-reason-edwards-a-supernatural-light/.

53. Jennifer A. Herdt, "Calvin's Legacy for Contemporary Reformed Natural Law," *Scottish Journal of Theology* 67, no. 4 (2014): 419.

54. An exact contemporary of Hutcheson, who wrote extensively on the concept, Edwards is known to have read "at least portions" of Hutcheson's writing. Stephen A. Wilson, "Jonathan Edwards's Virtue: Diverse Sources, Multiple Meanings, and the Lessons of History for Ethics," *Journal of Religious Ethics* 31, no. 2 (2003), 204.

55. Wilson, "Jonathan Edwards's Virtue," 205.

56. Jonathan Edwards, *The Nature of True Virtue*, 1755 (Ann Arbor: University of Michigan Press, 1960), 70.

57. Edwards, *Nature of True Virtue*, 70.

and inclinations," which "depend on particular laws of nature." These result in "certain affections and actions towards particular objects; which laws seem to be established chiefly for the preservation of mankind, and their comfortably subsisting in the world. These dispositions may be called instincts."[58] In short, human beings possess, naturally, a God-given "natural conscience" and "moral sense" which, together with our God-given natural instincts, dispositions, and inclinations, facilitate our well-being and the proper function of society. Although Edwards appears to have placed a great deal of confidence in these capacities, his discussion is theologically reverent and carefully nuanced. The natural instincts he describes are fundamentally oriented, he argues, toward benevolence, pity, and sympathy. The question the endorsement of these God-given capacities and instincts raises, however, is whether this is not another example of ushering a Trojan horse into the heart of Christian thought, leading persons to identify the deliverances of their immanent moral suppositions and natural instincts as reflecting God's purposes for the world and society—and where these do not require to be metamorphosed or reschematized by the gospel message.[59] Related questions are also raised by his account of the "approbation of justice and desert," which arises, he argues, "from a sense of the beauty of natural agreement and proportion."[60] Although he appears to commend the love of an enemy as "an evidence of a high degree of benevolence of temper," his account of punishment raises further questions as to whether his interpretation of humanity and human nature is informed at a foundational level by the one who alone is the true Adam and image of the Father, or whether this is driven by the "natural" instincts and associated "insights" of fallen humanity.[61]

One of the stains on the church in New England during the seventeenth century was the Salem witchcraft trials of 1692 and, in particular, the contribution of Cotton Mather to that tragic series of events. Suffice it to say, it would be hard to identify his attitude, as expressed in his speeches and letters at the time, as indicative of the mind of Christ. Although Edwards was not involved in these trials, questions should be asked about whether the sensibilities in his 1741 sermon "Sinners in the Hands of an Angry God" were not influenced by an interpretation of justice informed by deliverances of the moral sense and

58. Edwards, *Nature of True Virtue*, 75.

59. It is worth bearing in mind that, as Herdt argues, Calvin was particularly cautious about relying on the perceived deliverances of conscience and the natural instincts. Herdt, "Calvin's Legacy," 414–35.

60. Edwards, *Nature of True Virtue*, 59.

61. Edwards, *Nature of True Virtue*, 58.

natural instinct rather than the insight into God's purposes delivered by the incarnation. A key premise of the sermon is, as George Marsden summarizes, "God is a just judge who must condemn sinners because they are in rebellion against God and hence hate what is truly good."[62]

So what is the purpose of this all-too-summary excursus into the history of ideas? It is quite simply to draw attention to how profoundly influential the concept of the light of natural reason and related conceptions of an innate *sensus moralis* and moral instincts have been on the interpretation of God's overarching social, legal, and political purposes; we also observe their influence, in secularized forms, on the wider culture in the West and its approach to sociopolitical ethics and the framing of society's laws.

There is one obvious problem that emerges here. To appeal to the deliverances of natural reason assumes an epistemic base, and the claimed deliverances require to be distinguished from the deliverances of the culture that will inevitably shape the suppositions of its participants. To think, however, that reason can deliver a unitary set of neutral conclusions through reference to its own independent resources is as naive as the assumption that the history of philosophical reasoning is to be understood as a unitary expression of the outworking of reason—a supposition evident in recent Catholic thought.[63]

In sharp contrast to this, the recognition that God's self-disclosure in history has decisive significance involves the recognition that God intends to be known in this way. To recognize, in addition, that this self-disclosure redeems alienated minds is to recognize that our epistemic bases require to be transformed. That is, the suppositions, affiliations, and convictions that shape our interpretation of God and all things in relation to God require to be reconciled so that we can track God's purposes truthfully.[64] The implications of this for

---

62. George M. Marsden, *Jonathan Edwards: A Life* (New Haven: Yale University Press, 2003), 221-22. In this magisterial monograph, Marsden rightly emphasizes Edwards's concern to stress God's long-suffering grace. "What is often missed," Marsden argues, is that "being in the hands of God means for the moment you are being kept from burning in hell as you deserve. God in his amazing long-suffering is still giving you a chance; his hand is keeping you from falling" (222).

63. Precisely this assumption can be found in John Paul II's papal encyclical *Fides et Ratio*. For a pertinent analysis of these issues, see Alvin Plantinga's review of *Fides et Ratio*: "Faith and Reason," *Books and Culture* 5, no. 4 (July/August 1999): 32-35.

64. In his discussion of Kierkegaard's understanding of the "redemption of reason," Murray A. Rae comments, "The canons of reason are not as neutral as is often supposed but are themselves the product of a particular world view." Rae, *Kierkegaard's Vision of the Incarnation: By Faith Transformed* (Oxford: Clarendon, 1997), 113.

the widespread, subliminal assumption that our innate and moral instincts track God's moral purposes both naturally and reliably should be clear.

Why is this so important? First, it is inherently important that our understanding should be aligned with God's. That answer is sufficient! At the same time, it is evident that God's actions exhibit a concern for human flourishing and well-being and, indeed, for human community. Consequently, it is appropriate to consider the extent to which God's self-disclosure bears on the diversity of our epistemic bases and the alienation of our minds, not least because of the consequences of that diversity and alienation. One illustration of these is that appeals to the light of natural reason have resulted in mutually incompatible conclusions—with tragic results. A specific example is the diametrically opposite "readings" of nature to which this has given rise in the United States, on the one hand, and in South Africa, on the other. Famously, the Declaration of Independence (1776) affirms, "We hold these Truths to be self-evident, that all Men are created equal, that they are endowed by their Creator with certain unalienable Rights, that among these are Life, Liberty, and the Pursuit of Happiness."[65] In short, the natural-theological ground that straddled Thomas Jefferson's deism and the Reformed theology of the early Puritan settlers fed the conviction that, by the light of reason, it could be discerned to be self-evident that "all men are created equal"—and that this reflects the will of God.

In South Africa, by contrast, the Reformed theology of the Dutch Calvinists upheld apartheid on the grounds that it was a self-evident fact of nature that all persons were *not* created equal—that no such unalienable rights were endowed by the Creator. The decision, by whites, that whites should have voting and citizenship rights, but that "coloreds" and "blacks" should not, was perceived to reflect God's ordered purposes for the different tribes, races, and cultures of South Africa—what Paul Althaus had referred to as "orders of creation." In sum, parallel commitments to general revelation and the deliverances of natural reason had emerged from within the Reformed theological stable and yielded diametrically opposite conclusions. What this meant in the context of South Africa was that in a country of approaching forty million people, the power and the privileges (as these included voting rights and fair access to education, medical provision, and police protection) lay in the hands of 13 percent of the population whose defining qualification was the pigmentation of their skin—and where that pigmentation was perceived to be indicative of God's particular, racially exclusive purposes.

---

65. The Declaration of Independence (United States, 1776).

Now, it may be objected here that the differences are overstated in that "all men," as it appeared in the Declaration, did not actually mean "all persons."[66] It is not our concern here to defend the Declaration or, indeed, the deist theology and practices of Thomas Jefferson. What is relevant is the potential of similar approaches to natural theology, and the appeal to natural reason and moral instincts, to find divine endorsement for opposing political trajectories. Whereas the vision of Thomas Jefferson and the early Puritan fathers provided sufficient groundwork to uphold the American Civil Rights Movement in the 1950s and 1960s, parallel assumptions with respect to the grounding of theological claims were used by Calvinist theologians in South Africa to endorse the racist policies of the apartheid regime during that same period.[67] Similar natural theological assumptions have been applied to the role and rights of slaves, of women, and also of those of same-sex orientation. Significantly, in all these instances, forms of natural theology have been adopted by *both* sides of the relevant debates.

Do the inconsistencies and ambiguities in the perceived deliverances of natural reason and the reading of God's purpose constitute a repudiation of its use? Clearly not! Other considerations aside, that would itself be an inappropriate appeal to natural reason. It is important, therefore, to be clear where the problem lies. It does not lie with reason in the sense of rational argumentation. Rather, it lies with unwarranted appeals to "reason." More specifically, the claim to have discerned God's purposes "by the light of natural reason" too often amounts to claims as to "what one considers to be appropriate, rational or cogent, given one's particular, epistemic base." When asked by a young Canadian student about the role of reason in his theology, Barth replied, "I use it!"[68] Explaining his approach further to a group of students, he commented:

> Concerning *reason*, I want to say this: I will have nothing to do with the distrust of reason. I have great trust in reason. I am not a rationalist, but I

---

66. Slavery did not come to an end in the United States of America until eighty-nine years after the Declaration was signed, women did not receive the right to vote until 1920, Native Americans did not receive their voting rights until the Snyder Act of 1924, and segregation continued in the South until 1964.

67. See Douglas Bax, *A Different Gospel: A Critique of the Theology behind Apartheid* (n.p.: Presbyterian Church of South Africa, 1979), and John de Gruchy, *The Church Struggle in South Africa* (Grand Rapids: Eerdmans, 1979), esp. 199–236, for outstanding analyses of the theological and historical issues relating to the emergence and justification of apartheid in South Africa.

68. Joseph Mangina, *Karl Barth: Theologian of Christian Witness* (Louisville: Westminster John Knox, 2004), 49.

believe that the [sic] reason is a good gift of God and that we must make full use of it in theology. This is our praise of God, who has given us this gift to distinguish that two and two equals four instead of five. That is my rationalism! Some people want to make reason the abstract judge of all—and that is unreasonable![69]

It is interesting to note that Barth largely refrained from using the sociopolitical abuse of natural theology and its appeal to reason to argue against it. Barth is clear—the force of God's "No!" lies solely in God's "Yes!" If we are to say "No!" to a certain directionality of thought, our *reason* for doing so lies ultimately not in a pragmatic analysis of the problems and ambiguities that stem from it but by considering the nature and implications of that "Yes!" that characterizes God's Word to humanity. "Even knowledge of the impossibility of knowledge of the Word of God outside its reality is possible only on the presupposition of this real knowledge."[70] For the Christian theologian, the assessment of natural theology is to be undertaken "subsequently, *a posteriori*, exegetically."[71]

Is it possible that God provides direct natural knowledge of God's purposes? Barth's answer is clear! "There is talk of revelation outside the Bible too, and we have no reason to say that this is absolutely impossible."[72] The paramount question for Barth, however, concerns our response to the "Yes!" held forth in the incarnation. What are the implications of that "Yes!" for how we view "additional" words that are claimed to have been spoken independently of the Word become flesh? For Barth, true to the implications of Kierkegaard's argumentation, God's "Yes!" in Jesus Christ is not simply one "Yes!" among many other yeses and noes. If it were, then the criteria for assessing claimed additional words from God would be our own immanent criteria.[73] For Barth,

69. Karl Barth, *Table Talk*, in *Scottish Journal of Theology Occasional Papers* 10, ed. John D. Godsey (Edinburgh: Oliver and Boyd, 1963), 31 (emphasis original).

70. Barth, *Church Dogmatics* I/1, 197. "Auch die Erkenntnis der Unmoglichkeit der Erkenntnis des Wortes Gottes ausserhalb ihrer Wirklichkeit ist nur moglich unter Voraussetzung dieser wirklichen Erkenntnis." Barth, *Die Kirchliche Dogmatik* (Munich: Chr. Kaiser Verlag, 1932; and thereafter Zurich: EVZ, 1938–1965), I/1, 206.

71. Barth, *Church Dogmatics* I/1, 57–58; Barth, *Kirchliche Dogmatik* I/1, 58.

72. Barth, *Church Dogmatics* I/1, 331.

73. The language of the "immanent rationality" of the natural orders was explicit in the theology of the German Christians. In *Bekenntnis, Blut und Boden: Drei theologische Vorträge* (*Confession, Blood and Soil: Three Theological Lectures*), Werner Elert explains how we know when to obey or disobey secular authorities. In addressing this he argues that "we remain formally within the perimeters of divine law, which points us to the natural orders with their immanent rationality." *Bekenntnis, Blut und Boden: Drei theologische Vorträge*

the "Yes!" we receive in the incarnation is God's once and for all (*ephapax*) Word. One implication of this is that it is recognized and thus affirmed in its own light and not with recourse to prior immanent criteria. The condition for the recognition of that "Yes!" is given in and with that same Word, through the creative presence of the Holy Spirit. It is in the light of this one Word, therefore, that we are to "test the spirits" of our culture as well as any reference to deliverances by the light of natural reason.[74]

The Moral Conscience as a Twofold Point of Connection

So what are the implications of this for appeals to the light of the moral conscience? For Brunner, as for much of our Western tradition, the moral conscience was conceived, in continuity with the origins of the word, as an innate "with-knowing" (*conscientia*), with God, of God's law—a with-knowing that belonged, moreover, to our *humanum*.[75] As such, it constituted a point of connection (*Anknüpfungspunkt*) between the human and the divine that was also integral to the recognition of sin: "Only because men somehow know the will of God are they able to sin. A being which knew nothing of the law of God would be unable to sin."[76] Clearly, if we are to speak of a natural with-knowing, with God, of God's moral and legal purposes, we are again affirming something that goes beyond a formal capacity. It suggests that humanity in general possesses a concrete, material knowledge of God's will.

Unsurprisingly, Barth does not consider it the task of the theologian to identify points of connection within human nature by means of which God is able to communicate with us. For him, "revelation itself creates of itself the necessary point of contact in man."[77] It is no more appropriate to prioritize moral experience or the moral conscience as a point of contact than any other anthropological locus. Whole theological systems, Barth comments, have been

---

(Leipzig: Dörffling & Franke, 1934), 33. Cited by Green, *Lutherans against Hitler: The Untold Story* (St. Louis: Concordia, 2007), 215.

74. "Real rejection of natural theology can come about only in the fear of God." Barth, *No!*, 76. A further discussion of these issues can be found in Torrance, *Persons in Communion*, 23–25.

75. As indicated earlier, "conscience" translates the Latin *cum scientia* and Greek *suneidēsis*, both of which are literally translated "with knowing."

76. Brunner, *Nature and Grace*, 25.

77. Barth, *Church Dogmatics* I/1, 29.

built on particular loci which theologians choose to privilege for reasons he considers ill-conceived.

> The reason why some prefer one anthropological locus and others another has always been that each has thought or hoped he could best justify a specific synthesis of the relations between divine and human determination, whether indeterministic, dialectical or deterministic, in terms of the one anthropological locus or the other.[78]

Consequently, Barth's approach to the moral conscience requires to be seen within the context of his wider approach to the experience of God. And that contrasts profoundly not only with Brunner but also with the approaches of Schleiermacher, Ritschl, and Otto. Each sought to locate the essence of the Christian experience of God in some particular subjective capacity. The prioritization of the relevant capacity or mode of experience then served to shape the subsequent exposition of the essence of the Christian faith as a whole and, thus, its various doctrines. The effect of this is to build the exposition of Christian thought on a particular, immanent, formal capacity selected and prioritized by the relevant theologian. The consequences of this for the direction of theological thinking and for how the exposition of the faith is shaped do not require to be spelled out.

Four features of Barth's alternative approach reflect his commitment to a "movement of thought" that operates in the opposite direction. First, the focus in his exposition of the human experience of God is not experience of a general and abstract reality but of the God who transforms us in and through God's free act of self-communication. Significantly, therefore, his analysis of experience takes place within his discussion of the Word of God and not the other way around.[79] Human beings experience God because God determines to address them in a *transformative* event. This event generates acquaintance with the reality of God's Word such that that truth becomes a "determination" of the subject. Consequently, Barth sees "experience" as denoting the "determination of the existence" of the person who has this knowing acquaintance with the Word of God.[80] Second, the experience of God takes the form of *acknowledgment*—acknowledgment of God's free and concrete self-communication.[81]

---

78. Barth, *Church Dogmatics* I/1, 202.
79. "The Word of God and Experience," Barth, *Church Dogmatics* I/1, §6.3, 204–32.
80. Barth, *Church Dogmatics* I/1, 204.
81. Barth, *Church Dogmatics* I/1, 210–14.

Third, when God addresses the human subject, God addresses us in the second person as a "thou." In so doing, God addresses the person as a whole and thus our will, our emotions, and emphatically our reason. The resulting experience is not restricted, therefore, to any particular locus of experience. Finally, and as is implied above, the experience of God's address includes the provision of the conditions for its interpretation. The experience of God is not interpreted with reference to categories that have come from elsewhere. There is a unity of percept and concept in that experience.

In conclusion, although Barth never rules out the possibility that God can speak to a person through their "moral conscience," it is clear that to grasp God's moral purposes for our lives, we should look beyond the deliverances of a moral voice or set of instincts within, and we should certainly not make such deliverances the foundation for our interpretation of the gospel. Rather, to grasp Paul's emphasis on participation "in Christ" is to recognize that when we are given to share in his life—to have "that same mind" that was in Christ Jesus—we receive the condition for veridical with-knowing (*conscientia*), with God, of God's purposes both for ourselves and for others.[82] When this occurs our reasoning is set free from being its own light through being conformed and reconciled to the Light of the World.

Dogmatics, Apologetics, and the Challenge of the Grounding Question

Any attempt to advocate the KBT as we have outlined it is likely to invite distortive questions of the following form: Does revelation not presuppose *any innate capacity* in the light of which God's self-disclosure may be recognized and affirmed? Is there *no point of contact whatsoever* that might serve to ground

---

82. Phil. 2:5 NRSV. The doctrine of participation in Christ is central to Paul's theology and evident throughout Paul's letters; see, for example, 1 Cor. 1:9; Phil. 1:1. Parallel insights are integral to the argument in John's Gospel, especially John 14, 17. On Paul's theology of participation, see Douglas A. Campbell, "Participation and Faith in Paul," in *"In Christ" in Paul: Explorations in Paul's Theology of Union and Participation*, ed. Michael J. Thate, Kevin J. Vanhoozer, and Constantine R. Campbell, WUNT 2/384 (Tübingen: Mohr Siebeck, 2015), 37–60; Campbell, "A Participationist Eschatological Account of Justification: Further Reflections," *Revue Biblique* 125 (2018): 249–61. On participating in the mind of Christ, see Richard Hays, *The Moral Vision of the New Testament: A Contemporary Introduction to New Testament Ethics* (New York: HarperCollins, 1996), chap. 1, esp. 19–33. The *en Christō* conceptuality in Paul is closely related to the Johannine emphasis on "abiding" *in Christ*.

revelation and the discernment of God's purposes in the subject? Do fallen human creatures not possess *in any form* the conditions for understanding and appropriating God's revelation? Are we not able to presuppose *any common ground* shared with unbelievers and to which Christians can appeal in making decisions within the public, political, and ethical domains?

As we have seen, Kierkegaard argued that if the learner (with her immanent capacities) is the condition for the recognition and appropriation of the truth, then all she needs to do is to recollect, "because the condition for understanding [*forstaae*] the truth is like being able to ask about it—the condition and the question contain the conditioned and the answer."[83] For Kierkegaard, indeed, we are unable even to ask the question of Truth aright without God's help, that is, without the condition (which is faith). To ask after the Truth—that is, to ask after the one who *is* the Truth—is already to have been gifted with the faith to ask. Without that condition, we cannot even begin to know what we are asking.[84]

Barth is of the same view, and it is for precisely this reason that he interpreted theology as *Nachdenken* ("thinking after") in the context of faith. What Barth also saw was that when we seek to reverse the process and approach the theological task by assuming a prior, divinely endorsed, immanent frame of reference, this has potentially problematic implications for the scope of the divine address. If, for example, the point of contact for special revelation is a broader general revelation that includes (1) epistemic access to God's legal and ethical purposes, and (2) the capacity to interpret the teleology of race, gender, and sexual orientation, for example, then the door is opened for the church to endorse legislation on race and gender by assuming general epistemic access to God's purposes without any reference to so-called special revelation. This sets the scene for bracketing Jesus Christ out of consideration when it comes to thinking through fundamental questions of social and political policy, for example.

But if we put to one side the practical problems of separating eristic and dogmatic theology, is there not a proper place for supporting an apologetic approach along the lines that Brunner proposes? For Brunner, *theologia naturalis* is "of decisive importance for the dealings of Christians with unbelievers."[85] Eristic theology aims to challenge people's resistance to faith and has a distinct place in Christian outreach to the extent that it offers a more ad hominem approach than dogmatic theology.[86] For Brunner, reference to a point of con-

---

83. Kierkegaard, *Philosophical Fragments*, 14.

84. We are grateful to Murray Rae for his input here.

85. Brunner, *Nature and Grace*, 58.

86. Emil Brunner, "Die andere Aufgabe der Theologie," *Zwischen den Zeiten* 7 (1929): 269.

tact serves the church's witness by showing how the faith connects with those capacities and insights that define us.

Barth shared Brunner's missionary zeal but not his conclusions. In Barth's view, to ask how human knowledge of revelation is possible indicates doubt about whether revelation is actually known. To believe that we need to investigate human knowledge in the hope of gaining "insight into the possibility of knowledge of divine revelation" does not elevate confidence in revelation; it undermines it.[87] For Barth, the appropriate way to approach the knowability of Christian revelation is not to ask the *how* question but to ask, "What is true human knowledge of divine revelation?"[88] Questions of prolegomena "do not so much lead up to the real work of dogmatics as lead away from it."[89] When one seeks to appeal to general revelation as a *praeparatio evangelica* (evangelical preparation) for special revelation, the former will inevitably affirm *material* content that will not only be perceived as more foundational than that of special revelation but will serve to erode the *actual* content of God's self-disclosure.

For precisely the same reason, Barth objects to treating "creation" as a *vestibule* by which natural theology seeks to bring those outside the church into its midst. Why? Because Barth sees that the way we choose to construct the vestibule will inevitably, in practice, shape our interpretation and presentation of the Christian faith itself. The risk is that "God" will cease to be the triune God of the Christian faith, and creation will cease to be interpreted as the work of the Father, the Son, and the Holy Spirit to whom the whole work of creation must be attributed. He writes, "Knowledge of creation is knowledge of God and consequently *knowledge of faith* in the deepest and ultimate sense. It is not just a vestibule in which natural theology might find a place."[90]

For Barth, the word "creation" is not a synonym for "the world" or "the contingent order." "Creation" refers first and foremost to God's *action*. Consequently, if we are to inquire after God's purpose in this act, we are failing to be true to the Christian confession if we turn to natural theology or general revelation for answers. Why? Because at the center of the Christian confession we find, in its second article, "that in Jesus Christ we have to do with God Himself, with God the Creator, who became creature, who existed as a creature in time and space, here, there, at that time, just as we all exist. If this is true,

---

87. Barth, *Church Dogmatics* I/1, 29.
88. Barth, *Church Dogmatics* I/1, 29.
89. Barth, *Church Dogmatics* I/1, 29.
90. Karl Barth, *Dogmatics in Outline* (New York: Harper & Row, 1959), 52 (emphasis original).

and this is the presupposition everything starts with, that God was in Christ, then we have a place where creation stands before us in reality and becomes recognisable."[91] In the creative *dabar* become flesh, we have before us *in space and time* the key to understanding creation *as the intentional act of God*. In sum, for Barth, the historical is of decisive significance for understanding the identity of the Creator and God's creative purpose. Ultimately, the problem with natural theology and so-called general revelation is the extent to which they erode the doctrine of creation.

Apologetics and the Defense of the Faith

It is important to be clear that Barth is emphatically not opposed to the church's attempting to provide a defense of the faith. Quite the opposite! Both dogmatics and the church should "everywhere," he argues, speak "apologetically and polemically."[92] The question, however, is what form that defense should take. In Barth's view, "there has never been any effective apologetics or polemics of faith against unbelief except that which is not deliberately planned, which cannot possibly be planned, which simply happens as God Himself acknowledges the witness of faith."[93]

The temptation of theology and the church is to create vestibules and points of contact through which we can bring persons into the church and also convince the secular world to take faith seriously. For Barth, however, faith teaches us that access to the body of Christ is provided by the Holy Spirit, who works through the witness to Jesus Christ provided through the Word written and preached and, indeed, lived. It is not the place of human beings to arrogate to themselves the activity of the Holy Spirit by displacing the role of witness (through confession and proclamation) in favor of a program of self-vindicating argumentation. The recognition at the heart of the faith does not concern abstract or general truths but the very particular truth that in Jesus Christ, the Creator has established fellowship with us "here, there, at that time, just as we all exist."[94] For Barth, an apologetics that leads to confused assumptions about the nature of the truth that defines the Christian faith is not defending the faith!

In addition to the fear that eristics might allow false assumptions and distortions of the faith to enter through the back door, there were other reasons

---

91. Barth, *Dogmatics in Outline*, 53.
92. Barth, *Church Dogmatics* I/1, 30.
93. Barth, *Church Dogmatics* I/1, 30.
94. Barth, *Dogmatics in Outline*, 53.

why Barth was concerned about apologetic strategies.[95] First, in apologetics, faith can take unbelief so seriously that it fails to take itself seriously enough—and that is not an appropriate form of witness.[96] Moreover, it fails to take seriously the prejudice against the faith and the role that sin plays in unbelief.[97] Second, eristics generates the assumption that once its task is complete, "dogmatics will think that its conflict with unbelief has been brought to an end in the form of such prolegomena, and that it will thus lose the necessary awareness of the constant exposure to assault of all its statements."[98] The folly of every attempt to erect a "Great Wall of China"[99] to defend the faith is that it assumes that faith can be secured by such means. Again, it assumes too tame a view of unbelief—it thinks unbelief can be dealt with by arguing from premises that believers and unbelievers share in common. When one takes a backward look, however, from a redeemed perspective and with the eyes of faith, a very different take on the problem of unbelief emerges. Human alienation is seen to have *formal* implications that go far deeper than material arguments. Paul's reference to the hostility of our minds and his account of the remedy that is required suggests, to use a contemporary analogy, that we are processing reality with theologically dysfunctional software that flatters our self-understanding but generates erroneous interpretations of who God is and all things in relation to God.

Apologetics and Transformation

When Paul suggested that we require to be trans*formed* (lit. "metamorphosed") for the sake of discerning God's will, he wrote as one who saw himself as part of a "new creation," as participating within a new humanity.[100] This involved

95. There is a certain irony in that Emil Brunner, a dialectical theologian, should advocate eristics, given Arthur Schopenhauer's satirical work (1831) *Eristische Dialektik: Die Kunst, Recht zu behalten*, variously translated *Eristic Dialectic: The Art of Winning an Argument*, *The Art of Being Right: 38 Ways to Win an Argument*, or *The Art of Controversy*. Schopenhauer describes "Eristic Dialectic" as "the branch of knowledge which treats of the obstinacy natural to man. Eristic is only a harsher name for the same thing." *The Art of Controversy and Other Posthumous Papers*, trans T. Bailey Saunders (London: Swan Sonnenshein, 1896), 3-4.

96. Barth, *Church Dogmatics* I/1, 37.

97. Barth, *Church Dogmatics* I/1, 37.

98. Barth, *Church Dogmatics* I/1, 37.

99. The building of the Great Wall of China is obviously, he explains, "a thoroughly eristic enterprise" (Barth, *Church Dogmatics* I/1, 38).

100. 2 Cor. 5:17; Rom. 12:2. Paul uses the word *metamorphousthe*, meaning "Be transformed!"

nothing less than the transformation of our perception of God, of God's purposes for this world, and of the implications of this for our relationship with God and others, and specifically for how we serve God and others in this fallen world. What defined this new orientation could not be "schematized"[101] in the light of secular thought-forms or reduced to secular categories any more than new wine can be contained within old wineskins.[102] The challenge to any apologetic approach is that it is obliged to recognize those strands in the New Testament that indicate discontinuity between the old and the new, between our alienated and reconciled states. This is not to suggest there is no continuity between the two but rather that any continuity requires to be recognized retrospectively and not prospectively. The old, as this includes our old frameworks of thought, will be interpreted afresh and in a new light through the creative and transforming presence of the Holy Spirit.

The issue here comes to the fore when Barth challenges Brunner's suggestion that redemption is to be conceived as the repair or restoration of the old humanity.[103] Barth's response was impassioned.

> Is the change in the human situation through the revelation of God, of which 1 Corinthians 2 and Galatians 2 speak, really a *reparatio*, a restoration in the sense in which Brunner employs it: "It is not possible to repair what no longer exists. *But it is possible to repair a thing in such a way that one has to say this has become new*"? I must confess that I am quite flabbergasted by this sentence. Had one not better at this point break off the discussion as hopeless? Or should one hope for an angel from heaven who would call to Brunner through a silver trumpet of enormous dimensions that 2 Corinthians 5, 17, is not a mere phrase, which might just as well be applied to a motor-car that has come to grief and been successfully "repaired"?[104]

---

101. In Rom. 12:2, the Greek reads *mē suschēmatizesthe*, which means, literally, "Do not be schematized" (by the secular order).

102. Matt. 9:17; Mark 2:22; Luke 5:37–38.

103. As Helmut Gollwitzer has commented, Barth saw this as a regression to the kind of "reformism" that the Reformation rejected: "Justification and rebirth must be understood as revolution in the strict sense not as reform. In that sense the theology of the Reformers has stood the test in contrast to the anthropological reformism of scholasticism and Erasmian humanism, and in that sense Barth adhered to it. He attacked Emil Brunner so vigorously because in him he saw a regression to this reformism." Gollwitzer, "Kingdom of God and Socialism in the Theology of Karl Barth," in *Karl Barth and Radical Politics*, ed. and trans. George Hunsinger, 2nd ed. (Eugene, OR: Cascade, 2017), 65.

104. Barth, *No!*, 93 (emphasis original).

Any allusion by Paul to the metaphor of "repair" emphatically does not suggest, for Barth, that this is the kind of exercise in which the old humanity can appreciate the need for repair, let alone perform it on itself. That is because, in Barth's view, "the 'repair' consists in a *miracle* performed upon the human" such that she has become "a new human, a new creature."[105] And the passage to which Barth referred (2 Cor. 5) does not suggest in any way that the old is merely repaired or reformed: "If anyone is in Christ, there is a new creation: everything old has passed away; see, everything has become new!"[106]

For Barth, as for Kierkegaard, unbelief is not simply a neutral lack of information or the consequence of a gap in a person's reasoning that can be solved by means of argumentation from shared premises. Rather, as we have already pointed out, it denotes a form of alienation that has no grasp of what it means to share in the new and redeemed humanity. What is required, therefore, is not correction but conversion—a conversion that involves the bestowal of the perception, the orientation, and the epistemic base that is appropriate to participation in the new creation. Specifically, it means being part of a new humanity that lives *en Christo* and thereby (on the way to being) radically reoriented toward a new center that redefines their lives and their understanding.[107]

In sum, to suggest that persons possess a pure or formal faculty of reason that delivers, in and of itself, properly functional religious beliefs that possess a foundational place in the Christian confession is to believe a myth—and one that is far from insignificant. Not only is it false but it deceives us as to the nature of the Christian faith and blocks our understanding of it.

Addressing the Grounding Question

Is this to suggest that any attempt to provide an account of the mechanics and grounds of the faith is to question divine action? Is it appropriate to provide *any* account of the grounding of Christian affirmations that seeks to articulate it in a way that might "make sense" to the unbeliever? Does consideration of the grounding question *inevitably* undermine the New Testament emphasis that the creation of the new humanity and the transformed recognition of God's presence that attends this is miraculous?

105. Barth, *No!*, 93–94.
106. 2 Cor. 5:17 NRSV.
107. For a particularly insightful analysis of Kierkegaard's views here, see Rae, *Kierkegaard's Vision of the Incarnation*, chap. 6, "*Metanoia.*"

To answer these questions, we need to consider what the key New Testament metaphors imply. First, the recognition of Jesus's divine identity is something that cannot be delivered by "flesh and blood." Rather, it is "from above."[108] The provision of the relevant epistemic capacity or functionality (sight to the blind and ears to the deaf) suggests that recognition and confession are the result of a person's being reconstituted or, to draw on the Johannine metaphors, "born again from above" or "born of the Spirit" and enabled thereby to "see the kingdom of God."[109] Evidentialist or epistemologically internalist approaches, for example, are obliged to recognize that the thrust of the New Testament witness implies that human beings cannot overcome their rebellion and the associated blindness by purely philosophical means or by dint of some kind of intellectual exercise. To suggest that a person can be brought by argumentation to know and confess that Jesus is the Messiah or Immanuel would require an eccentric hermeneutic if it is to find support from the Synoptics, John, or, indeed, Paul.

As we shall argue at greater length in the next chapter, it is important to recognize that Christians do not require an answer to the grounding question to be secure in their faith, just as a woman looking at a face does not need to grasp the neuroscience of facial recognition to know she is looking at the face of her brother. Similarly, to be given the eyes to see is to recognize that we are able to see what is in front of us, even if we are unable to provide an account of the mechanics whereby this recognition is possible.[110]

So is there any reason at all to engage in the grounding question? There are at least three reasons why it remains justifiable to do so, all of which appear consonant both with the KBT, and, indeed, with the New Testament themes to which we have alluded.

First, gaining a deeper understanding of the nature of faith and the way in which God works to bring us to know God is inherently justifiable. Moreover, as we shall argue later, it is possible to engage with the grounding question in ways that do not attempt to bolster faith by looking sideways or inwards or by adopting a foundationalist approach. And it is also possible to do so without ignoring the epistemic consequences of sin or the fact that we live by faith and not on the basis of what we can demonstrate to be true.

108. Matt. 16:17.
109. John 3:3-7.
110. The briefest awareness of scientific research into face recognition will indicate just how difficult it is to make sense of a form of recognition that seems so basic and straightforward; see the research of David Perrett and his Perception Lab at http://www.perception lab.com.

Second, an understanding of the grounding question is pertinent to confirming the scope of the faith and what one can justifiably claim to know with the eyes of faith. That is, it may shed light on what kinds of recognition its distinctive grounds support and, at least as importantly, do *not* support. For example, how far does a theological account of the grounding of our faith in Jesus Christ ground further beliefs in, for example, the historical status of the creation narrative, the endorsement of certain ethical agendas, or the affirmation of an innate moral sense? In short, a consideration of what does and does not ground Christian convictions and how those grounds are to be understood can help to determine the scope and, consequently, nature of the church's obligations and responsibilities.

Third, to offer an account of the nature of faith and its implications for the grounding of Christian claims serves the witness of the church. That is, it can have an apologetic function in a way that does not attempt to establish that the faith can be secured by rationalistic strategies. Rather, it can bear witness that when a Christian is confident in her faith, this is not indicative of a *sacrificium intellectus* or the "arrogance and self-assurance" to which Barth objects.[111] For a Christian to be disinterested, however, in how she has come to hold the truth-claims that define her orientation to God and the world, and how she perceives the grounding of these, could undermine her effective witness.

When Kierkegaard determined, albeit after some deliberation, to make the authorship of the *Philosophical Fragments* pseudonymous and the author an agnostic, this reflected clarity in his mind that it was possible for the Christian to explore the grounding question in insightful ways—and ways that had an important *apologetic* function—without seeking to ground the Christian faith on neutral or universally demonstrable foundations. In no respect did Kierkegaard see that work as itself attempting to provide the condition for the recognition of the Truth or the teacher who defines Christian faith.

Christian Engagement in the Public Square

In chapter 4, we pointed to the problems deriving from the nature-grace model that Brunner affirmed—a model whose influence, like that of the Lutheran law-grace model, left the church ill-equipped to challenge the commitments of the "German Christians," the endorsement of apartheid by the Dutch Reformed Church in South Africa, and the challenges of segregation in the

---

111. Barth, *Church Dogmatics* I/1, 26.

American Deep South, not to mention racism more widely. Now the abuse of a doctrine does not, in and of itself, abrogate its proper use—*abusus non tollit usum*. What should be evident, however, is that the *grace-nature* approach, which, contra to the nature-grace model, interprets God's purposes for the contingent order ("nature") in the light of God's grace, can neither endorse nor justify sociopolitical dynamics of these kinds. On the grace-nature model, God's purposes are interpreted in the light of the one in whom there is neither Jew nor Aryan, black nor white, male nor female. This is not to suggest that this itself is the reason to endorse the grace-nature model. It simply draws attention to the fact that when we interpret God's creative purposes in the light of God's gracious self-disclosure in the incarnation and affirm the lordship of Christ over *every* area of life, not only is this faithful to the biblical and Nicene traditions but it also generates a radically inclusive vision of God's purposes for humanity. It was precisely such an emphasis that was upheld not only in the first thesis of the Barmen Declaration but also in the Belhar Confession (1986), drafted and adopted by the Dutch Reformed Mission Church in South Africa during the apartheid regime.

In recent years, however, there has been a resurgence of interest in natural law within Protestant circles. As Jennifer Herdt observes, this has been "driven by hopes of finding resources for moral agreement in the midst of a highly conflictual public sphere."[112] And it has done much, she comments, to uncover a "continuous tradition of distinctively Reformed natural law reflection, according to which knowledge of the natural moral law . . . is universally available to humanity in its fallen state and makes a stable secular order possible."[113] One effect of these recent developments in Reformed circles has been a renewed eagerness to revivify Emil Brunner's approach in the interests of legal and political ethics.[114] The Catholic political theorist Justin Buckley Dyer has joined in support of this, arguing that replicating Brunner's commitment to uphold

112. Herdt, "Calvin's Legacy," 415.
113. Herdt, "Calvin's Legacy," 414.
114. E.g., Grabill, *Rediscovering the Natural*; J. Daryl Charles, *Retrieving the Natural Law: A Return to Moral First Things* (Grand Rapids: Eerdmans, 2008); David Van Drunen, *Natural Law and the Two Kingdoms: A Study in the Development of Reformed Social Thought* (Grand Rapids: Eerdmans, 2010). Charles is particularly concerned with issues in bioethics and argues that a retrieval of natural law is necessary if Christians are to contribute to pressing ethical debates in the public square; Van Drunen seeks to associate the Reformed tradition with natural law and the associated "two kingdoms" doctrine. Herdt provides a lengthy list of further publications written with a similar goal in mind, most of which have emerged since 1990, by Timothy Beach-Verhey, Susan Schreiner, William Klempa, Allen Verhey, David Little, and others (Herdt, "Calvin's Legacy," 415n1).

the moral conscience and universal epistemic access to moral law is necessary if Christian theologians are not to abdicate the public square. "Today," Dyer writes, "after many years of Barthian hegemony, the tide of Protestant thought is moving toward reengagement with the natural law tradition."[115] The reasons he cites for this are threefold: first, a "gradual rapprochement" between Catholic and Protestant theologians that has generated an ecumenical "conversation about the ontological foundation of ethics"; second, the "nuanced ways" in which the Reformed tradition is reassessing the appropriation of the natural law tradition by the Reformers; and third, the fact that "evangelical political engagement in the United States has provided an occasion for evangelicals to work through broad questions of political theory, of which natural law traditionally has been a central component."[116] It may be worth noting that this was written in 2013 and, since then, questions have been raised about the nature of the political involvement of evangelicals in Western politics—specifically, why so many *reject* the suggestion that affirming the lordship of Jesus Christ should shape their commitments in the political sphere.[117]

In a 2014 article entitled "Calvin's Legacy for Contemporary Reformed Natural Law," Jennifer Herdt challenged those who draw on Reformed theology to justify appealing to natural law to clarify the nature of moral obligation in the public arena: "While a Reformed conception of natural law can undergird a general willingness to take part in public moral discourse aimed at constructing a just civic order, it should not be seen as a source of substantive action-guiding moral norms. It is simply not tailored to the task of providing concrete ethical knowledge." Moreover, she argues, Calvin's accounts both of human conscience and natural human instincts make it clear that he "never really expected it to do this kind of work."[118] As for the temptation to look to natural law discourse to "adjudicate controverted moral questions of our day," she suggests that "Reformed natural law reflection sets its eyes on this prize only at its own peril."[119] She then proceeds to expose the profoundly important differences between Calvin's account of natural law and the directives of the

---

115. Justin Buckley Dyer, "Lewis, Barth, and the Natural Law," *Journal of Church and State* 57, no. 1 (2015): 16.

116. Dyer, "Lewis, Barth, and the Natural Law," 16.

117. See Sarah Posner, *Unholy: Why White Evangelicals Worship at the Altar of Donald Trump* (New York: Random House, 2020). See also the monograph by the Reformed historian Kristin Kobes du Mez, *Jesus and John Wayne: How White Evangelicals Corrupted a Faith and Fractured a Nation* (New York: Liveright, 2020).

118. Herdt, "Calvin's Legacy," 417.

119. Herdt, "Calvin's Legacy," 418.

moral conscience, and that of Aquinas. For Calvin, she argues, "we should not seek directly to fathom an opaque supernatural reality. Rather we ought to obey God's clear directives."[120] He is also skeptical, she suggests, about what can be delivered by our instincts.

In order to address the issues here, it is important to be clear about the profound difference between the KBT and a radically different trajectory. As we have seen, Dyer supports an approach to engagement in the public square that utilizes natural law. What is important to appreciate is that this often goes hand in hand with an additional commitment to theological immanentism that has long been evident not only in Roman Catholic approaches to theological education but in Protestant approaches as well. There is a long-standing tradition of teaching "fundamental theology" in advance of any engagement with the historical foci of the Christian faith.[121] "Fundamental theology," which normally characterizes first year theology teaching in seminary, is intended to set the scene for the later teaching of "salvation" and "sacraments." This reflects a tradition evident in both Catholic and Protestant theological education of expounding the doctrine of God, theological epistemology, and theological method in advance of and, often, independently of engagement with the incarnation and the person and work of Christ. Suffice it to say, the consequence of approaching theology in this way inevitably downplays the theological significance of Christ's mediation of the knowledge of God and of God's creative purposes. It also has profound ramifications for how the doctrine of God is approached. Its effect is to dilute recognition of the decisive significance for theology of the historical.

Second, and running in parallel with this feature of theological education, is a further form of immanentism, namely, the scholastic nature-grace model that underpins "natural law" approaches to theology. As Dyer rightly recognizes, this model, which has characterized much Catholic theology, ethics,

---

120. Herdt, "Calvin's Legacy," 424.

121. Cf. David Tracy, "The Task of Fundamental Theology," *Journal of Religion* 54, no. 1 (January 1974): 13–34. Definitions of fundamental theology vary. Karl Rahner, for example, adopted a notion of a "formal-fundamental theology" and Bernard Lonergan "foundational theology" (13n1). Tracy, by contrast, considers the "two principal sources for theology" to be "the Christian fact and human experience," explaining that he opts for the concept "Christian fact" since "this does not imply (as do 'message' or 'kerygma' or 'tradition') that the fundamental theologian need be a believing member of the Christian community" (14n3). For Avery Dulles, "fundamental theology" concerns the exposition and analysis of "how God brings human beings to assent to His word." Avery Cardinal Dulles, "The Rebirth of Apologetics," *First Things*, May 2004.

and political theory, defines Brunner's "Reformed" approach to the relationship between nature and grace. So what precisely is the nature-grace model? Put simply, it refers to approaches that interpret grace in the light of nature or, more accurately, in the light of our prior "natural" *interpretations* of nature. Grace is then interpreted as God perfecting nature *as we have construed it.* Theological and, indeed, sociopolitical problems emerge when our *prior interpretations* of nature constitute the foundation for the interpretation of "perfecting grace." The effect of this is that God's reconciling self-disclosure and the nature of God's salvific purposes are interpreted in toto in the light of *prior,* "natural" interpretations of nature. The risk here is that the nature and implications of God's gracious self-disclosure and salvific engagement with humanity is submitted to the procrustean bed of our prior assumptions about nature and what is natural. Of course, those endorsing the nature-grace model are obliged to smuggle in a suitable reading of nature—the "perfection" of nature when conceived in Thomistic terms would be rather different from the "perfection" of nature were it conceived in Darwinian terms given the divergent teleological categories in play. The key question, therefore, for those who are committed to the nature-grace model concerns what counts as "natural" and how "nature" is to be defined. Does it assume a theistic or a deistic account of the natural order, and can we safely make that decision led by the "light of natural reason"? Is the true nature of "nature" apparent to all human beings? This is clearly pertinent if it is assumed that such an approach promises to provide a point of connection with humanity in general. Alternatively, might it not be the case that our interpretations of nature require to be redeemed if they are to be appropriate to the doctrine of creation, as discussed earlier?

As we have already suggested, the appeal of the nature-grace model in both Catholic and Reformed contexts is motivated, in part, by the conviction that there need to be universally accessible norms if we are to come to agreed ethical and political decisions in the secular domain or public square. Moreover, as we have also seen, a further appeal of this model is that it appears to support the notion that human beings know the divinely ordained dictates of natural, moral law in advance of so-called special revelation. The perceived benefit of that is that we have first an account of how human beings can be held to be morally responsible and thus accountable before God for their actions, and second an account of how we can assume common ground with non-Christians when it comes to creating, upholding, and enacting legislative, judicial, and penal systems within society at large.[122]

122. Herdt summarizes, "While Reformed reflection on natural law was hardly uniform

METANOIA AGAIN!

This brings us back, again, to the nature of repentance (metanoia). If the offer of God's forgiveness (and hence salvation) is conditional upon repentance for sin (as affirmed by the Western *ordo salutis*), then that suggests we must have some prior knowledge of sin. Clearly, if "ought" implies "can," persons cannot be regarded as either culpable for sin or obliged to repent if they do not recognize sin for what it is—that is, contravention of God's law. In short, this interpretation of repentance adds further support for the view that there must be universal and immanent knowledge of God's law and thus God's will.[123] But this raises a key question that is particularly pertinent to the KBT, namely, what precisely "metanoia" means. In Western thought, the interpretation of the word "metanoia" has been primarily deontic rather than noetic or "intellectual." Indeed, in the King James version of the New Testament, *metanoia* is translated "repentance" and its verbal cognate (*metanoeō*) is translated "repent" on twenty-two different occasions. It is not clear, however, that that translation is appropriate in every case.[124] This raises the question of whether the traditional translation of *metanoia* may have been skewed by subliminal assent to the nature-grace agenda with the result that the noetic or intellectual element—the "conversion" element—has been downplayed. In contrast to the Western tradition, the Greek Orthodox tradition interprets *metanoia* as denoting "a change of mind, a reorientation, a fundamental transformation of outlook, of man's vision of the world and of himself." That is, "repentance is not to be confused with mere remorse, with a self-regarding feeling of being sorry for a wrong done. . . . It is an invitation to new life, an opening up of new horizons, the gaining of a new vision."[125] Significantly, Luther also opposed the deontic interpretation, preferring, rather, to interpret it as "change of mind."[126] Such an interpretation finds support in the standard Greek-English Lexicon

---

in its details, there has been general agreement that knowledge of the natural moral law, though universally available to humanity in its fallen state, is not saving knowledge. It serves primarily to provide grounds for moral responsibility, rendering fallen human beings culpable for their sins. But it also makes a stable secular order possible" ("Calvin's Legacy," 416).

123. Rom. 2:12–16 is interpreted as providing support for this.

124. James Strong, *The Exhaustive Concordance of the Bible* (New York: Hunt & Eaton, 1894), s.v. "metanoia."

125. Greek Orthodox Archdiocese of America, "Repentance and Confession: Introduction," https://www.goarch.org/-/repentance-and-confession-introduction.

126. Martin Luther, Letter to John von Staupitz, May 30, 1518, in *Letters*, ed. and trans. Gottfried G. Krodel, vol. 48 of *Luther's Works*, ed. Jaroslav Pelikan and Helmut T. Lehmann, 55 vols. (Philadelphia: Fortress, 1963), part 1:64–70 (esp. 66–68).

of the New Testament (BDAG), which defines *metanoia* as a "change of mind" with its New Testament usage meaning "repentance, turning about, conversion," referencing "the positive side of repentance, as the beginning of a new relationship with God."[127] The association of repentance with the discernment of the kingdom of God further supports its interpretation as a transformation of mind whereby we are given to interpret God and God's creative purposes— and thus ourselves—in a new light and from a new perspective. Consequently, the context of its use in the New Testament suggests that *metanoia* should not be expounded by making recourse to the dictates of our natural or immanent sense of God's legal will and purposes. But what of the injunction to repent? Does that not imply an understanding of the need to do so? Its use in the imperative form in Mark 1 appears to suggest a performative element to the exhortation as when one says to a sleeping child "Wake up!"—when one exhorts a child to wake up, that does not imply the child is already awake and able, thereby, to respond by waking herself up. The same applies to the injunction "Believe!" (*pisteuete*), which does not suggest one comes to belief by virtue of an act of self upon self. The same also appears to apply to the use of the exhortation *metanoeite*.[128] In sum, it seems appropriate to interpret Mark 1:15 as meaning "The time is fulfilled, and the kingdom of God has come near; be transformed in your minds and believe in the good news!" The context of the exhortation is that the good news is simultaneously being presented to them in the person of Jesus. When the texts that feature *metanoiete* cease to be read in strongly deontic terms, it is no longer necessary to assume prior, immanent, and "natural" knowledge of God's moral and legal purposes. Indeed, the whole thrust of the gospel witness suggests that in meeting the person of Jesus and having God's purposes for us interpreted by means of his teaching, parables, and actions, persons are brought to interpret God's will aright by virtue of a metanoia in their thinking.

What this suggests is that when Kierkegaard argues that conversion—as this denotes the turn around that attends our being delivered from error—is integral to faith, and when Barth stresses similarly the importance of conversion and the theological "turnabout" necessary if God's purposes and relation-

127. Walter Bauer, *A Greek-English Lexicon of the New Testament and Other Early Christian Literature*, 3rd ed., rev. and ed. Frederick William Danker (Chicago: University of Chicago Press, 2000), s.v. "μετάνοια."

128. Mark 1:15. It is pertinent to consider the parallels here with Paul's injunction in Rom. 12:2, which reads "Do not be conformed [*mē suschēmatizesthe*] to this world but be transformed [*metamorphousthe*] by the renewing of your minds so that you might discern what is the will of God—what is good and acceptable and perfect."

ship to humanity are to be interpreted aright, both approaches go to the heart of the New Testament understanding of metanoia. The fundamental point is that only when we are delivered from error, and thereby redeemed from the misconstrual of God's law that characterizes our immanent assumptions, are we given to recognize God's purposes in truth.

There are thus two problematic claims we are challenging. First, there is the claim that, entirely independently of God's free self-disclosure as the Word become flesh, all human beings have natural, immanent, and successful epistemic access to God's purposes. This suggests there are two different acts of self-revelation on the part of God that deliver different conceptions of God's purposes. Second, there is the claim that natural epistemic access to God's legal and moral purposes is not only *prior* to but *foundational* to the transformed and reconciled epistemic access to God's grace and forgiveness that we receive in Jesus Christ through the Holy Spirit. One consequence of both of the above claims is that Jesus Christ no longer possesses decisive significance when it comes to interpreting God's fundamental purposes for human beings and how they should live. As should be clear, the attendant suppositions about God, God's will, and God's legal purposes constitute, therefore, a form of "fundamental theology" for which the historical does *not* possess decisive significance. Among the challenges that immediately present themselves here is the fact that to understand metanoia aright suggests, according to the New Testament witness, that God's historical engagement with humanity stands to transform and redeem our foundational theological assumptions rather than be interpreted in their light.

Nowhere is the distinction between the two approaches more relevant than when it comes to the interpretation of Jesus's injunctions exhorting us to love our neighbor and forgive our enemy "seventy times seven." The traditional Western approach has been to interpret these as *supererogatory* rather than as defining God's *original* and *fundamental* purpose for the nature and character of human relationships. What Jesus appears to be suggesting, however—not simply in what he said and in how he lived but in his interpretation of the law—is that human beings were created to love God and their neighbors as themselves, which includes the sustained and unconditional forgiveness of one's enemies. That is, Jesus's injunctions are not simply referring to works of supererogation, that is, works of extraordinary virtue that go beyond our moral obligations and duties to God as determined by natural law. Rather, Jesus is articulating God's will with respect to how we should live and how we should relate to God and to one another. And what it is imperative to appreciate here is that references to the "law" in the New Testament, not least in

Paul, are almost exclusively references to the Torah rather than "natural law" or the like. So when Jesus endorses a summary of the law as "Love God and your neighbor as yourself," he is expounding the heart of the Torah, as this defines God's will. Few would suggest that our natural consciences dictate that the law of nature informs us that we are to love God and our neighbors as ourselves, and that this means loving one's enemies unconditionally! The thrust of the New Testament suggests that knowledge of God's law is profoundly different from the kinds of moral dictates our immanent suppositions and moral instincts are likely to deliver. In his engagement with persons, Jesus sought to transform thought-forms that were *echthroi*[129] so that persons might come to discern God's purposes aright. Significantly, his ethical teaching was not maieutic.

THE IMPLICATIONS OF THE KIERKEGAARD-BARTH TRAJECTORY FOR SOCIOPOLITICAL ETHICS

We have seen that a pragmatic concern with theology's engagement in the public square is a primary motivator for the endorsement of immanentist or Socratic approaches. The nature of Barth's alternative direction of thinking with its attendant *ordo cognoscendi* finds lucid expression in three essays he wrote, the titles of which reverse the traditional nature-grace ordered pairings of law and gospel, justice and justification, and (reflecting the related "two kingdoms" doctrine) state and church. Rather, they are entitled "Gospel and Law" (1935), "Justification and Justice" (1938), and "Christian Community and Civil Community" (1946).[130]

The "turnabout" in understanding that he considers to be critically important is explained in the opening of his essay "Gospel and Law."

> If I chose the title, "*Law and Gospel*," I would have to speak in terms of the formula which has come to be taken almost for granted among us. But I should like immediately to call attention to the fact that I shall not speak about "law and Gospel" but about "*Gospel and Law*." . . . The nature of the

---

129. "Hostile" or "alienated"; see Col. 1:21.

130. First published as *Evangelium und Gesetz*, Theologische Existenz Heute 32 (Munich: Chr. Kaiser Verlag, 1935); *Rechtfertigung und Recht*, Theologische Studien 1 (Zollikon-Zurich: Evangelischer Verlag, 1938); and *Christengemeinde und Bürgergemeinde*, Theologische Studien 20 (Zollikon-Zurich: Evangelischer Verlag, 1946).

case is such that anyone who really and earnestly would first say Law and only then, presupposing this, say Gospel would not, no matter how good his intention, be speaking of the Law of *God* and therefore then certainly not of *his* Gospel. This usual way is, even in the most favorable case, enveloped in ambiguities of every sort.[131]

Citing Galatians 3:17, Barth reminds us the law follows the promise, adding, "It *must* follow the promise, but it must *follow* the promise."[132] The law is "hidden and enclosed in the ark of the covenant."[133] Although he rejects any identification of the law and the gospel, he is clear as to the epistemic implications of their interrelationship.

> The Gospel is not Law, just as the Law is not the Gospel; but because the Law is in the Gospel, from the Gospel, and points to the Gospel, we must first of all know about the Gospel in order to know about the Law, and not vice versa.[134]

For Barth, when we refer to law and grace, we are not referring to two words of God—one for humanity in general and one for Christians. There is one form of divine address to humanity, namely, the one Word made flesh, and the unity of grace and law lies in the fact that they are both "the one Word of God," which, in all its diversity, never ceases to be other than a word of grace—despite the fact that that word of grace may take the form of life (gospel) or judgment (law). So a word of God that had a very different content and meant we did not hear grace would not, therefore, be "a Word of the triune God."[135] The unity and diversity of gospel and law is ultimately knowable only in Jesus Christ as he is the content of the gospel.[136] For Barth, "the law is nothing else than the necessary *form of the Gospel*, whose content is grace."[137] Consequently, his rejection of attempts to ground theology in immanence could not be more clear. "A Gospel or a Law which we speak to ourselves, by virtue of our own ability

131. Karl Barth, "Gospel and Law," in *Community, State, and Church*, introd. Will Herberg (New York: Doubleday, 1960), 71 (emphasis original).

132. Barth, "Gospel and Law," 71 (emphasis original).

133. Barth, "Gospel and Law," 71.

134. Barth, "Gospel and Law," 72.

135. Barth, "Gospel and Law," 73.

136. See David L. Mueller, review of *Community, State, and Church*, by Karl Barth, introd. Will Herberg, *Church and State* 3, no. 1 (1961): 84–87.

137. Barth, "Gospel and Law," 80 (emphasis original).

and trusting in our own authority and credibility, would, as such, not be *God's* Word; it would not be *his* Gospel and it would not be *his* Law."[138]

Barth's essay "Justification and Justice" reflects the same direction of thought, but its focus is primarily on the relationship of church and state. The scene is set with an analysis of the authority of Jesus in comparison with that of Pilate, who represents the state. He then turns to consider Romans 13, which has been used so extensively by those in power to provide divine endorsement for their authority and to contain the reach of the lordship of Christ. As Barth argues, the exhortation in the chapter that relates to the role of the state "cannot possibly, if taken in its context, be regarded as an exceptional statement" that refers to the law of nature "because it is firmly embedded in a series of instructions all of which have as their presupposition and their aim the Christian existence as such."[139] For Barth, if theologians are to interpret the state aright, they must first understand the role of the church—and not the other way around. "The light which falls from the heavenly polis upon the earthly *ecclesia* is reflected in the light which illuminates the earthly polis from the earthly *ecclesia*, through their mutual relation."[140] What this means is that the church serves the state not by ceasing to be the church but by *being* the church in truth and thereby living from the one who is Lord over both, namely, Jesus Christ. In this way the church is to fulfill its service to the state by approaching questions of law and legislation from the recognition that here, as in other spheres of life, there are not two words from God but one Word. It is by serving the one Lord and reflecting that one Word in all its thinking that the church serves the state and fulfills its responsibilities to the state.

Barth's further essay on church and state is entitled "Christian Community and Civil Community." There his description of the state is candid. In stark contrast to any suggestion that it is anonymously or subliminally following God-given laws, he writes:

> The civil community embraces everyone living within its area. Its members share no common awareness of their relationship to God, and such an awareness cannot be an element in the legal system established by the civil community. No appeal can be made to the Word or Spirit of God in

---

138. Barth, "Gospel and Law," 72.

139. The original German title is *Rechtfertigung und Recht* ("Justification and Justice"). Published in English as Karl Barth, "Church and State," in *Community, State and Church*, introd. Herberg (New York: Doubleday, 1960), 134. References in the text will be to "Justification and Justice"; references in the note will cite "Church and State."

140. Barth, "Church and State," 135 (emphasis original).

the running of its affairs. The civil community as such is spiritually blind and ignorant. It has neither faith nor love nor hope. It has no creed and no gospel. Prayer is not part of its life, and its members are not brothers and sisters. As members of the civil community they can only ask, as Pilate asked: What is truth?[141]

The church, by contrast, is an "assembly" (*ekklesia*) with a common life defined by the one Spirit, the Holy Spirit, in obedience to the Word of God in Jesus Christ whom all have heard and "are all needing and eager to hear again."[142] The expression of their life as a Christian community is thus "the one faith, love, and hope by which they are all moved and sustained."[143] When the church is considered alongside the state, the latter is seen to have

> no safeguard or corrective against the danger of either neglecting or absolutizing itself and its particular system and thus in one way or the other destroying and annulling itself. One cannot in fact compare the Church with the State without realising how much weaker, poorer and more exposed to danger the human community is in the State than in the Church.[144]

In sum, when Barth examines law, justice, and the state, the pressure of interpretation runs from God's purposes for the church to God's purposes for the wider community. It is in the light of the incarnate Word, therefore, that God's purposes for that wider community—its well-being, its obligations, and the nature of its service—are to be discerned. Consequently, when God's historical engagement with humanity is recognized as having decisive significance for our understanding of God's purposes, this has radical implications for how we conceive of God's legal purposes, for our resulting conceptions of justice, and, indeed, for every facet of the role and duties of the state. This is a fortiori the case if it means, as Barth suggests it does, that God's relationship to humanity, and hence God's law, is to be interpreted in terms of "claim and demand": "From what God does for us, we infer what he wants *with* us and *from* us."[145] This requires to be interpreted in light of the fact that in all God's dealings with humanity, the *indicatives of grace* are prior to the *imperatives of law*. This

---

141. Karl Barth, "The Christian Community and the Civil Community," in *Community, State, and Church*, introd. Herberg (New York: Doubleday, 1960), 151.

142. Barth, "Christian Community," 150.

143. Barth, "Christian Community," 150.

144. Barth, "Christian Community," 151–52.

145. Barth, "Gospel and Law," 78 (emphasis original).

is evident not only in the New Testament but also in Exodus 20. The so-called Ten Commandments articulate obligations that stem from the *prior* statement recounting God's covenant faithfulness (v. 2). God's claim on God's people stems from God's historically enacted commitment to them; "I am the Lord your God, who brought you out of the land of Egypt" is followed by the "demands." Consequently, they could be summarized as "*Therefore*, have no other gods before me, and be faithful both to me and to all those to whom I am faithful!"

Barth's approach here faithfully reflects the fact that the whole structure of the Torah, that is, the law as we have it in the biblical witness, testifies that God's primary relationship to humanity requires to be conceived in covenantal rather than contractual (conditional) terms—that is, in terms of an unconditional and unconditioned *covenant* commitment rather than a conditional and conditioned *contractual* commitment to humanity. When, as in the nature-grace or the law-grace model, the imperatives of law are perceived as requiring to be affirmed in advance of and as foundational to the indicatives of grace, this risks making God's covenantal relationship with humanity, which is based in unconditional and unconditioned covenant faithfulness (*ḥesed*), into a contractual, conditional one—where God's grace becomes conditional upon and conditioned by the satisfaction of legal conditions.[146] The presentation of God's *ḥesed* cannot be interpreted in contractual terms.[147] Rather, *ḥesed* reflects the filial relationship between God and Israel, God's "child."[148]

Finally, what the presentation of the covenant, God's *ḥesed*, and the Torah affirms is the priority of the filial in God's purposes, over the legal or judicial. This again has clear ramifications for a theological understanding of society.

---

146. It is imperative, therefore, that the *descriptive* and the *prescriptive* "ifs" that appear throughout the Bible are not interpreted as *contractual* "ifs." An example of a *descriptive* "if" would be the following: "If you love me, you will obey my commandments" (John 14:15). This *describes* what is involved in loving God. An example of a *prescriptive* "if" would be "If you want to have a happy family life, do not beat and abuse your children!" Neither "if" suggests that the essence of our relationship to God or our families is contractual. Similarly, the "ifs" that appear throughout the Bible require to be read carefully so they are not taken as suggesting that God's relationship to Israel is essentially a contractual one.

147. Cristian Mihut insists that "*ḥesed* is a stable and permanent commitment to act lovingly toward Israel" that "fixed the contours of divine agency." Mihut, "Bearing Burdens and the Character of God in the Hebrew Bible," in *Character: New Directions from Philosophy, Psychology, and Theology*, ed. Christian Miller, R. Michael Furr, Angela Knobel, and William Fleeson (New York: Oxford University Press, 2015), 380–81. What this means is that God's commitment to forgive belongs to the very essence of who God is and God's relationship to Israel.

148. See Exod. 4:22.

Rather than defining community and society with recourse to unredeemed, immanent conceptions of God's law, contractual relations, and the requirements of "justice," the primary purposes for humanity, on the part of the only God whom Christians recognize, are irreducibly filial. Human beings are created as God's daughters and sons, and the framing of the penal system and all matters of legislation must be consonant with that. In short, God's purposes for humanity require to be defined with recourse to the righteousness of the Creator as it is manifest in the incarnate Son—the one through whom and for whom all things were created, and the one who both inaugurates and defines the new humanity as it represents God's vision for human relations. The Christian community is called therefore to image the triune God and thereby to image God's righteousness. The implications of this are clear: such a community will be committed to facilitating human flourishing as this includes the service of the poor, the sick, the elderly, and the marginalized, as well as those who are dysfunctional and those who are guilty, not least, those who are criminals and those whom society deems the worst of the worst. It is precisely this perception of God's purposes for humanity that defines the epistemic base of the Christian in her engagement with the public square. Consequently, support for policy decisions in local, national, and international politics; the endorsement of legislation at all levels; the enactment of penal policies; the approach to international relations; and, finally, every political affiliation must not only be determined accordingly but be seen to be justifiable on these grounds. This does not mean that there will invariably be certainty as to which specific policy should be endorsed but there should be absolute clarity as to the nature of the foundational commitments that inform and shape our thinking.

Now the objection is often made here that this risks imposing Christian morality on the non-Christian public. Two points might be made in response. First, there is no neutrality when it comes to framing legislation and, indeed, contributing to legal and political policy-making more widely. Everyone involved in the process makes judgments that reflect their epistemic base and the convictions and values integral to it. Indeed, it would not be rational for an atheist, therefore, to make her recommendations based on the assumption that God exists and has a particular purpose for humanity. Similarly, how could it be rational for a Christian to bracket out their faith and not bring all they know to the process of making the most effective and appropriate contribution they can? A violinist could perform a Brahms sonata using only three of the four fingers on her left hand. But why would she? Surely she would want to bring all the resources she can to bear on doing the job to her utmost ability! If a Christian knows that God exists, that God has established kinship with humanity in fulfillment of God's creative purposes, and that God desires to see the poor and the guilty loved, supported, and flourishing, it is surely rational that she should allow the knowledge of this to inform her contribution and arguments in the public square.

In sum, for Barth, following Kierkegaard, the incarnation is the decisive event of God's self-disclosure in history. It points to the one who simultaneously mediates not only *who God is* but *what it is to be human in truth*. If it really is the case that he is the sole mediator between God and humanity, the creative Logos *become flesh*, to be faithful to that fact involves allowing it to shape and, indeed, determine one's interpretation of God's purposes for humanity at large—and thus for society. For it is precisely in the incarnation that we find the mediation of God's telos for the contingent order (what could be described as God's "creation ordinances") as it defines God's moral and legal purposes. It is in the light of that same reality that the theologian is called to interpret the God-given responsibilities of the state. The incarnate Son alone constitutes the criterion for identifying whether a political program may or may not be endorsed as consonant with the will of God for the created order.

"EITHER-OR," OR "BOTH-AND"

Brunner argued that "through the preserving grace of God," the ordinances of creation are "*known* also to 'natural man' as ordinances that are necessary and somehow holy and are by him *respected* as such."[149] God's ordaining of marriage, for example, "is realised to some extent by men who are ignorant of the God revealed in Christ."[150] Although the believer understands these ordinances of creation better than the unbeliever, the unbeliever still understands them. Here, as we have seen, Brunner finds points of connection between the creature and the Creator, most specifically, the basic formal capacity of human beings that enables them to appropriate and recognize divine revelation. The perceived benefit of such an account is that by recognizing the existence of divinely ordained capacities such as instinct and reason, a broad answer can be provided to the grounding question. That is, it affirms the existence of a common foundation on the basis of which engagement in the public square and shared moral judgments are possible and shared conclusions can be held by both sides to be appropriate and properly grounded. What this approach assumes is that all human beings possess a hardwired and properly functional

---

149. Brunner, *Nature and Grace*, 31, quoted and discussed in Barth, *No!*, 85 (emphasis original).

150. Brunner, *Nature and Grace*, 30, quoted and discussed in Barth, *No!*, 85–86.

interpretive framework or series of axioms that sustain moral judgment and provide the basis on which Christians and non-Christians can come to shared ethical conclusions. It can be endorsed theologically, moreover, on the basis of the "like causes like" axiom. As we have already argued, such an innate capacity is also widely held to be key to the Christian understanding of repentance and, indeed, the recognition and appropriation of so-called special revelation.

Again, Barth's response is not to rule out a priori the possibility that human beings *may* have insights into how they should live. The problem that emerges, however, is simple: Who can be relied upon to make trustworthy adjudications as to what these claimed sociological deliverances or ordinances are? And how do they decide which axioms really *are* ordained by God and which are only *perceived* to be so ordained?

So important are the issues here, it is worth quoting Barth at length.

No doubt there are such things as moral and sociological axioms which seem to underlie the various customs, laws and usages of different peoples, and seem to appear in them with some regularity. And there certainly seems to be some connection between these axioms and the instinct and reason which both believers and unbelievers have indeed every reason to allow to function in the life of the community. But what are these axioms? Or who—among us, who are "sinners through and through"!—decides what they are? If we consulted instinct and reason, what might or might not be called matrimony? Do instinct and reason really tell us what is *the* form of matrimony which would then have to be acknowledged and proclaimed as a divine ordinance of creation? If we were chiefly concerned with the clarity and certainty of knowledge, would not the physical, biological and chemical "laws of nature" or certain axioms of mathematics have a much greater claim to being called ordinances of creation than those historico-social constants? And who or what raises these constants to the level of commandments, of binding and authoritative demands, which, as divine ordinances, they would obviously have to be? Instinct and reason? And what yardstick have we for measuring these sociological "ordinances of creation," arranging them in a little hierarchy and ascribing to one a greater, to the other a lesser, "dignity"? Do we as "believers" sit in the councils of God? Are we able to decide such a question? On the basis of instinct and reason one person may proclaim one thing to be an "ordinance of creation," another another thing—according to the liberal, conservative or revolutionary inclinations of each.[151]

151. Barth, *No!*, 86–87 (emphasis original).

He concludes: "Can such a claim be anything other than the rebellious establishment of some very private *Weltanschauung* [worldview] as a kind of papacy?"[152]

There can be few more graphic examples of the consequences of the utilization of natural theology and the perceived divine ordinances it delivers than the *Ansbacher Ratschlag* (Ansbach Counsel), which appeared in the same year that the Barth-Brunner debate took place.[153] This statement was intended as a repudiation of the Barmen Declaration that had been drafted by Karl Barth and adopted by the Confessing Church (May 29–31, 1934). The signatories of the Ansbach Counsel objected, in particular, to the first thesis of the Barmen Declaration, which reads as follows:

> Jesus Christ, as he is attested to us in Holy Scripture, is the one Word of God whom we have to hear, and whom we have to trust and obey in life and in death. We reject the false doctrine that the Church could and should recognize as a source of its proclamation, beyond and besides this one Word of God, yet other events, powers, historic figures and truths as God's revelation.[154]

The Ansbach Counsel, drafted less than two weeks after Barmen (on June 11, 1934), was signed by eight theologians and church leaders including, among others, the leading Lutheran theologians Werner Elert, who wrote it, and his Erlangen colleague Paul Althaus. It was also endorsed by Adolf Schlatter who, like Althaus, remains highly respected and influential among many conservative theologians. The document rejects what its authors perceived to be the narrowness of the Barmen Declaration's approach to revelation—a criticism that, unsurprisingly, was greeted with delight by the "German Christians" (*Deutsche Christen*).[155] The Ansbach Counsel deemed natural theology nec-

---

152. Barth, *No!*, 87 (emphasis original).

153. The *Ansbacher Ratschlag* is variously referred to as the Ansbach Counsel, the Ansbach Advice, and the Ansbach Mandate.

154. We are using here Douglas Bax's translation: "The Barmen Declaration: A New Translation," *Journal of Theology for Southern Africa* 47 (June 1984): 78–81.

155. Robert P. Ericksen, *Theologians under Hitler* (New Haven: Yale University Press, 1985), 88. Ericksen concludes his study by pointing out that "Kittel, Althaus and Hirsch were not isolated or eccentric individuals. . . . They were not extremists." Rather, their "assumptions, their concerns, and their conclusions represent a position that must have been common to many professors, theologians and pastors in Germany." Indeed, the views of a "large middle group in the university and church" would likely have resembled theirs (199). Although Paul Hinlicky has some useful corrections to make of Ericksen's important work (and sheds interesting light on the interpretation of Althaus), he strongly endorses

essary to create a proper place for political reasoning. Specifically, its authors endorse the notion that God had revealed his purposes for the natural order in the "family," the "people," and the "race," all of which were conceived in terms of blood relationship. It is the will of God, they argue, that we are all subordinate to this natural order. Consequently, the church had a "temporally specific" obligation to proclaim that *at that particular point in history*, the *law of God* included a special role for the national political order in Germany. The Counsel reads:

> The law, namely, the immutable will of God, encounters us in the total reality of our lives as they are brought into light by the revelation of God. It binds each in the position to which he has been called by God and commits us to the natural orders under which we are subjugated, such as family, Volk, race (i.e., blood relationship). . . . In that the will of God also meets us continually in our here and now, it binds us also to a specific historical moment of family, *Volk* and race, i.e., to a specific moment of their history.[156]

Two paragraphs later, it adds:

> We as believing Christians thank the Lord God that he has given to our people in its time of need the Führer as a "pious and faithful sovereign," and that he wants to prepare for us in the National Socialist system of government, good rule, a government with "discipline and honour." Accordingly, we know that we are responsible before God to assist the work of the Führer in our calling and in our station in life.[157]

In their view, the Nazi regime and its leader Adolf Hitler were ordained by God and faithfully disclosed, therefore, God's specific purpose at that point in

---

these conclusions. Hinlicky, *Before Auschwitz: What Christian Theology Must Learn from the Rise of Nazism* (Eugene, OR: Wipf & Stock, 2013), 15; on Althaus, 21–24. Hinlicky then goes on, however, to draw disturbing parallels between Germany in the 1930s and today's church—parallels that may be even more apparent in 2021 than they were in 2013.

156. Robert P. Ericksen, "The Political Theology of Paul Althaus: Nazi Supporter," *German Studies Review* 9, no. 3 (1986), 558. The full text of the *Ansbacher Ratschlag* can be found in Gerhard Niemoller, *Die erste Bekenntnissynode der Deutschen Evangelischen Kirche zu Barmen* (Göttingen: Vandenhoeck & Ruprecht, 1959), 1:144–45. We are grateful to Dr. Gotthelf Wiedermann for providing this translation.

157. Cited in Hugh Fogelman, *Christianity Uncovered: Viewed Through Open Eyes* (Bloomington, IN: AuthorHouse, 2012), 89 (translation corrected).

history.[158] It is as telling as it is shocking that none other than Paul Althaus, one of the signatories of the Counsel and one of the leading Luther scholars of the modern era, should have greeted Hitler's coming to power in 1933 as "a gift and miracle of God."[159] This went hand in hand with his conviction that the concept "the people" (*das Volk*) was an order of creation.[160]

As we have already mentioned, the fact that a particular approach to theology may be abused or misapplied does not mean it should necessarily be rejected. What the *Ansbacher Ratschlag* illustrates, however, is what can result when the direction of theological interpretation is reversed and our inherent instincts and readings of nature, of our nation, or of our race (and thereby the status of other races) are identified *as God-given* without considering whether they are consonant with, let alone warranted by, God's reconciling self-disclosure in Jesus Christ.

Barth's opponents will doubtless continue to question whether his approach leaves room for an adequate account of the role of the state, of justice, and of law, and space does not allow us to engage further with Barth's analysis of these three topics. What requires to be asked of the advocates of natural theology, however, is whether it possesses the means sufficiently to redress the ongoing potential of persons to appeal to it in the service of their own particular, political ends—an inclination that continues to this day.[161] In the light of the

158. The accompanying letter, signed by Hans Sommer, concluded with the words "With high esteem, Heil Hitler!"

159. Cited in Ericksen, "Paul Althaus," 547.

160. Althaus writes, "We may express our thankfulness and joyful readiness for that which manifests a will for the genuine brotherhood of blood brothers in our new order of the Volk. . . . We Christians know ourselves bound by God's will to the promotion of National Socialism, so that all members and ranks of the Volk will be ready for service and sacrifice to one another." Paul Althaus, *Kirche und Staat nach lutherische Lehre* (Leipzig: Deichertsche Verlagsbuchhandlung, 1935), 29. See Ericksen's discussion of Althaus's emphasis on the *Volk* in "Paul Althaus," 548–52.

161. See Paul Hinlicky's telling critique of Lowell C. Green's attempt to defend Elert's "new natural theology." *Before Auschwitz: What Christian Theology Must Learn from the Rise of Nazism* (Eugene, OR: Wipf & Stock, 2013), 59. In *Lutherans against Hitler: The Untold Story* (St. Louis: Concordia, 2007), Lowell Green refers to Elert's claim that the "new natural theology" he is advocating is not prior to but borne by the revelation of Christ and the faith that attends this (214). However, when it comes to the question as to how the "natural orders" and the "natural revelation in creation" are to be discerned, his answer is that "the Christian is to employ his God-given reason, which will counsel him to disobey the wicked demand of the state or even to take part in a revolution" (215). Again, we return to the problem of the ambiguities inherent in the so-called deliverances of reason and the fact that reason invariably operates from an epistemic base.

argumentation we have provided, we would conclude that the onus on any Christian "theology of politics" or "theology of political ethics" is to show that its claims are consistent with confessing the kinship the eternal has established in time, and through which God is reconciling the world—and not merely the church—to Godself.[162]

FROM SOLUTION TO PLIGHT

At the center of our discussion of the KBT has been the question of the directionality of Christian thought. The importance of this for Barth could barely have been made more explicit than when, following the conclusion of the Second World War, he was invited to give the inaugural keynote address at the first meeting of the World Council of Churches. This took place in Amsterdam on August 23, 1948. By then, the full horrors of the Holocaust were known, and the West was faced with the challenges posed by the communist (atheist) regime in the Soviet Union. Much of Europe, moreover, was seeking to recover from the devastating physical and economic destruction that was the legacy of the war. With this in mind, Reinhold Niebuhr and the organizing committee of the newly formed World Council of Churches invited Barth to give an address entitled "The Disorder of the World and God's Plan of Salvation." Although the proposed title was profoundly understandable, it exhibited the most profound failure to appreciate the whole thrust of Barth's prophetic theology. Barth's address, which he entitled "Beginning with Faith and not Fear," begins as follows:

> "The Disorder of the World—and God's Plan of Salvation." Right away, I should like to direct your attention to whether, in its entirety and in all of its several aspects, we ought not to regard and deal with this theme from back to front. It is said that we should seek first after the kingdom of God and God's righteousness, so that all those things of which we have need in view of the disorder of the world may then be added unto us. Why would, or why should, we not take this sequence seriously? God's "plan of salvation" is *above*, but the disorder of the world—and so also our concepts of its foundations, as well as our proposals and plans to oppose it—is all *below*. If it is to happen at all, the nature of this whole complex (as that includes the nature of our churches!) only becomes visible and tractable from up there, only

162. Cf. 2 Cor. 5:19.

from the perspective of God's plan of salvation downward—since there is no prospect or path upwards to God's plan of salvation from the perspective of the disorder of the world, or from the Christian analyses and hypotheses that we devote to it. We should not wish to begin down there in any of our concerns: not with the unity and disunity of our churches; not with the virtues and vices of Modern humanity; not with the nightmare scenario of a culture oriented solely around technology and intent solely on production; not with the confrontation of a godless West with a godless East; not with the looming threat of the atom bomb; and absolutely not with the few deliberations and interventions with which we all intend to deal with this calamity [*Unheil*].[163]

For Barth, the "Christian realism that is commanded of us" specifically requires us *not* to begin from below but to approach the relevant questions "in the right way." When we start from below, he argues, we assume the position of "having to act as though our beloved God had died"—as if there were no wisdom, justice, and plan of God's own "high above our entire Christian ecclesiastical existence." The assumption we make is that wisdom and justice are fulfilled in "our perspectives, insights, and prospects."[164] When we do this and then focus on the disorder of the world, we begin to emulate Peter who, when he looked at the storm and the waves, began to sink. The effect of this is to drive us to find solutions *outside* the gospel. For Barth, however, there is another alternative. We can have the courage to live as the body of Christ in truth.

The body of Christ really consists of such people as have, each in their own situations and ways, placed their entire hope and confidence exclusively upon Christ himself: on his unique work of reconciliation on the cross; on his resurrection as the sign of a new eon, already begun in him; on his Holy Spirit, through which he comforts his troubled community and also directs and corrects the world in completely different and vastly better ways than we have at our disposal; and finally, on his coming again in majesty, in

---

163. Karl Barth, "The Disorder of the World and God's Plan of Salvation," trans. Matthew A. Frost, https://www.academia.edu/38565248/_The_Disorder_of_the_World_and_Gods_Plan_of_Salvation_1948_Translation_, accessed October 20, 2021, p. 2. This is an edited translation of "Amsterdamer Fragen und Antworten," *Theologische Existentz heute* NF 15 (Munich: Chr. Kaiser Verlag, 1949), 3–10. Frost points out that the final word here, "rendered as 'calamity,' is *Unheil*, to which the obvious solution is *Heil*, salvation, framing Barth's point" (2n3).

164. Barth, "Disorder of the World," 3 (translation altered).

which the majestic redemption of the total creature that takes place in him will be revealed. The body of Christ lives exclusively out of, through, and toward this one who is indeed entirely present to it, but who as its Lord is also entirely superior to it.[165]

CONCLUSION

In this chapter we considered how we should interpret the theological, methodological, and epistemological grounds on which engagement with secular society takes place. With this in view, we assessed two contrasting styles of approach. The first assumes universal and immanent epistemic access to God's moral and legal purposes—an approach which, we suggested, can be viewed as an expression of the "nature-grace model." We argued that certain apologetic and eristic strategies operate along these same lines.

We then considered the implications of operating not by presupposing a universal and immanent grasp of God's purposes but from the recognition of the redemptive kinship that God has established in Jesus Christ and for which the historical has decisive significance. Our analysis of the Barth-Brunner debate and recent attempts to resurrect Brunner's arguments served to highlight the problematic theological implications of grounding the exposition of Christian theology and, indeed, the church's engagement with the secular world on the assumption of prior epistemic access to God's nature and moral purposes. What came to the fore was the fundamental importance of the *directionality* of Christian thought—of interpreting the nature of the world's problems in the light of God's redemptive purposes and not the other way around. This could not have been made more clear than in Barth's keynote address to the inaugural meeting of the World Council of Churches.

---

165. Barth, "Disorder of the World," 3–4 (translation altered).

Beyond Immanence

Our previous chapter sought to address the theological and sociopolitical problems posed by approaches to theology that assume immanence either materially or formally. Our analysis of the issues highlighted by the Barth-Brunner debate, and also contemporary attempts to resurrect central themes in Brunner, sought to show how a commitment to immanence can derive from an apologetic concern to find epistemological, ethical, and legislative common ground with the non-Christian world. This led us to consider the problems that stem from this, most of which result from the risk of reversing the direction of interpretation such that the mission and message of the church are reconceived in the light of commitments determined by the secular order.

The purpose of this chapter is to consider the implications of the Kierkegaard-Barth trajectory (KBT) for how we provide an account of the faith and the hope within. To this end, we shall start by considering Barth's account of the divine address and how God's speaking might take the form of human speech (or God-talk).

The Divine Address and Human God-talk

For Barth, the totality of the church's speech about God, and thus Christian theology as a whole, requires to be seen as a response to God's address. It derives from an initiating action that the God who is infinitely qualitatively different from human creatures has taken, rather than anything we initiate. It is not the result, therefore, of argumentation from first principles or anything in that neighborhood. Theology is the outcome of our being given to hear God's Word—a Word that cannot be anticipated and which is irreducibly bound up with events in human history. As such, theology takes place within a context of faith conceived in terms of participation within the body of Christ. As Barth puts it, while "already on the way, we give an account of the way which we tread."[1] There are three aspects to God's Word, as he interprets it, and his analysis of these is not only central to the first volume of his *Church Dogmatics*; it is key to his theology as a whole. The first aspect concerns the Word of God as God's revelation or self-disclosure and this finds its focus in the incarnation of the Word. The second is the Word interpreted as Holy Scripture. And the third is the proclaimed or preached Word through which God proclaims Godself—as God did through Moses, the prophets, and the apostles.[2] In proclamation, we are presented with "the presence and action of the Word of God."[3] Herein lies the key to understanding Scripture, which Barth views as recorded proclamation. Scripture is "the deposit of what was once proclamation by human lips," which the church recognized to be authoritative as "written proclamation."[4] At the core of Barth's account and key to all three aspects is the recognition that when we refer to the Word of God, we are referring to God speaking in person—the *Dei loquentis persona* (the person of the speaking God). This applies not least to the biblical witness on which the entire theological enterprise depends. "The Word of God is God Himself in Holy Scripture. For God once spoke as Lord to Moses and the prophets, to the Evangelists and apostles. And now through their written word He speaks as the same Lord to his Church."[5] It is this same Word that defines the task of the theologian as she is called to serve the life, witness, preaching, and mission of the church.

At the heart of Barth's exposition stands a question that not only occupied his mind as a preacher but that also played a central role in his entire theological project. How is it that the words of sinful, alienated human creatures can also be the Word of God? With this question, Barth launched his discussion of the mission of the church in a section entitled "The Word of God and the Word of Man in Preaching." If the Word of God is the basis of theology, then this requires us to ask not only how the God who is infinitely qualitatively

1. Karl Barth, *Church Dogmatics*, ed. Geoffrey W. Bromiley and Thomas F. Torrance, trans. Geoffrey W. Bromiley (Edinburgh: T&T Clark, 1956–1975), I/1, 43; Barth, *Die Kirchliche Dogmatik* (Munich: Chr. Kaiser Verlag, 1932; and thereafter Zurich: EVZ, 1938–1965), I/1, 43.

2. Barth describes it as "God's own proclamation" (*Church Dogmatics* I/2, 746).

3. Barth, *Church Dogmatics* I/2, 746.

4. Barth, *Church Dogmatics* I/1, 88. Barth also explains, however, that "in this similarity as phenomena . . . there is also to be found between Holy Scripture and present-day proclamation a dissimilarity in order, namely the supremacy, the absolutely constitutive significance of the former for the latter, the determination of the reality of present-day proclamation by its foundation upon Holy Scripture and its relation to this, the basic singling out of the written word of the prophets and apostles over all the later words of men which have been spoken and are to be spoken to-day in the Church" (*Church Dogmatics* I/1, 102).

5. Barth, *Church Dogmatics* I/2, 457.

different communicates Godself through human creatures and human words, but also how such human proclamation can be heard as God's Word. As might be anticipated from our discussion in chapter 5, Barth does not mince his words. "The attempt is made to speak of God with the intention that others shall hear of Him. This attempt and intention are as such impossible. God does not belong to the world."[6]

It is not possible to provide an answer couched in terms of any innate human capacity either to communicate or to hear God's self-proclamation.[7] Neither is explicable in terms of the spheres of "immanence" but solely in terms of the sphere of "transcendence," to borrow Kierkegaard's language.[8] What is communicated and what is heard is radically "new." It is not possible for others to hear God purely and simply on the basis of our direct speech about God. It is only possible for others to hear God if God *actually speaks* through our speech about God. If human proclamation takes place successfully, therefore, this is not the result of some capability that alienated humanity possesses, but the result of an act of pure grace—a "divine victory concealed in human failure, sovereignly availing itself of human failure."[9] Proclamation is not to be seen as taking place "naturally," therefore, or as the direct consequence of certain human actions. In the church's attempts to preach and testify to who God is, its hope lies in the fact that God will proclaim Godself through the church's proclamation: "It can only be hoped by faith in the foundation which God Himself has laid for the Church, that is, by faith in Jesus Christ."[10] For Barth, this means that "men are really able to speak of God, and to let others hear of Him."[11] To the extent that this happens, however, it requires to be understood as "a divine victory, a miracle."[12] It only happens as and when God graciously communicates Godself through the words of the one bearing witness.

6. Barth, *Church Dogmatics* I/2, 750.

7. Søren Kierkegaard, *Without Authority*, ed. and trans. Howard V. Hong and Edna H. Hong (Princeton: Princeton University Press, 1997), 96.

8. Kierkegaard, *Without Authority*, 94. The apostle, he insists, is required to proclaim that which is radically "new" and does not belong to the sphere of immanence. This newness also requires a person's apostolic role. "Prior to becoming an apostle, there is no potential possibility; every human being is essentially equally close to becoming that" (95). Becoming an apostle is not a development of any immanent capacity or potential. There are clear parallels between Kierkegaard's account of the role of the apostle and Barth's account of the nature of proclamation.

9. Barth, *Church Dogmatics* I/2, 751.

10. Barth, *Church Dogmatics* I/2, 751.

11. Barth, *Church Dogmatics* I/2, 751.

12. Barth, *Church Dogmatics* I/2, 751.

Proclamation is human speech in and by which God Himself speaks like a king through the mouth of his herald, and which is meant to be heard and accepted as speech in and by which God Himself speaks, and therefore heard and accepted in faith as divine decision concerning life and death, as divine judgment and pardon, eternal Law and eternal Gospel both together.[13]

So how can we be certain as to when true proclamation, namely, human proclamation through which God speaks, has taken place? For Barth, there is no mechanism to which we can appeal to ensure that proclamation will take place and has taken place. God's agency is not in our control, nor is it something that can be confirmed by human means. To understand, therefore, how God speaks in proclamation, we need to consider the nature of the Word of God. "The presupposition which makes proclamation proclamation and therewith makes the Church the Church is the Word of God."[14] As with revelation, to which we shall return later, there is, for Barth, an irreducibly Trinitarian "grammar" to proclamation that explains how alienated human subjects come to hear God's second-personal address mediated through human words.[15] Although Barth does not put it in quite this way, extrapolating from his account of revelation, we might say that God is the one who proclaims, God is the one who is proclaimed, and God is also the proclaimedness. That is, its being heard and appropriated is explicable solely in terms of the creative presence of the Holy Spirit. The miraculous nature of what takes place in proclamation means that any attempt to address the "how" of proclamation cannot provide an explanation that is more foundational than one that refers to God's action and, indeed, presence—it cannot penetrate to some deeper level of explanation.

This is certainly not to suggest that, within the church, a preacher can say *anything* in the hope that God will miraculously transform the speech into "proclamation"! The one who is called to preach and is set aside to serve the church seeks to be true to the gospel, yet always in the recognition that she does not and cannot "stand in" for God. She prays God will speak through her words while recognizing that disclosing God is not in her gift. That said, her desire that God will indeed speak through her words means she will be faithful to Scripture, to God's action and presence in history (to which Scrip-

13. Barth, *Church Dogmatics* I/1, 52.
14. Barth, *Church Dogmatics* I/1, 88.
15. The word "grammar" is the word used by Thomas F. Torrance in "The Basic Grammar of Theology," chap. 6 in *The Ground and Grammar of Theology: Consonance between Theology and Science* (Edinburgh: T&T Clark, 1980).

ture bears witness), and thus to the recorded proclamation that the church has singled out as Scripture because it recognizes it to be authoritative.

For Barth, the "temporal" reality of Scripture is the "bolt" that "shuts out Platonic *anamnesis*."[16] What Barth is suggesting here, like Kierkegaard, is that the temporal reality of God's self-proclamation has decisive significance, and its content cannot, therefore, be reduced to our "remembering" spiritual or moral truths that are universally, timelessly, and immanently known and hence recognizable. What is learned about God through God's self-disclosure is new.[17]

As we argued in chapter 5, Scripture and the creeds serve as ordained media—as "sign-posts to the Holy One" that point away from themselves to the personal reality of God. These are based on the fact that God reveals Godself in and through the medium of human speech.[18] This is not to suggest, however, that Scripture is to be conceived as a "third thing between God and man"—"a reality distinct from God that is as such the subject of revelation. This would imply that God would be unveilable for men, that God Himself would no longer need His revelation, or rather that God would be given up into the hands of man."[19] For Barth, the subject and object of revelation remains the personal reality of God.[20] To recognize Jesus Christ as God's Word is to recognize that God speaks but also that this speaking is always and invariably *personal* in nature. The God we know in Jesus Christ and through the witness of Scripture is an irreducibly personal reality—when God is revealed, God is revealed in an event of personal address.

The following summary of his own position may not be as analytically precise as one might wish, but it should nevertheless be clear what he is seeking to affirm and what he is determined to deny:

16. Barth, *Church Dogmatics* I/1, 101. The parallel here is to Climacus's demonstration that to hold that the historical has decisive significance for our relation to the Truth is incompatible with the Socratic.

17. "The apostle has something paradoxically new to bring, the newness of which, just because it is essentially paradoxical and not an anticipation pertaining to the development of the human race, continually remains" (Kierkegaard, *Without Authority*, 94). See also Stewart R. Sutherland's argument that "newness" is integral to revelation in "The Concept of Revelation," in *Religion, Reason and the Self: Essays in Honour of Hywel D. Lewis*, ed. Stewart R. Sutherland and T. A. Roberts (Cardiff: University of Wales Press, 1989), 43.

18. "Thus God does reveal Himself in statements, through the medium [*Mittel*] of speech, and indeed of human speech" (Barth, *Church Dogmatics* I/1, 142–43; *Kirchliche Dogmatik* I/1, 147).

19. Barth, *Church Dogmatics* I/1, 321. Cf. Kevin Diller, *Theology's Epistemological Dilemma: How Karl Barth and Alvin Plantinga Provide a Unified Response* (Downers Grove, IL: InterVarsity Press Academic, 2014), 45.

20. Barth, *Church Dogmatics* I/1, 136.

> God's Word is not a thing to be described nor a term to be defined. It is
> neither a matter nor an idea. . . . It is *the* truth as it is God's speaking person,
> *Dei loquentis persona*. It is not an objective reality. It is *the* objective reality,
> in that it is also subjective, the subjective that is God. God's Word means
> the speaking God. Certainly [*Gewiss*] God's Word is not just the formal
> possibility of divine speech. It is the fulfilled reality.[21]

Although revelation enables us to affirm innumerable true propositions about
God, Christian revelation cannot be reduced to the disclosure of these propositions. That is because no series of propositions can, in and of themselves,
disclose the God to whom they refer. There are, in other words, factors integral to revelation that are extrinsic to the meanings of these words and their
interpretation by our immanent thought processes. If we fail to recognize that,
we fail to recognize the personal element integral to God's address and which
cannot be communicated in an abstract form. This appears to be what Barth
is seeking to communicate, albeit in a somewhat abstruse way, when he insists
that the divine address always has "very specific objective content," that is,
"God always speaks a *concretissimum*."[22] To reiterate, divine revelation cannot
be reduced to the general communication of impersonal principles or general
truths. Rather, God addresses us personally as individuals in the context of a
concrete I-Thou relationship. "What God speaks is never known or true any-
where in abstraction from God Himself. It is known and true in and through
the fact that He Himself says it, that He is present in person in and with what
is said by Him."[23] The reality of God's Word cannot be abstracted or distilled,
therefore, from God's personal presence in revelation—God's addressing the
human subject as a "thou." If it is the case that when Scripture is read or
preached within the church, proclamation has successfully taken place, then
God has spoken through it as Lord of the process of revelation and has graciously given persons the ears to hear and the eyes to see their Lord.

In short, God's self-disclosure involves God's being freely and actively and
creatively present to the recipient. Second, and integral to this, God's address
includes the miracle of its being heard by the one spoken to. To draw on Gilbert Ryle's terminology, "self-revelation" and "disclosure" require to be treated
as "success words."[24] References to God's self-disclosure and revelation imply

21. Barth, *Church Dogmatics* I/1, 136 (translation altered; emphasis original); *Kirchliche Dogmatik* I/1, 141.
22. Barth, *Church Dogmatics* I/1, 136–37.
23. Barth, *Church Dogmatics* I/1, 137.
24. Ryle also speaks of "achievement words" and "got it words." Gilbert Ryle, *The Concept*

that the conditions for their taking place have been met. Where these conditions are indeed met, they are met *by God*. Here the outworking of Barth's Trinitarian account of revelation becomes clear. The Father addresses us in and through the person of the Son, the incarnate Word, and this Word is heard and recognized miraculously through the creative, reconciling, and transforming presence of the Holy Spirit. It is in recognition of this that the church has long prayed or sung in the context of worship, particularly at Pentecost, *Veni Creator Spiritus* ("Come, Creator Spirit").

What this means is that when Christian theology uses the word "revelation" to describe God's communication with God's creatures, the word undergoes a semantic shift from its ordinary everyday usage and takes on new and specific rules of use. The recipient "sees" and "hears" not by virtue of innate capacities or propensities but by the self-mediation of the Word through the activity of the Holy Spirit within the recipient. There is thus a form of discernment that is genuinely new and sui generis, a form of recognition of a unique reality that requires to be distinguished not only from the external furnishings of the contingent order but also from the innate furnishings of our minds and prior capacities. One consequence of this is that the words of the Bible are not to be identified per se with God's self-disclosure. They are to be understood as witness—they attest to it and proclaim it. Here Barth believes he is echoing Kierkegaard's thought as illustrated by his reference to the distinction Kierkegaard draws between an apostle and a genius; Barth explains by referring to Grünewald's portrayal of the crucifixion which hung above the desk at which he worked.

> At this point we cannot reflect assiduously enough on [Kierkegaard's 1847 essay "The Difference between a Genius and an Apostle"]. The model of the biblical witness in his unity of form is John the Baptist, who stands so notably at midpoint between the Old Testament and the New, between the prophets and the apostles: "There was a man sent from God, whose name was John. He came as a witness to testify to the light, so that all might believe through him. He himself was not the light, but he came to testify to the light"[25] [John 1:6–8; cf. 3:27–28]. In this connection one might recall John the Baptist in Grünewald's Crucifixion, especially his prodigious index finger. Could anyone point away from himself more impressively

---

of Mind (London: Hutchinson University Library, 1949), 149. See Roderick M. Chisholm's discussion of this in "Epistemic Statements and the Ethics of Belief," *Philosophy and Phenomenological Research* 16, no. 4 (1956): 455.

25. Barth cites this passage in Greek. We are using the NRSV translation.

and completely ("he must become greater, I must become less"[26])? And could anyone point more impressively and realistically than here to what is indicated? This is what the Fourth Evangelist wanted to say about this John, and therefore about another John, and therefore quite unmistakably about every "John."[27]

Barth's commitment to challenging the depersonalization of God's revelation has made his arguments controversial both with those who hold to an inerrantist doctrine of Scripture and with those who approach Scripture in Socratic ways, that is, where Scripture is seen as serving simply to remind us of what we already know immanently—moral or existential or spiritual truths, for example. The fundamental question for Barth, which we cannot sidestep, is simply this: "Why and in what respect does the biblical witness have authority?"[28] His answer is that its authority lies in its witness—"letting that other itself be its own authority"[29]—and in the Bible's refusal, therefore, to claim authority for itself independently of the one to whom it bears witness.

THE TRINITARIAN GRAMMAR OF REVELATION

It is important to recognize that in addressing the doctrine of the Word of God, Barth is also expounding the doctrine of God—specifically, the triune being of God.[30] Two key elements in Barth's approach quickly become clear. First, the revelation with which we are presented in the biblical witness refuses to allow itself to be interpreted as one revelation among many[31]—"it insists absolutely on being understood in its uniqueness" because "it insists absolutely on being understood in terms of its object, God."[32] Second, the form of revelation requires to be interpreted in the light of revelation itself and not in advance of it. As we have already seen, Barth spells this out in irreducibly Trinitarian terms:

---

26. Barth cites this passage in Latin—the words that John the Baptist appears to be uttering in Grünewald's famous painting.
27. Barth, *Church Dogmatics* I/1, 112 (translation altered).
28. Barth, *Church Dogmatics* I/1, 112.
29. Barth, *Church Dogmatics* I/1, 112.
30. Barth, *Church Dogmatics* I/1, 295.
31. Barth, *Church Dogmatics* I/1, 295.
32. Barth, *Church Dogmatics* I/1, 295.

God reveals Himself. He reveals Himself *through Himself.* He reveals *Himself.* If we really want to understand revelation in terms of its subject, i.e., God, then the first thing we have to realise is that this subject, God, the Revealer, is identical with His act in revelation and also identical with its effect.[33]

In most of the contexts in which we use the term "revelation" in everyday life, a straightforward distinction is assumed between the various components in an event of revelation. Suppose, for example, one chooses to reveal the color of one's handkerchief or the contents of a box. In such acts of disclosure, one can distinguish the *revealer* from the *property* or *object* that is revealed (e.g., the blueness of the handkerchief or the content of the box). Both of these, moreover, are assumed to be quite other than the *recipient* of the revelation. Furthermore, in normal parlance one distinguishes the *person* of the revealer from the *act* of revealing and from the *capacity* (e.g., color-perception) that is a property of the recipient and the means by which she recognizes what is revealed. On this model of the grammar of revelation, the assumption is that there is no essential ontological connection between the *revealer* and (1) what is revealed, (2) the recipient of the revelation, (3) the capacity by which the revealed information is appropriated. Given these common assumptions about the nature of revelation, the inclination among theologians is to assume that Christian "revelation" is similar in form, with the result that, too often, it is interpreted accordingly.

The consequence of this is that when God is interpreted as the *revealer*, then what is revealed is assumed to be true propositions of one kind or another—inerrant biblical propositions perhaps, or propositions expressing spiritual or moral truths, depending on the conservative or liberal affinities of the theologian.[34] The further assumption is then made that whatever is revealed must be recognizable as such by virtue of the natural capacities inherent within the subject. To make such an assumption inevitably returns us to the Socratic in that it assumes we already possess the relevant knowledge or ideas in the light of which we can "recognize" what is revealed. On this model of revelation, revealed truths, to the extent that they are recognizable by us, may also be perceived as "revealed" by other sources be they of a religious, philosophical, or ethical nature. Consequently, the revelation at the heart of the Christian faith becomes simply one instance of a generic series of revelations the content

---

33. Barth, *Church Dogmatics* I/1, 296 (emphasis original).

34. The former are more likely to think of revelation in propositional terms, and the latter in terms of moral or social ideals.

of which might equally be expressed in other religious or, indeed, nonreligious sources. This then raises the further question as to what the *criteria* are for determining what constitutes true revelation and what the status of these criteria is. Are these criteria of recognition *also* "revealed"? If so, what is the source of this revelation? If it is assumed that they are already possessed by us, that is, "given" within our immanent frame of reference, then we are back with the Socratic—with all the implications that result from this and which were exposed so brilliantly by Climacus in *Philosophical Fragments*.

What becomes clear in Barth's interpretation of the divine address is that he refuses to extrapolate from our normal use of the term "revelation" or, indeed, project such a model of revelation onto God's self-disclosure. For Barth, the shape or form of God's self-disclosure requires to be interpreted in the light of its actuality and not in advance of it. To do this is to recognize (1) that it is unique—"revelation" has a particular meaning in this context—(2) that it is irreducibly second-personal in character, and (3) that its logic or "grammar" is Trinitarian rather than functionally unitarian.[35]

For Kierkegaard, as we have emphasized throughout this volume, Christian revelation breaks with Socratic or immanentist approaches precisely because it recognizes that the teacher and the moment have *decisive significance* for our relationship to the Truth. As Climacus outlines, what follows from this is that the teacher communicates the truth by providing anew the subjective condition by which the learner is brought into relationship with the Truth. As Climacus makes clear, this constitutes a redemptive act in that it delivers the learner from her prior state, which requires to be interpreted as one of error. Although there may be partial analogies to such an interpretation of discovery in science, this event of redemptive revelation constitutes an *uniquum* in that it involves an epistemic event that is miraculous and that cannot, therefore, be interpreted in naturalistic or secular or idealist terms. To fail to appreciate this, and to attempt to reinterpret Christian knowing in ways governed by other forms of creaturely knowing, inevitably risks the functional rejection of God's self-disclosure.

As the KBT affirms, we are brought into relation with the Truth of God's revelation through the concrete and reconciling presence of the Holy Spirit.

---

35. "The common idea that one must follow the far too obvious and illuminating scheme: How do we know God? Does God exist? What is God? And only last of all: Who is our God? is in direct contradiction to the very important declarations that no one can then avoid making, about the actual and comprehensive significance of the doctrine of the Trinity" (Barth, *Church Dogmatics* I/1, 301).

Integral to the event of revelation is the provision in time of the condition through which we recognize God through God's personal self-disclosure. It is not only the revelation that possesses decisive significance for our relation to God; so too does the revealer (that is, the teacher), without whom the learner would not be brought into relation with the Truth. And so also does the re-vealedness, that is, the condition by means of which the teacher (or deliverer, to use Climacus's term) is recognized and heard.

> Thus it is God Himself, it is the same God in unimpaired unity, who accord-ing to the biblical understanding of revelation is the revealing God and the event of revelation and its effect on human beings.[36]

Barth's approach here led Jürgen Moltmann to argue that, far from challenging the usual rendering of the grammar of revelation, "Barth developed the doc-trine of the Trinity out of the logic of the concept of God's self-revelation."[37] Moltmann was not the first to suggest this. The same criticism of Barth had been made prior to the publication of *Church Dogmatics* I/1 and to which Barth responded as follows: "The serious or mocking charge has been brought against me that here is a grammatical and rationalistic proof of the Trinity, so that I am doing the very thing I attack elsewhere, namely, deriving the mysteries of revelation from the data of a generally discernible truth."[38] If it were possible to do that, Barth argues, then a doctrine of the Trinity could be constructed on the basis of a revelation claim made with respect to any other god or "supposed god." He responds, "Naturally, it is not my thought then, nor is it now, that the truth of the dogma of the Trinity can be derived from the general truth of such a formula."[39] Contrary to Moltmann's suspicions, it is clear from Barth's analysis that far from arguing *to* the doctrine of the Trinity, he is arguing *from* the doctrine of the Trinity and interpreting the form and structure of revelation in its light. For Barth, it is the biblical witness itself that suggests God's relationship with the world is Trinitarian in structure, and this applies a fortiori to the nature of divine revelation. Rather than working *to*

---

36. Barth, *Church Dogmatics* I/1, 299 (translation altered).

37. Jürgen Moltmann, *The Trinity and the Kingdom of God*, trans. Margaret Kohl (Lon-don: SCM, 1980), 140.

38. Barth, *Church Dogmatics* I/1, 296.

39. Barth, *Church Dogmatics* I/1, 296; *Kirchliche Dogmatik* I/1, 312. Cf. Alan J. Torrance, *Persons in Communion: An Essay on Trinitarian Description and Human Participation, with Special Reference to Volume One of Karl Barth's "Church Dogmatics"* (Edinburgh: T&T Clark, 1996), 250.

the doctrine of the Trinity *from* the doctrine of revelation, therefore, we are required to interpret both together.

One fundamentally important consequence of this is that the "very important term" "God" requires to be redefined in accordance with its referent so that it is "used in Church proclamation in a manner appropriate to the object which is also its norm." Barth continues, "The doctrine of the Trinity is what basically distinguishes the Christian doctrine of God as Christian, and therefore what already distinguishes the Christian concept of revelation as Christian, in contrast to all other possible doctrines of God or concepts of revelation."[40] Since the focus of Christian dogmatics is God and all things in relation to God, the doctrine of the Trinity is foundational to the dogmatic task. It constitutes the key to what Kevin Diller describes as Barth's "theo-foundationalism."[41] Still further, it constitutes the ground of Barth's challenge to those developments associated with the Enlightenment, which he confronted not only in the Neo-Kantian agenda of his theological teachers but also in Emil Brunner's eristic agenda and the way in which it utilized natural theology. What is surprising here is not Barth's decision to place the Trinity at the head of his *Church Dogmatics* but that this has not been the norm in traditional systematic theologies—Barth was, as he puts it, "adopting a very isolated position from the standpoint of dogmatic history."[42] This is indicative of the extent of the functionally unitarian pressures on the theological task. If the doctrine of God is not conceived in Trinitarian terms, it is all too easy for the church to float free from God's self-disclosure and embrace "religion" and whatever is deemed to be upheld by it.

THE KIERKEGAARD-BARTH TRAJECTORY AND THE THEOLOGISTIC FALLACY

A Trinitarian account of revelation conceived along these lines not only constitutes a decisive challenge to Socratic approaches to biblical theology; it also constitutes the most cogent alternative to them.[43] It does so, moreover, by

40. Barth, *Church Dogmatics* I/1, 301.
41. Diller, *Theology's Epistemological Dilemma*, 46, 87–88, 187. For his definition of the term, see 122n108.
42. Barth, *Church Dogmatics* I/1, 300.
43. This section reiterates in revised form part of the argumentation in Alan J. Torrance, "Can the Truth Be Learned? Redressing the 'Theologistic Fallacy' in Modern Biblical Scholarship," in *Scripture's Doctrine and Theology's Bible: How the New Testament Shapes Christian*

providing a coherent solution to one of the knottiest challenges confronting theology—namely, the place of historical biblical research in the task of Christian theology.[44]

Much contemporary biblical scholarship focuses on the contextual, sociological, literary, philosophical, and semantic/linguistic factors that shaped the biblical material. The assumption is that the historical, sociocultural, and religious contexts are important for understanding the meaning of the texts that are being interpreted. What is less clear, however, is whether such scholarship can, in and of itself, generate conclusions that extend beyond what the author may have meant by a particular statement when we bracket out the author's faith. Scholars who are interested in Pauline statements about God will want, quite rightly, to understand how Paul's writing reflects and interacts with the sociocultural influences of the time. At one level, this involves their understanding the semantic rules of use that were assumed in what was said. However, it also concerns the theological claims that Paul was making—that is, the truth-claims he was making about the God he believed he knew, whom he saw himself as worshiping, and whom he perceived as having specific purposes for the contingent order. In short, biblical scholarship is obliged to engage these theological claims.

The problem, however, is that the use of the term "theological" here is ambiguous, and this ambiguity has facilitated a widespread and seductive confusion. It can either mean "talk about 'god'" or it can mean "talk about God," that is, first-order claims about God. When there is confusion here, it can generate the unwarranted assumption that to report theological claims made by Paul is itself to engage in theology—and thus to make first-order theological claims about God. Now, if the purpose of the Bible is indeed to facilitate first-order theological claims, this raises a fundamental question. Under what conditions are we warranted in moving from *second-order* claims that *describe* Paul's theological claims to *first-order* theological statements that *prescribe* what we should believe? For example, how can we move from (P) "Paul claimed that God was in Christ reconciling the world to himself" to (P*) "God was in Christ reconciling the world to himself"? These are two radically different kinds of claim. The first is a claim about Paul ("Paul believed/affirmed

---

Dogmatics, ed. Markus Bockmuehl and Alan J. Torrance (Grand Rapids: Baker Academic, 2008), 143–64, copyright © 2008. Used by permission of Baker Academic, a division of Baker Publishing Group.

44. Too often, this is a question that generates a form of subliminal embarrassment over the use of biblical scholarship in the theological task. To find serious engagement with biblical scholarship on the part of philosophical theologians is unusual.

that God is X"), and the second is a claim about God ("God is X").[45] Unless we are clear about the justification for such a move, we are unable to provide an account of how biblical scholarship can have any bearing whatsoever on Christian theology.

The problem for biblical scholarship here is not dissimilar to what David Hume addressed in his exposé of what G. E. Moore would later refer to as the "naturalistic fallacy." In *A Treatise of Human Nature*, Hume made the following observation:

> In every system of morality, which I have hitherto met with, I have always remark'd, that the author proceeds for some time in the ordinary way of reasoning; . . . when of a sudden I am surpriz'd to find, that instead of the usual copulations of propositions, *is*, and *is not*, I meet with no proposition that is not connected with an *ought*, or an *ought not*. This change is imperceptible; but is however, of the last consequence. For as this *ought*, or *ought not*, expresses some new relation or affirmation, 'tis necessary that it shou'd be observ'd and explain'd; and at the same time that a reason shou'd be given, for what seems altogether inconceivable, how this new relation can be a deduction from others, which are entirely different from it.[46]

A parallel situation emerges when biblical scholars engaged in "neutral" historical research seek to draw theological conclusions. They adopt "ordinary ways of reasoning," when all "of a sudden" there occurs a change that is "imperceptible" but also "of the last consequence." That results when they move from second-order talk about God-talk (from the perspective of a religiously neutral academic discipline, god-talk-talk[47]) to first-order God-talk—that is, when

---

45. Although we would not formulate the problem in the same terms, Louis P. Pojman is grappling with related issues when, drawing on Kierkegaard, he argues, "Even supposing that the evidence for the historical claims of Christianity (e.g., the resurrection of Christ, his miracles, his teachings) was trustworthy, we would still not be entitled to infer from this that his metaphysical claims (e.g., that he was God's son, that those who believed in him would enjoy eternal life) were true. From the 'fact' that Jesus rose from the dead, we cannot infer that God raised him from the dead." He then adds, "To attempt metaphysical inferences from historic facts is to be guilty of what Lessing called a '*metabasis eis allo genos*,' an enormous categorical mistake." Louis P. Pojman, "Kierkegaard on Justification of Belief," *International Journal for Philosophy of Religion* 8, no. 2 (1977): 80.

46. David Hume, *A Treatise of Human Nature*, ed. David Fate Norton and Mary J. Norton (Oxford: Clarendon, 2007), bk. 3, pt. 1, sec. 1, p. 302 (emphasis original).

47. We are using lower case for "god-talk-talk" to emphasize the supposed religious neutrality of the community of academic biblical historians, some of whom may not believe that God exists.

they move from *descriptions* of claims made by biblical authors and the context of these claims to *prescriptions* as to what ought to be affirmed about God.

An example of this can be found in James Dunn's modern classic *Christology in the Making*.[48] This immensely influential monograph opens with the modest claim, "The following study is simply *a historical investigation into how and in what terms the doctrine of the incarnation first came to expression*."[49] Clearly, the reason Dunn deploys italics here is to emphasize that this is all he is seeking to do. He also explains that the volume "is not a philosophical essay on the concept of incarnation as such. . . . Nor is what follows an exercise in dogmatic theology."[50] His concern is simply "*to let the New Testament writers speak for themselves, to understand their words as they would have intended, to hear them as their first readers would have heard them*."[51] Again, he uses italics to emphasize the limited scope of this study. By the conclusion of the book, however, what Hume might have described as his "ordinary ways of [historical] reasoning" change all "of a sudden" in a manner that appears "imperceptible" to the author but which is yet "of the last consequence." His modest aims give way to first-order theological claims concerning what it is that we celebrate at Christmas, Easter, and Pentecost, culminating in the following quotation from Walter Kasper's *Jesus the Christ*: "In substance the trinitarian confession means that God in Jesus Christ has proved himself to be self-communicating love and that as such he is permanently among us in the Holy Spirit."[52] What becomes plain from this statement and its context is that Dunn has progressed to making prescriptive, dogmatic, or theological claims that he believes he has deduced from reflections on claims made by the church about the preexistence of Jesus Christ—reflections that bristle with philosophical assumptions concerning the nature of time, the concept of incarnation, divine intentionality, and so on. All this derives, ostensibly, from what was deemed to be a purely historical and theology-free investigation into the God-talk (or god-talk, if it is purely historical and theology-free) of the New Testament writers. What we have in actuality, however, is an explicit move in the conclusions of the book from god-talk-talk to God-talk. Without that move, one wonders whether the book would have been accepted so widely as an example of the kind of responsible biblical scholarship on which we can ground historically informed

---

48. James D. G. Dunn, *Christology in the Making: A New Testament Inquiry into the Origins of the Doctrine of the Incarnation* (London: SCM, 1980).

49. Dunn, *Christology*, 10 (emphasis original).

50. Dunn, *Christology*, 9.

51. Dunn, *Christology*, 9 (emphasis original).

52. Dunn, *Christology*, 268.

theological conclusions about the identity of Jesus Christ.[53] In sum, Dunn's argumentation leaves us asking about the justification he has for drawing any first-order theological conclusions at all.[54]

This brings us to a fundamental question. Under what conditions, if any, is it possible to move from second-order god-talk-talk (which characterizes much contemporary, academic biblical scholarship, of the kind that Dunn sets out to undertake) to first-order, Christian theological claims, namely, God-talk? If it is the case that the texts with which the historical scholar engages are recognized as *bearing witness* to God's engagement with the historical world, then she may be entitled to believe that studying this can lead to "successful" God-talk. That is, this may give her permission to believe that, under certain circumstances, she can draw first-order theological conclusions without succumbing to the fallacy outlined above.

To treat Paul, for example, as a witness in this sense is unlikely to be perceived within the academy as meeting the conditions of valid historical scholarship. It is not clear, however, why this should be the case. If it is possible that Paul was right in thinking that our minds require to be (miraculously) transformed in order to discern the very specific form of truth that stands at the heart of the Christian faith, then it is not clear how one can assess the validity or grounds of his argumentation without considering the truth-questions raised by these claims. Second, if a scholar were to approach Paul with the perception that he was indeed a witness to God's engagement with the world, this would not mean, of course, that she should ignore other historical or societal factors. It is clearly appropriate to recognize that Paul's letters constitute a witness that is nested within a particular context. If so, what he is saying cannot be adequately understood without taking into account the social, philosophical, political, and other historical factors and pressures together with the additional literary, semantic, and rhetorical elements that are integral to interpreting the argumentation of these texts. If so, it is clearly pertinent to a full understanding and interpretation of this witness to understand in as great a depth as possible all these factors.

53. By contrast, Richard Bauckham's more recent historical work facilitates theological engagement of a particularly constructive and cogent kind without making unwarranted moves of the kind we find in Dunn. See Richard Bauckham, *God Crucified: Monotheism and Christology in the New Testament* (Grand Rapids: Eerdmans, 1999). See also his *Jesus and the Eyewitnesses: The Gospels as Eyewitness Testimony* (Grand Rapids: Eerdmans, 2006).

54. C. Stephen Evans raises related questions about N. T. Wright's approach in "Methodological Naturalism in Historical Biblical Scholarship," in *Jesus and the Restoration of Israel: A Critical Assessment of N. T. Wright's Jesus and the Victory of God*, ed. Carey C. Newman (Downers Grove, IL: InterVarsity Press, 1999), 180–205.

There is a critically important question that this discussion raises, however. Under what conditions might a biblical historian be justified in regarding such texts as actual witness rather than simply perceived witness in the mind of their author? For a historian to recognize a text as constituting "actual" as opposed to "perceived" witness requires the historian to recognize the one to whom the text bears witness. To accommodate such a recognition within the historical task would require the historian herself to recognize that God has (miraculously, for both Kierkegaard and Barth) given her the eyes to recognize this witness for what it is. For the study of the biblical text to furnish theological conclusions therefore requires what we might refer to as a "third horizon" whereby scholarship does not simply involve a fusion (to use Gadamer's metaphor[55]) between our horizon and the horizon of the ancient author, but also a further third horizon—what Athanasius referred to as the "mind" (*phronēma*) or "scope" (*skopos*) or "perception" (*dianoia*) or, indeed, "worship" (*eusebeia*)[56] of the body of Christ.[57] This third horizon cannot be defined without reference to the kinship with the eternal God, which that same God has established in time.

Historians operating within the academic context may struggle to make sense of the notion of witness. It is not something that can be quantified or assessed using traditional academic techniques. However, what Kierkegaard and Barth saw with such clarity is that to bracket out the possibility of this element in the interpretation of Scripture is to assume either that the text is theologically irrelevant or that any "recognition" of theological truth must

55. Hans-Georg Gadamer, *Truth and Method*, rev. 2nd ed., trans. rev. Joel Weinsheimer and Donald G. Marshall (London: Continuum, 2004), especially 306–7. Regarding the place of language in the fusion of horizons, see 378–79.

56. See John Henry Newman, trans., *Four Discourses of S. Athanasius against the Arians*, in *Select Treatises of St. Athanasius*, trans. John Henry Newman (Oxford: James Parker, 1877), 2.18.43nI; available online, Newman Reader: Works of John Henry Newman, The National Institute for Newman Studies, 2007, https://www.newmanreader.org/works/athanasius/orig inal/discourse2-3.html#fnoteII.

57. Reference to a "third horizon" is an allusion to Hans-Georg Gadamer's concept of a *Horizontverschmelzung* (fusion of horizons) between our contemporary situation and the situation of those who lived at the time of the biblical authors. "Every finite present has its limitations. We define the concept of 'situation' by saying that it represents a standpoint that limits the possibility of vision. Hence essential to the concept of situation is the concept of 'horizon.' The horizon is the range of vision that includes everything that can be seen from a particular vantage point. . . . Working out the hermeneutical situation means acquiring the right horizon of inquiry for the questions evoked by the encounter with tradition" (Gadamer, *Truth and Method*, 301–2). What we are suggesting is that the very possibility of drawing theological conclusions requires us to make reference to a third "ecclesial" horizon whereby our "situation" is defined in terms of participation within the body of Christ, which is interpreted in turn by means of reference to the Holy Spirit.

stem from our own immanent capacities and abilities—that is, by Socratic means. As Climacus reminds us, if our theological conclusions are delivered exclusively by Socratic means, then the only kind of "theological" significance the Bible could possess would be *illustrative*—that is, where the text serves simply to remind us of what we already know subliminally to be true. Consequently, the Bible could not witness to anything *new*, such as that God is active in relation to particular persons in particular circumstances in time. It would not be possible on such an account to *recognize* Jesus, therefore, as having *decisive* significance for the theological task.

In contrast, Kierkegaard and Barth invite us to open the door to forms of biblical and historical scholarship that seek to be decisively theological—recognizing, for example, not only that Mark, Luke, and Paul *believed* they were witnesses to God's action, but that they *were* witnesses. This is emphatically not to bracket out engagement with the whole range of historical and sociological studies; but neither does it bracket out the further element that requires to be taken into consideration, namely, the theological witness borne through these texts. If biblical scholarship can accommodate this, then the conditions for the kind of historical scholarship that can generate theological affirmations will be met. That is, the conditions are met whereby biblical scholarship that is engaged in god-talk-talk can fuel first-order claims about God. So, under what conditions could this kind of theological interpretation of the biblical witness take place? The answer is simple. The relevant conditions are the same as those under which revelation can take place. Consequently, it is simply not possible for the scholar to establish a hermeneutical method that can deliver first-order God-talk in and of itself. It is to a consideration of the issues this raises that we shall turn now.

To summarize the argument so far, when religious claims made by historical figures (e.g., biblical authors) are taken as providing warrant for first-order claims about God in the present tense, then we are obliged to provide some account of what validates this move—that is, if we are not to commit that form of the naturalistic fallacy that we are referring to as the "theologistic fallacy." The theologistic fallacy refers to the unwarranted move from second-order god-talk-talk to God-talk. To recall our conclusions above, it is a problematic form of naturalistic theology whereby persons seek to argue from what is perceived to be an academically neutral analysis of ancient "god-talk" and its context to conclusions about what we *ought* to affirm about *God* in the present. If any such move is to be supported, it requires some kind of ontological and epistemological framework.

To reiterate, one of the primary reasons for the widespread failure to appreciate the radical and potentially fallacious nature of the move from second-order to first-order statements lies with a certain ambiguity in the way we use the word "theological." That is, the word has at least two different meanings. First, "theological" can mean "pertaining to the concept of 'god'"—for example, "Richard Dawkins made the theological claim that a loving god would not tolerate horrendous evil." Second, "theological" can denote (successful) reference to God. For example, "The theological claims she made shed light on God's purpose in the act of creation." In the second context, the statement is taken as referring successfully to the personal reality "God" and functions as an ostensive reference indexed to the person making the statement.

One of the most significant contributions of Kierkegaard and Barth is that, taken together, they spell out the conditions under which biblical scholarship can serve the theological task without falling foul of what we are referring to as the theologistic fallacy.[58] That is because their approaches generate a theological account of the conditions for God-talk where "theological" denotes successful theological reference, allowing the historical to have a decisive role. This means the biblical scholar can engage in theological interpretation that takes seriously social, philosophical, literary, and other historical factors without having to disguise situations in which their historical scholarship does not yield theologically relevant conclusions—for example, when their argumentation does not actually operate from socio-historico-religious *description*, or when they do not claim their conclusions constitute valid theological *prescription*.

How Barth's Trinitarian Approach Obviates the Theologistic Fallacy

Barth rejects what he refers to as the "far too obvious and illuminating scheme"[59] wherein the knowledge of God and the existence and nature of God are addressed prior to asking, Who is our God? To do so fails to recognize the "actual and comprehensive significance of the doctrine of the Trinity."[60]

---

58. It is noteworthy that two of the persons to have raised these fundamentally important issues with the greatest clarity are Kierkegaard scholars: Evans, "Methodological Naturalism," 180–205; Murray A. Rae, *History and Hermeneutics* (Edinburgh: T&T Clark, 2005).

59. Barth, *Church Dogmatics* I/1, 301.

60. Barth, *Church Dogmatics* I/1, 301.

When we ask the "who" question of the self-revealing God of the Bible, we find ourselves obliged to interpret God and the knowledge of God in irreducibly Trinitarian terms. As we have seen, for Barth, the doctrine of Christian revelation stands or falls with the doctrine of the Trinity.[61]

Fundamental to this is his insistence that the Word is identical with God as its own absolute ground.[62]

> According to Holy Scripture God's revelation is a ground which has no higher or deeper ground above or below it but is an absolute ground in itself, and therefore for humanity a court from which there can be no possible appeal to a higher court. Its reality and its truth do not rest on a superior reality and truth. They do not have to be actualised or validated as reality from this or any other point. They are not measured by the reality and truth found at this other point. They are not to be compared with any such nor judged and understood as reality and truth by reference to such. On the contrary, God's revelation has its reality and truth wholly and in every respect—both ontically and noetically—within itself.[63]

This represents Barth's rejection of theological approaches that are rooted in human immanence. For both Kierkegaard and Barth, the Christian theologian is presented with an unambiguous "either-or": either God has spoken to us in space-time, in which case the historical has decisive significance, or theology collapses into Socratic anamnesis. Both, moreover, are equally clear that to seek to accept or reject the faith from the standpoint of a higher or deeper (immanent) ground, is, by virtue of that fact, to deny it and, in doing so, Barth argues, to deny God's lordship in the self-authenticating and self-actualizing reality of God's self-disclosure. "Revelation is not made real and true by anything else, whether in itself or for us."[64] In revelation, God reveals Godself as the Lord, and this lordship is evident from the fact that the reality and truth of revelation are fully self-grounded. Revelation, therefore, "does not need any other actualisation or validation than that of its actual occurrence."[65] God's self-revelation requires to be conceived as "revelation through itself." It is a

---

61. Barth, *Church Dogmatics* I/1, 303.

62. Geoffrey W. Bromiley, *Introduction to the Theology of Karl Barth* (Grand Rapids: Eerdmans, 1979), 14.

63. Barth, *Church Dogmatics* I/1, 305 (translation altered).

64. Barth, *Church Dogmatics* I/1, 305.

65. Barth, *Church Dogmatics* I/1, 306.

self-authenticating and self-grounded reality and, from the perspective of our immanent assumptions, a "self-contained *novum*."[66]

Revelation is a self-unveiling on God's part where this "self-unveiling means that God does what human beings themselves cannot do in any sense or in any way: He makes Himself present, known and significant to them as God."[67] This unveiling means that God requires to be recognized as Lord "three times"—a statement Barth unpacks by means of the following definition: "Revelation in the Bible means the self-unveiling, imparted to humanity, of the God who by nature cannot be unveiled to human beings."[68] God's lordship is manifest first in that God unveils Godself to humans who are *unable, in and of themselves, to unveil God*. God's lordship is manifest a second time in that God is *inscrutable and not accessible to human purview*.[69] And, finally, God is Lord a third time in that God's self-unveiling is imparted to particular human individuals. God's self-revelation is neither generic nor a general revelation within the sphere of humanity. It is always an act of special revelation. There is, therefore, a *moment* of revelation in which God is Lord, that is, where God addresses "a specific person occupying a very specific place, a specific historical place."[70]

So God's self-disclosure does not dilute God's lordship; it confirms it. It is only because God is Lord over every facet of the process that God is revealed to human beings. Without God's being Lord "three times" in this unveiling, God-talk could ultimately be no more than the mythological projection of finite creaturely categories onto that which is epistemically inaccessible and inscrutable in its transcendence.[71] Importantly, to affirm God's lordship is also to affirm God's freedom: "God is free to reveal Himself or not to reveal Himself."[72]

---

66. Barth, *Church Dogmatics* I/1, 306.

67. Barth, *Church Dogmatics* I/1, 315. God reveals "his own *alter ego*" (*sein eigener Doppelgänger*) (*Church Dogmatics* I/1, 316; *Kirchliche Dogmatik* I/1, 333).

68. Barth, *Church Dogmatics* I/1, 315.

69. The *Deus revelatus* is the same God who is veiled and inscrutable—the *Deus absconditus* "to whom there is no path nor bridge, concerning whom we could not say nor have to say a single word if He did not of His own initiative meet us as the *Deus revelatus*" (Barth, *Church Dogmatics* I/1, 321).

70. Barth, *Church Dogmatics* I/1, 325 (translation altered). Barth immediately adds, "Part of the concept of the biblically attested revelation is that it is a historical event."

71. "Revelation encounters man on the presupposition and in confirmation of the fact that man's attempts to know God from his own standpoint are wholly and entirely futile" (Barth, *Church Dogmatics* I/2, 301).

72. Barth, *Church Dogmatics* I/1, 321.

HISTORY AND THE VEILEDNESS OF REVELATION

This leads Barth to address a widespread and serious confusion about what it means to affirm Christian revelation as *historical*. "Historical does not mean historically demonstrable or historically demonstrated. Hence it does not mean what is often meant by 'historical' (*historisch*)."[73] To suggest that the events of revelation attested in the Bible were "historical"—in the sense that they could be apprehended as such by "detached" academic scholarship— would be to discard the recognition of mystery in revelation. In a key section entitled "The Speech of God as the Mystery of God," Barth stresses that "we do not have the Word of God otherwise than in the mystery of its secularity."[74] When God speaks to a human being, the particular phenomena generated by the event of God's speaking are "secular." That is, the events through which God speaks do not "contain" God as if the Godhead were enclosed within a particular series of events. Here Barth reminds us that, *phenomenologically speaking*, the church may be perceived as merely a sociological entity and, similarly, preaching interpreted as merely human address—although neither the church nor preaching is reducible to these. Further still, Jesus Christ is the rabbi of Nazareth "who is hard to know historically and whose work, when He is known, might seem to be a little commonplace compared to more than one of the other founders of religions and even compared to some of the later representatives of His own religion."[75] In parallel with Kierkegaard's emphasis on the divine incognito and the offense of lowliness that we discussed in chapter 2, Barth continues, "Even the biblical miracles do not break through this wall of secularity."[76] Events in which God is involved in the historical order will always be open to being interpreted in different ways for the simple reason that "the veil is thick."[77]

Barth is certainly not suggesting that revelation is an additional layer that we choose to add to or project onto events of which the scientist can provide a full and all-embracing account. What he is eager to stress is that the divine speech to which the Bible attests has God as its subject. God cannot be subjected to scientific or historical investigation—so God cannot be regarded, therefore, as an additional factor to be included in a "scientific" or phenome-

---

73. Barth, *Church Dogmatics* I/1, 325.
74. Barth, *Church Dogmatics* I/1, 165.
75. Barth, *Church Dogmatics* I/1, 165.
76. Barth, *Church Dogmatics* I/1, 165.
77. Barth, *Church Dogmatics* I/1, 165.

nological account of God's historical self-disclosure. The content of revelation is inseparable from the triune God. If that were not the case, God would cease to be the living Lord in revelation, and what would be revealed would not be the person of the speaking God (*Dei loquentis persona*). Consequently, the historian, scientist, or biblical scholar who would treat God as an object of inquiry requires continually to be reminded that God never ceases to be the free subject of revelation—and any move to subsume God within a class of determinate objects under investigation constitutes a category mistake. No account of God's self-disclosure in history can afford to forget that God remains the free and transcendent Lord with respect to any self-unveiling and self-disclosure.

In sum, the beginning of Christian theology lies in recognizing God's lordship over all human knowing and God-talk, and that God's lordship in revelation requires to be conceived in irreducibly Trinitarian terms.

The Age-Old Challenge of Idealism, and Two Parallel Gulfs

In chapter 3, we argued that the father of myth theory, David Friedrich Strauss, exemplified what Climacus refers to as the "Socratic." On this view, the condition and criteria for the assessment of all truth-claims, not least those relating to the being and purposes of God, are immanent within our understanding—what we might refer to as "criterial immanentism." As we saw, the background of Strauss's arguments lay first in Leibniz's distinction between the necessary truths of reason (to which epistemic access is a priori) and contingent truths (to which epistemic access is a posteriori and mediated by means of sense perception), and second in Spinoza's related insistence that the truth of a historical narrative cannot provide knowledge of God. This led Lessing to determine that the "accidental truths of history can never become the proof for necessary truths of reason." There is a "broad and ugly ditch which I cannot get across, no matter how often and earnestly I have tried to make the leap."[78]

It is pertinent to our discussion here to revisit in greater depth the issues Lessing raises. Lessing's argument has been brilliantly analyzed by Gordon Michalson, who finds not one but three different gaps or ditches at the heart of Lessing's argument.

78. Gotthold Ephraim Lessing, *Philosophical and Theological Writings*, trans. and ed. Hugh Barr Nisbet (Cambridge: Cambridge University Press, 2005), 87.

The first gap, Michalson distills, is the "temporal gap" between historical events that were perceived by those who witnessed them as a proof of spirit and of power but which, given the passage of time, are not firsthand experiences and can only be regarded therefore as *reports* of a proof of spirit and of power. In Lessing's words, the "proof of the spirit and of power no longer has either spirit or power, but has sunk to the level of *human testimonies of spirit and power*."[79] He then adds, "Reports of fulfilled prophecies are not fulfilled prophecies; . . . reports of miracles are not miracles."[80] The effect of the temporal gap, therefore, is to deprive the miracles of their capacity to demonstrate God's miraculous power.

The second gap is a metaphysical one. Matthew Benton distinguishes three aspects to this gap.[81] First, there is what he terms the "rationalist" aspect, namely, the "uneasy conjunction of the particularity of contingent, historical truth as revelation with seemingly universal, necessary, religious truth."[82] The second aspect, which pertains to the most fundamental issue for Lessing, is the "modal" one. This is the ontological gap between historical truths on the one hand, which are contingent, and metaphysical truths on the other, which are deemed necessary. For Lessing, it is incoherent to confuse contingent historical truth-claims, which could be false, with metaphysical truth-claims about God, which are necessarily true. Third, there is what Benton refers to as the "dogmatic" aspect. This appears identical to the modal gap but pertains to the discontinuity between historical truths and Christological claims. This gap, he argues, "seem[s] to land one halfway between contingent truths and necessary truths," given that, as Michalson puts it, Christological claims are not "necessary truths" in the Leibnizian sense, and yet, despite that, they are still radically different from "normal historical assertions."[83]

The third ditch in Michalson's analysis concerns the problem of "religious appropriation," namely, the gap between what an individual can accept and the "dubious, strange, or fantastic" nature of the Christian message. How can

---

79. Lessing, *Philosophical and Theological Writings*, 84 (emphasis added).

80. Lessing, *Philosophical and Theological Writings*, 84.

81. Matthew A. Benton, "The Modal Gap: The Objective Problem of Lessing's Ditch(es) and Kierkegaard's Subjective Reply," *Religious Studies* 42, no. 1 (2006): 27–44.

82. Benton, "Modal Gap," 31.

83. Gordon E. Michalson, *Lessing's "Ugly Ditch": A Study of Theology and History* (University Park, PA: Penn State University Press, 1990), 11. We are drawing here on Benton's discussion in "Modal Gap," 30.

an individual possess the conditions necessary for "successfully apprehending, accepting, and perhaps even understanding the religious message"?[84]

The gaps that Lessing brings to the fore highlight challenges that will inevitably emerge if God's self-disclosure is located in space and time, that is, within history. What is important to appreciate here, however, is that this is no new discovery. Indeed, it is precisely this issue that lay at the heart of the Nicene debates! The Arians approached Christology in the light of the prior assumption of an infinite gap or gulf (*chōrismos*) between the divine, namely, that which is really Real (and hence necessarily unchanging[85]), and the realm of flux and change. Consequently, to suggest that the incarnate Son was "of one being with the Father" was simply incoherent for the simple reason that if the Son was begotten, then there was a time when he was not. Consequently, the Arians insisted that we are obliged to recognize that the incarnate Son belongs to the contingent order, as the first created being, *prōton ktisma*. This meant that, instead of affirming him as the one through whom *all things* were made, he was to be regarded as the one through whom *everything else* was made. This, however, posed a fundamental problem for Christian theology. What is arguably an infinite gap between the eternal divine order and the contingent temporal order (that is, between the noumenal and the phenomenal realms) generated an ontological gulf between God and the incarnate Son creating, in turn, an unbridgeable *epistemological* gap between humanity and God. If the Arians were correct, knowledge of the incarnate Son or Logos could not furnish knowledge of the Father. How could the incarnate Son or Word communicate anything whatsoever about the eternal God if the Son were a creature and thus belonged to the wrong side of that infinite ontological—and hence epistemological—gulf?

Athanasius spells out the implications of this gulf with ruthless consistency. If the Arians are right, then all our attempts to engage in theology (*theologein*) amount to nothing more than the mythological projection of creaturely thoughts (*muthologein*), whereby human creatures vainly project their own creaturely constructions onto an utterly transcendent reality that could not be known in truth (*alēthōs*). Moreover, despite the Arians' insistence on stressing the significance of this gulf (*chōrismos*), they assumed they had rea-

---

84. Michalson, *Lessing's "Ugly Ditch,"* 14–15. Cf. Benton, "Modal Gap," 30.

85. Parmenides and Plato drew attention to the incoherence of associating ultimate reality with change. That which is really Real cannot change because either it thereby acquires reality it was lacking, or it loses reality that it possessed. Either way, it is lacking reality.

sonably extensive epistemic access to what belonged to the other side of it. They knew, for example, what was and was not possible for God. Alasdair Heron comments:

> By a curious irony, on which Athanasius was not slow to remark, Arius seemed to possess a good deal of privileged information. But where had he got it from? Athanasius was in no doubt about the source: the Arians had fabricated this concept of the divine being out of their own minds, thus making their own intellects the measure of ultimate reality, and assigning to Christ, the Word-made-flesh, the place which their minds could make for him.[86]

For Athanasius, however, it was precisely the recognition that the incarnate Son is of one being (*homoousios*) with the Father that led creatures to believe they could refer to God or talk about God (*analogein* or *theologein*) truthfully (*alēthōs*). The incarnation means that finite human creatures can speak about God in a way that actually tracks the reality of God. Without God giving Godself to be known by creatures in this way, our god-talk can only collapse back into mythological speculation concerning a god with respect to whom we are literally agnostic (*agnōsis*). Consequently, we are left vainly projecting creaturely ideas across an infinite gulf onto that which we do not know—as we discussed in chapter 2, theology becomes what Kierkegaard refers to as "mythology in the proper sense, [which] is the creation of God in human form."[87] In sharp contrast to this mythologizing, the implications of affirming that the incarnate Logos is "of one being with the Father" are radical. T. F. Torrance summarizes Athanasius's view as follows: "Through the Word made flesh, we human beings with our created minds are enabled . . . to know and think of God in such a way that our knowledge and thought of him repose upon his divine reality."[88]

It is important to note, however, that, for Athanasius, the incarnation of the Word did not, in and of itself, solve the epistemological problem we have

---

86. Alasdair I. C. Heron, "*Homoousios* with the Father," in *The Incarnation: Ecumenical Studies in the Nicene-Constantinopolitan Creed, A.D. 381*, ed. Thomas F. Torrance (Edinburgh: Handsel Press, 1981), 70.

87. Søren Kierkegaard, *Søren Kierkegaard's Journals and Papers*, ed. and trans. Howard V. Hong and Edna H. Hong, asst. Gregor Malantschuk (Bloomington: Indiana University Press, 1967–1978), 3:2700.

88. Thomas F. Torrance, "Athanasius: A Study in the Foundations of Classical Theology," in *Theology in Reconciliation: Essays towards Evangelical and Catholic Unity in East and West* (Eugene, OR: Wipf & Stock, 1996), 239.

described. Central and, indeed, integral to Athanasius's response to the Arians is his affirmation that not only the Son but also the Holy Spirit is of one being (*homoousios*) with the Father. As he writes in his "Letters to Serapion," it is "madness [*mania*] to call him a creature. . . . For the whole Triad is one God"[89] and thus "rightly characterized as indivisible and of one nature."[90] As C. R. B. Shapland insists, for Athanasius, the Spirit's essential Godhead "is not an addendum artificially stitched onto his confession of the Son. The one doctrine springs naturally and inevitably from the other."[91] It is not possible to overstate the epistemological implications of Athanasius's insistence that the Son should not be divided from the Holy Spirit.[92] The incarnation of the Word does not constitute an event of divine revelation or self-disclosure *in and of itself*. It is only an event of *actual* (i.e., successful) *revelation* when it is *recognized* as such by the church, that is, when the Holy Spirit gives the church the eyes to recognize who Jesus Christ is. If the "revelation" has not been recognized, then nothing has been revealed—revelation has not taken place. The biblical witness, however, makes it clear that the recognition of God's presence is from God and involves our being reconstituted "from above."[93] Consequently, the essential condition by which sinful creatures can recognize the incarnate Word is the creative and reconciling presence of the Holy Spirit.[94] As Athanasius saw with unprecedented clarity, the biblical witness testifies to a twofold *homoousion*. Both the Son and the Holy Spirit are "of one being with the Father"—and it is purely by virtue of that twofold *homoousion*, the fact that both the incarnate Son and the Holy Spirit are divine, that we are given to know the eternal God in truth, and that God-talk can thus refer (*analogein*) truthfully (*alēthōs*) to the reality of God and not collapse back into confusing theology with creaturely mythology—what constitutes, for Athanasius, a form of insanity (*mania*).[95]

89. St. Athanasius, *Letters of Saint Athanasius concerning the Holy Spirit*, trans. C. R. B. Shapland (London: Epworth, 1951), 103.

90. Athanasius, *Letters of Saint Athanasius*, 106. The affirmation of the essential Godhead of the Spirit is expressed throughout these letters; see especially *Epistle* 1.17.

91. C. R. B. Shapland, introduction to *Letters of Saint Athanasius*, trans. C. R. B. Shapland, 35.

92. Athanasius, *Letters of Saint Athanasius*, 106.

93. Matt. 16:17; John 3:7.

94. See, for example, Athanasius's use of the Gospel of John and 1 Cor. 2 in *Letters of Saint Athanasius*, *Epistle* 1.6.

95. St. Athanasius, *Discourse 1: Against the Arians*, trans. John Henry Newman and Archibald Robertson, vol. 4 of *Nicene and Post-Nicene Fathers2*, ed. Philip Schaff and Henry Wace (Buffalo, NY: Christian Literature Publishing Co., 1892); rev. and ed. Kevin Knight, New Advent, 1.1, https://www.newadvent.org/fathers/28161.htm.

What should be eminently clear is that when Barth insisted that God's self-disclosure was to be conceived in irreducibly Trinitarian terms, he was reiterating the same fundamental insights that had characterized the thought of Athanasius and the Nicene fathers. What Athanasius had grasped, like Kierkegaard and Barth fifteen hundred years later, is that when the New Testament witness is interpreted in light of the categories the New Testament provides, it is possible to provide a coherent account of God-talk that is otherwise precluded by the infinite qualitative gulf between the divine and contingent orders and the associated epistemological gaps highlighted so effectively by Lessing.

It is simply mistaken, therefore, to think that the problem of the ontological and epistemological "gap" was not recognized until the Enlightenment, or, indeed, that the distinction between theology and mythology originated in the modern era with David Friedrich Strauss or Rudolf Bultmann or John Hick and his colleagues[96] and was generated by the discoveries of modern science by a humanity "come of age." The distinction between theology and mythology was made explicit by Athanasius and lay at the core of his defense of the Christian faith against those who would reformulate it to accommodate that infinitely broad ditch or, in the terminology of the fathers, "gulf of separation" (*chōrismos*) between God and the contingent order, between the eternal and the temporal; this gulf, which is unbridgeable by creatures, is what Kierkegaard and Barth would acknowledge as the infinite qualitative difference between God and humanity. Far from their believing in the incarnation on account of a failure to distinguish theology from mythology, the Nicene fathers recognized that the incarnation was the necessary condition of engaging in theology *as opposed to* mythology—the unwarranted projection of creaturely thought-forms onto a transcendent realm about which we are ultimately devoid of knowledge. For Athanasius, the construction of myths (*muthoplastia*) was the natural inclination of the unreconciled creaturely mind and precisely what Christian theology should and must repudiate.[97] In sum, it is through the incarnation of the Logos and through the creative power of the Holy Spirit that finite human creatures are enabled to recognize God's presence and thereby refer truthfully (*alēthōs*) to God engaging in faithful theological interpretation (*hermēneuein*) of the Scriptures.

---

96. We are referring here to the authors who contributed to John Hick, ed., *The Myth of God Incarnate* (London: SCM, 1976).

97. See Thomas F. Torrance, "The Logic and Analogic of Biblical and Theological Statements in the Greek Fathers," in *Theology in Reconstruction* (London: SCM, 1965), 30–45; Torrance, "Athanasius," 215–66.

Progressing beyond the Socratic in Biblical Scholarship

In chapter 3, we argued that, for Strauss, the primary contribution of the Gospels lay in the insight they provided into the workings of the mind (or "human consciousness"). As Tamar Ross summarizes:

> The Gospels represented an unconscious invention or myth which attempted to envision the Absolute in terms of images derived from sensible experience. They should be viewed as poetic renderings of man's desire to realize the immanent goal of Spirit in its journey toward the Hegelian Being-in-and-for-itself.[98]

The Gospels were interpreted, therefore, in terms of a Hegelian synthesis of the divine and the human where, as we argued in chapter 1, the union is perceived as finding its fullest expression in the Christian image of incarnation. To recall the quotation from Hegel, "the divine nature is the same as the human, and it is this unity that is beheld [in the incarnation of the divine being]."[99] In sum, for Hegel, Jesus Christ exemplifies a general union between God and humanity—the God-human union that is made apparent in Jesus Christ is true for all persons. In Strauss, as we saw in chapter 3, this resulted in the transfer of Christological attributes from the particular human Jesus to the universal, that is, to the "human race." The chilling results of this were spelled out in the dogmatic conclusions of his critical examination of the life of Jesus. Does the significance the church has attached to Jesus, Strauss asks, mean that we should attach exclusive value to that particular piece of history with its focus on the life of Jesus? No, it emphatically does not. "This is indeed not the mode in which Idea realizes itself; it is not wont to lavish all its fullness on one exemplar and be niggardly toward all others—to express itself perfectly in that one individual, and imperfectly in all the rest. Rather, it loves to distribute its riches among a multiplicity of exemplars that reciprocally complete each other in the alternate appearance and suppression of a series of individuals."[100] Strauss then asks whether this extension of Idea's realization beyond the partic-

---

98. Tamar Ross, "The Cognitive Value of Religious Truth Statements," in *Tamar Ross: Constructing Faith*, ed. Hava Tirosh-Samuelson and Aaron Hughes (Leiden: Brill, 2016), 44–45.

99. Georg Wilhelm Friedrich Hegel, *The Phenomenology of Spirit*, trans. Terry Pinkard (New York: Oxford University Press, 2018), 460.

100. David Friedrich Strauss, *The Life of Jesus, Critically Examined*, trans. George Eliot (London: SCM, 1973), 779–80.

ular Jesus constitutes a truer realization of Idea. He responds: "Is not the idea of the unity of the divine and human natures a real one in a far higher sense, when I regard the whole race of mankind as its realization, than when I single out one man as such a realization? Is not incarnation of God from eternity, a truer one than an incarnation limited to a particular point of time?"[101] The conclusions of his magnum opus concerning the "dogmatic import of the life of Jesus" are set out here with rigorous consistency:

> This is the key to the whole of Christology, that, as subject of the predicate which the Church assigns to Christ, we place, instead of an individual, an idea. . . . In an individual, a God-man, the properties and functions which the Church ascribes to Christ contradict themselves; in the idea of the race, they perfectly agree. Humanity is the union of the two natures—God become man, the infinite manifesting itself in the finite, and the finite spirit remembering its infinitude. . . . It is Humanity that dies, rises and ascends to heaven, for from the negation of its phenomenal life there ever proceeds a higher spiritual life. . . . This alone is the absolute sense of Christology. . . . The phenomenal history of the individual, says Hegel, is only a starting point for the mind.[102]

Here we have one of the most explicit and consistent expressions of a Socratic interpretation of Jesus resulting in the dehistoricization of the New Testament witness which is its inevitable outcome. As we argued in chapter 3, in the process of determining the essential meaning of the New Testament myths, Jesus is interpreted as exemplifying the "ideas" or "ideals" that the interpreter happens to perceive to be representative of the divine. Anthony Thiselton's comment about Lessing is pertinent here: "What the believer brings *to* history has become more important than how history constrains the believer."[103] Like Lessing, Strauss insisted that New Testament interpretation must departicularize and dehistoricize for the sake of theology, given that its function is to distill what is universal and timeless—namely, that which is perceived to express our perceptions of the divine. To reiterate, that which is historically particular can do no more than exemplify or illustrate those universal ideas or principles that we already know and which drive the interpretive process. So where precisely

---

101. Strauss, *Life of Jesus*, 779–80.
102. Strauss, *Life of Jesus*, 780.
103. Anthony C. Thiselton, review of *Lessing's "Ugly Ditch": A Study of Theology and History*, by Gordon E. Michalson, *Scottish Journal of Theology* 42, no. 2 (1989): 254.

is "revelation" located on this account? Quite simply, it is located within—in those suppositions, ideas, and assumptions immanent within the mind of the human interpreter.

Whereas Strauss assumed one form of idealism in his theological interpretation of the historical, Bultmann, as we have seen, assumed another. In both approaches, the New Testament accounts are demythologized in accordance with their respective philosophical and perceived "scientific" commitments. In the case of Bultmann, who wants to hold on to the notion of the divine address, this generates a tension. He writes, "In mythological thinking, the action of God, whether in nature, history, human fortune, or the inner life of the soul, is understood as an action which intervenes between the natural, or historical, or psychological course of events." He then goes on to explain that "a miracle, as an action of God, cannot be thought of as an event which happens on the level of secular (worldly) events. It is not visible, not capable of objective, scientific proof which is possible only within an objective view of the world."[104] That seems consistent. At the same time, however, he also holds that when the myths of the New Testament are demythologized, we come to recognize that although there is no sense in which our "inner life" is interrupted by the intervention of God, our personal relation with God can be made real "by the acting God who meets me in His Word."[105] This raises the obvious question as to how these claims can be reconciled. Bultmann suggests that God "meets us in His Word" while also confirming that that "meeting" cannot reflect any causal intervention on God's part with respect to our "inner life." As we saw in chapter 3, the answer is that we live (and clearly speak) *as if* the causal determinism the Neo-Kantian understanding of science requires us to affirm does not apply.

In sum, for two of the most influential figures in the theological interpretation of the New Testament over the last two centuries, theology requires a mode of demythologization that precludes a priori the possibility that God might freely determine to engage causally in a particular piece of human history or spatiotemporal event. For both, moreover, theology is the expression and outworking of prior idealist commitments couched in a Socratic episte-

---

104. Rudolf Bultmann, *Jesus Christ and Mythology* (New York: Scribner, 1958), 61. Early in the book, Bultmann reminds the reader that, in contrast with "mythological thinking," modern science and modern men and women "take it for granted that the course of nature and of history, like their own inner life and their practical life, is nowhere interrupted by the intervention of supernatural powers" (16).

105. Bultmann, *Jesus Christ and Mythology*, 59.

mology and operating with the hermeneutical assumptions and criteria such an epistemology prescribes.

What Athanasius, Kierkegaard, and Barth recognized was that the grounds of human God-talk repose on God's engaging with the contingent order in a manner that could not be predicted or anticipated from any grounds to which we have immanent access. What they also recognized was how radically this challenges the reduction of God-talk to the mythological projection of immanence, that is, of idealist assumptions (be they Hellenic, Hegelian, or Neo-Kantian). They do this by operating from an epistemic base that recognizes God's freedom and lordship over what would otherwise be deemed insuperable creaturely constraints. For them, the proclamation of the church testifies to our participation in the kinship that, contrary to anything that might have been contemplated let alone anticipated, the Eternal has established with creatures in time. All three, moreover, hold that the condition for the recognition of this kinship is also the result of miraculous divine action—because that moment of recognition is integral to the redemptive kinship that God has determined to establish in time.

In order to spell out the implications of such an approach, we shall now consider two developments in contemporary philosophy that, we shall argue, are consonant with the challenge the KBT presents to Socratic theological approaches. These concern the nature of knowledge and the function of the language used in the service of revelation.

Externalist Epistemology

Contemporary epistemology is defined in large measure by an ongoing debate between the representatives of two approaches to the definition of knowledge, namely, so-called internalist and externalist accounts.[106] The two approaches emerged out of a debate that resulted from the publication in June 1963 of one of the most famous papers in the history of modern philosophy: Edmund Gettier's short article "Is Justified True Belief Knowledge?"[107] In it, Gettier demonstrated by means of counter examples (now known as "Gettier cases") that

---

106. It should be noted that, during the course of recent debates, the nature of the internalist account has been reformulated to the point where the differences between the two accounts are less pronounced than they were initially.

107. Edmund L. Gettier, "Is Justified True Belief Knowledge?," *Analysis* 3, no. 6 (June 1963): 121–23.

the classical definition of knowledge as justified true belief was inadequate. This led philosophers to ask again how knowledge is to be defined, leading, in turn, to "internalist" and "externalist" solutions. Internalists maintain that for beliefs to be knowledge, they need not only to be true but also to be justified, where this justification is construed as "completely determined by a subject's internal states or reasons."[108] Externalists, by contrast, deny that knowledge is defined in terms of justification conceived in terms of the states or reasons internal to the knower. C. Stephen Evans explains the difference as follows:

> Rather than viewing knowledge as something that we must be able to certify by reflection on our own internal states of mind, the externalist thinks that knowledge is a matter of being properly related to external reality. We have knowledge not when we hold true beliefs by mere accident, but when those true beliefs in some way stem from an ability to "track" with reality. When our true beliefs are the result of reliable belief-forming mechanisms or are the product of faculties whose purpose is to help us reach truth and which are functioning properly in the right kind of environment, then such beliefs amount to knowledge.[109]

Our concern here is not to assess the ongoing philosophical arguments for or against the relevant options—nor, indeed, to seek to endorse a general epistemological account. Rather, our concern is to consider the implications of the New Testament witness for how we understand the nature of the knowing that defines Christian faith. In addition, it is also important to consider whether

---

108. Ted Poston, "Internalism and Externalism in Epistemology," *Internet Encyclopedia of Philosophy*, https://iep.utm.edu/int-ext/#H3. As C. Stephen Evans puts it, "From the perspective of externalism, it is clear that whether the warrant necessary for knowledge is present is not always something that can be determined by the knower simply by 'reflecting on his state of mind,' to use Roderick Chisholm's phrase." Evans, *Kierkegaard on Faith and the Self: Collected Essays* (Waco, TX: Baylor University Press, 2006), 189.

109. Evans, *Kierkegaard on Faith and the Self*, 18. See also Evans's particularly helpful analysis of the internalist-externalist epistemological debate and the challenges associated with internalist accounts in *The Historical Christ and the Jesus of Faith* (New York: Oxford University Press, 1996), 218–22. Ted Poston also provides a helpful definition of the externalist approach. For externalists, he argues, justification is not determined completely with reference to internal factors alone. Rather, "the facts that determine a belief's justification include external facts such as whether the belief is caused by the state of affairs that makes the belief true, whether the belief is counterfactually dependent on the states of affairs that make it true, whether the belief is produced by a reliable belief-producing process, or whether the belief is objectively likely to be true" (Poston, "Internalism and Externalism").

internalist assumptions may be part of the rationale for the endorsement of the immanentist approaches we have sought to critique.

Few modern Christian thinkers have devoted more energy to the fundamental questions of epistemology than Alvin Plantinga. One of the world's leading academic philosophers, he believes the Christian should approach every question, including philosophical questions, from their Christian epistemic base. Why would the Christian consider it appropriate to bracket out information she holds to be true and which bears on the assessment of such questions? It may come as no surprise, therefore, that his conclusions as to what makes true belief "knowledge" are particularly helpful when it comes to theological epistemology. Plantinga rejected the widely held assumption that what requires to be added to true beliefs to make them knowledge is "justification." Justification concerns the pursuit of duties and thereby concerns a different kind of question from what it is that makes true belief "knowledge." Plantinga refers to the factor that makes true belief "knowledge" as "warrant." This he explains by means of the concept of "proper epistemic function." Beliefs are warranted when they are produced by cognitive faculties that are (1) functioning properly, (2) operating in a cognitive environment similar to that for which they were designed, and (3) aimed at truth.[110] In short, we *know* that P is true when P *is* true, when we *believe* that P is true, and when our believing P is *warranted* by virtue of meeting the above criteria.

What is immediately clear is that the externalist account can make sense of the fact that a child can know the person looking at her is her mother, even though she may not be able to provide rational justification for what she knows. When it comes to theology, an externalist can make sense of the fact that in response to Peter's statement that Jesus was the Messiah,[111] we can say he knew who Jesus was, even though he might not have been able to provide sufficient evidence to confirm what he knew. Such an account can also make sense of the knowledge that characterizes participation within the body of

110. Alvin Plantinga's account is spelled out in *Warrant and Proper Function* (New York: Oxford University Press, 1993), where he provides the following provisional definition: "To a first approximation, we may say that a belief B has warrant for S if and only if the relevant segments (the segments involved in the production of B) are functioning properly in a cognitive environment sufficiently similar to that for which S's faculties are designed; and the modules of the design plan governing the production of B are (1) aimed at truth, and (2) such that there is a high objective probability that a belief formed in accordance with those modules (in that sort of cognitive environment) is true" (19).

111. "You are the Messiah, the Son of the living God" (Matt. 16:16 NRSV).

Christ. A church member whose educational background is limited may be able to say, "I know that my Redeemer liveth!" without being said to be either mistaken or lying when she makes that epistemic truth-claim. That is the case despite the fact that she may well be unable to provide sufficient evidence or rational argumentation for it. As Evans points out, "It is perfectly conceivable that true beliefs might be reliably produced in me, through my senses, my memory, or other basic cognitive faculties which were designed to produce true beliefs, without it being the case that I can provide much in the way of evidence for them."[112]

Such an account appears consistent, moreover, with the narrative of Peter's confession in Matthew 16:13–20.[113] When Simon Peter confesses who Jesus is, Jesus responds "Blessed are you, Simon son of Jonah! For flesh and blood has not revealed this to you, but my Father in heaven."[114] What Jesus suggests here is that the recognition was the result of an event of revelation that was from above and which flesh and blood could not deliver in and of themselves. In other words, this transformative perception was certainly not an event of Socratic anamnesis, nor was it a conclusion derived from the dutiful, rigorous, and informed assessment of the relevant evidence. In addition, it does not seem that Simon could check or confirm he knew who Jesus was by internal rational reflection. What applies to Peter applies no less to the membership of the body of Christ. The condition for the recognition that defines faith is the creative presence of the Holy Spirit. God causes an event of recognition in real time where this "moment" is not part of an evolutionary process. Rather, it requires to be interpreted as a *novum* that is of decisive significance for the believer's epistemic relationship with the Truth.

Robert Nozick argues that knowledge is a "real relationship to the facts" and a mode of "our connecting to reality."[115] The best way to make sense of knowledge, therefore, is to interpret the beliefs that constitute knowledge as "tracking" reality. The metaphor of tracking is central not only to his understanding of epistemology but also to his understanding of ethics. Without this kind of metaphor, Nozick considers it impossible to make any sense whatsoever of our relationship to the world. His discussion of epistemology concludes, "I find the

---

112. Evans, *Historical Christ*, 217.

113. A more condensed account of Peter's confession can be found in Mark 8:27–30 and Luke 9:18–21.

114. Matt. 16:17 NRSV.

115. Robert Nozick, *Philosophical Explanations* (Cambridge, MA: Belknap Press of Harvard University Press, 1981), 288.

account of knowledge as tracking illuminates and explains how knowledge is possible—something I did not understand before (though I didn't doubt that it was possible or, indeed, actual)."[116]

Whereas the general conditions of this tracking may be of interest to philosophers, what concerns our purposes here are the very specific conditions under which the human mind can be said to track the reality and act-in-being of God. So what are the implications of the discussion so far? If we appropriate Plantinga's approach and apply it to the truth-claim "Peter knew that Jesus was the Messiah," then it should be interpreted as entailing the following:[117]

1. Peter believed Jesus is the Messiah;
2. it is true Jesus is the Messiah;
3. Peter's believing was properly functional, operating in an appropriate cognitive environment, and aimed at truth; and
4. God enabled Peter to track God's activity in such a way that he was able to recognize who Jesus was.

Three further comments present a theological account of what is going on. First, Peter's ability to recognize (to track veridically) the messianic identity of Jesus indicates a properly functional cognitive environment generated by the Holy Spirit rather than one that is self-generating. It is not something that can be delivered by flesh and blood nor is it the straightforward outworking of immanent human capacities.

Second, Peter's recognition of the Messiah was not the acquisition of an additional true belief assimilated into his prior system of beliefs. This recognition involved the transformation of his system of beliefs. As such, it was the start of a redemptive metanoietic process that transformed his epistemic base in such a way that he would come to interpret his life and relationship to God and the world in a new way.

And third, to draw on a further New Testament metaphor, Peter was reconstituted from above ("born again") to become a new creature. In being brought into relationship with the Truth he was, thereby, delivered from an erroneous interpretation of reality—from what Kierkegaard presents as a

---

116. Nozick, *Philosophical Explanations*, 287–88.

117. As C. Stephen Evans rightly comments, "Kierkegaard would certainly stress far more than Plantinga that genuine religious faith is not simply intellectual assent to a proposition, but I do not think he would deny that faith contains cognitive content" (*Kierkegaard on Faith and the Self*, 171). There is a strongly personal element in Kierkegaard's understanding of our relationship to truth.

continual departing from the truth.[118] Those brought into relation with the Truth are given, therefore, to participate in a "new humanity," a "new creation" characterized by a transformed epistemic base that interprets the world from a new perspective—a perspective defined by the kinship the eternal God has established in time.

THE EXTERNALIST NATURE OF KIERKEGAARD'S AND BARTH'S ACCOUNTS

As we discussed in chapter 2, Kierkegaard's argument in *Philosophical Fragments* is that, on a Christian understanding of our relationship to the Truth, the teacher provides the condition for relationship to the Truth. That is, the teacher delivers the learner from error for proper epistemic function. In the moment of receiving this condition, the learner is brought into relationship with the Truth and thereby redeemed from the ongoing erroneous interpretation of reality. In this moment, a process of radical change or conversion takes place.

The account of Christian knowing that Kierkegaard presents through Climacus is consonant, therefore, both with the New Testament picture of our being given to know the Truth and with an externalist account of the epistemic relation that defines Christian faith.

Precisely the same applies to Barth—a feature that becomes evident in the parallels Kevin Diller draws between Barth's approach and the externalist epistemology of Alvin Plantinga.[119] For Barth, as we have seen, the fact that God can be proclaimed to human creatures, and that they can hear and recognize this proclamation, constitutes a miracle—what he refers to as a divine victory rather than a human accomplishment. The hearer only hears to the extent that she has been given the ears to hear—that is, the condition by means of which she is given to recognize the Truth and thereby brought into relationship with it. When Barth argues that "knowledge of God's Word becomes possible for human beings in the event of the reality of God's Word,"[120] he is affirming that the Holy Spirit constitutes the condition by means of which the human subject knows God in the divine miracle of God's free self-disclosure. It is thus not

---

118. Like C. Stephen Evans, we are taking the liberty of referring to Kierkegaard here rather than following the usual convention of referring to Climacus.

119. Diller, *Theology's Epistemological Dilemma*, 82.

120. Barth, *Church Dogmatics* I/1, 198 (translation altered).

possible to provide anything in the neighborhood of a Socratic or, indeed, an evidentialist account of God's self-disclosure. God is known through our being brought into relationship with the Truth by means of an act of reconciliation through which God establishes fellowship with alienated creatures *in time*— what is clearly perceived by Barth as God's establishment of the necessary cognitive environment in which alienated creatures are given to know God. Laurence BonJour argues that "a theory of justification is *internalist* if and only if it requires that all of the factors needed for a belief to be epistemically justified for a given person be *cognitively accessible* to that person, *internal* to his cognitive perspective."[121] What the foregoing discussion makes clear is that Barth's account does not meet the conditions described by Laurence BonJour. For Barth, the key factors that make a person's true beliefs "knowledge" are not accessible to her in the sense that internalists require. They lie with the miraculous activity of the Holy Spirit.

In sum, Barth adopts what would now be described as an externalist account of Christian knowing. The believer knows God by virtue of having true beliefs that constitute knowledge by means of the creative, transformative, and reconciling presence of the Holy Spirit (the revealedness). The resulting cognitive environment in which the believer finds herself is the body of Christ in which human creatures have been reconciled and thereby delivered from a state of alienation for proper epistemic function in relation to God. This is construed by Barth in terms of God's free action and lordship, creating anew what would otherwise be impossible. Knowledge of God is not a human achievement; it constitutes a miraculous and redemptive gift of grace.

Yet again, the continuity and parallels between the approaches of Kierkegaard as a philosopher and of Barth as a theologian are unambiguously clear.

Fred Dretske on Recognition and Entitlement

Kierkegaard's and Barth's interpretations of the Christian faith challenge not only a Socratic or idealist rendering; they also challenge "classical foundationalist" approaches. Classical foundationalism, as Plantinga defines it, is the view that for a belief to be basic, it has to be self-evident or incorrigible or

---

121. Laurence BonJour, "Externalism/Internalism," in *A Companion to Epistemology*, ed. Jonathan Dancy and Ernest Sosa (Cambridge, MA: Blackwell, 1992), 132, cited in Diller, *Theology's Epistemological Dilemma*, 82n72.

evident to the senses.[122] This approach is an expression of the Enlightenment ideal that we engage with the world from objective, detached, and certain grounds that enable us to guarantee certainty in our opinions and challenge spurious and superstitious claims.

By contrast, for both Kierkegaard and Barth, theology begins *coram Deo*—that is, within the context of the given personal relationship to the Truth established not by human beings but by God. To seek to detach oneself from this in order to attempt to reason from secure grounds is not only folly but also far from neutral. It is actively to break one's relationship to the Truth and return to an erroneous relationship with reality. From the perspective of the KBT, every facet of human life and experience requires to be understood with the eyes of faith and not from some secure foundation within the self, that is, it requires to be understood as an event of recognition that is properly basic—namely, the recognition of that kinship that alone constitutes the sure foundation for the interpretation not only of God but of all things in relation to God.

When Barth interprets Christian experience, therefore, he explicitly rejects any inclination to interpret experience in a "Cartesian" way from a basis in himself.[123] Rather, Christian experience requires to be understood ab initio as experience of the Word of God. Consequently, God is not to be treated as if God were an "object" experienced by virtue of natural capacities. In contrast to any such approach, Barth regards the essential form of Christian experience as "acknowledgment"—the acknowledgment of an event of personal address. This personal address does not merely include the subjective conditions by which such experience takes place; it also includes the conditions by means of which this unique form of experience is interpreted.[124]

122. For Plantinga the "fundamental principle" that defines classical foundationalism can be defined as follows: "A proposition p is properly basic for a person S if and only if p is either self-evident for S or incorrigible for S or evident to the senses for S." This, he explains, contains two claims, which are the following: "First, a proposition is properly basic if it is self-evident, incorrigible, or evident to the senses, and, second, a proposition is properly basic *only if* it meets this condition." The problematic claim, Plantinga argues, is the second rather than the first. Alvin Plantinga and Nicholas Wolterstorff, eds., *Faith and Rationality: Reason and Belief in God* (Notre Dame: University of Notre Dame Press, 1983), 59. See John Greco, "Plantinga, Foundationalism and the Charge of Self-Referential Incoherence," *Grazer Philosophische Studien* 31 (1988): 188.

123. Barth is eager to resist the ways in which "Cartesianism" can subtly be "brought back into theology as, so to say, an indirect Cartesianism, the Cartesianism of the believing Christian" (Barth, *Church Dogmatics* I/1, 213).

124. Barth, *Church Dogmatics* I/1, §6.3, 210–14.

If, however, we proceed to interpret the justification of Christian claims with recourse to an event of "recognition" and thus from within this given relationship, does this not short-circuit widely held and, indeed, justifiable assumptions about the obligations we have to justify the claims we make? If we claim, for example, that drinking orange juice while doing mental arithmetic provides immunity to COVID-19, there is a widespread assumption that we have an obligation to provide justification in the form of evidence for our claims, and that this justification must meet certain publicly acceptable criteria. The belief that Kierkegaard's approach short-circuits such obligations has led to the criticism that he opens the door to an irrational, subjectivistic fideism[125]—that he advocates a "leap of faith" that recklessly ignores questions about what we are entitled to claim to know and sidesteps the basic controls that ensure accountability in decision-making. J. L. Mackie, for example, describes Kierkegaard as advocating "a sort of intellectual Russian roulette."[126] More recently, Christopher Hitchens referred to Kierkegaard's "leap of faith" as "an imposture," given that "it has to go on and on being performed, in spite of mounting evidence to the contrary"—a process, he argues, that "leads to delusions and manias."[127] And Sam Harris comments, "Here we can see why Pascal's wager, Kierkegaard's leap of faith and other epistemological Ponzi schemes won't do."[128] Conservative Christians, moreover, have criticized Kierkegaard on similar grounds. Francis Schaeffer, for example, identified the ills of modern theology with a "line of despair" he traces to Kierkegaard's fideistic rejection of reason.[129] In response, those making such criticisms are operating on the basis of an unjustifiable misrepresentation (or "leap of faith" perhaps) since, as Alasdair McKinnon has shown conclusively, the phrase "leap of faith" does not appear in any of Kierkegaard's works, including his pseudonymous writings. In short, there is no clear record of Kierkegaard's ever

125. For a nuanced and informed discussion of the charge of fideism made against Kierkegaard, see the discussion of Kierkegaard in Richard Amesbury, "Fideism," in *Stanford Encyclopedia of Philosophy*, article published May 6, 2005, last modified February 5, 2022, https://plato.stanford.edu/entries/fideism/#2.2.

126. J. L. Mackie, *The Miracle of Theism: Arguments For and Against the Existence of God* (Oxford: Clarendon, 1982), 216.

127. Christopher Hitchens, *God Is Not Great: How Religion Poisons Everything* (New York: Warner Twelve, 2007), 102.

128. Sam Harris, "An Atheist Manifesto (2005)," in *Faith in Faithlessness: An Anthology of Atheism*, ed. Dimitrios I. Roussopoulos (Montreal: Black Rose Books, 2008), 247.

129. See Francis Schaeffer, *Escape from Reason* (Downers Grove, IL: InterVarsity Press, 1968), esp. the concluding section of chap. 3, entitled "Kierkegaard and the Line of Despair," and the opening section of chap. 4, "The Leap."

having used the expression.[130] He did use the language of "leap," but not in the sense of arbitrary volition. As C. Stephen Evans explains, what is required, in Kierkegaard's view, "is not an immoral attempt to manipulate my beliefs so as to make myself believe what I know is untrue. Rather, I am asked to transform myself so that I can be open to an encounter with the truth which will totally transform my life."[131]

The criticism that Kierkegaard is guilty of an ethically compromised volitionalism is traceable in part to the influence of a dogma, famously articulated by W. K. Clifford, that we have duties not to believe anything without sufficient reason (where "sufficient reason" implies publicly accessible evidence or demonstrable grounds).[132] Clifford developed arguments taken from John Locke,[133] concluding famously that "it is wrong always, everywhere, and for anyone to believe anything on insufficient evidence."[134] It is commonplace to point out that this maxim is self-referentially defeating, given that Clifford fails to offer (and is unlikely to be able to offer) "sufficient evidence" for this principle. Consequently, to accept it is to violate its own requirements. That is, the evidence suggests he is hoist with his own petard! Despite that, there are understandable concerns about whether, as Clifford suggested, we are not under a moral obligation to ensure that we are entitled to hold the beliefs we hold and are not simply flouting accountability to the truth. The concern is raised as to whether Kierkegaard's and Barth's externalist epistemology opens the door to an isolationist approach to religious claims—that is, whether the

130. See Alastair McKinnon, "Kierkegaard and the Leap of Faith," *Kierkegaardiana* 16 (1993): 107–25.

131. Evans, *Kierkegaard on Faith and the Self*, 309.

132. Cf. Andrew Chignell, "The Ethics of Belief," in *Stanford Encyclopedia of Philosophy*, published June 14, 2010, last modified March 5, 2018, https://plato.stanford.edu/entries /ethics-belief/.

133. "He that believes without having any Reason for believing, may be in love with his own Fancies; but neither seeks Truth as he ought, nor pays the Obedience due to his Maker, who would have him use those discerning Faculties he has given him, to keep him out of Mistake and Errour." John Locke, *An Essay Concerning Human Understanding* (1690) (Oxford: Clarendon, 1975), 687.

134. William Kingdon Clifford, "The Ethics of Belief," in *The Ethics of Belief Debate*, ed. Gerald D. McCarthy (Atlanta: Scholars Press, 1986), 24. Peter van Inwagen provides a diachronic version of Clifford's maxim, namely, "It is wrong always, everywhere, and for anyone to ignore evidence that is relevant to his beliefs, or to dismiss relevant evidence in a facile way." See Van Inwagen, "'It Is Wrong, Everywhere, Always, and for Anyone, to Believe Anything upon Insufficient Evidence,'" in *Faith, Freedom, and Rationality: Philosophy of Religion Today*, ed. Jeff Jordan and Daniel Howard-Snyder (Lanham, MD: Rowman & Littlefield, 1996), 145.

veracity of these claims can be checked, tested, and confirmed within the public domain. There is no need to point out the obvious potential for harm when people make unverifiable or unfalsifiable claims concerning the divine will. They are suggesting that their claims possess unquestionable authority.

As we have seen, Barth insists there is indeed a public domain wherein theological claims must be tested if they are to be regarded as scientific, and that is the church. The church is the context in which the conditions of this public relation to the truth are met. Consequently, that is the appropriate context in which questions of the veracity of theological and dogmatic claims, and thus our entitlement to believe and affirm them, are tested.

The desire to demonstrate our entitlement to hold Christian beliefs can lead theology in the direction of classical foundationalism, evidentialism, or Socratic idealism. A major appeal of these approaches is their capacity to demonstrate that one is or is not entitled to hold the beliefs one holds. However, certain recent philosophical developments provide a helpful way of reconsidering the perceived challenges here. These suggest that a person may be fully entitled to hold beliefs or judgments (and thus has an epistemic right to do so) even when these beliefs are unsupported by any evidence available to the person.[135] As Fred Dretske shows, we are often obliged to believe certain propositions (and are entitled to believe them) in circumstances when our epistemic right to do so is clearly *not* contingent upon our checking them by "some kind of sophisticated mental exercise" (Altschul).[136] He argues the case by means of a simple example: "I do not choose to believe my wife is sitting on the sofa when I see her there. Believing she is there when I see her there is not a voluntary act. I have no choice in the matter. I see that she's there and that's the end of it." He continues, "When I see that she is there, my belief that she is there is caused by the experience I have when I see her there. We describe this causal process—from perceptual experience to perceptual belief—by using a factive nominal, a that-clause, after the perceptual verb: I see that she is there. This is an involuntary, a non-intentional, outcome not just because I am caused to believe she is there, but because I am caused to believe it by events over which I have no direct control—my perceptual experiences."[137] Dretske

135. See Jon Altschul, "Epistemic Entitlement," in *Internet Encyclopedia of Philosophy*, accessed June 28, 2021, https://iep.utm.edu/ep-en/.

136. Altschul, "Epistemic Entitlement." Our exposition of Dretske draws on Altschul's lucid analysis here.

137. Fred Dretske, "Entitlement: Epistemic Rights without Epistemic Duties?," *Philosophy and Phenomenological Research* 60, no. 3 (2000): 599.

concludes, "I am entitled to accept the proposition that my wife is on the sofa when I am caused to believe she is on the sofa by seeing her there. When I see her there I don't need a justification for believing she is there. My right to believe she is there comes from another source."[138]

Peter's confession stemmed from his recognition of who Jesus was—a recognition, Matthew suggests, that was given by God. Given Matthew's interpretation, it was a recognition statement he was entitled to make, and where the epistemic rights lay in the fact that he was (nondeterministically[139]) caused to believe that Jesus was the Messiah. So, he believed not only that this confession tracked the true nature of the person who had addressed him but that this recognition was caused by that person and was an unavoidable response to who Jesus was. Jesus in turn confirmed Peter's confession as the recognition on which he would build his church, and the body of Christ is widely defined by that same recognition to the extent it is shared by its participants. The *entitlement* to make that confession lies in an event of personal recognition and acknowledgment. This recognition is actualized "from above" but takes place within a context of participation within the Body of Christ. There the hearer is subject to the proclamation, witness, testimony, confession, and worship that defines the church and in and through which the Holy Spirit gives persons the eyes to see and the ears to hear.

It might be objected that there is a clear difference between recognizing that Jesus is the Messiah and seeing that one's wife is sitting on the sofa. There is also a radical difference between both of these and the recognition that a piece of music has been written by Brahms, or a child's recognition that the face smiling at her is her mother's. What these latter two situations suggest is that, as Michael Polanyi argues, "*we can know more than we can tell.*"[140] Indeed, he also uses the example of face recognition: "We usually cannot tell how we recognize a face we know. So most of this knowledge cannot be put into words."[141] In short, it is not easy to explain how we recognize that the face we are looking at is our mother's, or that the music we are listening to was written by Brahms. The recognition may be immediate and straightforward but un-

---

138. Dretske, "Entitlement," 604.

139. We add "nondeterministically" to avoid any immediate association of this position with the kind of Calvinism that would interpret him as having been "programmed" to make the confession.

140. Michael Polanyi, *The Tacit Dimension* (Chicago: University of Chicago Press, 2009), 4 (emphasis original).

141. Polanyi, *Tacit Dimension*, 4.

derstanding how it happens is complex. So how might Peter (or Paul, following his experience on the road to Damascus) respond to being asked how he could recognize who Jesus was and, indeed, be sure that his confession was true? The only valid answer he could offer is that the certainty is "given" in the event of recognition—just as in the case of the child who recognizes that the woman in the green dress is her mother. The fact that she is certain that she has correctly recognized her mother is "given" in the moment of recognition. In Dretske's terms, when she sees her there, she does not need a form of justification for believing she is there. For the author of Matthew's Gospel, the givenness of Peter's recognition lies in the fact that God revealed it to him. This, however, raises obvious questions: Is Peter right? Did God *actually* give him the eyes to see? It is here that we are confronted with the offense at the heart of proclamation and, indeed, of the Christian faith in toto. The sole condition by which we can recognize that Peter's confession is true is that we too are given the eyes to recognize the identity of the Messiah. The recognition that Peter's confession is true is also grounded in the mediated—but no less miraculous—recognition of Jesus's identity. What applies to Peter applies to the church at all times and in all places. The necessary condition for the recognition that Jesus is the Messiah is the creative and reconciling presence of the Holy Spirit.

Semantic Externalism and Its Challenge of Descriptivist Theories of Reference

> When an oak nut is planted in a clay pot, the pot breaks; when new wine is poured into old leather bottles, they burst. What happens, then, when the god plants himself in the frailty of a human being if he does not become a new person and a new vessel![142]

We have emphasized that the transformation of humanity and the creation of a new humanity lie at the heart of the theology of the New Testament. This raises a further question, however. Is it appropriate to assume that our language naturally and inherently possesses the conceptual or semantic vessels by which to communicate the new wine, that is, the "reality of God's Word"? How far is the vocabulary and conceptual apparatus that human beings have to hand

---

142. Søren Kierkegaard, *Philosophical Fragments*, in *"Philosophical Fragments" and "Johannes Climacus,"* ed. and trans. Howard V. Hong and Edna H. Hong (Princeton: Princeton University Press, 1985), 34.

sufficient to articulate and, indeed, facilitate our "tracking" God? Pertinent to addressing this question is a further form of externalism that has come to the fore in the recent philosophical theological debate, namely, "semantic externalism." Although this has been shown by Linda Zagzebski to be relevant for the task of Christian ethics, little has been written concerning its bearing on theological language more generally or the question of analogy.[143] We shall now turn to consider this, albeit briefly.

In his famous essay "On Sense and Reference," Gottlob Frege argued for what is generally referred to as a "descriptivist theory of names." To say "Venus is the morning star" or that "the morning star is the evening star" requires to be distinguished from the empty tautology "Venus is Venus," even though both "the morning star" and "the evening star" refer to Venus. In other words, the claim that Venus is the morning star is not meaningless as would be the case if the "meaning" of the two expressions were simply the object to which they referred—namely, Venus. This is because, for Frege, different names or naming descriptions have different senses or meanings (*Bedeutungen*) even when their reference is identical. The different meanings denote different modes of designation of the reference—for example, "the morning star" designates Venus differently from "the evening star." So, on a descriptivist theory of reference (often referred to as the Frege-Russell view), "referring expressions such as definite descriptions and proper names are able to refer to some unique individual only because of some 'content' or description or characteristic which truly applies to the individual thing named or described which is the referent."[144]

This account was famously challenged by Saul Kripke in *Naming and Necessity*, in which he presented the case for a causal theory of reference.[145] In contrast to a purely descriptivist account, the causal theory of reference maintains that successful reference takes place when a particular individual enters into the historical account as a person of whom the speaker intended to predicate something.[146] In this way, the individual in the historical account *causes* the reference of the name used. As he points out, this means "the natural intuition

143. Linda Zagzebski, *Exemplarist Moral Theory* (Oxford: Oxford University Press, 2017), 13–14. See also Alan J. Torrance's discussion of Zagzebski's application of semantic externalism to Christian ethics in "Forgiveness and Christian Character: Reconciliation, Exemplarism and the Shape of Moral Theology," *Studies in Christian Ethics* 30, no. 3 (2017): 293–313.

144. James F. Harris, "The Causal Theory of Reference and Religious Language," *International Journal for Philosophy of Religion* 29, no. 2 (1991): 75.

145. Saul A. Kripke, *Naming and Necessity* (Cambridge, MA: Harvard University Press, 1980).

146. See Keith S. Donnellan, "Speaking of Nothing," *Philosophical Review* 83, no. 1 (1974): 16.

that the names of ordinary language are rigid designators can in fact be upheld."[147] Kripke thus provides an alternative account to the Frege-Russell view whereby reference to an individual is determined "causally" or "historically" by means of some original and actual encounter with the individual about whom the speaker is speaking. In order, therefore, to identify the referent of a name or other referring expression, "a story must be told—a story which traces the account of an individual being described in a certain way or being named a certain name back to the initial origin of the description or name."[148]

At least in certain contexts, therefore, the way in which a term refers requires to be explained with reference to an encounter with the one named. That is, the name functions because it has been claimed by an actor at a particular time and where this has, in turn, given rise to or is integral to a narrative. Since the major Western religions are narrative in character, Richard B. Miller asks about the relevance of the causal theory of reference for the philosophy of religion. This leads him in his conclusions to critique traditional philosophy of religion for holding two common assumptions: first, that "'God' must be defined before arguments for or against his existence can be evaluated," and second, that "the history of religious beliefs is irrelevant to their justification."[149] The traditional Western religions, he argues, "describe God interacting with human communities and revealing Himself to them from time to time. . . . 'God,' and similar names are used referentially to pick out the God of Abraham, Isaac and Jacob and not attributively to pick out whatever or whoever is omnipotent, etc."[150] On Miller's view, "if 'God' originates in encounters with some Entity, no matter how vaguely conceived, then That is God."[151] What this suggests is that, in Kierkegaardian terms, the historical has decisive *semantic* significance for the Judeo-Christian tradition over against Socratic accounts where the relevant terms refer to universally, timelessly, and immanently accessible descriptive concepts.

Whereas Kripke's causal-historical theory of reference applies specifically to names, Hilary Putnam extends the causal theory of reference to other kinds of terms, famously establishing that the reference of the term a person uses is not determined by the contents of a person's brain. In his famous "Twin Earth"

147. Kripke, *Naming and Necessity*, 5.

148. Harris, "Causal Theory," 76.

149. Richard B. Miller, "The Reference of 'God,'" *Faith and Philosophy: Journal of the Society of Christian Philosophers* 3, no. 1 (1986): 3.

150. Miller, "Reference of 'God,'" 10–11.

151. Miller, "Reference of 'God,'" 3.

thought experiment, Putnam supposes there are two near-identical planets. Not only are the surroundings identical but the inhabitants, the language they speak, and the psychological states of the inhabitants are also identical. The only difference is that on one planet ("Earth") water is composed of H_2O, whereas on the other ("Twin Earth") it is composed of XYZ. This raises the question whether Oscar and Twin Oscar mean the same thing when they use the term "water." Putnam uses this argument to conclude that the extension of the term "water" (that is, what it applies to) "is not a function of the psychological state of the speaker by itself."[152] He then provides a further, similar example where the extension of "aluminum" is "aluminum in the idiolect of Oscar1 and molybdenum in the idiolect of Oscar2."[153] Both are using the same term, and both share identical psychological states, but the extensions of the terms differ. This, again, shows that "the psychological state of the speaker does *not* determine the extension (*or* the 'meaning,' speaking preanalytically) of the word."[154] As he famously concludes, "Cut the pie any way you like, 'meanings' just ain't in the *head!*"[155] Now pertinent questions have since been raised by David Lewis, for example, as to whether there needs to be some kind of descriptive apparatus in addition to the causal relation between the speaker and the object.[156] That said, what Putnam illustrates is that the meaning of a particular term is not to be interpreted simply in light of the descriptive content in one's head or, indeed, the collective "heads" of the semantic community. The same term can be used appropriately and meaningfully of different referents even when the speaker is unaware of the difference. In short, the meaning of a term may be indexed to a piece of history, its context, and the associated narrative. There is, however, a further point to be made here. When the speaker is asked to define what a particular term refers to, her answer may change to accommodate scientific or other advances in understanding the precise nature of the reality to which she refers.

The theological implications of a causal theory of reference are significant. First, the history of God's engagement with humanity is not to be adapted to fit our immanent conceptualities and frames of reference. When the terms "Lord"

152. Hilary Putnam, "Meaning and Reference," *Journal of Philosophy* 70, no. 19 (1973): 702.

153. Putnam, "Meaning and Reference," 703 (emphasis removed).

154. Putnam, "Meaning and Reference," 703 (emphasis original).

155. Putnam, "Meaning and Reference," 704 (emphasis original).

156. David K. Lewis, "Putnam's Paradox," *Australasian Journal of Philosophy* 62, no. 3 (1984): 221–36.

or "Messiah" or "King" were used of Jesus, or when the term "God" was used of the one addressed as "Father" or "Abba," the relevant terminology was not adapted to fit the confines of a predetermined descriptive apparatus. Rather, their meaning was determined by a causal process in which the extensions of these terms were the agents. The meanings lie not in our heads, therefore, but with specific actors within the historical order.

Second, when the term "Messiah" (*Christos*), for example, came to name Jesus as its sole referent, it underwent a process of redefinition in light of the one whom it named and to whom it referred. The descriptive connotations associated with the term's original usage came to acquire new content. As we see in Matthew 16, the historical actor, the one named as the Messiah, reschematized the descriptive content associated with the term in such a way that the identity and purpose of the incarnate Son might be communicated accurately and the term serve to "track" him successfully.[157] This process of reschematization was, of course, one with which Peter wrestled, resulting in Jesus's challenging him in the most direct terms,[158] as we discussed earlier.

Again, our concern in introducing semantic externalism is not to encourage people to take sides in a philosophical debate between semantic internalists (who hold to the Frege-Russell view) and semantic externalists. Rather, it is to draw attention to the fact that the externalists' arguments about the nature of reference help to redress the influence within theology of what Miller refers to as "philosophers blinded by a descriptive theory of reference,"[159] and who are unable, therefore, to recognize the "historical validity of religion as essential rather than incidental."[160] Externalist arguments challenge the widely held assumption that the designation of the term "God" requires to be conceived exclusively in terms of a descriptive theory of reference, and that the attributes are to be understood as shaped neither by any causal action of God within history, nor by any specific way in which the designation of the term "God" functioned within the semantic community of the New Testament church. What the causal theory of reference helps us to articulate is that God discloses Godself as an actor within history and in doing so defines the reference of the term "God." Frege's descriptivist definition of reference defined the sense of a name as the mode of designation of its reference. The effect of our argument is to turn this around. God's self-disclosure means that the historical has decisive *semantic* significance. Consequently, the reference (or extension) of the term "God" re-

157. "Reschematized" is an allusion to Rom. 12:2, as discussed earlier.
158. See Matt. 16:21–23.
159. Miller, "Reference of 'God,'" 11.
160. Miller, "Reference of 'God,'" 11.

quires to be seen as the mode of designation of its sense rather than the other way around. It is in light of God's historical self-disclosure, therefore, that the sense or meaning of the term "God" requires to be defined or designated.

In sum, although the meaning of "externalism" in the epistemological context should not be confused with its use in semantics, both forms of "externalism" question the long-standing assumptions that rational reflection on the internal contents of our minds determines (1) the extent to which our Christian beliefs are warranted, and (2) the meaning of the language we use in the context of faith. Epistemic internalism and semantic internalism find themselves in tension with recognizing that the historical has decisive epistemological and semantic significance, and both, therefore, will struggle to grasp the full epistemic and semantic implications of the kinship that the Eternal has established in time.

Central to the Christian faith is the recognition that God is not only an actor within history but the Creator of space-time. This entails nothing less than that knowledge of the Creator—that is, of the one who explains the existence of the totality of the contingent order—is inseparable from knowledge of the God who acts within history to facilitate that knowledge. It also suggests that our prior and immanent assumptions concerning God's attributes and how God is to be described require to be transformed so that the reference of the terms we use faithfully track who God is in reality. The event of God's self-disclosure defines both who God is and how the term "God" functions. Consequently, the meaning of "God" in Christian theology can never be defined as the lowest common denominator in the diverse conceptions of the divine that characterize our philosophical and religious communities.

THE *DE RE* CHARACTER OF CHRISTIAN GOD-TALK

These distinctions help us to highlight the fact that Christian God-talk is fundamentally *de re* rather than *de dicto*. The distinction between *de dicto* and *de re* propositions is complex. Put simply, however, a *de dicto* assertion applies to a *dictum*, that is, to an abstract proposition, whereas a *de re* assertion applies to the *res*, that is, to the individual thing or reality to which the proposition refers. As André Gallois puts it,

> "*De dicto*" means "of, or concerning, a dictum," that is, something having representative content, such as a sentence, statement or proposition. "*De re*" means "of, or concerning, a thing." For example, a *de dicto* belief is a belief

that a bearer of representative content is true, while a *de re* belief is a belief concerning some thing, that it has a particular characteristic.[161]

As Gallois suggests, the distinction can apply to beliefs as well as propositions. Consider the following example: Julia goes to a sheepdog trial where all the participants own border collies. Standing beside her is a woman wearing an entrant's badge with "Susan" written on it. Julia and Susan have never spoken and do not know each other, but Julia believes Susan is the owner of a border collie. Julia's belief about Susan is a *de dicto* belief in that it is based on a dictum concerning the properties of the participants in the competition. That is, Julia's belief is not about a particular individual per se. It is essentially a belief concerning a property of the participants in general, one of whom is "Susan." Suppose, however, Julia were at a party and met Susan. During the course of conversation in which she refers to her daily exercise routine, Susan mentions to Julia that she owns a border collie. On this basis, Julia forms the *de re* belief that Susan owns a border collie. It is a *de re* belief in that it is a belief about the particular person, Susan, rather than a belief in an abstract proposition referring to a class of objects that includes "Susan."

Now consider the proposition "the person who holds the most IGFA bonefish records is one of Florida's leading breast cancer surgeons." One would not need to know who "the person who holds the most IGFA bonefish records" is in order to believe *de dicto* that that person is "one of Florida's leading breast cancer surgeons." Suppose, however, that "the person who holds the most IGFA bonefish records" were our friend, Jan Forszpaniak. Knowing that would enable us to believe *de re* of Jan not only that he is the person who holds the most IGFA bonefish records but that he is also one of Florida's leading breast cancer surgeons.[162]

What is important to appreciate here is how very different *de re* beliefs are from *de dicto* beliefs. Kevin Diller applies this distinction, in an insightful way, to the interpretation of Karl Barth.

Consider the proposition expressed by "God is omniscient." One may assert this proposition *de dicto*. One may form the *de dicto* belief with respect

---

161. This is André Gallois's definition in "De re/de dicto," in *Routledge Encyclopedia of Philosophy*, accessed May 27, 2021, https://www.rep.routledge.com/articles/thematic/de-re-de-dicto/v-1.

162. This example is a modification of one used by Kevin Diller in the doctoral thesis he submitted to the University of St Andrews. IGFA is the acronym for the "International Game Fish Association."

to the proper name "God" that it stands for a thing that has the property of omniscience. One may also form the *de re* belief of God, the personal being to which "God" refers, that *he* has the property of omniscience. *De re* belief, therefore, seems to require some knowing contact with the real referent(s) of the proposition. Since God's knowledge of himself is perfect, he is in the best position to form *de re* beliefs about himself with respect to true propositions referring to him. . . . It is clear that, for Barth, genuine human knowledge of God that comes by the self-revealing Word of God in the gift of faith involves not merely *de dicto* assertion, but *de re* belief.[163]

The effect of Barth's Trinitarian account of God's self-disclosure is that it enables human knowing to go beyond mere *de dicto* belief to yield warranted *de re* belief. Barth's insights here are anticipated in Kierkegaard. The Socratic may well be able to establish *de dicto* beliefs about God that are true. What the New Testament and the creeds of the church bear witness to, however, are *de re* assertions grounded in God's personal presence and engagement with humanity in time. What grounds these assertions are *de re* perceptions, that is, perceptions for which the historical has decisive significance. It is not simply the historical reality of Jesus Christ that has decisive significance here but also the free and creative presence of the Spirit in time. Both have decisive significance for the generation of *de re* beliefs about God. The focus of the faith is not mere, abstract *de dicto* propositions about God but the personal Reality of God and the Reality of the kinship that God has established with us. Is this to deny there are any *de dicto* elements to the experience? Certainly not!

Fred Dretske's understanding of tacit knowledge is pertinent here. When, in the experience of faith, the disciples and members of the body of Christ are given the eyes to see who Jesus is, they are given to know all sorts of things supported by the experience but which are also tacit. Tacit knowledge is knowing things that are supported by experience.[164] For example, if asked if our wives were wearing sunglasses at dinner last night, the answer would be a negative one based on our *de re* beliefs with respect to what we can remember seeing. Asked, however, if our wives were hovering a millimeter above their

163. Kevin Diller, "The Theology of Revelation and the Epistemology of Christian Belief: The Compatibility and Complementarity of the Theological Epistemologies of Karl Barth and Alvin Plantinga" (PhD diss., University of St. Andrews, 2008), 180, 181 (emphasis original), https://research-repository.st-andrews.ac.uk/handle/10023/497.

164. Cf. Fred Dretske, "What We See," Howison Lectures in Philosophy, 2007, https://gradlectures.berkeley.edu/lecture/what-we-see/.

respective chairs, the answer would also be negative. That is because our general experience of our wives is supported by *de dicto* beliefs, one of which is that, despite their many abilities, neither of them is able to suspend the laws of gravity in that way.

In the case of the identity of Jesus Christ, the process of unpacking the tacit knowledge supported by recognizing the identity of Jesus has taken place over centuries. The Nicene fathers, for example, unpacked tacit knowledge that was integral to but did not receive explicit expression within the New Testament. In contemporary theological discussion, the responses to certain theological questions may often be *de dicto*, in the sense that they are based on long-standing recognition statements that received creedal formulation. But any *de dicto* validity they might have remains contingent on their *de re* reference. What we need to appreciate here is that in every form of theological exposition the pressure must run from *de re* perceptions of the incarnate Word—supported by faith through the Spirit's mediation of the New Testament witness—to our theological formulations and not the other way around. To allow *de dicto* suppositions to redefine the Christian faith in ways that are not supported by—or, worse, are in tension with—these foundational *de re* perceptions is to disregard the kinship that God has established in time and thereby turn Christian confession and witness on its head.

Conclusion

This chapter began by asking how persons are brought into relationship with the Truth. Given the specific nature of Christian Truth, its communication and discovery cannot be conceived in terms of Socratic reflection. Nor can it be demonstrated on the basis of presuppositions immanent within us and accessed by rational reflection. On the KBT, the Truth is communicated by means of proclamation and witness. This is not to imply, however, that human beings either possess or are able to access the conditions for the recognition of that Truth by their own effort. For both Kierkegaard and Barth, Christian revelation is not something we can recognize on the basis of our immanent capacities alone. Rather, God provides through the creative presence of the Holy Spirit the condition for the recognition of God's self-disclosure as the Word become flesh. Scripture bears witness, indeed, to the fact that Christian revelation has an irreducibly Trinitarian grammar. God is the Revealer, that is, the author of revelation, God is the one revealed, the incarnate Word become flesh, and God is the Revealedness. God's address is heard and recognized, not simply on the basis of our inherent capacities, but miraculously through the transforming and reconciling presence of the Holy Spirit. Consequently, the recognition of God's self-disclosure is to be understood as the result of a redemptive act that transforms our categories of interpretation. This Trinitarian conception of God's self-disclosure in time addresses the fundamental, and insufficiently recognized, challenge of how we can move from second-order engagement with the biblical text (god-talk-talk) to first-order theological statement (God-talk) without falling foul of a form of the naturalistic fallacy to which we referred as the "theologistic fallacy."

With this in mind, we revisited the challenge of idealism in New Testament scholarship as exemplified in the Hegelian idealism that underpinned Strauss's approach and the Neo-Kantian form of idealism integral to Bultmann's approach. These two approaches illustrate the incompatibility of idealism with the very possibility that the historical might possess decisive theological significance. Second, they exemplify the attempt to sidestep the "gulf" that was assumed by Enlightenment thought to exist between historical and theological statements, and which motivated so many New Testament scholars to turn to the immanent for a solution.

The challenge of this gulf as it was famously analyzed by Lessing led in different ways to Strauss's myth theory, on the one hand, and Bultmann's program of demythologizing, on the other. We suggested that a related gulf at the heart of Hellenic thought also motivated the Nicene fathers to distinguish between mythology and theology, albeit drawing diametrically opposite conclusions. We saw that, for Athanasius, as also for Barth after him, it was precisely the doctrines of the Trinity and the incarnation that enabled Christian theology to affirm God's transcendence and God's freedom without collapsing God-talk into mythological projection.

The final section of the chapter examined how recent debates in philosophical epistemology and the philosophy of language help formulate the epistemological and semantic implications of the Kierkegaard-Barth trajectory. We argued that the epistemological and semantic implications of taking history seriously were best addressed by adopting not only epistemological externalism but also an externalist approach to theological semantics. A philosophy of language that recognizes a causal element to naming and reference is able to reflect the way in which the kinship that the eternal establishes in time serves to commandeer and redefine theological language enabling it to acquire a capacity to refer which the relevant language may not have possessed previously. Conversely, a descriptivist account of reference fails to recognize the decisive significance of the historical for theological semantics. This encourages a return to immanence with the resulting reversal in the direction of theological interpretation to which this leads.

The Christian testimony to God's engagement with humanity in space and time makes the defining claim that, by the grace of God, alienated and finite creatures are enabled both in their beliefs and in their language to "track" God's self-disclosure. Consequently, Christian beliefs and creedal statements require to be interpreted as fundamentally *de re* rather than *de dicto*. "God's Word is no mere thing; it is the living, personal and free God."[165] It is to the free and personal reality of the Logos that our words (*logoi*) bear witness. This is only possible because it is that same Word that both prescribes and reconciles the language we use.[166]

---

165. Barth, *Church Dogmatics* I/1, 198.

166. "Now they know that everything you have given me is from you; for the words [or language, *rhemata*] that you gave to me I have given to them, and they have received them and know in truth that I came from you; and they have believed that you sent me" (John 17:7-8 NRSV).

CONCLUSION

In 1925 August Messer and Anders Gemmer published their book entitled *Sören Kierkegaard und Karl Barth*.[1] In response to this publication, Barth commented to Eduard Thurneysen that he "[could] only grin painfully" at the notion of a book that focused on his relation to Kierkegaard.[2] So why risk giving Barth cause to look down on us with a painful grin? The reason is a recognition that certain defining arguments in their work have a decisive contribution to make to contemporary theology. This is because the challenges they confronted are the very same ones that the church must once again confront today. History is repeating itself, and so we have every reason to turn to these two thinkers to see what we can learn from them.

Our exposition of Kierkegaard and Barth explored the philosophical, theological, and contextual backdrop to their authorships. This exposed marked similarities between the religious, cultural, and philosophical challenges that each set out to address. It also highlighted the striking parallels between their responses. Chapters 1 and 3 considered the impact of three factors: first, the pedagogical assumptions that stemmed from the Enlightenment; second, the monist idealism of Hegel, on the one hand, and the Marburg Neo-Kantians on the other; and third, culturally defined religion—"Christianism" or cultural Protestantism. In both contexts, the respective cultures were shaping the church's agenda not only by determining what questions theology should address and how it should go about doing so but also by defining the theological answers that were given.

---

1. August Messer and Anders Gemmer, *Sören Kierkegaard und Karl Barth* (Stuttgart: Verlag Streder und Schöder, 1925).

2. Karl Barth, *Revolutionary Theology in the Making: Barth–Thurneysen Correspondence, 1914–1925*, trans. James D. Smart (Richmond, VA: John Knox, 1964), 1:232-33.

Of course, Kierkegaard and Barth were also unable to escape the influence of their respective contexts. Yet what distinguished their approaches was their shared insights into the key elements that enable Christian theology to transcend and, indeed, challenge the religious constructions and projections of our culture: (1) the *grounds* of Christian God-talk, (2) the *controls* on our interpretation of it, and (3) the *conditions* by which we engage in it. For both, it is only when all three are given, in a redemptive and revelatory initiative, that God's self-disclosure stands to be interpreted in its own light and on its own grounds. It is this alone that enables true revelation of who God is and who we are before God.

Central to their account of revelation was a shared recognition that the transcendent God, who is infinitely qualitatively different, has freely determined to address finite, alienated human creatures by establishing kinship with them *in time*. This address not only enables and prompts us but also obliges us to speak of God—to articulate who God is and to bear witness to God's purposes. For both of them, therefore, this kinship facilitates God-talk that is truly objective ("scientific," as Barth puts it) as opposed to god-talk that is determined by creaturely presumption, idle fancy, or criteria constructed with other ends in view. Both believed that the historical reality of the incarnation challenges us to rethink our religious, cultural, and sociopolitical affiliations, not least those defined by vested interests.

As well as drawing attention to the clear parallels between these thinkers, we have also given careful attention to Kierkegaard's influence on Barth, which we suggested was far greater than Barth himself appreciated. To demonstrate and examine this influence, chapter 2 expounded Kierkegaard's conceptions of "the infinite qualitative difference," "the divine incognito," "offense," "paradox," and "the moment," and then chapter 5 considered how Barth would commandeer and develop these concepts. At the same time, in our analysis of this influence, we also considered the reasons why Barth came to distance himself from certain elements in Kierkegaard's argumentation.

While we highlighted the direct influence of Kierkegaard on Barth, we recognize that much of the congruence between their approaches simply reflects a shared grasp of the theological, methodological, and epistemological affirmations of Nicene Christianity. We argued, for example, that the shared trajectory of Kierkegaard and Barth recovers insights that can be found in Athanasius, who anticipated their recognition of the epistemological implications of the incarnation. Far from a prescientific inability to distinguish between the incarnation and myth, Athanasius was explicit in distinguishing theology (*theologein*) from mythology (*muthologein*).[3] Indeed, he was clear that it is the incarnation of the Word that makes possible theology that is true (*alēthōs*) to the reality of God as opposed to those forms of *mania* (madness) that project creaturely "fantasy"[4] across an infinite gulf (*chōrismos*) onto a realm with respect to which we are ignorant (*agnōsis*).

In stark contrast, the idealist Hegel-Strauss and Kant-Bultmann trajectories interpreted the Gospels as prompting and inspiring theological insight while assuming that any identification of the being of God with a particular historical person must necessarily be either rejected as mythology or demythologized for the sake of theology. The irony here is how they themselves avoid "fashioning" the divine in the way that Athanasius rejected as "mythology."[5]

Kierkegaard and Barth, echoing Athanasius, recognized that it is precisely God's free decision to become incarnate and to be recognized (through the creative and reconciling presence of the Holy Spirit) that makes theology possible—that is, theology grounded in the objective reality of God rather than the fanciful projection of creaturely minds. When, moreover, God gives finite creatures the eyes and ears to recognize God's presence as the incarnate Logos, this constitutes a conversion. It turns the theologian around in a way that sets her free from slavery to culture, to philosophy, and to prior religious suppositions. Here the parallels between Kierkegaard's work in the *Philosophical Fragments* and Barth's in *Church Dogmatics* come to the fore. For both of them, this conversion and the subsequent about turn mean that our prior suppositions and affiliations are submitted to the critique of God's initiative in Jesus Christ rather than the other way around.

In considering the significance of the incarnation, we made extensive reference to the impact of culturally and politically constructed religion on events that have shaped the last two centuries—not only in Europe but also in North America, Southern Africa, and elsewhere. We drew attention to the long-standing complicity of god-talk in human suffering, not least, in acts of

3. St. Athanasius, *Contra Gentes and De Incarnatione*, ed. and trans. Edward W. Thomson (Oxford: Clarendon, 1971), §19, pp. 54–55. Specifically, he condemned those "called philosophers and wise men by the Greeks" who "fell to fashioning their gods" and "do not deny that their apparent gods are but forms and models of men and animals" (§19, p. 53).

4. St. Athanasius, *Discourse 1: Against the Arians*, trans. John Henry Newman and Archibald Robertson, vol. 4 of *Nicene and Post-Nicene Fathers*2, ed. Philip Schaff and Henry Wace (Buffalo, NY: Christian Literature Publishing Co., 1892); rev. and ed. Kevin Knight, New Advent, 1.24, https://www.newadvent.org/fathers/28161.htm.

5. See note 3 above.

oppression, exploitation, and racism. In the cases of the Crusades, the torture and execution of witches, slavery, and every facet of the Holocaust (to name a few instances), god-talk has been responsible for horrendous moral evil. Whereas the complicity of atheism in social evil is underplayed in our contemporary, secular rhetoric, it is imperative we not ignore the potential of religion and, indeed, Christian religion to go awry and be manipulated into serving oppressive, nationalistic and racist agendas.[6] For this reason, chapters 4 and 6 assessed the profound sociopolitical relevance of the KBT. This was seen to contrast dramatically with (immanent) assumptions about law, nature, reason, and god—specifically, we discussed appeals to "the moral sense," "moral instincts," "natural law," "general revelation," "the light of natural reason," "experience," and privileged "spiritual" capacities. Related to this, we also discussed the risks that Barth perceived as resulting from apologetic and eristic strategies. These start not with the kinship that God establishes with us in time but by our establishing a vestibule characterized by "points of connection" within the secular order from which to discern God's purposes. This attempt to ground the theological task in our own immanent assumptions inevitably displaces the God-humanward movement by prioritizing a human-Godward (godward) movement. The risk here is that God's self-disclosure in history is adapted to fit whatever secular procrustean bed we select as the control on our interpretation of God's revelation.

A growing awareness of the dangers of religion and an increasing bias toward secularism, especially in the West, have placed believers under increasing pressure to justify their beliefs and claims about God. The pressure increases when believers claim that their knowledge of God is delivered in and through privileged access to particular historical events. Part of the appeal of suggesting that epistemic access to God is universal and immanent, and does not require access to specific events in history, lies in the perception that such an account presents a less exclusive and more justifiable approach to knowledge of God. Our final chapter considered, therefore, how those who embrace the KBT might address questions relating to the justification of their God-talk, where knowledge of a particular historical event has decisive significance. This led us to consider the role of the Biblical witness, how it contributes to knowledge of God and whether (and under what conditions) "scientific" historical research might confirm the validity of its theological claims. This in turn raised questions about the grounding of claims that relate to God's involvement in his-

---

6. For further discussion of this point, see John Dickson's book *Bullies and Saints: An Honest Look at the Good and Evil of Christian History* (Grand Rapids: Zondervan, 2021).

tory—how such claims might be recognized to be true. Finally, we asked what kind of account might be provided of the nature of theological language here that does not reintroduce a conceptual immanentism by the back door. In addressing these questions, we argued that the KBT was consonant with an externalist approach not only to epistemology but also to semantics. To the extent that Christian believers know God, they do so because God has miraculously enabled the conditions to be met whereby their beliefs are not simply true but warranted. This led us to argue that the conditions under which we recognize God's presence in history are not conditions that we possess immanently or that we can awaken by means of some subjective strategy or technique. In tandem with this, we also argued that our language only (successfully) *refers* to God to the extent that God commandeers it in an act of self-naming and semantic self-designation within history. There is no descriptive capacity in our language which, in and of itself, can designate the God who is known in history. In sum, God's self-disclosure is a miraculous event that creates the conditions not only of proper epistemic function but also of proper semantic function, thereby enabling us to know God and to speak of God truthfully. This does not take place in an individualistic way. Rather, it takes place through the creation of a community characterized by testimony and proclamation— the community which the New Testament presents as the body of Christ and which is conceived as a new creation and a new humanity.

In conclusion, the KBT presents an account of God and the knowledge of God that recognizes the centrality of the incarnation and the full magnitude of its significance. It also presents us with the unambiguous *either-ors* that flow from this. To affirm God's triune self-disclosure in history precludes treating our immanent suppositions, agendas, and conceptualities as foundational— whether these are philosophical or religious, whether they are phenomenological or narratival, and whether they are ethical or sociopolitical. When theology takes place before God and affirms the God-humanward movement of God's grace, it recognizes the folly and vanity of constructing towers of Babel to help us reach God. It also recognizes that such attempts will foster the confusion that results from our disparate religious, philosophical, political, and ethical languages. In short, human-Godward or Socratic methodologies reflect a de facto repudiation of God's gracious movement toward us in Jesus Christ. To reject God's self-presentation, whether actively or passively, whether explicitly or subliminally, will result in our falling back on mythological constructs of our own. As Kierkegaard suggested, it is better for the Christian faith to be "well-hanged than ill-wed" to the idolatry of the immanent. More significantly, no constructions of the transcendent, shaped by natural dispositions, could possibly anticipate—let alone deliver—the radically inclusive vision of God and of God's reconciling purposes that is held forth in the incarnation. When the Christian church and its theologians have the courage and freedom to witness to the historical particularity of the gospel, their message becomes incomparably relevant to our divided, dysfunctional, and threatened world.

Bibliography

Søren Kierkegaard's Works

Buch des Richters: Seine Tagebücher 1833–1855 in Auswahl. Translated by Hermann Gottsched. Jena: Diederichs, 1905.

Der Augenblick. Translated by Christoph Schrempf. 2nd ed. Vol. 12 of *Gesammelte Werke*, edited and translated by Hermann Gottsched. Jena: Diederichs, 1909.

Philosophische Brocken / Abschließende unwissenschaftliche Nachschrift. Edited and translated by Hermann Gottsched and Christoph Schrempf. Vols. 6–7 of *Gesammelte Werke*, edited and translated by Hermann Gottsched and Christoph Schrempf. Jena: Diederichs, 1910.

Einübung in Christentum. Translated by Hermann Gottsched and Christoph Schrempf. Vol. 9 of *Gesammelte Werke*, edited and translated by Hermann Gottsched. Jena: Diederichs, 1912.

Erbauliche Reden. Edited and translated by Christoph Schrempf. Vols. 3–4. Jena: Diederichs, 1924–1929.

Søren Kierkegaard's Journals and Papers. Edited and translated by Howard V. Hong and Edna H. Hong, assisted by Gregor Malantschuk. 7 vols. Bloomington: Indiana University Press, 1967–1978.

The Concept of Anxiety. Edited and translated by Reidar Thomte. Princeton: Princeton University Press, 1980.

The Sickness unto Death: A Christian Psychological Exposition for Upbuilding and Awakening. Edited and translated by Howard V. Hong and Edna H. Hong. Princeton: Princeton University Press, 1980.

The Corsair Affair and Articles Related to the Writings. Translated by Howard V. Hong and Edna H. Hong. Princeton: Princeton University Press, 1982.

"Philosophical Fragments" and "Johannes Climacus." Edited and translated by Howard V. Hong and Edna H. Hong. Princeton: Princeton University Press, 1985.

Eighteen Upbuilding Discourses. Edited and translated by Howard V. Hong and Edna H. Hong. Princeton: Princeton University Press, 1990.

"For Self-Examination" and "Judge for Yourself!" Edited and translated by Howard V. Hong and Edna H. Hong. Princeton: Princeton University Press, 1990.

Practice in Christianity. Edited and translated by Howard V. Hong and Edna H. Hong. Princeton: Princeton University Press, 1991.

Concluding Unscientific Postscript to Philosophical Fragments. Edited and translated by Howard V. Hong and Edna H. Hong. 2 vols. Princeton: Princeton University Press, 1992.

Upbuilding Discourses in Various Spirits. Edited and translated by Howard V. Hong and Edna H. Hong. Princeton: Princeton University Press, 1993.

Works of Love. Edited and translated by Howard V. Hong and Edna H. Hong. Princeton: Princeton University Press, 1995.

"Christian Discourses" and "The Crisis and a Crisis in the Life of an Actress." Edited and translated by Howard V. Hong and Edna H. Hong. Princeton: Princeton University Press, 1997.

Without Authority. Edited and translated by Howard V. Hong and Edna H. Hong. Princeton: Princeton University Press, 1997.

The Book on Adler. Edited and translated by Howard V. Hong and Edna H. Hong. Princeton: Princeton University Press, 1998.

"The Moment" and Late Writings. Edited and translated by Howard V. Hong and Edna H. Hong. Princeton: Princeton University Press, 1998.

The Point of View for My Work as an Author. Edited and translated by Howard V. Hong and Edna H. Hong. Princeton: Princeton University Press, 1998.

"Prefaces" and "Writing Sampler." Edited and translated by Todd W. Nichol. Princeton: Princeton University Press, 1998.

Kierkegaard's Journals and Notebooks. Edited by Niels Jørgen Cappelørn, Alastair Hannay, David Kangas, Bruce H. Kirmmse, George Pattison, Vanessa Rumble, and K. Brian Söderquist. 11 vols. Princeton: Princeton University Press, 2007–2020.

KARL BARTH'S WORKS

The Epistle to the Romans. Translated by Edwyn C. Hoskyns. 6th ed. London: Oxford University Press, 1933. Originally published as *Der Römerbrief.* 2nd ed. Zurich: TVZ, 1922.

Theological Existence Today! A Plea for Theological Freedom. Translated by R. Birch
 Hoyle. London: Hodder and Stoughton, 1933.

No! Answer to Emil Brunner. In *Natural Theology: Comprising "Nature and Grace"
 by Professor Dr. Emil Brunner and the Reply "No!" by Dr. Karl Barth*, translated by Peter Fraenkel, with an introduction by John Baillie, 63–128. London: Centenary Press, 1946. Reprint, Eugene, OR: Wipf & Stock, 2002.

"The Disorder of the World and God's Plan of Salvation." Translated by Matthew A.
 Frost. Adapted from "Amsterdamer Fragen und Antworten," *Theologische
 Existentz heute* NF 15. Munich: Chr. Kaiser Verlag, 1949.

Das Geschenk der Freiheit: Grundlegung evangelischer Ethik. Theologische Studien
 39. Edited by Karl Barth. Zollikon-Zurich: Evangelischer Verlag, 1953.

Church Dogmatics. Edited by Geoffrey W. Bromiley and Thomas F. Torrance.
 Translated by Geoffrey W. Bromiley. 14 vols. Edinburgh: T&T Clark, 1956–
 1975. Originally published as *Die Kirchliche Dogmatik.* 13 vols. Munich: Chr.
 Kaiser Verlag, 1932; and thereafter Zurich: EVZ, 1938–1965.

Dogmatics in Outline. New York: Harper & Row, 1959.

"Church and Culture." In *Theology and Church: Shorter Writings, 1920–1928*, translated by Louise Pettibone Smith, 334–54. London: SCM, 1962.

"Church and Theology." In *Theology and Church: Shorter Writings, 1920–1928*,
 translated by Louise Pettibone Smith, 286–306. London: SCM, 1962.

Evangelical Theology: An Introduction. London: Weidenfeld and Nicolson, 1963.

Table Talk. In *Scottish Journal of Theology Occasional Papers* 10, edited by John D.
 Godsey. Edinburgh: Oliver and Boyd, 1963.

"The Church." In *God Here and Now*, translated by Paul M. van Buren, 61–85.
 London: Routledge & Kegan Paul, 1964.

*Revolutionary Theology in the Making: Barth–Thurneysen Correspondence, 1914–
 1925.* Translated by James D. Smart. Richmond, VA: John Knox, 1964. Originally published as *Karl Barth–Eduard Thurneysen: Briefwechsel.* Edited by
 Eduard Thurneysen. 2 vols. Zurich: TVZ, 1973.

"The Sovereignty of God's Word and the Decision of Faith." In *God Here and
 Now*, translated by Paul M. van Buren, 11–27. London: Routledge & Kegan
 Paul, 1964.

"Evangelical Theology in the 19th Century." In *The Humanity of God*, 11–33. London: Collins, Fontana, 1967.

"The Gift of Freedom: Foundation of Evangelical Ethics." In *The Humanity of God*,
 69–96. London: Collins, Fontana, 1967.

"The Humanity of God." In *The Humanity of God*, 37–65. London: Collins, Fontana, 1967.

"The Paradoxical Nature of the 'Positive Paradox.'" In *The Beginnings of Dialectic*

Theology, edited by James Robinson, translated by Keith Crim and Louis De Gratzia, 142–54. Richmond, VA: John Knox, 1968.

"The Christian Community and the Civil Community." In *Community, State and Church: Three Essays*, edited by Will Herberg, 149–89. New York: Doubleday, 1969. Originally published as *Christengemeinde und Bürgergemeinde*. Theologische Studien 20. Zollikon-Zurich: Evangelischer Verlag, 1946.

"Church and State" [Rechtfertigung und Recht]. In *Community, State, and Church: Three Essays*, edited by Will Herberg, 101–48. New York: Doubleday, 1969. Originally published as *Rechtfertigung und Recht*. Theologische Studien 1. Zollikon-Zurich: Evangelischer Verlag, 1938.

"Gospel and Law." In *Community, State, and Church: Three Essays*, edited by Will Herberg, 71–100. New York: Doubleday, 1969. Originally published as *Evangelium und Gesetz*. Theologische Existenz Heute 32. Munich: Chr. Kaiser Verlag, 1935.

"Kierkegaard and the Theologians." In *Fragments Grave and Gay*, edited by M. Rumscheidt, translated by Eric Mosbacher, 102–4. London: Fontana, 1971.

"A Thank You and a Bow: Kierkegaard's Reveille." In *Fragments Grave and Gay*, edited by M. Rumscheidt, translated by Eric Mosbacher, 95–101. London: Fontana, 1971. Originally published as "Dank und Reverenz." *Evangelische Theologie* 23 (1963): 337–42.

A Late Friendship: The Letters of Karl Barth and Carl Zuckmayer. Translated by Geoffrey W. Bromiley. Grand Rapids: Eerdmans, 1972.

Protestant Theology in the Nineteenth Century: Its Background & History. London: SCM, 1972.

The Christian Life: Church Dogmatics IV/4. Translated by Geoffrey W. Bromiley. Edinburgh: T&T Clark, 1981. Originally published as *Das christliche Leben: Die Kirchliche Dogmatik IV/4, Fragmente aus dem Nachlaß: Vorlesungen 1959–1961*. Zurich: TVZ, 1976.

Ethics. Edited by Dietrich Braun. Translated by Geoffrey W. Bromiley. Edinburgh: T&T Clark, 1981.

Karl Barth–Rudolf Bultmann Letters, 1922–1966. Edited by Bernd Jaspert and Geoffrey W. Bromiley. Grand Rapids: Eerdmans, 1981.

Letters, 1961–1968. Translated by Geoffrey W. Bromiley. Grand Rapids: Eerdmans, 1981.

The Theology of Schleiermacher: Lectures at Göttingen, Winter Semester of 1923–24. Translated by Geoffrey W. Bromiley. Edited by Dietrich Ritschl. Grand Rapids: Eerdmans, 1982.

The Göttingen Dogmatics: Instruction in the Christian Religion. Translated by

Geoffrey W. Bromiley. 1st English ed., edited by Hannelotte Reiffen. Grand Rapids: Eerdmans, 1991.

The Holy Spirit and the Christian Life: The Theological Basis of Ethics. Translated by R. Birch Hoyle. Louisville: Westminster John Knox, 1993.

God in Action: Theological Addresses. Eugene, OR: Wipf & Stock, 2005.

Secondary Literature and Other Works

Adams, Nicholas. *The Eclipse of Grace: Divine and Human Action in Hegel*. Oxford: Wiley-Blackwell, 2013.

Adams, Samuel V. *The Reality of God and Historical Method: Apocalyptic Theology in Conversation with N. T. Wright*. Downers Grove, IL: InterVarsity Press, 2015.

Altschul, Jon. "Epistemic Entitlement." *Internet Encyclopedia of Philosophy*. Accessed June 28, 2021. https://iep.utm.edu/ep-en/.

Amesbury, Richard. "Fideism." In *Stanford Encyclopedia of Philosophy*. Article published May 6, 2005; last modified February 5, 2022. https://plato.stanford .edu/entries/fideism/#2.2.

Anzinger, Herbert. *Glaube und kommunikative Praxis: Eine Studie zur vordialektischen Theologie Karl Barths*. Munich: Chr. Kaiser Verlag, 1991.

Appleby, R. Scott. *The Ambivalence of the Sacred: Religion, Violence, and Reconciliation*. Lanham, MD: Rowman and Littlefield, 2000.

Aquinas, Thomas. *On Creation* [*Quaestiones Disputatae de Potentia Dei*, Q.3]. Translated by S. C. Selner-Wright. Washington, DC: The Catholic University of America Press, 2011.

———. *Summa Contra Gentiles, Book 1: God*. Translated by Anton C. Pegis. Notre Dame: University of Notre Dame Press, reprinted 1975.

———. *Summa Theologiae*. London: Eyre & Spottiswoode; New York: McGraw-Hill, 1964–80.

———. "What Experience Teaches Us about God." In *Commentary on the Book of Job*, translated by Brian Mulladay, edited by Joseph Kenny, OP, chap. 12. https://isidore.co/aquinas/SSJob.htm.

Athanasius, St. *Contra Gentes and De Incarnatione*. Edited and translated by Edward W. Thomson. Oxford: Clarendon, 1971.

———. *Discourse 1: Against the Arians*. Translated by John Henry Newman and Archibald Robertson. Vol. 4 of *Nicene and Post-Nicene Fathers2*, edited by Philip Schaff and Henry Wace. Buffalo, NY: Christian Literature Publishing Co., 1892. Revised and edited by Kevin Knight, New Advent. https://www .newadvent.org/fathers/28161.htm.

————. *Letters of Saint Athanasius concerning the Holy Spirit.* Translated by C. R. B. Shapland. London: Epworth, 1951.

Baillie, John. *Our Knowledge of God.* London: Oxford University Press, 1939.

Balthasar, Hans Urs von. *The Theology of Karl Barth: Exposition and Interpretation.* Translated by Edward T. Oakes. San Francisco: Ignatius, 1992.

Barrett, Lee C. "Karl Barth: The Dialectic of Attraction and Repulsion." In *Kierkegaard's Influence on Theology, Tome I: German Protestant Theology*, edited by Jon Stewart, 1–41. Farnham: Ashgate, 2012.

Bartels, Cora. *Kierkegaard receptus I: Die theologiegeschichtliche Bedeutung der Kierkegaard–Rezeption Rudolf Bultmanns.* Göttingen: Vandenhoeck & Ruprecht, 2008.

————. *Kierkegaard receptus II: Die theologiegeschichtliche Bedeutung der Kierkegaard–Rezeption Rudolf Bultmanns.* Göttingen: Vandenhoeck & Ruprecht, 2011.

Bauckham, Richard. *God Crucified: Monotheism and Christology in the New Testament.* Grand Rapids: Eerdmans, 1999.

————. *Jesus and the Eyewitnesses: The Gospels as Eyewitness Testimony.* Grand Rapids: Eerdmans, 2006.

Bax, Douglas. "The Barmen Declaration: A New Translation." *Journal of Theology for Southern Africa* 47 (June 1984): 78–81.

————. *A Different Gospel: A Critique of the Theology behind Apartheid.* Presbyterian Church of South Africa, 1979.

Beck, Lewis White. "Neo-Kantianism." In *The Encyclopedia of Philosophy*, edited by Paul Edwards. New York: Macmillan and Free Press, 1967.

Beintker, Michael. *Die Dialektik in der "dialectischen Theologie" Karl Barths: Studien zur Entwicklung der Barthschen Theologie und zur Vorgeschichte der "Kirchlichen Dogmatick."* Munich: Chr. Kaiser Verlag, 1987.

Beiser, Frederick C. *Hermann Cohen: An Intellectual Biography.* Oxford: Oxford University Press, 2018.

Bender, Kimlyn J. "Søren Kierkegaard and Karl Barth: Reflections on a Relation and a Proposal for Future Investigation. " *International Journal of Systematic Theology* 17, no. 3 (2015): 296–318.

Benton, Matthew A. "The Modal Gap: The Objective Problem of Lessing's Ditch(es) and Kierkegaard's Subjective Reply." *Religious Studies* 42, no. 1 (2006): 27–44.

Bonhoeffer, Dietrich. *Berlin: 1932–1933.* Translated by Isabel Best and David Higgins. Vol. 12 of *Dietrich Bonhoeffer Works*, edited by Larry Rasmussen. Minneapolis: Fortress, 2009.

_____. *Christ the Center*. Translated by Edwin Robertson. New York: Harper & Row, 1978.

Bromiley, Geoffrey W. *Introduction to the Theology of Karl Barth*. Grand Rapids: Eerdmans, 1979.

Brunner, Emil. "Die andere Aufgabe der Theologie." *Zwischen den Zeiten* 7 (1929): 255–76.

_____. *Nature and Grace: A Contribution to the Discussion with Karl Barth*. In *Natural Theology*, edited by John Baillie, 15–62. London: Centenary Press, 1946.

_____. *Revelation and Reason: The Christian Doctrine of Faith and Knowledge*. Translated by Olive Wyon. Philadelphia: Westminster Press, 1946.

Bultmann, Rudolf. *Jesus Christ and Mythology*. New York: Scribner, 1958.

Busch, Eberhard. *Karl Barth: His Life from Letters and Autobiographical Texts*. Translated by John Bowden. Philadelphia: Fortress, 1976.

Calvin, John. *Commentaries on the Epistles of Paul the Apostle to the Philippians, Colossians, and Thessalonians*. Translated by John Pringle. Edinburgh: Calvin Translation Society, 1851.

_____. *The Deliverance of God: An Apocalyptic Rereading of Justification in Paul*. Grand Rapids: Eerdmans, 2009.

_____. *Institutes of the Christian Religion*. Edited by John T. McNeill. Translated by Ford Lewis Battles. 2 vols. Philadelphia: Westminster, 1960.

_____. *Praelectiones in librum prophetiarum Jeremiae et lamentationes*. 1576.

Campbell, Douglas A. "Participation and Faith in Paul." In *"In Christ" in Paul: Explorations in Paul's Theology of Union and Participation*, edited by Michael J. Thate, Kevin J. Vanhoozer, and Constantine R. Campbell, 37–60. WUNT 2/384. Tübingen: Mohr Siebeck, 2015.

_____. "A Participationist Eschatological Account of Justification: Further Reflections." *Revue Biblique* 125 (2018): 249–61.

_____. *Pauline Dogmatics: The Triumph of God's Love*. Grand Rapids: Eerdmans, 2020.

Campo, Mariano. "Natorp, Paul." In *The Encyclopedia of Philosophy*, edited by Paul Edwards. New York: Macmillan and Free Press, 1967.

Chalamet, Christophe. *Dialectical Theologians: Wilhelm Herrmann, Karl Barth, and Rudolf Bultmann*. Zurich: TVZ, 2005.

Charles, J. Daryl. *Retrieving the Natural Law: A Return to Moral First Things*. Grand Rapids: Eerdmans, 2008.

Chignell, Andrew. "The Ethics of Belief." In *Stanford Encyclopedia of Philosophy*. Article published June 14, 2010; last modified March 5, 2018. https://plato.stanford.edu/entries/ethics-belief/.

Chisholm, Roderick M. "Epistemic Statements and the Ethics of Belief." *Philosophy and Phenomenological Research* 16, no. 4 (June 1956): 447–60.

Clifford, William Kingdon. "The Ethics of Belief." In *The Ethics of Belief Debate*, edited by Gerald D. McCarthy, 19–36. Atlanta: Scholars Press, 1986.

Cochrane, Arthur C. "On the Anniversaries of Mozart, Kierkegaard and Barth." *Scottish Journal of Theology* 9 (1956): 251–63.

Come, Arnold B. *Kierkegaard as Theologian: Recovering My Self*. Montreal: McGill-Queen's University Press, 1997.

Congdon, David. "Dialectical Theology as Theology of Mission: Investigating the Origins of Karl Barth's Break with Liberalism." *International Journal of Systematic Theology* 16, no. 4 (2014): 390–413.

———. *The Mission of Demythologizing: Rudolf Bultmann's Dialectical Theology*. Minneapolis: Fortress, 2015.

Crisp, Oliver. *Approaching the Atonement: The Reconciling Work of Christ*. Downers Grove, IL: InterVarsity Press Academic, 2020.

Cyril of Alexandria. *De symbolo*. In *Cyril of Alexandria: Selected Letters*, edited and translated by Lionel R. Wickham. Oxford: Clarendon, 1983.

———. *On the Unity of Christ*. Translated by John Anthony McGuckin. Crestwood, NY: St. Vladimir's Seminary Press, 1995.

Dalferth, Ingolf. "Becoming a Christian according to the *Postscript*: Kierkegaard's Christian Hermeneutics of Existence." In *Kierkegaard Studies Yearbook 2005*, edited by N. J. Cappelørn and H. Deuser, 242–81. Berlin: Walter de Gruyter, 2005.

Dennison, William D. *The Young Bultmann: Context for His Understanding of God, 1884–1925*. New York: Peter Lang, 2008.

Descartes, René. *Discourse on the Method for Conducting One's Reason Well and for Seeking the Truth in the Sciences* [Discours de la Méthode pour bien conduire sa raison, et chercher la vérité dans les sciences]. 1637. Reprinted in *Philosophical Essays and Correspondence*, edited by Roger Ariew. Indianapolis: Hackett, 2000.

———. *Rules for the Direction of the Mind* [Regulae ad Directionem Ingenii]. 1701. Reprinted in *Philosophical Essays and Correspondence*, edited by Roger Ariew. Indianapolis: Hackett, 2000.

Dickson, John. *Bullies and Saints: An Honest Look at the Good and Evil of Christian History*. Grand Rapids: Zondervan, 2021.

Diller, Kevin. "Karl Barth and the Relationship between Philosophy and Theology." *Heythrop Journal* 51, no. 6 (2010): 1035–52.

———. "The Theology of Revelation and the Epistemology of Christian Belief: The Compatibility and Complementarity of the Theological Epistemologies of

Karl Barth and Alvin Plantinga." PhD diss., University of St. Andrews, 2008. https://research-repository.st-andrews.ac.uk/handle/10023/497.

———. *Theology's Epistemological Dilemma: How Karl Barth and Alvin Plantinga Provide a Unified Response.* Downers Grove, IL: InterVarsity Press Academic, 2014.

Donnellan, Keith S. "Speaking of Nothing." *Philosophical Review* 83, no. 1 (1974): 3–31.

Dorrien, Gary. *The Barthian Revolt in Modern Theology: Theology without Weapons.* Louisville: Westminster John Knox, 2000.

Dowey, Edward. *The Knowledge of God in Calvin's Theology.* New York: Columbia University Press, 1952; republished Grand Rapids: Eerdmans, 1994.

Dretske, Fred. "Entitlement: Epistemic Rights without Epistemic Duties?" *Philosophy and Phenomenological Research* 60, no. 3 (2000): 591–606.

———. "What We See." Howison Lectures in Philosophy, 2007. https://gradlectures.berkeley.edu/lecture/what-we-see/.

Dulles, Avery Cardinal. "The Rebirth of Apologetics." *First Things*, May, 2004. https://www.firstthings.com/article/2004/05/the-rebirth-of-apologetics.

Du Mez, Kristen Kobes. *Jesus and John Wayne: How White Evangelicals Corrupted a Faith and Fractured a Nation.* New York: Liveright, 2020.

Dunn, James D. G. *Christology in the Making: A New Testament Inquiry into the Origins of the Doctrine of the Incarnation.* London: SCM, 1980.

Dyer, Justin Buckley. "Lewis, Barth, and the Natural Law." *Journal of Church and State* 57, no. 1 (2015): 1–17.

Edwards, Aaron. "A Broken Engagement: Reassessing Barth's Relationship to Kierkegaard on the Grounds of Subjectivity and Preaching." *International Journal of Systematic Theology* 16, no. 1 (2014): 56–78.

———. "The Paradox of Dialectic: Clarifying the Use and Scope of Dialectic in Theology." *International Journal of Philosophy and Theology* 77 (2016): 273–306.

———. *A Theology of Preaching and Dialectic: Scriptural Tension, Heraldic Proclamation, and the Pneumatological Moment.* London: Bloomsbury T&T Clark, 2018.

Edwards, Jonathan. *The Nature of True Virtue.* 1755. Reprinted Ann Arbor: University of Michigan Press, 1960.

Elert, Werner. *Bekenntnis, Blut und Boden: Drei theologische Vorträge.* Leipzig: Dörffling & Franke, 1934.

Elton, Maria. "Moral Sense and Natural Reason." *Review of Metaphysics* 62, no. 1 (2008): 79–110.

Emerson, Michael, and Christian Smith. *Divided by Faith: Evangelical Religion and the Problem of Race in America.* Oxford: Oxford University Press, 2000.

Ericksen, Robert. *Complicity in the Holocaust: Churches and Universities in Nazi Germany*. New York: Cambridge University Press, 2012.

———. "The Political Theology of Paul Althaus: Nazi Supporter." *German Studies Review* 9, no. 3 (1986): 547–67.

———. *Theologians under Hitler*. New Haven: Yale University Press, 1985.

Evans, C. Stephen. *The Historical Christ and the Jesus of Faith*. New York: Oxford University Press, 1996.

———. "Kierkegaard, Natural Theology, and the Existence of God." In *Kierkegaard and Christian Faith*, edited by Paul Martens and C. Stephen Evans, 25–38. Waco, TX: Baylor University Press, 2016.

———. *Kierkegaard on Faith and the Self: Collected Essays*. Waco, TX: Baylor University Press, 2006.

———. *Kierkegaard's "Fragments" and "Postscript": The Religious Philosophy of Johannes Climacus*. Atlantic Highlands, NJ: Humanities Press, 1983.

———. "Methodological Naturalism in Historical Biblical Scholarship." In *Jesus and the Restoration of Israel: A Critical Assessment of N. T. Wright's Jesus and the Victory of God*, edited by Carey C. Newman, 180–205. Downers Grove, IL: InterVarsity Press, 1999.

———. *Passionate Reason: Making Sense of Kierkegaard's "Philosophical Fragments."* Indianapolis: Indiana University Press, 1992.

Fergusson, David. *Bultmann*. London: Geoffrey Chapman, 1992.

Ferreira, M. Jamie. "Faith and the Kierkegaardian Leap." In *The Cambridge Companion to Kierkegaard*, edited by Alastair Hannay and Gordon D. Marino, 207–34. Cambridge: Cambridge University Press, 1997.

Fogelman, Hugh. *Christianity Uncovered: Viewed Through Open Eyes*. Bloomington, IN: AuthorHouse, 2012.

Ford, David F. "Barth's Interpretation of the Bible." In *Karl Barth: Studies of His Theological Method*, edited by S. W. Sykes, 55–87. Oxford: Clarendon, 1979.

Ford, John C. "Natural Law and the Pursuit of Happiness." *Notre Dame Law Review* 26, no. 3 (1951): 429–61.

Friedlander, Henry. *The Origins of Nazi Genocide: From Euthanasia to the Final Solution*. Chapel Hill: University of North Carolina Press, 1997.

Gadamer, Hans-Georg. *Truth and Method*. 2nd rev. ed. Translated by Joel Weinsheimer and Donald G. Marshall. London: Continuum, 2004.

Gallois, André. "De re/de dicto." In *Routledge Encyclopedia of Philosophy*. Accessed May 27, 2021. https://www.rep.routledge.com/articles/thematic/de-re-de-dicto/v-1.

Garrison, Jim. *The Darkness of God: Theology after Hiroshima*. London: SCM, 1982.

Gavrilyuk, Paul. *The Suffering of the Impassible God: The Dialectics of Patristic Thought*. Oxford: Oxford University Press, 2004.

Gerlach, Wolfgang. *And the Witnesses Were Silent: The Confessing Church and the Persecution of the Jews*. Lincoln: University of Nebraska Press, 2000.

Gert, Bernard. *Morality: A New Justification of the Moral Rules*. New York: Oxford University Press, 1988.

Gettier, Edmund L. "Is Justified True Belief Knowledge?" *Analysis* 3, no. 6 (June 1963): 121–23.

Goldhagen, Daniel Jonah. *Hitler's Willing Executioners: Ordinary Germans and the Holocaust*. New York: Knopf, 1996.

Gollwitzer, Helmut. "Kingdom of God and Socialism in the Theology of Karl Barth." In *Karl Barth and Radical Politics*, edited by George Hunsinger, 77–120. Philadelphia: Westminster, 1976; 2nd ed. Eugene, OR: Cascade, 2017.

Gordon, Frank J. "Liberal German Churchmen and the First World War." *German Studies Review* 4, no. 1 (1981): 39–62. https://doi.org/10.2307/1428755.

Gouwens, David J. *Kierkegaard as Religious Thinker*. Cambridge: Cambridge University Press, 1996.

Grabill, Stephen. *Rediscovering the Natural Law in Reformed Theological Ethics*. Grand Rapids: Eerdmans, 2006.

Grant, Edward. *The Foundations of Modern Science in the Middle Ages*. Cambridge: Cambridge University Press, 1996.

———. *Physical Science in the Middle Ages*. New York: John Wiley, 1971.

Greco, John. "Plantinga, Foundationalism and the Charge of Self-Referential Incoherence." *Grazer Philosophische Studien* 31 (1988): 187–93.

Green, Lowell C. *Lutherans against Hitler: The Untold Story*. St. Louis: Concordia, 2007.

Greene, Robert A. "Instinct of Nature: Natural Law, Synderesis, and the Moral Sense." *Journal of the History of Ideas* 58, no. 2 (1997): 173–98.

Greggs, Tom. *Theology against Religion: Constructive Dialogues with Bonhoeffer and Barth*. London: T&T Clark, 2011.

Gruchy, John de. *The Church Struggle in South Africa*. Grand Rapids: Eerdmans, 1979.

Gunton, Colin E. *The Barth Lectures*. Edited by Paul H. Brazier. New York: T&T Clark, 2007.

———. *Becoming and Being: The Doctrine of God in Charles Hartshorne and Karl Barth*. 2nd ed. Eugene, OR: Wipf & Stock, 2011.

Hanna, Robert. "Supplement: The Togetherness Principle, Kant's Conceptualism, and Kant's Non-Conceptualism." In *Stanford Encyclopedia of Philosophy*.

Article published 2017. https://plato.stanford.edu/entries/kant-judgment
/supplement1.html.

Hannay, Alastair. *Kierkegaard: A Biography*. Cambridge: Cambridge University
Press, 2003.

Hannay, Alastair, and Gordon D. Marino. Introduction to *The Cambridge Companion to Kierkegaard*, edited by Alastair Hannay and Gordon D. Marino,
1–4. Cambridge: Cambridge University Press, 1997.

Harris, H. S. "Hegel's Correspondence Theory of Truth." *Bulletin of the Hegel Society of Great Britain* 29 (1994): 1–13.

Harris, James F. "The Causal Theory of Reference and Religious Language." *International Journal for Philosophy of Religion* 29, no. 2 (1991): 75–86.

Harris, Sam. "An Atheist Manifesto (2005)." In *Faith in Faithlessness: An Anthology of Atheism*, edited by Dimitrios I. Roussopoulos, 242–51. Montreal: Black
Rose Books, 2008.

Hartshorne, Charles. "The Dipolar Conception of Deity." *Review of Metaphysics*
21, no. 2 (1967): 282–84.

Hastings, Derek. *Catholicism and the Roots of Nazism: Religious Identity and National Socialism*. Oxford: Oxford University Press, 2010.

Hays, Richard. *The Moral Vision of the New Testament: A Contemporary Introduction to New Testament Ethics*. New York: HarperCollins, 1996.

Hector, Kevin. *Theology without Metaphysics: God, Language, and the Spirit of
Recognition*. Cambridge: Cambridge University Press, 2011.

Hegel, Georg Wilhelm Friedrich. *Encyclopedia of the Philosophical Sciences in Basic
Outline, Part I: Science of Logic*. Translated by Klaus Brinkmann and Daniel
Dahlstrom. Cambridge: Cambridge University Press, 2010.

———. *Hegel's Philosophy of Nature*. Translated by A. V. Miller. Oxford: Clarendon,
1970.

———. *Lectures on the Philosophy of Religion*. Vol. 1, *"Introduction" and "The Concept of Religion."* Edited and translated by Peter C. Hodgson. Berkeley: University of California Press, 1984.

———. *The Phenomenology of Mind*. Translated by J. B. Beillies. London: George
Allen & Unwin, 1949.

———. *The Phenomenology of Spirit*. Translated by Terry Pinkard. New York: Oxford University Press, 2018.

Heidegger, Martin. *Being and Time*. Translated by John Macquarrie and Edward
Robinson. New York: Harper & Row, 1962.

Herdt, Jennifer A. "Calvin's Legacy for Contemporary Reformed Natural Law."
Scottish Journal of Theology 67, no. 4 (2014): 414–35.

Heron, Alasdair I. C. *A Century of Protestant Theology*. Cambridge: Lutterworth Press, 1980.

———. "*Homoousios* with the Father." In *The Incarnation: Ecumenical Studies in the Nicene-Constantinopolitan Creed, A.D. 381*, edited by Thomas F. Torrance, 58–87. Edinburgh: Handsel Press, 1981.

Hick, John, ed. *The Myth of God Incarnate*. London: SCM, 1976.

Hinlicky, Paul. *Before Auschwitz: What Christian Theology Must Learn from the Rise of Nazism*. Eugene, OR: Wipf & Stock, 2013.

Hirsch, Emanuel. *Geschichte der neuern evangelischen Theologie im Zusammenhang mit den allgemeinen Bewegungen des europäischen Denkens*. Vols. 1–5. Gütersloh: Bertelsmann, 1949–1954.

———. *Kierkegaard-Studien*. Vols. 1–2. Gütersloh: 1933. Reprint, Vaduz, Liechtenstein: Topos Verlag, 1978.

Hitchens, Christopher. *God Is Not Great: How Religion Poisons Everything*. New York: Warner Twelve, 2007.

Hodgson, Peter. *Hegel and Christian Theology: A Reading of the Lectures of Philosophy of Religion*. Oxford: Oxford University Press, 2005.

Hughes, Carl S. *Kierkegaard and the Staging of Desire: Rhetoric and Performance in a Theology of Eros*. New York: Fordham University Press, 2014.

Hume, David. *A Treatise of Human Nature*. Edited by David Fate Norton and Mary J. Norton. Oxford: Clarendon, 2007.

Hunsinger, George. *How to Read Karl Barth: The Shape of His Theology*. New York: Oxford University Press, 1991.

———, ed. *Karl Barth and Radical Politics*. 2nd ed. Eugene, OR: Cascade, 2017.

Inwagen, Peter van. "'It Is Wrong, Everywhere, Always, and for Anyone, to Believe Anything upon Insufficient Evidence.'" In *Faith, Freedom, and Rationality: Philosophy of Religion Today*, edited by Jeff Jordan and Daniel Howard-Snyder, 137–53. Lanham, MD: Rowman & Littlefield, 1996.

Jenson, Matt. *The Gravity of Sin: Augustine, Luther and Barth on "homo incurvatus in se."* New York: T&T Clark, 2007.

Johnson, Keith. *Karl Barth and the Analogia Entis*. T&T Clark Studies in Systematic Theology. New York: T&T Clark, 2010.

Johnson, Roger A. *The Origins of Demythologizing: Philosophy and Historiography in the Theology of Rudolf Bultmann*. Leiden: Brill, 1974.

Jüngel, Eberhard. *God's Being Is in Becoming: The Trinitarian Being of God in the Theology of Karl Barth; A Paraphrase*. Translated by John B. Webster. London: Bloomsbury, 2001.

———. "Von der Dialektik zur Analogie: Die Schule Kierkegaards und der Einspruch Petersons." In *Barth-Studien*, 127–79. Zurich: Benziger Verlag. Reprint, Gütersloh: Gütersloher Verlagshaus Gerd Mohn, 1982.

Keeble, N. H. "C. S. Lewis, Richard Baxter, and 'Mere Christianity.'" *Christianity and Literature* 30, no. 3 (1981): 27–44.

Kerr, Fergus. "Rahner Retrospective III: Transcendence or Finitude." *New Blackfriars* 62 (1981): 370–79.

Kertzer, David. *The Pope and Mussolini: The Secret History of Pope Pius XI and the Rise of Fascism in Europe*. Oxford: Oxford University Press, 2014.

Kilby, Karen. *Karl Rahner: Theology and Philosophy*. London: Routledge, 2004.

Kilner, John. *Dignity and Destiny: Humanity in the Image of God*. Grand Rapids: Eerdmans, 2015.

Kirmmse, Bruce H. "The Thunderstorm: Kierkegaard's Ecclesiology." *Faith and Philosophy* 17, no. 1 (2000): 87–102.

Kooi, Cornelis van der. *Anfängliche Theologie: Der Denkweg des jungen Karl Barth (1909 bis 1927)*. Munich: Chr. Kaiser Verlag, 1987.

Kripke, Saul A. *Naming and Necessity*. Cambridge, MA: Harvard University Press, 1980.

Krötke, Wolf. "The Humanity of the Human Person in Karl Barth's Anthropology." Translated by Philip G. Ziegler. In *The Cambridge Companion to Karl Barth*, edited by John Webster, 159–76. Cambridge: Cambridge University Press, 2000.

Lane, Anthony N. S. *John Calvin: Student of the Church Fathers*. London: A&C Black, 1999.

Lessing, Gotthold Ephraim. *Lessing's Theological Writings*. Edited and translated by Henry Chadwick. Stanford: Stanford University Press, 1956.

———. *Philosophical and Theological Writings*. Translated and edited by Hugh Barr Nisbet. Cambridge: Cambridge University Press, 2005.

Lewis, C. S. *Mere Christianity*. London: Collins, 2012.

Lewis, David K. "Putnam's Paradox." *Australasian Journal of Philosophy* 62, no. 3 (1984): 221–36.

Lindberg, David C. "The Medieval Church Encounters the Classical Tradition: Saint Augustine, Roger Bacon, and the Handmaiden Metaphor." In *When Science and Christianity Meet*, edited by David C. Lindberg and Ronald L. Numbers, 7–32. Chicago: University of Chicago Press, 2003.

Locke, John. *An Essay Concerning Human Understanding, 1690*. Oxford. Clarendon, 1975.

———. *The Works of John Locke*. Vol. 7. London: Printed for Thomas Tegg, 1823.

Louth, Andrew. "Review of Alan J. Torrance, *Persons in Communion*." *Heythrop Journal* 42 (2001): 529–31.

Luther, Martin. Letter to John von Staupitz, May 30, 1518. In *Letters*, edited and translated by Gottfried G. Krodel. Vol. 48 of *Luther's Works*, edited by Jaroslav Pelikan and Helmut T. Lehmann, 65–70. 55 vols. Philadelphia: Fortress, 1963.

Mackie, J. L. *The Miracle of Theism: Arguments For and Against the Existence of God*. Oxford: Clarendon, 1982.

Malik, Habib. *Receiving Søren Kierkegaard: The Early Impact and Transmission of His Thought*. Washington, DC: Catholic University of America Press, 1997.

Mangina, Joseph. *Karl Barth: Theologian of Christian Witness*. Louisville: Westminster John Knox, 2004.

Marsden, George M. *Jonathan Edwards: A Life*. New Haven: Yale University Press, 2003.

Marshall, Bruce D. "Review of Alan J. Torrance, *Persons in Communion*." *Journal of Theological Studies* 50 (1999): 434–36.

Martensen, H. L. *Af mit Levnet: Meddelelser*. Copenhagen: Gylendal, 1882–83.

———. *Christian Dogmatics*. Translated by William Urwick. Edinburgh: T&T Clark, 1886.

———. *Christian Ethics: Special Part; Second Division: Social Ethics*. Translated by Sophia Taylor. Edinburgh: T&T Clark, 1882.

Martens, Paul, and C. Stephen Evans, eds. *Kierkegaard and Christian Faith*. Waco, TX: Baylor University Press, 2016.

Martens, Paul, and Tom Millay. "'The Changelessness of God' as Kierkegaard's Final Theodicy: God and the Gift of Suffering." *International Journal of Systematic Theology* 13, no. 2 (2011): 170–89.

Mather, Cotton. *A Man of Reason: A Brief Essay to Demonstrate That All Men Should Hearken to Reason* [. . .]. Boston, 1718. https://teachingamerican history.org/document/mather-a-man-of-reason-edwards-a-supernatural -light/.

McCormack, Bruce L. *Karl Barth's Critically Realistic Dialectical Theology: Its Genesis and Development, 1909–1936*. Oxford: Clarendon, 1995.

McInroy, Mark. "Karl Barth and Personalist Philosophy: A Critical Appropriation." *Scottish Journal of Theology* 64, no. 1 (2011): 45–63.

McKinnon, Alastair. "Barth's Relation to Kierkegaard: Some Further Light." *Canadian Journal of Theology* 13 (1967): 31–41.

———. "Kierkegaard and the Leap of Faith." *Kierkegaardiana* 16 (1993): 107–25.

Messer, August, and Anders Gemmer. *Sören Kierkegaard und Karl Barth*. Stuttgart: Verlag Streder und Schöder, 1925.

Michalson, Gordon E. *Lessing's "Ugly Ditch": A Study of Theology and History*. University Park, PA: Penn State University Press, 1990.

Mihut, Cristian. "Bearing Burdens and the Character of God in the Hebrew Bible." In *Character: New Directions from Philosophy, Psychology, and Theology*, edited by Christian Miller, R. Michael Furr, Angela Knobel, and William Fleeson, 368–92. New York: Oxford University Press, 2015.

Miller, Richard B. "The Reference of 'God.'" *Faith and Philosophy: Journal of the Society of Christian Philosophers* 3, no. 1 (1986): 3–15.

Moltmann, Jürgen. *The Future of Creation: Collected Essays*. Minneapolis: Fortress, 2007.

———. *The Trinity and the Kingdom of God*. Translated by Margaret Kohl. London: SCM, 1980.

Mondin, Battista. *The Principle of Analogy in Protestant and Catholic Theology*. The Hague: Martinus Nijhoff, 1963.

Mueller, David L. Review of *Community, State, and Church*, by Karl Barth, edited by Will Herberg. *Church and State* 3, no. 1 (1961): 84–87.

Mul, Jos de. "Das Schauspiel des Lebens: Wilhelm Dilthey and Historical Biography." *Revue Internationale de Philosophie* 226, no. 4 (2003): 407–24. https://www.cairn.info/revue-internationale-de-philosophie-2003-4-page-407.htm.

Mulgan, Tim. *Purpose in the Universe: The Moral and Metaphysical Case for Ananthropocentric Purposivism*. Oxford: Oxford University Press, 2015.

Newman, John Henry, trans. *Four Discourses of S. Athanasius against the Arians*. In *Select Treatises of St. Athanasius*, translated by John Henry Newman. Oxford: James Parker, 1877. Available online, Newman Reader: Works of John Henry Newman, The National Institute for Newman Studies, 2007. https://www.newmanreader.org/works/athanasius/original/index.html.

Niemoller, Gerhard. *Die erste Bekenntnissynode der Deutschen Evangelischen Kirche zu Barmen*. Vol. 1. Göttingen: Vandenhoeck & Ruprecht, 1959.

Nozick, Robert. *Philosophical Explanations*. Cambridge, MA: The Belknap Press of Harvard University Press, 1981.

Ogden, Schubert M. Introduction to *Existence and Faith: Shorter Writings of Rudolf Bultmann*, by Rudolf Bultmann. n.p.: Collins, 1964.

O'Grady, Colm. *The Church in Catholic Theology: Dialogue with Karl Barth*. London: G. Chapman, 1969.

———. *The Church in the Theology of Karl Barth*. London: G. Chapman, 1968.

Parker, T. H. L. *Calvin's Doctrine of the Knowledge of God*. Edinburgh: Oliver and Boyd, 1952. Republished, Eugene, OR: Wipf & Stock, 2015.

Pattison, George. *Kierkegaard and the Quest for Unambiguous Life: Between Romanticism and Modernism; Selected Essays*. Oxford: Oxford University Press, 2013.

———. *Kierkegaard and the Theology of the Nineteenth Century: The Paradox and the "Point of Contact."* Cambridge: Cambridge University Press, 2012.

———. *The Philosophy of Kierkegaard.* Montreal: McGill-Queen's University Press, 2005.

Peterson, Erik. *Theological Tractates.* Edited and translated by Michael Hollerich. Stanford: Stanford University Press, 2011.

Peterson, Ryan. *The* Imago Dei *as Human Identity: A Theological Interpretation.* Winona Lake, IN: Eisenbrauns, 2016.

Pierson, Daniel. "Thomas Aquinas on the Principle *Omne Agens Agit Sibi Simile.*" PhD diss., Catholic University of America, 2015.

Plantinga, Alvin. Review of *Fides et Ratio*: "Faith and Reason." *Books & Culture* 5, no. 4 (July/August 1999): 32–35.

———. *The Twin Pillars of Christian Scholarship.* The Stob Lectures. Grand Rapids: Calvin College, 1990.

———. *Warrant and Proper Function.* New York: Oxford University Press, 1993.

———. *Warranted Christian Belief.* New York: Oxford University Press, 2000.

Plantinga, Alvin, and Nicholas Wolterstorff, eds. *Faith and Rationality: Reason and Belief in God.* Notre Dame: University of Notre Dame Press, 1983.

Pojman, Louis P. "Kierkegaard on Justification of Belief." *International Journal for Philosophy of Religion* 8, no. 2 (1977): 75–93.

Polanyi, Michael. *The Tacit Dimension.* Chicago, IL: University of Chicago Press, 2009.

Posner, Sarah. *Unholy: Why White Evangelicals Worship at the Altar of Donald Trump.* New York: Random House, 2020.

Przywara, Erich. *Das Geheimnis Kierkegaards.* Munich: Verlag von R. Oldenbourg, 1929.

———. "Gott in uns oder über uns? (Immanenz und Transzendenz in heutigen Geistesleben)." *Stimmen der Zeit* 105 (1923): 343–62.

Putnam, Hilary. "Meaning and Reference." *Journal of Philosophy* 70, no. 19 (1973): 699–711.

Rae, Murray A. *History and Hermeneutics.* Edinburgh: T&T Clark, 2005.

———. *Kierkegaard's Vision of the Incarnation: By Faith Transformed.* Oxford: Clarendon, 1997.

Rahner, Karl. *Foundations of Christian Faith: An Introduction to the Idea of Christianity* ([New York?]: Crossroad Publishing, 1976; rev. ed., 1982.

Reddie, Richard. "The Church: Enslaver or Liberator?" Last modified February 17, 2011. BBC News. https://www.bbc.co.uk/history/british/abolition/church_and_slavery_article_01.shtml.

Rogers, A. K. "Plato's Theory of Forms." *The Philosophical Review* 44, no. 6 (Nov. 1935): 515–33.

Ross, Tamar. "The Cognitive Value of Religious Truth Statements." In *Tamar Ross: Constructing Faith*, edited by Hava Tirosh-Samuelson and Aaron Hughes, 41–86. Leiden: Brill, 2016.

Russell, Jeffrey Burton. *Inventing the Flat Earth: Columbus and Modern Historians*. Westport, CT: Praeger, 1997.

Ryle, Gilbert. *The Concept of Mind*. London: Hutchinson University Library, 1949.

Saltzman, Judy Deane. *Natorp's Philosophy of Religion within the Marburg Neo-Kantian Tradition*. New York: Georg Olms Verlag, 1981.

Schaeffer, Francis. *Escape from Reason*. Downers Grove, IL: InterVarsity Press, 1968.

Schopenhauer, Arthur. *The Art of Controversy and Other Posthumous Papers*. Translated by T. Bailey Saunders. London: Swan Sonnenshein, 1896.

Schreiber, Gerhard. "Christoph Schrempf: The 'Swabian Socrates' as Translator of Kierkegaard." Translated by David D. Possen. In *Kierkegaard's Influence on Theology, Tome I: German Protestant Theology*, edited by Jon Stewart, 275–319. Farnham: Ashgate, 2012.

Schröer, Henning. *Die Denkform der Paradoxalität als theologisches Problem: Eine Untersuchung zu Kierkegaard und der neueren Theologie als Beitrag zur theologischen Logik*. Göttingen: Vandenhoeck & Ruprecht, 1960.

Schulz, Heiko. "Die theologische Rezeption Kierkegaards in Deutschland und Dänemark: Notizen zu einer historischen Typologie." In *Kierkegaard Studies Yearbook 1999*, edited by N. J. Cappelørn and H. Deuser, 220–44. Berlin: Walter de Gruyter, 1999.

———. "From Barth to Tillich: Kierkegaard and the Dialectical Theologians." In *A Companion to Kierkegaard*, edited by Jon Stewart, 209–22. Oxford: Wiley-Blackwell, 2015.

———. "Germany and Austria: A Modest Head Start." In *Kierkegaard's International Reception, Tome I: Northern and Western Europe*, edited by Jon Stewart, 307–420. Farnham: Ashgate, 2009.

Searle, John. "The Storm over the University." *New York Review of Books* 37, no. 19 (Dec. 6, 1990): 34–42.

Shirer, William L. *The Rise and Fall of the Third Reich: A History of Nazi Germany*. London: Secker and Warburg, 1960.

Skidelsky, Edward. *Ernst Cassirer: The Last Philosopher of Culture*. Princeton: Princeton University Press, 2011.

Søe, Niels Hansen. "Karl Barth." In *The Legacy and Interpretation of Kierkegaard,*

Bibliotheca Kierkegaardiana, vol. 8, edited by Niels Thulstrup and M. M. Thulstrup, 224–37. Copenhagen: C. A. Reitzels Boghandel, 1981.

———. "Kierkegaard's Doctrine of the Paradox." Translated by Margaret Grieve. In *A Kierkegaard Critique: An International Selection of Essays Interpreting Kierkegaard*, edited by Howard A. Johnson and Niels Thulstrup, 207–27. Chicago: Henry Regnery Company, 1962.

Solberg, Mary M., ed. and trans. *A Church Undone: Documents from the German Christian Faith Movement, 1932–1940*. Minneapolis: Fortress, 2015.

Sponheim, Paul R. "Relational Transcendence in Divine Agency." In *International Kierkegaard Commentary: Practice in Christianity*, edited by Robert L. Perkins, 47–68. Macon: Mercer University Press, 2004.

Stewart, H. L. "The 'Reverent Agnosticism' of Karl Barth." *Harvard Theological Review* 43, no. 3 (1950): 215–32.

Stewart, Jon. *Kierkegaard's Relations to Hegel Reconsidered*. Cambridge: Cambridge University Press, 2003.

Strauss, David Friedrich. *The Life of Jesus, Critically Examined*. London: SCM, 1973.

Strong, James. *The Exhaustive Concordance of the Bible*. New York: Hunt & Eaton, 1894.

Sutherland, Stewart R. "The Concept of Revelation." In *Religion, Reason and the Self: Essays in Honour of Hywel D. Lewis*, edited by Stewart R. Sutherland and T. A. Roberts, 35–45. Cardiff: University of Wales Press, 1989.

Taylor, Charles. *A Secular Age*. Cambridge, MA: Belknap Press of Harvard University Press, 2007.

Taylor, Mark C. *Journeys to Selfhood: Hegel and Kierkegaard*. Berkeley: University of California Press, 1980.

Thielicke, Helmut. *The Evangelical Faith, I: Prolegomena; The Relation of Theology to Modern Thought Forms*. Grand Rapids: Eerdmans, 1974.

Thiselton, Anthony C. Review of *Lessing's "Ugly Ditch": A Study of Theology and History*, by Gordon E. Michalson, *Scottish Journal of Theology* 42, no. 2 (1989): 253–55.

———. *The Two Horizons: New Testament Hermeneutics and Philosophical Description with Special Reference to Heidegger, Bultmann, Gadamer, and Wittgenstein*. Grand Rapids: Eerdmans, 1980.

Thomas, John Heywood. "The Christology of Søren Kierkegaard and Karl Barth." *Hibbert Journal* 53, no. 3 (April 1955): 280–88.

Thulstrup, Niels. *Kierkegaard's Relation to Hegel*. Translated by George L. Stengren. Princeton: Princeton University Press, 1980.

Tietz, Christiane. *Karl Barth: A Life in Conflict*. Translated by Victoria J. Barnett. Oxford: Oxford University Press, 2021.

Torrance, Alan J. "*Auditio Fidei*: Where and How Does God Speak? Faith, Reason and the Question of Criteria." In *Reason and the Reasons of Faith*, edited by Paul Griffiths and Reinhard Hütter, 27–52. New York: T&T Clark, 2005.

———. "Can the Truth Be Learned? Redressing the 'Theologistic Fallacy' in Modern Biblical Scholarship." In *Scripture's Doctrine and Theology's Bible: How the New Testament Shapes Christian Dogmatics*, edited by Markus Bockmuehl and Alan J. Torrance, 143–64. Grand Rapids: Baker Academic, 2008.

———. "Christian Experience and Divine Revelation in the Theologies of Friedrich Schleiermacher and Karl Barth." In *Christian Experience in Theology and Life*, edited by I. Howard Marshall, 83–113. Edinburgh: Rutherford House Press, 1988.

———. "Forgiveness and Christian Character: Reconciliation, Exemplarism and the Shape of Moral Theology." *Studies in Christian Ethics* 30, no. 3 (2017): 293–313.

———. *Persons in Communion: An Essay on Trinitarian Description and Human Participation, With Special Reference to Volume One of Karl Barth's "Church Dogmatics."* Edinburgh: T&T Clark, 1996.

———. "The Theological Grounds for Advocating Forgiveness and Reconciliation in the Sociopolitical Realm." In *The Politics of Past Evil: Religion, Reconciliation, and the Dilemmas of Transitional Justice*, edited by Daniel Philpott, 45–86. Notre Dame: University of Notre Dame Press, 2006.

Torrance, Andrew B. "Beyond Existentialism: Kierkegaard on the Human Relationship with the God Who Is Wholly Other." *International Journal of Systematic Theology* 16, no. 3 (2014): 295–312.

———. "Creation: By, For, and Before God." In *The T&T Clark Companion to the Theology of Kierkegaard*, edited by David J. Gouwens and Aaron Edwards, 223–40. London: Bloomsbury T&T Clark, 2020.

———. "Kierkegaard on the Christian Response to the God Who Establishes Kinship with Us in Time." *Modern Theology* 32, no. 1 (2016): 60–83.

———. "Kierkegaard's Paradoxical Christology." In *The Vicarious Humanity of Christ and Ethics*, edited by Todd Speidell. Supplement, *Participatio*, vol. 5 (2019): 60–82.

Torrance, Thomas F. "Athanasius: A Study in the Foundations of Classical Theology." In *Theology in Reconciliation: Essays towards Evangelical and Catholic Unity in East and West*, 215–66. Eugene, OR: Wipf & Stock, 1996.

———. *The Ground and Grammar of Theology: Consonance between Theology and Science*. Edinburgh: T&T Clark, 1980.

———. *Karl Barth: An Introduction to His Early Theology, 1910–31*. London: SCM, 1962.

———. "The Logic and Analogic of Biblical and Theological Statements in the Greek Fathers." In *Theology in Reconstruction*, 30–45. London: SCM, 1965.

Tracy, David. "The Task of Fundamental Theology." *Journal of Religion* 54, no. 1 (January 1974): 13–34.

Turchin, Sean. *Introducing Christianity into Christendom: Investigating the Affinity between Søren Kierkegaard and the Early Thought of Karl Barth*. PhD diss., University of Edinburgh, 2011.

Tyrrell, George. *Christianity at the Crossroads*. London: Longmans, Green, 1909.

Vaihinger, Hans. *The Philosophy of "As If": A System of the Theoretical, Practical and Religious Fictions of Mankind*, translated by C. K. Ogden. 2nd ed. London: Routledge & Kegan Paul, 1935; first edition 1924.

———. "Karl Barths zweiter Römerbrief und seine Wirkungen." In *Karl Barth in Deutschland (1921–1935): Aufbruch-Klärung-Widerstand*, edited by Michael Beintker, Christian Link, and Michael Trowitzsch, 57–76. Zurich: TVZ, 2005.

VanDrunen, David. *Natural Law and the Two Kingdoms: A Study in the Development of Reformed Social Thought*. Grand Rapids: Eerdmans, 2010.

Verhey, Jeffrey. *The Spirit of 1914: Militarism, Myth, and Mobilization in Germany*. Cambridge: Cambridge University Press, 2000.

Walsh, Sylvia. *Living Christianly: Kierkegaard's Dialectic of Christian Existence*. University Park: Pennsylvania State University Press, 2005.

Walsh, W. H. *Kant's Criticism of Metaphysics*. Edinburgh: Edinburgh University Press, 1975.

Webster, John B. *Barth's Ethics of Reconciliation*. Cambridge: Cambridge University Press, 1995.

Weinandy, Thomas. "Cyril and the Mystery of the Incarnation." In *The Theology of Cyril of Alexandria*, edited by Thomas Weinandy and Daniel Keating, 23–54. Edinburgh: T&T Clark, 2003.

Wells, Ronald A. "Northern Ireland: A Study of Friendship, Forgiveness, and Reconciliation." In *The Politics of Past Evil: Religion, Reconciliation, and the Dilemmas of Transitional Justice*, edited by Daniel Philpott, 198–222. Notre Dame: University of Notre Dame Press, 2006.

Wells, William Walter. *The Influence of Kierkegaard on the Theology of Karl Barth*. PhD diss., University of Syracuse, 1970.

Westerholm, Martin. "Creation and the Appropriation of Modernity." *International Journal of Systematic Theology* 18, no. 2 (2016): 210–32.

———. *The Ordering of the Christian Mind: Karl Barth and Theological Rationality*. Oxford: Oxford University Press, 2015.

Wilke, Matthias. "Emanuel Hirsch: A German Dialogue with 'Saint Søren.'" In

Kierkegaard's Influence on Theology, Tome I: German Protestant Theology, edited by Jon Stewart, 156–84. Farnham: Ashgate, 2012.

Williams, Rowan. "Barth on the Triune God." In *Karl Barth: Studies of His Theological Method,* edited by S. W. Sykes, 147–93. Oxford: Clarendon, 1979.

Wilson, Stephen A. "Jonathan Edwards's Virtue: Diverse Sources, Multiple Meanings, and the Lessons of History for Ethics." *Journal of Religious Ethics* 31, no. 2 (2003): 201–28.

Wolterstorff, Nicholas. "The Reformed Tradition." In *A Companion to Philosophy of Religion,* edited by Philip L. Quinn and Charles Taliaferro, 165–70. Cambridge, MA: Blackwell, 1997.

Wright, N. T. *History and Eschatology: Jesus and the Promise of Natural Theology.* London: SPCK, 2019.

Yerkes, James. *The Christology of Hegel.* Missoula, MT: Scholars Press, 1978.

Zagzebski, Linda. *Exemplarist Moral Theory.* Oxford: Oxford University Press, 2017.

Ziegler, Philip. "Barth's Criticisms of Kierkegaard: A Striking Out at Phantoms?" *International Journal of Systematic Theology* 9, no. 4 (2007): 434–51.

———. "Christ for Us Today: Promeity in the Christologies of Bonhoeffer and Kierkegaard." *International Journal of Systematic Theology* 15, no. 1 (2013): 27–45.

Zuckmayer, Carl. *A Late Friendship: The Letters of Karl Barth and Carl Zuckmayer.* Translated by Geoffrey W. Bromiley. Grand Rapids: Eerdmans, 1972.

Index

"about turn," 134, 160–67, 287. *See also* metanoia

Adams, Marilyn McCord, 175

Adams, Nicholas, 33, 42

Adams, Samuel V., 160n44

Althaus, Paul, 147n4, 268, 297–99

Altschul, Jon, 344

Amesbury, Richard, 342n125

analogy, 185–89, 252–53, 347; of being, 186–87, 259, 261n39

Ansbach Counsel, 248, 297–99

Anselm, 165

anthropology, 7, 23, 43n34, 183, 185. *See also* theological anthropology

anthropomorphism, 194–98

anti-Semitism, 146, 147, 258, 260. *See also* racism

apologetics, 273–81

Aquinas. *See* Thomas Aquinas

Aristotle, 63n11, 115n28

Athanasius, 27, 142n126, 262, 319, 327–29, 330, 334, 355, 358–59

Augustine, 66n21

Baillie, John, 169

Balthasar, Hans Urs von, 223

Barmen Declaration, 123, 177, 248, 282, 297

Barrett, Lee, 6, 8–9, 194, 198, 217

Barth, Helene, 11

Barth, Karl: comparisons with Kierkegaard, 23–24, 111, 114, 115, 116, 117, 118, 125, 126, 150, 152, 162, 191, 195–98, 212, 217–18, 222, 224, 239–40, 242–43, 245, 246–47, 274, 307, 309, 321, 322, 324, 340, 341, 357–59; on philosophy, 173–75

Barth-Brunner debate, 247–62

Bauch, Bruno, 129n82

Bauckham, Richard, 318n53

Bax, Douglas, 269n67, 297n154

Baxter, Richard, 88

Bayle, Pierre, 66n21

Beach-Verhey, Timothy, 282n114

Beauvoir, Simone de, 109n12

Beck, Lewis White, 128, 129, 131n88

Beintker, Michael, 192n1, 237

Beiser, Frederick, 129

Benton, Matthew, 326

Berkouwer, Gerrit Cornelis, 178n113

Bethge, Eberhard, 119

Bible, the. *See* Scripture

biblical scholarship, 115–18, 168, 315–21, 331–34

Blatter, William D., 140n117

Blumhardt, Christoph, 123

Boethius, 189
Bonhoeffer, Dietrich, 89–90, 125–26, 147, 149
BonJour, Louis, 340
Brink, Gijsbert van den, 171n84
Bromiley, Geoffrey, 178, 183
Brunner, Emil, 25–26, 51, 109, 164n63, 188n147, 190, 246, 248, 249–58, 260, 261, 262, 271, 272, 274–75, 277n95, 278, 281, 282, 285, 295, 302, 314
Buber, Martin, 188n147
Bultmann, Rudolf, 3, 25, 26, 105, 117, 127, 131, 132, 133–41, 144, 330, 333, 355
Busch, Eberhard, 2n1, 121

Cajetan, Thomas, 252n13
Calvin, John, 167, 255–58, 259, 262, 265, 266n59, 283–84
Campbell, Douglas A., 136, 160n44, 164n61, 273n82
Campo, Mariano, 130
Cassirer, Ernst, 128
Catholic traditions, 115, 142, 148, 165, 258, 259, 267, 283, 284–85
causal theory of reference, 347–51
Chalamet, Christophe, 236–37
Charles, J. Daryl, 282n114
Chisholm, Roderick M., 308n24, 335n108
Choibalsan, Khorloogiin, 146n2
Christ. See Jesus Christ
Christian doctrine, 57–60, 87–92. See also Jesus Christ: and Christian doctrine; Jesus Christ: as teacher; theology; Trinity, doctrine of the
Christianity: in Denmark, 17, 18–19, 29–32, 41, 45–48, 49, 52, 54–56, 59, 64–65, 75, 76–77, 93, 100–101; in Germany, 106, 119, 120–22, 124–25,

147–48, 258–60, 297–99; and suffering, 31–32; in Switzerland, 123–25, 258–60
Christology. See Christian doctrine; incarnation; Jesus Christ
church, the, 20, 21, 41, 45, 46, 56, 110–11, 119, 120, 123, 159, 162, 176–77, 185, 187–88, 190, 200, 212–13, 234, 239, 248, 276, 281–85, 301–2, 305, 324, 334, 336–37, 340, 344, 345, 346, 353; and state, 291–92. See also Catholic traditions; Greek Orthodox traditions; Lutheran traditions; Reformed traditions
Clark, Gordon, 178
Clifford, W. K., 343
Cohen, Hermann, 127, 128–29, 130, 132, 139
community, 39–41, 55
Congdon, David, 128n74, 144n129
conscience, 154, 164–66, 251, 265–66, 271–73, 283–84, 289
counter-logos, 126, 149
covenant, 179–91, 293
creation, 8, 35, 62–70, 196, 203–6, 209–10, 215–17, 218–19, 224, 238–39, 240, 243, 244, 251–58, 275, 285, 295; and covenant, 180–81; out of nothing, 62–65; suffering of, 84, 254
Crisp, Oliver, 165n64
critical realism, 227–28
Cyril of Alexandria, 82, 83, 84, 85

Dalferth, Ingolf, 12n43
Danish Christianity. See Christianity: in Denmark
Deissmann, Adolf, 120n44
demythologization, 117, 134–35, 140, 162, 333. See also mythology

Dennison, William, 138–40, 141n119
Derrida, Jacques, 175
Descartes, René, 263–64
Dewey, John, 174n95
dialectic, 192n1
Dibelius, Otto, 122
Dickson, John, 360n6
Diem, Hermann, 119
differential calculus, 128
Diller, Kevin, 158–59, 163, 173–74, 314,
    339, 352–53
Dilthey, Wilhelm, 138n112
directionality, 158–79, 253, 260,
    261–62, 272–73, 299, 300–302
Dorner, Albert, 4
Dorrien, Gary, 250n4
Dowey, Edward, 255, 258
Dretske, Fred, 27, 344–45, 346, 353–54
Dryander, Ernst von, 122
Dulles, Avery, 284n121
Dunn, James D. G., 317–18
Dyer, Justin Buckley, 282–83, 284–85

education. *See* pedagogy
Edwards, Aaron, 7n28, 224n105, 242
Edwards, Jonathan, 265–67
Elert, Werner, 270n73, 297, 298,
    299n161
Elton, Maria, 263, 264
Emerson, Michael, 148n8
Enlightenment, the, 106, 107, 111–12,
    175
Ericksen, Robert, 259n32, 297n155
Eucken, Rudolf, 121
Evans, C. Stephen, 35–36, 82n100,
    97n157, 103n175, 152n18, 154, 155, 175,
    318n54, 321n58, 335, 337, 338n117,
    339n118, 343
experience, 108–10, 138–41, 272–73, 341

externalism: epistemological, 334–46,
    351; semantic, 346–51

faith, 12–13, 18, 20, 21, 22, 23, 38, 48, 49,
    56, 59, 67, 68, 70, 73–74, 79, 83, 92,
    94, 98, 99, 102–4, 109–10, 119–20, 132,
    133, 135–43, 203, 210, 211–13, 222–44,
    256, 274, 276, 277, 280–81, 337, 353;
    and fictional living, 137–43
Fergusson, David, 144n129
Fichte, Johann, 5
Ford, David, 125
Foucault, Michel, 175
foundationalism, 156, 280, 340–41
Franz Joseph I, 143n127
Frege, Gottlob, 347, 350
Friedlander, Henry, 259n30
Frost, Matthew A., 301n163

Gadamer, Hans-Georg, 319
Gallois, André, 351–52
Garrison, Jim, 254
Gavrilyuk, Paul, 84
Gemmer, Anders, 357
Gerlach, Wolfgang, 147n5
German Christianity. *See* Christianity:
    in Germany
Gert, Bernard, 248n1
Gettier, Edmund, 334–35
God: as absolute Spirit, 35; change-
    lessness of, 85–87; as Creator, 65–69,
    275–76, 294, 351; hiddenness of,
    73–75, 196–97; and humanity, 42–44,
    66–69, 225, 233, 236, 239, 240–41,
    250, 259, 262, 288, 292–93 (*see also*
    creation; image of God); objective
    reality of, 7, 24, 79, 110, 131, 132–33,
    140–41, 321; omnipotence of, 63–64,
    83–85; self-revelation of, 8, 20, 51,
    58, 59, 70, 77, 78, 83, 118, 119, 125, 126,

152, 153, 159–60, 169–70, 171–73, 174, 175, 195, 196, 197, 200, 201–22, 226, 227–29, 233, 234, 236, 240, 242–43, 244, 249, 251–55, 267, 268, 272–73, 275, 282, 285, 288, 295, 299, 304, 307, 308–9, 312, 313, 322–23, 325, 327, 339–40, 350–51, 353. *See also* Jesus Christ: as divine incognito; revelation

God-talk, 13, 42, 118, 147, 156, 157, 158, 164, 170–72, 190, 198, 253, 315–21, 323, 328, 330, 334, 351–54; theologistic fallacy, 320, 321–23

Goens, D. G., 121

Gogarten, Friedrich, 188n147

Gollwitzer, Helmut, 119, 278n103

Gordon, Frank, 121–22

Gottsched, Hermann, 4

Grabill, Stephen, 255n17

grace, 10–11, 17–18, 50, 95, 132, 133, 166–67, 182, 228–29, 230, 282, 285, 290, 292–93

Grant, Edward, 107n7

Greek Orthodox traditions, 286

Green, Lowell C., 299n161

Greene, Robert, 264

Greggs, Tom, 163n54

Gruchy, John de, 148n8, 269n67

Grünewald, Matthias, 309–10

Gunton, Colin E., 181n116

Hale, Matthew, 264

Hannay, Alastair, 115n28

Harnack, Adolf von, 115, 121

Harris, Sam, 342

Hartshorne, Charles, 181n116, 254n16

Hastings, Derek, 259n32

Hays, Richard, 273n82

Hector, Kevin, 13n48

Hegel, G. W. F., 28, 30, 32–44, 45, 55, 62n2, 70, 89, 96, 112, 127, 129, 133, 142, 175, 198, 208, 212n62, 226, 231, 243–44, 331, 332, 357

Hegelianism, 30, 32, 43, 76, 89, 93, 100, 239, 242, 243, 331; in Denmark, 44–48, 59, 64, 74, 76. *See also* idealisms: Hegelian

Heidegger, Martin, 134, 140, 169

Herbert, Edward, 264

Herdt, Jennifer, 265, 266n59, 282, 283–84, 285n122

Hermann, Wilhelm, 121, 132–33, 139–42

Heron, Alasdair, 328

Hess, Rudolf, 260n33

Hesse, Hermann, 147n5

Hick, John, 330

Himmler, Heinrich, 247

Hindenburg, Paul von, 122, 247

Hinlicky, Paul, 297n155, 299n161

Hirohito (emperor), 146

Hirsch, Emanuel, 5–7, 147n4, 190, 260–61, 297n155

history, 201–22, 244, 323, 324–27, 331–34; world history, 34–37, 40, 42, 93, 226

Hitchens, Christopher, 342

Hitler, Adolf, 122, 146, 247–48, 259, 260n33, 298, 299

Hodgson, Peter, 34n19

Holy Spirit, 21, 55, 83, 122, 167, 196, 200, 211, 212, 219, 221, 233, 234, 271, 276, 278, 292, 306, 309, 312, 329, 337, 338, 340, 345, 346, 353

Homer, 108n8

Hong, Edna H., 97n154, 102n174, 103n175, 194n2, 206n44

Hong, Howard V., 97n154, 102n174, 103n175, 194n2, 206n44

Hudson, Hal, 175

Hughes, Carl S., 237n155
humanisms, 13, 15, 47
Hume, David, 137n108, 175, 316
Hunsinger, George, 119, 241
Hutcheson, Francis, 264, 265n54

idealisms, 6, 13, 15, 47, 52, 79, 96, 97,
    100, 106–18, 142, 195, 334; Hegelian,
    52, 96, 116–17, 126, 127, 129, 133, 142,
    333, 334; Neo-Kantian, 117, 126,
    127–43, 150, 333, 334
image of God, 166, 184–85, 188, 250,
    252, 261, 262. *See also* God: and
    humanity; Jesus Christ: as image of
    God
immutability. *See* God: changelessness
    of
impassibility. *See* Jesus Christ: suffer-
    ing of
incarnation, 14, 36, 42, 43, 58, 70–72,
    82, 152, 153–57, 180, 187, 217, 221–22,
    236–37, 270–71, 275–76, 284, 294,
    295, 304, 327–29, 330, 331–32. *See also*
    Jesus Christ
individual, the, 39–41, 55–57, 138
infinite qualitative difference, 9–10,
    13–14, 69–70, 93, 95, 166, 186, 187,
    193–201, 217, 330
Inwagen, Peter van, 175, 343n134
Irving, Washington, 107n7

Jacobs, Helene, 147n5
Jefferson, Thomas, 268, 269
Jesus Christ, 6, 8, 12, 23, 46, 51, 53–54,
    58, 59–60, 179–80, 182–84, 187–88,
    196–97, 200, 211, 212–13, 226–27,
    244, 249, 273, 276, 290, 324, 353; and
    Christian doctrine, 89–92, 95–102;
    contemporaneity with, 102–4; as di-
    vine incognito, 10–11, 70–81, 83–84,
    197, 217–22; history of, 202–3; as

image of God, 185, 188, 217, 266, 295;
    as mediator, 9–10, 36, 44, 70, 92–104,
    195, 226–27, 243, 295; as Messiah,
    157n30, 170–71, 336–38, 345, 346, 350;
    as offense, 10–11, 75–81; as paradox,
    44, 81–94, 101, 215, 226, 229; suffering
    of, 83–85; as teacher, 99–102, 281,
    288; as Truth, 79, 100–102, 104. *See*
    also incarnation; resurrection
John Paul II, 267n63
Johnson, Keith, 187
Johnson, Roger, 127, 129n78, 131, 134,
    140n118, 142
Joyce, James, 108n8
Jüngel, Eberhard, 12, 171, 181n116
Justin, Eva, 259n30

Kant, Immanuel, 106, 108, 128, 129,
    130, 131, 137n108, 141, 142, 175, 208,
    244
Kasper, Walter, 317
Kerr, Fergus, 142n124
Kerrl, Hans, 259
Kertzer, David, 148
Kierkegaard, Søren: Anti-Climacus,
    7n25, 13, 30, 52, 53–54, 66, 67, 73,
    77–78, 80–81, 83–84, 100–101, 103;
    comparisons with Barth, 23–24, 111,
    114, 115, 116, 117, 118, 125, 126, 150, 152,
    162, 191, 195–98, 212, 217–18, 222,
    224, 239–40, 242–43, 245, 246–47,
    274, 307, 309, 321, 322, 324, 340, 341,
    357–59; H. H., 225–26, 227n115, 228,
    232; Johannes Climacus, 7n26, 11,
    38, 39, 40, 43n34, 46, 52–53, 63n11,
    70–72, 77, 95–99, 102, 103, 118, 150,
    152, 154, 157n31, 161, 201n24, 206,
    307n16, 312, 320, 325, 339n118; on
    philosophy, 175–76; pseudonyms,
    51–54; translations of, 4

Kierkegaard-Barth trajectory, 119, 143, 153–57, 170, 246–47, 262, 360–62
Kilby, Karen, 142n124
Kilner, John, 185
kinship, 13, 14, 75, 99, 111, 149–50, 167, 179–91, 334, 339, 341, 351, 354
Kittel, Gerhard, 147n4, 297n155
Klempa, William, 282n114
Klooster, Fred, 178
Kooi, Cornelis van der, 237
Kripke, Saul, 347–48
Krötke, Wolf, 22
Kulturprotestantismus, 20, 22, 121, 124, 150–51
Kutter, Hermann, 123, 124

Lahusen, Friedrich, 121
Lash, Nicholas, 142n123
law, 128, 131–33, 136–37, 139, 290, 292–93. *See also* natural law
law-grace model, 281, 293
Leibniz, Gottfried, 66n21, 106, 116, 325
Lessing, Gotthold Ephraim, 115n28, 116, 204, 316n45, 325–27, 330, 332, 355
Lewis, C. S., 88n124
Lewis, David, 349
"likeness" principle, 251–55, 259, 262, 296
Lindberg, David, 107n7
Little, David, 282n114
Locke, John, 106, 264, 343
Lonergan, Bernard, 284n121
Louth, Andrew, 171n84
Luther, Martin, 5, 22, 70, 150n11, 166, 286
Lutheran traditions, 18, 54, 59, 127, 132–33, 136, 142, 148, 258, 259; two kingdoms doctrine, 150–51

Mackie, J. L., 342
Mao Zedong, 146
Maréchal, Joseph, 142
Mariam, Mengistu Haile, 146n2
Marquardt, Friedrich-Wilhelm, 119
Marsden, George, 267
Marshall, Bruce D., 171n84
Martens, Paul, 31
Martensen, Hans Lassen, 28, 31n9, 44–46, 55, 90, 93, 240
Martyn, J. Louis, 160n44
Mather, Cotton, 264–65, 266
Maurice, F. D., 167
McCormack, Bruce, 16–17, 120n43, 142, 192n1, 201n24, 228
McInroy, Mark J., 188
McKinnon, Alastair, 2n1, 3, 342
mediation, 33–44, 76, 89
Merricks, Trenton, 175
Messer, August, 137n107, 357
metanoia, 160, 161, 165, 166–67, 261, 286–89, 338; semantic, 170–71. *See also* "about turn"
Meusel, Marga, 147
Michalson, Gordon, 325–27
Mihut, Cristian, 293n147
Millay, Tom, 31
Miller, Richard B., 348, 350
Milošović, Slobodan, 146n2
Moltmann, Jürgen, 152n15, 313
moment, the, 10–11, 206–14, 217, 323
Mondin, Battista, 252n13
Moore, G. E., 316
Moser, Paul, 175
Mozart, Amadeus, 261
Mul, Jos de, 138n112
Mulgan, Tim, 254
Müller, Ludwig, 147n4

Müller, Richard, 255n17

Mussolini, Benito, 148n7

Mynster, Bishop, 29n1, 31n9, 198

mythology, 65, 74, 75, 116, 117, 133–35, 234, 323, 325, 329–30, 333–34. *See also* demythologization

Nachdenken, 125, 126, 158–59, 160, 249, 274

nationalism, 120–23, 129, 146, 148, 262, 299

Natorp, Paul, 127, 130–31, 132, 139, 140

natural law, 282–85, 288, 289

natural theology, 154, 241, 249–62, 268–70, 274–75, 297–300

nature, 128, 268, 285, 299

nature-grace model, 164–65, 166, 284–85, 286, 293

Nazism, 15, 20, 21n68, 26, 122, 147–49, 185n37, 247–48, 258–60, 298–99

Niebuhr, Reinhold, 300

Niemoeller, Martin, 147

Nietzsche, Friedrich, 175

Nozick, Robert, 337–38

Numbers, Ronald, 107n7

objectification, 130–33, 134–35, 137, 138–40

objectivity, 12, 24, 37–39, 42, 49, 52

Ogden, Schubert, 134

O'Grady, Colm, 187n142

O'Neill, Aaron, 146n3

ordo salutis, 164–67, 286

Otto, Rudolf, 115, 272

pantheism, 34, 62

paradox, 35–36, 208, 209, 211, 217, 222–44. *See also* Jesus Christ: as paradox

Parker, T. H. L., 255–56, 258

Parmenides, 327n85

Pattison, George, 199n19

pedagogy, 107–8, 110, 111, 114, 161–62

Perkins, Robert, 32n13

Perrett, David, 280n110

Peter (apostle), 157n30, 170–71, 336–38, 345, 346, 350

Peterson, Erik, 235–36

Peterson, Ryan, 184n135

Pierson, Daniel, 251

Pius XI, 148

Plantinga, Alvin, 152n19, 174n95, 175, 267n63, 336, 338, 339, 340, 341n122

Plato, 97n154, 175, 253n14, 327n85

Pojman, Louis P., 316n45

Polanyi, Michael, 345

Pol Pot, 146n2

Pope, Alexander, 111, 114

Poston, Ted, 335n109

Pott, August, 122

preaching, 303–10, 324, 334

Przywara, Erich, 187, 223

Putnam, Hilary, 348–49

racism, 120, 146, 148, 258–59, 260, 262, 268, 269, 274, 282, 299. *See also* anti-Semitism

Rade, Paul Martin, 121

Rae, Murray A., 103n175, 161n45, 199n19, 267n64, 274n84, 279n107, 321n58

Ragaz, Leonhard, 123, 124

Rahner, Karl, 141–42, 284n121

Rea, Michael, 175

reality, 34, 36, 37–38, 40, 43, 127, 132, 137, 140–41, 196, 216, 228, 244, 335, 337, 338, 339, 341, 351–54

reason, 20, 33–34, 35, 43, 47, 49, 76–77, 80, 82, 86, 99, 101, 138, 160, 209–10, 218, 228, 232, 240, 244, 262, 263–71, 273, 285
reasonable religion, 106–15
Reddie, Richard, 146n3
Reformed traditions, 142, 148, 250, 255n17, 258–62, 265, 268, 269, 281, 282, 283
Religious Socialist movement, 123–25
repentance. See "about turn"; metanoia
resurrection, 204, 210, 212–13, 222
revelation, 16–18, 24, 39, 51, 58, 64, 76, 118, 139–40, 170, 171, 182, 200, 215, 219, 226, 227, 242, 244, 248–49, 252, 254–55, 258, 268, 270, 271, 273–74, 275, 285, 297, 306, 307, 308–9, 320, 322–25, 329, 333; Trinitarian grammar of, 306, 310–14. See also God: self-revelation of; Jesus Christ: as divine incognito; Trinity, doctrine of the
Riefenstahl, Leni, 247, 248
Ritschl, Albrecht, 115, 272
romanticisms, 6, 15, 47, 195
Rorty, Richard, 174n95, 175
Ross, Tamar, 331
Rumscheidt, Martin, 2n1
Russell, Jeffrey Burton, 107n7
Rutledge, Jonathan, 153n20
Ryle, Gilbert, 308

Schaeffer, Francis, 342
Schlatter, Adolf von, 120n44, 297
Schleiermacher, F. D. E., 112, 115, 141, 178, 199, 272
Schmithals, Walter, 134
Schmitz, Elizabeth, 147
Schopenhauer, Arthur, 277n95

Schreiner, Susan, 282n114
Schrempf, Christoph, 4, 5n16
Schrieber, Gerhard, 4
Schröer, Henning, 241
Schulz, Heiko, 4n13, 5
science, 43, 47, 107, 127, 130, 134, 135, 137, 139, 174, 216, 330, 333
Scripture, 19–20, 21, 24, 99–100, 111, 123, 136, 146, 154, 161–62, 196, 234, 241, 249, 276, 277–79, 280, 286–87, 288–89, 293, 304, 306–7, 308, 310, 330; and theology, 167–69, 315–21; as witness, 20, 167–68, 234, 276, 306–7, 309–10, 313, 318–20. See also biblical scholarship
Searle, John, 108n8
sensus divinitatis, 249, 256–57
sensus moralis, 249, 263–71
sexism and gender roles, 148–49, 262, 269, 274
sexual orientation, 262, 269, 274
Shakespeare, William, 144n128
Shapland, C. R. B., 329
sin, 11, 77, 97, 164, 165–66, 182, 216, 250–51, 256–58, 261, 271, 277, 280, 286
Skidelsky, Edward, 129
slavery, 146, 185n137, 269
Smith, Christian, 148n8
sociopolitics, 118–27, 146–49, 150–51, 184, 185, 190, 247–49, 258–63, 267, 281–85, 289–95, 296–300
Socrates, 96, 97n154, 99, 108n8, 114
Søe, Niels Hansen, 17n58
Söhngen, Gottlieb, 186–87
Solberg, Mary M., 147n4
Sommer, Hans, 299n158
Spinoza, Baruch, 116, 325
Spoendlin, W., 5n19, 121

Staewen, Gertrud, 147
Stalin, Joseph, 146
Stewart, H. L., 174
Stewart, Jon, 32n13
Strauss, David Friedrich, 25, 26, 116–17, 133, 325, 330, 331–33, 355
Stump, Eleonore, 175
Suarez, Francisco, 252n13
subjectivity, 7, 11–14, 24, 37–39
Sutherland, Stewart R., 171n82, 307n17
Swinburne, Richard, 175

Taylor, Charles, 201
theological anthropology, 179–91
theology, 157–79, 194–201, 219–20, 231–32, 233–40, 303; academic, 177–79, 184, 189–91; and the church, 176–77; "fundamental," 284, 288; and philosophy, 169–76; and Scripture, 167–69. *See also* Christian doctrine; God-talk; natural theology
Thielicke, Helmut, 163
Thiselton, Anthony, 131n88, 132, 134, 150, 332
Thomas Aquinas, 165n64, 175, 189, 251, 252–53, 254, 263, 264, 284
Thurneysen, Eduard, 5, 9, 206, 357
Tietz, Christiane, 90n130, 192n1
Tillich, Paul, 224n107
Torrance, Alan J., 125n67, 167n69, 271n74, 314n43, 347n143
Torrance, Andrew B., 7n26, 201n24
Torrance, Thomas F., 10, 306n15, 328
Tracy, David, 284n121
transformation, 277–79
Trinity, doctrine of the, 313–14, 321–23,

327–29. *See also* revelation: Trinitarian grammar of
Troeltsch, Ernst, 115
truth, 33–34, 38–39, 40–41, 43, 96–100, 109, 111, 114, 116, 160, 226, 241, 244, 274, 276, 312, 318
Truth, the, 13, 49, 50–51, 58, 96, 99, 111, 118, 206, 226, 241, 274, 281, 312–13, 337, 338–40, 341. *See also* Jesus Christ: as Truth
"turnabout." *See* "about turn"; metanoia
Tyrrell, George, 115

Vaihinger, Hans, 137–38
VanDrunen, David, 282n114
Van Til, Cornelius, 178
Verhey, Allen, 282n114

Walsh, Sylvia, 81
Webster, John B., 13n49, 15–16
Werkmeister, William, 131–32
Westerholm, Martin, 222–24, 233–34
Whitehead, Alfred North, 254n16
Wiedermann, Gotthelf, 298n156
Wilhelm II, 20n66, 120, 122n52, 133n95
Wilke, Matthias, 6
Williams, Rowan, 125
Wittgenstein, Ludwig, 108n8, 175
Wolff, Christian, 106–7, 137n108
Wolterstorff, Nicholas, 173, 175
Word of God, 303–10
Wright, N. T., 318n54

Zagzebski, Linda, 347
Ziegler, Philip, 3–4, 94n145
Zimmerman, Dean, 175
Zuckmeyer, Carl, 261n36